Peter H. Waddell

**Ossian and the Clyde, Fingal in Ireland, Oscar in Iceland**

Or, Ossian Historical and Authentic

Peter H. Waddell

**Ossian and the Clyde, Fingal in Ireland, Oscar in Iceland**
*Or, Ossian Historical and Authentic*

ISBN/EAN: 9783337318468

Printed in Europe, USA, Canada, Australia, Japan

Cover: Foto ©ninafisch / pixelio.de

More available books at **www.hansebooks.com**

# OSSIAN AND THE CLYDE

# FINGAL IN IRELAND

# Oscar in Iceland

OR

## OSSIAN HISTORICAL AND AUTHENTIC

BY

P. HATELY WADDELL, LL.D
MINISTER OF THE GOSPEL
EDITOR AND BIOGRAPHER OF ROBERT BURNS, TRANSLATOR OF THE PSALMS INTO SCOTCH,
AUTHOR OF "BEHOLD THE MAN," &c.

---

Glasgow:
JAMES MACLLHOSE, PUBLISHER TO THE UNIVERSITY
1875.

*All Rights Reserved.*

PUBLISHED BY
## JAMES MACLEHOSE, GLASGOW.

MACMILLAN & CO., LONDON.

| | |
|---|---|
| *London,* | *Hamilton, Adams, & Co.* |
| *Cambridge,* | *Macmillan & Co.* |
| *Edinburgh,* | *Edmonstone & Douglas.* |
| *Dublin,* | *W. H. Smith & Son.* |

MDCCCLXXV.

# PREFACE.

READERS who wish to know the worst that has been said of Ossian or his Translator, by the highest critical authorities in Great Britain, may consult at their leisure Dr. Johnson's *Journey to the Western Islands*, Boswell's *Tour to the Hebrides*, Pinkerton's *History of Scotland*, Vol. II., Laing's *Dissertation* on Ossian's Poems, also his edition of the *Poems of Ossian with Notes and Illustrations*, and Macaulay's *History of England*, chap. xiii.—in all of which, imaginary arguments have been advanced with studied contempt, and critical antipathies have been supplemented with insolence and scorn. Some secondary writers, who know nothing of the subject, may also be consulted; to whom such authorities were all-sufficient, and who had, or still have, a pleasure of their own, in rehearsing a century of abuse and blunders. As the present work conducts us to quite a different field of inquiry, from anything hitherto imagined by such critics, we shall reply to most of them by a line or two only, here and there, as our argument proceeds. When facts are known, this is all that will be required. The topography of Ossian, in short—which was a mystery to Johnson, to Pinkerton, to Laing, and a wilderness of error to MacPherson himself—will be found capable of identification at this hour, to its minutest features—in Scotland, in Ireland, in the Orkneys, and even in Iceland, by the light of Ossian's text alone reflected from the soil; and a veil of obscurity, for more than the first 250 years of our present era, will be removed alike from the surface and from the history of all these regions; which, for antagonists who boast of their own infallible erudition, and who weary us hitherto with oracular phrases, ought to be a rejoinder more than sufficient.

To do justice to Gibbon, who, if he could not entirely believe, dissented at least with diffidence, and expressed his doubts with magnanimity, as became a philosophic historian, it would be necessary to transcribe his words at greater length than the limits of a Preface will allow. Our readers must therefore consult the celebrated passage at large, in his *Decline and Fall of the Roman Empire*—Vol. I. chap. vi. We satisfy ourselves, now, by observing that it was partly to dispel the mists of which he complains, and establish the traditions in which he half believes, on principles of evidence and by critical researches never apparently anticipated by him, that the present work was undertaken: not to vindicate his doubtful faith, or in obedience to his inspiration, by any means; but from the clearest conviction of the truth of those traditions themselves. Whether Gibbon could have subscribed to the result of this inquiry, it would be impertinent to conjecture; but what Gibbon wished to see has been thus realised, and where Caracalla was defeated has at last been determined.

As for Laing, the most accomplished and unscrupulous of all MacPherson's adversaries, we shall have so many occasions to deal with his argument in detail, that quotation at present is unnecessary. On one point only, where a calumny against the Translator's character is unkindly insinuated by him, it affords us the utmost gratification to give direct and prominent reply:—

"His private character," says Laing, "may well be spared; and it is sufficient to observe that his morals were not such as to refute the charge which I have made, that, with a genius truly poetical, he was one of the first literary impostors in modern times."—*Preface* to Ossian, by Laing.

Whether this refers to habits of dissipation, as suggested by Mrs. Grant, in her *Letters from the Mountains;* or to some discreditable charge affecting MacPherson's honour as an agent for Government, we have no means, beyond this covert allusion, of deciding. But the fact now to be stated, and which is thus, for the first time, made public, is evidence to a character that could not be seriously depraved, and to principles that could hardly be immoral.

The comparative indigence of MacPherson's youth is known, and the difficulties he had to contend with in commencing life, as a student for the Church, may be conjectured. Laing indeed ungenerously proclaims all this, as a sort of presumption against him. He never, in fact, took license as a preacher, and therefore never reached the rank of a beneficed clergyman. His career stopped short at the school-room, and his utmost ambition then was to be a successful teacher; but even in this position, his emoluments were inadequate for his support, without occasional pecuniary assistance from friendly hands. Mr. ——, then a tenant farmer in the neighbourhood of Kingussie, was one of the friends who thus assisted MacPherson more than once, in the day of need; and the obligation, so far as he was concerned, was no more thought of. But when MacPherson returned after many years, an illustrious author and a monied man, to invest his fortune in an estate, and spend the remainder of his days at Belleville—which Laing caricatures, as another name for Selma—so far from forgeting these favours, he showed that he was neither unmindful of, nor ungrateful for such kindness. He not only received his old friend with conspicuous courtesy among other tenants on the rent-day—being now his landlord; but of his own accord desired him to select and enclose, from improvable pasture lands on the estate of Belleville, as much as he thought proper for a maintenance; to which he offered him, then and there, a freehold for life unconditionally. The offer so frankly made was not accepted by the gentleman in question, who had already determined to emigrate with his family—although that purpose was not ultimately carried into effect; but he often after regretted his declinature of the proffered advantage. Information of an act so creditable to MacPherson we have, on the authority of a living representative of the person himself to whom the offer was made; and our informant can substantiate the statement.

As to the actual worth of the bequest proposed, we cannot, of course, at this date, presume to speak with certainty—land, in the meantime, having risen so much in value; but the land in question was of excellent soil, and is now producing as good crops as the best in the neighbourhood. Without, therefore, attaching undue importance to the fact thus recorded, or attempting in any way to exaggerate its moral merit, we can hardly recognise it as the act of a " profligate," or a " ruffian," or a " cheat ;" and it would require much more than Johnson's authority to convince us, that the man who thus offered to repay, with spontaneous benevolence, the unknown obligations of his youth had been a practised liar from the beginning, and an irreclaimable impostor to the end. We do not believe it possible, in fact, that a virtue of this kind could have survived untarnished a life of money-making fraud and unrighteous gain, or even of sensuality and selfishness, in any man. The government of Pensacola, and the agency of Arcot, and the profits of *Ossian*, if they had been the triumphs of falsehood or the reward of sin, would have obliterated, long before the purchase of Belleville, all recollection of favours once received by the poor teacher at Ruthven and the penniless student of Kingussie. Critics, therefore, in the meantime, who can see nothing but forgery in the translation of Ossian, must remember that MacPherson, as a man, was thus honourable to a very rare degree; and that the mere inventor, as they affirm, of such lofty attributes for Fingal had the best model of the noblest virtues in himself, during a whole lifetime of alleged unflinching dishonesty.

In conclusion, the Author has now to return his best thanks to the friendly correspondents, clerical and others, whose names appear from time to time in course of the work, for the prompt and courteous assistance they have afforded him in prosecuting his researches; and to explain (1.) that the maps have been constructed by himself, partly from the Ordnance Survey and partly from a careful personal examination of the ground; (2.) that the various woodcuts representing scenes or objects, have all been made from sketches taken on the spot, except where otherwise stated; and that the whole were transferred to wood with the utmost accuracy for the engraver, under the Author's immediate inspection, by a member of his own family.

ELMGROVE PLACE.
GLASGOW, August, 1874.

### Part First.

# OSSIAN AND THE CLYDE.
## ARRAN AND THE FRITH.

# CONTENTS.

PAGE

CHAPTER I.—The "many-streamed" Clyde—Surface of Scotland—Geographical Survey of the Intersecting Friths—Certain Aspects pre-supposed in Ossian, ... ... ... ... ... ... ... ... 9

CHAPTER II.—Geology of the Clyde—Marine Deposits at Stobcross, and Neighbourhood, ... ... ... ... 14

CHAPTER III.—Date of High Levels in the Clyde—Survey of Frith from Girvan to Paisley, and from Arran to Cardross—Etymological Evidence in Names, from Girvan to Renfrew and Rutherglen; from Sanda to Arran, to Garscadden, to Sandyford, ... ... ... ... ... ... ... ... ... ... 20
Compare also Part Fourth, Chapter V.

CHAPTER IV.—Navigation of the Clyde—Letters of First Series in Local Press—Question of Canoes—*Carthon, Colna-donna, Cathlin of Clutha, Calthon and Colmal*, incidentally illustrated—Passage by Sea from Lochgilphead to Crinan implied—Was Balclutha at Dunglass or Rutherglen?—Reply to "SAXO"—His Letter in Appendix, ... ... ... ... ... ... ... ... ... ... ... ... 31
Compare as above, Part Fourth, Chapter V.

# ILLUSTRATIONS.

OSSIAN'S TOMB, open (FRONTISPIECE).
COAST OUTLINES, Dumbarton to Bute. ... ... 12
What GLASGOW might seem in OSSIAN'S day, ... ... 13
STOBCROSS and FINNIESTON HOUSE, in decay, ... ... 16
STOBCROSS, Heliotype I. of Marine Deposits, ... ... 19
STOBCROSS, Heliotype II. ,, ,, ... ... 20

# ARRAN AND THE FRITH.

## CHAPTER I.

### THE MANY-STREAMED CLYDE.

To say that Scotland from the Tweed to the Orkneys, with its endless variety of outline—its multiform rocky ridges, precipitous cliffs, and angular mountains; its deep ravines, sullen lochs, bounding cataracts and rivers; swelling uplands, barren moors, and rich alluvial straths—has been the creation of volcanic forces, enriched, harmonised and clothed by deluges of aquatic deposits, far beyond the memory of man, can be nothing new to the geologist, or even strange to the unscientific intelligent reader. That it has even been the theatre of active volcanic eruptions may be easily shown, and all doubt in any one's mind on the subject satisfactorily removed, by pointing to the most conspicuous extinct volcanic cones still prominent in the Island, and to the other isolated monuments of volcanic action strewed everywhere over its surface. The Tap-o'-Noth in Aberdeenshire, Ben-Lawers in Perthshire, the Lomonds apparently, in Fifeshire, the opposing Laws certainly of Largo and North Berwick on the Forth, and the Goatfell ridge of Arran in the Clyde, have been the miniature Vesuviuses and Ætnas of the Country. Arthur's-Seat, St. Leonard's and the Salisbury Crags; the corresponding, although smaller ridges of the Lesser Cumbrae and adjoining headlands, and the final step of Drumadoon Point on the verge of the Atlantic, —all of similar formation and precisely similar form—bespeak the underground march of some volcanic Titan, across the waist of the Island from east to west, heaving up to cool the blazing fuel in his path; whilst the Bass Rock on the one side and Ailsa Craig on the other, with Dumbarton or Dumbuck for a resting place half-way, mark the limits of his journey. Stirling Castle, Abbey Craig, Craig Forth and the Trossachs may indicate a divergent line to the north-west, from the starting point at Edinburgh; whilst the Grampian range from Montrose to Benlomond makes a magnificent parallel to the southern earth work of the Lammermoors and Lowthers, in the middle zig-zag of Scotland.

At what date these operations were concluded, or at what expense of time and energy in the reconstructive progress of the universe, and with what precise materials in every case, it is not the purpose of the present treatise to determine; but the appearance of the intermediate straths, and more especially of the Clyde, as one of the most conspicuous scenes of Ossianic history, and the theme of at least one third of Ossianic poetry, must be carefully examined, and the date of their formation ascertained with some approximation, if possible, to certainty. That both the Forth and the Clyde have been immense fiords at some remote period, penetrating nearly half-way in opposite directions through the country, and prevented from cutting it in two only by the intervening ridge with a watershed respectively to east and west, must be obvious at a glance to almost any traveller by canal or railway, and more and more obvious to any pedestrian at leisure, on his way between Glasgow and Falkirk. The Forth, from the east, must have occupied in two great floods of inundation comparatively shallow, except in their central streams, the whole expanse of grange-land through which the windings of that river far beyond Stirling are now seen, on the one hand; and the less extensive, but still considerable valley from Falkirk to Kilsyth, through which the Carron and the Bonny Water now flow, on the other—Stirling Castle being as a headland or promontory between them. The Clyde on the west, of nearly the same dimensions, but with innumerable ramifications in its tidal flow, and a bewildering multitude of islands, would reach as a fiord, shallow at the sides but sufficiently deep in the centre to be regarded as in every sense of the word an inland sea, with varying breadth as the hills approached or receded, from Dumbarton to beyond Rutherglen or Bothwell. The two friths, with the short intervening ridge from Maryhill to Cumbernauld between them, would thus form another zig-zag, not of rocks and mountains, but of watery parallels, across the Island, and practically separate its inhabitants into two distinct nationalities, with sufficient ground of defence, by walls or bulwarks, for or against invading forces.

The Frith of Clyde, as every excavation for miles east, west, and south of Glasgow now shows, and as the accumulating bank between Cardross and Port-Glasgow demonstrates, must have occupied an enormous plain of sand, interlaced and bounded with solid fields of the finest clay, and ribbed or walled with the purest sandstone. From the Kilpatrick to the Gleniffer Braes, from Jordanhill to Camphill, from Garnethill to Cathkin Braes, and from Camlachie ridge to Bothwell, this deposit of intermingled clay and sand, the sand predominating and overtopping, would diffuse itself; and the water would be spread, with its shallowest and by far its widest expanse between Glasgow, Pollokshaws, and Paisley. But with every recession of the tide that immense plain of sand would become partially visible, as the bed of the Solway still does, and the frith would thus come to be known and designated among our Scandinavian ancestors, allies, or adversaries, as the Sandy fiord—a name still traceable as Sandyford, in the western suburbs of Glasgow, the very point at which the character of the beach and bottom would be most conspicuous, and from which the widest view of the intervening expanse could be obtained. In the meantime, every prominent elevation, now a hill or ridge occupied with trees and terraces, colleges, cathedrals and churches, would be a naked island, and every headland a precipitous rock; every tributary stream, from the Cart to the Kelvin and the Calder, would be a small estuary, and every adjacent hollow would be a marsh. Blythswood-hill would be a clayey peak, packed with boulders; Garnet-hill, the Rottenrow, and Garngad, three unattractive ridges, rough with stones; Langside an island, possibly verdant; Erskine submerged, Dumbarton rock a double-headed islet, and Cardross a tongue-land from Dumbartonshire. Ardmore and Roseneath Points, now rich with verdure and waving with trees, would then be invisible; Roseneath itself a mere circular peninsula, tacked like an emerald, by a link of rock, to the solid land; Ardenslate and Hafton, all but separated from Dunoon; Bute divided by Kilchattan bay, at Kingarth; Portincross cut off from the shore, and Arran intersected by deep and rocky inlets, or scooped into wider bays. Loch-Winnoch and Loch-Lomond, at the date in question, would be inland seas—the Cart, the Gryfe, and the Leven, as rivers, gone. The Atlantic from beyond, between Ayr and Irvine, swallowing up their feeble streams, would cover the entire expanse of sandy desert nearly up to Kilmarnock, with a dangerous creek between Inverkip and Greenock, and a natural marine canal along the present line of railway from Bishopton to Ardrossan; of which canal obvious traces still remain in the intermediate lochs and rivers. The whole coast line would be shorn of verdure to the very cliffs, from Ardgowan to Port-Glasgow; and the whole extent of Renfrewshire from Kilbirnie to the Cloch, with the Cunningham of Ayrshire, would be separated from the rest—Dundonald, perhaps, remaining as the only noticeable headland on the southern shore. A distribution, or as it may rather be called, an absorption of the surface so violent as this, may seem almost incredible to the modern observer and dweller among its beauties—to the inhabitant of cities, and the voyager in ships; but the sectional views, photographic illustrations, and other proofs about to be submitted to the reader, will demonstrate not only the truth of it, but the certainty that it must in part at least have been traceable since the beginning of the Christian era. At that date too, there must have been a busy population in the region—boat-builders, sailors and soldiers, poets and musicians, on the banks of the Clyde; cities of a sort, fortresses and strongholds, long since crumbled into dust; with kings and queens, whose dynasties are extinct for ever. But geology, and not statistics, must for the present occupy our attention; and we shall be satisfied therefore, in conclusion of these remarks, to observe that navigation by canoes, or larger

DUMBARTON ROCK, FROM THE SOUTH.

ROSENEATH POINT, FROM THE SOUTH-WEST.

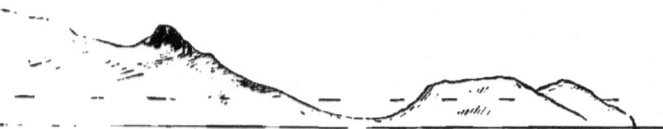

DUNLOSKIN HILL, FROM DUNOON PIER.

KILCHATTAN BAY, BUTE, FROM OFF LARGS.

The straight lines in the above sketches indicate the present sea level; the broken lines, its presumable level, at the date in question.

vessels if they had then existed, would be easy, so far as depth and expanse of water were concerned, from Bothwell to Lochlong—the only obstacle being the bewildering multiplicity of islands and intricacy of the channels. Any tributary current followed up might lead the navigator astray for hours; and the tiniest thread of blue in a mist might conduct him to destructive shoals, or to endless marshes. And that such was the fact, we learn from the oldest reputed authority on the subject. Ossian, as yet but a hypothetical witness, speaks nevertheless like a man who was acquainted with the region, and accustomed to navigate the river. The "streamy," or the "winding Clyde," are its appropriate epithets; and "the winding of his own dark streams," with "rushy desarts" by its banks, are its distinguishing characteristics—terms, in the mouth of a poet, as accurately descriptive as the most scientific phraseology could be, and suggestive enough to indicate besides that a subsidence of the water, along the highest levels and in the distant creeks or bays, as between Paisley and Cathcart, was already in progress. James MacPherson certainly did not dream of this, when he translated the original.

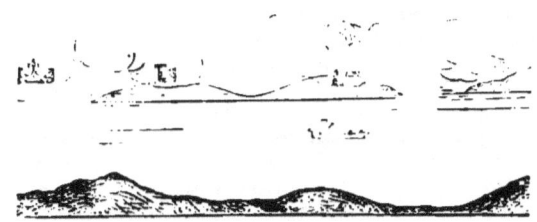

WHAT GLASGOW MIGHT SEEM TO OSSIAN IN HIS DAY.

## CHAPTER II.

### GEOLOGY OF THE CLYDE.

THE general descriptive outline of the old geographical features of the Clyde, attempted in the foregoing chapter, could be applicable to the Forth only as regards expanse of water at the date supposed. Of islands, other than those still visible on its surface, there would be comparatively few in that frith; and no intricacies of navigation, except in the valley of the Carron. To these, however, our attention will be more minutely directed hereafter, and for the present we return to the Geological survey of the great western estuary.

By far the widest extent of level land in the upper frith of Clyde—that is, from Dunglass or Dumbuck to Bothwell—would lie then, as it still lies, to the south of the river, between Paisley and Cambuslang. The widest level on the north side, with a few trifling elevations, would be from the Broomielaw of Glasgow to Barrowfield or Tolcross: and the whole of this region, as every brickmaker, builder, and railway contractor knows, consists almost entirely of pure sea sand to any depth, with occasional layers of coarse gravel, interlaced with the finest clay in dykes or fields of equal depth, and bounded by the firmest freestone, as in the quarries of Giffnock and Possil. The elevations which interrupt it are chiefly of boulder clay, coarse and unmanageable, as in the "hills" so called about Glasgow; whilst the mineral deposits at greater depths are of coal and iron. This trough of the Clyde has in process of time been covered with innumerable layers of alluvial soil, remarkable in many places for its strength and fertility, but diminishing on the heights to feeble sand or bleak and barren till. The river, notwithstanding all these changes of subsidence and accumulation, seems to have adhered pretty much to its original main channel, and flows now perhaps, with a few restrictions and short cuts below Glasgow, very nearly in the same track on which it glided imperceptible, as an under current of the ocean, two thousand years ago. Indeed, the building of cities, the construction of harbours, the excavation of docks; the deepening, the dyking, the directing and utilising of its waters in every way, within the last fifty years, have done more to divert it from its native path than the lapse of so many centuries; but always, as now, the general trend of its current has been close to the northern shore.

Within our own recollection, its deepest and most picturesque turn was underneath the magnificent old trees, but lately felled, between the Point-house and the end of Lover's Loan at Kelvinhaugh; where at full tide it was barely possible to find a passage on foot between the margin of the water and the overhanging hedge, scooped and washed to its very roots by the river; and in flood-tides or spates, it was not possible at all Between the uppermost of these points and Glasgow, there was scope enough on the banks in general; but almost every winter, when the river "came down," the low-lying lands of Stobcross, Finnieston, and Lancefield—except where carefully embanked—were submerged, and in the very highest floods the whole lower parts of the city, with the Fleshers'-haugh and even portions of the Upper Green, were inundated as far as to Rutherglen bridge, and farther. The highest of these, within the memory of the present generation, touched a point still marked by a brass memorial plate (on which the lettering, we regret to observe, has been totally obliterated) several feet above the level of Glasgow Jail door south; whilst an older flood, still higher apparently, has been recorded by an inscription, *not* obliterated, on the rocks at Bothwell Castle.

This whole northern bank, now within the precincts of the city, from the east end of Monteith Row to the western limits of Stobcross—by the Trongate, Argyle Street, and Stobcross Street—was then defined by a long low ridge, here and there subsiding to a level, but reaching a considerable elevation at Cranstonhill and Stobcross. This ridge throughout is almost entirely of sand and gravel, with belts of clay and occasional boulders, as already described. Not a new house can be built, or a sewer opened, or even a street repaired, without demonstrating this; but some recent railway operations on the lands of Stobcross, more especially on the highest part of the ridge there, called Stobcross hill, have disclosed some marine formations of sand and gravel so beautifully mixed, and leaning on a bank of solid clay so strong and deep, as to place the united action of sea and river—of tidal wave outside and of alluvial current inside—in conjunction at the spot, beyond question or dispute. These formations, exclusive of the solid clay, which may have been partly accumulated by the river, partly by some Arctic drift, are or rather were, July 1872—for they no longer exist in their integrity, if they now exist at all—of three distinct characters: (1.) Of pure unmixed sea sand in extensive layers both broad and deep, low down, or in magnificent massive blocks heaped high up, as in photograph No. II., like some prospective precipice. (2.) Of sea channel round and rough, or fine and small, of every tint and colour, from yellow to the palest blue, stored together as in mountains, leaning back on the clay and solidified by the pressure of its own weight. (3.) Where these were intermingled in successive layers, and piled with regularity of action beyond the finest art, deepest lay the pebbles of the greatest size or weight, and over these it might be some hundred layers of sand; another bed of pebbles, smaller than the deepest, succeeded to this, and then more layers of sand; and so on, diminishing in weight and size, but with increasing tenuity of deposit and delicacy of divine workmanship, till a loose coat of shingle smoothed all in and overtopped the whole. In a few individual spots, the layers of sand lay packed in basins scooped out by the eddies of the tide; in others, they seemed to have been kneaded with the finest clay, and melted or bent under the action of rain, with a curve like plaster; and at one particular point, where the clay itself formed tiny layers among the sand, they stood out when first discovered, like slips of paper among ton-weights of flour, tough enough to be gently separated, but crumbling in the hand like dust, when rubbed or rudely removed. Such flakes, in their original condition, could have been but films on the surface of the water in some steady pool, or were suspended in a cream-like solution, and gently dropped in the deadest calm. As a matter of geological curiosity, it should be farther observed that a thin layer of partially carbonised and inflammable matter ran transversely through the sand, staining it around as if with iron, at a depth varying from 1 to 30 feet below the surface; and indicated most probably the deposit of some burnt-out moss by the Clyde in flood, brought down on the stream from its upper reaches.

The line of these formations was from east to west, along the track of the present railway on its southern side—their range, as hitherto disclosed, being about one third of a mile, their depth on an average about 40 feet, their breadth from the clay dyke outwards about 180, and their surface level proximately from 80 to 90 or 100 above low water in the Clyde. The ridge they thus composed sloped rapidly down, but with a graceful sweep—as having been fashioned by the gradual subsidence of the stream, or by the action of waves from the south-west in conflict with the stream—to the old level of the haugh now filled up with output, or scooped away for docks, but formerly occupied as pasturage or garden ground, and subject, as already stated, to frequent inundations of the river; and it was covered with a thin top-dressing, or layer of black artificial soil, averaging from less than 6 to about 8 inches deep, gradually increased to that slight depth by manure and tillage, and therefore not more than a hundred years old at the utmost. The half decayed roots, or skeleton roots, of small trees and shrubs were yet discoverable in 1872, slanting outwards in the sand towards the river; and might either have maintained for their branches a short-lived precarious existence on the bank before cultivation reached it, or have been lodged there at still remoter periods by the passing flood. The probability is, that the entire ridge was clothed along its shingly top with brooms or alders, as far upwards as Glasgow Bridge; and so the name of Broomielaw, its then appropriate designation, was transferred to the harbour which now occupies its place.* How the "law," or highest part of the ridge there, was disposed of at the formation of the harbour may now be uncertain; but it is not impossible that it was removed, in the same way as Stobcross ridge has lately been, to fill up some hollow on the banks adjacent. This conjecture is, indeed, so far supported by a fact within the Author's knowledge—that in digging the foundation of Howard Street Church, to be then occupied by his own congregation—only a little to the eastward of the Broomielaw—an old brick building, apparently some workshop, was discovered many feet below the present surface. The bricks were of antiquated mould, and the superincumbent mass was chiefly of sea sand; which could not, therefore, have been deposited in that hollow so recently by the river itself, but must have been carted, either from the foundation of other houses long ago, or from some ridge in the neighbourhood, such as the Broomielaw ridge would be.

Formations similar to those above described, but purely marine, the present writer has also personally examined in the moor beyond the Manse at Dunoon in Argyllshire, and by the sea shore at Girvan in Ayrshire; and he has no doubt that many such may be met with at intervals along the coasts of the frith, or in the trough of the Clyde, on both sides, from Ballantrae to Bothwell. Anything so beautiful, however, as those at Stobcross he has neither seen nor imagined; yet their fragility was so great, that a night's rain would obliterate the distinctest tracery among them, and a fortnight's storm, or even the thrust of a walking-stick, would dissolve an apparent precipice. For this reason, he was anxious to secure not only some records of their evanescent beauty, but some unquestionable evidence of their existence, before accident destroyed them; but only by the utmost vigilance in unpropitious weather, and among surrounding interruptions, could succeed to any degree in this object. What had been perfect at nightfall

---

* Of the larger sorts of trees—planes, elms, beeches, saughs, and limes—which once decorated the slopes from Stobcross to the Clyde, planted most probably by the Orrs of Barrowfield, proprietors of the soil long since, and which still flourished in the Author's boyhood, but all now subverted or felled, except half-a-dozen leafless stems in the neighbourhood of the old mansion; or of the summer-house or "Temple," which terminated the pleasure walk along the ridge, and which must have commanded one of the finest views on the Clyde, before steamboats and building yards or factories were invented, and which forty years ago, in the days of the Philipses, was a holiday rendezvous for the boys and girls of the two neighbouring families; or of the market gardens and dairies, which occupied the intervening space, now razed and vanished—we need say nothing. These extended not to Ossian; were but the works and monuments of later years: and the accompanying sketch from photograph, No. 1., of Stobcross house and of Finnieston house, forlorn, but still respectable-looking in their decadence, among railway excavations and adjoining chaos, must say all that need be said on the subject.

Forsan, et haec olim meminisse juvabit.

was often a wreck in the morning, and the most exquisite work of centuries thus perished before it could be transferred to the lens. In such circumstances, fewer and less perfect copies of these interesting formations were obtained than would otherwise have been possible; but such as they are, and with all the indistinctness of reproduction, he submits them to scrutiny, in proof that his own descriptions are no exaggeration of the fact.

No. I., sketch on wood from a photograph, represents an excavation on the track of railway between the clay dyke on one side (to the reader's left hand) and the marine formations on the other, near their commencement eastward, with sea stones scattered on the foreground, at a depth of 40 feet or thereby from the surface; Stobcross house on the middle view line, and the gable of Finnieston house on a lower level, with Verreville old glass-work cone, in the distance. It is chiefly to show the general elevation of the ridge, above the bed of the Clyde, that this view is introduced; for as a woodcut it cannot represent the geological features of the ground, nor were these by any means so interesting, being mostly of clay, at the point selected. The portion from which the remaining illustrations were taken rose above Stobcross, as high as the level of the chimneys.

FROM STOBCROSS, LOOKING TOWARDS GLASGOW.

No. II., heliotype, as described, represents a miniature rock of possibly 300 layers, about 12 feet high in itself, and 50 feet above the level of the Clyde, rising from a bed of the roughest channel in the centre of the ridge 200 paces westward, and facing to south-west, but in an exposed situation. A portion of this beautiful structure fell—about half-way up, as a microscope will show—the night before the view was taken; and in less than a week afterwards it was a total ruin. It has since been swept off in progress of railway operations.

No. III., also a heliotype, represents the upper portion of a somewhat solider cliff, and of much finer sand than the above, about 200 paces farther west, in a more sheltered situation; where, being undisturbed by accident or the weather, it had contracted a smoother surface which threw the descending rain off, but was in reality equally perishable. It was, in fact, all that remained distinguishable, after a fortnight's hurricane, in a series of still more beautiful cliffs, full of the most exquisite net-work of cross formations and gossamer deposits of clay and sand, which had all rushed down in shapeless ruins, or been strewed in impalpable powder along the surface by the passing wind, in the interval. The extreme range of this particular formation, as discernible at the date, was about 300 feet, its height as represented about 20 feet, and its greatest elevation above the level of the Clyde at low water from 80 to 90 feet.

Without presuming from such data to draw any dogmatical conclusion as to the antiquity of these formations, it must be obvious from their very fragility that they could not be old. Without the slight covering of artificial soil, indeed, with which they had been recently clothed, they would long ago have been scattered by the winds, or trodden out of shape by the foot of man, as heaps on the open shore. In this view of their accidental preservation, they may be said to have been the creations of yesterday, scarcely dry from the touches of the tide. A thousand years more, in favourable circumstances, might have made them something like sandstone, and two thousand more might possibly have converted them to rock; but to judge of them by their condition as recently disclosed, soluble by the slightest rain and transferable by the very winds, Giffnock and Possil might be five, or ten, or twenty, or fifty times as old. In any view, they must have been comparatively recent; and other circumstances concurring to support the conclusion, we may be justified in assuming that the topmost layers at least could not have been deposited much earlier than the commencement of the Christian era, if so early as that. But additional evidence of other sorts is required to substantiate this theory, and we shall now proceed to consider it.

## CHAPTER III.

#### DATE OF HIGH LEVELS IN THE CLYDE.

I. IN adducing proofs confirmatory of the conclusion arrived at in the preceding chapter, we may now consider first the obviously recent character of the geological deposits in the region. Thus (1.) All the embayed land on the eastern shore of the frith, from Ballantrae or Girvan to Kilmarnock, is either of very late acquisition, almost within the memory of man, or contains deposits in the shape of shells and other marine products, of common and still extant formations. To the comparatively recent occupation of arable shore lands and links at Girvan, for example, any inhabitant of the district, from observation or from tradition, can bear witness. A certain portion of the town itself indeed, called the Flushes, was long subject to inundation, and was only finally reclaimed and consolidated by artificial labour accidentally bestowed in the winter of 1854. The rabbit warrens at Turnberry, and every intermediate farm along the coast, and those about Prestwick beyond Ayr, speak plainly enough of their own origin; and the almost barren reach of sand, strewed everywhere with sea plants and shore grass for miles around, thence towards Irvine and Kilmarnock, is obvious to all travellers by railway between Ayr and Glasgow. The river Ayr itself flowed originally in another channel towards the sea, than it now does; and the Irvine, for many miles upward, must have been at no very remote period the central stream of an expanded fiord. Any one standing on the Craigie-hill at Kilmarnock, and looking westward to the frith, will have no longer much doubt on the matter; yet more conclusive proof may be obtained, the farther we advance inland. "I have collected," says the Rev. Alex. M'Bride, of North Bute, whose valuable testimony in another department of evidence we shall have occasion more fully to quote— "I have collected the *recent shells* of the frith about 200 yards from the railway station at Paisley, about 2 feet under the surface, overlying the glacial or brick clay; and in that clay, 15 feet beneath the surface, I have collected the arctic shells of the glacial era," &c. So also, with respect to the extent of the frith, the latest surveys (1873) by members of the Geological Society of Glasgow may be quoted, as the reader will find by comparing extract in Appendix. In connection with which, to look back for a moment from Paisley to Girvan, where our present survey begins, we find that all this theory, founded originally on general superficial observation only, has now been confirmed, since these very pages were in type, by facts the most incontrovertible. It is but within the last few weeks or months, as we learn, that in sinking wells throughout that burgh, in streets on its highest level, beds of cockle shells upon sea sand, at the depth of 12 or 15 feet, under soil of alluvial deposits intermixed with soft yellow clay and an occasional layer of fresh water channel as if after a flood, have been penetrated —in one case, so abundant that they were thrown up in shovelfuls to the surface and carried away as curiosities by the people ; and that in another case, at a slightly lower level, a thick layer of the finest vegetable mould or peat moss, at the depth of 8 or 10 feet, was pierced in comparatively close proximity to the sea. Now, although the cockle as a living bivalve has been almost extirpated on the coast at Girvan, yet within the memory of men not more than sixty years old it used to be found, and had been so common there, that a small hollow on the shore, not far from the deposit above referred to, was called the cockle loch : and although, in like manner, the hills immediately to the east of the town, and nearer to which the layer of peat was discovered, have long since been stripped of their timber, they were formerly so well clothed with a certain kind of wood that one of them is still called the Saugh-hill; from which most probably, or from some decayed forest at their base, swept down by the torrents—of which one, called the Downe Burn, still flows in the neighbourhood—and deposited on the shore, the vegetable debris must have been lodged which was but yesterday disturbed by excavation for a supply of water to the inhabitants. Such changes, therefore, cannot have been much more remote than the date already fixed for them in the preceding pages ; and as discoveries of the same kind in shells and sand are by no means confined to the precincts of the town, but extend up the whole valley of the Girvan wherever wells are sunk, the conclusion is irresistible that the bed of that river has been a fiord from the present sea line, and with all the characteristics of the modern coast, to beyond Dailly, and a tidal-stream most probably to Crosshill or Blairquhan at the commencement of our own era. To reason farther on the subject would be superfluous, for to doubt it in the face of such facts would be absurd.

(2.) To the same effect, as regards the deposit of shells, we may farther state on the authority of eye-witnesses, that on the opposite shore of the frith, in the Island of Arran, three quarters of a mile at least from the present sea line there, and fully 20 feet above it, shells may be found in the creeks and hollows of the land—as at Lagg, for example—precisely similar to those which are still common on the beach, intermingled also with fragments of arctic shells among the deeper clay, but not to be confounded with them. Such marine deposits, even 20 feet above the present level of the sea, might imply a depth of water 50 or 100 feet above that level at the date of their formation. Much farther up, but on the same side of the estuary, the acquired lands on the shore between Cardross and Dumbarton, which are yearly increasing by the recession of the tide, are crowded in every corner with the purest sea channel of all modern tints, and with similar tribes of shells. These, in fact, are turned up by the ploughshare in every furrow, and might be removed from the ground, it is said, with little sifting, in almost any numbers. So impregnated is the soil with these peculiar deposits in that immediate neighbourhood, indeed, that any new-ploughed fields, or mole-hills thrown up among the grass, appear after a night's rain as if they had been sprinkled with lime or snow. But without urging such minuteness of proof, although it abounds everywhere, a glance at the frith from the hill-side above Port-Glasgow, or from the heights of Kilmahew above Cardross, will satisfy any intelligent observer that the Clyde must be an ebbing fiord. Surveyed from such levels, it seems to be steadily decaying. Its shores are oozy terraces of increasing breadth, its banks are recently deserted sea-cliffs fringed with wood, its waters are a weakening tide; and closer inspection confirms this rather saddening impression. The Vale of Leven, as seen from Dumbarton Rock, or even from the railway station at Dumbarton, is but a reclaimed swamp; Erskine, Ardmore, and Roseneath, as you traverse the line, look like new-born petty peninsulas emerging from the waters; and the verge of the river in many places, for miles in extent, is found to be accumulated soil, the work of yesterday, which an inundation of twenty feet would restore again to the dominion of the sea. To look at all this, with whatever sentiments of regret, satisfaction, or surprise, and to believe that the Clyde is now—even by many scores of feet in depth, and thousands of feet in breadth—what it was at the commencement of the Christian era, is impossible. Acres, miles, and whole parishes of arable land have been gained; but the river itself is disappearing "from the midst of the earth."

II. A few miscellaneous facts, not strictly in the province of geology, but sufficiently connected with its proofs to be arranged under that head, may now be mentioned; and some of these, in their bearing on dates and levels, are perhaps the most conclusive of all. Such, for example, as (1.) the stranding and wreck of a vessel on the parapet beach of Arran, considerably above the present level of the shore, on a point which is still designated from the event, not far from Lagg, and not more than, if so much as, a hundred years ago. (2.) The sailing of boats, and the lading of goods in that neighbourhood, within the memory of persons still living, where sheep and cattle now graze. (3.) The finding of a ship's anchor several hundred paces inland from the beach, in one of the eastern bays of the same island; and more notably, of another, said to be about 2 tons weight and 2 feet below the surface, beyond Oscar's reputed grave at Glenree, a mile and a half at least from the present shore line. How such a relique of maritime traffic came there at all has been a problem to many, for few have been bold enough to imagine that the sea ever ranged so high. Yet if it was carried and hidden there, since the date of Oscar's burial, it must still have been from the fiord of Sliddery which flowed in the neighbourhood; and the hiding of such a treasure, say fifty feet high on a barren hill-side, must have been without any assignable object whatever in the doing of it. (4.) That there is still pointed out on the opposite coast at Ardrossan, and not far from the gate of the old castle, a rock, now considerably inland, to which, in the memory of the last generation, fishermen used to moor their boats. (5.) And finally, that canoes of various sizes have been found everywhere in the strath of the Clyde, many feet under its present surface; most notably in recent times, by the side of the river at Erskine, and in certain low-lying thoroughfares of Glasgow. All which particulars, it must now be observed—from the discovery of shells and canoes on the banks of the river, to the wreck of ships, the disinterring of anchors, and the mooring of skiffs far above its present level, and at so many different points on both sides of the frith—although we had nothing more to add to them, would go far to substantiate the theory in question, that the waters of the Clyde as a fiord, at no very remote date, were at least as high as the marine formations at Stobcross. That the whole frith, in short, has been steadily retreating for a thousand years or more, and is still retreating—slowly in a certain sense, yet perceptibly in a lifetime—may be relied on as a physical fact. The difficulty of preserving its channel clear of accumulations, as between Cardross and Port-Glasgow, and of equalising the depth of the river bed above that, is not wholly owing to the increasing sewage of cities, or the deposits of floods. The water itself is receding; and a day is certainly coming, although it may be far distant, when the stream of the Clyde may either be reduced to a comparative rivulet, or will require to be deepened to a dead canal; and any one who chooses, on a calm day at low tide, to look steadily down on the frith from Lunderston hill towards the Bullwood of Dunoon, will see the commencement of an eliptical or horseshoe fall, marked by the ripple of the water on a ledge of rocks underneath, which at last, like Connal Ferry on Loch-Etive, if the recession of the ocean does not cease, will be impassable. On the other hand, there may be a return of the ocean by equally slow degrees, or even by more rapid movements, to its old level; in which case, all the land hitherto gained and the cities built on its deserted territory, would be submerged: which the occasional inundations of the tide—most notably during the present winter of 1873, by which houses have been filled, streets covered, and railroads destroyed along the coast—very clearly demonstrate to be no impossibility. In the meantime a recession has occurred, by which the surface of the Island has been perceptibly increased, and its geography materially altered. How this recession has been, or still is occasioned—whether by the actual withdrawing of the sea from certain shores, or by the rise of the land, or both; or by the gradual absorption or evaporation of all aqueous matter on the globe, as many believe, in preparation for its ultimate destruction by fire—is not within the province of our present inquiry to discuss. It is with the fact alone we have to do, which in the Frith of Clyde, and on the coast line of Scotland east and west, is obvious ; and more particularly with the date of it progressively, which, at the average rate of somewhat less than one inch in the year for the last two thousand years, or thereby, seems to be indisputable.

III. Besides these geological proofs, there is yet another sort of evidence equally strong, to illustrate and confirm our position, in the etymological traditions of the region; from which, however, we must be content to select only such designations of points and places, here and there, as will determine incontrovertibly the assumed level of the waters at the date in question. The point farthest south already referred to, and most intimately known to the present writer, with which therefore it will be most convenient again to begin, is the valley of the Girvan— itself a name of Celtic origin—still a river, in its upper reaches, of devious course, and liable to wide inundations ; but which, as we have just seen, must have extended inland as a fiord, from the present shore line to beyond the village of Dailly. This fiord was narrowed at the sea, exactly opposite Ailsa Craig, by two distinct Knocs, or small elevations, at the mouth of it—one of them on the south, where the Town-hall of Girvan now stands, an abrupt peninsula called *Knoc-Oisshon* or *Knoc-Usshon*, translated hill-of-the-ocean by some, and by others hill-of-justice, as if it were *Knoc-Cuish;* the other affording long ago some passage by the shore on the north, hence called *Knoc-a-balloch*, vulgarly Knoc-a-valley, or hill-of-the-pass. About the Celtic origin of these names there can be no doubt, or that the points they still designate were the boundaries of the Girvan fiord seaward when they were adopted; but as no nearer approximation can be found to *Knoc-Oisshon* or *Knoc-Usshon*, with the sense of ocean attached, than *Knoc-Aigean*, which is by no means identical; and as the earls of Carrick, by whom alone justice was administered in the district, had no existence either as serfs or rulers at the time when such a name must have been bestowed, it would be satisfactory to learn farther from Celtic scholars whether *Knoc-Oisshon* be not after all a corruption of *Knoc-Ossian*, and might not as well be translated Ossian's hill accordingly. In the meantime, we shall be satisfied with remarking that many or most of the local names in the valley itself are of modern origin, whilst those on the heights and ridges, or promontories which shoot into it, are Celtic—indicating thus two distinct ranges of occupation by two distinct races of inhabitants in the process of its formation; the older occupying the only then accessible land, and the younger the richer low-lying haughs disclosed at a later period by the subsidence of the waters. Under the head of geology at this point, however, we may farther add that the sea bank formations, such as those of Knoc-a-balloch, on the coast from Girvan to Turnberry correspond precisely to those along the shore on the South End of Arran opposite; and that, on both sides of the frith, they still show a remarkable external resemblance to what the now obliterated ridge at Stobcross on the Clyde once was. These, it may be yet farther observed, are all removed, both in Ayrshire and in Arran, to equal distances, varying from 20 to 300 paces inland, from the present shore line.

We cross now to Arran itself for corresponding etymological testimony, and find it if possible still clearer there. The whole South End of that Island, as hereafter more minutely will be described, is bounded by a parapet of bank formations obviously marine, broken here and there with rocky scaurs, and penetrated with deep and sometimes tortuous inlets. One of the deepest and most tortuous of these, with basins, straits, and shallows of its own, has been the little fiord, now only the water or burn of Lagg—girdled and floored with flat or jagged rocks, and scooped into bays at every sudden turn. These have all been converted by time and culture into romantic precipices or fruitful haughs, and an inn as beautiful and picturesque as any Alpine hospice might delude the unobservant tourist to believe that it had been always so. But the sea has been there, the very herds of Proteus have disported there, and ships from the ocean have been harboured there, if not within the memory of man, at least within the range of tradition by the people, and the limits of their spoken tongue at the present moment. In what is still the Lagg-burn below the inn was the ship's pool, or ship's ridge—*getthin-a-lang*, pronounced *getthin-a-loigh*—where a ship, sailing down with the tide from the harbour above, grounded in her passage on the point; and in the howe of Lagg, considerably above the inn, and now within or adjacent to the Glebe lands of Kilmorie, was the seals' pool, or *Lagg-an-roan*, where these amphibia, once common in the frith, and still to be met with occasionally about the Craig or on the rocks at Turnberry, used to bask in sunshine between the cliffs, or regale themselves on salmon in the shallows. " Names," says Rev. Mr. M'Bride, to whose valuable testimony we again recur, and who is no less distinguished as a Celtic scholar than as a geologist and antiquarian—who was, moreover, born at the manse of Kilmorie, and is intimately acquainted with every spot in the neighbourhood—" names have a wonderful vitality. They are, in fact, amphibious; water won't drown them, and they won't die for the want of it. . . At the era in question, I think there is proof that the valley through which that burn [the

Lagg-burn] flows, was a fiord to beyond the church of Kilmorie. Standing at the point where the road to the church and manse strikes off at right angles from the main road to Claonaidh, and looking down the valley towards Lagg, you look down upon an amphitheatre bounded on all sides by steep sloping braes and precipitous boulder clay cliffs; through which the river has cut its channel. That amphitheatre is a dead level, and very little above that of the sea—[10 or 20 feet, we suspect] and at the time that the valley of the Clyde was a fiord up to Bothwell, it was a saltwater loch communicating with the sea, through a narrow gorge at Lagg. The name of that amphitheatre is *Lagg-an-rean, i.e.* the seals' hollow or den. It was quite the sort of place that seals would choose to disport themselves in, when it was connected with the sea." Testimony so clear seems to be entirely conclusive, but we might stray round the whole island and collect similar evidence at every creek or from every headland, embodied in the very language of Ossian, or at least identified with the tongue of his people.

But if the Clyde was thus familiar as the ocean among the crevices of Arran, at a date when he might have lived and flourished, have we any evidence that the ocean was known as a lake or as a fiord at Bothwell, for example, or among the distant reaches of the Clyde, at the same period? This question is by no means of incidental, but of essential importance; for Arran, being not only an island, but evidently the scene of many a volcanic shock, might have been raised in the course of centuries above its original level, whilst the coast of the mainland adjacent, much more at the distance of seventy or eighty miles, remained unmoved; and thus the shore lines of the region might be different, although the level of the ocean was the same. But if the two extremes of that region, thus connected or contiguous by nature, shall be found connected also by human speech of the same type at the outermost limits of the level, then every point between them would be included as submerged at the same moment to a given line; every channel would be filled up to a given depth, every adjacent marsh would be flooded, and every lake and minor stream swallowed up within a given range, as part and parcel of a great inland sea:—and so far from being doubtful or deficient, the sort of evidence required is superabundant on the very point in question. "You are right," says Mr. M‘Bride again, referring to Letter No. I. of second series, on Navigation of the Clyde (p. 46), " in saying that in the days of Ossian the Clyde was a Loch at Rutherglen. In fact, the Clyde was then a fiord; Cambuslang was the Greenock of the Clyde, and Rutherglen the natural mole that formed the harbour. How prove this? *Cambus* means a bay, and *lang* a ship: *Ruth* is a point of land jutting out into the sea, *jar* [pronounce *eer*] is west, and *glen* a valley,—Ruth-er-glen, the point of the west valley. Cambuslang lies inosculated to the east of it, and protected by it from the wind blowing up the frith from the west. Under shelter of Rutherglen, vessels could lie in smooth water during westerly gales." Again, says our reverend and esteemed correspondent, "when returning last week [September, 1871] from Edinburgh, by the new line *via* Coatbridge, I observed, before passing the Clyde above Rutherglen, a station called Carmyle. Looking down the river towards Glasgow, the whole valley as far as the eye could reach, was a dead level. Now what is the meaning of Carmyle, or Garmyle? You will find the same name near Port-Glasgow, on the banks of the river; and again, in the Lough of Belfast. It is *Gear* short, and *Mull*, pronounced *Moyle*—which means a bare elevation, generally projecting seaward. Gear-myle, or Garmyle, is thus the Short-Mull, or elevated seaward projection [in the channel of the river, that is, which must then have been a sea.] Finally, the names of places in the strath or valley [of the Clyde] are Cymric, whilst those on the rising ground above it, and which before the elevation of the land formed the shore ground, are Gaelig—thus Renfrew is Cymric, whilst Rutherglen and Blantyre are Gaelig—the former on the *raised* ground, the latter on the *rising* ground behind and above it. All this shows that, during the Celtic era, the valley or strath of the Clyde was a fiord to above Bothwell-Bridge or at Blantyre; and that the rises of the land took place previous to the settlement of the Strath-Clyde Britons in the district"—that is, before Dumbarton or Dunbriton was occupied as a fortress, or at least received that name. To which it may be added, that opposite Renfrew, and about a mile and a half from the river as it now flows, is Garscadden, which is also Gaelig, and signifies the bight or enclosure of coarse herring; being a retreat between two hills, where that sort of fish must have spawned when the brine of the frith reached it. Whether the fish now peculiar to Loch-Lomond, and so much resembling a herring as to be called the fresh-water herring, is but the herring in reality, secluded and degenerate there since that old arm of the sea became a fresh-water lake, is uncertain; but as Loch-Lomond at its highest was but 20 feet above the level of the frith in 1772, and was then confined by frequent accumulations of earth and stones in the Leven, which Golborne the engineer proposed to cut through—see Pennant's *Tour in Scotland*, Vol. II.—and which might easily have prevented the escape of herring once left in the lake above, there is much probability in the conjecture. The lake, of course, would for some time retain its original saltness, and the fish might thus by degrees become adapted, both in constitution and in habits, to the change; on which supposition, the very existence of such a fish there, and nowhere else, is the clearest evidence that Loch-Lomond itself was once a part of the sea, and that its separation from the frith was by the rising of the intermediate land suddenly. But however this may be, certain it is, that *Sgadan* in the Gaelig—corrupted by Lowland tongues, as we see, to *Scadden*—is synonymous with *Sidon* or *Zidon* in the Phœnician dialect, being so pronounced; and that Sidon, or the City of herring—the Herring-town of Canaan, in fact—was so called from the multitudes of that fish caught there; and, notwithstanding all its maritime splendour, might well be associated with Tyre in its doom by the Prophet, that it should once more be reduced to its original obscurity, and become "a place for the spreading of nets," by the shore at least, if not "in the midst, of the sea:"—on which subject the reader is referred for much interesting information to the Epitome of ancient Irish History, from the *Chronicles of Eri*, in the Appendix. In the meantime, as incidental to our present inquiry, it may here be remarked, not only that Garscadden, or Garsgadan, among the hills on one side of the frith, must have been so called, when the site of Renfrew on the level ground opposite was submerged; but also that the most distinguished names associated by Ossian with Clutha or the Clyde have still permanent connection with the course of that river, and carry us up the stream for many miles beyond the limits of the present estuary, to the very line, and almost to the spot to which our geological researches conduct us. Thus Carthon, Cathmol, and Cathlin are personages of importance in Ossian's poems connected with the Clyde, and suggest without a moment's hesitation the Cart, Cathcart, and Cathkin.

IV. Only one additional argument under this head, but one which, from its peculiarity, may be thus separately classified, the Author thinks proper at present to introduce; and in so doing must premise that, although personally he believes much in its correctness, he does not rely on it in support of Ossian's authenticity, in any way other or farther than as a mere illustrative probability. It has already been suggested in connection with the marine formations at Stobcross and the immense deposits of sea sand there, that Sandyford as the name of a suburb in the neighbourhood of these deposits, and at a point where their extent as boundaries of the frith long ago would be most conspicuous, might be nothing more than a corruption of Sandy-fiord, indicating thus in its very origin, if correctly derived, both the character of the Clyde as a frith at the point in question, and the fact that Norwegian sailors, or pirates and adventurers—the Duthmocarglos of their day—may have visited its shores. He is aware that another derivation, purely local, may be suggested for this name—viz., that it indicated not a frith, but a *ford* in the neighbourhood. If so, then it may be replied, (1) that such ford must have been either in the Clyde or in the Kelvin. If in the Kelvin, no trace of any ford deserving the designation of Sandy is to be found in that river for miles around the spot in question, if any where in its course at all; and if in the Clyde, then the Clyde must have been almost as broad as a frith and as shallow as the Solway, at the time when such a ford as the Sandy-ford was recognisable there. (2) That it is not unreasonable to suppose that the name was originally Sandy-fiord, as now maintained; but that in process of time, as the river receded and a ford became possible, the name was corrupted, or purposely adapted to express the physical change which had occurred in the aspects and conditions of the place before the eyes of the inhabitants themselves. In verification of which, the testimony of an intelligent neutral witness, exactly one hundred years ago, may here be quoted—

"The city of Glasgow till very lately," says Pennant in 1772, "was perfectly tantalized with its river: the water was shallow, the channel much too wide for the usual quantity of water that flowed down, and the navigation interrupted by twelve remarkable shoals. The second inconveniency continually increased by the wearing away of the banks, caused by the prevalence of the South-west winds that blow here, and often with much violence, during more than half the year: thus what is got in breadth, is lost in depth; and shoals are formed by the loss of water in the more contracted bed. Spring-tides do not flow above three feet, or neap tides above one, at *Broomy-law-quay*, close to the town; so that in dry seasons lighters are detained there for several weeks, or are prevented from arriving there, to the great detriment of the city."—*Tour in Scotland*, Vol. II.

But such phenomena could never have occurred in any river which had not also been a frith, with decreasing water and a sandy bottom from side to side. Pennant's observations on the Clyde indeed, from Glasgow to Dumbarton, might be quoted with the greatest propriety in corroboration of all that has hitherto been advanced in these pages on the character of that river as a decaying fiord, if additional evidence was required; but it seems unnecessary farther. In any case, there must have been water there shallow enough to disclose the sand, or there could have been no passage with any such name at Sandyford.

The only point conceded here would be the presumed Scandinavian origin of the name itself; but that cannot be given up without farther argument in its favour. Such a name as Sandyford, or Sandy-fiord, is not confined to Glasgow or to Scotland. It may be found on the Norwegian coast at the present moment, as the name of a small seaport. In the custom-house entries at Grangemouth for March 17, 1872, as quoted in the daily papers, we find the term express— "Arrived, Henriette, from Sandy-fjord;" and for August 9th, same year, the name a little differently spelt—"Arrived, Draupner, Sandi-fjord." This Sandyfiord, as almost all northern names are, is doubtless a descriptive name, and if our Sandyford has, or ever had, a similar descriptive signification, its origin can no longer be doubtful. But is it possible, it may still be objected, that any Norwegian crew, ever landed or stranded in the Clyde, could bestow such a designation on the frith? It is not, at least, *im*possible. A Dutch crew, wrecked in the Forth, not only named but created the fishing port of Buckhaven in Fifeshire, and maintain by their descendants an exclusive sort of existence there till the present day, with much material prosperity; and the survivors of a war-ship's crew in the Armada, wrecked on the shore at Portincross on the Clyde, have left the impress of their features at least, and perhaps of their language also, among the population of that neighbourhood. The soldiers of Cromwell garrisoned at Inverness have bequeathed a purer dialect of English to the inhabitants of that town, by mixture with their own, than is to be found elsewhere in Great Britain, north or south. The people of the Orkneys and Shetlands deny that they are Scotch, and maintain a speech of their own in spite of public intercourse with us; whilst there is hardly a spot on the eastern coast of our Scottish mainland, where Danish and Norwegian appellations do not abound. Such considerations in this argument are not to be forgotten or ignored; but what is still more to the point, and almost conclusive, is that the first land visible in the frith, by which its whole extent westward may be measured, and where Norwegian pirates entering its waters might first disembark and reconnoitre—as, in point of fact, they did—is the Island of Sanda. It was their key to the navigation of a frith remarkable for sand through its whole extent, and was itself the Sanda or Sand-oe, the Island of the sandy [bay], the recognised landmark and resting place of their expeditions. In confirmation of the above theory, it has been ascertained that this island in Gaelig is called Evhan, or Avhen—Latinised by Buchanan, *Avena*—and contains an excellent harbour of refuge capable of accommodating sixty sail of considerable tonnage, hence called *Avena portuosa* by him in his history; and that *Sanda* is not a Gaelig, but a Scandinavian word, most probably applied to the island by Norwegian pirates, who were accustomed to take refuge or refit there before entering the frith for plunder. Such information, obtained subsequently to the Author's written theory on the subject, although not conclusive in itself, is at least strongly confirmatory of his views; which he would not now be quite inclined to surrender without the clearest evidence of their incorrectness. To pursue this inquiry a single step farther, he may also state that he does not by any means forget that Evhan is supposed to be but the corruption of *Havin*, another Norwegian or Danish term, signifying harbour—" *Sanda*, or *Avoyn* or Island of Harbours, so called," says Pennant, " from its being the station of the Danish fleets, while that nation possessed the Hebrides;" "the Dean of the Isles calls it *Avoyn* fra the armies of Denmark, callit in their leid, *Havin*," &c., which, if correct, would be an additional corroboration of his argument. But it seems equally possible, in his own opinion, that Evhan, Evhon, or Avoyn, is a double corruption of *I-thon* or Isle of the Waves—first by the Norwegians, who confounded that name with Havin, because the island itself was indeed their haven; and then by Buchanan or the Monks, who translated it from them *Avena*—all parties being alike unconscious of its original Celtic signification. On this point, however, and on the piratical uses of the island as referred to by Ossian, much more will hereafter require to be said. For the present, and in conclusion of our etymological researches, it may be sufficient to observe, that Ossian is presumably the oldest, if not the only extant authority, from whom we derive any consistent information at the date supposed with respect to these Norwegian allies or invaders. In his poems, their otherwise pre-historic expeditions and achievements are either directly described or referred to; and it is impossible to understand, or at least to enjoy the continuity of his recitals, on any other hypothesis.

In addition to the more strictly scientific proofs, geological and etymological, which have just been submitted to the reader, others of an antiquarian order, equally valuable, might still be cited in corroboration of our fundamental theory as to the levels of the Clyde; but as these are more numerous, and interwoven more intimately both with the letter of the text and with the critical investigation of its authenticity, we shall reserve them to be adduced as circumstances require, for the elucidation of the subject.

## CHAPTER IV.

**NAVIGATION OF THE CLYDE—LETTERS OF FIRST SERIES, WITH ADDITIONS.**

In proceeding now more directly to the question of Ossian's authenticity, the Author thinks it advisable to follow the order of discussion in which the theory was first suggested to him, by quoting the substance of certain Letters of his own which appeared in a local paper, with such additional remarks or slight adaptations, here and there, as have been since found necessary to carry out, or to complete the argument.

The first of these letters, occasioned by a review of the late elegant valuable edition and retranslation of Ossian by the Rev. Archibald Clerk, of Kilmallie, is as follows :—

ELMGROVE PLACE, *March* 23, 1871.

SIR,—I observe, by two notices in [your columns] lately, that a new translation of "Ossian," by the Rev. Mr. Clerk, of Kilmallie, at the instance of so distinguished a patron as the Marquis of Bute, has just appeared, and, from what your reviewer admits, I presume the work has much to recommend it. Being no Gaelig scholar, I cannot pretend to be a judge of the comparative accuracy of the old and new translations, but I am glad that the appearance of the new version has revived the question of Ossian's authenticity. For my own part, I am a believer in that authenticity by instinct, much in the same way as I should believe in the authenticity of the Gospels, whatever MM. Strauss and Renan might advance to impugn them. The "Sermon on the Mount" and the "Lord's Prayer" are out of our reach. No man now living, or that has lived since the days of Christ, could have written, spoken, or imagined these. They go utterly beyond our poor modern patchwork existence, and, like all true words of God, take the universe in. On the same principle, although the subject matter be entirely different, I would rely on the authenticity of Ossian, whatever Dr. Johnson and his supporters might think or say to the contrary. Neither MacPherson, nor any man that has lived for the last thousand or fifteen hundred years, could have fabricated such poems. As good or better, of a different sort, men may have written in the interval, but not of the same sort. The tone, the character, the construction of the poems themselves; their lofty, unequivocal humanity; the pure morality, the childlike tenderness and pathos, the inartistic yet consummate art, the condensed and comprehensive action; the grand glowing figures, borrowed in a mass from earth and sky, before carbon and sewage had infected them or dimmed their glory; and the unique phraseology, possible only when the law of public speech was that of few words and well chosen, which pervades them all, testify so plainly to primitive conditions of life, of manners, and of moral principles in their author, that the reader must be as the owl at mid-day who can seriously doubt them. Nothing tenderer than the death of Carthon can be imagined, but it belongs not to these later ages of ours at all; nothing sublimer than the "Address to the Sun" has yet been discovered in Milton, Shakespear, or Homer—I might even say in Moses, if it were not likely to be misunderstood. But why should we not frankly avow what is manifest? Yet there are men who will call Moses himself and Homer, as well as Ossian, forgeries, in these days of the higher critical analysis!

Hateful Twaddle

There is evidence, however, of a plainer sort on the very page, which may be more conclusive to many of your readers than the questionable oracle of instinct to which I am content to appeal; and as it is connected in more than one instance with the Clyde, perhaps you will allow me space enough in this, and, if required, in another letter, to quote it. There are at least four poems in which the Clyde is referred to, and in three of them the condition of the Clyde, as a navigable river, is indirectly illustrated. *Carthon* is one of these. About twenty years before the story begins, Clessammor in his "bounding ship" was driven by a storm into the frith, and took refuge at Balclutha, on the river. That Balclutha was on the very stream of the Clyde is obvious, for its ruins "removed the river from its place;" and that it was immediately below some lofty ridge is also obvious, for the people "fled along the hill" in the day of its overthrow. But it was also near enough the sea, or the sea came near enough to it to be distinctly visible, for Clessammor "plunged into the stream of Clutha" in his flight, yet his "white sails rose over the waves, and he bounded on the dark blue sea," at the same moment. Balclutha, then, was either where Dunglass now stands—or far above Dunglass. But what is of more consequence for the present is, that the river was then navigated by ships, and that ships also were constructed on its margin; for when the poem begins, Carthon, the young king of Balclutha, appears with a whole fleet of war vessels on the coast of Morven to avenge his grandfather's wrongs. These ships of his, therefore, whatever they were—galleys or canoes—must have been built or congregated in the very bight of the river at Bowling. That such ships were capable of carrying considerable sail, and of making long and dangerous voyages, is plain enough from scores of passages in Ossian; that the canvas they carried was square, and slung equally before the wind, is also plain, for when "the wind roared behind them," they were always at its mercy, and when it met them ahead, they could never tack. "Often did I turn my ship," says Clessammor (to get back to Balclutha for his bride), "but the winds of the east prevailed." From such indications, we may conclude fairly enough that these "dark-bosomed, bounding ships" were but long canoes, and unmanageable almost except before the wind—although swift enough then.

But the mode of their construction on the western coast, four or five generations before Ossian's own time, is minutely detailed by him in another poem of more historic importance than *Carthon*. One of the aged bards in *Temora*, describing the first voyage of the Bolgae, or Belgae, into Ireland from the British coast of Inis-huna, in "the times of his fathers," is made to say of Larthon, the chief of Inis-huna, "He mounts the wave on his own dark oak, in Cluba's ridgy bay. That oak which he cut from Lumon to bound along the sea. The maids turned their eyes away, lest the king should be lowly laid, for never had they seen a ship, dark rider of the wave." This might have been some three or four hundred years before Carthon's time; but in Carthon's own time these very ships, "dark riders of the wave," were as numerous on the Clyde, between Renfrew and Dumbarton, as fishing boats or skiffs now are in the harbour at Greenock. Now, I need hardly remind your readers, Mr. Editor, that specimens of such simple craft were disinterred only the other summer from the silt of the river in the deepening operations at Erskine, and no doubt many more might be found in that neighbourhood, if we had occasion to look for them. Another sort of marine architecture has since superseded all these, and several sorts of shipbuilding have doubtless intervened and superseded one another on the Clyde, between the date of their construction and that of the "Black Prince" or the

E

"Iona," but there they once were undoubtedly, equipped and manned. So also have myrtles, and laurels, and fuchsias, and rhododendrons, and araucarias, and crystal palaces with rare exotics, by a process the very reverse, superseded the magnificent oaks which were then grander and more numerous along the banks of the Clyde, in Ayrshire, in Argyllshire, and throughout the Hebrides, than their decaying remains still are in the forest of Cadzow; and another population, too, has superseded the men and women of those days, who, if they were alive again, would have no need to fear comparison with us; and it is just within the limits of possibility that MacPherson, or somebody else shrewd enough, might imagine all this, and people the Clyde at random with fleets of ships and hosts of heroes, by a grand poetical forgery in Ossian's name; but by what conceivable chance did he congregate this fleet in Bowling Bay, or sink those canoes at Erskine more than a hundred years before they were discovered on the very spot?

In continuation of these remarks, but before any additional geological or other evidence had been procured, which would have enabled the writer to assert his position and extend his views with much greater confidence, the following letter by him, founded entirely on antiquarian discoveries and on the text of Ossian himself as represented by MacPherson, appeared:—

ELMGROVE PLACE, *March* 27, 1871.

SIR,—Resuming the question of navigation on the Clyde according to Ossian, as bearing on the ulterior question of his own authenticity, I shall enumerate, in the first place, the several instances of passage beyond the limits of the Frith into the Western Ocean narrated by him, and then consider what these imply, or how they can be accounted for.

1. There is the drift of Clessammor in his own ship alone into the river Clyde, as we have seen, and his escape thence to the Hebrides again by sea; and twenty years afterwards the invasion of Morven with a fleet by Carthon:—"We beheld the distant fleet. Like the mist of ocean they came, and poured their youth upon the coast." If the accepted interpretation of Ossian's geography be correct, this fleet, when it was seen from Cona, must have been somewhere on the Appin coast, at the confluence of Loch-Linnhe and Loch-Leven.

2. In *Colna-Dona*, old Carul of Col-amon tells us he pursued Duthmocarglos, "a dweller of ocean's wind"—which seems to mean a pirate of the channel—from "Clutha's winding waters" along the sea, till night deceived him on the deep, and he sailed on unconscious of his route till he came to Fingal's palace at Selma. Being a native of what we now call Stirlingshire, he was comparatively ignorant of the Clyde, and hence his unexpected betrayal.

3. In *Cathlin of Clutha*, Duthcarmor, another pirate of the channel, murders "Cathmol of Clutha, by the winding of his own dark streams," and carries off Cathlin, his daughter, to the Bay of Cluba, on the west coast, by night, whence she escapes in disguise, and comes in a solitary ship to Morven as a suppliant to Fingal, the recognised redresser of all wrongs, for help and revenge.

4. In *Calthon and Colmal*, we have yet another suppliant in disguise, but accompanied by her lover. They come all the way together from Balteutha, on the Tweed, to Selma, in the Hebrides, for help to redeem a brother from impending death. Such help is accorded by Fingal, under the guidance of his son Ossian, and they return to the rescue, but in vain. This is by far the most extraordinary journey of them all, and must be looked at separately for a moment. How did these young persons travel? By Nithsdale to the Ayrshire coast, and thence by ship to Morven? Or by Clydesdale to the frith, and so by ship, or otherwise, to their destination? By Clydesdale most probably, inasmuch as the youth had been born and still had friends residing there. How, then, as to the frith? It must either have been by ship, round the Mull of Cantyre, or partly by ship and partly by land, as at Tarbert on Loch-Fyne, or by some shorter sea passage, as we shall immediately inquire. But in whatever way, if Teutha were the Tweed, as it seems to be, the expedition is almost incredible, and might tempt one to reject the whole story as a fabrication. Yet it can be no fabrication, for two obvious reasons—First, that a journey so absolutely improbable would never have been forged by any one who knew the region, without an explanation or apology interwoven; witchcraft, or some miraculous agency, would certainly have been employed to facilitate the action, or at least the nearest way pointed out. Storytellers of the Middle Ages, or the mock-heroic Gaelig bards of Ireland, who claimed to be the rivals of Ossian, would not have been able to move a step without such help. Scott himself, in the region of avowed romance, would not have ventured on such an episode otherwise; Dick Turpin's celebrated ride to York does not come up to it. But not a word of explanation, nor the slightest hint of the conveyance required, is vouchsafed. Second, in a forgery, the destined victim for whose relief the expedition was undertaken would certainly have been spared and delivered; but he dies an inevitable death, in sight of the very friends who come to relieve him. To these we may add a third, as regards MacPherson himself, viz., that if he was the author of the forgery, he might have redeemed it from such extravagance by explaining that Teutha was the Teith and not the Tweed; yet he expressly identifies the name with that of the border river. The journey of these two suppliants, then, still remains to be accounted for. To suppose that from the Clyde they went round Cantyre, and so north to the Hebrides, and that Ossian returned with them by the same route, when life and

death depended on their expedition, is absurd ; and to suppose that a girl clad in armour, and dragging a useless spear behind her, could traverse such a distance, through moors and over mountains, wholly on foot, is worse than absurd. The wanderers took ship undoubtedly much higher up the Clyde than Dumbarton, much higher even than Glasgow, and found a swifter and an easier passage somehow to Selma than by the Mull of Cantyre.

But, at this point, it is now proper to observe that no explanation whatever is vouchsafed concerning any of these voyages, more than concerning that from the Tweed. The travellers all come and go as if there was no mystery of any kind about their motions, but everybody then living understood distinctly how their passage was made. " By Tarbert and Loch-Fyne, of course," the reader will exclaim ; " there could be no other way ; and their ships would be hauled across the isthmus, as the fishermen of later ages hauled their boats." But that could not be the route in every case. Old Carul, pursuing Duthmocarglos, and deceived by darkness in the frith, sailed on without knowing it to Morven. Did he follow Duthmocarglos, then, from Rutherglen or Renfrew, to Stranraer in a single day, and, there losing sight of him, double the opposite headland, and so, through all the perils of a night voyage among the Hebrides, to Selma ? The possibility of such an involuntary cruise cannot be denied, but it seems highly improbable. Is it not more likely that Duthmocarglos, being a " dweller of the ocean wind," and well acquainted with every turn of the Clyde, misled his pursuer about the Cumbraes or among the Kyles of Bute; where, getting involved in the shades of night, the East Country man would be hopelessly entangled in Loch-Fyne, and, by some natural exit, no longer existing, drift westward and northward, keeping always on the coast, till he got finally embayed at Morven ? But what natural exit could there be that would account for this? None certainly to MacPherson's knowledge, or to the knowledge of any poetical impostor within the last 500 years, or he would assuredly have named it. Yet it was not impossible by any means at the supposed date in question, as I shall now endeavour to suggest.

1. The Clyde is called by Ossian invariably the "streamy," or the "winding," or the " dark winding Clyde," and once indirectly, as to its banks, the "rushy;" not so much because it received more tributaries than any other large river known to him, as because the stream itself was divided into many tortuous branches, and the current lost in lakes. This we know was the character of the Clyde within the memory of man. From Erskine to Govan it was little better than a tidal marsh full of reeds and rushes, with currents obscurely flowing among considerable islands, on which flocks of sea-gull hovered and settled. Ships before that were built at Renfrew on the old main branch of the Clyde, now a stagnant ditch ; and so close to the houses there, that a vessel once swerving on

the stocks, her bowsprit or yard broke a window in the manse—a curious tradition, which I have no doubt is correct, having heard it in detail from a former minister of that parish. At all events, county maps, so late as the beginning of the century, give the Clyde as an estuary up to Glasgow, and the Cart as a smaller estuary up to Paisley; and I have been informed that certain older maps (which, however, I have not seen) give the appearance of an estuary to the Clyde as far south-west as Loch-Winnoch, and that in these the Gryfe, or Black Cart water, totally disappears. In confirmation of all which, I may remind your readers that a canoe, similar to those at Erskine, was disinterred some years ago near the foot of the Saltmarket in this city.

2. In connection with these facts, it is obvious that the whole lower grounds on which Glasgow now stands, with the Fleshers' Haugh, and even much of the High Green, must have been, at no very remote historical date, under water. Dumbarton rock, a thousand or fifteen hundred years ago, must have been entirely insulated, with the river Leven like another frith on its eastern side, and the sea "rolling darkly blue," as Ossian describes it, from where the church at Cardross now stands to the opposite cliffs at Langbank, or even higher, when the town of Dumbarton would be nowhere, and Balclutha was on the sides of Dumbuck. If so, and we have no reason to doubt it, then there was corresponding breadth and depth of water in the Gareloch, in the Holy-Loch, and Loch-Fyne. Certain it is, that in the glacial period icebergs with their load of boulders, like crystal decanters with a cargo of pebbles, were afloat in the Gareloch. I have myself counted not fewer than 90 of these huge blocks in a mass together—the burden, doubtless, of some iceberg which had swung in from the south-east, and grounded above Fernicarie. In those days the ridge between the Gareloch and Loch-Long would be a mere step, and the moor at Poltalloch, through which the Crinan Canal now runs, between Lochgilphead and the Western Ocean, would be deep and quiet water. I am far from imagining that the poems of Ossian have any such remote antiquity, or that Scotland was so far submerged in his day. Historical and geological epochs are not to be confounded. But your readers will please observe at the same time, that at whatever period the sea began to retire, the low land between Lochgilphead and the Western Ocean would be longest under water, and, for anything we know to the contrary, might have been quite navigable for canoes or ships scooped from trunks of oak, in the days of Ossian and Fingal. Without absolutely affirming that this was so, I may at least suppose it is not beyond the bounds of credibility in connection with known facts; and then every apparent contradiction or improbability in Ossian, of the kind now in question, is explained. He was under no necessity to describe a voyage which all men at that time knew as well as tourists now know the most

celebrated route to Oban; and no insurmountable difficulty remains in reconciling his narratives. By this route, Carthon could have reached Loch-Linnhe with all his fleet in comparative ease and safety, and still seem to have come from the ocean; Carul might have drifted through it in a night without danger, to the shore at Selma; and Calthon and Colmal could reach Morven sooner from the Tweed by that line than by any other, more especially if they took ship above Glasgow.

3. Perhaps I may be demanding too much in all this, for the actual levels are not before me for the required depth of water at Lochgilphead or Tarbert. If so, the theory must be abandoned, and the voyagers allowed to make their own way by Cantyre. On the other hand, if there was no real Ossian, but only James MacPherson, at the age of twenty, to contrive the whole, then he must have been not only a poet such as men have never seen, but a geologist far in advance of his own day, and a craftsman in soothsaying beyond all precedent, to attempt such a series of fabrications, with the geography of Scotland and of the Clyde in particular, before him, as it was in 1760, without so much as one syllable of explanation on his own part, or one fragment of contrivance—the easiest thing in the world—to reconcile or recommend them. And if MacPherson did not thus invent, certainly no man for five hundred years before him could; and the farther back always the more impossible, till we reach an epoch in which the geology and the geography, the water and the wood, the history and the native inspirations of the country coincided. Truth, then, required no explanation, and poetry, like the subject, sprung spontaneous from the soil. About the actual date of Ossian, however, I say nothing; or about the possibility of interpolations here and there, of a word or a line, which may be admitted without affecting the authenticity of the whole. MacPherson himself gives the middle of the third century as the proximate date; but from all that appears on the surface, except in an isolated passage which may possibly be an interpolation, it might be even beyond that.

The reader is now aware, from what has already been advanced under the head of Geology in preceding Chapters, how satisfactorily all this question of ocean levels in the Clyde has been established. Many additional proofs, if required, might easily be quoted in support of it—especially as to the tidal flow of lochs connected with the frith, such as the Holy-Loch, Loch-Goil, Loch-Long, and Loch-Fyne, all similar to Loch-Gilp. Loch-Long, for example, at no very remote period, must have been deep water a mile and more beyond the high-way at Arrochar; where an alluvial deposit of vegetable matter, of which the strata can still be counted, lies plainly extended as a beautiful valley, from 15 to 36 inches deep of soil on the old bed of the sea. The only point requiring farther consideration is the precise locality of Balclutha. Some plausible, if not convincing, reasons from the text will by and by be adduced, to show that it was even as high up as Rutherglen; but as such an assumption for the present might seem extravagant, that ruined fortress may be left, as hypothetically suggested, about or above Dumbuck; and the reader may be well assured it could not have been lower on the frith. It should also be observed that, although Renfrew is quoted in the preceding letters, as a limit or point of departure, the word is only used as a well-known name to indicate a neighbourhood; for Renfrew itself, as we have seen, could not then exist—the very site where it now stands being, at the date in question, deep under water. In the interval, however, and whilst the argument was still in this hypothetical condition, a correspondent in the same paper, who signed himself "Saxo," thought proper to object to it in specific terms. That gentleman's communication will be found in Appendix; but for the benefit of readers now who may entertain similar doubts on the subject, and by way of anticipating such objections once for all on the threshold of inquiry, as much of the Author's reply as seems necessary for that purpose is subjoined, with which the present chapter on the Navigation of the Clyde at the date supposed may conclude :—

ELMGROVE PLACE, *April* 4, 1871.

SIR,— . . . Your correspondent ["Saxo"] in his letter of the 28th ult., honours me by summarising the whole of my first communication under two heads, [of which he] scouts the one and ridicules the other. To take the slightest of these matters, then, first. I did not make the building or the finding of canoes on the Clyde a superior argument to that of instinct in the case, but entirely supplementary for the benefit of others, as your correspondent, if he chooses, may see. Nor was it the building or finding of canoes at random—here, there, or anywhere —on which I relied; but their proved construction exactly as Ossian describes it, and their recent discovery on the very spot on which, according to Ossian, they should be found—such discovery being more than a hundred years since the publication of his reputed poems. This, I maintain, is corroborative evidence in support of my instinctive faith in his authenticity, whatever your correspondent may think to the contrary; and yet my faith in that authenticity would have been just as firm, although no such discovery had occurred. Further, under this head, the gentleman refers to some canoe with a " cork plug in the bottom " as having been found, he believes, in MacPherson's day, and which, according to Mr. Geikie, " must have come from the latitudes of Spain, southern France, or Italy," from which he seems to infer that there could be no such boat-building on the Clyde as Ossian describes, or his reference to such a boat at all is quite irrelevant. Now, suppose I took it in my head to say that the canoe in question with its " cork plug " came from Carthage, or from Tyre or Sidon, or was picked up on the way by Phœnicians in their passage through the Mediterranean to the coast of Cornwall, could the gentleman disprove that? If not, will he be frank enough to admit it? Then thereby, whether he admits it or no, hangs another theory of mine about the antiquity of Ossian, with which, however, I shall not for the present annoy him. Again, because a stone hatchet was found in a third canoe, your correspondent infers that the people of that day knew nothing of the metals, and, therefore, Ossian from beginning to end must be an imposture; which is rather precipitate logic for one who talks with an air about " syllogistic forms," &c. I might as well say that, because the Egyptians long ago used a sharp Ethiopic stone in their embalming process, where a modern operator would certainly employ the finest scalpel, they knew nothing of knives; or because the Caledonians preferred shells for drinking at their feasts, they had no other festive gear. In short, there is no end to such absurd argumentation; because neither hammer nor axe was heard at the building of Solomon's Temple, the Jews knew nothing of such implements! But the multiplication of " celts " has been such a sore subject for antiquaries lately—almost as bad, I am told, as the "*Prætorium*" at Kinprunes and the " lang ladle "—that I shall not press it more directly. At the same time, I would like to know how trees, sufficiently large for canoes, were felled in those days, for the process requires consideration; and that implements of some kind were used we learn incidentally from Ossian, who, when such implements were awanting for a similar purpose, " tore an oak from its hill, and raised a flame on high." If MacPherson was an impostor, therefore, he must have seen the difficulty.

But with respect to the foundation of my faith in the authenticity of Ossian, which is so ridiculous in your correspondent's eyes, I need hardly explain to anybody but himself, that by instinct in such a case I mean moral instinct or intuition; which may be called intellectual or even critical, according to its exercise or cultivation—mere animal instinct, surely, for either prose or poetry, being quite out of the question here. Is there no such faculty, then, in the human soul as the power of discerning between good and evil, or between true and false, real or unreal, in its own creations? According to your correspondent himself, the higher moral qualities so obvious in the poems of Ossian are proofs of their falsehood, since no such qualities could have been known among untutored savages—robbers of cattle and stealers of wives—before the promulgation of Christianity. How, then, did Dr. Johnson, or your correspondent, or anybody else, discover this, if not by the very faculty to which I refer, only exerted through a medium of prejudice and suspicion? They seem to see a want of harmony or truthfulness there, which nothing but some instinct in themselves could discover. " Could such purity and tenderness," they cry, " come out of a heathen Highland Nazareth?" To which I can only answer, that the Gospel came out of Nazareth itself. Besides, it does not follow that everybody in Ossian's day was like Ossian. On the contrary, both heroes and heroines of his receive more than half their poetical grandeur from him; which, however, is an entirely different question from that of his authenticity. But the objection itself, founded on the superior morals of Christendom, is surely most unfortunate in an age when the morality of our largest Christian communities has become a scandal to Christ; and when the revelations of the race-course, the Divorce Court, and the Stock Exchange (established, one may say, in the very heart of the Church), seem to be actually annihilating all Christianity. What would Caractacus and Boadicea respectively think of some of their own descendants in 1871? But my instinct, your correspondent will persist, enables me to determine authenticity and antiquity together; proximately, why not? There are interpolated lines in Homer—what led any man first to suspect them? Emendations are being made every day on our highest classic authors—what can justify any scholar in suggesting these? The unity of Homer has been impugned—what discerning faculty in any critic of his originated this doubt? If the text in such cases had been uniform, natural, and clear, the instinct of suspicion could never have been roused, and the idea of interpolation or improvement would have been scouted as impertinent and insane. To carry the argument still higher, there are said to be fictitious Gospels, spurious dialogues of Plato, patchwork plays of Shakespear; and to demonstrate the unreliable character of such works may, perhaps, require elaborate critical analysis—but what first suggested doubts of their reliability? Had the works in question been in absolute conformity of thought and diction with the ascertained originals of their respective alleged or reputed authors, the natural instinct of every reader would have confirmed them, and no intermeddling critical authority on earth would be allowed to displace them, false and all as they might be, but on one condition—the accidental discovery of their falsehood as an undeniable matter of fact; with which reason, however, on which your correspondent depends, could have nothing to do, and which would be resisted to the uttermost by every intelligent reader as perhaps a worse imposture. Where such evidence is allowable at all, is only where the subject is suspicious; and where such suspicion is very clear and strong, no evidence whatever may be required. The "Titus Andronicus," for example, was that play as it now stands the work of Shakespear? Assuredly not. How do I know? How does any man know? How did a child of nine years old like Robert Burns, when the reading of that play convulsed him with rage, and he threatened to throw the book in the fire if it was not taken out of the house—I say, how did this child know, but by instinct, that the work was horrible, which nothing a man like William Shake-

F

spear ever wrote could be? Critical inquiry may have confirmed this judgment or not, but independently of all such inquiry the testimony of the soul is against that work; it can no more be Shakespear's own, as it stands, than a pinchbeck sovereign tainted with verdigris, or a pewter shilling, can be the coinage of the mint. On the same principle, false Gospels are consigned to oblivion; and spurious dialogues, and letters, and epistles, from their own inherent inferiority, are discarded. Why, then, on this principle also, but applied in the opposite direction, should I not accept with confidence, as upon the whole genuine, what has been presented to the world in the name of Ossian, when my critical instinct warrants me? All men may not have the same faculty of judging, or they may not cultivate it, which is a matter, I think, to be much regretted, even for their own sakes. On the other hand, the faculty in myself may be over-cultivated, too much relied upon, perhaps, and therefore apt to mislead me in a case like this—a possibility which I do not deny; but the burden of such an admission does not rest with me. Those who deliberately accuse MacPherson of falsehood; who cannot see, or do not choose to see, the inherent harmony and splendour of Ossian, and then denounce the whole as an impudent forgery in face of the translator's reiterated protest—these are the judges who, in common course of logical law, are bound to produce their proofs.

It may be allowable for the writer now to state, in conclusion of this incidental matter, that he adheres, if possible, with more assured confidence than ever to the truth of these views and principles as regards both Ossian, Moses, and the Gospels. No genuine work of God or man, he firmly believes, can be long or ultimately mistaken. Local newspapers and their correspondents may, and often do, err, but nature in her witness-bearing cannot.

**END OF PART FIRST.**

## Part Second.

# GEOGRAPHICAL, TRADITIONAL,
### AND
# ANTIQUARIAN.

# CONTENTS.

PAGE

CHAPTER I.—Revelations in Island of Arran—Letters of Second Series to Press—Arran and Loch-Fyne—Headquarters of Fingal between Morven and Ullin—Sepulchral Mounds on South Shore of Arran—Ossian's Tomb—Final Measurements and Details of, at Clachaig, ... ... ... ... ... ... ... ... 45

CHAPTER II.—Revelations in Arran continued—Letters of Second Series continued—Poem of *Berrathon* illustrated—Heart-shaped Cromlech—Malvina's Grave, Drumadoon—Theory of Immortality by Fire—Traditions of Malvina's Death in Neighbourhood, ... ... ... ... ... ... ... ... 59

CHAPTER III.—Revelations in Arran continued—Simplicity of the People—Mixing-up of Irish Fables with the Text of Ossian—Burial of Oscar—Anticipations of Malvina's Death in *Croma*—Particulars of Oscar's Interment—Measurement of his Grave, ... ... ... ... ... ... ... ... ... 73
    Note in Reply to Laing, on Malvina's identity ... ... ... ... ... ... ... 84

CHAPTER IV.—Revelations in Arran concluded—Fingal's Grave—Claims of other Sites, as at Killin, considered—Traditions of his Death at Carriefiun, hence so-called—His Age and Circumstances at the time—Graves of his Kindred, ... ... ... ... ... ... ... ... ... ... ... 85

## ILLUSTRATIONS.

| | |
|---|---:|
| OSSIAN'S TOMB, Ground Plan, ... ... ... ... ... | 54 |
| OSSIAN'S TOMB, View of, with Ailsa Craig in the distance, ... | 57 |
| RONAN'S CAVE, now King's Cove, ... ... ... ... | 63 |
| TORLUTHA, now DRUMADOON, from the North ... ... | 67 |
| MAP OF ARRAN, South End, ... ... ... ... ... | 72 |
| OSCAR'S GRAVE, Ground Plan, ... ... ... ... ... | 81 |
| OSCAR'S GRAVE—MALVINA'S GRAVE, ... ... ... | 83 |
| FINGAL'S GRAVE, looking North, ... ... ... ... | 89 |
| FINGAL'S GRAVE, looking South, ... ... ... ... | 91 |
| GUIDE to FINGAL'S GRAVE, ... ... ... ... ... | 96 |

# ISLAND OF ARRAN.

## CHAPTER I.

**REVELATIONS IN THE ISLAND OF ARRAN—LETTERS OF SECOND SERIES.**

In the month of July succeeding the date of this correspondence, the Author had the pleasure of visiting in his holidays the Island of Arran, where revelations in geology, in monumental reliqnes, and in tradition, affecting the authenticity of Ossian, were afforded him of so striking a character as both to confirm and enlarge all his previous convictions on the subject. These, so far as they could then with certainty be embodied, he communicated to the public, in a Second Series of Letters through the local press; from which he now makes the following extracts, omitting or postponing, where indicated, only a few sentences already anticipated, or requiring to be slightly remodelled in harmony with subsequent discoveries.

ELMGROVE PLACE, *August* 25, 1871.

SIR,—When I last addressed you on this subject I had no idea of recurring to it again. Since that date, however, a good deal of additional information has accumulated in my hands; and as much of it has been obtained by personal observation or inquiry on the spot during some weeks' late residence in Arran, and so far as I am aware is entirely new to the public, I have to beg the favour of space for a letter or two to make the facts known. The supplementary evidence of Ossian's authenticity thus acquired may be divided into geographical, traditional, and antiquarian, and to present the whole as distinctly as possible to your readers, I shall make a corresponding allotment of these communications. For the present, therefore, and by way of introduction to what follows, I shall confine myself exclusively to the new geographical evidence in support of my own previous argument, which, as some of your readers may remember, was to the effect that there might possibly have been in Ossian's day a passage by sea at flood-tide between Lochgilphead and the Western Ocean, and that this was the line of communication for Fingal and his heroes between Morven and the Clyde.

The lower or extreme south end of Arran, as many of your readers are doubtless aware, distinguished from the other or higher end, is a large irregular plain, bounded east and west from Struey to Corrycraivy by considerable ridges, intersected here and there with small ravines or water courses, and terminating seaward in a steep grassy bank or parapet, broken with an occasional cliff, but so uniform for the most part where it follows the shore, that it might be defined and measured to a hand's breath. This may be said to extend from Whiting Bay to King's Cove, except where a shallow or a promontory intervenes, and was the original sea-line of the island. Where the small rivers debouch, the parapet follows them up equally on both sides, as at Lagg and Sliddery, till it dies away in the interior; and from river to river there are now fertile fields between the parapet and the shore, partly formed by alluvial deposits, doubtless, from the rivers themselves, but chiefly by the subsiding of the sea. Nearly the whole of the extensive district thus defined was at one time covered with magnificent wood, including oaks of the highest growth, of which remains are still found in the mosses, and the little rivers must have been navigable as estuaries for at least a mile inwards from the shore. All this, of course, is now changed. Not an old tree worth speaking of is to be met with in the whole lower end of the island, and the rivers, except in winter, are fordable on foot close to their very junction with the sea. How long, then, is it since these changes occurred? There were woods all around in the days of Robert Bruce, and even much later. From Corrycraivy to Struey, a distance of some eight or ten miles, was an uninterrupted forest of trees so numerous and large as to have been celebrated in a proverb. Climate, cultivation, and natural decay may have removed all these; but such causes could not affect the rivers and the shore. How long have their channels been lessening, and the shore beyond them extending? The change has no doubt been gradual, but the date of its ascertained progress is by no means so remote as your readers may suppose. . . . Five hundred years ago, or less [as detailed in Part First, Chap. I., p. 10, and IV., pp. 24, 37,] the sea would be nearly up to the parapet already spoken of; a thousand years ago, these rivers would be little estuaries; fifteen hundred or two thousand years ago, South Arran would be far intersected with narrow lochs. Flood-tide, then, on the shore at Arran would make the Clyde like a lake at Rutherglen, and might even carry a canoe with ease over the level lands between Lochgilphead and the Western Ocean; and so the most formidable geographical difficulties in Ossian, as in former letters I endeavoured to show, may be explained.

But is there any evidence that this line of communication with the North Hebrides was ever so employed? Those who are at all familiar with the remains and traditions of antiquity in Arran, more especially on the south-west side of it, will require no details from me to remind them that Fingal's name and Fingal's exploits, and the exploits of Fingal's following, dogs and heroes, are associated with almost every cairn, monolith, and circle. No guide-book to Arran would be complete without some mention of these. But there is one in particular, having no special reference to tides or sea lines, and therefore all the more important in its circumstantial bearing, to which, in support of my present argument, I must direct attention. Your readers may be aware that two of Fingal's most conspicuous enterprises were certain expeditions to the North of Ireland to assist his allies there. Now, a voyage to Ireland from Morven by the outer channel in the open sea, or with a rest for refitting at Islay, if required, would be indisputably the most natural, indeed the only imaginable course, unless an easier or a safer passage was known by the inland lakes; and what are the traditional facts of the case? In Headrick's *Arran*, in a letter from the Rev. John Stewart, Kilbride, dated January, 1805, we have the following statement :—" It is believed here that Fingal took Arran for a resting-place on his going to assist his allies in Ireland, having come down Loch-Fyne in boats or birlings. He landed at Machrie, where there was a fine natural harbour, which I showed you, and resided in the Coves on Drumadoon shore. . . . On Fingal's returning from Ireland, he spent some considerable time in hunting." Here, then, are two distinct occasions, going and coming, on which Fingal must have used the passage by Loch-Fyne. But he might have had his boats carried over from Crinan to Lochgilphead. Of course, he might; but with the open sea before him to the west, was this conceivable? Or he might have had two fleets—one at Crinan and another at Lochgilphead, and could march from the one to the other. If so, he must have been well supplied with supernumerary transports, and fonder of transhipments than most modern commanders would be, when a straight course, with a favourable breeze, would have carried him to Ireland in half the time. Or finally, what did the people of Arran in the last century know about the matter at all? Perhaps this tradition was invented to bolster up MacPherson's forgery? This latter supposition is just as likely as that Mr. Stewart's letter in 1805 was invented to support my theory in 1871; but another quotation from the same volume, which, on account of its peculiar interest, I shall give entire, will not only satisfy your readers on that subject, but settle the question of Ossian's authenticity itself, it may be hoped, beyond further dispute. Says Rev. Dr. M'Kinnon, under same date, in reply to Dr. Johnson's objection that there was not a book in the Gaelig language an hundred years old—" The good Doctor should have been better informed before he ventured to make such an assertion, for in the Duke of Argyll's library at Inveraray there is a book, elegantly printed in the Gaelic language, as early as the year 1567; and in the 19th page of that book, the author, Mr. John Carsuel, superintendent of the clergy in Argyllshire, laments, with pious sorrow, that the generality of the people under his pastoral care were so much occupied in singing and repeating the songs of their old bards, particularly those that celebrated the valorous deeds of Fingal and his heroes, that they entirely neglected the Scriptures and everything relating to religion. The whole of this is composed in very pure Gaelic; but particularly, the dedication to the Earl of Argyll is written with more classical purity and elegance than any composition I ever saw, either written or printed, in that language. This is not hearsay evidence, my friend, for the last time I was at Inveraray I read the book from beginning to end, and in the course of the evening repeated to the Duke a summary of its contents, for which his Grace thanked me in his usual mild and polite manner, observing that he never before had met with any person who could give him any information with regard to the subject-matter of that book, though he had showed it to many whom he thought good Gaelic scholars." If the people of Argyllshire, then, at such a remote date were acquainted with these poems, why should the people of Arran have been ignorant? On the contrary, Mr. Stewart, as above, distinctly states that his own father, "when a young man, heard his [Ossian's] poems repeated by the old people, the same that are recorded by MacPherson, making some allowance for little alterations," such as might easily occur in different districts. These ancient reciters, therefore, in Mr. Stewart's father's youth, must have known the originals of Ossian long before MacPherson published; and the still remoter worshippers in Argyllshire, of whom Mr. Carsuel complains, must have had them transmitted to their keeping more than two hundred years before MacPherson was born. Further discussion is surely unnecessary; the argument seems to be unanswerable: yet more interesting matter, as regards Ossian himself, is in hand.

By way of supplement to this letter, it may be convenient now to state that Loch-Fyne, more accurately Loch-Fyn or Loch-Fiun, that is Fingal's Loch, was the name appropriated to this important estuary by the people, in commemoration of the hero's frequent voyages by that route, to Ireland and elsewhere, from his residence at Morven. This origin of the name is reported and maintained by tradition among the inhabitants of Arran; and indeed, there can be no serious doubt of its reality. Many other scenes of Fingal's exploits and expeditions, as we shall by and by see, retain the trace of his presence in their modern designations; but in this particular instance, the correctness of tradition has been confirmed so explicitly by Pinkerton—one of the most contemptuous unbelievers in Ossian—that the aptness of his unconscious testimony on the point is amusing. The estuary in question, it appears, was known to the Romans at the commencement of the Christian era, and for nearly two hundred years after, as the *Lelamonius Sinus*, or Lelamonian Gulf. Tacitus, in his *Agricola*, describes the inhabitants of North Britain beyond the Forth and Tay, 85 A.D., as Caledonians: "Ptolemy," says Pinkerton, "40 years after marks the people of this part of Britain by the same name;" and "in 150 A.D., knew nothing of a new name." But the limits of this people he expressly defines, so late apparently as 160 A.D., for he was then alive, as "from the *Lelamonius Sinus* to the frith of *Varar*," which Pinkerton, in the same breath with his own quotation, identifies respectively with "Loch-Fyn" (so spelt by him in his innocent forgetfulness) and the "Murray Frith:" for which change of designation after 160 A.D. no reason is assigned, although the reason is obvious both in the name itself, and in the fact that, immediately after the date in question, Fin, Fyn, Fiun, or Fingal began to navigate that lake, hitherto called Lelamonius, as the most convenient route for his warlike expeditions. We borrow thus from the hands of our most accomplished adversary, and return again, with increasing confidence and faith, to Arran.

ELMGROVE PLACE, *September* 4, 1871.

SIR,—In pursuing our investigations about Ossian, we come now to consider the bearing of certain traditions on the subject, and more particularly, as I hope to show, on the interesting questions of his own life, death, and burial. I need hardly remind your readers that on the great level moor to the west, between the Shiskin and the Brodick roads, in Arran, called Machrie Muir, are several Druidical circles and other monumental stones. All who have been in the neighbourhood, or who have looked at any antiquarian guide-book that treats of Arran—Pennant, Headrick, M'Arthur, Landsborough, or the Statistical Account of Scotland—must be aware of the fact. The great antiquity of these remains is certain; their Druidical or Scandinavian origin is probable; but by recent excavations, at the late Duke of Hamilton's expense, conducted by Dr. Bryce of this city, it has been distinctly ascertained that they were used, possibly at a later date, for funereal purposes—cists, urns, skulls, and among other objects of interest, a female ornament in bronze, having been discovered underneath or beside them. But they are connected also, by invariable tradition, with Fingal— one of them, for instance, being called his "cauldron seat," another "his judgment seat," another the "panel's stone," &c.,* much of which is undoubtedly mere imagination. Nearer to Blackwater-foot, however, is a place of indubitable sepulture, alone and separate, in the form of a large cromlech, which on excavation was proved to contain an urn of unbaked earth full of burned bones; and this, by tradition, was the tomb of Ossian's daughter, or rather, perhaps, of his daughter-in-law that would have been, had Oscar lived, and who constantly

* We learn, for example, on good authority in the *Highlander*, that what is commonly called Fingal's Cauldron-Seat is a mistranslation from the Gaelig for Fingal's Seat by Right, as head of the people.

attended him. In visiting this spot I was unluckily without a guide at the moment, and so could not quite assure myself of its identity; but if the cromlech in question stands in a quiet, verdant recess of the shore, below a bosky bank, and at a point where two lines—one from Blackwater-foot, and another from Drumadoon farm—would cross nearly at right angles, then it might very well be distinguished once for all as the heart-shaped cromlech, the upper slab being almost of that form—a curious and beautiful coincidence, if the fact be so that it was the burying-place of Malvina. But as some of these traditions and discoveries, however reasonable they may appear, may still be no better than fables or misinterpreted facts, I shall risk no theory at all in connection with them for the present. One thing, however, remains indisputable—that is, as indisputable as unvarying tradition can make it; as indisputable as the traditions of Palestine or Babylon—that many of Fingal's people, children or followers of his, died and were buried there. This has been rehearsed by the fathers to the children, from children to children's children, so distinctly and invariably, that Johnson and Gibbon themselves would be staggered into some sort of faith by it; in a word, the death and burial of the Patriarchs is not more certain. But to identify the spot where these events—so interesting in themselves, and for ever memorable as the remotest landmarks in the history of British literature—occurred, is the point still at issue.

Along the south end of Arran, close by the shore, is a series of monumental mounds, among the largest and most perfect of their kind in the island, time immemorial reputed to be the graves of giants or Fingalian heroes, and held sacred by the peasantry on the pain of supernatural mischief or death. One of these on Margreeach Farm, by the Sliddery Burn, as we learn from Headrick, was bored long ago by some daring islander, who discovered a bone of huge dimensions in it; but which, from apprehension of the consequences, he was induced quietly to restore. This tumulus, like many others of the same sort in the Highlands, has a smaller mound attached, in which the dog of the giant hero, slain to accompany him to the fields of his Elysium, is supposed to be laid. The probability, however, according to Headrick, is, that the large mound is the grave of many heroes interred together after battle, and the smaller mound the grave of their dogs—a dog for every hero—interred for company along with them; a supposition which has since been confirmed to some extent by the opening of a corresponding tumulus at Torlin, about two miles and a half to the eastward, which M'Arthur informs us (p. 22 of his *Arran*) " is intersected from east to west by a row of vaults, consisting each of six unhewn slabs from five to eight feet square. These vaults were filled with human bones, some of which were cleft, as if from the blow of an axe or hatchet. This cairn was partially removed some years ago by a modern Goth, who rifled the cells of their contents and strewed them over his fields," &c. The perpetrator of this unnecessary outrage, we further learn from the same authority, was struck with horror at the thought of his own sacrilege, and finally met with a violent accidental death in his distraction, which the people of the district interpreted, of course, as a judgment on his profanity. However this might be, the character of the mound, as the collective burying-place of heroes slain in battle, most probably defending the shore from invaders, has been determined beyond doubt. But there is another mound, of a different shape and character, on a neighbouring farm, about half-way between the two above specified, but rather nearer Torlin than Margreeach, to which public attention has never hitherto been directed—which does not, indeed, seem to have been known either to Pennant or to Headrick, and is certainly not referred to by any other authority I have seen. Headrick, however, incidentally states (p. 150) that "the old men here have many traditions about Fiun and Ossian, whom they represent as the last of his race. But they rather believe them to have been giants and necromancers, than men of ordinary stature who acquired celebrity by the exertion of their natural powers;" which seems clearly to indicate two things—(1.) that Fingal and Ossian were the great themes of tradition on the identical ground in question —that is, from Margreeach to Torlin and the neighbourhood; and (2.) that popular fear of their supernatural power protected such graves from violation, in case the remains of either should be disturbed. But Margreeach and Torlin being practically disposed of as scenes of collective sepulture, the intervening tomb at Clachaig alone remains to be accounted for; and the reader must now be distinctly informed that tradition not only assigns the south end of Arran as the scene of Ossian's death, but specifies Clachaig itself as the very spot where it occurred. This tradition, floating about in the region for generations, has been briefly summarised in the Statistical Account of Scotland, 1845, by Rev. Alexander M'Bride, North Bute—from whose report of Kilmorie parish (p. 51, Buteshire) the following extract must suffice :—" Rev. William Shaw, author of the first Gaelic grammar and dictionary that were published, was born at Clachaig, in this parish. . . . . As it claims to be the birth-place of the first Celtic scholar, so also it claims to be the death-place of the first Celtic bard. Ossian is said to have died here." And here, both as a matter of course, and because he had no living representative to claim him, he would also be interred, yet not without the utmost solemnity of sepulture, we may be sure, though by the hands of comparative strangers. Up to the date in question, however, no steps had been taken to ascertain the fact.

Clachaig, as we have just seen, lies more than half-way between Margreeach and Torlin, by the shore; and the farm-house itself, tenanted now for two generations by gentlemen of enterprise and intelligence from Renfrewshire, stands about a gunshot inland from the verge of the parapet, or old sea line, already spoken of. At more than one point along the margin of this parapet are places of interment in cists or cairns, but all of a second-rate order; and one in particular, so comparatively recent as still to be pointed out as the resting-place of some unfortunate seamen drowned on the coast below. But apart from all these, and close to Clachaig House, is a much larger double mound, distinct and lofty, like a small Danish camp, of oval form; held not only in the utmost traditional veneration by the natives, but protected from violation by traditional prophecies of death to whosoever should disturb it. One adventurous person, more than two generations ago, who dared to turn the turf of the upper round, was repelled, it is said, by the glare of two terrible eyes from beneath; and Mr. Speirs himself, the present tenant's father, when proceeding to excavate on the same spot, was actually deterred by the prayers and entreaties of the assembled people, imploring him to forbear, for that instant death would be the penalty of his sacrilege. Shortly after the publication of the Statistical Account, however, and stimulated by the reference to Clachaig as the scene of Ossian's death, above quoted, Mr. Speirs's son, succeeding to the tack, resolved to know the utmost of this mysterious tomb, and boldly recommenced operations from the top.

These operations resulted in discoveries at the time sufficient to satisfy Mr. Speirs that his conjectures about the important character of the burying place were correct; and as reported by him to the present writer they were detailed in succeeding portions of the above letter. But as this investigation took place more than twenty-five years ago, and no accurate measurements at the moment were made, it was possible Mr. Speirs's memory might have deceived him. On the Author's second visit to Arran therefore, the summer following, Mr. Speirs courteously volunteered to re-open the grave, that an opportunity for the minutest survey might be afforded. On that occasion, the evening of July 8th, 1872, a considerable number of friends, both ladies and gentlemen, including the Rev. Charles Stewart of Kilmorie, and the Author's own family, accompanied Mr. Speirs to the ground; when, all preliminaries having been carefully accomplished by workmen in attendance, under Mr. Speirs's direction, the spot of interment was again uncovered, with the assistance or in the sight of all present, and the following exact details were taken:—Upper tombstone, a coarse whitish flag much stained by earth and slightly corroded on the surface, measured 5 ft. 2 in. by 3 ft. 6 in. and 5 to 6 inches in thickness—being considerably *less* than Mr. Speirs had imagined; cist underneath, on which it lay flat, as a covering, 3 ft.

8 in. by 1 ft. 9 in. within, and 18 inches deep—being considerably *larger* than supposed, and not of one stone as conjectured by Mr. Speirs, but of four square slabs from 2 to 3 inches thick, neatly smoothed and jointed, sunk edgeways in the solid clay as a floor—the whole, by rough measurement, being 4 feet by 2 over all. This enclosure, during the lapse of more than twenty-five years since its first opening, when it contained only fine grey dust—of which a small specimen was long carefully preserved—had got partially filled with the finest portions of the adjacent soil, washed in by the rains through chinks between the lid and the edges, but still preserved among its contents a few distinct particles or fragments of black calcined earth or ashes, which were examined and removed. No trace of anything else, monumental or other, on the most careful scrutiny, being found, the soil was again filled in, and the tombstone replaced reverentially as before. The rough sketch on title page, taken by the Author at the time, represents the general aspect of the grave when thus opened. The turf was afterwards replaced, and the surface, as far as possible, restored to its original level.

In addition to these particulars, however, many others, of a most interesting and suggestive character, disclosed by subsequent measurement of the entire tomb, have yet to be specified. The cist itself, as above described, seems to have been adopted as a unit of proportion for the whole. The tomb, as the reader will observe by the annexed representations, although apparently only a *double*, is in reality a triple mound of terraces, diminishing in depth, but rising by pretty equal slopes from one another to a level top. These, as might be expected, have suffered here and there in their outline, from accidents and the waste of time, so that in certain lights or from certain points of view in the landscape, they seem to blend. The lowest indeed, which is of course the largest and closely adjoining on the field, has been considerably curtailed on one side for a garden, and more recently on the other by some unwarrantable excavations for material to repair the high road—an encroachment wisely interdicted by Mr Speirs at his own expense, but, so far as it has gone, irremediable. Even the topmost round, although in best preservation, has lost a little of its surface either by ancient violence or in the various attempts which have been made to explore it: notwithstanding all which, they are distinctly traceable as represented on the accompanying ground plan; and, as the reader will perceive, they are all ovals of equal symmetrical proportions.

In the uppermost, as already explained, about 18 inches below the original surface, and reaching 18 inches farther down, lies the cist under its tombstone; about 4 ft. by 2 over all, built into the solid clay as a foundation, in the very middle of the oval. But this upper mound or terrace containing the cist, measured on its top, is 24 ft. long by 18 broad—that is, six times the length

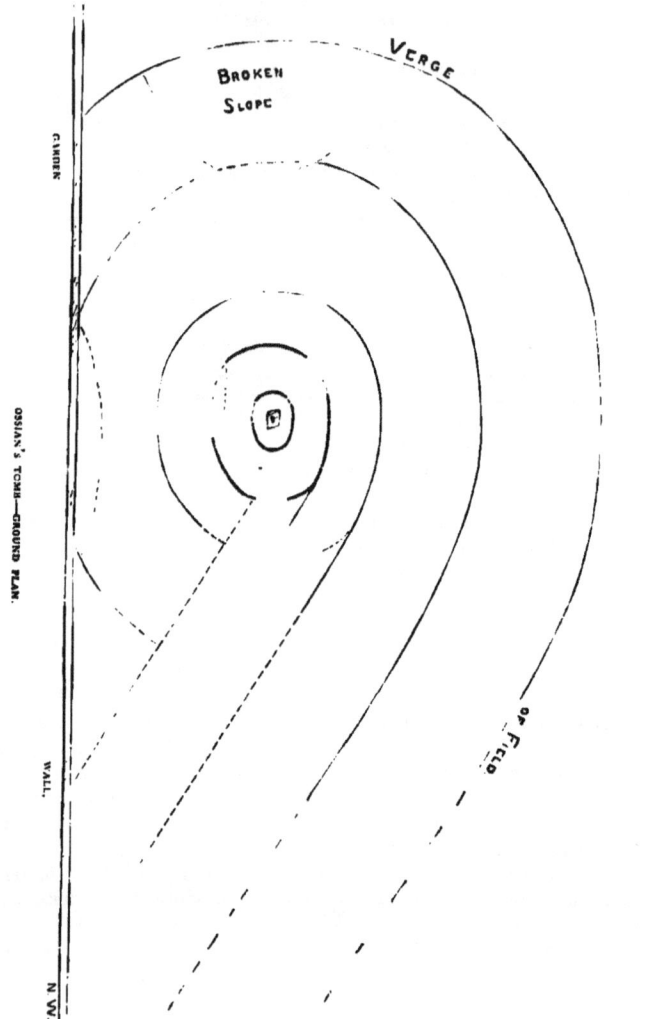

and nine times the breadth of the cist; the round or terrace immediately underlying this, by top measurement also, is 72 ft. long by 54 broad—that is, three times 24 and three times 18, or nine times the size of the one above it; and the lowest of all, to where it terminates in field or garden, is 200 ft. long by 90 broad—that is, nearly three times 72 long, being drawn out with a sweep at one end for an entrance, now cut off by the garden wall, and shortened a little at the other for a finish, where the excavations above referred to have been made—and five times 18 broad. Still farther, these terraces of symmetrical dimensions are also symmetrically disposed, not irregularly, but with arithmetical accuracy, around the cist, N.W. and S.E., as blunted ovals around an oblong centre; tapering a little at one end to harmonize with the entrance which sweeps round to north, and flattened at the other to harmonize with the finish, but equal at the sides; the height of the whole to its topmost level being 18 ft. above the level of the adjoining field, and its surface originally horizontal with the ocean. The unit of proportion in all these arrangements, as we have seen, was the cist, in nice adaptation to the reduced dimensions of a presumably gigantic human body, being as 4 to 7 and 2 to 3; but the unit of measurement throughout has been the human foot, of 12 inches long, applied to the surface of the soil; and it seems almost impossible to believe that such proportions could have occurred by accident, or could even have been devised without the nicest art. The original mound or foundation terrace, which is of rough consolidated gravel mixed with clay, may have been natural, doubtless; but the terrace immediately above it must have been shaped to correspond; whilst the uppermost of all is not only artificial, but has been elaborately constructed of boulders lodged in the clay, to protect the remains of the dead, and to finish the structure in symmetrical proportion to the whole. The entire surface has then been covered with the richest soil in the neighbourhood to the depth of 10 or 12 inches, which in the lapse of ages has clothed itself with fine verdure; and so the outline of the monument, although exposed to the accidents of time and the waste of centuries, is distinctly traceable thus after 1500 years. To complete the impression which an object like this can hardly fail to produce on the mind even of the most unbelieving and unimaginative reader, it is only necessary farther to state that the tomb itself must have originally projected in verdant solitude towards the ocean from the skirts or bosom of an immense forest of lofty oaks, and had for counterpart in the immediate neighbourhood a small deep lake on the verge of the wood, girdled with its giant stems, and overhung like a mirror with its branches. This lake which once glistened in the hollow between Clachaig and Lagg, by the very roadside there, has been drained within the memory of man; trunks and roots of great trees, chiefly oak, having been disembedded from its recesses; and its site is now covered alternately with clovered pasture and waving corn. All that yet remains, therefore, of nature as it then was, or of human life, labour and sympathy, to testify to the passage of the "dark brown years" over Clachaig, is this monument of veneration for individual rank and greatness. Shortly after writing the above, the Author observed in some local papers an interesting account of a corresponding discovery in the adjoining Island of Bute, and at a still more recent date, of similar discoveries in the Island of Cumbrae also; for which, however, he must refer the reader to the Appendix, and now resumes quotation from his letter on the tomb at Clachaig as follows—

That this has been the burying-place of some distinguished chief or hero of the remotest times, as Ossian was, is certain; or of some priest or prophet, or poet, or of one who combined all or most of these characters in himself, as Ossian pre-eminently did among his fellow-countrymen, is at least highly probable, from the very maledictions which protected the grave; and these considerations, combined with the fact that it has been discovered not only in Clachaig, where tradition points to his interment, but within a hundred paces of the door where his death took place, render such a conclusion almost irresistible. In refutation of this, it may, of course, be alleged that Ossian gave orders to Oscar for his own interment in terms expressly different—"Remember, my son, to place this sword, this bow, and the horn of my deer, within that dark and narrow house, whose mark is one grey stone;" but it may as easily be replied—that Ossian was not fated, as he hoped, to die on the field, nor was Oscar fated to survive him; and the terms of his sepulture, being unknown to strangers, could never be fulfilled. The very object, indeed, of his journey from Glencoe to Arran seems to have been to die and be buried at Clachaig. Without some such motive why should he, blind and disconsolate, with no companion but an adopted daughter to guide or cheer him, have undertaken such a pilgrimage? Yet the motive and the circumstances both were full of the purest poetry. By that very route from Morven, long years ago, and to this very point at Clachaig on his way to Ireland on that memorable expedition, came Fingal with his host, Ossian himself, as "king of many songs," their marshal and their bard. At Machrie, as we know, they disembarked and rested; by Glenscordale and Glenree the chiefs at least might hunt to Clachaig, for their dogs were with them; and at the *Cletes*, or at the harbour of Lagg between the *Cletes*, they would embark again. By that route assuredly, if not by the fiord at Sliddery, they would return, as the nearest and the best from Ireland. Fingal and his sons would hunt by Glenree and Glenscordale again, and again re-embark at Machrie. Ossian, as the poet hero, was triumphant then; Oscar, the heir of his father's fame and the sharer of

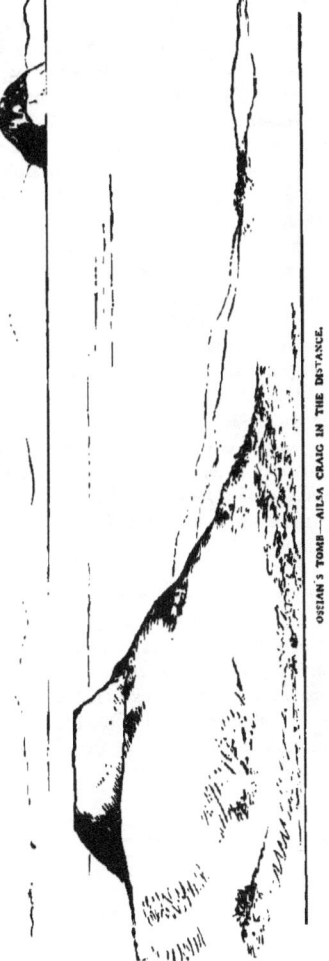

OSSIAN'S TOMB—AILSA CRAIG IN THE DISTANCE.

his father's deeds, was living then; and the "white-armed daughter of Toscar," Malvina, loved him. Now, Ossian will return by the self-same route, and to the self-same spot, to die. Malvina droops at Machrie; but the aged minstrel journeys on, till the roar of the sea on the beach at Clachaig stops him. Here, the last of his race, he must bid eternal farewell to earth and ocean. Fingal and the rest of them are gone—all ceased from battle; Evirallin and Oscar, wife and son, and Malvina, but yesterday a small heap of dust beneath a cromlech, are gone—all in the clouds before him. Dark and sightless, but not tearless, he turns southward to the deep blue sea, of which he so often sang, which his own and his father's oak-built ships, and Oscar's too, had ploughed; and beyond that sea, in fancy, towards Ireland he gazes, where he won by sword and song the dark-haired Evirallin for his bride; to whose coasts he had been welcomed with joy as an ally and deliverer afterwards, and from which he had returned triumphant to the very beach where he now stands, but which he never again shall see. He gazes hopeless, and turning, as it were, a second time to Oscar, reiterates—"I have no love to leave to the care of my son, for graceful Evirallin is no more, the lovely daughter of Branno." His course of song is finished, and he waits with patience what higher obsequies than those of a mere battlefield the love and admiration of his fellow-countrymen may accord him. Higher these may be than any that Oscar and Malvina could have provided, but not more dear. All this, of course, may be pronounced a dream, and I shall not too earnestly insist on it; but there is a reality of nature in it also, or I am much mistaken, which neither criticism nor scepticism will undo.

Such was the Author's original theory on this subject—both as to Ossian's final journey to Clachaig, and as to the various routes adopted by him and by his people, in going and coming to and from Ireland; which farther inquiry and subsequent revelations, both by text and tradition, as the reader shall immediately see, have not only confirmed but extended to the most convincing proof of Ossian's own life and authenticity, and of the life and history of the most distinguished personages connected with him by family relationship and by song.

## CHAPTER II.

#### REVELATIONS IN ARRAN CONTINUED—MALVINA'S GRAVE.

IN following up the thread of revelation thus casually discovered in Arran, we must be guided now not only by the tissue of tradition itself, as it runs among the feet of the people, and from point to point on the very surface of the island; but by the text of Ossian as well, with which it becomes indissolubly interwoven, illuminating every word, as it winds its own way back into the past, beyond the imagination of translators and critics, and receiving from the text in turn strength and continuity beyond all previous conjecture, till it weaves itself into a consistent web of history worthy of the solemnest investigation. With slight enough presentiment of such possibility at the moment of this first discovery, the Author nevertheless turned instinctively to Ossian himself, and in the concluding words of his sublime soliloquies, found not only all that was required to confirm the tradition of his death, but more revelation in the way of important historical fact than had yet been imagined in the annals of the country. A fragment or two of these discoveries were communicated as heretofore in letters to the Press, the remainder being reserved for subsequent publication in the present form; but in immediate connection with what has already been advanced, the following additional extracts, as the foundation of all possible argument on the subject, must now be introduced, displacing for the moment a previous letter on the Altars and Tombstones of the period, which may be reproduced with more propriety hereafter.

ELMGROVE PLACE, *September* 14, 1871.

SIR,—My dream of Ossian's final journey to Arran and of his musings on the shore at Clachaig, of Malvina's death at Machrie and her burial at Drumadoon, "was not all a dream," as more careful collation of his text than I then had time or space for will now show. That his last thoughts were of Oscar and Ryno, his beloved son and youngest brother, who both fell on the field at different dates in Ireland, and that their names were the last on his lips, the reader may learn at his leisure from the closing lines of *Berrathon*; that this poem itself, the concluding hymn of his life, was inspired by the death of Malvina; that her death took place where it did, in his company, by surprise or suddenly, and that Ossian himself in his grief would fain have died along with her and slept on the moor at Machrie, had the Fates decreed it so, is equally clear on his own authority. But that Malvina herself, as well as Ossian, had a personal motive for revisiting Arran, and, as his adopted daughter, might even urge him to go when his house was extinct in Morven—in short, that Malvina was born at Drumadoon and hunted in the woods at Machrie, where Oscar saw her, and whither she returned to die—has probably never been suspected, yet may be easily proved; and because James MacPherson's absolute integrity as a translator may be proved along with it, there is a double motive to undertake the proof. But with MacPherson's integrity, Ossian's own authenticity and reliability, as a contemporaneous witness and actor in the remotest history of Scotland and Ireland, will be established also, and thus interests of the very highest moment accumulate to justify the prosecution of the proof. In present circumstances, however, only a summary of one part of it can be attempted.

1. In the first place, then, *Berrathon*, now so called, although no such name originally belonged to it, was Ossian's final hymn—the prelude, in fact, to his own death and apotheosis; and must have been composed by him far to the south of Glencoe, with his face to the west, on the verge of the frith, surrounded by woods, and with a dark lake behind him. According to invariable local tradition, this must have been somewhere in Arran, and nowhere else.

2. The scene of Malvina's death and the very site of her tomb are specified in the poem; their latitude and longitude, in fact, are incidentally given with an accuracy that may astonish unbelievers. A breeze from above Glencoe, due north, and "a cloud from the dusky west"—that is, from the horizon beyond Campbeltown, where the clouds seem always to gather, and from which they drift, are to converge or pass over it. But two lines drawn, one from Glencoe straight southward and the other from a little above Campbeltown eastward, will converge at right angles on the Arran shore, between Drumadoon and Blackwaterfoot exactly.

3. The breeze of sympathetic sorrow from the north is sent by Fingal from his airy palace above Glencoe, where Malvina's spirit joins him; and the cloud from the west brings the spirit of her father, the generous Toscar of Lutha, to brood over his daughter's grave, and to console with visions of glory the sightless Seer himself—the last of his race—who now laments her premature departure. Who, then, was this Toscar, and where was the Lutha of which he once was lord? The Toscar here spoken of was Ossian's earliest friend, and "the narrow plain of Lutha" would be the last scene of Fingal's rendezvous on his great expedition to Ireland—that is, it was in the immediate neighbourhood of Machrie, where he disembarked, where he feasted and hunted, and from which again (by Glenscordale most probably) he rejoined his ships. A little clearer identification, however, of this important locality, in the interests alike of history

and of poetry, is required. According to Ossian himself, in the poem above cited, it was a narrow plain, with a lovely field, by a swift river, with a great stone, which seems to have been a landmark even then, called "The Stone of Mora;" with a dark lake and deep oak woods in the neighbourhood, having a steep rocky precipice and huge moss-covered fortress—Tor-lutha, to the seaward or west of it, close on the shore; all this, it must be remembered, where two lines, one from Glencoe and the other from above Campbeltown, would meet. A reader who knows anything whatever of the region, or who chooses even to look at an atlas, will have no more doubt on the subject. But for the benefit of those who may not have seen it, and therefore cannot imagine it, the following verification may be adduced :—" The Vale of Shiskin is intersected by a rivulet called the Blackwater, which has cut a passage to itself through a bar of rocks where it joins the sea. Here it has formed a small harbour for boats, which is the ferrying place from Campbeltown in Kintyre, distant about twelve miles. Before the water cut this channel through the rock, the vale behind must have been an extensive lake; and in high floods it still overflows considerable tracts of excellent soil."—(Headrick, p. 151.) Here the river, and the lake, and the lovely field, and the narrow plain, are all equally accounted for; but I must further observe that, before this bar of rock was forced, whether by floods or by an earthquake, the stream would be a *rapid* where there is now a basin and a waterfall; hence the descriptive designation applied to it by Ossian, of Lutha, which means the swift darting river. The ancient moss-covered fortress of Drumadoon, a little to the north of it, called Tor-lutha by the poet—that is, the lofty keep or court of the rapids—of which only the foundation now remains, is admitted universally to have been one of the earliest and most important strongholds in the West of Scotland, the residence of powerful chiefs and a place of refuge for the people; and the appellation of Tor-lutha—Tor being one of the oldest and commonest prefixes on the south-west coast of Arran for all similar elevations where justice was administered—is almost sufficient of itself to determine its whereabouts. Tor-nan-uain, Tor-lin, Tor-chaistel, Tor-daimh, Tor-beg, *Tor-lutha*, Tor-righ, and Tor-more, would complete the circle of such defences on that corner of the island. The precipice or "rock" on which it stood is a whinstone columnar cliff, about 300 feet in perpendicular height; and the materials of which it was built, being enormous blocks of granite, imply labour almost beyond belief in its construction. "The Stone," by pre-eminence, "of Mora," among the bare blasted oaks by the side of the lake, where Ossian wished to die, is obviously the monolith at Tor-*more*, the Great Seat of Justice, on Machrie; and as for the oaks and the woods themselves, "there is a tradition," says Pennant, "that in old times the shores were covered with woods (oak woods, as we elsewhere learn), and this was the habitable part." In his own day it was "an extensive plain of good ground, but quite in a state of nature." If still further verification, however, should be required, the reader will find, near the end of the second book of *Fingal*, that Toscar's own sister, who had fled to a great cave in the neighbourhood, frequented by hunters, and hung round with implements of war and of the chase, to escape the importunities of a man she hated, was accidentally slain by the man she loved when she came out in disguise to meet him on his return from hunting in Mora. He was afterwards slain himself near the same spot, by voluntarily exposing his breast to the arrows of piratical invaders; and "he sleeps with his loved Galvina at the noise of the sounding surge. Their green tombs are seen by the mariner when he bounds on the waves of the north;" and antiquarians, if they choose to explore, may yet discover them, for there they lie buried by the shore of the sea as surely as the tide flows. But this cave, frequented by the lovers and hung with trophies of the chase, between Mora and the beach, is so evidently what is now called "King's Cove" that scarcely a word is required to prove it; yet a word in confirmation may be quoted:—"The sides of the cave," says Headrick, "exhibit innumerable small figures, equally rude, representing dogs chasing stags, and men shooting arrows at them," &c.—Galvina fell by an arrow, and her lover was returning from the chase of a stag; and "the people here believe these figures to be representations of various exploits of Fiun (that is, Fingal) and his heroes in the chase." Finally, to conclude this part of the proof, Machrie, by tradition still extant in poetry, was the scene of a Norwegian invasion repelled by Fingal, in which the chiefs of the neighbourhood assisted him, and in which, according to the text of our author, Toscar's sister's lover voluntarily fell.

4. But clouds are not like mathematical lines—length without breadth or thickness. The "cloud from the dusky west," with Toscar's spirit in its bosom, might be a mile to the north or to the south of Drumadoon, or it might cover half the region—are there no clearer indications of the spot? There are; but even if there were not, the spirit of Toscar, as a matter of course, would be in the centre of the drift, and, however far that might stretch to north or south, would still be above the grave. The site of the grave itself, however, is minutely specified:—"It rises yonder beneath the rock, at the blue stream of Lutha:" that is, on the shore line between the precipice of Drumadoon and the river of the Blackwater—the identical spot where the heart-shaped cromlech, already referred to as the tomb of Ossian's daughter, is to be seen. But all these names are now changed, it may still be said; so are other names in this world, of much greater importance, and reasons sufficient for the change are obvious.

CHAP. II.] MALVINA'S GRAVE. 63

The "Cove." Entrance. The "Stable."
BONAN'S CAVE, NOW KING'S COVE.

The Lutha, that was a blue rapid in Ossian's day, is now a waterfall and a pool, dark with moss drainage, which it could not have been till the woods were destroyed—is, in fact, the *Black*water; the lake from which it flowed, to whose melancholy sound Ossian responded disconsolate, has been emptied, most likely by means of an earthquake; the woods that surrounded the lake, among which he hid himself in grief, or which covered the shore where he wandered, have fallen; "the narrow plain" has thus been converted to "an extensive plain," or great fertile strath; and Tor-lutha, with its mossy walls on Drumadoon, is now levelled with the surface; above all, "the sons of little men" have succeeded, who changed the scene and were entitled to designate its features as they pleased, in their own more recent language. But the great "Stone of Mora" remains untouched, and the cromlech remains, not untouched but comparatively sacred; and the ruins of Tor-lutha remain, a wonder to the men of our day; and "the rock" remains, and the cave, sanctified as the hiding place of a still greater hero than Fingal. To restore the woods, in fact, and the lake, is all that is needed to produce immediate and irresistible conviction.

Here, then, beyond a doubt, in the palace of her fathers, was Malvina born; here in the woods, when Oscar passed and repassed, she was a huntress; here, when he returned from Ireland in triumph, she would be betrothed to him; here, when his shrouded corse arrived from his last expedition, she would receive it with tears, and follow by and by, as a widowed bride, in his father's train to Cona; thither again, with the sightless old man, she would return to die of grief, or to fall by accident, and be lamented and entombed. We learn, indeed, from another poem, that as Ossian's future daughter-in-law, Malvina was at Morven before, and so must have returned to Tor-lutha twice—the second time to die. Of *Berrathon* itself, from which these particulars are gathered, I say nothing. It is worthy not less of Shakespear, or Homer, than of Ossian. Let those who can appreciate the loftiest productions of human genius, or who care for the most exquisite embodiment of grief and love, open their eyes and look at it. It is with facts and traditions only I have now to do, and the identification of localities; and it is some satisfaction to find that so minute an analysis is reliable. By these investigations a new light of truth, as well as of beauty, seems to shine in Ossian. His works are like a new revelation, the history of Scotland is like a new book, and the sea-beaten shores and barren wastes of Scotland are like a new creation.

Why, then, was not all this known long ago? Because men, perhaps, did not look with their own eyes at the facts of the case, or at the letter of the text before them; never had their attention turned in that way with such an object, or persistently ignored the testimony of tradition that has been pointing without intermission for centuries to the spot. By this neglect, both poetry, history, geography, and geology, have been losers. That the inland lake of Ossian's day has been drained by some rupture or subsidence in the bed of the river at its junction with the sea is geologically certain, and that this has occurred since the date of Ossian's death is historically certain. It may possibly, indeed, have been much later; and I am inclined to believe that the whole surrounding region would be equally depressed at the time, for King's Cove is obviously on a lower level than it could have been when Bruce and Fingal frequented it, and the face of Drumadoon has been splintered. But however all this may be, it is clear and yet more strange, and yet more fortunate than strange, that MacPherson himself knew nothing of it; knew nothing of the traditions of Arran, knew nothing apparently of Arran itself; certainly nothing of the region in question, or he could have been at no loss to identify the scene of this poem, which he gives up in despair. "It is impossible," he says, "at this distance of time, to ascertain where the scene here described lies. Tradition is silent on that head, and there is nothing in the poem from which a conjecture can be drawn." The simplicity and frankness of this avowal are worth a thousand protestations in his favour. In his second edition, 1763, this note is retained; but in his revised and final edition, ten years later, as if the subject was still inscrutable, and no further light could be obtained, it is omitted. If Machrie, Drumadoon, and Blackwater had been familiar to him, he could have explained all; if they had even been described to him in the meantime, he would have referred to them on chance; if he had actually forged a poem in Ossian's name adapted to such scenery, and in connection with every object of water, wood, and stone, on the surface, it would have been utterly impossible for him to be silent in relation to it. But he evidently knew no more of the scene than if it was not in Scotland, and could, therefore, as little be guilty of fabrication in the poems ascribed to Ossian as the writer of this letter could have been of a conspiracy to invent the Koran. Does any man in his senses, beyond the bedlam of Grub Street, with such evidence of unconsciousness before him, persist in accusing MacPherson of forgery?—then he will have to maintain that theory in the face of facts and declarations as clear and consistent as any in the whole history of literature, and, considering their antiquity, much clearer than many others of the same sort in the history of the world. . . . . . .

In pursuance and confirmation of the above, the Author subsequently addressed a letter to the Press, of date January 1st, 1872, from which the following passages may be quoted—with a few words introduced in brackets, where new evidence has accidentally accrued since the date in question.

. . . . . . From correspondence with which I have been favoured since the conclusion of that argument, I might adduce much additional proof of the correctness of the theory then advanced by me about the scene of that poem —*Berrathon*, and of Malvina's grave, but shall content myself with the following: —Mr. Bannatyne, of the Royal Academy, Inverness, a native of Arran, and an accomplished Gaelig scholar, writes to say that, in corroboration of my statements, he could point out to any geologist with perfect ease the entire space occupied by the lake long ago in the vale of Shisken; and remembers the stump of a decayed tree in that neighbourhood, the remains of the ancient forest once there, still rooted on the soil, and described by him as " enormous "—so large as to have been a sort of castle or redoubt for schoolboys, who used to scale its sides and drive nails into it. Further, in the immediate vicinity of the grave itself, between that and Drumadoon, as I understand him to say, or thereabouts, he saw the trunk of another tree disembedded from the moss at peat-casting, some 10 feet in circumference. When in full growth and girth, say fifteen hundred or a thousand years ago, a tree like that might be four or five feet in diameter, though this is but a guess; yet under such an oak might Ossian in his darkness well sit when the smoke of Malvina's burial rose, and hang his harp, as he actually says he did, among its decaying branches. [That such forests have so recently fallen, may be doubted by the reader; but that such peat, which is the product of their ruin, " is most probably the growth of a recent time," the reader who does doubt may satisfy himself by consulting the latest edition of Dr. Bryce's *Arran*, p. 211, whose geological researches in that very neighbourhood had certainly no reference to the authenticity of Ossian.] Still further, Mr. Bannatyne informs me that the walls of Drumadoon—" Tor-lutha "—were in many places ten feet thick, in others six and eight; and I should be glad to learn, with proof, by what foreign or domestic siege, then or since, such a stronghold was levelled with the ground. It seems much more likely that it fell by no siege, but, like the walls of Jericho, by an earthquake—the same earthquake that splintered the rock on which it stood, and that emptied the adjoining lake which flanked it; and the same sort of earthquake that divided the Jordan over against Jericho, fifteen hundred years still farther back. There were no priests with their horns, at Drumadoon, to be sure; no miracle, nor even the foreknowledge of a miracle; but there was a prophet with his harp, the singer and seer of his age, the last and most gifted of his race, lamenting and foretelling with his latest breath the approaching degeneracy of his people. With respect to the burial itself, Mr. Bannatyne thinks that, according to tradition also, it was by burning of the remains; which not only corresponds with the discovery of a cinerary urn in the tomb, but seems to suggest an entirely

CHAP. II.]   MALVINA'S GRAVE.   67

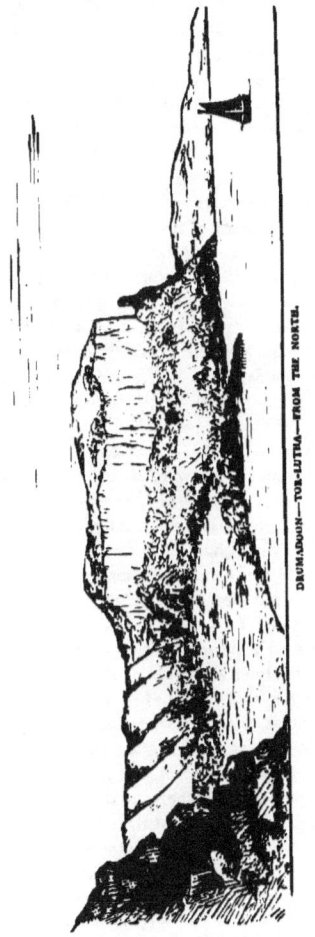

DRUMADOON—TOR-LUTRA—FROM THE NORTH.

new reading of a great part of the poem, and a sublime interpretation of its theology. In the light of this simple fact, it is easy to see that the poem itself, in its introduction, describes the very process of burning, and the rise of Malvina's soul in gentle flame to its airy dwelling place in the clouds. Nay, further, it is impossible almost not to believe that the process of incremation itself was founded on the still higher philosophy that the body should return to the dust as it was, and the spirit, purified and freed by fire, should return again to the infinite bosom of God, or of the atmosphere of God, who gave it. "Thou hast left us in darkness, first of the maids of Lutha! We sit at the rock, and there is no voice; no light but the meteor of fire. Soon hast thou set, Malvina, daughter of generous Toscar! But thou *risest* like the beam of the east, among the spirits of thy friends, where they sit in their stormy halls, the chambers of the thunder. . . . . . . . The lesser heroes, with a thousand meteors, light the airy hall. Malvina rises in the midst; a blush is on her cheek: she beholds the unknown faces of her fathers, and turns aside her humid eyes." "Why shinest thou, so soon, on our clouds, (says her father immediately afterwards, bending from his cloud as it drifts "from the dusky west," and catches illumination from her blazing tomb) O lovely *light* of Lutha?" If the interpretation I thus suggest have any truth in it at all—and it seems to me to be not only true but sublime, exquisitely sublime, in the very beauty of its truthfulness—then MacPherson, so far as this poem is concerned, knew nothing of it; as translator, had not the dimmest perception of it; talks only of the "beam of light" as a "metaphor" running "throughout the paragraph"—and thus unconsciously confounds the whole. In this view of the matter, his integrity, about which we are inquiring, becomes a question of secondary importance altogether. It is not his honesty so much as his capacity that is now on trial; or, rather, it is the divine and solemn sense of a poetico-religious philosophy that is at last opening out before us, whose principles are as old as the foundations of the world.*

But to proceed, further and finally, Mr. Bannatyne incidentally informs me that, according to tradition, the lady who died and was so interred on the spot was spoken of by the people of that neighbourhood as the "Queen-daughter of Fingal"—a peculiar designation, and of the greatest interest in relation to the present argument. Tradition elsewhere in the island, as we have seen, bears that she was the daughter, not of Fingal, but of Ossian; and I have already shown from Ossian's own text that she was neither, but only the prospective daughter-in-law of the one, and the adopted grand-daughter of the other. But

---

* The reader will find the whole of this interesting subject more fully evolved, and the idea traced to its origin, in a subsequent portion of the work—Part Fifth, Chapter VIII, Religious Faiths, &c.

Ossian was Fingal's immediate heir, and Oscar, her betrothed husband, his heir-apparent. Ossian's own wife, Evirallin, who would have been Queen-daughter to Fingal in reality, was long ago dead; and Malvina, therefore, as his grandson's betrothed bride, would assume the vacant title—would be acknowledged, in fact, by affectionate courtesy, as Princess-Royal of the House of Morven. This endearing distinction, bestowed and preserved by the people, explains and harmonises everything, and is the last required link in completion of the argument; for Fingal himself, in *Temora*, speaks of Oscar as his SON—" My sons fall by degrees: Fingal shall be the last of his race. . . . . . . I shall sit a grey cloud in my hall, nor shall I hear the return of a son in the midst of his sounding arms;" and Malvina's spirit, as we have just seen, when it soars from the funeral pyre to Fingal's heaven, "beholds the unknown faces of her fathers," though her father himself was not there—coincidences, at distant dates, of which MacPherson was quite oblivious, but which no forger would have overlooked for a moment. Nor was this principle of domestic and political adoption then a novelty among the nations of the world—Romans, Greeks, Hebrews, and Egyptians acted upon it; and Moses, who had the offer of its advantages, " refused to be called the son of Pharaoh's daughter:" all which would have been uppermost in the mind of an inventor to whom the materials were patent; yet MacPherson has forgotten it all.

Now, the local evidence and the evidence of tradition thus adduced, as well as all that has previously been advanced, was a blank to MacPherson; the scene of the poem itself, and the philosophy it contains, were mysteries to which he had no clue. I am, perhaps, the first commentator on the text of Ossian who has had the satisfaction of explaining this, and of adducing such proofs not only of MacPherson's innocence, but of his ignorance; of innocence founded on ignorance the most complete—ignorance enough, and more than enough, to disqualify him for any sort of work in relation to the poem in question, but the work of the humblest translator: and this I must reiterate as a fact, before another word is spoken, for I mean to prosecute the matter; and will neither forget it myself, nor allow your readers to forget it; nor allow any detractor of MacPherson's fame to forget it, or to impugn it, or deny it, till this argument is finished.

In support of which position, and in conclusion of these remarks on the identity of Malvina's tomb, and yet more touching illustration of the text of Ossian in relation to it, the following traditions accidentally obtained in Arran, more than six months after the date of the foregoing letter, must be added.

1. According to the rehearsal of one of the oldest and best authorities on such subjects in the island, now deceased, but still quoted by his grandson Mr. Peter

Downie, teacher of the Assembly's School at Sliddery, Malvohr or Malvina's death occurred with insult or by violence from men of some neighbouring tribe, whilst she was hunting or passing through the woods between Corriecraivy and Drumadoon. Hence, obviously, the sudden and inexplicable departure of his daughter lamented by Ossian, and so mysteriously described by his attendant, as too sad to be detailed—"I saw the daughters of the bow. I asked about Malvina, but they answered not. They turned their faces away; their darkness covered their beauty." Hence also the "blush upon her cheek," and hence the "turning aside of her humid eyes" in presence of her unknown glorified kindred—an allusion unsurpassed, for delicate pathos, in any poetry.

2. To avenge her death a battle of retaliation was fixed to be fought between her own kinsmen on the one side, and the men of the guilty tribe on the other ; and the scene selected for this engagement is still pointed out on a low ridge— the lowest ridge on the horizon, between Corriecraivy and the district of Drumadoon, looking northward from Mr. Donald Downie's farm at Corriecraivy. But on the eve of battle a flag of truce was seen approaching borne by a female, who proved to be no other than Malvina's sister, and on her supplication the hostile parties separated without bloodshed. Farther particulars of this strange and beautiful incident Mr. Downie does not now remember, but in his grandfather's time, and in his grandfather's lips, the tradition in all its details was perfect. Now this messenger of peace and of forgiveness in her sister's quarrel, the reader will observe, must have come direct from the region of Drumadoon, across the lake in a barge, or by the rapids at Blackwaterfoot, and thence by the lowest range of the intervening hills towards the anticipated rendezvous ; for it was only by such a route she could reach the scene of intended conflict in time, or be discovered at a distance approaching by the men of Corriecraivy—a circumstance which determines almost precisely the place of Malvina's residence ; whilst the alleged existence of such a sister, who had companions like herself doubtless surviving, explains not only how these are represented as lamenting in silence and sorrow at her loss, but how they are described as "daughters of the bow" frequenting the woods in the neighbourhood, and returning disconsolate from the very scene of her death. In short, had a tradition like this been invented on purpose to illustrate the poem of *Berrathon*, or to support the present writer in his theories concerning it, it could not have been more apposite or beautiful ; but those who preserved it knew nothing of *Berrathon*, and James MacPherson, the translator of that poem, and who actually conferred that very designation upon it, knew least of all.

3. But why should Malvina, even in company with her sisters, have been wandering in the woods of Corriecraivy? or why should the men of Corrie-

craivy have been guilty of such cruelty? or, such being the case, how did Ossian but a few days afterwards, old and infirm as he was, attempt a passage through the hostile region to Clachaig? To these questions it must suffice for the present, by way of anticipation, to reply briefly thus—(1.) That according to tradition Oscar was buried in that neighbourhood, where his grave is still shown; which would be the strongest inducement in the world for Malvina to revisit it, either alone or in company, after an absence of several years. (2.) That she had a vision of Oscar in the clouds which seemed to rise from his grave, beckoning her towards him and forewarning her of her approaching end; in obedience to which she would be secretly and instinctively disposed to wander near it. This affecting circumstance is narrated in the introduction to *Croma*, which must have been written on the spot, and but a few days before the sad accident. (3.) Whatever apprehensions of this kind she may have had as to death itself, she might have no foreknowledge of its character: and although the men of Corriecraivy were at feud with the friends of Fingal—were in fact the reputed murderers of Fingal, whose burying place is still identified on their coast— and so might have been disposed to offer violence to Malvina, such an opportunity occurring; yet, as Malvina, according to farther tradition, was marching with her father-in-law at the head of an armed force on their way to Ireland at the time, she might have less fear than otherwise in traversing the region. (4.) And finally, as regards Ossian himself, that the truce so bravely and humanely established by Malvina's sister at the moment when her death was to be avenged, with the very enemies who had slain her, would afford him a safe conduct through their territory, and was not improbably devised by the heroine with such a pacific object in view.

But details of so much importance require minuter investigation, and the authority on which they rest must be well considered. In the argument of this chapter, however, and wherever else the names may hereafter occur, the reader will please to remember that the Lutha of Ossian is the Blackwater of to-day, that the Tor-lutha of Ossian is the Drumadoon of to-day, and that the dark lake of Ossian, with its decaying oaks, is now the valley of Shisken. Corriecraivy, whatever its designation may then have been, is Corriecraivy still; and extends, with a bold irregular sweep along the shore, from a mile beyond Sliddery westward to the south-west point of Arran. It is now a cultivated district, but was once, as its name implies, a deep hollow forest, or "cauldron of trees." In these, and some other researches, as regards the geography of Ossian, the accompanying map may be consulted with advantage.

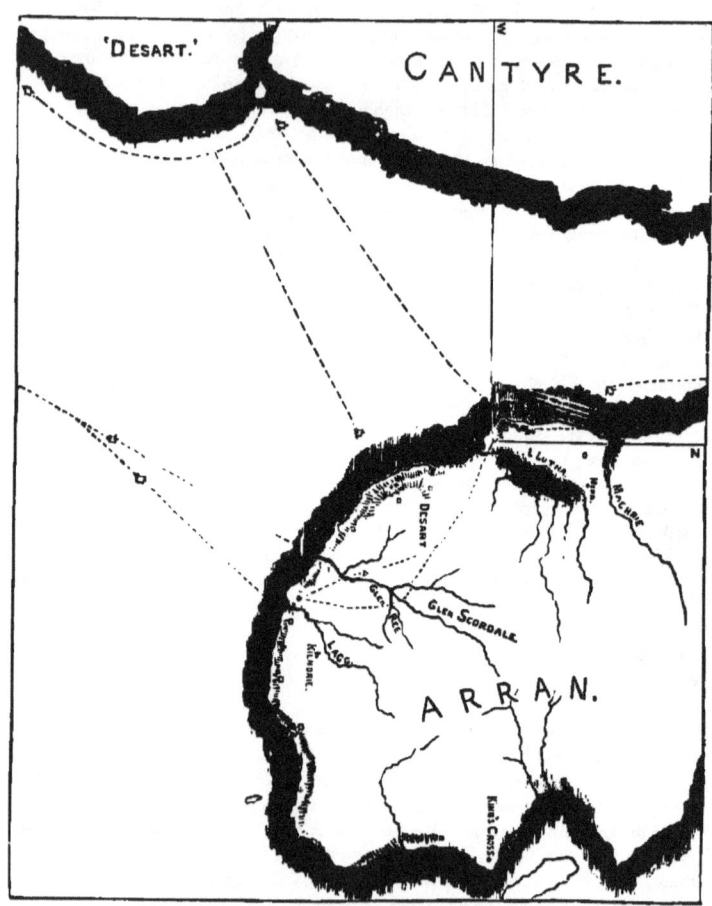

SOUTH END OF ARRAN—POSITION OF MALVINA'S GRAVE.

## CHAPTER III.

#### REVELATIONS IN ARRAN CONTINUED—OSCAR'S GRAVE.

THE reader has already had opportunities of observing that traditions recorded on the authority of natives regarding the residence and exploits of Fingalian heroes in Arran, and of their intercourse with Ireland, correspond as accurately with the text of Ossian as if they had been quoted from MacPherson; and additional opportunities of the same kind will immediately be afforded. Yet the persons now, in the end of the nineteenth century, possessed of this knowledge and communicating these details, know nothing of the original as a book, or even of the translation. The source of their information and belief is exclusively the memory of ages, preserved in substance, although sometimes exaggerated in details or mixed with the recital of more recent horrors not to be found in any book, and transmitted thus from generation to generation at fireside gatherings in the winter evenings. Authorship, or the study of literature in any form, has not yet penetrated their primitive intellectual sphere: even newspapers have not enlightened them, nor criticism, as common as the air, disturbed their faith in the past. Their dim conceptions of time itself, their unconscious confusion of eras, and their total misapprehension of character and the simplest figures of speech, are sufficient proofs of their absolute unacquaintedness with any text, even of the very author in whose existence they believe, and with the most important facts in whose personal history they are familiar; whose own words their traditions confirm, and on whose achievements as recorded in song their fireside gossip reflects the clearest elucidation. A few of them, in the last generation, were more fully masters of these details; could and did rehearse entire poems, and believed in them as enthusiastically as they rehearsed them, whether they understood them or not; and individuals of the class, educated now at college for the pulpit, or the bar, or the academy, and who have not lost their old associations with the soil in the whirl of the outside world, are not only qualified to understand, but are often the most discriminating critics of the text. But in the humbler half-educated, or rather un-educated mass, whose traditions are still the truest, or at least the clearest, it is tradition solely and not intelligence, certainly not the intelligence of books, that predominates. For them " the dark brown years " are still strangely indefinite periods, and the finest figures of poetry, the highest speculations or faiths of the poetic soul, are but idle dreams or lying vanities. Thus Ossian lived in " the days lang syne "—that is, on more definite inquiry, "from fifty to five hundred years ago—maybe about the Bruce's time, after or before him; and was the greatest liar of his age"—that is, described men poetically as clouds, or trees, or giants, or as ridges of fire in battle, with weapons of sunshine or of lightning; saw spirits in the air, or heard them in the winds, or encountered and overcame them in the storm; or detailed, with the loftiest figures of poetic phraseology, achievements beyond the comprehension of the vulgar: and so, for these and similar reasons, or possibly because his name has got confounded in their imaginations with the name and exploits of some Irish imitator in the priestly fabulous era, beyond all human credibility or even sane romance, "to be as great a liar as Ossian" has become a proverb among these people.* According to one respectable informant, who, however, does not believe in the truth of his own narratives, or at least cannot comprehend them, "there was some wonderful type of birds at that time to be occasionally found in the island, called *vohns*—in shape and size like clouds, sailing aloft on extended wings, or settling for a rest on the surface; the men also were of corresponding size in those days, no man now could say how large—lived by the arrow and the bow, and could shoot these *vohns;* on some unfortunate occasion, Fingal's favourite dog Bran, officiously eager to assist his giant master, raised one of them too soon for Fingal to obtain a shot at it; whereupon Bran was chastised, and in disdain forsook his master, and never returned, to Fingal's inexpressible regret, who would rather have had his right arm struck off by the shoulder than have lost such a dog," &c.—a story which either implies the occasional visit of birds like the condor and albatross to Arran, or intimates more probably some gross misapprehension of the text of Ossian; who represents his heroes discomfitting the spirits of evil which dwelt in or took the shape of clouds, by thrusting at them with a spear or sword, or perhaps now

---

\* These observations, made on the spot in Arran, July, 1872, confirm in a remarkable way the opinions of MacPherson on the same subject more than a hundred years before. In a note to "Temora, an Epic Poem", p. 144, original Edition 1763, we find the following:—"The poetical hyperboles of Ossian were afterwards taken in the literal sense by the ignorant vulgar; and they firmly believed that Fingal and his heroes were of a gigantic stature. There are many extravagant fictions, founded upon the circumstance of Fingal leaping at once over the river Lubar. Many of them are handed down in tradition. The Irish compositions concerning Fingal invariably speak of him as a giant. Of these Hibernian poems there are now many in my hands. From the language, and allusions to the times in which they were writ, I should fix the date of their composition in the fifteenth and sixteenth centuries," &c. When it is considered that the traditions on which MacPherson's remarks are founded were entirely of the North, and that similar absurd traditions borrowed from Ireland and current in Arran were totally unknown to him, the singularity of the correspondence adverted to becomes still more striking: it amounts, in fact, to an argument. Many similar preposterous stories, of the size and strength of Fingal, might easily be quoted from the vulgar in Arran—for some of which, compare Headrick; the only difference now being, that in the nineteenth century the people do not believe them.

and then by the discharge of an arrow, which, piercing their atmospheric disguise, put them to flight. How such unsophisticated readers would interpret "The Ancient Mariner" of Coleridge, with its shooting of the albatross and the dismal experience which ensued; or even the Song of Solomon with its oriental exaggerations of size and beauty, to which the exactest parallels might be quoted from Ossian, need not now be insisted on. Before the eyes of these simple people, Fingal still " sits a grey cloud in his hall;" Toscar still floats across the frith, or leans on his spear of mist from the middle heavens; and Malvina in reality, queen-daughter and victim, ascends in a wreath of smoke from the cromlech. They literally "see men as trees walking" in their own traditions, although they do not understand, and cannot believe such phenomena. Could any finer unconscious testimony be imagined to the authenticity of a text neither read nor seen, but only rehearsed and misinterpreted for fifteen hundred years? or to the substantial honesty of an unknown comparatively modern translation representing it?

In addition to which, however, we have the narration of facts they do understand, and which they assert with implicit confidence. Cloud or no cloud, Fingal subsisted by the arrow and the bow; had a dog called Bran, of surpassing strength and fleetness, but occasionally too prompt for his master; made many an expedition to Ireland; lived till he was an old man half blind, and died or fell at Corriefiun, and was interred there. Ossian, according to the same authority, was the last surviving son of this same Fingal; traversed Arran also repeatedly, on expeditions of love or war, to Ireland; passed through by Glenscordale on such occasions, from Machrie to the *Cletes* at Clachaig, where he took ship; was married to the daughter of an Irish chief, and had a son by her whose name was Oscar, and who was killed in Ireland, or brought a corpse to Arran, and buried in Glenree; had a daughter or a daughter-in-law, Malvina or Malvohr, resident at Drumadoon, and much beloved by him; witnessed this daughter's untimely death by accident or violence, and assisted at her burial, which was by the burning of her remains, as we have seen, and their interment in an urn or pot under a cromlech still extant at Drumadoon; thence finally, on his way to Ireland, old and blind, he passed through Glenscordale as heretofore, and by Glenree—the spot where his son was buried, for shipping at the *Cletes* of Clachaig, where he died and was interred:—all in literal conformity with a text which they the narrators never saw, and which MacPherson himself, in geographical and historical details like many of the foregoing, did not even understand and has utterly misinterpreted. But such people are illiterate peasants, it may be said, and do not themselves believe in the truthfulness of Ossian. So much the better, is the obvious reply: for their unlearned, unprejudiced, and often confused rehearsals of the simplest matters of fact which they do believe, are still the truest confirmations and the finest illustrations of his sublimest poetry.

On some of these traditions, however, in the way of supplementary evidence and not without a special interest of their own, although hitherto irrelevant, we are now at liberty to bestow exacter attention. The two of greatest importance and authority, on which the concurrence of the people is uniform, and which bear most directly on the authenticity of the text, are those which relate respectively to the death and burial of Oscar, and to the death or murder of Fingal, already anticipated; to some more detailed investigation of which we shall, therefore, dedicate the present and following chapters.

Fingal's death, so far as we are aware, has not been celebrated in Ossian as now known, for which we may find a natural reason by and by, in certain traditions regarding it; but Oscar's death by treachery in Ireland, and the embarkation of his body for burial in Scotland, have been very fully narrated, with the pathos of grief and of moral triumph, in the Poem of *Temora*, B. I. The dying hero is there represented as requesting to be buried with the accustomed solemnities at home—" Ossian, carry me to my hills! Raise the stones of my renown. Place the horn of the deer, and my sword, within my narrow dwelling. The torrent, hereafter, may raise the earth: the hunter may find the steel, and say 'This has been Oscar's sword.'" But Ossian's help could not be dispensed with in the war, and the obsequies were therefore entrusted to the care of Ullin, one of the royal bards, by the express command of Fingal. "'Ullin, my aged bard, take the ship of the king. Carry Oscar to Selma of harps. Let the daughters of Morven weep.' . . . . Ullin raised his white sails: the wind of the south came forth: he bounded on the waves towards Selma. I remained in my grief, but my words were not heard," &c. Whether such interment ever took place on the shores of Selma as originally intended, we are not informed; and the indefiniteness with which the subject is abandoned, as it were, seems to indicate that it did not: but that the remains were conveyed to Scotland, is beyond doubt. The point of embarkation, as the reader will find by referring to the poem, was at Lena, or Moi-Lena, in Ullin, on the north-east coast of Ireland; and the invariable route for Scotland, thence, was to the south end of Arran. There were two natural harbours there, of considerable depth and capacity, as the reader has already been informed in a previous chapter. One of these was near Clachaig on the Lagg, and the other at Sliddery a little to the west; which penetrated the island as a frith—first in a basin, and then in a straight line, so deep and equal between its walls of rock as in many places to resemble a canal—for fully a mile and a half inland, and terminated thus about three miles nearer Tor-lutha than the harbour at Clachaig did. On return voyages, therefore, persons coming from Ireland with that destination in view, as the Fingalians always had, and in ships that could not tack, would naturally prefer this landing place on the island; and in the circumstances of the case described, with a " south wind in his white sails," and with such a sad and difficult consignment as the mortal remains of a murdered chief, which had to be carried still farther, it was not only natural but absolutely certain that an aged navigator like Ullin should prefer it as the deepest, most accessible, and securest port. Sailing up the equal channel thus with his sacred burden, as far as the tide would permit—which might be half way between the present bridges on the river, or a little farther—he would anchor on the western bank as being still nearest to Tor-lutha, and there disembark his crew. Many considerations—most obviously his own age, the difficulty of farther transportation for the body without help, and the possible decomposition of the remains—might combine to suggest immediate interment; and interment would accordingly take place on the hill side, and at the very spot, where the tomb of Oscar son of Ossian, (to distinguish him from another Oscar, son of Caruth), by the authority of tradition time immemorial, is pointed out, nearly opposite the entrance of Glenree. The hero's favourite dog, which to a certainty would follow his remains as his destined associate in another world, would then be immolated and buried beside him, as the custom was; where, in fact, it is said still to lie, with a humble headstone of its own adjacent. It may farther be observed, as a probable incident on the occasion, that from the point in question a message might be carried across the hills, or rather up the glen—in less than two hours, the distance being not more than five miles—to Tor-lutha, where Malvina lived; who might thus, with her sisters or friends, attend the obsequies of her betrothed husband, and chant the coronach of grief and praise at his funeral. In point of fact, however, such message as we here suppose was not required, being anticipated by Malvina herself in a sort of dream, and she was present at the funeral in reality without any verbal summons. This affecting circumstance has been recorded by Ossian in a minor poem of which only a fragment remains, presented by MacPherson in a note to *Temora*, B. VIII.

. . . . . " The greatest, and perhaps the most interesting part of the poem," he says, " is lost. What remains is a soliloquy of Malvina, the daughter of Toscar, so often mentioned in Ossian's compositions. She, sitting alone in the vale of Moi-lutha, is represented as descrying, at a distance, the ship which carried the body of Oscar to Morven. ' Malvina is like the bow of the shower in the secret valley of streams; it is bright, but the drops of heaven are rolling in its blended light. They say that I am fair within my locks, but on my brightness is the wandering of tears. Darkness flies over my soul, as the dusky wave of the breeze along the grass of Lutha. Yet have not the roes failed me, when I moved between the hills. Pleasant, beneath my white hand, arose the sound of harps. What then, daughter of Lutha, travels over thy soul, like the dreary path of a ghost along the nightly beam ? Should the young warrior fall, in the roar of his troubled fields! Young virgins of Lutha, arise; call back the wandering thoughts of Malvina. Awake the voice of the harp, along my echoing vale. Then shall my soul come forth, like a light from the gates of the morn, when clouds are rolled around them with their broken sides. Dweller of my thoughts by night, whose form ascends in troubled fields, why dost thou stir up my soul, thou far-distant son of the king? Is that the ship of my love, its dark course thro' the ridges of ocean? How art thou so sudden, Oscar, from the heath of shields?' The rest of this poem, it is said," continues the translator, "consisted of a dialogue between Ullin and Malvina, wherein the distress of the latter is carried to the highest pitch."

Of the fragment thus strangely preserved and commented on by MacPherson, who could know nothing of its real import, for he knew nothing of Arran, the present writer was himself ignorant by oversight at the time when the above remarks on Oscar's burial, and corresponding incidental remarks on the same subject in preceding chapter, were recorded; and its accidental discovery, when subsequently transcribing these for the press, has produced an impression on his own mind as vivid and indelible as the fulfilment of a prophecy. According to this fragment, Malvina at Drumadoon, startled by a vision in some reverie of her own, looks out from the coast towards Ireland, and descries the ship of her lover approaching unexpectedly; she rushes through the hills with her companions to anticipate its arrival in the fiord of Sliddery, or at Glenree, where she finds Ullin disembarking, who narrates the story of her irreparable loss; and so her grief, at the funeral of her betrothed, finds vent in lamentation at his grave. No corroboration, we think, could be clearer; and a single word of explanation now, as to the geographical possibilities of the case, seems to be all that is required to produce absolute certainty of conviction on the subject.

From Moi-lutha, otherwise Tor-lutha, now Drumadoon—where Malvina in her day-dream of sorrow and apprehension, conjuring up scenes of bereavement for herself only too real, as we know, in Ireland, is supposed to be thus watching the tide—any ship of reasonable size, approaching the Island of Arran from the south, could be easily descried at a distance of 20 miles; more especially if its course, as represented, was from Sanda to Sliddery. On a clear day indeed, the very point, as by compass, on the Irish coast from which it sailed, could be distinguished at a distance of 40 miles; and its ominous solitary approach thence towards Arran, continuously traced, by one who was nervously apprehensive of evil tidings. As it drew nearer to the shore, with signals of death, it might be distinctly recognised, and its arrival in the well-known port anticipated without difficulty, by a walk of less than two hours through the intervening hills, which would bring the passenger exactly to Glenree. But this very process of watching from Drumadoon; of sorrowful and apprehensive discovery, of hasty departure to ascertain the cause of such a voyage from Ireland, when her hero should have been victorious on the field; and the agonised meeting of the widowed bride with the aged harper in charge of her lover's remains, on the spot where his grave is still shown, are the subject matter of the entire poem in question—apparently unknown to the people of Arran, and transferred by MacPherson in his ignorance to Morven. It may be accepted therefore, as an indisputable historical verity, authenticated by every variety of evidence—geographical, traditional, and poetical —that Oscar, slain in Ireland, was thus conveyed to, and buried in, the vale of Sliddery; and that Malvina his betrothed, from the vale of Shisken, forewarned by such a dream, was chief mourner at his funeral.

That she lingered about this spot continually, or at least frequented it often, and met with her own death by accident or violence in the neighbourhood, is certain also, both by tradition and by the letter of the text. The Poem of *Berrathon*, as already explained, confirms that fact; and the introduction to *Croma*, which must have been written immediately before, in which she laments his absence on the ground, and hears him crying to her from the very grave in anticipation of her own departure, illustrates the prophetic yearning of her grief with a pathos that can hardly be rivalled; and converts the whole region from Shisken to Sliddery and Clachaig, into a scene of real romance in suffering, in sorrow, and in sepulture, consecrated by the last efforts of the sublimest poetic genius.

"It was the voice of my love! few are his visits to the dreams of Malvina! Open your airy halls, ye fathers of mighty Toscar: unfold the gates of your clouds; the steps of Malvina's departure are near. I have heard a voice in my dream: I feel the fluttering of my soul. Why didst thou come, O blast, from the dark-rolling of the lake? [That lake was the lake of Shisken or Lutha, and the blast which passed over it would come straight from Glenree; nearly opposite to which, on the side nearest to Drumadoon, but a little to the south, was the grave of Oscar—whose rising shade would be thus caught by the breeze, and dissipated in the vale of Shisken.] Thy rustling wing was in the trees; the dream of Malvina departed. But she beheld her love, when his robe of mist flew on the wind. The beam of the sun was on his skirts; they glittered like the gold of the stranger. [A colour which would certainly be reflected by any wreath of mist from Glenree in the rays of the rising sun, to an observer at Drumadoon or in Shisken.] It was the voice of my love! few are his visits to my dreams! But thou dwellest in the soul of Malvina, son of the mighty Ossian. My sighs arise with the beam of the east; my tears descend with the drops of night. [The east to her was beyond Glenree, the west was in the ocean.] I was a lovely tree in thy presence, Oscar, with all my branches round me; but thy death came like a blast from the desart, and laid my green head low. [That desart would be the range of the Brown hills between Drumadoon and Sliddery—one of the bleakest in all Arran, and across which the first tidings of her lover's death would come. The woods also about Drumadoon were then beginning to fall, and Malvina herself might have seen some of them overthrown.] The spring returned with its showers, but no no leaf of mine arose. [More than one spring had passed since his death occurred.] The virgins saw me silent in the hall [that is, of Tor-lutha;] and they touched the harp of joy. The tear was on the cheek of Malvina; the virgins beheld me in my grief. Why art thou sad, they said, thou first of the maids of Lutha? Was he lovely as the beam of the morning, and stately in thy sight?"

Thus sings she in her sorrow, looking towards the very scene of Oscar's burial, and foreseeing her own departure thence—not a word in her soliloquy misplaced, as the reader will observe by the explanations introduced in brackets, or a figure in her speech misdirected: to whom her father-in-law in his blindness, yet cognisant of all the circumstances of her bereavement, thus replies.

"Pleasant is thy song in Ossian's ear, daughter of streamy Lutha! Thou hast heard the music of departed bards [of Ullin and his retinue, to wit, who brought her lover home a corpse—long since departed] in the dreams of thy rest, when sleep fell on thine eyes, at the murmur of Moruth [that is, the great stream—now Sliddery water, then the fiord of Sliddery and one of the largest in the island—on the banks of which, to the west, as we have seen, Oscar was buried; and where the hunting grounds are celebrated to this day as having been frequented by Malvina.] When thou didst return from the chase, in the day of the sun, [the vale of Sliddery, which in its upper range is called Glenscordale, runs nearly due south, and in the heat of the day is entirely filled with sun-light] thou hast heard the music of the bards, and thy song is lovely. It is lovely, O Malvina, but it melts the soul. There is a joy in grief, when peace dwells in the breast of the sad. But sorrow wastes the mournful, thou daughter of Toscar, and their days are few!"—Introduction to *Croma*.

O Johnson, Pinkerton, Macaulay, and the rest—to say that this was all bombast and a lie! But you knew nothing of Arran: you never traversed the vale of Shisken, nor surveyed its monuments, nor considered its geography; nor heard the rustle of the winds, in your imagination, among its prostrate woods; nor glanced on the surge of its departed lake, nor compared its traditions with the text of Ossian: yet neither did MacPherson, whom you have accused of falsehood and forgery; he was equally ignorant of it all. How strange you now look, confronted with him thus; how strange he himself looks, in the bewilderment of unexpected victory at the grave of Oscar, and by the tomb of Malvina; with the ghosts of fifteen hundred years ago, awoke from the dead, to enlighten and convict you—yourselves now ghosts, like them—in the pride of your unbelief!

Ossian still survives, you perceive, in spite of your infidelity; Oscar and Malvina have certainly lived, and loved and died; deeds of assassination were done in Ireland, deeds of violence occurred at home, and sepulchres were dug in Arran—not always in Morven, as your friend MacPherson believed, which was only his error of ignorance; and funeral chants of the tenderest pathos, with instinctive yearnings for immortality beyond them, were then heard in Shisken. As regards Ossian and his people, the facts of the case are so. Even the possibility of reply is foreclosed, by the verdict of the whole landscape around you. The earth, the water, the wind, and very clouds are agreed about it. The sunbeam from the east, beyond the grave at Glenree there, glances golden rebuke on your dull calumnies, and the ebbing fiord of Sliddery carries your vaunted authority to sea. The fine drawn light which shimmers thus, through so many centuries, on fallen forests, wasted lakes, and mouldering dead, dispels the last obstruction of your scorn—and our controversy with you is ended.

GROUND PLAN OF OSCAR'S GRAVE.

The grave itself around which so many associations cluster, and from which so many arguments emerge, now partially sunk or hollowed by decay and the action of the weather, lies S.E. and N.W. on the hillside above the river, within the limits of Margareeach farm. It measures, as in the foregoing ground plan, about 18 feet in length by 4 feet 4 inches in breadth, over all; enclosed between two rows of rude, unhewn and irregular, but massive flags deep on edge; with a still larger triangular flag, not less than 6 feet by 4 feet 6 inches, for headstone, towards the setting sun—in which position also, being highest up the hill, which is very steep at the place, it protects the grave from inundation by descending rains. The other end has been left open, most probably for a similar reason, that any rain, accumulated in the hollow, might escape. Some of the stones, as the reader will perceive, have been slightly displaced by accident, or subsidence of the ground; but none of them have been removed or injured.

Thus entombed and protected, interred by Ullin and lamented by Malvina, sleeps Oscar, son of Ossian; and his resting-place has been preserved sacred by the veneration of all occupiers of the soil, amidst surrounding cultivation, to the present hour—the small stones gathered from the field where his remains are laid being heaped around or within it, as a sort of modern cairn, to prevent accidental violation; and they should never be disturbed, from henceforth.

In the accompanying sketches—the one of Oscar's, the other of Malvina's tomb—taken by the Author on the spot, the graves of this devoted pair are represented with as much fidelity as possible, both as to their relative size and their appearance. The sleepers below, at the distance of a few miles from each other, the reader may now be well assured, were important historical personages in their day—true prince and true princess, genuine son and daughter of our oldest veritable royalty; a brave loyal man, and an accomplished devoted woman, believers in love, in honour, and in immortality; who fell sacrifices both to their own affectionate trust in the truth of others, and to the highest moral instinct of reverence for human duty. "They were lovely and pleasant in their lives," as life then was—full of manifold trials and sorrows, with triumphs and consolations of its own; "and in their death, they were not *far* divided."

OSCAR'S GRAVE.

MALVINA'S GRAVE.

## NOTES IN REPLY TO LAING.
### EVIRALLIN AND MALVINA.

We have not hitherto had an opportunity of replying directly to one of the most accomplished adversaries of MacPherson—Mr. Malcolm Laing—who republished the poems of Ossian in 1805, as the Poetical Works of MacPherson, with notes and commentaries of his own; nor do we intend to encumber our text itself by frequent reference to his authority. Where opportunities, however, occur hereafter as now, we shall quote and reply to his criticisms at the conclusion of separate chapters. According to this learned commentator on the supposed forgeries of MacPherson, there was never either a real Evirallin or a genuine Malvina; but both of these beautiful characters were manufactured out of one and the same worthless personage in an old Irish ballad, called Ossian's Courtship of Evirallin; who in the one case, it seems, "solicited, or rather despised the old bard;" and in the other was "converted into Malvina, the daughter of Toscar, and Oscar's mistress, a fictitious personage, for which there is no foundation, even in tradition."—Vol. I. p. 122. Mr. Laing, of course, was never in Arran; or he could not, with his ears open, have made such an allegation. But even if the miserable suggestion had been true, how profoundly has the world since been indebted to MacPherson for such a transformation! Mr. Laing should have thought of that. A little farther on, pp. 538, 539, &c.—in commenting on the passage from *Croma*, prophetic of Malvina's death, which we have just been illustrating from the very landscape in Arran where it was spoken, he endeavours to show that it was a piece of patchwork, not from an old Irish ballad at all, but from Solomon's Song, Thomson's Seasons, Pope's Iliad, 2 Timothy, Paradise Lost, I. and II., Solomon's Song again, Pope's Iliad again, Psalms of David, Solomon's Song a third time, Virgil's Æneid, Mason's Elfrida, &c., &c.; all woven together, a word here and another there from each, to finish the picture! But by spending half an hour at Drumadoon, standing on Malvina's grave, and with a copy of Ossian in his hand, the reader now, without more trouble or assistance, may realise every word of it. Finally, says Laing, Vol. II. p. 198, "Malvina is admitted to the airy hall of Fingal, without either mist or song; and no explanation is given of the situation of the dead," &c. That is, Mr. Laing understood as little as MacPherson about the burial of Malvina—either where, or how, or when it took place, or any circumstance whatever, accidental or ceremonial, connected with it. All that, however, has now been made plain; and thus not only Mr. Laing's theory of elaborate patchwork and splendid transformation, but his calumnies and his accusations alike, perish.

## CHAPTER IV.

**REVELATIONS IN ARRAN CONCLUDED—FINGAL'S GRAVE.**

FOR the place and circumstances of Fingal's death and burial, the traditions of Arran, supported by inferences from the text of Ossian, are our sole authority. From Ossian himself, as represented by MacPherson, no direct information, so far as we are aware, can be obtained on these points; although the clearest light is reflected by him on Fingal's demise itself, both by melancholy anticipations of it as then fast approaching, and yet more melancholy allusions to its having occurred, as a great and irreparable calamity. In these allusions one characteristic prevails—the idea of waste immortality, of glory half obscured, and of power diminished or intermitting in its grandeur, like a watery column or a spendthrift hurricane in the heavens; and if traditions in Arran are to be relied on, Ossian might have reasons of filial pride and sorrow both for this silence of his own in regard to the death, and for such melancholy associations in connection with it. In this view of the matter, indeed, his text may be regarded as rather corroborative than otherwise of the traditions; and as the reliability of these in other important cases has already been established, they deserve respectful consideration at least in the present.

It must be premised, however, in the first place, that there are other traditions in Scotland on the same subject, and a different resting-place claimed for the remains of Fingal. Pennant, in his Scottish Tour, is the first authority, perhaps, who makes a formal record with some detail of particulars on the matter; but after him, the same tradition is alluded to by the Rev. Patrick Stewart of Killin, in his contribution to Sir John Sinclair's Statistical Account of Scotland. According to Pennant, Killin is but a corruption of *Kil-Fiun*, or the burying-place of Fin; and Fin-larig, or Fin's-pass, in that immediate neighbourhood, is some corroboration of the local idea that Fingal did occasionally traverse the district—which we not only do not doubt, but have the best reason for believing, as the reader shall hereafter see. But how Fingal came to be killed and buried there, tradition does not show; and in point of fact, if any reliance is to be placed on Pennant's derivation of the name, Fingal must have had many burying-places in Scotland, for there are many Killins, and one among the rest in Arran. The statement, however, as originally made by Pennant, with his usual shrewdness and descriptive simplicity, had much to recommend it; and in default of any reliable information, the present writer was disposed to accept it as final, till minuter inquiries and personal examination of the spot entirely dissipated that faith. (1.) In the first place, Killin looks much more like a corruption of *Kill-lan*, the burying-place of a Celtic St. John, who was famous in that neighbourhood; and this derivation of the word would be indubitable, if there was not a tradition that the saint in question was buried at Dull—so called from the fact that the Dhulls, or twisted withes, on which his remains were borne, gave way at that spot; and that his body now rests there, under the floor of some chapel consecrated to his memory. (2.) If this tradition be correct, the grave pointed out as Fingal's, a little to the west of the town, cannot be St. Ian's;—but it is at least in the immediate precincts, if not within the very limits of the oldest ecclesiastical burying-ground there, and in close proximity to an ancient gallow-knowe, or place of execution. (3.) The grave itself, now shown, is obviously fictitious; and cannot possibly be the same as that referred to below, which was opened and explored by Mr. Stewart. It is not a mound, but a paltry ridge, a few feet in length, and not more than a few inches in height above the surrounding meadow—less conspicuous, indeed, than the grave of a peasant would now be in a decent cemetery. About shoulder-length in this lair, counting up from the foot, stands half thrown back a rude headstone block, grey enough undoubtedly, and apparently of softish whin, but not larger than those most commonly used for corners to dry-stone dykes in many parts of the country. The headstone for Oscar's dog, in fact, is a much more imposing monument. Pennant's legend, after this investigation, had very much the look of a fable, accepted second-hand most probably for some garrulous native in the district; and a reference to the Statistical Account of Scotland, in which an authoritative entry on the subject occurs, was sufficient to disabuse the present writer's mind of all farther faith in the entertaining Englishman's recital, even before anything in Arran purporting to be Fingal's grave had been seen by him. "A small eminence in the neighbourhood of the village of Killin," says the Rev. P. Stewart, "has accordingly been pointed out as his [Fingal's] grave; but on being opened some years ago, no vestige appeared of any persons having been interred there."—Vol. xvii., p. 368. It might, no doubt, have been opened before, and all traces of interment abstracted; as Pennant, with some obvious confusion of particulars about another grave in Glenalmond, seems to imply. But this robbery, if it ever occurred, as alleged, in General Wade's time, when the Highland roads were being constructed, must have been but a few years comparatively before Mr. Stewart's incumbency, and should have been fresher in the memories of the people than the tradition of the interment itself, which could not have been much less than 1500 years before the date in question. It is impossible, in short, for any antiquarian who has looked at a burial-place like Ossian's and Oscar's in their rude sublimity and grandeur, to believe that such a heap of meadow grass between a church-yard and a gallow-knowe at Killin ever covered the remains of a man like Fingal. Some Highland cateran of later days, from the Trosachs, with some similar real or affected name, may have been "justified" and buried there; but Fingal—the last generalissimo-king of Scotland, great-grandson of Trenmor, and father of Ossian—lies nearer his own kindred in the dust, or is at least sleeping solemnly elsewhere.*

As compared with Ossian's tomb, however, which is artistically sublime, or even with Oscar's, which is grand in its rudeness, the burying-place assigned to Fingal in Arran has specifically little but its own simplicity to distinguish it. On the west coast of the island, about three quarters of a mile beyond the extreme precipitous point where the road from Corriecraivy turns abruptly north to the Kilpatrick coves; or more exactly, half way between the two highest intermediate points on the long reach of road there, about sixty paces from the opening of a cattle-path called the "Queys' Slap" to the shore, and nine paces up from the road itself, in the lowest hollow of the hill-side, almost directly opposite the mouth of Campbeltown Loch, S.W.—is the verdant expanse of grassy heath fringed with heather, where his ashes are said to repose. The whole adjacent hill, for more than a mile in extent, is strewed so closely from top to bottom with enormous granite blocks, chiefly flat, but of every form and dimension, bleached white and bare in the tempests, as to resemble a graveyard of Titans; and these, by their multitude and size, might well dwarf the proportions of any ordinary human monument erected in the midst of them. But the space around the grave has been carefully cleared, apparently on purpose, and the two huge blocks, either left or placed there to mark its limits, are by a few minutes' steady observation easily distinguished; and once seen, will remain for ever distinguishable, even in imagination, from the chaos of volcanic ruin around them. No doubt at all about the sense or propriety of their position can ever again arise in the observer's mind. These blocks are respectively—the south-west or square one, as represented in the adjoining wood-cut, about 6 ft. long by 4 ft. broad and 3 ft. high; the other, like a lion couched, about 5 ft. 6 in. square, also by 3 ft. high—not less, in solid measurement above ground; and the space they mark out is a level heath, with a gentle rise to the hill above and a slope more irregular to the road below, which separates it from the verge of the precipitous cliff that

---

* Since writing the above, the Author has been informed that the stone at Killin is not now in its original position, and that the grave as now shown is actually fictitious. So much the worse for all tradition concerning it. The granite blocks in Arran, represented on the adjoining page, are treated with more reverence: both because the people, by invariable faith amounting almost to superstition, believe in them, and because they could not be so easily rifled with by surface-men and tenants.

fences up the Corrie from the sea. By a strange enough coincidence, they are very nearly in one and the same straight line from Drumadoon to Sanda; and the spectator, by standing between them and looking in opposite directions north and south, can realise at a glance the entire route from Morven to Ireland, and comprehend at once the natural order and propriety of all expeditions by Arran between the two extremes. Looking north over Drumadoon, the opening of Loch-Fyne is discernible, and thence in imagination, by a direct line, the view stretches on to Morven; south, between Sanda and Cantyre, the Fairheads of Ulster on the coast of Ireland, and more dimly to the east the range of mountains near Lough-Larne, are visible—between which and Morven, the tomb is almost equidistant; whilst right opposite to westward, as already indicated, lies Campbeltown Loch, of which more hereafter: nor is there any other point on the coast of Arran from which the same sort of survey, including so many important landmarks for the geography of Ossian, can be obtained.

The space between these monumental stones, which thus face one another N.E. and S.W., is 34 ft. exactly; of indefinite breadth, according to the fancy of the spectator; clothed with short grass, and decorated only with the waxen heath-bell and the smallest bright specks of the golden starwort. Here and there, through the surface, the tops of some underlying stones, as if of a subterranean cairn covering the remains, are indistinctly traceable—and this is all: large enough, simple and solemn enough, in its solitude and quiet grandeur, for the resting-place of a royal hero. A little to the north of it, but at a respectable distance—72 paces or thereby, has been an inferior grave with a single small headstone; and 50 paces farther on in the same line, another sepulchral enclosure of six triangular stones in a broken semicircular sweep, dedicated possibly to the memory of some attendants who may have fallen in fight; but both by comparison so insignificant as hardly to deserve being mentioned, except with a view to identify the spot, and to bear their own part as they stand, in confirmation of tradition. One of these, the intermediate one, has been dug into, and so left in ruin; the other as above described, in semicircle, may possibly have lost as many stones as would have completed the circle, but seems otherwise to be intact. Fingal's, so far as is known and as its very appearance testifies, has never been violated or disturbed by any human agency. The sheep alone now traverse its surface, and nibble down the grass to an equal level; but the "wild roes" once fed upon it; and Ossian in those days sat often beside it, and with filial hand, in his blindness, measured its smooth turf. "I hear not thy distant voice on Cona. My eyes perceive thee not. Often, forlorn and dark, I sit at thy tomb; and feel it with my hands. When I think I hear thy voice, it is but the blast of the desart." Compare *Fingal*, end of B. III. with end of B. V.

FINGAL'S GRAVE—LOOKING NORTH—DRUMADOON IN THE DISTANCE.

The region around and below it, towards the shore, is a sort of semispherical hollow, not much above the old sea line—so that landing in the neighbourhood would then be easy; and it is still called *Corrie-Fiun*, or Fingal's Corrie, in commemoration of his unlucky disembarkation and destruction there. The expedition from which he was returning has been variously described as on the coast of Ireland, or of Cantyre; or from Cantyre, as intermediate, on his way from Ireland—more likely to be the case; but however this might be, he had either been unexpectedly encountered by some hostile tribe on his arrival, or mistaken by friends as an invader, suddenly assailed and ignominiously discomfitted and slain, in the decline of a gigantic manhood. Tradition is clear on this, tradition is emphatic on this; and in the absence of all other information—in the significant silence of Ossian himself, who in pain and humiliation might distrust his own genius even to refer to it, it is some satisfaction to obtain a glimpse of the hero's fall on a shore where so many of his kindred are buried. On the supposition that these traditional accounts are true, and that the facts have been all as represented, of which there can be no reasonable doubt, we have two more additional and powerful links of association, in the graves of Oscar and Fingal, to bring Ossian back from Morven, with feeble step and blind, to be laid himself in his own sepulchre, among the ashes of his people.

It will not be allowed, however, to assume all this, or even any part of it, without evidence more direct than the traditions of the natives; which require, indeed, to be investigated always, and carefully collated with the text. Is there proof, it may be said, that Fingal was in Ireland at the time? that he was so inadequately attended at the time? or so aged as to be unable to make good his own landing, on a shore with which he was so intimately acquainted? In replying to these difficulties, we find the amplest confirmation of tradition, in this as in other cases, from the very mouth of Ossian; as if tradition, in fact, by the consent of ages, had been founded unconsciously on his songs and poems.

The reader will find, on this particular occasion, by consulting *Temora*— (1.) That Fingal was in the North of Ireland immediately preceding his death; (2.) that he was then so far advanced in life as to resign all authority in the field; and (3.) that he must have left the coast of Ireland on his homeward route, with nothing more than a personal retinue, for the army he commanded was left behind. In B. I. of that poem, he is described as 'aged,' as 'a gray cloud,' as in the 'midst of his darkening years,' as 'beginning to be alone, and dreading the fall of his renown.' In B. II., as requiring the assistance of his son; again as 'beginning to be alone,' with 'darkness gathering on the last of his days,' and 'near the steps of his departure.' In B. III., as the poem proceeds, he is represented as 'leaning on an oak,' 'brightening in the last of his fields,' 'his grey

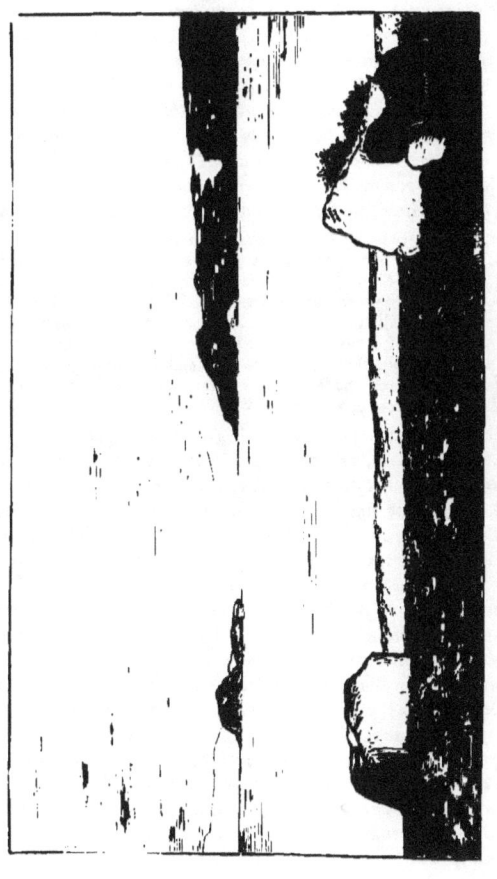

FINGAL'S GRAVE—LOOKING SOUTH—SANDA IN THE DISTANCE.

hair on the breeze.' "Stand, Ossian," he cries, "near thy father, by the falling stream. Raise the voice, O bards ; Morven, move beneath the sound. It is my latter field ; clothe it over with light." In B. VI., Ossian "beholds the foe round the aged, and the wasting away of his fame. Thou art left alone in the field, grey-haired king of Selma." In B. VIII., when the crisis of the campaign approaches, he enters battle with the presentiment that it is for the last time— "if there my standard shall float on wind, over Lubar's gleaming course, then has not Fingal failed in the last of his fields." He is successful, however ; but victory achieved, he resigns his spear, the hereditary spear of Trenmor, to Ossian, and retires for ever from the field, leaving Ossian generalissimo in his room.

"Ossian, thou hast the spear of Fingal : it is not the staff of a boy with which he strews the thistle round, young wanderer of the field. No ; it is the lance of the mighty, with which they stretched forth their hands to death. Look to thy fathers, my son ; they are awful beams. With morning, lead Ferad-Artho forth to the echoing halls of Temora. Remind him of the kings of Erin ; the stately forms of old. Let not the fallen be forgot, they are mighty in the field. Let Carril pour his song, that the kings may rejoice in their mist. To-morrow I spread my sails to Selma's shaded walls ; where streamy Duthula winds through the seats of roes."—*Temora*, end of B. VIII.

In these circumstances, therefore, aged, grey-haired, and now approaching his latter end ; without arms, sword or spear, and with probably a very small following, as on a peaceful voyage ; Fingal, at the close of the campaign in Moi-lena, left Ireland for the last time on his return to Selma. But his route, for convenience, might be by the coast of Cantyre ; most certainly, it must have been by the Island of Arran ; and if, in landing on the southern shore there, he should have been mistaken or opposed by unfriendly natives, his untimely, or at least obscure and unhonoured death might thus occur on the spot. In point of fact, as we have seen, according to tradition, it did so occur then and there ; and the few followers who accompanied him, being slain in his defence, were buried also at a little distance from him there, where their tombs seem still to be indicated by the circles or monoliths above referred to, and are so identified by the people.

In reply to this, it may, of course, be urged that a man, so old as Fingal in *Temora* is represented to have been, could never have performed the exploits ascribed to him in that poem—an objection which MacPherson anticipated ; and by the most extraordinary calculation, founded as he says upon tradition, has endeavoured to show that, at the date in question, Fingal's age, in face of all that has been quoted from the poem itself, " was just fifty-six years ;" and in face of his own calculation elsewhere, founded on historical data, that it could not have been less than ninety-two! These self-contradictory conclusions are to be found respectively in his notes to *Temora*, end of B. VIII., and in his summaries to *Comala* and the *War of Caros*. In the note to *Temora*, his computation is that Fingal was but 18 at the birth of Ossian; that Ossian was the same age at the birth of Oscar, and that Oscar was about 20 at the time of his own death, = 56. But Oscar, who was slain in *Temora*, was alive at the *War of Caros*—was, in fact, the hero of that campaign; and Fingal in the poem of *Comala*, before Ossian was born, and who, therefore, could not be much under 17 at the time, defeats Caracul on the Carron. According to MacPherson's own showing, however, and as we shall by and by see was undoubtedly the case, Caracul was identical with Caracalla, and Caros with Carausius. But Caracalla's defeat, according to all contemporaneous history, could not have been later than 211 A.D.; nor the defeat of Carausius, before 285 A.D.—which gives a difference of 74. To this, 16 or 17 must be added at least, for the age of Fingal, and perhaps another year for the interval between Oscar's victory on Crona and his death at Temora; so that Fingal's age, who was present on both occasions, would be 74 + 18 = 92. How little reliance is to be placed on MacPherson's conjectures after a contradiction like this, preserved in his own editions to the end, is obvious; and how unconscious of all dishonesty he must have been in thus contradicting himself, when the alteration of a word or two in either of the poems would have prevented it, must be still more obvious. There was an absurd, almost incredible oversight here, but no forgery. Ossian, in fact, alone is consistent and reliable. Fingal is described by him as a very old man in the campaign of Temora, and all intermediate dates, when fairly ascertained, correspond: yet nothing on the one hand is ascribed to him in *Temora*, which, with due allowance for poetic and filial exaggeration of great exploits, might not have been achieved by him. On the contrary, his action throughout is characterised both by the prudence, and the conscious approaching infirmities, of old age; and nothing, on the other hand, is unlikely in the tradition that such a man, with all his magnificent physical endowments, but without arms or followers, might perish by violence on the open shore. Men, in fact, were giants in those days—not supernatural in size, as foolishly imagined by the vulgar; but still gigantic, in strength and physical development—as Ossian distinctly asserts; and as the discovery of their remains, and the very dimensions of their graves at this day, in Arran and elsewhere on the western coasts of Scotland, prove—of which the reader will find some illustrations in the Appendix; and in other regions too, within the verge of the Christian era, there were men of corresponding vitality. Fingal, living a life in the simplicity of nature, and inured to hardship from his youth, does deeds at the age of 92 at which men in their decadence now wonder; and John the Divine, originally a fisherman in Galilee, but two hundred years before that, escapes from captivity in Patmos and indites the "Revelation" apparently at 96. A still more wonderful coincidence occurs a thousand years earlier, in the case of Solomon; who, according to Josephus, ascended the throne at the age of 14, was husband and father at the age of 16, reigned 80 years, and after a life of unparalleled sensuality died at the age of 94. But even giants are not immortal; the latter day for all will come: and Ossian himself, who must have been 65 or 70 years of age at least, in the campaign of Temora, returns to Arran—first from Ireland, and finally from Morven—as to his long home. Without father, without mother, without wife or son; without brother, almost without kindred, or with a widowed daughter-in-law alone to cheer him, in "the dark brown years" of sorrow and bereavement which were beginning to close thickly around, he returns and dies.

"But age is now on my tongue; and my soul has failed. I hear sometimes the ghosts of bards, and learn their pleasant song. But memory fails in my mind. I hear the call of years. They say, as they pass along, why does Ossian sing? Soon shall he lie in the narrow house, and no bard shall raise his fame. Roll on, ye dark brown years, for ye bring no joy on your course. Let the tomb open to Ossian, for his strength has failed. The sons of song are gone to rest; my voice remains like a blast, that roars lonely on a sea-surrounded rock, after the winds are laid. The dark moss whistles there, and the distant mariner sees the waving trees."—*Songs of Selma.*

"The time of my fading is near, and the blast that shall scatter my leaves. To-morrow shall the traveller come; he that saw me in my beauty shall come: his eyes will search the field, but they will not find me! So shall they search in vain for the voice of Cona, after it has failed in the field. The hunter shall come forth in the morning, and the voice of my harp shall not be heard. 'Where is the son of car-borne Fingal?' The tear will be on his cheek. Then come thou, O Malvina, with all thy music, come: lay Ossian in the plain of Lutha: let his tomb rise in the lovely field."—*Dying Hymn* [in Arran.]

But Malvina herself was already gone, and Ossian must now be buried, a few miles farther south than the plain of Lutha, by the hand of comparative strangers. The son of Alpin, it is true, himself a younger bard, who knew all the history of his father's house, and was privileged to be the personal attendant of the poet; who had reported Malvina's death to him, when no one else had courage to mention that calamity; and who was honoured, beyond doubt, to rehearse the Dying Hymn, now called *Berrathon*, in which it was commemorated, and thus to preserve the record of it to posterity:—this youth alone, besides the soldiery of Morven on their way to Ireland, was with him, and might preside at his obsequies in Clachaig, or chant the requiem of his soul at the tomb. All else, beloved and related, were gone; their monuments only were extant around him. "The fame of my former actions is ceased; and I sit forlorn at the tombs of my friends."—*Fingal*, B. VI. Oscar and his dog were asleep, in their lonely sepulchres, at the sound of Moruth; Fingal, between his giant blocks, lay prone on the volcanic ridge—his head to Morven, and his feet to Ireland—on the verge of the ocean; Malvina, in the ashes of her urn, reposed by the brink of Lutha; her own father Toscar, it may be presumed, and her mother Colnadona, from Col-amon, lay not far distant; her father's sister at least, as we know, Galvina the unfortunate, and her luckless lover Comal, also slept, a little farther northward, in their own "green tombs, at the noise of the sounding surge." Fillan and Ryno, in the meantime, victims of war, "lay peaceful" on the banks of the Lubar in Ullin—almost within eye-shot of their father Fingal's grave; and Bosmina, their sister, had departed. Only one death more was needed, to complete the extinction of his race; and one other burial in Arran, to consecrate its soil for ever. Ossian, therefore, has come hither to die; and the son of Alpin shall superintend his funeral—shall consecrate his lofty resting-place at least, with the funeral dirge, and carry back the news of his death to Morven.

In summing up these traditions of the dead, it seems impossible again to look at such monuments of their long-doubtful existence without wonder and reverence, not unmixed with a feeling of sorrowful admiration and love. Apart altogether from their connection with literature, their preservation for nearly two thousand years with almost no injury but what our own hands, in verification of their claims, have inflicted on them, makes them venerable; their magnitude and rude artistic beauty, as the workmanship of reputed savages, makes them objects of devout curiosity; but connected, as they undoubtedly are, with the oldest and sublimest literature of a great nation, united indissolubly with the remotest action of its earlier life, and reflecting as they do the light of absolute certainty on such a past, as unmoved landmarks and unbiassed chronicles to establish or correct its history, their value is almost inestimable. It is doubtful, indeed, whether Great Britain contains in any corner of it, and within so small a compass, monuments of the same age or of equal grandeur and importance. The tombs of Palestine alone have corresponding interest for the world.

END OF PART SECOND.

"The Desart."

The Brown Hills.

Leac-a-Breac, or the Stone-speckled Mountain.

| N. | 60 Paces from "Query' Slap." | Road. | "Query' Slap." | S. |

Fingal's Grave

Corrie-Fiun.

Sea Shore opposite Campbeltown-Loch.

For Readers who may be also Tourists, the above diagram will be of service.

## Part Third.

# FINGAL IN IRELAND.

## THE SCOTS IN IRELAND.

# CONTENTS.

## SECTION FIRST.

|  | PAGE |
|---|---|
| CHAPTER I.—*Fingal* and *Temora*: Analysis of Scene—Ullin, Moi-Lena, Cromla, The Lubar, &c., | 99 |
| CHAPTER II.—*Fingal* and *Temora* (continued): Verification of Scenes above mentioned, … … | 108 |
| CHAPTER III.—Fingal in Ireland: Objections considered—Irish Bards—MacPherson's bewilderment explained—No Scene in Ireland corresponds to Moi-Lena but valley of the Six-Mile-Water, … … … | 125 |
| NOTES in reply to Laing: I. Gelchossa and Lamdearg—II. Cuthullin's Shield at Tura—III. Oscar's death at Temora, … … … … … … … … … … … … … … | 134 |
| CHAPTER IV.—Lake Lego—Lough-Neagh: *Death of Cuthullin*—Poem analysed—Scene determined—Origin, Position, and Characteristics of Lough N., signification of name, and identity with Lake Lego established, | 137 |

## SECTION SECOND.

|  | PAGE |
|---|---|
| CHAPTER V.—The Scots in Ireland: Dynasty of Conar—Origin and Limits of its Sovereignty—Temora not Tara in Meath, but Connor in Antrim, … … … … … … … … … … | 149 |
| NOTES from O'Donovan: I. The Lubar identified—II. Fall of Foldath—III. Foldath's Grave, … … | 164 |
| CHAPTER VI.—Scots in Ireland (continued): Emigration from the Solway—Larthon lands at Ardglass, … | 171 |

## ILLUSTRATIONS.

|  | PAGE |
|---|---|
| Full Page Map of ULLIN and INISHUNA, | 124 |

# FINGAL IN IRELAND.

## SECTION FIRST.

### CHAPTER I.

#### CAMPAIGNS IN *FINGAL* AND *TEMORA*.

IN turning attention at last to this much controverted topic, which will be found replete with interest both critical and antiquarian, the reader must be informed in advance that it is far from being critical and antiquarian solely. It will afford, indeed, the clearest evidence of that sort to the authenticity of Ossian, and the honesty or ignorance of MacPherson—which have first of all to be established; but beyond these points, when fairly proved, it will conduct us by the plainest paths of historical revelation into many of the most important, and certainly the very oldest, details of our national existence. That the argument, therefore, may proceed without flaw or prejudice, it will be necessary, in prosecuting the inquiry, to adhere exclusively as well as rigidly to the text of Ossian as represented by MacPherson, making no farther account of MacPherson himself than as avowed translator; and of how little account beyond that his authority must prove, will soon be made apparent to the reader.

The two greatest works ascribed to Ossian, as the world is aware—greatest in extent, in poetical elaboration, and in historical interest—are the Epic poems of *Fingal* and *Temora*; and they both refer to Ireland. In *Fingal*, we have a spirited dramatic narration of the first great expedition of relief by the Caledonian king, to his relatives and allies in a certain region of that Island; and in *Temora*, a corresponding account of his last expedition. In *Fingal*, the invaders are Norse or Norwegians; in *Temora*, they are usurpers from Erin; and in both expeditions Fingal is victorious, repelling the invaders in one case and subduing the usurpers in the other. There was before these, also, an earlier expedition in Fingal's youth, which is introduced as an episode in *Temora*, and interwoven with the general history by inference alone. Of this, however, for the present, we can make no separate analysis. It is with the two larger poems complete in themselves, of which the scenes are the same and can be easily defined in the text, we are now concerned; and to identify the action of both with the hitherto unknown verities of history and geography, our present argument is addressed.

On the supposition, then, that two such poems, detailing affairs of such importance in the ancient intercommunity of nations, were forgeries by MacPherson in the middle of the eighteenth century, it must be surprising to the dullest unbeliever in their truth, that the author of these forgeries can give us no farther information of their geographical groundwork than that it was somewhere in Ulster; and yet more surprising, that the plainest indications in the poems themselves, determining their localities, are misunderstood or overlooked by him. He perceives, indeed, that the scene of both poems is the same, or nearly the same; and that the general action, therefore, is confined to a comparatively small space. Guided by his knowledge of the Gaelig language, he determines also that Ulster and Connaught are represented in the poems, and that certain mountains, lakes, and rivers, as he believes, in both provinces, are specified by name. Such names he translates, but identifies with nothing now known in the geography of the country. The provinces themselves, in which something corresponding to these names should be found, are only indicated, not defined, and may be of any extent whatever. The deficiency thus obviously felt is filled up with annotations, critical and traditional, on the various topics suggested by the text—such as the customs of the people, or the genealogy of the actors—and which are valuable or entertaining, but commit their author to nothing, and in a controversy like the present must be dismissed as irrelevant. That there may be no room for doubt, however, on such an important preliminary as the translator's inability to assign any known region as the immediate scene of action in either poem, the following abstract of all the geographical information communicated by him in his notes to *Fingal* and *Temora* is subjoined :—

The scene, he says, which is nearly the same in both, lies on the heath of *Lena*, and the mountain *Cromla* on the coast of Ulster.

*Atha* is a "shallow river" in Connaught;

*Tura*, . . . . a castle on the coast of Ulster;

*Slimora*, a hill in Connaught;

*Alnecma*, or *Alnecmacht*, the ancient name of Connaught;

*Ullin*, still the Irish name of the Province of Ulster;

*Ul-Erin*, "guide to Ireland," name of a star;

*Lego*, or *Li-ego*, "Lake of disease," a lake in Connaught, into which the river Lara emptied itself—a fact thus according to MacPherson, in his notes, which the reader will find to be the very reverse of what appears in his own translation.

These annotations occur in his first edition; to which in his final edition, ten years later, he adds—

*Cromleach*, or *Cromla*, signified a place of worship among the Druids;
*Erin*, "Western Isle," .... means Ireland;
*Inisfail*, "Island of the Fa-il, or Falans;" and
*Lubhar*, or *Labhar*, "loud, noisy"—a river in Ulster:

This, so far as appears, is the sum of all information, conjectural or real, on the geography of the two great epics vouchsafed by their translator. Considering that Ulster and Connaught represent nearly one-half of all Ireland, containing together about 15,378 square miles, of above 200 miles in length and about 100 in breadth, with a seaboard of almost infinite irregularity—in bays, creeks, and indentations beyond number; and contain rivers, streams, brooks, woods, valleys and mountains, if not absolutely innumerable, at least too numerous to be identified; and on the other hand, that the scene described in *Fingal* and *Temora* does not exceed some 5 miles square, with a comparatively small mountain stream in the centre of it, which here and there might be bounded over with the help of a spear,—it may be safely said that no information could be more insufficient or unsatisfactory; and that if any forger had designed expressly to bewilder his readers and screen himself from critical detection, he could not have been more indefinite. Yet MacPherson obviously gives us all the information in his power; and it may be demonstrated from the text itself, that the ground he describes, with all its principal features unchanged, is still traceable on an average atlas in a region he never dreamt of, and with a minuteness of correspondence in many respects to the most trivial descriptive terms in the poems in question, which would have delighted or confounded him, if he had been able to realise the facts —in one instance so little realised, that he seems to be tracing a river backwards to the sea, which is flowing inland from its source on an outlying mountain.

Setting aside, therefore, his own meagre and inconclusive geographical details, except where it may be necessary to contradict or correct them, and adhering exclusively, as proposed, to the letter of the text, the following explanatory remarks have to be made, on the threshold of our inquiry:—(1.) That in the poems of *Fingal* and *Temora*, ERIN, although sometimes figuratively applied as a name to the whole island, means generally the south and south-west provinces of the kingdom of Ireland, as contradistinguished from the north and north-east; a signification attached to it still by the native population from Dublin southward, who regard the people of the north as hereditary national intruders— "cold and black." (2.) That ULLIN, in its application by Ossian, is restricted exclusively to the north-east; does not seem by any means to be co-extensive with Ulster, as MacPherson represents it, or to include much more geographically than the County of Antrim: and (3.) that ALNECMA, or ALNECMACHT, may be equivalent to Connaught, but has no definite limits assigned to it; was applied generally, as a sort of comprehensive title, to the country west of Ullin, and was included occasionally under the wider designation of Erin.

The scene of *Fingal* and *Temora*, therefore, being in the kingdom of Ullin; and the expeditions themselves celebrated in these poems being for the restoration of that kingdom to its lawful dynasty of Caledonian princes, murdered or dethroned by usurpers from Alnecma and Erin; must be sought for, beyond doubt, if it exists anywhere at all, on the coast of Antrim or in that neighbourhood: and in Antrim itself, within a few miles of the shore at a given point, every feature of the region described in the poems, with many particulars confirmatory beyond imagination of their various details, may yet be discovered.

In reproducing the scenes in question we shall, in the present chapter, arrange their principal outlines from the text, under such heads as may be most convenient for subsequent comparison with geographical authorities; and shall then proceed, in the chapter immediately following, to verify their identity by that means, with occasional quotations where it may seem necessary.

#### SCENE OF ACTION AS REPRESENTED IN THE TEXT.

I. GENERAL ASPECT.—The scene of action in both poems, as MacPherson correctly observes, is almost identical—the only difference in fact being, that the scene of *Fingal* is enlarged in *Temora*, as the nature of the action required. In *Fingal*, invaders from the sea are to be driven back to the shore; but in *Temora*, usurpers from the interior are to be confronted: the progress of the action, therefore, in the one poem is to eastward, in the other to westward, on the same plain. It seems to begin, by an accident, a little farther north also in *Temora* than in *Fingal*; but it is vividly and repeatedly represented in both, as at first upon a heath, or Lena proper, on the shore, at the head of a bay stretching inland, "where its blue waters tumbled in the bosom of echoing woods;" and then upon a larger heath, or Moi-lena, as the name implies, which extends at the close much farther west, till it becomes a valley of considerable dimensions, traversed by a mountain stream called the Lubar, with a "hundred" tributary rills after rain; and bounded south and north by two mountain ranges meeting in a point on the shore at the head of the bay, and so closely adjoining there that the leaders of the opposing armies may distinguish one another on the opposing hills, and issue orders with precision to their respective hosts on the plain below. Where the mountain ranges thus meet there is a narrow defile, traversed by another and a smaller stream in an opposite direction—that is, to seaward; which defile is to be carefully guarded, for by it an invading army on the shore might either advance or retreat with advantage, but which might be held by one or two brave men against a thousand. The most serious conflicts, however, occur inland—some of them, far inland—and crowds of slain are represented as being entombed afterwards in the greater valley, or Moi-lena, towards the setting sun ; whilst Fingal, with a small retinue, is re-embarking for Scotland, near the foot of said defile, on the shore at Lena. The bay itself, by which access to this strath or valley is afforded from the ocean on the east, is called indifferently the Bay of Lena, or of Moi-lena, as the destination of the voyagers, friends or foes, might be ; but it was apparently the natural landing place, and afforded the safest harbourage " in its bosom of echoing woods," for all who were bound to Ullin from the Clyde—with this disadvantage, however, that it had a rock or rocks in the offing, on which shipwreck before a gale from the north was a danger to be seriously apprehended.

II. SOUTH SIDE.—Of the mountain ranges now specified, one called Cromla heads up to the bay on the east, slopes down to the sea on the south, and stretches far to westward inland ; is of moderate height, with steeps to the north—not higher, however, than can be easily ascended and re-ascended, and crossed over to the sea, in the course of an afternoon or evening ; is crowned on the summit with a comparatively level heath, in which to the eastward is a small lake or tarn, called "the lake of roes," and which is once the scene of a chase; is covered on its northern slopes with groves and brushwood ; is intersected everywhere with ravines and torrents, which burst forth after rain, and leap over moss-covered rocks ; is pierced with many considerable caves to the westward, in which Druids lodge, and fugitives from battle hide themselves, and ghosts of the slain confabulate. Near one of these in particular, and in close proximity to the lake above mentioned, is a rivulet remarkable for its noise—where Muirne or Morna, the beloved daughter of Cormac, fell a victim to the revenge of a rejected lover, and perished " in the cave of the rock, at the oak of the noisy streams," beside the circle of stones where a Druid dwelt : " Why in the circle of stones ; in the cave of the rock, alone? The stream murmurs hoarsely. The old tree's groan is in the wind. The lake is troubled before thee ; and dark are the clouds of the sky ! But thou art like snow on the heath ; and thy hair like the mist of Cromla, when it curls on the rocks ; and it shines to the beam of the west : "—indications of locality and position, every syllable of which, as the reader will by and by find, is significant.—*Fingal*, original Edition, B. I.

In the same neighbourhood, apparently on the same spot, or very near it, at a later date, another lady, called Sulmalla, takes refuge, whilst the object of her ambitious love falls by the hand of Fingal on the plain below. She believes that she sees him on the mountain, " when the sun looks from the rocks of the west," and "the mists of the lake arise." It is but the spirit of Cathmor, however, as the Druid "in his mossy cave," "near his own loud stream," "under his echoing tree," when "his eyes had failed," "leaning forward on his staff," had informed her: "It was the spirit of Cathmor, stalking large, a gleaming form. He sunk by the hollow stream, that roared between the hills."—*Temora*, BB. VII. VIII. Farther, this southern range has lower spurs here and there on its northern slopes, running out into a plain where the armies contend—one of which to the east called Mora, a heathy ridge with projecting rocks, is easily occupied by Fingal as a vantage ground of observation; and another, apparently at some distance to the west or north-west, called Dora, shines "yellow" in the setting sun. Beyond this ridge to southward, close on the shore of the sea, but at right angles from the bay in which the invading forces land, and at no great distance westward from the lake above mentioned, lies Tura, the seat of Cuthullin (and before him, of other princes also—of the lady Muirne's father, Cormac, for example), with its "mossy towers" and a dreary cave of its own—"beside a stream of roaring foam, his cave is in a rock," "the dreary cave of Tura," "the cave of his grief"—a spot which seems to be easily accessible to messengers and warriors, and even to women, by crossing the mountain from the north, as if the distance were but an evening's walk, with the setting sun glittering behind them. "The sun is bright on his armour: Connal slowly strode behind. They sunk behind the hill [implying that they had crossed it,] like two pillars of the fire of night; when winds pursue them over the mountain, and the flaming heath resounds."—*Fingal*, B. V. This motion is to southward, and towards the cave above described—points, in the scene of both poems, to be carefully noted by the reader now for his greater satisfaction afterwards.

III. NORTH SIDE.—The other ridge, as we have seen, runs inland also from nearly the same point on the shore, but at a sharp angle with Cromla—that is, westward or north-westward; and through the triangular plain thus formed, flows the Lubar, which springs from the side of Crommal, a "misty top" in the northern ridge and apparently near the sea. The Lubar, therefore, must have been an inland-flowing stream; and the valley through which it thus flows to westward, between the ridges, is celebrated for the richness of its pasture, the greenness of its verdure, and the beauty of its cattle, especially of its bulls and horses. The river itself seems everywhere remarkable for the grandeur of the oaks on its banks, the mossy rocks which interrupt it, the dripping caves by which it murmurs, the monumental stones which mark its course, and the rapidity and force of its current throughout. One red oak in particular, three upright stones commemorating covenants—one called "the stone of Lubar"—and a cave in a ledge of rock, where a dying hero, Fillan the son of Fingal, is laid, are designated by the poet as conspicuous objects in connection with important events in battle. On the farther side of the range from which this river issues—that is, to the northward of it, flows another stream, through a similar valley, and in a similar direction, called the Lavath; and the palace of Conar, the first Caledonian prince of Ullin, is not far distant—called *Ti-mór-ri*, or Temora, as in the title of the poem; but not to be confounded with *Teac-mór*, much less with *Tobrad*, or Tara, the traditional palace of the supreme kings of Ireland on the plains of Meath—of which more in succeeding chapters, and in Appendix.

IV. EAST AND WEST; or Eastward and Westward: for it is only by the rays of the sun, their original direction and reflection at certain points in the landscape, and at a given season of the year, as described in the poems, that we can determine the bearings; which seem to be more exactly north-east and south-west, than east and west, by the compass—so that north and south, as hitherto indefinitely employed, will have a slight variation accordingly. With this explanation, it is now to be noted that the whole scene above described is illuminated, from the east or eastward, by the first rays of morning light over the ocean— "High Cromla's head of clouds is grey: morning trembles on the half-enlightened ocean."—*Fingal*, B. II. "Morning is grey on Cromla: the sons of the sea ascend," that is, from their ships.—B. III. "The faint beam of the morning came over the waters of Ullin."—B. IV. "Now like a dark and stormy cloud, edged round with the red lightning of heaven, flying westward from the morning's beam, the king of Selma removed. . . . High on Cromla's height he sat, waving the lightning of his sword, and as he waved, we moved."—B. IV. "Brightening in his fame, the king strode [from Cromla, the southern ridge] to Lubar's sounding oak [northward], where it bent from its rock over the bright tumbling stream. Beneath it, is a narrow plain, and the sound of the fount of the rock. Here the standard of Morven poured its wreaths on the wind, to mark the way of Ferad-Artho from his secret vale [still farther north]. Bright, from his parted west, the sun of heaven looked abroad. The hero saw his people, and heard their shouts of joy. In broken ridges round, they glittered to the beam."—*Temora*, B. VIII. The sun still shining thus "from his parted west," as in the above quotation—that is obviously, after leaving the west; or, in other words, from the north-west—intimates conclusively that the action of the poem was in summer; and the fact that a severe thunderstorm with torrents of rain is described as having occurred but a few hours before, after which "the hundred streams of Moi-lena shone," and "the blue columns of mist slow rose against the glittering hill," seems to determine the date about the end of July or beginning of August. All which indications of locality and motion and reflected light, in the early autumnal months, so vivid and exact, in connection with previous data, demonstrate unequivocally that the bay of Moi-lena, "with its blue-tumbling waters embosomed in echoing woods," was on the north-east coast of Ireland; and that the ridge of Cromla from which Fingal stepped north into the evening sunshine, and which warriors crossed over to the south with backs to the setting sun, ran westward or south-westward inland; with another sea-coast, where Tura lay, facing to the south or south-east beyond it. This seems to be mathematically, as well as geographically certain; which the landmarks and bearings of the scene, as incidentally suggested by the poet, with pictorial precision, confirm, if such confirmation is necessary. (1.) There seems to be some island, or small peninsula, in the offing; by which the harbour is sheltered, and on which invaders, in their first attempt, might land. "The king, whose ships of many groves could carry off thine isle! So little is thy green-hilled Ullin to him who rules the stormy waves."* *Fingal*, B. II.—words which could never be intended by any sane man, much less an ambassador, to apply to the whole of Ireland; but might, with some vain-glorious boastful license, be spoken of an insular offshoot—such as Isle Maghee, when the mainland, as we are informed, was partially concealed by a mist. (2.) From a point over the sea, in advance of Cromla, and therefore close upon the shore, a scout looking north-eastward—for in any other direction it would be impossible to look—can discover "the ships, the ships of the lonely isle! There Fingal comes, the first of men, the breaker of shields: the waves foam before his black prows. His masts with sails are like groves in clouds."—*Fingal*, B. II. (3.) "But the night is gathering around, where now are the ships of Fingal? Here let us pass the hours of darkness, and wish for the moon of heaven."—*Ibid.* Besides which, a storm begins—"the winds came down on the woods: the torrents rushed from the rocks: rain gathered round the head of Cromla; and the red stars trembled between the flying clouds."—*Ibid.* But a rock in the harbour, or at the entrance to the harbour, is most dangerous of all, and whilst Fingal is rapidly approaching in the storm, Cuthullin on Cromla prays—"shew thy face from a cloud, O moon; light his white sails on the wave of the night; and if any strong spirit of heaven sits on that low-hung cloud; turn his dark ships from the rock, thou rider of the storm!"—*Ibid.*, B. III.

V. And finally: The whole scene we have now been describing has been crowded, during several expeditions, from east to west, with the graves of innumerable dead. The valley of the Lubar, in fact, and the very spurs of the mountains adjoining, were made fields of sepulture—filled with the green tombs of the nameless, and the cairns or cromlechs of the mighty vanquished—includ-

---

* In his final edition, MacPherson reads *Erin* for *Ullin*; which makes the boast still more insane.

ing kings, and princes, and sons of Fingal. To quote every passage that might be cited in illustration of this, would be to occupy pages of our text; therefore, a few references only can be allowed. (1.) Besides the three standing or pillar stones by Lubar, already referred to—one ancient, one erected by Ossian, and the third by Fingal to commemorate covenants, there were several others of the same sort, monumental or sepulchral. (2.) There was an ancient tomb already in existence called Lamdearg's, but in reality to the memory of himself and of Ullin his rival, and of Gelchossa, the object of their love—near the head of the valley, on a spur of Cromla; in or near which, other heroes—one of them Ryno, a son of Fingal, and the other Orla, a Norwegian slain by Fingal—were interred as an honour, not very far from the lake already mentioned, there. (3.) There was a special tomb to Cairbar, the usurping king, raised by a hundred heroes in one night, in the valley of the Lubar, "where three stones lift their grey heads, beneath a bending oak." (4.) The tombs of the unnumbered dead spreading and multiplying westward, still westward, as the valley widened and the conflicts raged. "Fillan poured the flight of Erin before him, over the echoing heath." Again, "Fillan hung forward on their steps; he strewed with dead the heath. . . Or, striding amid the ridgy strife, he pours the deaths of thousands forth." *Temora*, B. V:—all this in addition to previous slaughter, both in the present and in the two former expeditions by Fingal, and to corresponding slaughter on his own side. "The virgins wept, by the streams of Ullin. They looked to the mist of the hill; no hunter descended from its folds. Silence darkened in the land: blasts sighed lonely on the grassy tombs."—*Temora*, B. II. "Faint glimmers the moon on Moi-lena, through the broad-headed groves of the hill. Raise stones, beneath its beams," cries Fingal, "to all the fallen in war. Though no chiefs were they, yet their hands were strong in fight. They were my rock in danger: the mountain from which I spread my eagle wings. Thence am I renowned: Carril, forget not the low!"—B. III. "Malthos, I am revenged," cries Foldath, a very different character, in his death pangs. "I was not peaceful in the field. Raise the tombs of those I have slain, around my narrow house. Often shall I forsake the blast, to rejoice above their graves; when I behold them spread around, with their long whistling grass."—B. V.

The whole valley, in short, during these three expeditions, and others recorded elsewhere, was made a Gehenna; and if the ploughshare has not utterly rased them, the Moi-lena of Ossian may be recognised at this day as distinctly by the graves of the dead and by "the dry bones in its valley," running westward from the shore, as by any other marks of its identity.

## CHAPTER II.

CAMPAIGNS IN *FINGAL* AND *TEMORA* CONTINUED.

VERIFICATION FROM GEOGRAPHICAL AUTHORITIES.

IT must already be obvious to all who are acquainted with the neighbourhood, that in the outline we have just attempted, of what thousands believe to be a mere imaginary scene from the forgeries of an impostor, we have in reality been depicting one of the most familiar on the coast of Ireland—the bay of Lough-Larne, to wit, and the whole surrounding region; with the valley of the Six-mile-water between its romantic ridges widening as it goes, and the Six-mile-water itself flowing westward in the sunbeams, through its wooded prairies, to Lough-Neagh. Many details, however, will be required not only to establish this identity to the satisfaction of others, but even to unfold it to its full extent for those who may never hitherto have looked at that locality, or even dreamt of it, as the scene of Ossianic poems; and in producing these details, by reference to the recognised authority of geographical surveys, gazetteers, and topographical dictionaries—to which Ossian and MacPherson were presumably alike unknown—we shall arrange them, as far as possible, under the same heads as those already adopted in our analysis from the text, that proof, by direct comparison of all particulars, may be most easily available.

I. GENERAL ASPECT.—As to its general aspect, then, in the first place, that the scene at large, with its most important relative bearings, may to some extent be realised—a glance at any atlas, the older the better, will immediately instruct us that **Lough-Larne** is an arm of the sea in County Antrim of Ulster, on the north-east coast of Ireland, formed by what was once an island, and is still a peninsula, called Island or Isle Maghee—about ten miles long—closing-in the ocean from the east; and that this projecting tongue of land, as both its name and configuration imply, was certainly at no very remote geological epoch an island, the reader must distinctly bear in mind. In point of fact, it is represented as such, in Horsley's *Britannia Antiqua*, at the date of the Roman occupation—that is, about the beginning of the Christian era. The lake, or lough itself, thus formed, is a magnificent natural harbour, winding inland; but at the entrance there is a cluster of rocks, beautiful to look at, although dangerous to come near, called the Nine Maidens—which might be particularly inimical to voyagers like Fingal, whose ships before the wind, and at its mercy in a northern gale, were approaching the harbour: "and if any strong spirit of heaven sits on that low-hung cloud; turn his dark ships from the rock, thou rider of the storm!" The view from near the head of this lake to seaward is due north-north-east, and comprehends not only a dim outline of Arran and Ayrshire in the distance, but a tolerably distinct view of Ailsa Craig—that "lonely isle," or "perch of the Clyde," as seamen to the present day call it; and possibly, at a given angle, of Sanda to the westward, another "lonely isle"—between which two landmarks or beacons of the frith the ships of Fingal, approaching Ireland from Arran, would inevitably sail, as directly as the wind could carry them, and between which from Lough-Larne they would first be visible. Hence the words of the scout who so reports them, describing their actual position at the moment, as speakers in Ossian always do—"the ships of the lonely isle!"—or "isles;" —and hence Fingal's designation, rehearsed in Norway, as "chief of the lonely isles." "The entrance of Lough-Larne," says the *Parliamentary Gazetteer*, "with the Nine Maidens or Whillan Rocks in the offing, forms a softly pleasing image. Black Cave Head, a little north of the entrance of the harbour, frowns darkly on the ocean beneath; and Island Maghee, stretching along the east side of the lough, appears a charmingly cultivated expanse enclosed by 'the bright blue sea,' and gently wooing the eye away to a distant view of the rocky hills and varied isles of the coast of Scotland."

The time required to accomplish a voyage, from where Fingal is first reported, to the harbour of Lough-Larne, with ships of a single sail, the distance being about 60 miles, could not be much less than six or eight hours; so that, if sighted on the evening of one day, he might reach his destination, by the help of some "strong spirit of heaven," early on the morning of the next, as described. "Now, from the grey mist of the ocean, the white-sailed ships of Fingal appear. High is the grove of their masts as they nod, by turns, on the rolling waves."— *Fingal*, B. III. Nor was Fingal the only Scottish ally, or Swaran, perhaps, the only invader who made use of Lough-Larne to effect a landing in Ireland. It was on this very spot Edward Bruce disembarked with an army of six thousand, in his chivalrous enterprise to relieve Ireland from English domination, and to constitute it an independent kingdom; in which he was actually crowned king of the Island, but shortly afterwards fell in battle, against ten times his numbers, on the coast of Dundalk. Lough-Larne, in short, as a natural harbour, was the nearest and best port on that coast, spacious and always accessible, from the Clyde; the only port it may be said, indeed, at the remote date in question—for Belfast Lough, in Ossian's days, would terminate in a swamp, and Belfast itself had no existence. Fingal, it is certain, must have sailed into Lough-Larne with a fleet at least three times in his life; and the Danish or Norwegian pirate kings once, if not oftener before—although to "carry off" Isle Maghee to Norway with them, on their departure, was a feat they did not accomplish.

II. SOUTH SIDE.—1. The coast all around Lough-Larne is hilly, rock-bound, and precipitous—at some points, sublimely so; but the ridge we have more immediately in view at present is that which stretches from the head of the bay south-westward, by the shore of Belfast Lough, at right angles, or thereby, with Lough-Larne. This ridge, which extends with no other interruption than an occasional ravine, to beyond Belfast, is from 500 to 1100 feet in height; generally level on the summit with a moorland surface, and not exceeding a mile in mean breadth—so that it might easily be crossed and recrossed in the course of an afternoon or evening, by pedestrians, male or female, accustomed to the chase, as the ridge of Cromla was crossed in the poems of Ossian. It has some elevated points, however, and many peculiar features, including caves and waterfalls, and a lonely tarn or mountain lake on its eastern declivity, overlooking Lough-Larne—all which require attentive consideration. "There are also various natural caverns" in the region, says the *Topographical Dictionary*, "of which the most remarkable are those of the picturesque mountain called Cave Hill;" which rises "with alternately intricate and mural acclivity," says the *Parliamentary Gazetteer*, to "a height of 1064 feet," according to others, 1100. Within a mile or two of Carrick-Fergus, to the north-east of Belfast, and about half-way to Lough-Larne, is another lofty peak of the same range, called Slieve-True; but the highest of all, Mount Divis, is to the west, where it reaches an elevation of 1567 feet; "and as the rock of the frontier uplands" of all these mountains "is chiefly white and grey indurated chalk, containing nodules of flint," the reflection of the sun's rays from all exposed points must be unusually brilliant; as if such a fact had been recorded expressly to confirm Ossian's allusion to Morna, in *Fingal*, B. I.—"But thou art like snow on the heath; and thy hair like the mist of Cromla, when it curls on the rocks; and it shines to the beam of the west." Farther, a village called Doh-ar—now Do-agh—set down in one of the oldest geographical surveys of the country, seems to rest on the slope of a steep opposing hill, north-east of Mount Divis and the Cave Hill. But Dora, from which Doh-ar by the slightest transposition may be derived, is a mountain side, in *Temora*, visible to the westward from a certain point on the Cromla range: so that, seen from the eastern extremity of the entire range, "the setting sun," now as then, may be literally "yellow on Dora, [when] grey evening begins to descend" on all the surrounding plain. The precise position of Dora, as now identified with Doagh, may be incidentally determined otherwise, as the reader will by and by find, on a comparison of certain quotations, in a succeeding chapter; but the fact is thus referred to in passing, as one of the many minute coincidences which occur, beyond all previous calculation, to fix the locality in question, and to demonstrate the authenticity of the writer as an eye-witness of everything he describes. The motions of Fingal and his people in the valley of the Six-mile-water, east of the village of Doagh, are now almost as easily recognisable in virtue of this single identification, as the evolutions of a brigade on the heath at Aldershot.—*Temora*, BB. I. II.

2. With respect to the caves, however, so frequently mentioned by Ossian as characteristic of the Cromla, and so conspicuously numerous and beautiful in the Larne and Belfast range, we must be a little more minute in our inquiries.

"Amongst the most curious reliques of antiquity," says the *Topographical Dictionary* already quoted, "are the caves in various places [of this range] formed in the earth and in the hard limestone rock. Of the former, three were discovered in 1792 at Wolf-Hill, the largest of which is 8 yards long and 1 yard wide, with four small chambers diverging from it; on the side of a small hill in the townland of Ballymargy is one of larger dimensions, and in a more perfect state, with two entrances; and near Hannahstown is one still larger, which since 1798 has been closed, having at that time been a place of concealment for arms. Three large caves, which give name to the mountain called Cave Hill, are all formed in the perpendicular face of an immense range of basaltic rock; the lowest is 21 feet long, 18 wide, and from 7 to 10 in height; above this is another, 10 feet long, 7 wide, and 6 in height; and above that is a third, said to be divided into two unequal parts, each of which is more extensive than the largest of the other caves; but the ascent is so dangerous that few venture to visit it. The large ramparts of earth, called raths or forts, are also numerous; of these the most extensive, called MacArt's fort, is on the summit of Cave Hill, protected on one side by a precipice and on the other by a single ditch of great depth, and a vallum of large dimensions. . . . . Near the base of Squires hill are many smaller raths, and two of large dimensions, almost on the summit of the Black Mountain"—of which, hereafter.

But as we travel thus eastward along the shore by Carrick-Fergus, whereabouts by calculation, or between that and Belfast, "the dreary cave of Tura," "beside a stream of roaring foam . . . in a rock," should be found, we reach the Woodburn-water. Being a mountain stream, "formed by the union of two rivulets about two miles above the town [that is, among the hills to the north of it], on each of which is a picturesque cascade," "this river, after rain, rises considerably, and runs with great rapidity." It is interrupted also by other cascades in its descent, during which it has been estimated to afford many hundred feet of unemployed waterfall. But at the lowest fall, " a little south-west of Carrick-Fergus, are two caves hewn in a rock; . . they can be entered with some difficulty, but are not spacious"—dreary enough, in short, by the " roaring foam."

Besides the caverns, natural and artificial, now enumerated—some of which, it must be observed, have been but recently discovered; there may be others in the same region not yet discovered or not authentically described, for the whole range is full of them. But of those thus distinctly specified, and all in the very neighbourhood where the cave of Tura should be found, more than one, upon inspection, might be identified with ease as the possible, if not the probable, retreat of Cuthullin, on the evening of his discomfiture in *Fingal.*

3. The point, however, most distinguishable in our present inquiry, for the identification of this range with the Cromla of Ossian, remains yet to be noted. " A loftily situated lake of about 90 acres in extent, lies in the north-east corner of the parish," [Carrick-Fergus,] and about three miles north of the town. " It occupies the summit of an eminence" from 500 to 550 feet above the level of the sea, and is " supposed to be fed by a central spring." It is described generally as a moorland tarn, about a mile in diameter; country around waste, but the lake itself a resort of numerous wild fowl in winter. "A glen called the ' Noisy Vale ' lies in the vicinity" of this lake, " and has its name from a small rill which falls with much violence into an aperture of the ground, and becomes so mysteriously subterranean that its subsequent identity is matter of mere conjecture. Sulla-tober, or the Sallow-well, supposed, but not known, to be the rill of the ' Noisy Vale,' springs from beneath a limestone rock about 1½ miles north of the town" [that is, nearly on the summit of the ridge]; and in the neighbourhood are " circles," one in particular at Stony-glen, supposed to be " the foundations of monastic cells"— but, with equal probability, we may add, once occupied by Druids. When the reader has compared the geographical site thus quoted for the lake on the ridge of the mountain overlooking Lough-Larne, and the "Noisy Vale" with its " mysteriously subterranean stream," with the position already ascertained from the text of Ossian for " the lake of roes" on Cromla, beside the " noisy streams" and the cave of the Druid; and where, at a later date, the spirit of Cathmor " sunk by the hollow stream that roared between the hills," and disappeared in it—he will have little hesitation in admitting that we have our eye on the spot at last. If the slightest doubt should remain, however, it may be enough to state (1.) that the lake is called Lough-Mourne or Morne—the very name of the lady, to a letter, who perished in the cave beside it, when its mist rose cold on the barren heath around; (2.) that the Sulla-tober, now translated Sallow-well, might as well be translated Sulla's or Sulmalla's well, in honour of the princess who took refuge with the blind and aged Druid there, when her royal lover was in conflict with Fingal; (3.) and finally, that " the Orland-water, which descends from Lough-Mourne, and falls into the bay [of Carrick-Fergus] at the eastern suburb of the town," may as well have been so named from Orla the Norwegian, who was slain in battle by Fingal, and interred with Ryno his son beside lady Muirne and her lovers in a " green tomb"

then extant, and not far distant from the spot, as from any other person or cause. Other interpretations of these names may, no doubt, be attempted in ignorance of the facts now critically established, which we may by and by have an opportunity of considering; but in the meantime, we have thus three or four distinct designations connected with a locality which is geographically identical with that described in Ossian, and with which the same names are associated by him; and it may fairly be questioned whether any more perfect coincidence, as between the text of a disputed author and the most indisputable verities of the soil, can be produced in the whole range of human literature, sacred and profane;—a coincidence, it must farther be observed, utterly unknown to the translator of the text in question. The scene of Saul's suicide on Gilboa, or Hagar's fountain in the wilderness, will never be more clearly established.

4. But how, it may be objected, do these rivers run chiefly to the sea, when the rivers in Ossian have already been represented as running chiefly inland? There are other rivers, it may be replied, more important than these, which do run inland as Ossian has described them, and as will be immediately explained. These are but subordinate rivers, and correspond precisely to the smaller streams incidentally mentioned by him; but even with respect to these, it must be observed in the words of the *Gazetteer*—to whose unsolicited and involuntary testimony, oblivious of Ossian, we are so much indebted, that "the chief stream," the Woodburn-water presumably—on which the cave of Tura, somewhere on the southern side of the range, as we have already seen, almost certainly lay—"has all its course in the *interior*, and terminates a brief distance west of the town [Carrick-Fergus]; and it [the mountain range from which the stream issues] is rich in landscape, wood, cascade, cave, villa, and factory, and anciently was overlooked by an abbey." By one of the tributaries of that stream, or by one of the three others in the neighbourhood—" his own loud stream" of the Noisy Vale, or the Orland, or the Sulla-tober—by one of these assuredly, the Druid then mused in his blindness, not anticipating abbeys; and to its dreary caves of difficult access, Cuthullin, "sad and slow," with his back to the evening sun, "retired from his hill" to hide himself for shame after his defeat in battle, little dreaming of the profanation of factories, or of the splendours and comforts of domestic habitations, in succeeding centuries. Here Fingal at midnight "took his deathful spear, and struck the deeply-sounding shield," at which poor Sulmalla trembled, "and the screams of fowl," not yet assembled at their winter rendezvous on the lake, "are heard in the desart, as each flew frighted on his blast;" here he ascended from the plain after victory, to recover and console his desponding friend; here the chase of the dark-brown hinds began, at the sound of the horn, with a "thousand dogs, grey-bounding through the heath," and

P

continued eastward to the lake—that same little lake, of a mile in diameter—"the lake of roes" and resort of wild fowl, on the ridge of Cromla; here "one deer fell at the tomb of Ryno," and "the grief of Fingal returned. He saw how peaceful lay the stone of him who was the first at the chase," but who slept now with Orla by "the green tomb" of Ullin and Lamderg, near the lake of the lady Muirne—the same lake still—with its mantle of mist, on the treeless waste of the mountain. It seems all so distinct and clear, so concise and consecutive, that even the blindest objector, with the mere feel of instinct, may realise it.

5. But Cromla and Tura, the most conspicuous names in both poems, where are they to be found? On this point we have first to remind our readers, that according to MacPherson's unsolicited definition already quoted, and which any good Gaelig dictionary may confirm, Cromla, *lit.* Cromleach, "signified a place of worship among the Druids;" but "is here the proper name of a hill on the coast of Ullin or Ulster;" and then to state (1.) that on the northern slope of the Larne and Belfast range "near Cairngrainey, to the north-east of the old road from Belfast to Temple-Patrick, is the cromlech most worthy of especial notice—it has several table stones resting on numerous upright ones; and near it is a large mount, also several fortified posts, different from all others in the county," &c. (2.) That at the east end of the ridge in Island Maghee, and close upon the shore, is another cromlech, if not quite so large, at least quite as remarkable, crowned with a huge "rocking stone," so wonderfully poised that its lapse into the sea has been feared by doubtful antiquarians, and surrounded with numerous Druidical remains on the surface. (3.) That on Slieve-True, which overhangs the caves on the Woodburn-water about the centre of the range—and which, by the transposition of a single letter, seems to be identical in name, as well as in position, with Slieve-Tura—is a magnificent cairn; and all around, along the ridge from east to west, are indubitable proofs, by "circles, cairns, caves, and cromlechs," of Druidical occupation. Is it wonderful, then, that a range of mountains which has been literally inhabited by Druids; which begins on the verge of the ocean with a cromlech, and ends towards the setting sun with a cromlech—the most magnificent and curious in the whole Island; and which has been everywhere the scene of Druidical residence and worship, should have been called the Cromlech or the Cromla range, before Fingal was born? It would have been more wonderful, indeed, if any other name had been applied to it; and that the name did so originate from the cromlech at its eastern extremity, may be gathered from the very text of *Fingal* itself. When Cuthullin, in that poem, summons his heroes to resist the invasion of Swaran, his shield is struck "at Tura's rustling gate" westward, and the defenders of Ullin flock eastward to his standard on the coast. "The sounds of crashing

arms ascend: the grey dogs howl between: unequal bursts the song of battle;" and so loud is the universal din, that "rocking Cromla echoes round"—which may mean either literally, that the rocking stone of the cromlech on the shore, so delicately balanced, vibrated with the echoes of the war; or that the hill overhanging, so called from the rocking stone, seemed to shake with the reverberations of the sound. In either case, it seems almost incredible that Mac-Pherson, when interpreting and commenting on the very words now quoted, should have had no suspicion of their real significance, or should have been so ignorant of the most celebrated antiquities of Ireland as never to have glanced at the neighbourhood. Yet such ignorance and simplicity are unquestionable. Besides, the root of the word itself—*Cruim*, which he never attempts to trace, is preserved by the unconscious people to this hour, at the other end of the ridge, in the name of Crumlin, a town a mile or so to the north-west of where the grandest cromlech still stands. Thus we have Cromla to the east, and Crumlin to the west, at opposite extremities of the same range, corresponding in all other respects, geographical and antiquarian, to the Cromla of Ossian; with Slieve-True, or Slieve-Tura, precisely where it should be, about the middle—and further argument on the subject of its identity would be superfluous; would be ridiculous indeed, if equally surprising revelations to identify the river Lubar and the valley of Moi-lena were not awaiting us in the region beyond. We turn, therefore, for final confirmation, to the northern ridge, and to the valley of the Six-mile-water, which expands between.

III. NORTH SIDE.—As Ossian himself, or his translator, says little specifically of this northern ridge, we have fewer opportunities of identification; but what occurs in the text is amply and literally confirmed. The Lubar, we are expressly informed, flowed with a bound from the side of Crommal of the "misty top;" and beyond that ridge, to the northward, flowed another stream of a similar character, in a cave or in a vale by which lay Ferad-Artho, the heir of Conar's throne, in hiding, till the usurpers had been expelled. "Crommal, with woody rocks and misty top, the field of winds, pours forth to sight blue Lubar's streamy roar. Behind it rolls clear winding Lavath, in the still vale of deer. A cave is dark in a rock; above it strong-winged eagles dwell, broad-headed oaks, before it, sound in Cluna's wind. Within, in his locks of youth, is Ferad-Artho, blue-eyed king, the son of broad-shielded Cairbar, from Ullin of the roes."—*Temora*, B. VIII. The relative position of the two streams, therefore, at their source, is thus made unmistakeable. But farther, of the Lubar we learn, that although swift and furious, it was confined by rocks in a narrow channel—so narrow, that Fingal on a certain occasion, by the help of his spear, bounded over it: "he bounded on his spear over Lubar, and struck his echoing shield."—*Ibid*.

1. It may be observed, in the first place, in passing, that all the highest points in the northern range which bounds the coast above Larne and runs inland with numerous spurs, are called Tops till the present day, and the mountain from which the Six-mile-water springs is one of the highest. The name of Crommallin itself is still found on the same range a little farther north, as the designation of a particular hill; but unless it could be shown that such designation applied to the entire range from Lough-Larne along the coast, the coincidence might be objected to as a trifle. It is certain, however, that it is a geographical peculiarity of the whole range that it skirts the coast, and that all its principal streams flow inland. Of these, the Six-mile-water is the chief, and the Glenwherry-water to the north of it, with a ridge between, and numerous caves or ravines running to the shore, in which a fugitive might lodge, is only second in importance. Let the reader now first recall Ossian's description of the Lubar, and then read what follows from neutral authorities on its modern representative, after fifteen hundred hypothetical years of warfare, agricultural improvement, mechanical adaptations and changes of nature in every aspect, incidental to manufacturing requirements, have contributed to efface or transform it.

The Lubar, as its name implies, is "the loud or noisy"—that is, the rapid impetuous stream interrupted by rocks, rushing headlong among crags and caves, and expending its energy everywhere in its current. It flows first from a mountain, then through a heath, and at last, augmented by a hundred rills after rain, sweeps through a valley to the west, diversified throughout with rocks and trees, and clothed over all with the richest verdure. Besides which, caves and recesses on its banks are constantly alluded to; in one of which, poor Fillan, from the strife of battle, is laid down to die—"Ossian, I begin to fail. Lay me in that hollow rock; raise no stone above; lest one should ask about my fame. . . . . I laid him in the hollow rock, at the roar of the nightly stream."—*Temora*, B. VI. Such is an outline of the river near which so many conflicts took place, and on whose banks so many affecting incidents occurred. "The rapidity of these, [the Six-mile-water, the Glenwherry, and the Braid] and the smaller rivers," says the *Topographical Dictionary*, "renders their banks peculiarly advantageous sites for bleach-greens, cotton mills, and flour and corn mills," and the waters of these rivers, especially of the Six-mile-water, have been so utilised; but not even such adaptation of its current could destroy its beauty, or subvert its original character. "Travellers," say Mr. and Mrs. Hall in their Tour of Ireland, "can form no idea whatever of the graceful recesses of this sylvan spot. It is unrivalled in its way—trees, rocks, banks, and paths, screened from the sun and terminating in vistas, reveal the country around. . . . . The waters *rush* to their trained courses, and set at work the machinery of these mighty mills.

.. It would be impossible to describe the varied, yet continued beauty of this scene." Farther, of its pasture and produce in cattle, for which the Lubar was celebrated in Ossian, it may be sufficient to refer to Blaeu's general testimony in his Atlas, that in his day the country around was occupied by the most luxuriant woods or richest prairies, intersected by innumerable streams. Pasture so rich, that sheep would burst of it, if allowed to eat their fill. Cattle various and numerous, including horses of a peculiar ambling gait, "which we call *hobies*"\*
—and which, in this respect, correspond to those described by Ossian as indigenous to that country; "the high-maned, broad-breasted, proud, *wide-leaping*, strong steed of the hill. . . . The thin-maned, high-headed, strong-hoofed, fleet, bounding son of the hill. . . . The steeds, that like wreaths of mist, fly over the streamy vales!" And for other cattle then known, we have a type of them in "the spotted bull," which each of the rival chiefs claimed as his own. "But ah! why ever lowed the bull on Golbun's echoing heath? They saw him leaping like snow: the wrath of the chiefs returned! On Lubar's grassy banks they fought, and Grudar, like a sunbeam, fell."—*Fingal*, B. I. Finally, of the Six-mile-water, as a river, it may be observed that in one atlas, of more minuteness than the rest, no fewer than eight or ten double tributaries are represented as conducting their adjacent rills from the mountains to swell its stream; and a number so great, thought worthy of representation, may fairly be doubled in detail. In the Ordnance Survey of 1865, we can enumerate forty-five in all; so that fifteen hundred years ago, before cultivation had united or destroyed them, they might well be three-fold in reality; and then the "hundred" streams of the Lubar, after a thunderstorm on Cromla, would be no exaggeration—so minutely do all circumstances, correctly noted and faithfully recorded, tally with the text. Yet this very river of Lubar, we must remember, so powerful in its course, was but a rivulet in its earlier stages at the foot of the mountain, where most of the battles were fought; or flowed through the plain between such narrow chinks of rock, that Fingal, with the help of his spear, could bound across its waters. A feat like this by a man of 92 was construed into a miracle, as we have seen, by the ignorant vulgar, to the discredit of Ossian; and has been quoted by the wise and learned as an incredible absurdity, sufficient not only to compromise his fame, but to disprove his authenticity—both parties being equally ignorant of the fact, having imagined the Lubar to be some navigable river like the Shannon or the Clyde. Compare Note on p. 74, and the argument on Fingal's age, p. 93. It was but an effort of native agility, in fact, for a magnificent athlete, even in the decline of life; and its record, as a mere incident of the campaign, indicates

---

\* Hence the English *Hoby-horse*, which imitated their action,

more clearly, than pages of elaborate description could, the size and character of the river itself where the leap was made. Let the Six-mile-water be carefully searched—say from Ballyclare eastward, where rocks confine its course—and if milldams or sluices have not swamped it, the very spot may yet be found.—See *Temora*, BB. VI. VIII.

2. With respect to the valley beyond, and the stream which intersects it, which we may be bold enough now, perhaps, to identify with the Lavath, it may be sufficient for general recognition, after what has been already said, to quote the words of the *Parliamentary Gazetteer*—" The valley of the Six-mile-water, the most southerly of the noticeable westward openings among the hills, is a fine expanse of beauty and cultivation. . . . . The valleys of the Glenwherry and the Broad [or Braid] rivers, farther north, though of less extent and attraction, expand beyond the limits of Glens, and possess the amenities of verdure, cereal crop, and wood." We have already noticed that these valleys, that of the Glenwherry in particular, are so " infracted with ravines and caves" towards the sea, that any fugitive might safely be concealed in them, as Ferad-Artho was in the caves of Lavath. But we farther learn from the text of Ossian, that the Temora or Royal house of the Caledonian dynasty, of which Conar was the founder and Ferad-Artho the present heir, was somewhere in that neighbourhood, apparently to the south-west of this stream; and by reference to our geographical authorities we are expressly instructed, as if the words had been so written on purpose, that the village of Connor, on the Glenwherry westward, has near it one of those Great Forts or " Folkmote," of which specimens are found throughout Ireland, " with outworks exactly resembling that at Dromore ;" which has " a treble fosse on the north side and a strong outpost to the south, continued in a regular glacis to the water's edge." Such fortified places, used both for the residence of the chiefs, for the administration of justice, and for the protection of the people in danger, were similar, it should appear, to the Scottish Tors—such as Tor-lutha in Arran, of the same date; and this in particular at Connor, like the other at Dromore, would be Royal house or Temora enough for a petty sovereign on Irish soil at the commencement of the Christian era. In the way of special identification, therefore, all that could be desired, and more than could have been imagined, has been ascertained, to the farthest geographical limits northward, of Ossian's descriptions in *Fingal* and *Temora*. To be able to point out that dark cave in a rock, at the gorge of Cluna, where Ferad-Artho lodged—with its old eagle-eyries above, and its broad-headed oaks before, would complete the miracle of recognition. Friends on Glenwherry-water should look for it now, for assuredly the cave, as described, is or has been there.

IV. EAST AND WEST; or Eastward and Westward.—But the valley of the

Lubar itself, as we have seen, was signalised by repeated conflicts during three warlike expeditions, and is spoken of as having been the scene of slaughter and the site of tombs, beyond number. The valley, we have already shown, ran westward, expanding in its progress, and the slaughter of the flying foe extended as they fled; so that many of their tombs, if still in existence, may be looked for between Lough-Larne and Lough-Neagh, if the valley of the Six-mile-water, as we suppose, be the valley of Moi-lena. Besides which, there were ancient tombs described as landmarks on the scene, and tombs of the last generation consecrated in the memory of survivors or celebrated in the recital of bards, and pillar stones in commemoration of covenants. To verify this, a quotation here and there from the best statistical authorities on the region seems to be all that is required. "There are numerous barrows," says the *Topographical Dictionary*, "or tumuli, scattered over the face of the [country at Carrick-Fergus]; of which some have been opened and found to contain rude urns, ashes, and human bones. The largest of these, which are chiefly sepulchral, is called *Duncrue*, or the 'Fortress of blood'"—in which, or in another closely resembling, at Carrick-Fergus, "have been found several curious Danish trumpets." "At Slieve-True is a cairn 77 yards in circumference and 20 feet in height. A little towards the west of the same mountain is another of nearly equal dimensions, and about a mile to north-west is a third exactly similar"—which brings us close, as the reader will observe, to the valley of the Six-mile-water. "Raths, barrows, and cairns," says the *Parliamentary Gazetteer*, "are numerous on the hills;" . . . "cairns, cromlechs, pillar stones, raths, and earthen mounds, all strictly similar to those which prevail from Belfast Lough to Meath—[of which, hereafter] abound along the whole coast, and occur somewhat numerously in the interior . . . . all of which are rude, and indicate the work of quite a barbarous people. . . . . Raths and mounds are so plentiful, that no fewer than 237 have been enumerated in the two parishes of Killead, or Killeagh, and Muckamore"—both in the valley of the Six-mile-water, adjacent to one another, and stretching eastward from the shores of Lough-Neagh towards Lough-Larne, as well as north and south across the breadth of the valley—that is, through the very centre of the strath, in all directions, where the slaughter occurred. "Of mounts, forts, and intrenchments," says the *Topographical Dictionary*, "there is every variety which exists in Ireland; and so numerous are they, that the parishes of Killead and Muckamore alone contain 230 [?237, as quoted above], defended by one or more ramparts; and ten mounts, two containing caves—of which that called Donald's Mount is a fine specimen of this kind of earthwork." The whole region, in fact, seems to be filled with them; and in the two parishes just specified, in the very heart of the valley and with nothing but a stream between them, on the banks of which the fury of battle in three successive campaigns must have raged, their multitude, although matter of notoriety, would have been otherwise incredible. Further evidence in this department of our inquiry, it may be presumed, will be unnecessary. The only matter which seems to need a word of explanation is the construction of these raths, or earth mounds—by some supposed to be graves, and by others small temporary fortifications with trenches and outworks. That two parishes alone, in close proximity and in a comparatively small valley, should contain 237 fortifications of any kind may well perplex the shrewdest antiquaries who look only at the raths themselves, or at the "arrow heads and curious Danish trumpets, and brass and bronze implements of war" occasionally found within them, or even at the "rude urns and human bones" which are disinterred from their fosses. That the raths are there is certain, that many of them are encircled with ramparts and trenches may be true, and that human bones and Danish or Norwegian reliques, especially of war, have been disinterred or discovered among them, is highly probable; that some of them were even temporary forts, or fortified camps to shelter the belligerents, and were defended by their holders to the death, is not denied. All these admissions, however, will not account for their numbers, still less for the aggregation of so many of them in so small a space. The distribution of 237 forts on the frontier, or coast line of a whole province, would have been a miracle of military defence among savages; their accumulation in the centre of a single valley only a few miles square, is unaccountable and absurd. But if the reader will now recall the request of Foldath, as already quoted from B. V. of *Temora*, to raise the tombs of those he had slain, around his own narrow house, that he might often forsake the blast and rejoice above their graves, when he beheld them spread around with their long whistling grass; and will consider, at the same time, not only that many such tombs surrounded by common graves may have been erected to savage chiefs like him in a war of three generations on the same field, but that these would include to a certainty the remains alike of Scotch and Irish, and of Danes and Norwegians, who did fight with arrows, who did carry swords of brass or of bronze in battle, and did use trumpets most likely of a curious form—he will find the mystery of the raths and their contents more easily explained. There is, in fact, no other explanation. All this, however, implies the frank admission not only of Ossian's authenticity, but of Ossian's truth; of his honesty, accuracy, and minute descriptive fidelity—which it has not been convenient hitherto for antiquarians or critics, much less for historians or geographers, to acknowledge.

One point alone now, of the entire disputed region, remains to be identified—that defile to the east by which the enemy might surprise the defenders, or by which they might retreat and escape if their invasion was unsuccessful; the defile of the "narrow way," where two brave men might withstand a thousand. This defile seems to have been the eastern limit of "the heath of Lena," within which to the westward it was an open plain; and from some advantageous point in this defile, most probably, the earliest glimpse of Fingal's approaching fleet might be obtained by the scouts without encountering the enemy; but here certainly, after his own first defeat, Cuthullin with Calmar determined to remain alone and defend the pass to death, against advancing invaders. "When the battle is over, search for us in this narrow way: for near this rock we shall fall, in the stream of the battle of thousands." It was to be the Thermopylæ, in fact, of Moi-lena; and fortunately for the conclusion of our present argument, its identification may be brief and simple. Concerning a village in a certain pass, at the spot required, "it stands," says the *Parliamentary Gazetteer*, "in a romantic dell 3½ miles southwest of Larne. . . The road through [the Glen], though nearly two miles shorter than the other between Larne and Carrick-Fergus, is seldom travelled; for it is generally steep and rugged, and in particular, it makes a dive nearly impracticable for ordinary conveyances into the dell." Such precipitous descent, however, though impracticable for ordinary conveyances in the nineteenth century, might be most suitable for an armed surprise or for an obstinate defence at any time, as well as at the date supposed, more especially as it was two miles nearer the then scene of action than any other way in the neighbourhood. It is farther described as a "pleasant glen, through which a mountain stream takes its course into Lough-Larne"—which Cuthullin, by melancholy anticipation, refers to, both literally and figuratively, as "the stream of the battle of thousands," in which he and his friend were to fall;\* and which MacPherson, in a note to *Temora*, B. V., by some strange, almost unaccountable inadvertence, already glanced at, seems to confound with the Lubar, giving that river thus apparently a double course, east and west, at the same moment. The name of this village in the pass has been alternately the Glynnès, the Glinus, or more anciently Glenoe —a designation which has again been revived in geographical surveys. Glynnès or Glinus, applied to the village, is the obvious corruption of Glin-house or Glenhouse, that is, the house of the Glen—as Stennis or Sten-house, in Orkney, is the house of the standing stones: but Glenoe is Leno or Lena, with a G prefixed, equivalent to Glen-leno; and indicates thus, by its traditional usage, the precise limits of the old "heath of Lena," where the "open meadow space," as Mac-

---

\* The position seems to be that of a rock projecting into the stream, which would strengthen the defile and enable the defenders to meet the assailants with advantage. Robert Bruce undertook a similar feat single-handed, with fewer exaggerations of poetry but with more success against an army of pursuers, on a flagstone rock in the Burn above Penkill, in the parish of Dailly, Ayrshire.

Pherson translates it, on which all the battles were fought, terminated in a passage to the sea. By a still more marvellous coincidence, the spot was yet more anciently Glencoe, as if the stream which pours through it had once been a "Cona," or as if Ossian had bequeathed such a name to the romantic defile from some fancied resemblance in the scene to his native vale. This, however, would be too fine a dream in philology, and need not be persisted in. Glencoe remains distinct, inscribed on the surface; and that this Glynn, or Glen, or Glencoe, was the veritable pass of Lena with its "narrow way," seems as indisputably certain as anything in geography or philology can be.

From this point, therefore, thus definitely fixed, turning our faces once more in the opposite direction, about two miles off to the westward on the southern range, where Fingal took his place on "Mora" to direct the battle and survey the plain, we find a hill sloping north called Slimero, or Slieve-Mora—that is, the hill of Mora; with two prominences on its eastern side, Upper Carneal and Lower Carneal, recognisable as the very spot where he stood—being identical in position, and all but a letter in name also, with the Cormuil or Cormul of *Temora*. "On Mora stood the king in arms: mist flies round his buckler broad, as aloft it hung on a bough, on Cormul's mossy rock."—*Temora*, B. III. A little farther still, where the plain begins to widen, and so becomes *Moi*-lena, or the greater plain, on which the campaigns were ultimately decided, we have Moylusk or Malusky, in which the root of the old designation, descriptive and poetic, is retained. To the north of which we find Dora—first as Doh-ar, then as Do-agh—still glittering where it should be, in the setting sun; and still farther west, as our footsteps approach Lough-Neagh, we come upon Moi-lena itself, the designation of a modern manor there, at the present hour; whilst in the space between, there are the parish lands of Ballylinny—that is, Balla-Linny, or the fortified township of Lena—occupying half the region: so that the names, and very syllables, most familiar in Ossian, are thus literally strewed along the ground. The people, indeed, for reasons hereafter to be explained, have abandoned all sympathy with Fingal, and forgotten the traditions of his fame. They have involved them in incredible superstitions and transferred them to unrecognisable ground, or have suffered them insensibly to perish like a foreign dream. But the names associated with his exploits, and which illustrate the scene of his triumphs, still linger on their lips, and are written legibly down on the surveys of their country, although they perceive it not. That so many fragments of language—not mere syllables, but entire words, changed only by the transposition of a letter, as in the tongue of a kindred people—should thus be found adhering to the soil after a lapse of fifteen hundred years, and assigned by that people unconsciously to those precise features of the scene which may otherwise be identified as the very points of the whole region in question to which they should belong, is surely significant beyond the necessity of exaggeration; and in review of such accumulated evidence, spontaneously accruing at every step of our argument, philological, geographical, and antiquarian, the process of verification and the question of authenticity alike may be considered as affirmatively closed. Yet there will be murmurs against the admission of the whole theory as too wonderful to be believed, or even formal objections to its conclusiveness as a thing beyond such evidence to prove; and these obstacles to its frank recognition, however easily disposed of, must be fully considered and removed. The writer has been too much surprised, indeed, at the clearness of his own discoveries, to be offended at surprise in others; and is willing, therefore, not only to reply to, but even to imagine the most frivolous or obstinate objections against a result of deliberate inquiry so convincingly plain : and that the fullest opportunity for considering these objections may be afforded, he shall transfer the whole remaining inquiry to a separate chapter. Before proceeding, however, there is a single passage, in which the names of all the most prominent localities already enumerated occur in regular succession, from Tura westward to rocking Cromla eastward, that may be quoted and compared with the accompanying map, for the reader's satisfaction. The words in CAPITALS and *italics* are those to be specially noted, and the order in which they occur is also to be remarked. A chase, it should be stated, was in progress on Cromla, from Tura to the lake of roes, when news of Swaran's landing on the coast was communicated to Cuthullin.

"'Go, Fithil's son,' cries he, 'and take my spear. Strike the sounding shield of Cathbait. It hangs at TURA's rustling gate: the sound of peace is not its voice. My heroes shall hear on the *hill.*' He went and struck the bossy shield. The hills and their rocks reply. The sound spread *along* the wood: deer *start* by the LAKE OF ROES. Curach leapt from the *sounding rock;* and Connal of the bloody spear. . . The son of Favi leaves the dark brown hind. It is the shield of war, said Ronnar! The shield of Cuthullin, said Lugar: Son of the sea, put on thy arms! [A sort of interjectional address to Swaran, as if he could hear it.] Calmar, lift thy sounding steel! Puno, horrid hero, rise! Cairbar, from thy red tree of CROMLA! Bend thy white knee, O Eth; and *descend* from the streams of LENA. Ca-olt, stretch thy white side, as thou movest along the whistling *heath* of MORA. . . They came like streams *from* the mountains; each rushed roaring from his hill;" . . and finally, when "on LENA's dusky *heath* they stood, like mist that shades the hills of autumn," then "unequally bursts the song of battle, and *rocking* CROMLA echoes round."—*Fingal;* B. I.

All this, the reader will observe, must have happened within a space so limited, that the sound of a shield at Tura's gate was heard along the ridge of Cromla; and when the heroes assembled on the plain below they confronted Swaran to the east, among the very rocks on the shore of the bay of Lena.

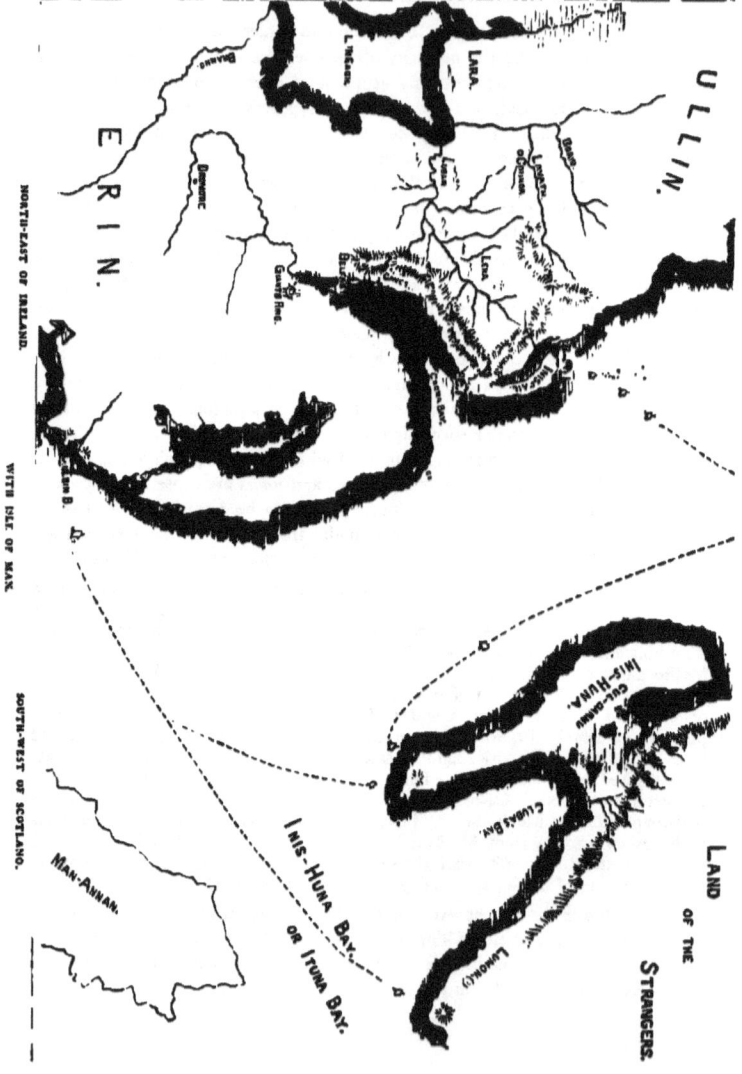

## CHAPTER III.

#### FINGAL IN IRELAND CONTINUED—OBJECTIONS CONSIDERED.

The first objection, both as to weight and relevancy, and which will be urged with vehemence by hundreds against all that has hitherto been advanced, is the tenor of Irish traditions on the same subject—the existence of an Irish Fingal, for example, of an Irish Ossian, and of an Irish Oscar and others, with legendary lore attached to their names, in many respects different from ours; and if these traditions in prose or poetry, it may be said, should be at variance with the details of our present argument, what then? The first step, then, as a matter of course, will be to ascertain the value of these traditions, on the supposition that they are in conflict with proved realities or the facts of nature; and to deal with them accordingly, by selecting from, rejecting, or attempting to harmonise their relations, as the case may be.

I. It is to this inquiry, therefore, in the first place, we now address ourselves; premising only that, although there is no doubt much truth in ancient Irish history, as we shall by and by show; there is also, by the admission of Irishmen themselves, much obvious fable—on which, therefore, where it is beyond the limits of our present subject, neither argument nor loss of time need be bestowed. It is to that only which claims to be genuine and relevant we can attend, and shall endeavour to satisfy the reader in regard to it, as much by explaining its origin as by exposing its unquestionable character. If the present work, indeed, had been a treatise on the historical antiquities of Ireland, one of the most interesting and intricate, although by no means inextricable problems in the course of it, would have been to separate between the true and the false of this whole legendary lore, and to apportion the credit or responsibility of faithful tradition or chimerical invention connected with it, accordingly. It is only in so far, however, as Irish fables have been fabricated out of Ossian, or from materials to be found in him, in contradiction to himself, to the discredit of his fame, and the falsification of history in some important respects at his era, that their origin need now be traced, or their authority investigated at all. What is true in Irish history beyond that period shall be briefly summarised, from what seem to be the most reliable sources, in a separate page hereafter, at its proper place in our Appendix; and the reader, for many reasons, may find the digest referred to worthy of his most deliberate attention; although any critical controversy, for the discrimination of particulars in that field, would be out of proportion here.

But to proceed—1. By reference to the Glossary, under the term *Bardh*, our readers will observe that there were three distinct and well recognised orders of Public Poets, or Poet-spokesmen, among the Celtic people both of Scotland and Ireland—the *Pri-vardhs*, or more correctly in the plural number, the *Pri-vairdh*, the *Pos-vairdh*, and the *Aruy-vairdh;* besides which there were other distinctions also. The entire profession, indeed, might be arranged in a three-fold order of three, as follows:—

(1.) As to rank—the Authors, Inventors, or Poets proper, with whom originated the discovery in science, the theme in poetry, or the inspiration in speech; the Teachers, Reciters, or Rehearsers, who were restricted to the text of the Authors; and lastly, the Ensigns, Exhibitors, or Actors.

(2.) As to functions—The Chroniclers, the Eulogists, the Heralds; who delivered embassies, recited the praises of heroes, stimulated the troops in battle, and even rallied them in retreat.

(3.) As to the subject matter of their compositions—The grand Epic writers, who spoke always in the presence of kings and princes, as Ossian himself did; the Moralists and Lyrists, who were patronised by the gentry; the Satirists, Epigrammatists and Jesters, who addressed the mob.

Individual men, it may be presumed, as their gifts or ambition prompted them, would aspire to unite in themselves several of these independent distinctions—as, in point of fact, they did; to which not a few of them added magic and medicine—hence called *Vaidhs* or physicians, whence the Latins derived their *Vates*. But among all ranks of the Order, poetry, with music in some form, was an art; in which they studied proficiency as in a branch of learning, and graduated with honours in it, as Doctors in the Schools. The title for a graduate in poetry, as well as in medicine or magic, was Ollamh or Ollaw, and the head of the fraternity was called Ard-Ollamh, or Doctor-in-Chief. According to Toland, there were often at one time not fewer than 1000 such graduates of all classes on the roll of poets in Ireland; so that Ossian's "hundred bards," so frequently referred to, might be no exaggeration after all. For the present however, we must be satisfied to remark, that the two first ranks of each class here specified are distinctly recognisable in the text of Ossian, and are there represented, for Scotland and Ireland both, by men of dignity, gravity, and importance; skilled in music, as well as gifted with poetic genius; intrusted with all embassies, treaties, and proclamations, and everywhere reverenced as sacred in the presence alike of the people and their kings. But no man of the third rank, as to subject at least, seems to be traceable in his pages. If such foolish talkers and jesters were known to him, they were known only to be ignored as unworthy of notice among their brethren. In succeeding generations, however, as the types of little men, they multiplied exceedingly in Ireland, and extorted a contemptible livelihood by the prostitution of whatever gifts they had; until at last, being patronised in vast numbers—by rival chiefs, most probably, or by rival factions—they became such a nuisance in that kingdom, that according to Toland, himself an Irishman, a sumptuary law for their repression or banishment was enacted.

"These bards are not yet quite extinct," says he, "there being of them in Wales, in the Highlands of Scotland, and in Ireland: nor did any country in the world abound like the last with this sort of men, whose licentious panegyrics or satyrs have not a little contributed to breed confusion in the Irish History. There were often at a time a thousand Ollaws or graduate poets, besides a proportionable number of inferior Rhymers, who all of 'em liv'd most of the year on free cost: and what out of fear of their railing, or love of their flattery, nobody durst deny them anything, be it armor, fewel, horse, mantle, or the like; which grew into a general custom, whereof the Poets did not fail to take the advantage. The great men, out of self-love and interest, incouraged no other kind of Learning, especially after they profest Christianity: the good regulation, under which they were in the time of Druidism, as then in some manner belonging to the Temples, having been destroyed with that religion. In a small time they became such a grievance, that several attemts were made to rid the nation of them; and, which is something comical (what at least our present poets would not extraordinarily like), the orders for banishing them were always to the Highlands of Scotland; while they were as often harbor'd in Ulster, till upon promise of amendment (of their manners I mean, and not of their poetry) they were permitted to return to the other Provinces. At last, in a general national assembly, or Parliament, at Drumcat, in the country we now call the County of Londonderry, under AIDUS ANMIREUS, the 11th Christian King, in the year 597, where was also present AIDUS King of Scotland, and the great COLUMBA, it was decreed: that for the better preservation of their History, Genealogies, and the purity of their Language, the supreme Monarch and the subordinate Kings, with every Lord of a Cantred, should entertain a poet of his own (no more being allowed by antient law in the Iland), and that upon each of these and their posterity a portion of land, free from all duties, shou'd be settl'd for ever; that, for incouraging the Learning these Poets and Antiquaries profest, public schools should be appointed and indow'd, under the national inspection; and that the Monarch's own Bard shou'd be ARCH-POET, and have super-intendency over the rest."— *Toland's Works—Druids:* l. pp. 27, 28. London: 1747.

Poetical appreciation of the Highlands of Scotland seems to have considerably advanced, not only since the edict above narrated was issued, but even since Mr. Toland's day; an act of banishment to that region for ill-behaved poets in our own happier times, however comical in itself and unpleasant for the people of the district, being most likely first of all to increase the actual numbers of the banishable squad. But with respect to the statement itself, as a piece of historical evidence, the reader will observe—(1.) That, having emanated innocently from its shrewd but loquacious author in 1718—that is, 20 years before MacPherson was born, and more than 40 before his translation of Ossian appeared, it could by no chronological possibility have any connection with that work; much less, being issued by an Irishman, could it have been devised at any time to support it. (2.) That in consequence of the edict in question, the pestiferous impostors alluded to, having a natural dread of banishment to Scotland, took refuge from its penalties in Ulster; that is precisely where Fingal and his people, a few centuries before, were known, and where his principal campaigns were conducted. In this region, therefore, where "they were harbor'd" by the natives, they would naturally obtain from their countrymen traditional exaggerated or imperfect accounts of his proceedings; and, by exercising their own peculiar gifts of travesty and imposture, would produce still more exaggerated, often scandalous and incredible stories in the name of Ossian, with respect to to Fingal and the rest; turning all to the credit of their hospitable entertainers, or to the honour of their country at large—not only transforming that hero himself into an Irishman, but ascribing to him, and to his followers or friends, the most preposterous capabilities and achievements. New Fingals, Ossians, and Oscars, in fact, who had no real existence, were invented by them, with the grossest and even the most indecent fables attached to their names. That these names, therefore, and a few important dates in the genuine history, should have been retained in such fables, was a matter of course; for it was on these very names and dates, adhering for centuries after Ossian's day to the soil of Ulster, that the fables themselves were founded—and, in so far, they are incidental proofs of his accuracy; but the details associated with them by these legendary liars are, for the most part, so contradictory and grotesque, as to be incredible or worthless. (3.) And lastly, that Toland himself, knowing nothing of the true Ossian, which had not as yet, by nearly half a century, appeared; and being therefore equally ignorant of the history of Fingal as recorded there, accepted to some extent, with a sort of solemn credulity, the ridiculous inventions and pseudo-narrations of these banished bards. He believed, for example, on their authority, that Fingal, Cuthullin, and the other Scoto-Celts were Irishmen; and that Cormac was supreme King of Ireland in Fingal's day, and had his palace at Tara in Meath—in which last error, he was indeed the more excusable, forasmuch as MacPherson himself, with Ossian's own text to guide him, was nevertheless induced to accept, as a matter of fact, the same absurdity. All which transactions and occurrences being thus simply collated, and traced, on the admission of an Irish writer who lived before MacPherson, to a date so close to the epoch of Ossian, leave almost as little doubt about the origin of these fables as if their individual authors had acknowledged the fraud. In short, it is plain beyond all reasonable controversy, that it was by these infamous traders in eulogy and bombast, in scurrility and scandal, and in misrepresentation generally; whose presence in the south was a plague, and who were banished beyond its frontiers by sumptuary edict; that the legendary lore of Ireland in post-Ossianic ages was corrupted, and the credit of its genuine annals destroyed, for a morsel of bread.

2. A single illustration of these fables, incidentally quoted by Toland, being much to our present purpose, may perhaps be reproduced with advantage here, both to satisfy the reader of the justice of our remarks, and to explain how the simplest facts became the foundation of elaborate scandals. There are certain Druidical edifices, it should appear, very common in Ireland, for which an origin in romance connected with Fingal was to be invented or found.

"The vulgar Irish," says Toland, "call these Altars DERMOT *and* GRANIA'S *Bed*. This last was the Daughter of King CORMAC ULFHADA, and Wife to FIN MACCUIL; from whom, as invincible a General and Champion as he's reported to have been, she took it in her head (as women will sometimes have such fancies) to run away with a nobleman call'd DERMOT O'DUVNY: but being pursu'd everywhere, the ignorant country people say they were intertain'd a night in every quarter-land or village of Ireland; where the inhabitants sympathising with their affections, and doing to others what they would be done unto, made these beds both for their resting and hiding place. The poets, you may imagine, have not been wanting to imbellish this story: and hence it appears, that the Druids were planted as thick as Parish Priests, nay much thicker."—*Toland, Ibid.* p. 95.

So much, on Toland's own authority, for what the poets were not wanting to embellish, and so much also for the style of their embellishment itself—the only germs of fact in the story being that the lady's name was Ros-crana, corrupted to Grania; that she was a daughter of Cormac MacConar's, and fled with her father to a cave on the coast of Ullin, to escape the solicitations of his enemy Colculla, whom Fingal, coming to their rescue, met and slew; on which occasion Roscrana was given in marriage to Fingal, her kinsman as well as her deliverer, and left Ireland with him on his return to Morven almost the next day. To this extent, tradition and the truth, with some slight variations, agree. Her sudden departure, however, in this inexplicable manner, seems to have been a mystery to the popular imagination, and by the assistance of the "poets" became the groundwork of this preposterous fable; referring to which most probably, although he does not expressly name it, MacPherson, in a note to *Temora*, B. IV., with admirable simplicity says, "The Irish bards relate strange fictions concerning this princess. Their stories, however, concerning Fingal, if they mean him by *Fion MacCombal*, are so inconsistent and notoriously fabulous, that they do not deserve to be mentioned; for they evidently bear, along with them, the marks of late invention." That the bards did refer to Fingal is obvious enough, from what Toland says, although

MacPherson may well be excused for doubting it; and how they obtained and corrupted their traditions, we have also endeavoured to explain, although MacPherson seems not to have been aware of it. Roscrana, as our readers may remember, was the mother of Ossian—who, if not her only, was certainly her most distinguished son; and whoever recalls the reverential glimpses of her we obtain in his pages, will understand how to appreciate both the libellous work of the legend-mongers of Ireland, and the taste of the people who could believe it.

3. Such were the first-fruits of their inauspicious exile in Ulster, exaggerated and adorned doubtless, after the same fashion, in the process of transmission, by the priestly rhymers of succeeding generations; who added fable upon fable to gratify the vanity of a credulous people, and exalt what they called the honour of the nation: and it is to James MacPherson the world of letters, far beyond the limits of Ulster, is now indebted, for having rescued the authentic annals of the period, in so far as they are connected with the names of Fingal and Ossian or those of their real contemporaries, by the lips of a veritable chronicler and truly inspired bard, and for having separated them for ever from the fabrications of such mercenary scoundrels. Ossian, in his unique simplicity and grandeur, in his truthfulness to nature and to fact—in his very adherence to geographical positions hitherto unknown, and which, but for his own accuracy of description, would never have been known—requires no support of theirs, although support by them is involuntarily rendered; and can never suffer the slightest depreciation from their accumulated falsehoods.

In conclusion, it is obvious that the traditions of Ireland, which either thus ignore the reality of a Scottish Fingal and Ossian altogether; or substitute in their place another Fingal and another Ossian, with fabulous impossibilities of existence attached to them—outraging, in fact, the very limits and laws of nature; cannot be accepted, any more than MacPherson's notes and commentaries, when these are at fault. They are self-excluded by their own claims, in such an argument as this. It is with the text of a book which is denied, and with the geographical features of the country which cannot be denied—with these alone, we have to do. If these should coincide generally, their coincidence would be in our favour; if they should coincide to such an extent as to confirm and illustrate one another, to the minutest particular of their respective details; and even so as to give a new sense to obscure passages of the text, and new beauty or interest to well-known features of the landscape, as they evidently do; the coincidence must be accepted as conclusive. The text will then have been established by the testimony of nature beyond all contradiction, and will remain immutable, although the scenes to which it refers should hereafter be dislocated by earthquakes—as scenes already referred to have literally been. To all this, if the traditions of the country in question conform, it will be only so much additional evidence in its favour; if they should not conform, being known and proved, in other respects, to be false, they must without farther ceremony be rejected.

II. But if all this was so, it may be again demanded, how should MacPherson have been ignorant of the fact? This ignorance on given points, we have already had occasion to glance at with astonishment; but in reply to the general objection, it may be answered without difficulty—(1.) That Macpherson was not an eye-witness of the scenes described, and could never have written the poems; was only an innocent and admiring translator, giving word for word to the best of his ability, although the result should be unconsciously to compromise himself in many ways, as an antiquarian and a scholar. (2.) That he knew nothing, as has already been shown, of the traditions of Arran, and very little apparently of the geography of Ireland; and was therefore incapable of turning either to account —fortunately so far, for his own credit, in respect of his disputed honesty. (3.) That as a commentator on the text, he did not suspect the altered levels of the ocean, or the possibility of a passage from the north by way of Loch-Fyne to the coast of Ireland; and was misled from the beginning as to Fingal's route, which he assumed to be always beyond or through the sounds of the Hebrides. Fingal, indeed, in his youth, when he sailed for the first time to Erin by the guidance of a star, may possibly have adopted that route, although even this is uncertain; but in all subsequent expeditions he took the safer and directer passage of the inland lochs, refreshing at Arran, and resuming his voyage southward thence, between Ailsa Craig and Sanda—from which point indeed, without star or compass, his ultimate destination would be visible. MacPherson, however, as we have repeatedly observed, did not know—did not even dream of this: saw Fingal, in his own imagination, always on the Atlantic, beyond Islay and Mull, or disembarking his troops on the north-west coast of Ireland, in Lough-Swilly or Lough-Foyle; but being unable to trace their progress farther, or reconcile the geography of that region with the text before him, he abandoned them there as beyond his cognisance; disguised his own ignorance of their whereabouts, by the use of indefinite terms, such as Erin, Ulster, and Connaught; and left his readers, like himself, in bewilderment as to their actual destination. Cromla, for him, was a mountain among the hundreds of Ullin; Moi-lena was an unknown strath, and the Lubar a magician's river, running backwards and forwards to the sea. If he knew more than this, he has carefully concealed it in his notes to Ossian; but his ignorance is so obvious in his own attempts at explanation, that we are bound to credit him with total unconsciousness in the matter. Such obscurity, it may be hoped, has now been finally dispelled, and the actual position of these localities, as well as of many others, determined in the geography of the world. In which process, not only the authenticity of Ossian, but his truthfulness to fact—which is of equal importance—has been established also; and it will be at the peril of discredit to himself for any student of history hereafter to ignore, or, without the clearest evidence to the contrary, to deny it.

III. And finally, it may be objected that some other scene in Ireland may correspond as well to the disputed text in question, as the region between Larne and Lough-Neagh, and so all our illustrations be in vain:—to which it may again be replied, that in matter of fact such double correspondence is incredible; no other such scene exists. No mountain range full of caves and cromlechs, between two arms of the sea at right angles to one another east and south; with a lake on its summit and subterranean streams adjoining, or with a valley to the north full of graves, and a rushing river flowing westward; a defile to the east that might be defended by two brave men against an army; and a glimpse, to seaward, of Scotland, with solitary isles in the distance—is anywhere to be seen or traced, in any map or survey of the country. If it exists, let it be defined and illustrated and collated with the text, and the claims of the region now specified will be frankly withdrawn—but not the authenticity of Ossian. Such double correspondence of nature (which, for the present, must be held impossible) with the text of a disputed book would prove nothing more, than that the scenery of a picturesque island may perhaps repeat itself. No such repetition, we are confidently convinced, can ever be established; but if it could, it would be only so much more in MacPherson's favour, that a choice of two similar scenes, of necessity notorious in themselves from their very resemblance to each other, being possible to illustrate a forgery, the alleged author of the forgery himself knew nothing of either; did not even hint the possibility that one or other, or anything corresponding to them, could ever be traced. Such simplicity is incomprehensible, except on the supposition of conscious ignorance, and yet more conscious honesty on the part of accused. The only matter of wonder seems to be, that antiquarians and critics with such a region before them for a hundred years, and with the text of Ossian to explain it, should ever have had any difficulty in understanding the one or in believing the other. The true difficulty, indeed, is to understand the one without the other. For his own part, the present writer must candidly avow, that although the scenes of *Fingal* and *Temora* were clear enough to his own mind long before he consulted an atlas or gazetteer on the subject, yet the minuteness and beauty of correspondence revealed, by a careful comparison of such authorities with the text, overwhelmed him with surprise. The geography of Ireland seemed scarcely to have been known to him before, in its romantic significance. Ossian, in fact, became its truest exponent—as graphic in his descriptions as Walter Scott, more minute and reliable in his very details than surveys and gazetteers. All obscurity about the region under the light of his text vanished, and all hesitation about the authenticity of his text was dispelled for ever by an intelligent look at the landscape. He believes, therefore, that the genuineness of Ossian in these the most important works, as well as in other minor works ascribed to him, may be considered an established fact —historical, geographical, and literal—in all its bearings; and that his poems, when divested of the mere hyperboles of speech and poetic utterance, are henceforth entitled to be regarded and relied on, if rightly understood, as authentic records in the history of the nation—more venerable for age than anything we possess besides, and a thousand times more vivid and beautiful than anything of the sort in the archives of Britain.

Besides all these hypothetical objections, however, to certain aspects of the argument, it must be obvious that an important geographical feature of the region in question remains still to be accounted for—the existence and whereabouts of Lough-Neagh. Could Ossian be ignorant of it? Did Ossian ever see it? Does Ossian refer to it? That a great body of water to the westward, called Lake-Lego, was intimately known to him, and frequently referred to by him indirectly in the poems now under discussion, is certain; but the head-quarters of the expeditions celebrated in these poems never reached it, and no operations of consequence took place upon its banks. If the lake referred to be Lough-Neagh, the fliers from battle and their pursuers might come in sight of it, and considerable slaughter in this way undoubtedly took place not far from it; but Fingal and his chiefs remained fighting and manœuvring always to the east of it, and were probably never more than half-way from Lough-Larne towards it. Its existence, therefore, as a part of the country occupied and described, is never recognised; but, on the strictest principles of purely dramatic narrative, is totally excluded. In episodes and digressions, however, or by figurative allusions, it is frequently introduced; so often, indeed, and with signs of such intimate acquaintance by the poet and his friends, that its name becomes one of the most familiar in both epics. In a solitary instance, it seems also to be referred to without name—as a " reedy lake " in the neighbourhood of Lena:—" Hereafter shall the traveller meet their dark, thick mist on Lena, where it wanders with their ghosts, beside the reedy lake."—*Temora*, B. III. But as the identification of this lake—whether as the reedy lake, or as Lake-Lego—will require minute geographical inquiry and the careful analysis of one other poem at least, besides *Fingal* and *Temora*, it must be reserved for a separate chapter : in the meantime, the reader's attention is invited to a note or two on the intervening pages, in reply to Laing and his supposed confutations of MacPherson.

## NOTES IN REPLY TO LAING.

### I. MOI-LENA—GELCHOSSA AND LAMDERG.

In relation to the tombs of Lamderg and Gelchossa—*Fingal*, B. V.—and the details of Irish fable on the subject, Laing, in his notes on the place, refers to a tradition in Toland—*Druids*, 23, 55, 56—in which all the names introduced by Ossian occur; and from this fable MacPherson is alleged to have constructed the whole episode of Gelchossa, and to have turned her grave "into the tomb of Lamderg, the common burial place, in which Ullin, Lamderg, Gelchossa, Ryno, and Orla, are all interred." He then proceeds:—

"The discovery of Gelchossa's Mount in Inisoen, and of Lamderg's Mountain, between Buncranach and Fathan, in the county of Donnegal, ascertains the intended scene of Fingal; viz. the Peninsula of Inisoen between Loch-Swilly and Loch-Foyle. But Moi-Lena, where the battles are fought upon landing, is a part of King's County, in the Province of Leinster; and an inland district, in the very centre of Ireland, is transferred to the shores of the most northern extremity of the Province of Ulster. The 'cause of this strange mistake," he says, "was explained in the *Journal des Savans*, 1764—. . . . 'Sous le titre de *Cath-Moigh-Lena*, c'est a dire, *l'Histoire de la battaille de la Champ de Lena*: Memoire de M. de C. [onor] au sujet des Poems de M. MacPherson'"—and then concludes, "The battle of Moi-Lena is an Irish romance, which MacPherson had certainly seen, and in searching the map for the situation of Gelchossa's Mount, and Lamderg's Hill, on the west side of Inisoen, as described by Toland, he probably mistook Maline, at the extremity of the Peninsula, for the field of Moi-Lena."

And thus, according to our ingenious critic, the story of Gelchossa and the campaign of Moi-Lena have been mixed up, and converted into the poem of *Fingal* by the genius of a lying impostor, at the age of 18; and transferred by him, in his ignorance of geography, from Tullamore to Londonderry. In other words, Toland and the Irish Rhymers, M. de Conor and the French Savans, Laing and MacPherson himself, were all equally and alike ignorant of the facts of the case. Ossian alone, as represented by MacPherson, is the true authority. There may, indeed, have been two native traditions about Gelchossa and Lamderg, but the difference between them is this—that the tradition accepted or invented by the Rhymers is a Druidical absurdity, divided between the Counties of Londonderry and Donegal; whereas the tradition accepted by Ossian, hundreds of years before, relates to a melancholy but simple matter of fact, which occurred on the hillside within a mile or two of Carrick-Fergus, and on the very verge of Moi-Lena, in the valley of the Six-mile-water—hitherto unknown, not even suspected, by Laing or MacPherson or O'Connor, as the veritable scene of *Fingal* and *Temora*.

### II. CUTHULLIN'S SHIELD AT TURA.

In his note to the passage, already quoted by us at the end of preceding chapter from *Fingal*, B. I., Laing suggests (1.) that the whole piece is a literal imitation from the well-known poem of *Hardyknute*, itself a forgery; and (2.) that the names of certain personages introduced—such as "Crugal, Lugar, Favi, Puno, dreadful hero! are fictitions names of the translator's invention." If this were really the case, their introduction was certainly no great proof of the inventor's taste. But the learned critic forgets that the passage contains the names of places and objects in regular succession, as well as the names of heroes; and that these are not to be found either at Tullamore or at Londonderry, or anywhere else in Ireland, but between Belfast and Larne, where neither Laing nor MacPherson ever dreamt of looking for them. The whole scene in its integrity, even to the minutest geographical detail, is now before the reader; and on comparison he will find, not only that the various points enumerated occur along the Belfast range as regularly as the stations on a line of railway, but that the sound of the shield at Tura must have traversed them all with the precision and speed of a telegraph. Laing was, no doubt, a most accomplished commentator, as well as a most ingenious critic, with immense resources of parallel passages at command to support his theory of plagiarism; but it is possible for the most ingenious critic with all his resources, when ignorant of facts, to imagine too much. Laing, if it had been possible for him in 1805, might as well have asserted that *Fingal* was to be a prophecy, and that the poor young schoolmaster of Ruthven, in his dreams of the future, had foreseen the days of electric telegraphy. The transference of Tullamore to Londonderry, and the fabrication of *Fingal* out of Irish Druidical romances and the Ballad of *Hardyknute*, may therefore be abandoned.

### III. OSCAR'S DEATH AT TEMORA.

In the following note on the death of Oscar, as in *Temora*, B. I.—we have a somewhat different account from that which MacPherson gives us of the Irish ballad on the subject, in so far as the voyage of Fingal and the name of Albion are concerned—which name Laing affirms should be Allen in Leinster, and not Albion at all. If so, there must certainly have been two versions of the ballad, for MacPherson in his own note quotes the word Albion expressly twice, where such a mistake could serve no purpose whatever of imposture. For the rest, when the reader has examined the quotation and compared it with facts already now in his possession, he will be better able to judge for himself of its critical value as regards the honesty of MacPherson and the authenticity of Ossian.

"The Irish ballad on the death of Oscar, which MacPherson has described and quoted, is the sole foundation for the epic poem of *Temora*, and the only poem upon the subject that has ever been discovered in the Highlands of Scotland. . . . . But the first book of *Temora* exhausts the ballad, from which the invitation to the feast at Tara, and the proposed exchange of spears, are adopted; and Cairbar threatens to hunt and carry the spoils next day from *Almhuin*, Oscar to hunt and carry the spoils next day to *Almhuin*; not to *Albion*, as misquoted by MacPherson, but the hill of *Allen* in Leinster, the residence of Fingal, within a few miles of Tara and of the pass of Gabhra where the battle was fought. Oscar made a prodigious slaughter in the battle, which was fought next day; and when pierced through the body with a poisoned, or seven-barbed spear, thrown by Cairbar, he fell upon his knee, as in the

Temora, pierced Cairbar's forehead with a nine-barbed spear, and with another which he hurled, slew young Artho, Cairbar's son. Fingal arrives in his ships, not, as MacPherson asserts, from Scotland, but from a voyage to Rome. Oscar, while still alive, is carried, on the shields of his attendants, to his grandfather's house; evidently to Almhuin, not to Albion; and the Irish ballad, from which these circumstances are taken, was undoubtedly the only original that ever came to the translator's hands."

This note appeared in Laing's so-called edition of "MacPherson's Poetical Works" in 1805, and many of our readers may be aware that, contrary to his implied prediction, the remaining seven Books of *Temora* in the Gaelig language, ascribed to Ossian, were subsequently discovered, and the entire poem published along with *Fingal* and others in an authorised edition at Edinburgh in 1818—the very year, as it happened, of his death. But even if this had not been the case, we have to remind our readers (1.) that the scene of Ossian's *Temora* has now been identified, where neither Laing nor MacPherson imagined; that the spot where Oscar was treacherously slain may yet be found on Glenwherry-water; that the circumstances of his burial in Arran have been proved, and that his sepulchre there is with us until this day. (2.) That Fingal's expedition, as described in this poem, was certainly from Scotland and from nowhere else; that the point of his departure from Arran, either at Sliddery or Lagg, may be verified; and that the scene of his own death and burial, when he returned, has also been ascertained—all which circumstances were utterly unknown to MacPherson, although certainly known to the people. (3.) We may be allowed to remark, also, that the character of the Irish romance itself—which, after all, would be but a fractional part of the whole—with its outrageous atrocities of seven-barbed and nine-barbed, or poisoned spears; its palace for Fingal at Tara, and its voyage of Fingal from Rome—why not from Jerusalem?—sufficiently betrays its origin, as the work of priestly rhymers or lying sennachies in the middle ages, in a trial of strength between Leinster and Ulster for the fabrication of the greatest falsehood in honour of their respective provinces. The only remark worth adding is, that the bold introduction of Tara in this ballad may have bewildered MacPherson, who knew of no other Temora—but of this we shall inquire in the text, hereafter. In conclusion, we profess ourselves infinitely indebted to Mr. Laing's work for enabling us to put an end for ever to his own ingenious calumnies, which thus perish in the very repetition of them in the face of facts and traditions of which, with all his scholarship, he knew nothing.

## CHAPTER IV.

LAKE-LEGO—LOUGH-NEAGH.

THE two poems, *Fingal* and *Temora*, with their episodes, have hitherto been the exclusive sources of information on which we have relied. Two other poems, however, much smaller, and mere supplements to the greater epics, remain to be examined; and to make assurance of the geographical position already identified doubly sure, a brief analysis of one of these seems desirable.

I. The *Death of Cuthullin*, historically, is a supplement to *Fingal*; *Darthula*, in like manner, is a supplement to the *Death of Cuthullin*; and *Temora*, the record of the last great expedition to Ireland, concludes the series. The poems themselves, greater and smaller, are inseparably connected—being interwoven with one another, by allusions to the same scenes and the same actors—and illustrate one another by descriptive references to succeeding events on the same ground. Cuthullin, as we already know, was regent for Conar's dynasty in Ullin before Fingal's arrival; but after Fingal's departure, he was slain by an arrow in the last moment of victory, somewhere between Lake-Lego and the stream of Lara, where also he was interred, with much solemnity, under a mound. To assist in this fatal campaign, three other Scotchmen of distinction, Nathos, Althos, and Ardan, brothers, with their respective followings, arrive, but too late to be of service to Cuthullin: they can only avenge his death, and return again to the coast at Tura where he had formerly lived. These allies from Scotland " come from the sea to Tura's bay;" they seek in vain for Cuthullin at Tura—he was gone, and " the halls of Tura were silent." They then march north or north-westward to Lego's lake, to Lara's stream, and to the palace of Temora; but the king, as well as Cuthullin, has been already slain. Sad they return again " in their grief towards Tura's sounding bay," to re-embark; but in their return they pass by Selàma, where Darthula, sole daughter and surviving child of the chieftain there, becomes enamoured of Nathos and prepares to fly with him to Scotland, that she may escape the hateful solicitations of Cairbar, the murderer of her father, and the murderous usurper of the throne. They take ship accordingly, but a north wind meets them in their flight; " Erin stretches its green head into the sea beyond them, and Tura's bay [again] receives the ship." Here their position on the shore, where they take refuge, is exactly defined as among rocks at the foot of a mountain ridge, with a torrent from Cromla on the north dashing down behind them; the open sea or bay, to the south, beside them; and the coast along the shore, with an easy passage over the hill to Lena—from

s

which they may be, and finally are, overtaken—eastward before them. One of the caves of Tura is again pointed out from the shore, as in a rock; the towers of Tura, with a dim light burning, are visible beyond it; and the fortress of Selàma is distinctly noted as among the hills, in the forsaken distance, westward. It would perhaps be impossible by any mere incidental collocation of phrases, indicating points of the compass and describing geographical positions, more clearly to define Carrick-Fergus bay. Latitude, longitude, and superficial scenery could hardly make it plainer. One might almost lay his finger on the spot to westward of the town at this moment, on which the unhappy fugitives were overtaken and slain by the jealous monster who pursued them. This point, therefore, being now identified beyond dispute, it is only farther necessary to remind the reader that one of the great raths, possibly Duncrue, in the neighbourhood of Carrick-Fergus, may indicate the position of the "Halls of Tura;" and that the extensive fort already described, called MacArt's fort, on the summit of Cave-Hill, "protected on one side by a precipice, and on the other by a single ditch of great depth and a vallum of large dimensions," is almost certainly the very Selma or Selàma from which Darthula, in despair and terror, took flight; and so proceed, on the same principles as hitherto, to identify Lake-Lego.

1. Lake-Lego, or its shores, we find incidentally specified or referred to, at least six times in *Fingal*, nine times in *Temora*, fifteen times in *Death of Cuthullin*, and twice or thrice in *Darthula*; in most of which cases it is distinguished by characteristics ascribed to no other in the neighbourhood. It is filled along its shores with reeds, so large and numerous that the masts of a fleet are once compared to them; it has a sable surge, and emits pestilential vapours; it is wood-skirted, and large enough to have more than one princely district on its banks, and with a gulf or corner at its northern extremity projecting inland, across which the sound of the war-horn may be heard. Rivers flow into it, and one at least, to the north, flows out of it, or the lake itself becomes a stream there. It has been frozen frequently, and floods from it in winter, when the ice breaks up, endanger the inhabitants in that direction. It requires a journey from Lena to pass to the south of it, a journey from Tura by the mountains to pass to the north of it, a journey to pass from one end to the other of it, and it has a plain large enough on its eastern side to afford scope to armies for battle and pursuit. It seems to be west of the province of Ullin, and to border on Alnecma beyond; has been the scene of revelry among chiefs, and of rivalry among bards, in which Ossian was a partaker; but is haunted by the spirits of the discontented dead, and is spoken of with apprehension as the source of disease. As already intimated, it has no direct dramatic connection with the campaigns of Fingal on the Lubar, although once and again the spirits of the dead emerge from its mists, as if close

at hand, to survey the scene and watch the progress of the conflict; but it has the directest connection with the death of Cuthullin, who, marching from Tura, encamps at its northern extremity, fights southward along its eastern shores, falls, and is entombed on its borders. Other indications of its locality, similar to the above, might easily be quoted, but these for the present may suffice; and to reason from these, as arguments afforded by the text itself, to ascertain its proximity to Lena, to Tura, to Temora, and the other points already identified by geographical evidence in Ulster, requires no great ingenuity.

(1.) The spirit of Conar, rolled by a north-western breeze from its utmost extremity northwards, is seen to hover over the grave of Fingal's son, who had fallen on Lena southwards, in the cause of his house; but if, as MacPherson instructs us, this celebrated lake was in the province of Connaught, and if Connaught was identical with the province which is now known by that name, there could be no other body of water there—and by preference, the nearest—than Lough-Allen (not Bog of Allen, in Leinster), corresponding to it; and it seems irrational that the spirit of a king of Ullin should take refuge on a lake in the land of his enemies, and return in an instant by a zigzag circuitous route, first north, then east, then south-east, from a distant and questionable scene of repose, whose distance was thus three-fold multiplied, to console the ghost of a relative who lay buried at his own door, if there was any other lake on the confines of his kingdom, where his soul could be accommodated as a spectator of the battle, nearer home. Besides which, the peculiar terms of reference employed seem to bring it close at hand on the west, as if Ossian saw the mist rising in which the spirit of Conar rolls—"when the gates of the west are closed on the sun's eagle eye." In addition to which, still farther, it must be observed that the stream which flows into Lough-Allen flows from the north, and the stream which flows out of it is the Shannon, which flows southward from the lake—conditions the very reverse of those which are specified of Lego.

(2.) We find it expressly spoken of as near enough for the ghosts, which frequented its clouds, to hear the voice of Carril on the Lubar chaunting their praise; and not too far to permit them to gather around him in an instant to enjoy the consolation of his theme—which, at the distance of a hundred miles, would have been a poetical, as well as a practical impossibility, too gross for the imagination of a man like Ossian, so entirely truthful in his most vivid representations, to have employed, or even tolerated, for a moment. Those who conceive of him otherwise have never studied his works, or have utterly misunderstood his genius. The fairies of Shakespear were unknown to him: only clouds and whirlwinds rolling mists, which must have time to travel, and which sometimes traverse the whole breadth of the Island, are admitted to the action of his poems

—dreams and mental visions of the night alone excepted, which like glimpses of the moon, or "the swift-winged arrows of light," are present in an instant.

(3.) It seems to be near enough to be *heard* from where the armies are encamped, as if the sound of it was familiar—"like the noise of the Lake of Lego, when its waters shrink in the days of frost, and all its bursting ice resounds;" not as if the season were winter then—for it was the end of summer, as we have seen; but as if the sound of such a change were well enough known to all who had occasion to visit that country, and could be referred to with intelligence.

(4.) It was not more than an afternoon's march north-west of Tura and west of Temora, to its northern extremity at Lara; but southward from Lara, along its eastern shore, it must have been a full day's journey, for an embassy is required to come and go between the armies encamped on that side of it—Torlath's marching down from the south, and Cuthullin's bivouacked in the north, with some great arm of the lake shooting eastward between them; across which, as they approach to conflict, the horns of Torlath's trumpeters are heard. To the east of it also, and to the south of Temora, somewhere between that and the valley of the Lubar, is a mountain, or a mountain range, called Slimora, of which nothing more precise is yet known than that it was wood-covered and conspicuous as a sort of landmark in the region, and not to be confounded with the other Mora, now Slimero, to the south-east, on which Fingal's head-quarters were pitched in his own campaigns. But if Tura was at Carrick-Fergus, as we have seen, and Temora at Connor, the geographical position of Lake-Lego, whose extent and extremities are thus defined, is already certain. Slimora might be Slievemeset, or some other point in the Donegore range, between Tura and Temora; but Lego itself was Lough-Neagh, and the Bay of Antrim in that lake the interposing gulf between the armies.

2. Again, with respect to its tributaries and outflows, or other lakes adjoining, we gather from the text of the various poems now in question, as already stated—

(1.) That at the west end of Lena—that is, of the valley of the Six-mile-water—there was a "reedy lake," name not specified, from which the mists of the dead arose. If this lake was identical with Lego, as the characteristic of reeds may imply, then it was identical also with Lough-Neagh; but if not, then it was certainly identical with Lough-Beg, otherwise Portmore—a small round lake in the immediate neighbourhood of Lough-Neagh, and at the date in question most probably a part of, or at least connected with it, as its name of Portmore, or the great harbour, seems still to show.

(2.) That to the south or south-west there was a region called Branno, with a chief called Branno—Ossian's own father-in-law; and that in this region there were the "streams of Branno," which most probably flowed into it.

(3.) About the north, we have more distinct information. Some district there called Lara, to the west of Temora, apparently populous and with rich pastures, but subject to inundations, seems to suffer most from these when the ice breaks up on Lego; so that the outflow of the lake must have been to northward, and the land in that neighbourhood low-lying or level—" when its waters shrink, in the days of frost, and all its bursting ice resounds: the people of Lara look to heaven, and foresee the storm."—*Temora*, B. II. In this valley seem to be many streams, some of which may flow into Lego; but the principal stream, which is of the same name, Lara, undoubtedly flows out from Lego; for Lego itself, where the river is discharged, gets the name of a stream, as if the lake and the river were blended, and the mists from Lego spread wide along that stream, following its course among marshes northward.

(4.) And finally, wherever this outflow of the lake, in or at Lara, might be, it was not far west from Temora. " He dwelt with Cormac [young king of Ullin] in windy Temora, when Semo's son [Cuthullin] fell at Lego's stream." . . . " Battles are fought at Lego: the sword of Nathos [friend of Cuthullin] prevails. Soon shalt thou behold him in thy halls, king of Temora of groves!"—*Temora*, B. I. It was from this point also, with a change of wind, striding " from blast to blast," which " at times rolled him together—but the form returned again," that Conar came southward, " with bending eyes and dark-winding locks of mist," to brood in sympathy " on the grave of Fillan, at blue-winding Lubar."—*Temora*, B. VII.

3. All which conditions being taken into account, and the site of Temora near the village of Connor on the Glenwherry-water, as already determined in a preceding chapter, being remembered—it must be obvious that no lake in all Ireland corresponds to this lake but Lough-Neagh, and that Lough-Neagh in all its geographical bearings corresponds exactly. Long ago, it must have had the marshes, still the " low-lying valley," of the Lagan, or La-an, adjacent; with the tributaries of the Branno, still water of the Upper Bann, and of the Black-water westward, flowing into it on the south. Then, as now, to the north, its " only outlet would be the Lower Bann, which being obstructed by weirs and rocks prevents the free egress of the water, and causes the surrounding country to be injuriously inundated in winter"—*Topographical Dictionary;* when " the people of Lara look to heaven and foresee the storm." Then, as now, it might well accommodate many friendly or even hostile tribes along its shores, partitioned among rival chiefs, and maintaining a savage independence—for " it is the largest lake in the British islands, and is chiefly in the County of Antrim, but extends into several others"—Tyrone, Armagh, Londonderry, and Down. It is, in fact, an inland sea, being, according to the Ordnance Survey, " about 20 British miles

in length from north-east to south-west, about 12 miles in extreme breadth from east to west, 80 miles in circumference, and comprises about 154 square miles." Then, as now, although never remarkable for wood, it might well be woodskirted, even more richly than it is, and might abound with reeds on its northern shores, where the water overflowed in marshes—for in 1663, according to Blaeu, it was still "surrounded by the most luxuriant woods or richest prairies, intersected with innumerable streams;" and still farther north, on the Lower Bann by Glencolkein, it afforded, at the same date, "shelter to the insular Scotch freebooters [remnants of the older inhabitants] by reason of the dense forests and almost inaccessible marshes there (*des marests fort difficiles*)." Then, more certainly than now, notwithstanding its immense size, it might be occasionally frozen over, for in the last and present centuries such a phenomenon has thrice occurred —"This vast expanse of water," says the *Topographical Dictionary*, "was frozen in 1739 and 1784, and in 1814 the ice was sufficiently thick for Col. Heyland to ride from Crumlin-water foot to Ram's Island;" that is, nearly across the corner of it—which island, it may be remarked, "is the only one of importance on the lake, and contains the remains of a Round Tower." Finally, the mists which then overhung its waters, or were floated from its shores along the rivers and valleys in autumn, might well be productive of disease—for the climate of Ireland generally, according to Blaeu, and therefore much more of such a region as this, was "very moist, generating all sorts of rheums and fluxes (*des flux de ventre*) especially among strangers; for which," however, then, as well as in the days of Fingal when the "shell of joy" went round, the natives had, as they still have, a sovereign antidote "in an excellent *eau-de-vie;* which is drier and not so hot as ours," called "usquebah,"—literally, *uisge-beatha*, the water of life —which neutralised the injurious effects of the too moist atmosphere.

In short, there is not a single feature in all Ossian's incidental descriptions, dropped or reiterated by so many speakers, of this remarkable lake, that may not be paralleled with the minutest precision from statistical accounts and surveys of Lough-Neagh, both in the past and present centuries. Even that which seems most incredible, the blackness of its surge and the murky hue, if not the poisonous character, of its exhalations, may be explained on authority independent of his, yet coinciding with his text to a miracle. The commonly received geographical theory of its formation is, that the confluence of the Bann, the Black-water, the Six-mile-water, the Glenwherry-water, and other minor streams, in a hollow, by degrees constituted the lake; which to a certain extent, and now that all other causes are removed, may be true. But the fact that the Bann, flowing into the lake from the south, re-appears at the north, and affords the only visible outlet for the accumulated waters of so many other rivers besides itself, seems to imply that there may or might be some other means of absorption, and that the levels of the area occupied by the lake were not always the same. According to the Ordnance Survey, it is only 48 feet above the level of the sea at low water, and Belfast on the Lagan is not above 6, deriving its very name from the fact "that it was *Ball-fosaght*, or the town with a ditch or foss, which from its low situation were anciently constructed round the town, to protect it from the tide."—*Topographical Dictionary.* The valley of the Lagan, on which it stands, must have been a saline lake for miles inland, and the channel of the river, fordable at low water, is crossed by a long low-level narrow bridge of 21 arches, erected in 1686; below which, it expands into the estuary almost at dead level, through which a new cut for navigation has recently been made, and an artificial island of great extent created by simply shutting out the tide. Belfast Lough, therefore, at one time, must have been not only much broader, but much higher, than it now is; at which date, the tide, then 20 or 30 feet above its present level, would be up to the very foot of the mountains; Belfast itself would be nowhere as yet; and the waters of the ocean would be within a few miles of the southern extremity of Lough-Neagh: as if in confirmation of which theory, there is a distinct tradition to the effect that that lake "was formed in the year 62 by an irruption of the sea." Its very appearance, indeed, seems to justify the tradition—"It resembles a sea," says Blaeu in 1663, "if the sweetness of its waters did not forbid the idea." But its waters might not be always sweet, as they now are; on the contrary, the probability is that it was once a bitter gulf with waters of Marah fermenting around, and that it was the very putrefaction and effervescence of rank vegetable matter, submerged and rotting under the stagnant tide, which constituted it thus in Ossian's day a dark and pestilential marsh, with "sable surge" and curling vapour breathing death; if the vapours alluded to were not occasionally mingled also with sulphureous smoke, through the chinks of a surface that had been rent by volcanic agents not entirely dormant at the date in question. That there might even have been some subterranean communication, now closed, between the lake and the sea, is not impossible. Its surface, as already stated, is only 48 feet above the level of the sea at low water; but its depth in the centre is 45 feet, that is only 3 feet above the same level, which would be more than covered by the rising of the tide; so that when the sea itself was 20 or 30 feet higher than it now is, the communication, if it existed, would be regular and constant. On these suppositions, Milton has not more correctly described

> The gulf profound, as that Serbonian bog
> Twixt Damiata and Mount Cassius old,

connected with the Mediterranean and once strongly impregnated with asphalt, than Ossian has in his own vivid and truthful fashion, from actual observation, this *Lacus Sirbonis* of his remoter day, in "the dark rolling of its waters, with their sable surge"—the only difference being, that when the connection between the Serbonian Bog and the Mediterranean ceased, there being no influx of water from the surface to maintain it, that lake dried up; whereas the constant drainage of the neighbourhood by multitudinous streams into Lough-Neagh not only preserves it, but has ultimately sweetened its waters.

II. Nor are these suppositions merely: everything goes to confirm the theory, as founded on fact. The waters of the lake, now purified, are at some places medicinal, at others indued with petrifying power—in both cases, supposed to be connected with the soil; and throughout all the ridges of the surrounding country, already described—indeed, through the whole County of Antrim between the lake and the sea—are springs of saline and sulphureous elements, acting as most powerful drugs. "There are numerous mineral springs," says the *Topographical Dictionary;* " one near Ballycastle is chalybeate, another aluminous and vitriolic, and a third on Knocklaid mountain, chalybeate; at Kilroot, there is a nitrous water of a purgative quality; and near Carrick-Fergus are two salt springs, one at Bellahill and the other in Island Maghee." It cannot be surprising, therefore, that the vapours of a lake which must have combined many of these elements should once have been injurious, when too highly impregnated with some of them; although now the very waters from which they were exhaled, rectified by time and absorption, or by the continual influx of purer streams, are actually beneficial. And that all this was the result of volcanic agency, is just as certain as tradition and the concurrence of the unconscious text can make it; for that more than one great earthquake in this very region, followed by minor ones, with subterranean thunder, took place before Ossian's day, moving the mountains and terrifying the people, is clear. Nay, that such earthquakes were comparatively common in Scotland and Ireland about the commencement of the Christian era, if not later, incidental allusions to them in the text of Ossian demonstrate—" He lay like a shattered rock which Cromla shakes from its shaggy side, when the green vallied Erin shakes its mountains from sea to sea"—*Temora*, B. I.; that is, from Belfast Lough to Lough-Foyle—the very track in which Lough-Neagh now lies. "The sound of their steps is like thunder in the bosom of the ground, when the rocking hills shake their groves, and not a blast pours from the darkened sky!"—*Temora*, B. II.—phenomena of which Ossian, or the writer of these words, whoever he was, must certainly have been a living witness. We look in vain through all the records of modern geographical or geological transactions, for anything to compare with such descriptions in suggestive pictorial precision, commemorating without attempting to explain such sublime occurrences in nature, as events to be noted in the poet's soul and employed as mere poetic imagery, before men had investigated or systematised them as the results of a force in the universe. Yet MacPherson has been accused with insolent contempt, by men like Laing and Macaulay, of having forged or fabricated passages like these, although he could not even guess the scene of such phenomena within a hundred statute miles of the reality; and did not remember, which a forger in the circumstances would never have forgotten, that the alleged volcanic formation of Lough-Neagh took place at the very commencement of those remarkable geological changes in the south of Europe which began with an earthquake in 63 that injured many cities in Italy, and ended with the eruption of Vesuvius in 79, when Herculaneum and Pompeii "were consumed or buried;" or that a lake like Avernus, although "now a cheerful and salubrious spot, once exhaled mephitic vapours . . and gases as destructive of animal life, as those suffocating vapours given out by Lake Quilotoa . . . by which whole herds of cattle on its shores were killed."—*Lyell's Geology*, Vol. II. Quilotoa, indeed, emitted such vapours in 1797, which was many years too late for MacPherson to have quoted it; but Avernus was known to every schoolboy, and was older than Ossian.

III. All that now remains to be determined, therefore, for the complete identification of this lake and of the river Lara connected with it, is the origin and signification of their names. Although almost every proper name in Gaelig, as in other primitive tongues, has some descriptive sense, it is not always possible with complete accuracy to trace this; and in the present case, MacPherson explains only one of the names in question, leaving the other totally unexplained, in a note of considerable length to his first edition; of which he omits in his final edition the explanatory part, either as if he was doubtful of it, or did not consider it necessary. From the part thus omitted we make the following quotation:—" Lego, so often mentioned by Ossian, was a lake in Connaught, into which the river Lara emptied itself. . . . . . The signification of Lego [Gaelic Li-Ego] is the *Lake of Disease*, probably so called on account of the morasses which surrounded it."—*Temora*, B. VII. Of the Lara, as we have said, no interpretation is afforded; but the idea that it flowed *into* Lake-Lego is assumed as obvious, which we have already demonstrated to be false. To dispose of this term, therefore, in the first place, by some derivation of our own, is allowable in the circumstances; and as the word Lara is the name of a district as well as of a river, its signification must have had primary reference to the region through which that river flowed—for it is not the Lara of the region, but Lara of the streams, that is most frequently mentioned. The reader has already been informed that the vale of Moi-Lena was celebrated for its breed

T

of horses, minutely and poetically described in *Fingal* as swift, superb, and powerful, even to a proverb; and such horses could not have been produced without the utmost attention to their breeding. It should be nothing surprising, therefore, if some district near the royal residence, and as far removed as possible from the scene of frequent campaigns, were referred to in Ossian as the ground where such animals were reared—it would be surprising, indeed, if it were not. But the royal residence, or Temora, as we have already seen, was in the very heart of Ullin, near the village of Connor, on the banks of the Glenwherry, northward; and according to our geography, Lara would be a little to the west of this, where minor streams were numerous, and the pasture, in consequence, luxuriant; where the royal stud, therefore, might be nursed in safety till their strength was adequate for the fatigues of war. But Larach, or Larah, contracted Lara, as a proper name, means the region abounding with mares. The valley through which the river of that name, therefore, flowed would be the stock-region of the household cavalry of Ullin, where "sons of the wind," like Sithfadda and Sronnal, were trained, and yoked to "the car of gems." No other derivation seems requisite, and no other could be in more perfect harmony with the context of both poems; but as MacPherson does not suggest it, does not seem even to have imagined it, his credit, for honesty and unconsciousness alike, remains.

With respect to Lego or *Li-ego*, as the lake of disease, it may be incompetent for a philologist, without practical knowledge of the language, to object to such a derivation, and it must be accepted for the present, on MacPherson's authority, as good. But the most careful scrutiny of the best Gaelig Lexicons to be found will compel us to correct his orthography. No such word as *ego* is discoverable there; but *aog*, which by simple transposition becomes *ago*, *eag*, *eig*, and *eug*, all signifying death, are distinctly legible. *Li* seems to be some half obsolete word, and means a flood or sea, otherwise written *Lighe*—so that these two terms, with the '*n* of possessive affinity interposed, signifying the Flood of Death, or of Disease, will give us *Lighe-'n-Eag*, as near an approach to Lough-Neagh as the most fastidious philologist could reasonably demand. But Lough-Neagh itself, in one of the oldest geographical treatises on the region extant, already quoted—viz., Blaeu's of 1663—is described in the letterpress as the *Lac-d'-Eaugh*, or the Lake of Eaugh, equivalent to the Gaelig *Lighe-'n-Eagh*; an orthography which makes it plain that the 'n prefixed to the descriptive term is but a significant particle even in the modern designation, representing the possessive case; and Lough-Neagh is thus really the Lough-of-Eagh or Eag—the Lake of Disease or Death, and the veritable Lego, or Li-ago, of Ossian. Whatever the true meaning, then, of the terms in question may be—Lake of Disease, or Lake of Death—it seems impossible to dispute longer about its identity.

But it must be further remarked, that this designation is common to the whole surrounding region. There is Reagh, now Castlereagh, and Iv-eagh Upper and Iv-eagh Lower, both adjoining the lake; and Killead or Killeagh, a parish on its eastern shore, already mentioned as part of the valley of dry bones—the scene where so many deaths occurred, and where so many tombs attest the slaughter—that practical Gehenna of the district; and finally there is Antrim, originally Antreagh, in the neighbourhood of Muckamore the contiguous parish, in which, as in Killead, so many similar monuments of sepulture are extant. How, then, comes this designation to be so frequent there? Either because there were other marshes in the low-lying land between Lake-Lego and the sea, as fatal to the inhabitants by their exhalations as the great source of pestilence itself—which corresponds precisely with the geological characteristics of the ground already specified, including by pre-eminence the Lagan; or because the word *Eagh* had some other sense—had, in short, a double sense—equally appropriate to the region. In point of fact, we find that *Ligheach*, or *Ligheachan*, means the flooded region, or the region that had been subjected to floods, the country of inundations; than which no other term could well be more descriptive of the country in which these names are found—Lough-Neagh itself, the first volcanic flood and origin of them all, included; in confirmation of which it may be mentioned, that according to some authorities on the subject Antrim, or Antruim, originally Antrim-Eagh, means the habitation on the flood, traceable as far back as 495 —that is, within a hundred and fifty, or say two hundred years of the Ossianic era; and applied to that town most probably on account of its close proximity to the great Eagh, or flood of Lough-Neagh, in the neighbourhood. We have thus, then, a compound descriptive designation in Lake-Lego, of which not a letter need be lost, intimating as clearly as human language can that the neighbourhood of Lough-Neagh was pestilential, and pestilential because it was Lough-Neagh; that it was the region of death because it was the region of volcanic floods, and of disease because it was covered with the exhalations of marshes. Such is the information we obtain, geological, statistical, and physical, derived by so plain a process from the text of Ossian, concerning the now beautiful region around, and to the north of, Belfast; confirmed by geological surveys and Parliamentary Gazetteers, more than a hundred years subsequent to the translation of that text by a man who transferred the entire scene in his simplicity to the backgrounds of Connaught. Every point being thus minutely identified, from the hiding-places of the living in the caves of the rocks to the burial-places of the dead on the fields of battle, it remains only now, by way of realising the whole, to remind the reader that in this romantic valley, beginning from Glenoe near the head of Lough-Larne and expanding along the course of the Six-mile-water to the modern Moi-Lena on the shores of Lough-Neagh, the two great campaigns of Fingal on behalf of the dynasty of Conar, first against Norwegian invaders and then against usurping Irish, were fought; that the campaign of Cuthullin took place in the interval, somewhere in the district of Moilinny, near the head of Antrim Bay—but whether to the north or south of it, is uncertain—along the borders of the lake, where he routed the hostile Irish under Torlath, but fell, as the King of Israel did, by an arrow shot "at a venture" in the fight, "like the sting of death in a blast," and lies buried under the tomb of his fame, among the slain in Muckamore or on the borders thereof; that Cairbar the tyrant, succeeding or outmarching his own lieutenant Torlath, pushed on to Temora at Connor, and smote the boy-king there in the beauty of his golden locks, with the sword of the assassin; that he was afterwards slain by Oscar, who was himself perishing by treachery in the very act of vengeance; that Cathmor, the noble brother of this bloody usurper, but fighting in his unrighteous cause, fell on the fourth day thereafter in battle, on the banks of the Six-mile-water, by the hand of Fingal—who thus restored the dynasty of his father's house in the person of Ferad-Artho to the throne of Ullin, and returned again to Scotland himself, where he fell by accident or violence on the shores of Arran: and that all this, by the plainest laws of human evidence, is as certain as that the Crown Princes of England were murdered by their uncle in the Tower of London; that Richard III., thus wallowing like a boar in the blood of his kindred, was slain at last on the field of Bosworth; and that the wars of the Roses, between York and Lancaster, were consummated and finished in the triumph of Henry VII.—and has been narrated by Ossian with a poetic force and truthfulness to nature, as touching as the finest delineations of Shakespear. The people of the district, indeed, among whom all traditions seem to have perished, do not now recognise these facts; and critics who deny the existence of Ossian cannot be expected, without reflection, to believe them; but the testimony of the mountains and valleys, of the rivers and lakes, remains, and the geography of the region itself is their incontrovertible evidence.

What the practical personal acquaintance of Ossian with this region was, and how far his knowledge of Ireland and its people extended beyond; or whether he and his friends penetrated more to southward, remains yet to be considered, before the historical aspect of the subject can be fairly realised. This inquiry, as the reader has doubtless observed, we have already been anticipating by many casual hints in our progress, but the details demand separate investigation and analysis; to which, therefore, we shall proceed, under a distinct Section.

# FINGAL IN IRELAND.

## SECTION SECOND.

### CHAPTER V.

#### THE SCOTS IN IRELAND—DYNASTY OF TRENMOR.

It may prevent some confusion in our farther inquiry, in which names must now be as landmarks, to observe before beginning, that there are many instances of different persons with the same name being introduced by Ossian, not merely as actors in his Epics, but as historical personages of importance in the nations or races to which he refers. This fact alone would be an argument of some weight in support of his authenticity, if we still required to prove that; for no fabricator of such poems would have encumbered himself or perplexed his readers with the repetition of names, the same to a letter, for many different persons, if the exigencies of history and fact had not compelled him. It is not, however, in the way of argument, but solely as a matter of convenience, that we now refer to the circumstance. There are two Cormacs, for example, great-grandfather and great-grandson, of the race of Trenmor, and, therefore, relatives of Fingal; and a third Cormac, in no way apparently related to them. There are also two Cairbars, one the legitimate king of Ullin, grandfather of the younger Cormac; the other, an enemy and a usurper, from the south or south-west, of an entirely different lineage. Besides whom, there seems to be a third Cairbar, who perishes, rushing in a frenzy of grief and rage for the death of his daughter, against the Norse—with whom, therefore, we have no concern as a permanent actor in the campaigns. There were two Ullins, one an aged bard —with whom we are already acquainted, as the conductor of funeral obsequies for Oscar; the other, a young chieftain; besides Ullin, equivalent to Antrim or a portion of Ulster, the province of the Scottish kings. There are two Arthos, half brothers, sons of Cairbar MacCormac by his first and second wives; for the elder brother being reported dead, according to tradition, when the younger was born, the younger was thus named Fer-ad-Artho—almost as exactly as the Latins would say *Vir-ad*-Artho—or a man in place of Artho, as Seth was so named by his mother "instead of Abel, whom Cain slew." Besides which instances of iteration, most perplexing in the casual reading of the text, there are also certain names of localities of doubtful or indefinite application—such even as Erin itself, Inisfail, and Alnecma—which require to be defined or limited, that the places or regions referred to may be more easily recognised; and to these also, in due time, sufficient attention will be devoted.

In the midst of all this apparent uncertainty, however, there was but one Fingal, son of Comhal and king of Morven; one Ossian, son of Fingal; and one Oscar, son of Ossian, recognised as actors or historical personages at the time. If we take into account the early Irish, or later mediæval romances, there was indeed another Fingal, another Ossian, and another Oscar; all very different from the real men of these names—types of a nationality exaggerated, distorted, and confused by the imaginations or traditions of priests and bards, to an excess of monstrosity unworthy the genius of a poetic people; and no more to be relied on, or even looked at, in the way of history, than Gog and Magog of the city of London. Such figments, as we have elsewhere explained, grew out of the credulity and vanity of the southern Irish, fostered and embodied by the ambition of their bards, to supply the place of real historical characters that belonged to another nation and another epoch. They were not only not Ossian's, being a thousand years later than any production of his, but were utterly inconceivable by a man like him. For him there was but one Fingal, his father, son of Comhal; and one Oscar, his own son, by Evirallin, daughter of Branno. What related to these and to himself, the intermediate link between them, was matter of fact to him; what related to their allies, and friends or foes, in Ireland, was matter of history to him; and the various enterprises, expeditions, achievements, victories—deaths, sorrows, triumphs, and bereavements incidental to these, were themes of poetry to him. The monstrous absurdities invented in later ages, and palmed upon the world in his name, for the exaltation of his enemies, are devices of which he was of necessity as innocent and unconscious as if he had never lived. It was to supplant or discredit him, in fact, that such inventions were concocted; but the very grossness of their fabrication has defeated that end. It is entirely, therefore, to his own poetic histories, to the letter and details of his own text, and to the various relationships traceable among his heroes, we must now attend, if any real acquaintance with the history of the Scots in Ireland is to be attained by us, notwithstanding all that has been alleged to the contrary.

1. A concise and accurate enough summary of this interesting chronological epoch drawn from the poems themselves, may be found in MacPherson's epitome of the subject in his dissertation on Ossian, with this sole deduction from its authority—that he confounds Ullin with all Ulster, Alnecma with Connaught, and Erin with the whole of Ireland. The Scotch kings are thus made by him

to be supreme in Ireland before the appearance of Fingal; to be driven by revolt into the Province of Ulster, and to be reinstated again in supreme power by the timely assistance of Fingal. This error, as the reader is aware, originated in MacPherson's misconception of the geographical limits of the region described by Ossian. If he had been able to define that region correctly, he could never have made this mistake, however much an occasional ambiguous phrase in the text might seem to favour it. It is true, that from among the kings of these minor nationalities the supreme kings of Ireland were long regularly chosen, and that the kings of Ullin, raised thus in turn to the highest sovereignty, had been really the most distinguished and influential on that exalted roll—as the language of Fingal, at the conclusion of *Temora*, implies:—"Remind him [Ferad-Artho] of the kings of Erin; the stately forms of old." But at the date now in question, there seems to have been no supreme head acknowledged among them. They were acting all independently, or by league, against some neighbour, as their several interests or ambition prompted them; and whatever dormant or disputed claim there may have been on the part of Ullin to sovereignty, and however much the rest of Ireland might have been disposed to resist it, especially when represented by a Scotchman, no such claim is either alluded to or presupposed in the text of Ossian. Of this, however, we shall inquire presently. In the meantime, the reader must observe that Ossian's Ullin was the County of Antrim, discovered and occupied by the Scots of Arran and Argyle, in the days of his own great-grand-father; by them maintained as they found it an independent principality, with its palace or Temora at Connor, and various frontier strongholds, such as Tura and Selàma, along its southern sea-board on the Bay of Belfast; and secured from invasion westward by the "sable surge" of Lough-Neagh, and the torrents or marshes of the Lower Bann. Alnecma was the province immediately adjoining this, west and south-westward beyond Lough-Neagh, where it might extend indefinitely to the uttermost wilds of Connaught and the shores of the Atlantic; but was neither to be identified with Connaught, nor measured by it, as it has been by MacPherson. This region also, as we have said, had kings and a population of its own. Erin, properly so called (although the name is sometimes extended poetically to the whole Island, as contradistinguished from Lochlin and other foreign countries) was the remaining southern portion of Ireland, occupied along its eastern shore, from Dundalk to Dublin at least, by the Bolgae or Firbolgs from Britain, who penetrated inland; and by the aboriginal or oldest known inhabitants of the Island, southward—for a most interesting account of whom, on what seems to be the only reliable authority now extant, called the Chronicles of Eri, our readers are referred to the Appendix. The people of these two regions, Erin and Alnecma, south and south-west, were in constant league against the Scots of Ullin, with a view most probably of sharing the sovereignty between them; and during the continuance of the war, which seems to have lasted for four or five generations at least, their council chamber was the Cave of Moma, otherwise Muma—to the present writer as yet unknown, but glanced at also, by way of recognition, in the Appendix; their head-quarters Atha, or the region of shallow waters, apparently about Armagh; and the line of their incursions through the intervening regions, by the valleys of the Upper Bann and of the Lagan, between the head of Belfast Lough and Lough-Neagh, into the fertile plain of the Six-mile-water, where almost all the decisive battles of the period were fought. About the time of which we are now inquiring, the chief representative, or petty king of Alnecma was Cairbar, son of Borbar-Duthul; and the chief of Erin, Cathmor his brother—Firbolgs by descent from the coast of Britain, but natives of Ireland and with Irish blood in their veins; who being both slain, the one by Oscar and the other by Fingal, and their Irish forces, called the "Sons of Erin," utterly routed, hostilities for a season were suspended; and the authority of the Scottish kings was confirmed in Ullin, if not even extended beyond the bounds of that province, into Alnecma and Erin themselves.

II. The origin of these internecine wars, according to Ossian, was an act of abduction with consent of the lady, like another Helen of Troy, by Crothar, one of the chiefs of Alnecma; who carried off Conlama, daughter of Cathmin, one of the aboriginal Celtic princes of Ullin. This must have occurred near the village of Dora, already identified with Doagh—p. 110—as the reader will now easily perceive by the following incidental quotation, in which the very syllables of the modern designation are combined and preserved:—

"He pursued the chase in Ullin: on the moss-covered top of Drumardo. From the wood looked the daughter of Cathmin, the blue-rolling eye of Conlama. . . . . The love of Crothar rose. He brought the white-bosomed maid to Atha. Bards raise the song in her presence; and joy dwelt round the daughter of Ullin."—*Temora*, B. II.

But the ridge above Doagh, on the Six-mile-water, is Drum-ad-arragh to the present day; which may either be a mere modern corruption of Drum-ad-dora; or in combination at least with Doagh, pronounced Dogh, will give Drum-ad-ard-dogh—that is, the ridge of the hill above Doagh = Drum-ard-do, contracted Drumardo. From this point to Armagh it would be an easy march, or chase, or flight of about 30 miles, through the pleasantest valleys; and thus, by this much frequented and now celebrated strath, the visit of Crothar from Atha might take place, and the abduction of Conlama from Dora followed: to avenge which insult Turloch, the chief to whom she was betrothed—and whose name, also, is preserved in Turloughstown on an adjacent ridge, to this day—pursued with the design of reclaiming her. Her husband's brother, Cormul, rose to meet him, but was slain. Her husband himself then rose, and rolled back the foe from Alnecma, returning victorious to Atha " midst the joy of Conlama" there. But the war of reprisals was not finished: " Battle on battle comes; blood is poured on blood; the tombs of the valiant rise"—along the valleys of the Bann and the Lagan, still traceable in hundreds of raths and monumental cairns precisely similar to those along the valley of the Six-mile-water, through the whole intervening region between Dundalk and Armagh. The same people fought there, in short, and buried their dead in the same fashion. Finally comes Conar, son of Trenmor and brother of Trathal, from Morven, to espouse the quarrel of his kindred. " He poured his might along Green Erin"—that is, south-westward up the valley of the Bann. " The sons of Bolga fled. . . . Crothar met him in battle, . . . . but Alnecma's warriors also fled. The King of Atha [Crothar] slowly retired, in the grief of his soul. He afterwards shone in the south, [that is, beyond or towards Athlone]; but dim, as the sun of autumn."—*Temora*, B. II. In consequence of this victory, or in preparation for the contest, Conar seems to have been elected king of Ullin by the petty chiefs there, and was invested with the traditional spear of royalty by them; with some pretensions, perhaps, to sovereignty in Alnecma, if he should succeed in his enterprise. But Alnecma was only chastised, not conquered by Conar. Reprisals on their side again succeed, and Cormac MacConar, that is Cormac I., driven to extremity by their incursions in Ullin, appeals for help to Morven. Fingal, then a youth, and but newly seated on the throne, sends Duthcaron, his own old preceptor in the art of war, with Connal, Duthcaron's son, his companion, to assist. In company with them, Cormac himself takes the field westward; but they are totally routed by Colculla, then generalissimo of Alnecma, and Duthcaron himself is slain. Connal, however, escapes, and returns with intelligence of the disaster to Morven. Fingal in person then repairs, on his first expedition, to retrieve the fortunes of his aged relative. He finds Cormac in hidings on the shore, with his daughter Roscrana, in a cave, and Colculla with his people approaching. He demands Roscrana in marriage; he totally defeats Colculla, re-establishes Cormac on the throne, and returns with Roscrana to Morven, and she becomes the mother of Ossian.

This Cormac was succeeded by his own son Cairbar, in whose reign, or in that of Artho his son, comparative tranquillity must have prevailed; for Ossian, then grown up, made an expedition through the district to Branno—that is, to the very frontiers of Alnecma in the valley of the Upper Bann—to claim the hand of Evirallin for himself; which he won in a duel of eight to eight against a rival, called also Cormac, whom he smote and slew by cutting off his head. This victory secured him a bride, whose own gentleness was in beautiful contrast to the savagery around her; and who, although devoted to Ossian, seems to have reflected on the whole scene with pain and sorrow. Such a contest, indeed, enjoined by her own father, even in the brief interval of peace, bespeaks the ferocity of the age; yet was not a whit more savage than the free and gentle passage of arms at Ashby, when Ivanhoe fought for Rowena; or the horrid lists on the North Inch at Perth, where Harry of the Wynd, according to romance, contended for the Glover's daughter—the only essential difference being that Ossian was a heathen, a poet, and a hero, as well as a more successful champion driven by necessity to mortal combat in the lists of love.

Time rolls on, and Evirallin dies; but Oscar her son has been born, and has already been distinguished in the field; Cormac the younger has ascended the throne in boyhood, and Cuthullin of Skye has been appointed regent during his minority—when an invasion of Danes or Norwegians, under Swaran, occurs. Fingal, again appealed to for help, arrives, attended and assisted by all his sons, including Ossian, and by Oscar, his grandson. Swaran is defeated on Lena, and the crisis of invasion is turned; in celebration of which success, young Cormac, in the fulness of his heart, bestows the "spear of Temora," as a gift, on Oscar. But a new attempt by the southern Irish under Cairbar, the Firbolg, now king of Atha, to seize the throne of Ullin and to subjugate that province, is made. His friend, or lieutenant, Torlath, marches northward, as we have seen, by the eastern shore of Lough-Neagh towards Temora at Connor; but is encountered, defeated, and slain by Cuthullin the regent there, who himself falls afterwards in battle. Cairbar, as we have also seen, outmarches his lieutenant, reaches Temora, murders young Cormac, and completes the usurpation; at which crisis, Fingal and his sons again appear. Oscar dies, but Cairbar and his brother Cathmor, the royal representatives of Erin and Alnecma, perish; and the dynasty of Conar in Ullin is reinstated in the person of Ferad-Artho, half-uncle to young Cormac II., and grandson to Cormac I. Fingal then retires, but Ossian remains for a season to re-establish his relative on the throne—which finishes the connection of the Scots with Ireland, so far as the history of their expeditions has been preserved by Ossian, and so far as Fingal's own life is concerned; who in returning to Morven by Cantyre, as we have shown, was surprised and murdered on the shores of Arran. But in all this epitome, it is obvious that that connection never extended beyond Armagh, or some indefinite line from east to west in that neighbourhood—certainly never beyond Ulster; nor does Ossian seem to know much, if anything, of Ireland farther south than this, but by the reports of the people, or by the traditions of the bards who met him in friendly rivalry, or at the "feast of shells," in the intervals of battle. The scene of Scotch occupation and of Scottish supremacy in Ireland, therefore, from the days of Conar and many generations before that, to the days of Ferad-Artho inclusive, was confined entirely to the County Antrim; and it is astonishing that MacPherson, by any effort of imagination, even in partial ignorance of the facts, should have extended it farther. To believe, as he seems sincerely to have done, that a handful of Scotchmen from the Hebrides should have risen to supreme power, and conquered the allegiance of all Ireland in a single generation, or even in a century, was so extravagant a faith, that it is almost incomprehensible how it could ever be entertained by him. It is true, indeed, that when Conar came his renown was before him:—"His battles were on every coast; a thousand streams rolled down the blood of his foes; his fame filled Green Erin, like a pleasant gale." But his election was to the throne of his own people only, the Scots in Ullin. "The nations gathered in Ullin, and they blessed the king"— not the king of Ireland, but "the king of the race of their fathers, from the Land of Selma." To oppose his election even there, "the chiefs of the South were gathered in their pride. In the horrid cave of Moma, they mixed their secret words." .... "'Why should Conar reign,' they said," as a new intruder to chastise us—"'the son of resounding Morven?'" They resolved accordingly to invade Ullin, as we have now seen. "They came forth like the streams of the desert, with the roar of their hundred tribes. Conar was a rock before them; broken they rolled, on every side. But often they returned, and the sons of Selma fell. The king stood among the tombs of his warriors; he darkly bent his mournful face. . . . When Trathal came, in his strength, his brother from cloudy Morven." . . . Then, "he lightened forward in battle, till Bolga yielded at her streams."—*Temora*, B. II. It is some apology, of course, that the word Erin should have been employed by Ossian in the passage above quoted; but besides that it does not necessarily include more than the north of Leinster, if so much, where the term occurs, the use of it implies only fame and not sovereignty for Conar there; and all that follows indicates distinctly that his sovereignty even in Ullin was disputed as dangerous, and usurpation, if possible, determined on where he was legitimate king.

III. It is farther true, that the throne to which Conar was thus called, is represented by Ossian as of the highest antiquity, and the "spear of Temora," symbolic of royalty, as the heirloom of an hundred kings; but this antiquity was exclusively among the Scots, as a separate nationality in the North of Ireland; besides which, MacPherson himself interprets this very boast as mere poetic hyperbole, and thus unconsciously cuts away the foundation of his own faith. How innocent, therefore, he must have been of all forgery or imposture in the matter, is obvious. The loudest insulters of his honesty, indeed—Johnson himself, philologist and critic; Laing, with all his learning; and Macaulay, statesman and historian—were not more ignorant of the now indubitable facts of the case, than he was. But as regards the supposed origin of the Scottish people from the soil or population of Ireland, his words first printed in 1763, in the clearness of his own personal conviction, may yet be quoted with the triumph of ascertained truth—" The favourite chimera, that Ireland is the mother country of the Scots is totally subverted and ruined. The fictions concerning the antiquities of that country, which were forming for ages, and growing as they came down, on the hands of successive *seanachies* and *fileas*, are found at last to be the spurious brood of modern and ignorant ages."—*Dissertation.*

To understand more fully, however, all the relations of the time, and to trace the history of the period and the people, on Lord Macaulay's own principles of living memory in the representatives of successive generations, as far back as the testimony of men in Ossian's own day and with whom he was conversant will carry us, we must separate the traditions or recitals of his contemporaries from the record of facts known to himself, and authenticated by him as eyewitness of their reality. Lord Macaulay, who so unscrupulously assailed MacPherson when beyond the hearing of reproach, and ridiculed with easy scorn poetry too sublime, perhaps, for his own sympathy, does not himself now live, any more than MacPherson's other numerous detractors, to impugn this; but any advocate of his lordship's faith, who feels disposed, may reply to it at leisure. The present writer is too distinctly assured of the correctness of his own conclusions to be much concerned in the matter, and shall be prepared, henceforth, either rightly to interpret silence or patiently to investigate doubts. Sneers and contempt, from intelligent readers, will by and by be impossible, he hopes.

1. With respect to the throne of Ullin, universally reputed ancient; and the spear symbolic of its sovereignty, delivered first to Conar and finally bequeathed to Oscar; challenged again in Oscar's hand by Cairbar the usurper, who desired to obtain it as the type of warlike supremacy, and declared explicitly to have been " the pride of an hundred kings" and " the death of heroes of old "—it is by no means certain that " *Hundred* here," as MacPherson suggests, "is an indefinite number, and only intended to express a great many;" or that the phrase thus employed was hyperbolical. Conar, it is clear, succeeded to a throne already long established, not of all Ireland indeed, but of a petty kingdom in the north of it; and the spear which he then assumed and handed down to his posterity was an object of veneration to the people, and of kingly pride to its possessors, which no representative of royalty but a child would ever have parted with to another. Through how many hands it may actually have passed before it

was bestowed on Oscar, cannot, of course, with certainty be now determined; but one hundred being specified by living witnesses, who must have received information from other living witnesses in turn through an indefinite period to justify that statement, and the deaths among royal inheritors being not only violent but frequent, it is quite possible that so many as a hundred may actually have wielded it, without implying an improbable antiquity. During Fingal's own lifetime, much less than a century, no fewer than eight transfers may be specified, with a possible ninth or tenth, which would give ten on an average to the century; and if that ratio be taken as reasonable, the entire list of possessors would carry the spear or its substitute back for a thousand years; which, from the date in question at Ossian's day, would fix the origin of this independent monarchy about 714 B.C.—that is, about 126 years before the destruction of Jerusalem by Nebuchadrezzar. But there is a tradition at least among Irish chroniclers,* that a certain ship's crew of Israelitish emigrants of the tribe of Dan, fleeing from their native country in Tiglath Pileser's time, settled in this very region shortly before that date; and that subsequently, when Jerusalem had been destroyed and the desolation of their country was complete, another small colony of fugitives from Judea, bringing many reliques of value from the ruined Temple with them, were stranded in their ship near Carrick-Fergus rock about 570 B.C. On their arrival, these second emigrants found the neighbouring region already occupied by an independent tribe, including their brethren of Dan, with a sovereign of their own, who was solemnly ordained to power on a Druidical stone set apart for the purpose, and with Druidical ceremonies; but whom they persuaded to accept the *Lia-Fail* or Stone of Destiny, supposed to be Jacob's pillow, which they brought with them in their ship, as substitute for the Druidical foundation of sovereignty. This stone, it is farther maintained, on the same authority,† was carried to Scotland by Fergus I. when he emigrated from Ulster thither; and has ever since been a royal coronation seat, first at Scone and now at Westminster, for the sovereigns of Scotland and of Great Britain. All this tradition, it must be observed, is entirely independent of Ossian; but however the truth of it may be, it is certain that Cairbar of Atha, after his usurpation, and when threatened with vengeance by Oscar, took refuge "behind his stone" near Temora, as if there a sort of sanctuary which he carried with him to maintain his power, on the same principle on which Edward I. removed the Stone of Scone from Scotland, to remove power. Nothing is said in the tradition, so far as we are aware, con-

---

\* Compare *Cambrensis Eversus*, Professor Kelly's Edition, Maynooth, Vol. I., as quoted by J. B. Barnett, in *Jewish Chronicle*, September 13, 1872.

† Barnett in *Jewish Chronicle*, August 2 and 23, and September 13, 1872; see also Note in Appendix —In connection with Chronicles of Erl.

cerning any sacred spear; but a people who had a royal stone of Druidical consecration for their kings at the date supposed, might as well have had some warlike sceptre in the shape of a spear as a symbol of independent power, quite as early; and as Cairbar already possessed the one, it was most natural he should desire to possess the other, that his title to sovereignty might be complete in the eyes of the people. The spear in question came ultimately into Ossian's hands—"I took the spear of Temora," he says—B. VI.; along with the spear of Trenmor immediately afterwards—"Father of heroes, Trenmor, dweller of eddying winds! I give thy spear to Ossian; let thine eye rejoice:"—Fingal, in B. VIII. He was thus personally invested with the symbols of royal power over both the branches of his race; and the terms of veneration in which these reliques are referred to by him seem to indicate that he regarded them, together with his harp, as the most sacred possessions in the world.

2. Who the people themselves were, and of what origin, who then inhabited the north-east corner of Ireland, is not difficult to decide—if the Chronicles of Eri, to which we have already referred, and of which the reader will find a summary in the Appendix, are to be depended on. It is worth observing, however, although only in passing, that the first Israelitish settlers on the coast were called the *Tuatha de Dannan*, or tribe of Dan-ish men; and that two of Ossian's heroes resident on the very spot, after a lapse of presumably seven hundred years, are called Tuathal and Damman respectively—designations which may have been derived by inheritance from these strangers, although the words have also a descriptive meaning. But that the occupants of the soil among whom these Dannan settled, and by whom they were ultimately absorbed, were of Celtic origin is clear, for they spoke the language of Ossian; that they were themselves also emigrants from Scotland, and looked with faith and veneration to the Celts of Scotland both as friends and allies, and as kindred of the parent stock, is equally clear, for they appealed to them directly on every occasion of danger, for help in war alike against Norwegians and Irish, and for kingly administration of their domestic affairs in difficulties and disorders—and when Conar appeared, "they blessed the king, the king of the race of their fathers, from the land of Selma." Their very reverence for the symbolic spear was a point of significant resemblance between them. Trenmor's spear was an heirloom of royalty and power in Fingal's hands, and by him transferred with the solemnest ceremonies and injunctions to Ossian already in possession of the spear of Temora, as that spear had been transferred from hand to hand by a hundred heroes. Scotland, in short, was to them their fatherland, and the race of Trenmor their natural and perpetual allies. Their music, their poetry, their arts, such as they were; their traditions and their religion were the same; their blood was intermixed by mar-

riage, and their history identified by the same exploits; and when longer possession of the soil in Ireland became impossible for them, or the *amor patriæ* induced them to return, they returned in a body under Fergus and Lorne to the land from which their forefathers had emigrated, bringing their traditions and their poetry, and perhaps their coronation stone, with them—leaving nothing but their name to the region, which was called the Land of the Scots for long centuries after their departure, and the specific names they had attached to the soil still recognisable in the text of Ossian, as witnesses of their former occupation; or a few degenerate souls, perhaps, in the rear of their exodus, to become serfs and freebooters among the marshes of Lough-Neagh—a theory of occupation during more than a thousand years, of emigration and of re-emigration, which is actually borne out by the oldest geographical surveys, and still older traditions of the country: for the district thus identified with Ullin retained the name of Scotland in Blaeu's time—1663, and had been occupied, according to ancient Irish authors, by the Caledonians or Scots from time immemorial; and thence Fergus, the youngest representative of Trenmor's line, made his expedition, according to some in the end of the fifth, according to others in the beginning of the sixth, century, to reconquer a portion of his father's fatherland. That same district of Ullin, however, since his departure, has been all re-peopled again, partly by Irish, partly by English, but chiefly by another immigration of Scotsmen, who have identified themselves once more with the very soil their Celtic progenitors so long ago occupied; but in whose memories, recent and almost foreign, all tradition of former occupation has been obliterated, and not even the scene of their forefathers' triumphs and royal administration, although proved by the very names every day in their mouths, is suspected by them. Fingal in Ireland is now fainter than a dream to them; the voice of Ossian is weaker than an echo; and the bleachfields of the Six-mile-water have washed out alike the blood of Cormac and Cairbar, of Oscar, of Cathmor, and Cuthullin.

IV. But the extent and application of such names as Erin and Inisfail to the same or different subjects, of Alnecma and even of Temora, so frequently introduced in these poems, remain yet to be considered. Can we then limit and define these, or even correctly translate them? it may be asked; and in reply to this question, which is certainly of importance not only as regards the authenticity of Ossian, but as regards the geography of Ireland itself, hitherto so much misunderstood, satisfactory explanations are indispensable.

1. Of Erin and Alnecma we have already practically disposed; and now with respect to Inisfail, which MacPherson confounds with Erin—that is, according to his own theory, with all Ireland—it may be confidently affirmed that, in Ossian's mouth, it had no such signification. The reader who has leisure to collate the

poem of *Fingal*, or even the first Book of it, in which Inisfail is most distinctly referred to, will discover without much difficulty that it was identical (1.) certainly, with Ullin or Ulster; and (2.) probably, by limitation, with Isle Maghee. Two passages alone, of others we might as easily quote, if space permitted, will enable us to determine this. "'Hail,' said Cuthullin, 'sons of the narrow vales! Hail, ye hunters of the deer! Another sport is drawing near: it is like the dark rolling of that wave on the coast. Shall we fight, ye sons of war; or yield green Inisfail to Lochlin?'"—*Fingal*, B. I. But Cuthullin was only regent of Ulster, and could with difficulty, if at all, maintain his ground there; not only against foreign invaders in front, but against the sons of Erin themselves in rear. The narrow vales, therefore, of which he speaks, were those only over which he had authority—those of the Braid and Glenwherry waters to the north, and of the smaller glens adjacent; or even those on the slopes of Cromla, including Isle Maghee itself—whose warriors had assembled at his own summons from Tura, as we have seen, to resist the invasion of Swaran on their coast. He could yield no more than he possessed, and that was barely the Province of Ullin. But, on the other hand, if he yielded Isle Maghee, which was the point of Swaran's present attack, and to which Swaran was still confined—then Ullin itself might be lost, beyond the hope of re-conquest.

Nor was this the only occasion on which Norse invaders had disembarked on the same spot. "'In other days,' Carril replies, 'came the Sons of Ocean to Erin. A thousand vessels bounded over the waves to Ullin's lovely plains. The sons of Inisfail arose to meet the race of dark brown shields,'" &c.—*Ibid*. Here the number and subordination of terms in regular order, with a certain and appropriate limitation of their sense, seems to make everything distinct and unmistakeable. (1.) Erin for the whole of Ireland, as opposed to Lochlin or Norway, from which the invaders came; (2.) Ullin, or Ulster, that province of Ireland on the shores of which they disembarked; and (3.) Inisfail, some island on the coast of Ullin where their landing was effected, and where the people first rose to repel them. With such local applications as these to guide us, so natural and explicit, we can have very little doubt about the region intended, or even about the subdivisions of it thus specified. Inisfail—so called, for what reason we shall immediately inquire—in its most limited signification, was properly Isle Maghee, once a populous offshoot of Ulster; Inisfail, in its more extended sense, was equivalent to Ullin—itself a peninsula to this hour, and in Ossian's day all but an island, cut off from Erin by Belfast Lough, Lough-Neagh, and the Lower Bann; and Erin, wherever it occurs in this Book of *Fingal*, and sometimes possibly elsewhere, is but a generic term—not so much for the rest of Ireland, or for all Ireland, in contradistinction to Ullin; as for any part of Ireland, with its green vales, in contradistinction to Lochlin, or the Kingdom of Snow. There may be exceptional cases, in which Inisfail itself seems to be used in the same sense, as if applied to all Ireland; but in such cases the speakers will be found to be strangers, and not persons acquainted with the region, or to whom the proper distinction of its names was known.

To these conclusions it may, of course, be objected that the derivation of the word itself, as given by MacPherson, and quoted already (p. 101) at the commencement of our present inquiry—" *Inis-Fail*, the Island of the Fa-il or Falans," the name of a colony which first settled in Ireland—is proof sufficient that it was originally applied to the whole Island; but it may be more easily replied (1.) that no such colony can be traced to Ireland, and no such name was ever elsewhere applied to it, in Ossian's day. Its original inhabitants were called *Cloden* in reproach, or the lowest sons of the soil, by its first foreign invaders the *Dannan*, who dispossessed and enslaved them. The Sons of *Er*, in turn, superseded these Dannan, and gave their own name of Er-i, or Er-in to the Island—as the reader will find explained in our Appendix. Subsequently, a colony of Bolgae settled on its eastern shore from the opposite coast of Britain, when and where, we shall forthwith determine; and finally, the Hebridean Scots of Trenmor's day took possession of Ulster: among all which no name corresponding in the least to Fail or Falan is discoverable. (2.) That a more probable derivation of the word Inisfail is from *Inis* and *Fail*, or the Island of Destiny; so called from *Lia-Fail*, the Stone of Destiny, on which the kings of Ulster, from a given date, were invariably crowned, and which seems to have been preserved, as we have seen, at their own palace of Temora. In which case, Inisfail itself, as a designation, would include all Ullin, where that stone was kept; and by limitation might be applied to Isle Maghee, where the " rocking stone" of the cromlech was so conspicuous, as a monument and symbol alike of Druidical power. It is a curious corroboration of this view, that the translator of the Chronicles of Eri gives the same derivation of the word incidentally in his preface, although he does not refer to the stone; but he extends the term, as MacPherson does, to the whole Island—in which we cannot agree with him, so far as Ossian is concerned.

2. With respect to Temora, as employed by Ossian, we have already ascertained beyond reasonable controversy that it was the conventional name of some house or palace occupied by the kings of Ullin, a little east from Lough-Neagh on the Glenwherry-water; and most probably identical with Connor, or with the remains of a royal residence there, still traceable on the surface. MacPherson, on the other hand, translates and explains it as " Ti'-mór-ri', *the house of the great king*—the name of the royal palace of the supreme kings of Ireland;" and seems thus to identify it either with Teacmor, or with Tara, on the plains of Meath:

x

notwithstanding which definition, however, he seems at a loss where to locate it finally; for in the advertisement to *Temora* he says " that poem had its name from Temora, the royal palace of the first Irish kings of the Caledonian race, in the Province of Ulster." Without attempting to account for this contradiction, it must be sufficient for us, in present circumstances, to correct the obvious error involved in it; and so far as MacPherson's identification of the term with Teacmor is concerned, it may be enough (1.) to quote the words of his own translation at the end of the poem referred to—" With morning lead Ferad-Artho forth to the echoing halls of Temora:" that is, according to his own theory, " with morning lead him through the whole range of the enemy's country, to the echoing halls of a palace nearly one hundred miles distant." But (2.) in so translating *Ti'-mór-ri'*, MacPherson makes an etymological error. That combination of syllables is really equivalent to Tigh-mor righ, not to Tigh mor-righ; and means the great house or palace of the king, not the palace or house of the great king; so, at least, it might be translated with equal if not with greater propriety than otherwise.* (3.) He mistakes also the title of the supreme kings of Ireland, which was *Ard-righ*, or Ardri, the High king; never *Mor-righ*—which would be questionable Gaelig besides, for *Righ-mor*—or the Great king. (4.) In point of fact, the precise name of the palace in Meath was only *Tigh-mor*, or Teacmor, the great house, or royal official residence where the Ardris in succession, during their occupancy of the throne, dwelt, or were expected to dwell. *Righ* was never added to it, for *righ* was a subordinate title, confined to the kings or princes of the provinces; and to have called it Tigh-mor-righ would thus have been a derogation from its rank, as palace of all Ireland. To call it Tigh-mor-Ardri, indeed, might have been admissible, as a mere form of speech, but it would have been also a redundancy. Besides, it is not what Ossian says, and was possibly never heard of in the language. Tigh-mor-righ, or Temora, on the other hand, if properly translated, was not only legitimate but correct, as a designation for the palace of a petty sovereign, such as Conar and the Cormacs were in Ullin. There might be, and there were, Temoras in Ulster and Leinster, in Connaught and Munster, for their own respective kings—one of them, at least, as we shall hereafter see, rivalling in splendour the imperial palace in Meath; but there was only one Teacmor in Ireland, the residence of its sovereigns. (5.) *Tobrad*, corrupted to Tara—so strangely confounded, both by Clerk and MacPherson, with Temora—was not a palace, properly so called. It was the

---

* Clerk confirms the translation now suggested, but adds " it is generally written *Teamhair*, ' pleasant;' or *Teamhra, Teamhair-rath*, ' pleasant circle,' ' fortification' or ' dwelling,' modernised into the well-known Tara, the palace of the King of Ireland." In a certain Edition, Berwick, 1795, *Ti'-mor-rath*, or the House of Good Fortune, is suggested by the Editor as a more probable derivation.

## THE SCOTS IN IRELAND.

high place or hill of Election, where the supreme kings were regularly chosen, and where justice was publicly administered, after solemn proclamation, by them. It was situated in Meath also, not far from the town now called Trim; and the Tigh-mor or Teacmor, where the Ardris resided whilst they reigned, was in close proximity. But Tobrad, or Tara, does not occur in Ossian as a proper name, and the place itself seems not only never to have been seen by him, but to have been utterly unknown to him—the most conclusive proof imaginable that he was never much farther south than the line of Armagh; and the only house at all comparable to Teacmor, he could see there, would be the rival palace in that northern capital of the Island—most probably identical with Atha, but never specified by him in any other way than as the residence of an enemy and a usurper, who was constantly invading Ullin. By consulting Appendix, under the head of Armagh in the Chronicles of Eri, the reader will obtain more light on this interesting subject than can conveniently be communicated at the present stage of our inquiries; to which, therefore, we refer, and conclude by remarking (6.) and finally, that there was no hereditary spear either in Teacmor or at Tara in Meath, whatever there might be at Temora in Ullin. On the contrary, the sole indications of supreme authority there were the Asion or crown, and the royal mantle—of which Ossian, however, takes no notice, never having seen them; and so far from any spear being held as a symbol of sovereignty at Tara, all arms whatever were forbidden on that neutral consecrated ground; and more than one instance is on record, in which proceedings were absolutely suspended until arms, inadvertently or surreptitiously introduced, were carried out and deposited elsewhere.

We have only farther to add, in conclusion of our present summary, that all these matters seem to have been unknown to MacPherson; who, by the mistranslation of a single word in his simplicity, has not only misled himself and his readers, but has misrepresented the details of two important historical epics, and confounded every element of Irish history, already sufficiently confused in all that related to its connection with Scotland. Nor is it less surprising that the very author from whom such particulars have now been obtained, and who laughs at the ignorance of MacPherson, should never himself have condescended to look at Ossian. He fancies only that MacPherson made Temora out of Teacmor to please the English ear, but inquires no farther into such an obvious error; and thus between two translators—one of Ossian, and the other of the Chronicles of Eri; one Scotch, and the other Irish; one misinformed, and the other indifferent—the credit, the sense, the accuracy, and the very authenticity have been jeopardised, of one of the sublimest poets and most truthful historians that ever lived or spoke.

## NOTES FROM O'DONOVAN.

### 1. TUATHAL TEACHTMHAR—GELCHOSSA'S FATHER.

Long after the foregoing pages had been written, and even after they were in type, an incidental confirmation of their truth, so singularly conclusive, occurred, that the particulars of it seem to demand special record here. The Tuathal referred to in the preceding chapter, in so far as we can judge from the text of Ossian alone, might have been some influential chief, possibly even a king, in Ullin; whose residence there was at Selma or Selàma, on the Cromla range, and therefore, according to our geography, somewhere to the west or north-west of Carrick-l'ergus. He was father of the Gelchossa already mentioned, and his name occurs, with some encomiums, in the episode of her death.—*Fingal*, B. V. Compare Note in reply to Laing, p. 134. We elsewhere learn (MacPherson's *Fragments*, 1760) that his surname was Teachtmhar, pronounced Teachvar; and that his entire designation, of Tuathal Teachtmhar, means the surly but fortunate man. This descriptive addition of Teachtmhar, however, might be otherwise translated, and according to O'Donovan means the Legitimate. At the date of his daughter's death, he does not seem to have been alive, although we have no account in Ossian either where or how he died, or whether any male representative survived him. According to Irish tradition, on the other hand, he was both a prince in Leinster and the sovereign of Ireland, whose chief residence was at Treamhainn, near Mullingar, in Westmeath. By one authority he is said to have been succeeded on the throne by Feidhlimidh Reachtmhar, his son; by another it is alleged that there was no such succession at all, but that the man by whom he was slain—Mal, of Ulster—was elected King of Ireland in his room. The native authorities are thus obviously at such variance on the subject, as to be practically unreliable. In Ossian, neither one tradition nor the other is mentioned; but Gelchossa the daughter, alone, is represented as residing, apparently with some retinue, at Selma—which may have been her father's palace in Ullin, although he had another in Leinster. That he maintained royal rank of some sort and somewhere, need not, however, be controverted; for in Fingal's day, the same Selma where he once resided was occupied by Colla, whose line also dies out in a daughter, and who is expressly styled "the King of Selàma." Reckoning back, therefore, from the era of Fingal's expedition against Swaran, in terms of the episode of Gelchossa's death, her father's death must have occurred most probably in the same neighbourhood, and at least four generations from the date of recital—including Ryno, a youth, at whose interment the recital takes place; Ossian, himself beyond sixty years of age, who listens; Fingal, their father, not less than eighty-five, by whom the recital is invited; and Gelchossa, whose death is the subject of recital by old Ullin—beyond whom, dead or alive, was Tuathal her father. On the usual average calculation, therefore, of 30 years to a generation, we have thus 120 years to be deducted from the date of *Fingal*, *circa* 280 A.D.; which will leave 160 A.D., as the date of Tuathal's death. These matters being premised, as approximately certain from the text of Ossian, we have now to quote from O'Donovan's *Annals* the following record by the "Four Masters," with some notes of his own on the subject, under the head of Tuathal:

"The Age of Christ, 106. Tuathal Teachtmhar,*y* after having been thirty years in the sovereignty of Ireland, was slain by Mal, son of Rochraidhe, King of Ulster, in Magh-Line, at Moin-an-chatha, in Dal-Araidhe, where the two rivers, Ollar and Ollarbha,*z* spring. Ceann-gubha is the name of the hill on which he was killed, as this quatrain proves:—

> Ollar and Ollarbha,
> Ceann-gubha,*a* lordly, noble,
> Are not names given without a cause,
> The day that Tuathal was killed. —*Annals*, I., p. 99.

[NOTES.]

*y Tuathal Teachtmhar:* i.e. Tuathal the Legitimate. Flann synchronizes this monarch with the Roman Emperor, Adrian; and Tighernach, who gives him a reign of thirty years, says that he was slain in the last year of Antoninus Pius by Mal. Now Adrian reigned from the death of Trajan A.D. 117, to A.D. 138, when he was succeeded by Antoninus Pius, who reigned till 161. Therefore Tuathal's death occurred in 160, which shows that the chronology of the Four Masters is antedated by many years.

*z The two rivers, Ollar and Ollarbha*—The names of these two rivers are now obsolete, but there can be no doubt as to their modern names. The Ollar is the Six-mile-water, and the Ollarbha is the Larne-water. The Larne river rises by two heads in the parish of Ballynure; the Six-mile-water, in the parish of Ballycor, a little south-west of Shane's Hill: after a course of about 100 perches, it becomes the boundary between the parish of Kilwaughter, as well as between the baronies of Upper Glenarm and Upper Antrim. Following the direction of a ravine, which runs down the face of the hill, it arrives at the townland of Headwood, in Kilwaughter parish, near the place where the three baronies of Upper Glenarm and Upper Antrim and Lower Belfast [meet]. In this townland there is a spot where a branch of the Six-mile-water can be turned into the Larne river; and here is a large bog, probably the *Moin-an-catha*, or Battle-bog, mentioned in the text, lying between the two rivers. On the face of Ballyboley Hill, about a quarter of a mile to the west, is a place called *Carndoo;* and here, under the brow of the hill, is a pile consisting of several huge stones, ranged in an irregular circle; the space within being chiefly occupied by six upright stones, disposed in pairs, and supporting two blocks above five feet long, and from two to three feet square, laid horizontally upon them. . . . *a Cran-gubha:* i.e. Head, or Hill of grief. This is doubtlessly Ballyboley Hill, and Tuathal's monument is the pile at Carndoo above described.—O'Donovan's *Annals*, Edit. 1856, Vol. I., pp. 100, 101

What is most remarkable here, in the first place, is the absolute agreement of our own previous calculations from the text of Ossian, as to date, with the corrected chronology of the "Four Masters" by O'Donovan, founded on the concurrent testimony of other chroniclers. Had Tuathal's death, for example, been ascertained, according to the "Four Masters," at 106 A.D., then on our supposition that only four generations had intervened between that and the death of Ryno, Gelchossa must have been fifty-five or sixty years of age when she died, which is absurd. It may be urged, of course, that five generations intervened, which would reduce her age to twenty-five or thirty; but of this there is no proof, and it is still improbable: much more improbable would it be, to imagine six generations. It is not, however, between O'Donovan and the "Four Masters" we have to decide. Whichever of these authorities be adopted as the true one, our own calculation, as with four generations in the one case or with six in the other, would correspond. Nor is this all. Adhering to the interval of four generations or thereby, which we believe to be the correct one, then by a similar process of calculation, substituting Trenmor's race for Tuathal's, and still reckoning from the epoch of Fingal, we have young Cormac II., who was murdered, and Artho his father; Cairbar, father of Artho as well as of Ferad-Artho; and Cormac I., the father of Cairbar—four generations; the remotest of which, by its unprecedented duration, more than compensates for the shortness of the last. Beyond these, but immediately preceding, was Conar, the first Scottish king in Ullin; who must, therefore, have been contemporaneous with Tuathal, and was most probably his successor in the precarious sovereignty of that province; but took Temora for his residence there—hence called Connor—and left Gelchossa in possession of her father's residence at Selma. It was by a son of Cairbar's, in fact—apparently the same above named, as the grandson of Conar—whose own palace was in the plain between Selma and Temora, that her lover Lamderg in a duel was slain; and thus every point in the chronology of the period, as deducible from the text of Ossian, synchronizes with data rightly ascertained in the best independent historical authorities extant.

For the rest, the reader has now only to substitute the name of Lubhar for Ollar—which seems, indeed, but an easy corruption of it—to be convinced that the Notes on which we are now commenting are unconscious supplements to the text of Ossian. The scene of Gelchossa's death within a few hundred paces of her father's tomb, and her interment there with Lamderg and Ullin her rival lovers, exactly where we have already ascertained it, on the northern slope of the Cromla and *not* at Londonderry, is now indisputable as a matter of fact; the campaigns of Fingal and the death of Ryno are localised beyond doubt; the Battle-bog, or heath of Lena, on the Six-mile-water—where Orla, and Foldath, and Cathmor fell—is also measured and defined as by the links of a surveyor's chain; and the whole surrounding scenery, in hill and dale and river, grouped, as we have seen it grouped in the pages of *Fingal* and *Temora*. No consilience of induction, to use the favourite modern logical phrase, could be more perfect; no argument more conclusive or unimpeachable. We do not, indeed, thank Dr. O'Donovan for this; but we must be allowed to congratulate ourselves. That a man like O'Donovan should have been professor of Celtic in Belfast College for years, with all the antiquarian and literary lore of the nation at his command; should have paced the valley of the Six-mile-water with the minuteness and precision of a surveyor, and, with the very words of Ossian in his mouth, should have failed to trace the battlefields of Moi-Lena and the Lubhar—is a mystery in literary oversight more wonderful than the cunningest forgery. O'Donovan, in fact, with all his erudition, knew nothing of the contents of Ossian. He set Ossian aside without reading him apparently, as a worthless fiction, on the sole authority of Pinkerton and the jaunty allegation of Moore. So much the more discreditable to O'Donovan's unquestioned scholarship. Yet he saw with his own eyes and heard with his own ears, unconsciously, from other sources, what Ossian with ten times more accuracy and pictorial effect narrates and describes in his suspected epics. And thus it happens, that the most accomplished Irish scholar that ever lived becomes an involuntary witness to the literal truth of a disputed text, much older than the written annals of his own nation; by which the very dates in its remotest chronology, as we see, may be rectified, and the most romantic incidents in its history localised and detailed.

How, then, it may be objected, does it happen that no reliable trace of such facts as those narrated in Ossian is to be met with in these Irish chronicles? and that only incidental proof of them can be obtained from such chronicles? For the most obvious reason, already stated or implied—that the Scots in Ireland, as Ossian represents them, were but a colony of foreigners; occupants and lords of a corner, and never sovereigns of the Island. The Irish from the first disputed their settlement, even in Ullin; and, after their expulsion, transferred the achievements of their kings and heroes to the credit of their own monarchs—that no record, if possible, should ever be found of such unwelcome intruders on the soil. Fingal they transformed into Cormac's lieutenant of militia, and located him in a palace near Dublin, or sent him on embassies to Rome, in their own imaginations; they slew Oscar at Gabhra, with a poisoned spear; and converted Ossian himself into a monstrous incoherent liar, to complete the delusion. What Ossian really narrates, they never accurately heard—O'Donovan himself will not hear it; what MacPherson translates, they will never heartily believe, although it really enhances their own history—O'Donovan superciliously scouts it. Even MacPherson's own countrymen, to increase the wrong and aggravate the folly, have stigmatised him as an impostor, because they understood not his text. Alas for our guides in history! If proofs like these from adversaries themselves, and such arguments as we are now adducing from their own scrutiny of the ground; almost literally with "tongues in trees, books in the running brooks, sermons in stones," or at least in monuments, "and good," that is, truth "in everything," have not some slight convincing power, the case for them may well be abandoned as hopeless. One thing, however, is now certain, and must be repeated—that the Scots in Ireland were a separate people, and the Celts or Caledonians of Argyllshire and the Hebrides, in Ullin, were a distinct and independent nationality.

## II. THE FALL OF FOLDATH.

In Chapter I. of the present Part, near the end, p. 107, and in Chapter II. of the same Part, p. 120, the reader will find consecutive allusions to the death and burial of a conspicuous, but by no means attractive personage called Foldath, one of the "sons of Erin," and a usurping conspirator from Moma, in the campaign of Temora; who desires to be buried in the midst of the dead he had slaughtered, that he might "forsake the blast to rejoice above their graves, when he beheld them spread around with their long whistling grass."—*Temora*, B. V. By a note on the passage we are informed that Foldath was induced to join the war in hope of distinction, and by a false augury as to his own death. He was to fall by the "*Clon-cath* or reflected beam of Moruth," which meant the sword of Fillan, youngest, and a favourite surviving son of Fingal; but was misunderstood by Foldath to mean some harmless or impossible agency. What is chiefly of importance however, is that he did so fall, to westward of Lena on the Six-mile-water, by the hand of Fillan, in the campaign of Temora; which must have been fought, as we conclude, not earlier than 285 A.D.—possibly in the autumn of that very year. In connection with facts thus ascertained, we quote again, as follows, from the "Four Masters:"—

"Age of Christ, 285. Fothadh was one year over Ireland. Fothadh Cairp-theach was slain by Fothadh Airgtheach. Fothadh Airgtheach was afterwards slain in the battle of Ollarbha[d] in Magh-Line, by Caeilte."[e]—*Annals*, I., p. 121.

[d] "Tighernach does not mention either of these Fothadhs as monarchs of Ireland, evidently because he regarded them as usurpers. . . . . . [e] Caeilte MacRonan, the foster-son, and favourite of the celebrated Irish General, Finn MacCumhail."—O'Donovan's Notes to above.—*Ibid.*

The reader, we presume, need hardly be informed that the Fothadh here mentioned by the "Four Masters" is identical with the Foldath of Ossian; and that, for the reasons assigned, his name has been disguised by some, and entirely omitted by other chroniclers of his own nation. It might be mispronounced also in Ossian's hearing, to whom he was otherwise a stranger, and who knew only that he was a dangerous and bloody conspirator from Moma, in the war against the Scotch of Ullin. It is more important to observe (1.) that his character is represented by the Irish themselves precisely as Ossian represents it—in point of fact, he seems to have been not only a conspirator and a usurper, but a fratricide; and that his death occurred at the very time and place, and by the hand of a son, or foster-son as was supposed, of Fingal's, as already ascertained from the text of Ossian—that is, on the heath of Lena, somewhere between the Larne and Six-mile-water, 285 A.D. (2.) That the Irish have been misinformed, or have wilfully misinformed themselves, as to the name and parentage of Fillan. It so happens, as we shall hereafter show, that Fillan, son of Fingal by his second wife Clatho, was born near Drumadoon in Arran, and most probably in the Cave of Ronan there—now King's Cove, as we shall also show—which Fingal and his people frequented much, during his visits to that island; and this fact having been confusedly reported that he was the "Son of the Cave," gave origin to the reproach that he was a son of Ronan, adopted by Fingal in his old age to save the honour of his family and the credit of Clatho. He is elsewhere, as we see, called Fillan of Moruth—that is, of Sliddery-water in Arran; because he was not only born in Ronan's cave, but nursed and educated in the same neighbourhood. By this curious coincidence, the identity of Fillan with Caeilte MacRonan, as the youthful hero by whom Foldath was slain, is established beyond dispute, and the last link of evidence to the authenticity and truth of Ossian is thus acquired from the very lips of his adversaries. The whole passage, in fact, looks like an unconscious quotation from Ossian to illustrate or supplement his own text, by men who had already rejected Ossian as a fable, and knew nothing either of Fingal or of Fillan, or of the cave of Ronan, as represented there. (3.) It is only necessary farther to remark that the omission of Fothadh, that is, of Foldath's name, by Tighernach, on the ground that he was a usurper, is in perfect consonance with and explains our own theory of similar omissions, or worse perversions, by the Irish chroniclers and bards—compare Chap. III., p. 125—of all that related to Fingal and the Scots in Ullin. The whole race of Trenmor, in short, were intruders; and were either thus to be turned to account by appropriating their achievements for others, or to be ignored and misrepresented entirely by imputations of falsehood, cowardice, or bastardy, as might best suit the purpose of the inventors. Even on their own showing, and without any information of the truth from Ossian, if Fothadh was a usurper in Munster, and Fingal generalissimo in Leinster, why should Fothadh be slain beyond Carrick-Fergus in Ulster by a foster-son of Fingal's, within sight of Ailsa Craig or the coast of Scotland? But Fingal, it may be said, according to the same tradition, was already dead, having got himself treacherously murdered by a fisherman some years before on the Boyne-water, where he had retired in his old age—283 A.D.—to spend the remainder of his life in seclusion. True: but it is also true that, according to the other tradition already quoted, he was still in the prime of life on an embassy to Rome, from which he returned in time to see Oscar die at Gabhra, in 296; and it is farther true that according to certain other accounts, which need hardly now be specified,—" Ossian [in one of these called *Son* of Oscar!] lived three hundred years, Gaul four hundred years, and Fingal himself fifty-two tens of years (five hundred and twenty years):"—Laing, Vol. II., p. 262: any, or all of which contradictions Laing and O'Donovan would possibly rather have admitted than the authenticity of *Fingal* and *Temora*, although the scenes of these poems have been unconsciously identified by one of themselves nearly a hundred years after

Y

the date of their publication. Why should argument about these Irish annals, as they are called, be prosecuted farther; except to expose their own incoherence, or to rectify them, in so far as they may be capable of such rectification, from the text of Ossian himself? Only one illustration more shall be added.

### III. FOTHADH'S GRAVE.

—" For a very curious account of the identification of the tomb of Fothadh Airgtheach near this river [the Larne river]," says O'Donovan, " see Petrie's *Inquiry into the Origin and Uses of the Round Towers of Ireland;*" but on referring to the work in question, Edit. 1845, we find at pp. 108–9, that O'Donovan has either misquoted or misunderstood the author. In point of fact, the tomb there spoken of was not identified by Petrie, but only described by him from the text of an Irish chronicle on the subject, in which Caeilte is a speaker. Caeilte, by his own account (time and place, however, correctly given), shot his spear at Fothadh with such force from a round stone, that it passed through his body entirely, and buried itself in the earth beyond so deep that the shaft was torn from the socket, and the head remained hidden in the ground!—like a rocket, in fact, through the sides of an iron-clad. The tomb, he then goes on to say, contained the body in a stone cist, with two silver rings, and two bracelets, and a silver torque on the chest; and finally, that the cairn had a pillar of red sandstone beside it, with a fine inscription on the end in Gaelig, signifying—

" EOCHAID AIRGTHEACH HERE."

This child's tale is related by Caeilte to Fingal in person, who is passing for the moment *incognito* as Mongan, and modestly refuses to be addressed by his own foster-son as the illustrious Finn!

To think that an accomplished scholar like O'Donovan should accept such a story as genuine, in preference to the simple narrative of Ossian, which he rejects as a fable! " Foldath fell on his shield: the spear of Fillan pierced the king. Nor looked the youth on the fallen, but onward rolled the war. . . . 'Raise the tombs of those I have slain, around my narrow house. Often shall I forsake the blast to rejoice above their graves; when I behold them spread around with their long whistling grass.'" According to O'Donovan, this account, so natural, so characteristic of the speaker, and so savagely pathetic, is a fable; according to O'Donovan, the other account, with its " curious" details, is true! Surely miracles of literary credulity, and of national self-complacency, will never cease.

## CHAPTER VI.

THE SCOTS IN IRELAND (CONTINUED)—EMIGRATION FROM THE SOLWAY.

HAVING thus summarised, and to some extent detailed, the first settlement of Hebridean Scots in Ullin, with as much of their history, and of the vicissitudes of their dynasty established there, as seems to have been known to Ossian, or has at least been recorded by him in celebrating the expeditions of his father and of his forefathers, it remains for us now, before quitting our researches in Ireland, to inquire whether any, and what other, emigrants from Britain known to him had ever effected a similar settlement in the Island.

I. A certain race of men, clearly distinguishable from his own, although speaking unquestionably the same language, and with whom he often came in contact or collision as the sons or soldiers of Erin; clearly distinguishable also from the people of Alnecma, although in league with them; seem to be traceable in his text as then inhabiting the region between Belfast Lough and the Boyne Water. These were called the Bolgae; and it is the fact of their settlement in Ireland, how and when, which has yet to be ascertained. The only accurate information on the subject, anywhere to be hoped for, is still through Ossian, and chiefly in his epic of *Temora*. It occurs incidentally in an episode there, and is founded on the testimony of others with whom he had intercourse, and who by tradition among themselves preserved a record of the fact; in which respect it is not only equally entitled to credit with any other statement in history, but is freer from all suspicion of partiality than it might be supposed to be, if it had been directly introduced by himself for the honour of his nation. To some brief details in this interesting and important matter, therefore, we shall now proceed.

1. Pinkerton, whose great object, as the reader is aware, was to establish the Gothic origin of the Scotch, and to invalidate not only the authority of Ossian but the nationality of the Celts, and to reduce the Celtic population of Scotland to identity with the wild Irish of Connaught, is constrained beyond himself to admit the immigration of the Bolgae, somewhere or somehow, into Ireland; but when, where, or how, he seems unable of his own authority to determine. An appeal to the text of *Temora*, with anything like intelligent reading, would have decided this difficulty for him conclusively; but the same text would also have established the independent origin of the Celtic Scots, and so have subverted his theory. He dismisses Ossian, therefore, as a frantic dream, or wicked imposture in the name of history; will not even condescend to investigate the text

of Ossian where it seems to throw light on the subject, but wilfully confounds MacPherson's commentaries with the text, as if they were one and the same, on the assumption that MacPherson was the author of both; and finally, in the heat of his aversion, misquotes the name of a mountain or of a mountain range, as if it were the name of a man—"The single ship," says he, "invented by Lumon with which he effects a settlement in Ireland!"—Lumon, in fact, being the hill from which the oak for that ship was felled, and Larthon, or Learthon, the bold and skilful adventurer by whom it was manned and sailed. The most amusing part of his self-contradiction, however, is that after having cleared away all the obvious imposture and error connected with the subject in the native Irish legends, he agrees with Ptolemy the geographer, that the settlement of these Bolgae or Belgae in Ireland could not have been earlier than 300 B.C., possibly later; but how much later, he does not affirm—without Ossian's help, indeed, he could not. Yet so close is the approximation he thus unconsciously makes to the very date incidentally assigned by Ossian, that they almost correspond. In point of fact, according to Ossian, the first Bolgic settler on the east coast of Ireland was the Larthon of Lumon already referred to; who came and returned frequently to his native country on the British coast, carrying with him, doubtless, on each new voyage to his adopted home, fellow emigrants from that side of the channel. These expeditions were made in a ship or canoe, as we have seen in a former chapter, scooped by himself from an oak on Lumon, which was the first that ever hoisted sail or "called the winds" on that shore—himself the earliest navigator. Among the descendants of this man in Ireland were Cairbar and Cathmor, the brother kings of Alnecma, already signalized—the one as a usurper, and the other as an unwilling auxiliary of his brother's guilty cause—in the days of Fingal. These personages are traced back in our hearing, by two generations beyond themselves, towards their progenitor Larthon—their own father, Borbar-duthul, having lived so long as to be blind of age—yet we do not reach Larthon. Finally, Fonar, an aged bard who in turn takes up the recital, recalls the traditions of *his* fathers, thus reaching a century at least still farther back; and from them recounts, as from living successive witnesses, the first expedition of Larthon from the shores of Lumon, and his settlement in Ireland: on which occasion, slumbering in a cave, Larthon sees in a vision, but not like Macbeth's, the princes of his race in succession arising before him; in commemoration of which he builds a hall on the spot, and begins to establish his colony. But antiquity like this, traced clearly through his own and three other generations—one of them being nearly of a century in duration, with several intervening lost; to the first of whom the very art of shipbuilding in Great Britain from solid oak is traced, in terms of a discovery—will give us at least 500 years back from the recital in question, which takes place in *Temora*, B. VII., presumably about 285 A.D.; so that the expedition of Larthon of Lumon, the leader of these Firbolgs to Ireland, must have occurred from 220 to 250, B.C., if not earlier. By this calculation, which he disdained to make, and which now, perhaps, is for the first time made, or thought of, Mr. Pinkerton's conjecture from the statement of Ptolemy is confirmed: but his credit for candour and intelligence as a historian, in denying the existence of Ossian, without even collating his text, is at the same time destroyed. Out of his own mouth of mockery, and by help of the very authority he ridicules and despises, this intolerant boaster is both justified and condemned.

2. Ptolemy, who could know nothing of Ossian, puts the settlement of the Bolgae on the south-east of Ireland; and MacPherson himself, who seems to be quite uncertain on the subject, not correctly interpreting the geography of Ossian, and relying apparently on Ptolemy to guide him, puts the voyage of Larthon from Inis-huna as from "that part of South Britain which is over against the Irish coast," wisely indefinite. It appears, however, from the text of *Temora*, B. VII., that the expedition started from under Lumon range in the ridgy bay of Cluba, in or near the territory of Inis-huna; and terminated after more than a day's voyage, interrupted by the fogs of night, in the bay of Culbin—that is, in the bay "Behind the hill"—on the opposite Irish coast, and "in the bosom of its echoing woods;" from which we may conclude, that that bay was both limited in extent and closed in from the sea by some woody eminence. Here was also the horrid cave of Duthuma, where Larthon slept and had his vision of the future. From the text of another poem, *Cathlin of Clutha*, it appears farther incidentally that Lumon itself was in a rock-bound frith, with its side to the sun-beams—that is, probably, on the north side of the frith; and four days' sail from Morven; which, by comparison with *Temora*, B. IV., at the beginning, would be about two days' sail beyond some point in the frith of Clyde from which Ireland comes first in view. In other words, it was twice as far from Morven, as from Morven to the south end of Arran. But the only frith opposite the Irish coast, rock-bound and divided by ridges on the north running into the sea, so as to contain many minor friths or bays, and at the distance thus specified from Morven, is the Solway; which in the *Britannia Antiqua* of Horsley, and the oldest geographical authorities on the region, is expressly designated Ituna. The bay nearest Ireland, on the north side of that frith, is the Bay of Luce or *Leus*—most probably so called from the *glistening* of its waters in the sun; but which we may by and by be able to identify with that of Cluba, by peculiarities discoverable in no other estuary on the coast.

It is precisely at this point, however, that the most interesting problem in our present geographical inquiry occurs. The region itself is represented in Ossian distinctly and invariably, as a kingdom; but the word Inis-huna, the reader will observe, is really the designation of an island, or of some peninsula so nearly approaching the character of an island, as in common descriptive phraseology to deserve that name; as Isle-Maghee, for example, on the coast of Ireland, or the peninsula of Roseneath, long ago, in the frith of Clyde. Inis-huna, in fact, means the Green-Island; of which I-tuna itself, the name adopted by the Romans, is but a contraction—as I-thon and I-thona, elsewhere in the text, are but contractions of Inis-thon and Inis-thona. It is farther obvious that the frith of Inis-huna, or I-tuna, now the Solway, was so called by the Celts, and by the Romans of the period from them, in connection with the island of that name; which must, therefore, have had some close geographical relation to it, most probably at its entrance. But no such island now appears on any atlas representing the region—none, certainly, worthy to be called a kingdom, or to be the acknowledged residence even of a petty prince. It must be farther observed, however, that there was a bay more closely connected with Inis-huna, than the open frith—the ridgy Bay of Cluba; into which and out of which, Fingal and Ossian seem to sail without impediment to and from Inis-huna, as if it actually coasted the inner side of the island. It is impossible to tell from any cursory reading of the text—it would be difficult, indeed, even after the most careful reading, to say whether, in so entering and departing, it was from north or south, or from both indifferently, as the winds and their destination required. On one occasion, Fingal seems to have sailed *out* of it northward, as if with a favourable breeze, from whichever side he entered; on another, Ossian seems to have sailed *into* it in similar circumstances, whether he returned by the same route or not. All we know for certain is, that it was a ridgy bay; that a mountain range called Lumon overhung it on one side; and that Inis-huna, as an island, must of necessity have been to seaward—that is, most probably to westward, of it.

3. With these explanations before him, if the reader will now in imagination connect Loch-Ryan and the Bay of Luce, he will find that the "Hammerhead" of Wigtownshire outside, otherwise called the Rhinns—sometimes the "Beak"—of Galloway, and large enough to have been a handsome principality or petty kingdom in those days, must have been identical with Inis-huna. Nor will much imagination on his part be required to realise such a change: for after what we have already seen of coast lines in Arran and the frith of Clyde, as well as in Ireland, the isolation of the Rhinns from the mainland of Galloway by the junction of these two lakes about the date in question, may be assumed as mere matter of physical certainty, and should rather have been added to our previous list of proofs, than made a subject requiring proof itself in the present instance; for every point delineated on the Ordnance Survey, and every name connected

with the intervening ground, proclaims it. It is only by degrees, however, that such discoveries grow upon us; and in connection with our present object of identification, it is more desirable, perhaps, to adduce such proof in detail, that both the region and the text may be illustrated together. The most obvious particulars are as follows:—(1.) In Blaeu's Atlas, 1663, the detached headland called the Rhinns is distinctly spoken of as "all but an island," and is even so represented—the Bay of Luce passing obliquely eastward beyond the head of Loch-Ryan. Besides which, the names of other points on the same side of the Solway—such as the Isle of Whithorn and St. Mary's Isle, which still retain the express appellation of islands although connected with the mainland—seem to imply a higher level of the tide there formerly, than now obtains. (2.) The Sands of Loch-Ryan and the Sands of Luce—which, like the Clyde itself, are ebbing fiords—bring the estuaries themselves at least two miles nearer than the tide now does; up to these limits, therefore, they must once have flowed, possibly still flow; and the space between them, thus reduced to five miles in length, is almost a dead level. (3.) On this level tract, in so short a distance, there are no fewer than nine or ten lochs of various dimensions, with additional bogs and marshes—one of these being now converted into arable land, called the Lochans —thus attesting the presence, not long ago, of much water there. (4.) There is but one noticeable rising ground on the whole space, about 100 feet high at its highest level, a little south of Stranraer, which is called Inis or the Inch, to this day, and gives its name to the adjoining parish; which has thus been originally the parish of the Island—that is, of the only spot above the level of the waters when the two estuaries met. (5.) All the names on the level ground, except this of Inch, or the Island, are of lowland, almost recent origin; whilst those on the rising ground above, on both sides, are Gaelig. Among which latter on the west side, strange to say—that is, on the Inis-huna side—we find an Aughter Lure, which is but the modern corruption of Aughter Lear, some designation connected with the sea; and on a gentle eminence immediately below, we find Culhorn, now seat of Earl Stair, which, both from its position, and the very sound of the name, must be identical with the Culdarnu of Ossian, where Fingal killed the boar in its woods, that terror of the region, on his first visit to Inis-huna. (6.) Readers of *Guy Mannering* will remember the description there given of the shores of the Solway—they present, in fact, a continuous girdle of rocks, alternately shelving, precipitous, overhanging, fantastic, or terrible, and pierced everywhere with caverns, deep, gloomy, or romantic—which might well justify the application of such a term as "ridgy" to the whole frith, independently of the numerous promontories which divide it into creeks or bays. But in following up the east shore of the Bay of Luce along the level tract now described, we count no fewer than sixteen distinct ridges in that space alone; each with a torrent, on either side of it, rushing down into the valley. Some of these ridges rise, a little to the background, as high as 700 feet, and they all come down as precipitous headlands on the hollow. When the hollow itself, therefore, was filled with the tide—was in fact, as it must have been, an arm of the sea; and when we take into account the additional number of ridges that would then be contiguous along the eastern shore, amounting to not fewer than twenty-nine, each with its torrent and ravine adjacent, we shall have forty-five in all; and must see with how much more propriety this bay of Luce might be called the ridgy bay, than any other estuary on the west of Scotland; and with what singular pictorial, as well as poetic, truthfulness it might be said of it, that "Lumon came forward in mist. In winds were its hundred groves. Sunbeams marked at times its brown side. White leapt the foamy streams from all its echoing rocks." The ridge, in fact, is a great elevated waste, with a frontier of Titanic rock-work to the west; and, from its brown heathy aspect at the present hour, is called The Moors of Galloway—although doubtless, in every recess, long ago, it was clothed or filled up with forests. Whether this be, indeed, the very Lumon range we are in search of, or whether that should be sought on the Inis-huna side of the isthmus, is perhaps a little uncertain; but what seems, for the present, to be almost conclusive on the subject is, that the most northerly ridge of all on the Loch-Ryan side, at the entrance of Glenapp, is called Fin-ard—that is, Fingal's point; the point to which he might most naturally direct his course in expeditions from Arran—which is, indeed, one of the landmarks at this moment for Loch-Ryan, from Lagg and Sliddery; and the last and highest point on the Solway side is a lofty peak, from which the whole intermediate channel, with the Isle of Man and the Irish coast in the distance, may be easily surveyed, and from which most easily also a returning mariner might be descried. "Nor did he forget green-headed Lumon; he often bounded over his seas, to where white-handed Flathal looked from the hill of roes. Lumon of the foamy streams, thou risest in Fonar's soul." The "brown-sided" ridge to the north, and the "green-headed" peak to the south, in these descriptions respectively, correspond sufficiently well to the actual features of the range we have just been surveying, from the entrance of Loch-Ryan to the Cape of Barhullion at Whithorn. On this supposition, the kingdom of Inis-huna under Larthon, 250 years, at least, B.C., and under Conmor in Ossian's day, 286 A.D., must have included the Moors and the Machers, as well as the Rhinns of Galloway—that is, a portion of the mainland, as well as the island where their chief residence seems to have been; between which, access would be comparatively easy by means of the small islands or inches, already referred to, in the straits; and yet comparative

safety might be ensured at the capital, by vigorously defending the passage.
(7.) All that remains yet to be added, is that the entire region now described—east, west, north, and south—of the Rhinns on one side and the Moors and Machers on the other, is covered with cairns, moats, tumuli, Tors, and standing stones—precisely similar to those in Arran and the north of Ireland; all apparently of corresponding dates, although, from their great multitude, these may vary; and some of them, even on recent examination, have been found to contain human remains of gigantic proportions. At Loch-Doon in Ayrshire, to the north-east, canoes also, similar to the ship of Larthon as described in the text, were accidentally raised from the lake a few years ago, and are still in preservation there; whilst the name of Fingal himself is distinctly traceable by such local designations as Fintrakin-Loch, due eastward, on the very verge of the Roman Road near Closeburn, beyond the Nith in Dumfriesshire; and north-eastward by Loch-Doon, from Finard point on Loch-Ryan to Finglass Loch or the Fin-lochs, and thence to Fingland or Finglen, with standing stones or cairns on his track, towards the same road on its progress by Lanark to the Clyde at Rutherglen—Entrekin at Ayr, and Entrekin-path between Fingland and Fintrakin, being probably but a corruption of the same. Of such routes, however, and of the extent of Fingal's exploratory marches inland from north and west, we shall have occasion to treat more explicitly hereafter. In the meantime, it may be presumed, nothing farther need be said to satisfy the reader that the Rhinns of Galloway must have been the Island of Inis-huna; that the Bay of Luce was part, at least, of Cluba's ridgy bay; and that Larthon of Lumon, in his first expedition to Ireland, sailed, amidst the wonder and apprehension of his people on the shore, from Whithorn or from Port-Mona.

II. The only objection to the whole of this, is that the Romans do not specify such particulars; and that they call Loch-Ryan Rerigonius, although they call the Solway Ituna. To which it may be replied, that Ossian himself calls a certain creek in the Bay of Cluba Rathcol, which seems, indeed, to be near the northern entrance of it; and that the town Rerigonium of the Romans, a little east of Stranraer, was probably situated on the very creek in question—the root syllables at least of all three names—Ra, Rer, and Raer—being almost equivalent. Besides, if the sea had begun to retire about the date of their occupation, there might be a sufficient isthmus at low water between the opposite lochs or bays to justify separate names; so that the one would be designated Ryan or Rerigonius, whilst the other retained its original designation of Ituna, transferred and extended by them to the entire frith.

It is not without considerable satisfaction the author has attained a conclusion on this subject so distinct, and it may be hoped convincing. If he could determine with equal certainty the very point from which Larthon sailed, he should hold the investigation, as regards the Scottish side of the Channel, complete. This, however, may as yet be impossible. We have, indeed, as already suggested, the Whithorn Cape or Burrow Head, and the Cape of the Rhinns or Mull of Galloway, to choose between—each with a hill or hills corresponding, in many respects, to Lumon; and between these alone, our selection lies. All that can be done, in guiding our choice, is to mention as a matter of suggestive coincidence, that on the south-western extremity of the Rhinns, as indicated in the Map, p. 124, two considerable elevations are to be found, one called Cairn-mon, the other Dun-man, most probably a corruption of Dunmon—one of which may possibly be identical with the Lu-mon of Ossian; if we ought not rather, for other reasons, to adhere to Barhullion on the Whithorn side. But whilst this minor detail, for the present, may remain a little in doubt, the writer flatters himself that everything, even to a foot of ground, will be made incontrovertibly clear as to the point of arrival by this heroic adventurer, and of his actual disembarkation, on the coast of Ireland.

1. The reader has already been informed how far distant, by time occupied in sailing, the point of Lumon must have been from Morven and from Arran respectively—about four days' sail from the one, and about two from the other, on average computation; and, by consulting an atlas at his leisure, may realise both the geographical position, relative to Arran, of the Bay of Luce, and how exactly the distance of its eastern headland—which seems rather to favour the idea that Lumon was identical with Barhullion—from the points in question, remote and intermediate, has been defined; at a date when there were no atlases, and nothing but the stars and winds, and the space traversed between the rising and setting of the sun, to determine drifts and distances. The time occupied by Larthon in his first voyage to the Bay of Culbin, somewhere opposite on the Irish coast, is more indefinitely stated. But it was more than one day, his progress having been impeded by mists; and his course was directed by Ton-thena, some south or south-westerly star, which was occasionally seen through the bad weather. With such data to guide us, we find the bay most accessible on the Irish coast for such a voyager would be Dundrum Bay, with a choice of Strangford-Lough to the north, and of Dundalk Bay to the south of it. Strangford-Lough is of proverbially difficult approach, besides that it would imply a turn at the entrance, which a navigator who had never used sails before would be most unlikely to attempt; and Dundalk seems too distant for the time allowed. The probability, therefore, is that somewhere in Dundrum Bay was Larthon's destination from the Solway, for Dundrum Bay itself has much too wide a sweep of shore to be identified with such a creek as Culbin. At the northern extremity,

however, of this great expanse are several creeks or minor bays, in one of which —nearest to Scotland, and from which the mountain ranges of the Solway may be discerned—the minutest local characteristics assigned by Ossian to the Bay of Culbin may be recognised; a fact of which the present writer was ignorant when the above hypothesis was framed. The following extracts from Lewis's *Topographical Dictionary* of Ireland, under the head of Ardglass, County Down, will put the reader in possession of all that can be required in the way of evidence on such a point, to produce absolute conviction:—

"The town [of Ardglass] is pleasantly and advantageously situated on the eastern coast, and on the side of a hill overlooking the sea, and is well known to mariners by two conspicuous hills, one on the west called the Ward of Ardglass, and the other on the east called the Ward of Ardtole. . . . It derives its name, signifying in the Irish language 'The High Green,' from a lofty green hill of conical form, called the Ward, and situated to the west of the town. From the remains of several castles, it appears to have been formerly a place of some importance, . . . now one of the most fashionable watering-places in the north of Ireland. . . . . The green banks of Ardtole and Ringfad, on the north and south sides of the bay, overhang the sea, where ships of the largest burden can approach within an oar's length of the bold and precipitous rocks that line the coast"—from which it appears that the bay itself is "behind" these hills. "There is a harbour admirably adapted for trade and steam navigation; . . . . and an inner harbour, . . . . for the accommodation of fishing vessels. It is called Kimmersport, and is capable of accommodating a great number of fishing boats, exclusively of other vessels of 100 tons burden; but the sea recedes from it [now] at low water. . . . . The outer pier, forming a break-water, affords a beautiful promenade, embracing fine views of the Isle and Calf of Man. . . . . From the Ward of Ardglass is a delightful prospect extending from 30 to 40 miles over a fertile country. On the south-west, beyond Killough and the beautiful Bay of Dundrum, are seen the lofty mountains of Mourne rising in sublime grandeur; on the east, the Isle of Man, and on the north-east the Ayrshire [? Galloway] mountains of Scotland, in distant perspective, appearing to rise from the ocean and embracing with their extended arch more than one-half of the horizon;"—and finally, "In Ardtole Creek, on the north-east side of the bay, is a natural cavern with a large entrance, which gradually contracts into a narrow fissure in the rock, scarcely admitting one person to creep through it; the elevation is very great; from which circumstance the townland probably derived its name Ardtole, signifying 'High Hole.' Some persons have penetrated a considerable way into this cavern, but no one has explored it fully." With respect to the people and trade of the place, we are farther informed that it has been a resort of traders since the days of Henry IV.; that the people are hereditary fishermen, having no other employment; and that Ardglass is the common centre of their traffic—to which boats resort "from Donaghadee, Carlingford, the Skerries, Dublin, Arklow, and the Isle of Man, but principally from Penzance on the coast of Cornwall."

We have thus (1.) Culbin, or the "Bay behind the hills;" (2.) the hills themselves, which are a landmark to mariners; (3.) the outer and the inner harbour "in their bosom of echoing woods," frequented by fishermen with their tiny craft for generations; (4.) by a sort of miraculous conformity, "the horrid cave of Duthuma" unexplored to the present hour, from which the ghosts of the future in dreamy exhalations emerged, to reassure the exhausted and adventurous visitant of its recesses; and (5.) the sight of Scotland with the peaks of Galloway from which he had sailed, and by which he was guided home again so often; and of the Isle of Man for a beacon, or for an occasional resting-place—all concentrated here on the very shore where he must have landed, and from which his children marched westward to their predestined seats of sovereignty on the Bann or beyond it, on a line already proved as the limit of the Ossianic campaigns and the probable centre of the Bolgic territory. No evidence on the point, as a question in geography, could be imagined clearer. At the distance, indeed, of fifteen hundred years, it is perhaps unexampled in the minute accuracy of its statistical correspondence to an outline of poetic hints. The only wonder is, that neither Pinkerton with his prejudiced learning, nor MacPherson himself, who was bound to ransack the world for proofs, should have been aware of it; and thus Ossian, equally beyond the suspicion of his translator and the cavils of his enemies, is borne out as authentic, to the minutest letter of his historical recitals on the subject. How poor, after examination and cross-examination like this, on his unaltered text, seem all the quibbles of learned critics, antiquarians, and linguists.

2. Yet farther proof of the same sort may be adduced from another unconscious witness, himself an Irishman already quoted, and who wrote before MacPherson was born. Larthon, or *Learthon*, as our translator explains, means a wave of the sea; and was a name figuratively applied to the early navigator whose expedition to Ireland we are now commenting on. This man, according to our theory, must have had the Isle of Man for a landmark at least, in his voyages between the Solway and Ardglass; and would, therefore, in all probability establish permanent relations with it, as an intermediate station, if for no other purpose than to refresh himself and refit, in his expeditions. Without knowing anything of Ossian, much less of what has since and now been written—

"I will not fail," says Toland, "doing justice to the memory of the great Hero and Legislator of the Iland, MANANNAN; reported after the manner of those ages to have been the Son of LEAR,* or the God of the Sea, from his extraordinary skill in navigation and commerce. . . Who, from his instruction by the Druids, was reputed a consummate magician, and was indeed most happy in stratagems of war both by land and sea. Mr. SACHEVERELL, except

---

* MANANNAN MHAC-LEIR: thus in Toland's Irish. But the name is still common as MacLure, vulgarly MacLare, along the western coast from Girvan to Stranraer and the Rhinns of Galloway.

in affirming MANANNAN (whom he misnames MANNAN) to have been the *father, founder, and legislator of the Iland*, is out in everything he says concerning him: for instead of living about the beginning of the fifth century, he liv'd as many centuries before CHRIST; and so cou'd not be contemporary with PATRIC, the Apostle of Man as well as Ireland. Neither was MANANNAN the son of a King of Ulster, nor yet the brother of FERGUS II. King of Scotland: and as for his not being able to get any information what became of him, I have already told that he was killed in Ireland, and by whom"—by one ULLIN, to wit, "near Galway."—History of *Druids*, pp. 66, 67.

Here, then, with almost as much completeness in the history of the individual, as already in the description of the scene, we have (1.) the skill, the daring, and the capacity of the explorer—of the shipbuilder, in short, and of the sailor; for how otherwise could this hero have received from admiring posterity the honour of such a title, as Son of the Sea, or of the God of the Sea? (2.) We have next the voyage to Man from some distant coast beyond; for how could he be the "father and founder," as well as legislator of the Island, if he had not himself been a colonist at first? (3.) We have then some voyage to Ireland by him on the coast opposite to Man, and his exploration of the country inland; for how otherwise could he have been killed on the confines of Galway—either city, or county—if he had not so landed, and advanced? We have even the confirmation of his dream, in his reputation as a magician. (4.) And finally, we have the proximate date, presumable but not affirmed, as about 500 B.C. Could the reader believe such a coincidence between tradition and the text of a disputed author, as to time, place, and designation, character, and destiny—unknown, overlooked, or forgotten by all concerned—as possible at the distance of two thousand three hundred years or thereby, with respect to any one personage hitherto considered mythical, if it had not been thus explicitly afforded by such a witness? The only point of difference, in fact, between so remarkable a tradition and the letter of the text, is the slight variation between Wave of the sea, and Son of the Sea, or of the God of the Sea—between Lear-thon and Mac-Lear—in the allegorical distinction of the hero; a difference which does not in the least affect the identity of the man, and rather confirms the independent authority of both accounts. All difference beyond that is but abbreviation or omission. The "ridgy bay of Cluba," for example, and the "horrid cave of Duthuma," which limit and define the voyage, are both awanting, and fortunately so; for Laing, with a kind of perverse ingenuity, omitting half the story told by Toland, insists that MacPherson plagiarised the rest, and identifies Inis-huna with the Isle of Man. The Isle of Man, in fact, is not even glanced at by MacPherson; who intimates expressly and repeatedly that Inis-huna was the ancient name of that part of South Britain which is next to the Irish coast; nay, farther, that the coast of Ireland to which it was next or opposite must have been somewhere between Dublin and Wexford, although he cannot tell where. That all this theory of his was a dream, we have endeavoured to demonstrate; and it is certain, at least, that neither Laing nor MacPherson had the slightest idea that the Rhinns of Galloway on the one hand, or the cave of Ardglass on the other, would ever be quoted as they now are, in verification of Ossian.

III. The Bolgae, thus settled as emigrants on the Irish coast from the shores of the Solway, were fellow-countrymen and allies of Fingal himself, as we learn by repeated allusions to him and to his people, in the poems now under review. In *Cathlin of Clutha*, for example, Ossian and Oscar, in pursuit of a ravisher from the Clyde, overtook him in a grassy glen called Rathcol, on the shores of the ridgy bay near Lumon, elsewhere called Cluba's bay—which we presume to be identical with the Bay of Luce—and are thus introduced to hospitalities at the palace of Conmor, father of Sulmalla and king of that region; Sulmalla herself, in her father's absence, being hostess. From this princess afterwards, in the poem of her name which immediately follows, they receive traditional accounts of Fingal's ancient friendship for her father's house, and of his exploits in the neighbourhood; especially in the killing of a wild boar in the woods of Culdarnu, which had committed much devastation there, and had even caused loss of life among the youths of the country sent out to destroy him. Fingal's action in this affair was highly characteristic, and his presence as a royal hero had inspired profound admiration among the fair of Lumon.

"'Not unknown,' I said, 'at the streams is he, the father of our race. Fingal has been heard of at Cluba, blue-eyed daughter of kings. Nor only at Cona's stream, is Ossian and Oscar known. Foes trembled at our voice, and shrunk in other lands.' 'Not unmarked,' said the maid, 'by Sulmulla, is the shield of Morven's king. It hangs high, in Conmor's hall, in memory of the past; when Fingal came to Cluba, in the days of other years. Loud roared the boar of Culdarnu, in the midst of his rocks and woods. Inis-huna sent her youths, but they failed; and virgins wept over tombs. Careless went the king to Culdarnu. On his spear rolled the strength of the woods. He was bright, they said, in his locks, the first of mortal men. Nor at the feast were heard his words. His deeds passed from his soul of fire, like the rolling of vapours from the face of the wandering sun. Not careless looked the blue eyes of Cluba on his stately steps. In white bosoms rose the King of Selma, in midst of their thoughts by night. But the winds bore the stranger to the echoing vales of his roes. Nor lost to other lands was he, like a meteor that sinks in a cloud. He came forth, at times, in his brightness, to the distant dwelling of foes. His fame came, like the sound of winds, to Cluba's woody vale."—*Sulmalla of Lumon*.

The reader will find how naturally all this corresponds with our idea that Loch-Ryan was in the bay of Cluba, and that Culhorn is identical with Culdarnu.

We extract this passage entire, for the admirable description it affords of Fingal in his youth, both physically and morally; and for the indication it gives of his extending fame at home and abroad. But besides these recent and traditional friendships with the house of Morven, the people of Inis-huna, and of the Wigtownshire coast generally, were allied to Fingal by language and habits at least, if not strictly by blood; and seem to have received both him and his as kindred of the same nationality, although their descendants in Ireland had become the enemies of his race, and ultimately provoked the bloodiest campaigns by their savage incursions.

But whether Celts of the race of Trenmor in Ullin, or Bolgae reigning in Atha and practical sovereigns of the intermediate region, these two tribes were of Scottish origin alike, and actually emigrants or colonists—the one from the north-west, the other from the south-west coast of Scotland—invited as allies, or stimulated by the thirst of adventure. Up till Fingal's time, friendly enough relations seem always to have been maintained and alliances carried out, both between the Hebridean Scots and their fellow-countrymen in Ullin and between the Bolgae of Ireland and their brethren on the Solway, as incidents in *Temora*, and in *Sulmalla of Lumon*, explain. But in the course of centuries, the chief remaining portion of the latter race seems either to have followed their leaders into Ireland, or to have sunk into insignificance on their native coast; for according to the most reliable subsequent authorities, the Piks took possession of that country, and a new military kingdom, called Bernicia, was established between the Forth and the Solway by Ida from Jutland with an army of Angles, in 547 A.D.; among which changes of inhabitants and of government, their individuality and independence disappear.\* Even before Ossian's visit, as recorded in *Cathlin of Clutha*, one petty dynasty had been extinguished. "Here, midst the waving of oaks, were the dwellings of the kings of old. But silence, for many darkbrown years, had settled in grassy Rathcol; for the race of heroes had failed along the pleasant vale:" and at the very moment of his arrival, danger was threatening the whole monarchy of Inis-huna from the east. "Darkness dwells in Cluba of harps," says Sulmalla, in anxiety: "The race of kings is distant far. In battle is Conmor of spears; and Lormor, king of streams. Nor darkening alone are they; a beam from other lands is nigh: the friend of strangers in Atha, the troubler of the field"—Cathmor, to wit, her kinsman and lover from Ireland; who was then assisting her father to repel the Romans most probably, or their allies, making head against the Galvidian Scots along the Solway, by that very road of theirs through Dumfriesshire, where Fingal, as we have seen, confronted or surveyed them more than fifty years before. Thus came "darkness," ad-

---

\* Compare Bede as quoted by Pinkerton, *History of Scotland*, Vol. I., p. 327.

vancing, on the race of Conmor, in spite of all confederate protests and endeavours to prevent it. Lormor, it seems, according to tradition, succeeded to his father's throne, and may have maintained it for a time in comparative independence; but nothing could long avert the approaching doom of extinction, and the new name of Galloway itself was at last imposed on the region.*

With respect to the native Irish, among whom these Bolgae had settled, and by intermixture with whom their blood was unquestionably much affected; or who still occupied in their natural, semi-civilised condition, the south and southwest of the Island, hence called the Wild Irish—whence they were derived, how they were governed, or what had been their history as a people, we find no direct information in Ossian. It is to the Chronicles of Eri, already referred to, we must have recourse for this. Ossian knew them only by their own name, as "Sons of Erin" employed in the ranks of the Bolgae, represented here and there by some native chief from the wilds of Alnecma—of intractable disposition like themselves, stimulating them constantly to revenge or outrage, and falling at their head with imprecations of hate; and how exactly all this is borne out by the letter of their own chronicles, the reader will be enabled in due time to judge. They had evidently been subjugated somehow by the Bolgae, who must, therefore, have multiplied on their adopted soil, or been considerably reinforced from the Solway, as above explained. But their history, beyond that, is a blank to Ossian; and so far as their claims to antiquity and civilisation are concerned, we must consult themselves.

* The only source from which any information on this interesting subject could have been obtained was a poem of Ossian's in MacPherson's hands at the date of his last publication, and referred to by him in a note at the end of *Temora*. Sulmalla seems to have occupied a prominent place, as heroine, in that narrative; but no details are given; and the poem itself, so far as we are aware, has never been published. Galloway, or *Gallovidia*, a name unknown to Ossian, is understood to mean the country of the Irish tributary Gael; and must have been applied to the region, on the supposition that its more recent inhabitants—hence called Novantae, or new comers—were a colony from Ireland. In point of fact, as we have seen, they were but returned emigrants, with Irish affinities, and doubtless also with Irish blood in their veins. It may be worth noticing, in conclusion, that the *Oppidum Rerigonium*, or town of Rerigon, as contradistinguished from the *Sinus Rerigonius*, or bay of Rerigon, is written expressly by one important authority with a t—Retigonium; which looks not unlike a corruption of the root syllable in Ossian's *Ruth*-col. Pinkerton cannot understand this variation, and prefers Rerigon.

END OF PART THIRD.

### Part Fourth.

# FINGAL IN SCOTLAND.

## STIRLINGSHIRE

AND

## LAND OF THE STRANGERS.

# CONTENTS.

                                                                                                                                                    PAGE
CHAPTER I.—Fingal and his People in Stirlingshire: Their Expeditions against the Romans—*Comala, Colna-dona, War of Caros, Carthon, Cathloda*—Poems analysed, and Scenes, as described by Ossian, determined,   167

CHAPTER II.—Fingal and his People in Stirlingshire (continued):—Identification of certain Scenes above described—The Carron—The Kelvin or Col-avon—Colzium or Colam—The Crona or Bonny Water—The Gathered Heap—The Roman Road and Wall, &c.,   ...   ...   ...   ...   ...   ...   199

CHAPTER III.—Fingal and his People in Stirlingshire (continued):—Explorations from Kilsyth to the Carron—Comàla's Rock—The Place of Renown—View from Tomfin—The Ardvens of Stirlingshire,   ...   ...   210

CHAPTER IV.—Fingal and his People in the Land of the Strangers:—Routes and Boundaries—from Morven to Castlecary, thence, by Fannyside Lochs and Coul-hill, to the Clyde,   ...   ...   ...   ...   226

CHAPTER V.—Fingal and his People in the Land of the Strangers (continued):—Rutherglen, Balclutha, Cathkin and the Clyde—Route from near Innerkip along Southern Shore of the Frith by Fingalton, to Balclutha, &c.—Character and Campaigns of Fingal,   ...   ...   ...   ...   ...   ...   238

## ILLUSTRATIONS.

ROMAN FORT at Confluence of Carun and Crona,   ...   ...   195
ROMAN EAGLE found in the Wall,   ...   ...   ...   198
COMALA'S ROCK,   ...   ...   ...   ...   ...   ...   216
ARDVENS from Tomfin,   ...   ...   ...   ...   ...   223
VIEW from Finglen,   ...   ...   ...   ...   ...   225
CANOES and WAR-CLUB at Bowling,   ...   ...   ...   256

# FINGAL IN SCOTLAND.

## CHAPTER I

FINGAL AND HIS PEOPLE IN STIRLINGSHIRE—THEIR EXPEDITIONS AGAINST THE ROMANS, &c.

ANALYSIS OF TEXT.

WITH a basis of geographical certainty so broad and so well established, both in Ireland and in the West of Scotland, to guide us in tracing the progress of Fingal and realising the descriptions of Ossian, we might be justified in accepting all further details, rightly understood, as unquestionable; and in some cases, where the action lies abroad, we must be content with such alternative. But as there are several poems still to be investigated, of which the scenes lie at the very door, and notwithstanding the numerous changes which have occurred on the surface since Ossian's day may still be recognised, it will add considerably to the conclusiveness of our whole argument to identify these, and will give an interest to the history of Scotland beyond what we are accustomed to attach to it, if we can illustrate them now, at the distance of eighteen hundred years, more clearly than has hitherto been possible.

I. The poems in question are *Comala*, *Colna-dona*, and the *War of Caros*, with parts of *Carthon* and of *Cathloda* incidentally related; of which pieces, the three first are of chief importance to our present argument, and refer exclusively to Fingal's alleged wars with the Romans, or with some distinguished foreign enemies in the valley of the Carron. To adopt, then, the same mode of illustration as hitherto, we shall first analyse the subject-matter of these poetical narrations as presented to us in the text, and then endeavour to confirm or explain it from the existing geographical features of the region to which the poems refer.

1. In *Comala*, which is a strictly dramatic rehearsal, and, according to Mac-Pherson, was "perhaps presented" as such "before the chiefs upon solemn occasions," we have the history of an Orkney princess in love with Fingal on his first return from Norway; who follows him in disguise as a boy-warrior

first to Morven, and then as his affianced bride, with her maids of honour in attendance, in his expedition against Caracul, who is called "King of the World." Caracul is defeated, his cavalry scattered, and "the wings of his pride" driven back to other lands. Fingal returns in triumph up the valley of the Crona, to the spot where Comala waits; but a false report of his death in battle, wickedly announced by his own herald to Comala, overwhelms her, and she dies of apprehension or terror at the first glimpse of him in the moonlight, when he arrives. This is the second disappointment in love, by the sudden death of an intended wife, which Fingal was doomed to lament before his marriage with Roscrana. The events thus detailed in the poem before us take place fully three days' march from Morven, and somewhere in the joint valley of the Carron and the Crona; but from the peculiar style of dramatic narrative employed, it would be difficult to determine precisely where, if we had not some assistance from the text of the others. Three names, however, distinctly recognisable, are introduced—Carun, on whose banks the battle was fought, beyond the knowledge and far beyond the vision of Comala; Crona, some stream in the neighbourhood, flowing towards the Carun; and Ardven, a mountain, or peak of some mountain range, not very remote. If Comala, as it seems, followed Fingal only so far towards the field, not knowing "that he went to war," and rested with her attendants on the banks of the Crona whilst the battle was in progress by the Carun— "He left me at the chase alone: I knew not that he went to war: he said he would return with the night"—then Crona must have been considerably westward of Carun at that point, and Ardven some conspicuous hill, or shoulder of a hill, still farther west, where her maids had been pursuing the chase, but from which they descend to prepare the feast of triumph on a rock, and call her in vain from watching forlorn by the stream—Says one to the other, "come from Crona's banks. Lay down the bow and take the harp; let the night come on with songs, and our joy be great on Ardven."

These points in succession must have been all to the west or north-westward of each other, and at a few miles' distance—the first from the last; for Fingal on his return in the evening, from the banks of the Carun to the slopes of Ardven, finds Comala dead or dying on his way beside the rock of Crona, and the fire of the feast neglected "ascending" on another rock, if not on another and higher portion of the same rock, in the immediate neighbourhood.

2. Some years after this, during which his first expedition to Ireland occurs and his marriage with Roscrana, and whilst Ossian their son was still a youth, Fingal had made another successful campaign in the same neighbourhood; had routed his foes, most probably the southern Britons supported by the Romans from beyond the Wall, at Crona; and in the poem of *Colna-dona* sends Ossian

and his young friend Toscar of Lutha in Arran, to erect a stone of victory on the spot where this new triumph had been achieved. Being as yet mere lads, and unacquainted with the region, they " move beneath the voice of the king," that is, by his orders and directions to guide them, "to Crona of the streams;" and so, "attended by three bards with songs," and with "three bossy shields borne before them," they reach the field, where the ceremony of commemoration, by placing a stone, with trophies of war underneath it, is accomplished. This occupies the afternoon and evening of the first day, and must have been by the verge of the river where it flowed through a marsh, for it was "by Crona's mossy course Fingal had scattered his foes," and the stone was taken from the very "ooze" in which their "blood hung curdled." It must have been some little distance also beyond where Comala died, for she sat by a rock on the brink of the stream when it was still a mountain torrent, and much nearer to Ardven. From this marsh they return next day by special invitation to Col-amon, the residence of Carul, a little westward; which they must have passed the day before, on their way to Crona, else Carul could not have seen them. Here they spend a night in the "Hall of harps," at "the oak of feasts," in the midst of the utmost hospitality—through which Colna-dona shines, and captivates the heart of Toscar; or in listening to the tales of other years from Carul himself, who had once visited Selma as a stranger in his ship from the Clyde, and had seen Roscrana there, the mother of Ossian and the light of Cormac's race. In the morning the two youths, for recreation, "awake the woods, and hang forward," that is eastward, "on the path of the roes," by Crona, and return again up its vale to Col-amon. They are encountered by a stranger from the woods in the disguise of a warrior; who proves to be Colna-dona mutually enamoured of Toscar, to whom her love is thus revealed. The poem here abruptly terminates, much of it being lost; but it should appear that Colna-dona was married to Toscar and became the mother of Malvina—to whom Ossian therefore was doubly attached, as the daughter of his friend and the betrothed bride of his own beloved son Oscar.

In this narrative, the Crona only is mentioned, and not the Carun; but the Col-amon, another river "of troubled streams, dark wanderer of distant vales," is introduced, a little more to the westward. Beside this river, near its source, is the fortress of Col-amon, where Carul resides; and Carul himself, as we have seen, had made a hostile voyage in a ship of his own on the Clyde, which drifted westward to Selma about the time that Ossian was born. The Col-amon, therefore, must have been some stream that, through marshes or other impediments, and by distant vales, could conduct him thither, yet at its source was in close proximity to the Crona. As a matter of mere speculative geography, this is clear.

3. Finally, in the *War of Caros*, as years roll on and the third generation has arisen, we have an early triumph of Oscar's narrated, over Caros "king of ships," between the Crona and the Carun. Caros had arrived with his fleet in the neighbourhood, at some entrenchment or "gathered heap" of his own on the north bank of that river, "spreading the wings of his pride," and surveying Oscar's position with fear, from behind the stones of his rampart. Oscar, by a bard, challenges him to abandon both fleet and camp and come to battle in the open plain between the rivers; and in the meantime summons his own people around him on the Crona, from their headquarters westward at Ardven. Caros declines this challenge, and will not cross the Carun. Oscar then listens to the story of Hidallan, whose falsehood had occasioned Comala's death in the same neighbourhood; and, to prepare himself for the possibility of a conflict, retires to commune with the ghosts of his fathers on Ardven—which he seems to ascend from north-east, for the "half-enlightened moon sinks dim and red behind it"—that is, to south-west; and a heath with aged oaks spreads around, "where feeble voices are heard" and "the meteors of night are setting," which completes the solitude of the situation. His people, now assembled to the eastward, are left to keep watch on the enemy from the banks of Crona; but song and the shell prevail, and Caros, eluding their vigilance or taking advantage of their neglect, crosses the Carun during night with his cavalry, to surround or surprise them. Oscar, returning from Ardven, encounters or discovers him in the grey of the morning; stands defiantly alone, to confront him; and with a voice of thunder, which is echoed for miles around, shouts to awake his own people. This post of his was where "a green vale surrounded a tomb which rose in the times of old, and where little hills lifted their heads at a distance." His voice, thus suddenly heard, awakes the people of Caros first, who rush to overwhelm Oscar; but he boldly and with success, exaggerated perhaps by paternal admiration in the poem, withstands their onset.

"The voice reached his people at Crona; they came like a hundred streams. The warriors of Caros fled, and Oscar remained like a rock left by the ebbing sea. Then dark and deep, with all his steeds, Caros rolled his might along: the little streams are lost in his course; and the earth is rocking round."

From which it would appear that the ground was boggy, and shook with the tread of retreating cavalry. The whole scene, in fact, is so vividly minute in representation that it is impossible, with any reasonable attention to the text, to misconceive or to misplace it.

In this narrative, as the reader observes, we have the same three points of the landscape specified, and nearly in the same relation—Carun to the north of the present position, and Crona to the south or south-west of it, with Ardven to the west of both, but approached more from the north than heretofore; from which it is obvious, that the Carun itself, on which Oscar had his eye and from which he expected a surprise, must have been to that side of it. We have this additional intelligence, also, that the sea was in the neighbourhood, with accommodation sufficient for a fleet and even for the disembarkation of cavalry. From other poems we learn incidentally that the region now represented had been the scene of many a previous conflict with the "strangers," or with the "kings of the world." One triumph of Fingal's is recorded in *Carthon*—most probably the same which he sent Ossian afterwards to commemorate, as described in *Colna-dona*—from which he returned a distinguished victor; when, to celebrate his arrival, "a thousand lights from the strangers' land rose in the midst of the people:" correctly explained by MacPherson to be "wax lights carried, among other booty, from the Roman province." In the same poem Clessammor, recounting the exploits of Comhal's youth, Fingal's father, says—"Often did we pass over Carun to the land of the strangers: our swords returned, not unstained with blood: nor did the kings of the world rejoice." And at a still earlier date we find, in *Cathloda*, Duan II., a convention of the petty States assembled at Colglan-Crona, in mutual jealousy and distraction, to resist the aggression of these "strangers;" on which occasion, Trenmor, the type of wisdom, modesty, and courage, is elected commander-in-chief, and becomes practical dictator in the field—an honour maintained without loss of credit or dignity through the succeeding generations of his race; in which limited sense, as we shall hereafter learn, he was first king of Caledonia; and this title, with the same limitations, descended to his sons.

"From their hundred streams came the tribes, to grassy Colglan-Crona. Their chiefs were before them. Each strove to lead the war. Their swords were often half unsheathed. Red rolled their eyes of rage. Separate they stood, and hummed their surly songs—'Why should they yield to each other? their fathers were equal in war.' Trenmor was there, with his people, stately in youthful locks. He saw the advancing foe. The grief of his soul arose. He bade the chiefs to lead, by turns: they led, but they were rolled away. From his own mossy hill, blue-shielded Trenmor came down. He led wide-skirted battle, [by turning the enemy's flank] and the strangers failed. Around him the dark-browed warriors came: they struck the shield of joy. Like a pleasant gale, [after that] the words of power rushed forth from Selma of Kings. But the chiefs led by turns, in war, till mighty danger rose: then was the hour of the king [so chosen, and entrusted with supreme temporary power] to conquer in the field."—*Cathloda*, D. II.

The "grassy Colglan-Crona" where this league was sworn, and the first election of a generalissimo king was made, must have been somewhere between the Crona and the Col-amon—of which two names the word itself may be a compound; and thus we have references, from the text of not fewer than five separate poems, to identify the most important features of the region.*

II. But it is necessary, before adducing proof of their identity, to ascertain how far MacPherson himself was acquainted with the scenes so distinctly recognisable in his own translation. He knew, certainly, that the Carun was the Carron, and that Ossian refers to some line of defence—a wall, or other military work—by the Romans, in its neighbourhood. He was correct, also, in his supposition that these invaders were referred to by him as "kings of the world;" that the "wings of their pride" were the expanded eagles on their standards, of which a specimen, brass gilt, has been discovered in the wall; and finally, that Caros, as "king of ships," was identical with Carausius, intrusted with the command of the Roman Fleet, A.D. 284; and in like manner, that Caracul was identical with Caracalla, who commanded in Great Britain, as his father's lieutenant and prospective successor, A.D. 208-11—although this latter identification has been objected to by distinguished authorities, and has indeed been insisted on as one of the clearest proofs of his dishonesty. It was most unlikely, it has been said, in the first place, that the Romans should ever adopt such a nickname as Caracul, or the "fierce eyed," from savages like Fingal for one of their Emperors; in reply to which, it has simply to be stated that Ossian makes no such allegation, neither does MacPherson. The charge, therefore, so far as they are concerned, is false and invalid in the very terms of it; and in conceding, or seeming to concede the truth of it to Laing, Dr. Graham conceded by far too much. But it is farther objected that, as the name Caracalla, or man with the cloak, had not been invented, or at least applied to the son of Severus by the Romans themselves, till several—perhaps, four—years after the date of Fingal's alleged victory, it is absurd to suppose that Ossian, or Fingal either, could have heard it at the time. Gibbon, and after him, Laing reiterates this objection; to which it may as reasonably be replied, that Ossian could not have been the author of the poem because he was not then born. MacPherson himself, indeed, anticipates this objection, and replies to it in his first edition; which it is surprising neither Gibbon nor Laing should observe. The date of the poem, in fact, in which Caracul is mentioned, might have been fifty or even seventy years later than

---

* By some strange editorial misreading, this word Colglan-Crona has been converted to Colgan-Cona in Stewart's Gaelig Edition, 1818; in accordance with which, we must suppose that whilst the tribes are assembled to resist an aggression at the Carron, they are transported in a moment to finish their councils in the wilds of Glenco, and return again to the combat. Through the officious intermeddling of his friends, or the ignorance of his Editors, Ossian is thus made not only to contradict himself, but to rehearse incredible absurdities. In this respect, MacPherson's edition and translation are superior to all others, being intelligible and consistent, however imperfect his own acquaintance may have been with the geography of his subject.

the victory it celebrates; during which time, it is obvious that the people of Fingal having heard Caracalla's name, which they did not understand, and having a name of their own corresponding to it all but a letter, might apply that name in jest for their own gratification to a man whom they both hated and despised, and who, for anything we know to the contrary, may have had some peculiarity of vision besides to justify the sarcasm; and they might so speak of him to Ossian, who would adopt the name on the authority of his kindred, and introduce it accordingly in his drama. The persons through whom such information might have reached Ossian were, according to MacPherson, "the Christians whom the persecution under Dioclesian had driven beyond the pale of the Roman Empire;" and there is nothing, as we shall by and by see, at all improbable in the supposition. Or finally, as Clerk ingeniously suggests, Caracul, although translated by MacPherson " fierce eyed," might as well be translated "short tunic," and might really have been applied to the son of Severus by Fingal himself, before it was applied by the Romans. In confirmation of which, although Clerk does not observe it, we may add that Caracalla, the nickname in question, is expressly quoted in our best Latin dictionaries as a "Gallic word," introduced into the language of Rome when the garment which it described was introduced among the people. The objection itself, indeed, as Mr. Clerk justly observes, is frivolous—it may well be called foolish; but his own argument, by the retranslation of Caracul as "short tunic," seems to be quite conclusive: for if the son of Severus appeared with a tunic of that kind, as very likely he did, at the battle of the Carron, Fingal to a certainty would dubb him "scant skirt" as he fled from the charge. "Raise, ye bards of the song, the wars of the streamy Carun: Caracul has fled from mine arms along the fields of his pride: he sets far distant, like a meteor that encloses a spirit of night."—*Comala.* Our best congratulations are due to the reverend translator for this happy amendment; which we have the more satisfaction in now offering, as we shall have occasion to differ from him, perhaps, on certain points of greater importance to be investigated hereafter.

MacPherson's identification of Caracul with Caracalla, therefore, as it is reasonable on other grounds, and may be confirmed by an allusion in the text besides, cannot be objected to on these. But the knowledge of all the preceding facts, however easily acquired in Stirlingshire, was not sufficient to enable him to construct three poems such as those now quoted, much less to interweave them with two or three more, including a variety of personages and events of which he knew nothing, relating to regions he never dreamt of, and extending in their united narrative over a period of two hundred and fifty years; and that he was not only destitute of all other knowledge in the case, but did not even understand the bearing of the text and of his own admirable translation, may be demonstrated by the simplest evidence from that translation itself.

1. He misapprehends entirely the position of Caros as to the Roman Wall, from which he represents him as sallying. To sally from the Wall on Oscar, Caros must have crossed the Crona, and not the Carun. Caros, in fact, was north of the Carun as well as of the Wall; and the "gathered heap" behind which he took refuge, and from which he surveyed the field, when he found himself intercepted by Oscar, must have been some fortified station or temporary camp on the Roman Road at Larbert; and he retained that position in defence, with the river between himself and Oscar. The Roman Road, itself, indeed, which, according to Nimmo, consisted of several layers of earth and stones thrown together one upon another as they came to hand, the uppermost very large, and was generally about twelve feet in breadth, raised in the middle and with a deep foundation, would correspond sufficiently well to the "gathered heap" of Ossian without any additional work—although some such work, as a terminus on the bank of a navigable river, was highly probable there. In point of fact, since the above hypothesis was finished, we learn incidentally from Gordon's *Itinerarium*, 1726, that an artificial *tumulus*, or Mound of Observation, had been built by Agricola on the very spot in the year 80 or 82—that is, more than 200 years before Caros or Carausius arrived. "About a mile farther east," he says—and on the north side of the Carron, as we have now been insisting—" at a place called *Larber-bridge*, upon the same Isthmus, I met with another artificial *Tumulus*, like what in England they call a *Barrow*, and is the last round mount to be seen on the whole track"—to which, therefore, of necessity, Caros would betake himself when storm-sted in the river. It must also be farther observed, that such forts were constructed with a raised platform inside, so that the garrison on watch could look over the rampart. "'What does Caros, king of ships?' said the son of the now mournful Ossian. 'Spreads he the wings of his pride?' 'He spreads them, Oscar,' replied the bard; 'but it is behind his gathered heap. He looks over his stones with fear, and beholds thee terrible, as the ghost of night that rolls the wave to his ships.'" Nothing as to the invader's position, between the frith and the fort—driven from the one by a storm, and reconnoitering from the other in doubt—could be more explicit. The very ground where Caros then stood, although now covered with rubbish, might be identified. Oscar himself, on the other hand, was protected in rear by the Crona which flowed eastward between him and the Wall, as well as by the Carun in front, from the risk of any sudden surprise; and was confident enough in the security of his place to challenge the enemy "to leave the rolling of his wave," that is, either to disembark, or to cross the Carun, or both, and

## FINGAL IN SCOTLAND.

to meet him in the plain between—a challenge which Caros, from behind "his gathered heap," declined, till the darkness of night should screen his passage. MacPherson, in his note, unaccountably reverses all this, and thus utterly bewilders both himself and the reader; when a glance at Gordon's work—which should have been sufficiently familiar to him as an antiquarian, having been published only a dozen years before he was born—would not only have enabled him as an editor to avoid this error, but would have assisted him, had he been an impostor, to harmonize contradictory details. The extraordinary correspondence, indeed, between the topographical discoveries of Gordon and the minutest points of descriptive phraseology in the text of Ossian—which did not appear for thirty-six years afterwards, and of which, therefore, he could know nothing—and the absolute ignorance of MacPherson himself on the subject, is one of the most convincing coincidences in the whole argument.

ROMAN FORT AT CONFLUENCE OF CARUN AND CRONA.

2. He gives no explanation either of the proximity of the sea, or of the arrival of Caros with cavalry and a fleet; where or how they had disembarked, or could disembark; what "rolling wave" it was, which protected them; or how it was possible for them, by any strategical manœuvre to leave ships and ramparts at the same moment, or to cross the Carun in so doing. Such a feat was impossible for Caros, if he was anywhere behind the Wall; it was hardly possible, indeed, for Oscar's herald to reach him there with such a challenge—the Carun itself, according to MacPherson's supposition, with about two miles of marshy ground, and at least one other river of considerable size, intervening. But Caros, as we have just seen, had been driven up the frith; "the ghost of night was rolling the wave to his ships;" the wind was roaring around the sides of Ardven, and meteors were seen flitting on the heath around. He was before a storm, in short, and had drifted to the nearest harbour, with the intention, doubtless, of reaching the Wall, when he was intercepted and repulsed by Oscar. Where

this occurred, we shall immediately see; but that MacPherson did not even imagine this, has been shown. According to his interpretation, Caros was comfortably entrenched behind the Wall, when in reality he was only meditating an escape from an untenable strategical position, towards it.

3. In Carul's episode, in *Colna-dona*, of his own adventure on the Clyde, not the slightest hint is afforded how such a voyage was possible. Yet the most unreflecting reader must be struck with the absurdity, of a prince from the heart of Stirlingshire pursuing a pirate full sail on the Clyde, if no communication by water existed between. This palpable apparent impossibility elicits neither explanation nor apology. It does not even seem to occur to MacPherson that the Col-amon, or *Col-avhain*, with its "troubled streams in distant vales," by which alone such communication could be effected, was identical not only in name, which is obvious, but in every other particular—source, course, and character —with the river Kelvin.

4. In commenting on the story of Hidallan from Balva, in the *War of Caros*, he attempts an explanation of the scene, founded on a similarity of terms, without reflecting on the consequences. "This is perhaps that small stream," he says, "still retaining the name of Balva, which runs through the romantic valley of Glentivar in Stirlingshire. Balva signifies *a silent stream*; and Glentivar, *the sequestered vale*." But we are expressly told in the sequel of that story, as narrated by Ryno in the poem above named, (1.) that Hidallan was a young chieftain, and an honorary ally of Fingal's, from the north, in his expedition against Caracul at Carun; (2.) that being dismissed by Fingal from his service, in consequence of his false report to Comala which occasioned her death, he returned to his father's halls at Balva, which he reached after three days' solitary travel from the camp at Crona; (3.) that "his name remained on the rocks of Cona," that is Glenco, in Oscar's day, who had "often seen the streams of his hills"—which facts, recorded in the text of the same poem and on the same page, are to be reconciled with the idea that Balva was a quiet stream in a sequestered vale of Stirlingshire. The absurdity of this self-contradiction is too obvious. It belongs not to forgery, but to the simplicity of error in attempting to explain by accidental coincidence what was otherwise inexplicable at the moment. An inventor would have omitted the passage, as of no use to him at all; and that MacPherson should have retained it in the circumstances to speak for itself, as it may hereafter do, was the clearest proof of his integrity.

5. And finally, he knows nothing of the Ardven of Stirlingshire, although he so translates the word—does not even attempt to recognise it, or to distinguish it in any way from the Ardven at Selma in Argyllshire; knows only that it was some "hill, within sight of Caracul's army." This indifference or obscurity in

an early translator, however, who still adhered conscientiously to his own rendering as correct, is perhaps the less astonishing, inasmuch as the most recent successor in the same field leaves the difficulty equally unexplained, or tries only to avoid it by occasionally superseding the terms. For Ardven and Morven in *Comala*, for example, Clerk substitutes here and there "the great mountains," "the great Bens," "the heathy height;" "for unquestionably," he says, "this is the true meaning, and the Gaelic gives not the slightest authority for confining Fingal's dominions to the district now known as Morven. Their only acknowledged boundaries were the 'great Bens.'" Whether MacPherson so understood it or not, there seems to be no advantage, and certainly no improvement, in thus abolishing the proper names; for all these Ardvens were local—may still be pointed out on the map, and would undoubtedly have been localised by MacPherson had he only known where to find them. Clerk does not, indeed, supersede them all. With respect to Morven, in particular, "I have retained it in some instances," he says, " both because I am unwilling to break up associations so firmly established as those connecting Fingal with the kingdom of Morven, and also because Morven is a much more manageable word in a line than the ' great mountains.' "—*Notes to Comala.* If this be true of Morven, the same may be said of Ardven; but in any case, Mr. Clerk was bound to use a little more vigilance before obliterating such important landmarks with a touch of his quill. In point of fact, had he observed more accurately the various contexts in which that name occurs, he would have found that, according to MacPherson, there are three Ardvens distinctly recognisable in Ossian. There may possibly be two Morvens also, as Mr. Clerk insists; but it is necessary to remark with precision, that MacPherson, as a translator, nowhere justifies the idea. One of the Ardvens was certainly in Morven proper, although it may be the least distinguishable of the three; another, we shall by and by find, is conspicuous in Arran; and the third, which has now to be identified, is in Stirlingshire. It would be strange, indeed, if any single mountain could be discovered in Morven, or anywhere else, in which the characteristics, much more the bearings of three separate hills so widely distant could be found together; and it is probably as much to this confusion of three prominent localities with one, or with one another, as to any other cause, that the difficulty of understanding, or even of believing Ossian, is to be attributed—a difficulty which Mr. Clerk's partial retranslation of terms is by no means sufficient to obviate. MacPherson's phraseology on the one hand, is far too explicit to be so easily set aside; and Clerk's theory, on the other, that Fingal's kingdom was co-extensive with the " great Bens" is not only untenable in fact, but at variance with every text in question. Fingal, as a king, was supreme only in his own territory of Morven. In his expeditions as an ally to Ireland, he passes through Arran as a friend; and in Stirlingshire he appears as generalissimo, with the same authority as Trenmor's, to lead the united Caledonian tribes to war—which being finished, they disperse. But in Stirlingshire we find an old independent prince, Carul, still jealous of his local dignity, and even in collision with Fingal; still called a king on Crona, and not afraid to contract alliances with the strangers, or South Britons, on his own responsibility—as the reader may learn by consulting the poems now under review. What the geographical limits of Morven proper itself might be, is not so easily determined; but that Selma, the capital, was fully three days' journey from the Carron, we have seen; and that it was eighteen hours' sail, at least, from the Orkneys, we shall hereafter see—so that its centre, somewhere on the Argyllshire coast, may be reasonably conjectured. It is with the geography of Stirlingshire, however, or of the region between the Forth and Clyde, as known to Ossian, we have now more particularly to do; and having thus completed our analysis of the text as regards the somewhat complicated scenes of *Comala*, *Colna-dona*, and the *War of Caros*, which are all to be found within the limits in question, we are in a position to identify these more easily by topographical survey, and to observe how distinctly every reference by Ossian to the landscape may be traced to its own peculiar feature of the field—river, rock, and ruin.

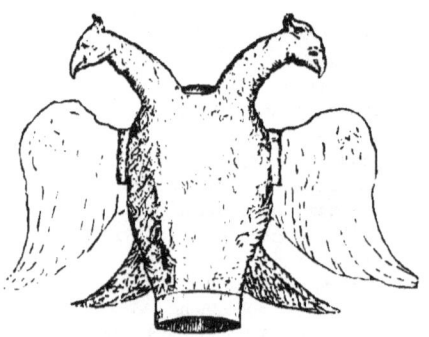

"The wings of their pride."
ROMAN EAGLE FOUND IN THE WALL.
(*Wings Restored.*)

## CHAPTER II.

**FINGAL AND HIS PEOPLE IN STIRLINGSHIRE (CONTINUED)—IDENTIFICATION OF LOCALITIES.**

I. In what has already been advanced, in the course of our analysis, on the long-unquestioned misapprehensions of the translator and consequent unbelief of the public, in relation to such an important region as the isthmus between the Forth and Clyde, a good many points of proof have of necessity been anticipated; but the identification of the localities in dispute or doubt must be more fully established, than by mere inferential evidence. The minutest details, in fact, as well as the general outline of the country must be attentively considered; and the first point of consequence to be determined, as the groundwork of much that has to follow, is the proximate level of the ocean at the date assumed.

1. By geological observations already submitted to the reader, the level of the Clyde at a comparatively recent period has been established as from 80 to 100 feet above its present low-water range. By the same evidence, the level of the Forth as a tidal frith—except on the supposition that the plane of the Island as from east to west has been altered, of which there is no proof—must be accepted as having been identical with that of the Clyde at a date corresponding. On this indisputable theory, when the Clyde was a fiord at Rutherglen, the Forth would be a fiord beyond Stirling in the Carse, and the Carron a minor fiord, or at least a navigable river, beyond Larbert or Dunipace; and that this was certainly the case within a known geological epoch, is determined by the discovery of marine deposits of recent type everywhere in the region—among which, the skeleton of a whale at Lecropt, disclosed many years ago; fragments of a similar skeleton, dug up in 1864 on the lands of Cornton between Stirling and the Bridge of Allan; thousands of oyster shells in sand and shingle almost annually laid bare, and glistening in the sunshine on the banks of that river after every flood, at Bridge of Allan itself, still within the tidal flow; and endless banks of sea sand and gravel from Falkirk to Borrowstoness eastward, and from Larbert to Stirling within sight of the railway northward—all now verdant with pasture —may be mentioned as proofs beyond cavil. The very names on the rivers bear testimony to the slow recession of the tide. Stirling-*shore* on the Forth, where it still flows deep near the town; and Carron-*shore* on the Carron, where an old anchor has just been disinterred—compare notice in Appendix—are witnesses in our own language that the sea has been recently there, where crops now flourish;

and the discovery of a canoe deep-sunk on the banks of the Carron, corresponding in many respects to those discovered recently on the Clyde at Erskine, demonstrates that the navigation of that river as a fiord, not in the stream only, but in tidal water on the banks of it, was familiar to our ancestors at a date when the fabrication of such vessels was possible. It is amusing to reflect that this latter piece of evidence comes directly from the hands of Mr. Pinkerton, who is so blinded by his own prepossessions as not to see the bearing of it. He thus describes that interesting relique, and endeavours to account for its origin—" In the year 1726, under several strata of earths and fossils, was found in the bank of the Carron a large boat, 36 feet long and 4½ broad; made of one entire piece of oak, and well polished both within and without. From the number of strata, Sir John Clerk thought it an antediluvian boat; but that jest apart, these strata certainly show it very old; and it is most probable," he adds with characteristic prejudice, "that it was Pikish, because found in the country of the Piks."— *History of Scotland*, Vol. I., p. 275. Very old, of course, it must have been, though not of necessity so old as Mr. Pinkerton imagines. But whatever its age might be, if our Pictish ancestors on the eastern coast could construct such a vessel at any date before the era of modern civilisation, why should not their fellow-countrymen on the western coast, who depended almost entirely on ships for locomotion, have been able to construct others similar, at the same date? MacPherson seems to have known nothing of this canoe, yet according to his translation, ships innumerable of the sort were navigating the western waters at the commencement of the Christian era; and the first ship of the kind among the Bolgae, as we have seen, was built, or rather scooped and rigged in the Solway, about 250 years before that. Such evidence of Celtic progress, however, was inadmissible by Mr. Pinkerton, who had pronounced Ossian a fable and MacPherson an impostor; yet the canoe was there, an indisputable reality on the banks of the Carron, and it is just possible that the Romans themselves might have been the temporary possessors of such a craft, for the transport of stores and cavalry at the reparation of the Wall by Carausius; nay, that the very canoe in question was thus employed at the War of Caros, and stranded there in the flight of the invaders, or by the storm that drove them "rolling" up the frith.

2. But the most conclusive proofs as to date for the levels of the sea at that time, on opposite sides of the Island, have yet to be quoted, as under—

(1.) Scotland beyond the friths is described by Beda, even in his own day, as a sort of separate island, and its inhabitants as transmarine in the days of the Romans, "not because they were out of Britain, but because they were distant from the possessions of the Britons, two arms of the sea being interjacent"—a sort of figure that could not have been employed with the slightest propriety by any historian in recent centuries; and that it was not altogether a figure, what immediately follows will prove—for (2.) a gap occurs in the Roman Wall, or rather between two stations on the Wall—Simmerton and Balmulzie, on the Kelvin; where a lake or marsh of nearly a mile broad, through which that river must have flowed, remains unoccupied—either because it was impossible to build in it, or because such a precaution, from the depth of the water, was unnecessary. At which point also, to a magnificent fortification on the east side, characterised by Gordon in his *Itinerarium* as a city, situated on the Balmulzie ridge overlooking and commanding the marsh, water was conveyed under ground in stone conduits from the Kelvin; which could not have been the case, if the surface level of the river had been nearly as low as it now is. The conduits in question are described by Gordon, as familiarly known to the people of the district in his day—*circa*, 1726. (3.) That a similar gap, not in the Wall, but in the Roman Road already described, from the Wall at Rough-Castle by Camelon to Stirling, occurs on the Carron at Larbert. The road approached the Carron there at a frightful precipice, but must have reached the water edge by a slope; at the foot of which, in 1773, the foundation stones of some pier or harbour were dug out of the river. It re-appears again on a rising ground near Larbert House, about a quarter of a mile to the north-west, from which it passes on to Stirling in a line which was then probably on the verge of the frith, although now several miles inland; and finally crosses the Forth at Drip, which must have been the nearest available route for such a communication by land into Perthshire. Larbert, therefore, would then be a tidal harbour, and much of the intervening ground between the Carron and the Roman Wall would be a tidal marsh. (4.) And finally, a little below Larbert, as we learn from Nimmo,

"The track of the old bed" of the river, "is still visible. The high and circling banks upon the south side give to this valley the appearance of a spacious bay; and as tradition goes, there was once a harbour here. Nor does the tradition appear altogether groundless: pieces of broken anchors have been found there in the memory of people yet alive [1777], and the stream tides would still flow near the place, if they were not kept back by the great damhead built across the river at Stenhouse. There is reason, too, to believe that the frith flowed considerably higher in former ages than it does at present; so that there is no improbability in supposing that, at least, small craft might have advanced thus far."—*History of Stirlingshire*, Vol. I., p. 74.

The above facts in such striking coincidence with the text of the poems now under consideration, as other facts in similar cases have also been, were entirely unknown to the present writer when his analysis of the text was made, and are not less surprising to himself than they must be to the reader. By their quotation, however, which could no longer be delayed, the reader is now in circumstances to understand distinctly how Caros should have been moored in the Carron, and how a challenge could be sent to him from the south side of that river "to leave the rolling of his wave" and advance; and that this was his position in reality, the day before his defeat, shall in due time be established.

The dates now quoted, the reader must observe, are from the commencement of the Christian era to the end of the third century at least—that is, from the days of Trenmor to the death of Ossian; and include every other date for Scotland, Ireland, and Norway, implied in the course of his poetic narratives. The date of tradition for the harbour in Carron is indeed much later, if proof of later high-levels in the Frith of Forth were required. Our investigations, however, extend only to what can be proved as geologically certain in the third century, and we have clear enough evidence for that period without relying on tradition; but tradition supported by discoveries so distinct, on the very spot, or within a mile of it, to which the text refers, corroborates our theory and includes all.

3. When the Clyde, then, was a fiord at Rutherglen, there would be, on the west side of the Island in the first place, by the most accurate measurement now possible, from 10 to 20 feet of clear water in the Colamon, *Colambain*, or Kelvin, at Maryhill, and a tidal flow beyond that for several miles inland. When there was a marsh or lake at Balmulzie bridge, deep enough and broad enough to interrupt or supersede the Roman Wall, and divert its course for more than a mile, and from which water might be drawn in conduits to a station on the neighbouring ridge, there would be level water, with lakes and marshes intervening, to Kilsyth; and if Carul then lived in that neighbourhood, as we shall immediately show, he had free navigation from the heart of Stirlingshire, through troubled waters in the first instance, but afterwards by a deep and beautiful, though tortuous fiord, "through distant vales," to the open frith—a geographical possibility undreamt of by MacPherson, but as certain as the flowing of the tide. Through all this region, the Col-amon is expressly described by Ossian as a "dark wanderer"—that is, winding with a dark or invisible stream through marshy meadows and shallow lakes, in which its current was lost or flowed imperceptibly; and that the Kelvin was, and must have been such a river at the date in question, the names along its lower banks—the Garscubes, the Garbraids, and Garriochs, still indicate; and the remains of lakes, and marshes or bogs everywhere discernible, both by name and by appearance, through its entire upper course, to beyond Kirkintilloch, incontestibly prove. If any support of an interpretation so natural should be required, it may be enough to state that what MacPherson renders "dark" Clerk translates "blind," with as little knowledge as MacPherson that the epithet was intended for the Kelvin—than which, however, no other could be more appropriate for the course, and very aspect, of that river in its

upper reaches. "It is conjectured," says the Editor of Nimmo, "that the whole vale of Kelvin was anciently a morass, impassable even in boats;" and at a certain intermediate date, it was undoubtedly so, although not in the days of Carul; who had sufficient water to float him, or who knew better how to thread his way through its "blind, dark wanderings."

The higher we now ascend, the clearer its identification becomes. The Colamon, at first, according to the poet, was a stream of "troubled waters" with its "course between trees," near a fortress of the same name—the residence of that very Carul who navigated the Clyde, and of his daughter Colna-dona. But the Kelvin also, where it leaves the Bonny Water, must have dashed furiously through a deep and densely-wooded ravine till near the beginning of the present century, when its waters were accumulated in a reservoir to maintain the canal; above which reservoir, however, it still retains its character of a torrent; and at the western extremity of which, on the brink of a neighbouring ravine and tributary, shrouded in the last remains of an ancient forest, are or were the ruins of old Castle Colzam—represented still by Colzium House, the residence of one of the oldest and most distinguished families in the county. The existence of such a castle, indeed, although matter of geographical certainty, had been well nigh lost sight of in the neighbourhood, till the waterspout of 1865 removed the accumulated artificial soil, and disclosed it to the foundation. Its whereabouts, therefore, on the north bank of the Kelvin near its source, can no longer be a matter of dubiety; but by the mere quotation of such names in connection with that river at its source, their identity with those in Ossian becomes apparent. Colzium, or Colzam, as it stands written in our oldest atlases, requires only to be read or pronounced to be accepted at once for Colamon, being, in fact, the two first syllables of that word, abbreviated by those who received it only from tradition; and Col-amhain itself—that is, either the stream of Colam, or the stream of the narrow glen—softened and contracted as in such cases was invariable, becomes Col-amon or Col-avon, as the speech of the people inclined; which by one step farther in the same process of softening by lowland tongues becomes Colvain or Kelvin—the river of the region to this day; narrowest at its rise, and widest or blindest in its original course, of all in the district. It seems strange that two such authorities as Clerk and MacPherson, in their derivation of this word, about the sound of which there can be no dispute, should both omit the intermediate syllable *am*, retained in Colzam but dropt in Kelvin, by immemorial use and wont of the people. There must have been some reason for this—why the first and second syllables of the written word should have been kept for the *place*, and the first and third for the *river*—which one or other of these distinguished translators, had either of them known to what place and river the name applied, would certainly have endeavoured to explain. A sufficient account of the matter, we hope, may by and by be suggested, in which all the syllables alike shall have their own significance; but the particulars of such derivation must be reserved for our Glossary in the Appendix.

A coincidence so remarkable throughout, of localities and names, and with an alphabetical minuteness so surprising, where everything else corresponds, would alone be sufficient to determine the identity now required; and how MacPherson should have overlooked it, or how Clerk should not have observed it, is unaccountable on any other supposition than that of the fundamental error, committed by the one and followed by the other, of looking southwards instead of northwards, and so inverting the whole scene. "Col-amon," says MacPherson, with the utmost simplicity—and Clerk nowhere contradicts him—"was in the neighbourhood of Agricola's Wall towards the south;" where, however, he does not attempt to identify it—where, indeed, there was nothing to correspond; and whilst he is thus idly surveying the country from Castlecary to the Clyde on the south, both Colzium or Colzam and the Kelvin, which were really "in the neighbourhood of Agricola's Wall" to the north, escape his observation, and are excluded from his geography as completely as if they had never existed.

II. An outflow for the water-shed of the isthmus between the Forth and the Clyde westward, contemporaneous with the building of the Roman Wall, being thus established in the Kelvin; and that river itself, both in character and name, having been identified with the Col-amon—an outflow to the eastward, and its identification with the Crona, remains now to be proved; and then all the essential difficulties of the problem, by which a key to the history of Scotland at the commencement of the Christian era may be furnished, shall have been solved. About the mere geography of the problem, fortunately, there can be no doubt; and about the accuracy of Ossian, in every syllable of his own regarding it, as the reader will very soon see, there is triumphant certainty.

1. Dullator Bog—in which many of the cavalry of the Covenanters under Baillie, in their flight from the battle of Kilsyth, 1645, were engulphed; but which has since been drained, partly by the passage of the canal and partly by trenches hereafter to be described—at a level of 160 feet above the Forth, represents the top level of the opposite friths when they actually met, and when Scotland beyond was literally an island. This must have been long before the invasion of the Romans, however, as their works beyond the Carron show. But the valley through which the eastern frith receded from that level is still open and distinct, shorter and compacter than the valley of the Kelvin; and through this valley the Crona, of necessity, towards the adjacent valley of the Carron—and thence, towards the sea—as the text of Ossian explicitly informs us, must

have flowed. There can be no doubt, therefore, either about the water-shed of the isthmus through this channel, or about the modern representative of that celebrated stream: yet strange to say, MacPherson knows nothing of it, and the only man who names it at a venture, Nimmo in his *History of Stirlingshire*, draws back from his assertion as if it were a dangerous liberty of thought. "Here about, too," says he, "we are directed to look for the stream of Crona, so much celebrated in the ancient compositions of the Gaelic Bard; but we find ourselves now treading upon very uncertain ground, and know not where to find that stream, if it was not the Water of Bonny, which runs in the near neighbourhood of the Roman Wall, and discharges itself into the Carron opposite to Dunipace," &c.—Vol. I., p. 79. The cause of this uncertainty on his part, and of MacPherson's obscurity alike, was MacPherson's own blunder about the position of Caros behind his "gathered heap." That entrenchment, as we have seen, according to Ossian in the text, was at Larbert beyond the Carron to the north; according to MacPherson in his note, it was at Rough-Castle or Castlecary, beyond the Wall to the south; and thus the geography of the whole region was inverted. According to MacPherson, the Crona must then be sought for at Bannockburn or nowhere, and the text of Ossian in the *War of Caros* becomes inexplicable— even more inexplicable than in *Fingal* and *Temora*, as it hitherto confessedly has been. To accept the Crona for what it is, the Bonny Water; and to put Caros where he must have been, at Larbert, restores not only harmony and sense, but geographical and historical truth to every word of the poems in question.

Thus—(1.) The Col-amon flows westward, as we have seen, for many miles, through distant devious vales, till it joins the Clyde, precisely as the Kelvin does; whereas the Crona flows eastward till it joins the Carun at the distance of only a few miles, as the Bonny Water, flowing towards the Carron, does. (2.) The Crona was thus to Oscar's rear, when his front was to Caros on the Carun; so would the Bonny Water be, if the campaign were fought again to-morrow on the same ground. (3.) Fingal and Oscar alike return up the valley of the Crona from the banks of the Carun to near the head of the Col-amon in a few hours, on the evening respectively of two different days; but the highway from Denny to Kilsyth at the present moment is, and from time immemorial has been by the Bonny Water valley, and from Carron banks to the Kelvin head, is but an evening's walk. (4.) The Crona rises somewhere in close proximity to the Col-amon —insomuch that the reader, whilst tracing either of them up to its source, comes unexpectedly and mysteriously on the other, flowing in an opposite direction; but the Bonny Water and the Kelvin do, in fact, spring from the same source, and flow together in one stream for more than two miles to the point of their separation north-east of Kilsyth. This circumstance alone, indeed, would be sufficient to identify the rivers, for they are the only streams in all that region, if not in all Scotland, so strangely related. Their point of separation, moreover, is on the mountain's verge, as incidentally specified in *Temora*. " On Crona, said the bards, there bursts a stream by night. It swells in its own dark course, till morning's early beam. Then comes it white from the hill with the rocks and their hundred groves. Far be my steps from Crona: death is tumbling there." B. III. In this remarkable distant allusion, made on the coast of Ireland, the features of the scene at Colzium or at Banton are as accurately described, as if Ossian had been standing on the spot. The name of one of the twin-born rivers, indeed, is transferred by a figure of speech common enough in poetry, but quite unperceived by MacPherson, to the mountain from which they both spring—as elsewhere, unperceived also, the combination of Col-glan-Crona is employed to designate the valley; but their united course on its ridge, to the point where sunshine first catches them, could not have been more accurately represented; and whoever has seen the Kelvin in flood, when it separates from its sister-current and dashes down its precipice to the west, or who can imagine what it must have been before its waters were absorbed in the reservoir at Colzam, will be able not only to identify the ground, but to determine almost the spot from which Ossian surveyed it—for proof of which, we refer to the Appendix.

2. In tracing these rivers, however, the reader must observe that what is now called the source of the Kelvin is but a trench, draining off westward half the water from the entire original bog; and in like manner, that the source of the Bonny is a corresponding trench draining the other and more important half eastward, each into the proper channel of the respective streams; which have still the common source above referred to, parting right and left from a single fountain, much higher up the hill—the whole marsh thus drained having in a great measure been created by their natural accumulation, time immemorial, in the hollow. These trenches, through their entire extent, run parallel with the canal, and have been cut also from a common summit almost imperceptible, called Kelvin-head, which is marked by a post in the ground nearly due south in the valley from the true source on the hill; so that by a curious coincidence, the points of departure both high and low for these historical rivers correspond; and the watersheds of Scotland, both natural and artificial, on this its most remarkable isthmus and "laighest neck," are in one and the same straight line sweeping down from the hill at right angles or thereby to all the great tracks of communication that have ever existed—Wall, Canal, and Railway—between the opposite friths. It is still farther to be observed that the Kelvin, after being arrested in the gorge at Colzium to assist in creating a reservoir there, has suffered yet greater violence in being checked and diverted at a lower level, to become a feeder to the canal,

so that probably not a tenth part of its original current ever reaches its original channel, except after heavy floods or when discharged again at distant openings from sluices in the canal. In like manner, also, the Bonny Water, for economical purposes, has been conducted, as we shall see, first to a mill pond at Orchard, and then behind a long dyke of earth to some tank at a distillery near Wyndford, fully ten feet above its natural course in the marsh, but is ultimately restored again to its channel without any loss, and reaches the Carron nearly as full as it could ever be, according to the season, although not so broad. These relations will be more easily understood by a glance at the accompanying map, and the reader will then perceive that Ossian's route from the west till within sight of Colzam on the Kelvin, would be first along the north bank of the river-marsh as represented, and then by the brink of the gorge where the reservoir now surges; but where a false step then, for himself or for his retinue, might have been fatal. That he was made fully alive to this danger on his first visit, when he had still to inquire his way, with shield-bearers and bards before him; and that it was vividly impressed on his mind by some occurrence at the moment, is obvious from the sort of allusion he afterwards makes to it in *Temora*, as already quoted—and where, as if still shrinking from the recollection of it as recalled by the bards, he says, with expressive horror—" Far be my foot from Crona: death is tumbling there!" Even to-day, on the comparatively broad and well made road which skirts the reservoir on the south along the verge of the precipice, although sufficiently romantic, it requires caution to walk; and at many points, in mist or darkness, a slight deviation might be attended with much risk. On the opposite side, however, where Carul's residence of Colzam was situated, and along which the heralds would proceed with Carul's invitation to the " Hall of harps" for Ossian and his friend; and by which Colna-dona herself, next morning, encountered them at the chase, there could never be any serious danger, by night or day. There was, indeed, a similar risk to be encountered, a little farther to the east, almost if not quite so imminent; to which allusion might also be implied, as we shall hereafter find; but all this, as a matter of course, Ossian himself would ascertain by degrees. As a stranger at first, in the poem of *Colna-dona*, he appears in ignorance of the fact, and seems to have acquired the knowledge of it, in some way, at the hazard of his life: which danger, however, being for the present surmounted or escaped, his route would then be, by a few steps forward, on the Crona itself—either eastward, as we are inclined to believe, towards the accustomed rendezvous, called afterwards Tomfin, and so directly down; or southwards at first in a slanting direction, along the brink of the river still flowing in a marsh, to where " Fingal had scattered his foes," and where " their blood hung curdled in its ooze." Any other passage for him

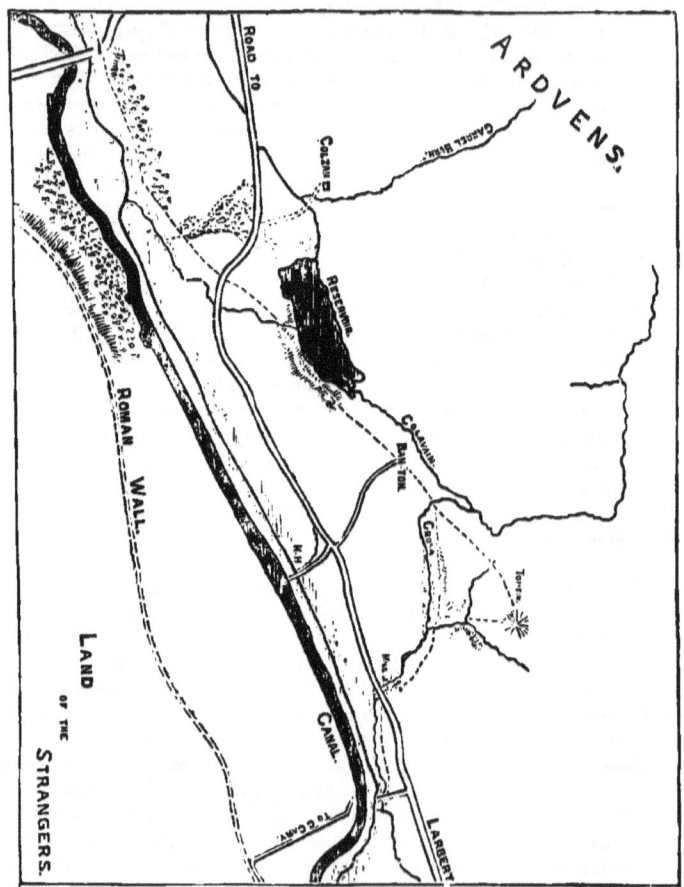

on foot than this by the valley of the Kelvin, as the reader must perceive, would be impossible, for the whole intermediate ground, now drained and cultivated, was then an impracticable marsh. But in corroboration of these particulars, and of many others most intimately connected with the region, we have so much interesting evidence to adduce from actual observation, that it must be reserved for a separate chapter. The whole of what has now been submitted to the reader, indeed, both in the present and in the preceding chapter, when fairly written out, seemed to the writer himself not only in such plain conformity with the text of Ossian, but in such obvious harmony with the details of all atlases ancient and modern, that he resolved to visit and survey the region for his own satisfaction—to test all assumed bearings, and to reconnoitre all supposed localities; to sight the hills, and trace the streams; but above all, to seek for the stone which Ossian had erected, and for the rock where Comala died, being confident he could lay his finger on them if they still existed there. No suitable opportunity, however, for such an elaborate survey occurred until the autumn of last year, being more than twelve months after his manuscript was finished— a delay which he does not now regret; inasmuch as the evidence obtained was made clearer. In the beginning of August, 1873, accordingly, he began these short exploratory tours, accompanied by friends, to assist and verify his observations. Their first excursion, August 6th, included a general survey of the Kilsyth hills, from near Nether Croy by the banks of the canal to the reservoir at Colzium, and by Banton to Tomfin; thence returning, by the mineral railroad to the canal at what is called Kelvin-head, and so along by the marsh to Wyndford; in which comparatively brief walk, notwithstanding all the surface changes already described, the writer had the satisfaction of tracing, as he believed, so clearly the footsteps of Ossian and his people, from the head of the Col-amon, and by the banks of the Crona on its lowest level, to where two grey stones appeared at the point where Fingal must have scattered his foes— that the search became too fascinating by far to be left imperfect, and its results promised to be too important to be neglected or concealed. It seemed all so like a dream, in fact—among coal-pits, railroads, and canals; yet in such veritable accordance with the letter of a book read and interpreted long months before, that nothing short of the most definite assurance in the matter could satisfy his curiosity. Ossian himself seemed to rise at every footstep, and to beckon him to come on and see. Another expedition was therefore resolved upon, the details of which shall now be recorded, with as near an approach to journalistic precision as the character of the present work will allow; by which, it is hoped, the nature and importance of the discoveries effected will be better realised, than by a mere general summary or outline.

2 D

## CHAPTER III.

### FINGAL AND HIS PEOPLE IN STIRLINGSHIRE (CONTINUED)—EXPLORATIONS FROM KILSYTH TO THE CARRON.

I. It was by the oozy brink of the Crona, then, where it sunk into the marshy vale, that Ossian in company with his friend Toscar, on the expedition already described and still alluded to, raised a stone to commemorate his father's victory and "bade it speak to other years;" and it was by a rock on the same Crona, but a little farther up and above the ooze, where the stream was still a torrent, and near another rock on which fire might be kindled, and therefore presumably low and flat, within sight of Fingal's rendezvous on the one hand and still within sight of the Roman Wall, or of the valley between, on the other, that Comala, many years before, had died of apprehension and grief: which events being thus associated with that river, and fixed respectively at given points on its course by the letter of the text, it was the present writer's object, guided solely by his reading of the text, to ascertain whether the rude monuments commemorating such events, or connected with them according to the text, had a corresponding existence in nature.

1. To reach the assigned localities he was bound, as a matter of course, to adopt the Bard's own route, as far as it might now be practicable and as he himself understood it; and therefore on this second excursion, August 20th, with the text religiously before him—instead of following the canal as on the former occasion, he crossed both the canal and the Kelvin, at Auchensterrie bridge on the road to Kilsyth; and, turning immediately to the right, crossed the mineral railway track adjoining also, where he found, as was anxiously hoped for, a country road—more like an avenue, indeed, than a road—leading eastward by the river, but partially barred against public traffic, with a sculptured intimation on the barricade, that it was a "Private Road to Colzium." Nothing could have been more appropriate there, for it was in fact a royal road, and might have been as correctly described as Ossian's Road to Colzam—so exactly must the whole of that well-made track lie over the very footsteps of the poet. Except, indeed, where some slight cutting has been made to ease the ascent, or to shorten a turn where the subsidence of the water now permits it, this private road to Colzium must be almost the precise line—accidentally resumed, or unconsciously maintained by use and wont—on which Ossian at the age of 17 first travelled to Col-

amon, with a retinue of bards and shield-bearers, to commemorate his father's victory on Crona. The rock at Auchensterrie, under whose overhanging cliffs he passed, has indeed been quarried, and the hill-side beyond has been rifled for mineral ores; the old oak woods, also, have long ago been felled, except where a solitary tree still attests their former growth, and the ridge has been partially cleared, or converted into run-rig for cotters; but the young coppice sprung from its ancient root, overhangs the traveller as he journeys on, the brook from its recesses brawls under his feet, and the rugged crags, yet untouched by cultivation, project at every turn to remind him of its original condition. This on his left, and over his head, going eastward. On his right, and at the distance of some 500 paces to the south, rise the woods of Nether Croy from loftier rocks, larger also and leafier for the hour—screening the range of old Roman earthworks on the height, to which Ossian in filial triumph might look over; and between these wooded margins, once clothed with forest stems worth speaking of, lies the marsh now drained and cultivated, but as distinctly defined as it ever was, with the canal on its farther side absorbing part of it, and the Kelvin degraded to a trench, darker and sadder than ever, still flowing in its bosom—all less changed by far, than it might have been by the slightest touch of an earthquake, such as we have described at Drumadoon; and all, in its essential features, as Ossian might have seen it, and as a single winter's flood, or a breach in the canal, or the bursting of the reservoir, in a few hours' time would make it again. The canal not being visible in fact, and the quarry with its adjuncts lost sight of behind, the scene but for modern cultivation, and hayricks standing where old Carul's canoes once swam, is almost yet what it must then have been; and when the present woods shall have attained maturity, if the Kelvin was luckily in flood, the reader might traverse this road and quote Ossian's words to the river, without the slightest effort of imagination to assure him that they were really once spoken there—nay, in all the circumstances of the case, looking westward to the Clyde to which it flows, it would be more difficult for him not to quote them, than to doubt the quotation when made—" Col-amon of troubled streams, dark wanderer of distant vales, I behold thy course between trees, near Carul's echoing halls." Even now, he may follow this track to the highway eastward, and so to the reservoir or to Colzium House itself, where Carul's halls once stood, as certain that he follows the footsteps of Ossian, or walks within sight of them at least, as if the poet and his retinue were still hovering like shadows on the path, or flitting in the woods before him. At one point only he might hesitate for a moment—where the empty channel of an old tributary to the Kelvin has been converted into a splendid avenue, the tributary having been drawn off towards the north; but Ossian himself might have hesitated there too, when it was a torrent and not an avenue, not knowing precisely whether it was tributary or stream. He might hesitate and follow it, wisely enough, for it would lead him to the same destination; or he might cross it and go on, which Ossian probably did, for the flood in the marsh "between trees" was still to guide him, and he walked "beneath the voice of the king." Onwards and upwards, then, the procession would move, till Col-amon was sighted; and Carul's scouts, on the verge of the ravine, would report his arrival to their aged chieftain. This route, so natural and obvious to-day as the most beautiful approach to Colzium, and in a certain sense exclusive, was sketched and mapped from the text alone as Ossian's road, the reader must again be reminded, and was ready for representation as on the accompanying page, before a step of the present survey had been taken.

2. At Colzium or Colzam, on the afternoon of Ossian's arrival, there was no delay, although his passage to the eastward was known. Following his footsteps, therefore, and leaving Colzium on the left behind, we pursue our journey. He walks on the cliffs before us, and higher than we now can reach; our path lies by the brink of the reservoir, on a well made road, half down the cliffs, the reservoir itself being from 35 to 40 feet deep below us. But we learn from his own words, as we journey on, that in passing down the stream of the Crona from its source—of which we yet know nothing, having formerly only crossed it and made a circuit by the line of railway from Banton to the canal—it should be found "swelling" first "in its own dark course," and shortly after lost among accumulated rocks; and that at a given point on its eastern bank, from which the first view of the valley towards Castlecary in front could be had, and the last view of Tomfin in the rear, there should be found one large flat rock on the ridge, like a forest-hearth, on which fire could be kindled; and most probably also in close proximity, if the rock itself in question did not bound the stream, another rock or rocks on the same side overhanging the stream, in shelter of which a belated traveller might recline, or a stranger looking anxiously towards the valley might take up a position. By these rocks—by the hearth-stone or table-rock in particular, on its eastern bank—if not removed by violence, not only might the river be identified, but the very spot where Comala died might also be ascertained; passing beyond which through some dangerous gorge, the stream should then flow into the valley and be lost for a while like the Kelvin, in the oozy marsh of the isthmus; from which it should again re-appear, and be distinctly traceable as the Bonny Water.

II. Such explanations—founded on the express letter of the text in *Temora*, in *Colna-dona*, and in *Comala*—having then, as now, been made, long before the place could be seen or its present character imagined, were all minutely verified on nearer approach. 1. For about half a mile or more from its source, the river had originally flowed through marshes, which have since been converted by drainage into summer meadows; in threading its way through which it was yet almost imperceptible, and immediately after escaping from which it began to be involved among rocks or huge solitary boulders—its entire eastern bank, not long ago a heath, being crowded with them. It had then been conducted by force among splintered fragments of these to a mill-pond, and thence, by the usual artificial means to a mill-wheel, near the mansion house of Orchard; but precisely at the point where its natural course was resumed, and partially occupied by overflow from the sluices, the remains of an old quarried whinstone rock, which when entire must have overhung its eastern side, were discernible; and about a hundred paces southward on the same side, on the summit of the slope, and at a point where the valley towards Castlecary was first disclosed in front and where Tomfin was still visible in rear, with an Ardven itself in the background as it should be, the TABLE ROCK untouched, deep and solid on the heathy ridge, appeared—on which a fire might well be kindled that should roast three deer and be a beacon besides in the darkness, and where the anxious friends of warriors doing battle in the vale would most naturally and certainly expect them. A discovery like this, so precise and perfect, on the banks of the river and at the spot in question, had it not been made in express submission to the "voice of the king's" son, and by following his footsteps, might have seemed a mere trick of the soil to impose upon enthusiasts; but being so made, and at a distance of more than sixteen centuries since he himself stood there, it seemed little less than miraculous in support of his disputed authenticity.

2. The rock thus strangely, yet so easily and certainly identified, projects considerably above the surface, on which the grass, however, by cultivation, has increased. When the soil was a heath, as Ossian represents it, and as it must very recently have been—if not also partially covered with brushwood—the rock might be fully two feet above the level, at its highest part; but even now, as it emerges, with verdure interwoven in its seams, it measures 18 feet by 9, and on its upper face, sloping slightly to the sun, is as smooth as a hearthstone. On this slope the fire would ascend, and by the slope itself the light of the fire would be more distinctly projected on the valley. The banks of the river on both sides, immediately adjoining, have been lined with corresponding blocks, part of the underlying dyke. Many of these have doubtless been removed, in the progress of improvement; but others, jammed together in the water-way, still almost obstruct its course, which in consequence is absolutely impassable but by dangerous climbing, until the site of the old quarry has again been reached going upwards. There, the stream has been delayed in a marsh

before plunging through the crevices beneath; and these, when the banks were in their natural condition, steep and rugged, must have been the bottom of a precipitous ravine, where "death," when the Crona was in flood, might be "tumbling," as well as in the gorge at Colzam. There, then, "Comala sits forlorn!" watching among the rocks. "She turns her blue-rolling eyes towards the field of his promise. Where art thou, O Fingal, for the night is gathering around?" There, on the rocky hearth, her feast for him is preparing—"Comala has slain three deer on Ardven, and the fire ascends on the rock: go to the feast of Comala, king of the woody Morven!" Yonder comes Fingal, or Fingal's ghost in his steel, from the slaughter of his foes, himself supposed to be fallen. "It is Fingal in the crowd of his ghosts! why dost thou come, my love, to frighten and to please my soul?" "Look from thy rocks, my love," cries he; "and let me hear the voice of Comala." But there below the rock she dies, of terror and apprehension. "Descend ye light mists from high; ye moonbeams, lift her soul! Pale lies the maid at the rock! Comala is no more!"

3. Had this been all discovered, we must again repeat, before the text was read, and had the reading of the text but followed in reasonable conformity, the coincidence would have been astonishing, if not absolutely convincing. But when the text itself rightly read was the only guide, and by the truthfulness of its letter alone took the reader to the spot—where every syllable and reference was verified by the surviving features of the soil; and would yet more fully have been verified, if these in the meantime had not been touched—what more, in the way of evidence or illustration, could be imagined or desired? Yet much more was implied here, than the reader at first may apprehend. The melancholy mischance described occurred at least eighteen months before Ossian was born, and it was in his 17th year he first visited the neighbourhood—that is, nearly twenty years from the date of Comala's death. But it is impossible he could have described it with such minute topographical accuracy, and with such truthful pictorial reference to the general aspects of the scene, had he not actually surveyed the ground. The story of his father's grief, the rumour of Hidallan's perfidy, and his own poetical instinct combined would naturally lead him to the place with which such a tragedy was connected; and thus upon his earliest expedition to the Crona, and following the windings of its marshy stream till they issued among rocks, as he had been told to do, he would pause on his errand where the princess died, before he descended farther towards the vale. There were two or more opportunities, indeed, for such homage; for the visit we thus imagine might occur either on the afternoon of the first, or on the morning of the third day, when he and Toscar "hung forward on the path of the roes," or on both; and the terms employed, descriptive of the scene, are in strict con-

formity with the supposition that he had more than once reconnoitred the field. He saw it beyond doubt, both where the river was swelling "in its own dark course, till morning's early beam," and also where it came "white from the hill, with the rocks and their hundred groves"—words which, if possible, are more applicable to the upper marshes of the Bonny Water than to those of the Kelvin; where the stream above the mill-pond at Orchard would swell, and may still swell, in prolonged obscurity, and where overhanging precipices of rock with the scanty remnants of "their hundred groves" at Tomfin, among pasture lands and boggy hay-fields, still signalise the region. Besides, as Crona was a name applied equally to the river and to that part of the range from which it flowed, it is possible that the words so descriptive of hidden danger may have applied equally also to both rivers, sprung so strangely from the same source on its verge, and characterised alike by their sudden descent southward—that is, towards "the morning's beam"—through latent ravines or precipitous chinks; which, before the hand of modern science, in the construction of reservoirs and mill-ponds, reached them, must have been ominous, if not dangerous enough. Certain at all events it is, that it was along the rocky ridge between Banton and Tomfin, still at many points inaccessible to culture, above the upper marshes of the Bonny Water, that Ossian and Toscar from Col-amon "with morning awoke the woods, and hung forward on the path of the roes," when Colna-dona in disguise encountered them. Certain also it might be shown to be, although it is not now of this we are inquiring, that it was on the same ridge Comala herself, with her attendant maids and the two grey dogs, pursued the chase, and drove her quarry to bay, or pierced them in their downward flight, at the very stone where the fire was kindled; for there, precisely there, when "the chase was over; no noise on Ardven but the torrent's roar"—Comala sat forlorn. "Two grey dogs near shake their rough ears, and catch the flying breeze. Her red cheek [as if flushed with recent exertion] rests on her arm, and the mountain wind is in her hair. She turns her blue-rolling eyes towards the field of his promise [that is, towards the vale by Castlecary and the Carron, through which Fingal should return.] Where art thou, O Fingal, for the night is gathering around?" Then "ascends the fire on the rock," which must therefore have been near, in preparation for the feast, and as a beacon to guide him to the spot. All this is plain; but with respect to Ossian and Toscar it is equally plain, that either in their morning's chase over the same ground, or the afternoon before on their solemn errand, or on both occasions, they might visit Comala's rock together, to mark the scene with all its surroundings, and silently, on Ossian's part at least, to propitiate her ghost with the poet's vow of immortality. If they saw it also by moonlight, in returning from their work of commemoration on the evening of the first day—which they might easily do, for they were occupied till night-fall—the whole aspect of the place, as then presented, would be precisely as it was when Comala died—when "meteors rolled around the maid, and moonbeams lifted her soul." Here, then, by this identical rock—

COMALA'S ROCK ON THE CRONA

and inspired by such associations, Ossian himself must have stood—grander in every circumstance than Byron at Loch-na-gar; for Byron wanted both the love and the simplicity as well as the surroundings and antagonists of Ossian, the very kings of the world themselves being in discomfiture before the son of Fingal. Here he must have stood, looking eastward and downward across the oozy plain to Castlecary, whither the Romans in retreat had fled; and down the ridge, with bards and shield-bearers before him, he would stride to the scene of victory. Following his footsteps, therefore, as far as highways and modern enclosures will permit us, till we strike the line of the marsh below, and keeping the object of his errand attentively in view, we come without difficulty or much deviation, by a few minutes' walk, to where the two grey stones already specified are found, by the brink of the bog at Wyndford, and where the Bonny Water again re-appears.

4. Confident enough that the reader now accompanies us so far, we proceed more attentively to inspect these reliques. They remain right and left on opposite sides of the road from the highway to the canal at the point now named— the road itself, by a strange coincidence, having been cut equally through between, without touching them. The stone to the east, with pyramidal point, seems to be much smaller than the other, but is deeply imbedded in the soil; which, as Ossian describes, has been literally "raised" around it. That to the west, which measures fully 8 feet long by 3½ feet broad and thick, is a sort of oblong column, cylindrical through waste at the top; and has fallen, when the bank on which it stood by the brink of the marsh was cut away to make a dyke for the water. The water itself, no longer in the marsh, flows a few feet in front of them both behind a hedge, in its present artificial course, to the Ban-

kier distillery eastward. It was underneath this large stone presumably, which is more like a monument than the other, that Ossian " placed at intervals three bosses from the shields of foes," and " Toscar laid a dagger in earth, a mail of sounding steel;" but if any remnants of these warlike deposits survived at the date of its fall, they would probably be thrown aside at the moment, or lost in the dyke as rubbish. It is very unlikely, however, that any fragments of rude iron, much more bosses from a shield or shields of hide, would remain recognisable for more than 1640 years in such a situation, and in constant contact, as they must have been, with stagnate water in an oozy bed. But why TWO such stones, it may be said, when only one was required and has been described? Because one may have been pitched by Fingal himself to identify the spot for Ossian, or before he had resolved to send Ossian at all—which is, indeed, implied, for the place is called " the place of renown;" or because some other event of the same kind, which is not impossible, may have occurred on the same spot requiring some sort of commemoration also—which would increase its renown. Bankier, in fact, or White-Castle, described by Gordon in 1726 as one of the finest old Roman forts between the Forth and Clyde, north of the Wall, was in the immediate neighbourhood beyond; and, if then occupied by the Romans, would be the most natural base of operations for them against the advancing Caledonians; from which, on the other hand, it would be Trenmor's and Comhal's chief object to expel them. The place would thus become the scene of many a conflict, and in consequence would become also a " place of renown," in strict conformity with allusions in the text, even before Fingal was born. But that it was the scene of Fingal's own triumph as celebrated in *Colnadona*, and of the flight of the Romans or their allies, A.D. 228 or thereby, is indubitable; and that one or other of these rude monumental blocks—the fallen one, most probably—still marks the place where Ossian stood, as well as the field where Fingal fought, may be accepted with almost as much certainty as if the reader had seen them erected. They were sought for there, like Comala's rock above—one of them, at least—according to the letter of his text, and there they were both found. Thus " beneath the voice of the king" in the most literal sense of the words, and in sole reliance on the truth of his own descriptions, after the lapse of so many centuries with all their changes, have scenes of romance in princely love and of triumph in the wars of Scotland been identified among the most unlikely of all modern surroundings, yet infinitely more interesting in themselves than those of the most cunningly devised fable.

" By Crona's mossy course, Fingal had scattered his foes: he had rolled away the strangers, like a troubled sea. We came to the place of renown: from the mountains descended night. I tore an oak from its hill, and raised a flame on high. I bade my fathers to look down, from the clouds of their hall; for at the fame of their race, they brighten in the wind. I took a stone from the stream, amidst the song of the bards. The blood of Fingal's foes hung curdled in its ooze. Beneath, I placed, at intervals, three bosses from the shields of foes, as rose or fell the sound of Ullin's nightly song. Toscar laid a dagger in earth, a mail of sounding steel. We raised the mould around the stone, and bade it speak to other years"—

And speak it shall, O Ossian, whilst type and the page endure!

"Speak to the feeble, O stone, after Selma's race have failed! Prone from the stormy night, the traveller shall lay him by thy side: [it was large enough, therefore, to afford such shelter, as its measurement also shows:] thy whistling moss shall sound in his dreams; the years that were past shall return. Battles rise before him, blue-shielded kings descend to war: the darkened moon looks from heaven, on the troubled field. He shall burst with morning, from dreams, and see the tombs of warriors round. He shall ask about the stone, and the aged will reply, ' This grey stone was raised by Ossian, a chief of other years!"

The aged in its neighbourhood, alas! seem to know little, and the most learned in the nation still less, of its place or history—but the STONE is there; and there, has been "the place of renown;" and " the tombs of warriors" are also there, if the aspect of that ground does not greatly deceive us. It looks more, indeed, like an extended tumulus broken down by continued cultivation, or a scene of promiscuous interment after some great slaughter, than an ordinary ridge on the field. Even without any sign to suggest such an origin, or the neighbourhood of Bankier to explain it, it might challenge at least an attentive glance from the antiquarian in passing; but with such a ruin and two such monuments adjoining, its real character cannot be very doubtful.

5. Still more, however, is connected with this discovery than we have yet made apparent. The reader may remember, as an incidental fact, that although the scene of *Colna-dona* is in some important respects the same as that of *Comala*, and nearly the same as that of the *War of Caros*, the river Carun, common to both of these, is neither introduced nor named in it. This fact, however, though only incidental, is highly significant. For (1.) an impostor, or even a careless historian who had once got the Crona and the Carun associated in his narrative, without realising or discriminating their geographical relations, would be certain to name the one at random wherever he introduced the other; and therefore we may fairly conclude that the author of *Colna-dona* was not only not an impostor, but a faithful observer of facts and a conscientious describer of localities. If Mac-Pherson, for example, had been the author, knowing nothing of the ground, he would certainly have introduced the Carun as a mere finish to the scenery of the Crona; but Ossian in *Colna-dona* never sees the Carun, therefore Ossian does not even refer to it. But (2.) if Ossian, from "the place of renown," where he

erected the trophy described in that poem, did not see the Carun, then the spot where he stood, and even the track that he followed eastward the second morning thereafter, "on the path of the roes," must have been so far up the Crona that the south-eastern slope of the Ardvens intervened to prevent that view. The farthest point in question, therefore, reached by Ossian in that expedition, could have been little, if at all, beyond Bankier; nor could it have been on Bankier itself, for the roes were in the woods and not at the castle; and the stone, although it was erected, "or reared on high" upon the bank, was still by the ooze of the river and not on the hill top. From all which it is clear, that "the place of renown" where Fingal had scattered his foes, and where Ossian commemorated that victory, must have been a little to the west of Bankier—that is, it must have been on the very ground at Wyndford, where the monumental stones above described have been actually discovered.

But it was through this region, and by these triumphal landmarks, that Fingal travelled, along the very ridge where Comala, on her rocky hearth, had that feast for him prepared. What his ordinary route, therefore, must have been from Tomfin to the Crona, then down the Crona to the Carun, and so back, is thus as clearly established as any geographical fact can be in the campaigns of the Island. Bruce's place at Bannockburn, or James's march to Flodden; the relative positions of Cavaliers and Covenanters, at Drumclog; the march of the Highlanders to the battle of Kilsyth, on Fingal's ancient track; or the loss of Baillie's cavalry in Dullator-bog, less than a mile from the spot in question—these, however certain, are not more clearly defined. On the same line of march, or near it, but at a later date, we find Oscar moving eastward to defy Carausius; and by the same process of investigation, founded on the text alone, the very scene of their conflict may be identified. You recognise it without difficulty, even on a distant survey, by features in the landscape, which all the changes occasioned by agriculture, coal-mining, canal and railway operations, and the very shifting of the river itself, have not obliterated. To make sure of "the mossy rock of Crona"—if it were not still Comala's rock, where Ossian in imagination sees him stand—you must go forward to investigate. But there it was, or is, before you, if it has not yet been shattered, you are certain. Looking back through the haze of night, and the smoke of kilns or the dull red glare of coke furnaces, which now take the place of oaks that once "burned to the wind" in camps, you see "the ghosts of Ardven pass through the beam. . . . Comala is half unseen on her meteor, and Hidallan is sullen and dim." But there, you say without doubt, in the triangular strath between the Carron and the Bonny Water above their confluence, to which that natural ford in the Carron, most suitable for the passage of men and horses, conducts near Dunipace—there, the encounter must have been. "The tomb which arose in times of old," where Oscar stood, "and raised thrice his terrible voice," may be altered or gone; but the "little hills which lift their heads at a distance, and stretch their old trees to the wind" are still there—one of them so close to the Carron as to have been encroached on by the stream, and the other not so far distant that they might not both have been surrounded by it, as Ossian seems to imply; and if so, then Arthur's Oven might be the tomb. If the river has much altered its course, indeed, to the south, as we know by the testimony of Buchanan it has done, it may even now be flowing through the identical spot where Oscar stood. But the boggy ground along which Caros fled lies still to the north-west, and "the small streams which were lost in his course" flow still into the Carron. He could not escape to the east or south, you now perceive, for the people of Oscar were before him; and even if he had broken their ranks with a rush, the Crona was still to cross, which, with their rallying forces in his rear, would have been almost an impossible achievement. He might have taken the Roman road to Camelon at first, no doubt, and so round to Castlecary by a retrograde movement in flank, instead of crossing the ford at Dunipace in front; but that would have been too great a detour; besides which, he had store-ships at Larbert to think of, which could not be removed in the storm, and would have been plundered in his absence. In short, there was no alternative—Oscar and his people, who intervened between him and the Wall, must be disposed of somehow, by surprise or by circumvention, on which he seems to have resolved; in attempting which, however, although it was his only real strategy in the case, his own discomfiture by the vigilance of his antagonist, descending from Ardven at the dawn, became inevitable.

On the same spot apparently, or very near it, about seventy years before, Fingal defeated Caracul—the day that Comala died—with this difference only in their positions, that Caracul was advancing from the south, and was driven back with ignominious rout through the Roman Wall; and here Trenmor, as generalissimo king of the Caledonians, withstood the incursion of the South Britons at a still earlier date. The ground, indeed, as the only free passage from south to north, has been the scene of many a conflict for national liberty, although not always with similar success. Here Wallace, deserted by the nobility of Scotland, was defeated in 1298; but a royal convert to the cause of freedom was that night made on the banks of the Carron, who was destined to tread Fingal's very footsteps again in Arran, to live by the chase in Fingal's forests there, and to lodge in the recesses of Fingal's caves; who redeemed all the damage of that overthrow by his own final victory at Bannockburn—greater than any yet achieved by Oscar, Fingal, or Trenmor—but a few miles beyond.

III. The Carron, the Bonny Water, and the Kelvin are thus obviously the historic streams of the region. If there were others corresponding, to distract the choice of a geographer or to complicate our ideas of the text, a decision might be more difficult; but there are no others, so that the identity of these respectively, with Ossian's rivers in front of the Roman Wall, is unquestionable. The only other point on this field, hitherto as perplexing as the course of rivers, to determine, is the locality of an Ardven in Stirlingshire corresponding to the Ardven or Ardvens of Ossian, in *Comala* and the *War of Caros*. Without recapitulating proof to show that this Ardven was really a proper name, or the name of a mountain or of a mountain-range, or of peaks in a mountain-range, in the neighbourhood; we shall be satisfied now, before adducing evidence, to recall the reader's attention for a moment to our analysis of the poems in question, and the outline of the scene as there presented from the text. (1.) Fingal, it may be remembered, returns from the Carun *up* the Crona to his temporary head-quarters somewhere on Ardven, near which Comala in anxiety was expecting him. (2.) Ossian, from the Col-amon or Col-avhain, now identified in the opposite direction as the Kelvin, goes *down* the Crona towards the Carun, although he neither reaches nor even comes in sight of that stream; and returns thence again by the Crona to Col-amon Hall—which must, therefore, have been somewhere on Ardven also, being on the very route by which Fingal had already returned thither—"no noise on Ardven, but the torrent's roar." And (3.) Oscar, from the banks of the Carun, east or north-eastward, ascends the same Ardven, but at a considerable distance, from the other side; or possibly from "the place of renown," by a circuit round the ridge, to the north—which would bring him also to the position assigned him. The Ardven in view, therefore, to which they all thus resorted from opposite points of the same region, and from the banks of the same rivers, so far from being anywhere in Morven, must have been some extensive ridge, with many peaks in the course of it, between these rivers; that is, between the Kelvin and the Bonny Water on one side, and the Carron itself on the other.

1. The reader who now consults an atlas, or is at all familiar with the district, will perceive without farther assistance that the range of the Campsie and Kilsyth hills corresponds exactly to the ridge in question; but it is necessary to observe, for more absolute certainty in the way of identification, that this range consists—as may be found by reference to the Ordnance Survey—of no fewer than 35 separate elevations, three or four only of which are represented in our map of the district; but all originally, and most of them still, designated by descriptive terms in the Gaelig language. The first of these to eastward, a little apart from the rest, and about 700 feet high, called Myot Hill—that is,

the soft, smooth, or grassy Hill of Honour—is a crested eminence of singularly elegant formation, with a shoulder projecting to the west, and as a point of observation in battle was every way suitable for a king; is, in fact, most probably the "mossy hill" occupied by Trenmor in his first conflict with the Romans or their allies, and overlooks the battlefield of Oscar and Caros: from which the ridge broadens and rises westward up to its highest level beyond Campsie, at an elevation of nearly 2000 feet. About the centre of the range is a lofty peak conspicuous alike by shape and height—being rather conical at top, and not less than 1870 feet high—overlooking Kilsyth, at some distance, from behind, called the Meikle Bin or Ben, which is but a semi-translation into Lowland Scotch, of Mor-ven. Behind this again, that is yet farther to the north, is another similar elevation, 1446 feet high, called the Little Bin or Ben; so that the whole range, including so many of these and extending from east to west nearly 15 miles, by whatever local name now distinguished—of Campsie, Kilsyth, or Strathblane—might most appropriately be called either the Ardven range, the Morven range, or as Clerk translates it, the "Great Mountain" range, of Stirlingshire; whilst any peak more prominent than the rest—the Meikle Bin itself, by preference, on which snow lies till the end of May or the beginning of June—"was he white as the snow of Ardven?" says Comala—might with equal propriety be called Ardven, as Ossian in fact does so call it, extending that name, however, both to the entire range and to several other points as well, as they approach the respective scenes of action. No geographical definition, indeed, could be clearer; and the closer the hills are surveyed and their various bearings distinguished, the more artistic and appropriate will such descriptive glances be found. They seem to be all one Ardven, when looked at from a distance; but when the spectator has penetrated their recesses, they divide and multiply and change their outlines, and blend and separate in endless and beautiful variety. You seem to be only on a slope at first, in which nothing remarkable could be looked for; but you find yourself suddenly among deep glens and lofty ridges, diversified with rocks and rivers and moorland wastes, with numerous passes so plainly defined that there can be no mistaking of them, and which, carefully followed, would conduct you without much difficulty from the Forth to Loch-Tay or Loch-Lomond. The view from Tomfin in particular—from which Fingal, Ossian, and Oscar, as well as Comhal and Trenmor, must frequently have seen them—includes so much that is both picturesque in itself, and geographically interesting otherwise, that it is impossible to look at it for a moment with a volume of Ossian in your hand, without being assured that it was a point both of rendezvous and observation for himself and for all his people. To the west, rise three of the Ardvens, with a magnificent strathlike pass between them on which Fingal's fol-

## FINGAL IN SCOTLAND.

lowers have assuredly marched; to the south and south-east, in succession, are the Roman Wall, the fort of Castlecary, and the distant reaches of the Crona and the Carun; whilst close in front, at the very foot of the eminence, Comala's death-scene and the "place of renown" present themselves to the eye. This view alone, it seemed to the writer as he stood there, and took the compass of it leisurely in, from west to east and from north to south, was enough to convince any reasonable gainsayer that Ossian himself must have surveyed it, and transferred every aspect of it to his memory for reproduction in immortal verse. Not a single allusion to it is misplaced, or a feature of it misrepresented in his reference.

ARDVENS FROM TOMFIN.

2. Still further eastward on the range, where it begins to decline on the Carron, and where Myot with its mossy ridge rises separate from the rest, we are able to realise more distinctly again what we have already descried in the valley. By following this slope a little round to the north, if we knew only the right level to hit, we should find the whereabouts of Oscar's communing with the ghosts of his fathers, who had often fought in its neighbourhood, and were supposed still to haunt its heights. At that point, he would have the forest of Torwood, then in its glory, on his left; the smaller forest of Haggs, on his right; and the scene of his approaching victory as already described, in the heathy plain of Dunipace or Denny, strewed with scattered oaks, at his feet, and illuminated all night with flashes of lightning. We might imagine, at least, the track on which he descended, "thoughtful and dark" from converse with the dead, on Tarduff or the Darrach hill, at grey dawn to battle. Or if Myot itself was the scene of that interview with his fathers, which is not impossible, it would be still less difficult to find him, for there unquestionably Trenmor stood, our oldest generalissimo king, face to face with the invading strangers; thence Comhal drove the Romans headlong, through a breach in their own Wall,

to beyond Castlecary; and thence Caracul fled before Fingal, and "spread the wings of his pride in other lands."

Such then would Ardven be, and still is, in most essential respects, where it rises from between the Carron and the Crona. To the west, it is divided first by two important passes, of which one, called the Campsie or Craw-glen, double, leads north-east towards Fintry; and the other called Finglen, that is, Fingal's glen—a long, smooth, narrow defile—leads north-west towards Killearn and Loch-Lomond. Still farther to the west, the range terminates abruptly on the valley of the Blane at an angle to the north, in a range remarkable for its bold picturesqueness, called the Strathblane Hills; in which two of the most prominent elevations, Dumfin or Fingal's Hill, and Dumgoyne or the Hill of wounds—indicating most probably some conflict there—are visible as landmarks for miles around, from south and west, up the valley of the Blane towards Campsie. Such names, it is obvious, and many others similar, adhering still to the most prominent features of the region, point all to the occupation of the territory in some way by Fingal and his people; to which the invariable tradition of the country, time immemorial, corresponds. The Finglen, in fact—pronounced by the natives Fing-len—is the recognised haunt of the old Celtic giants, who long ago used to invade the low-lying lands of Stirlingshire; the place in which they halted, or through which they came and went, in those remote pre-historic expeditions of theirs. Its opening to the south, with the valley of the Kelvin in the distance, is faintly but correctly represented in the accompanying wood-cut; and the reader's attention will by and by be more explicitly directed to the coherence of all these particulars among themselves, and with the text of Ossian.

The modern distinction of the Campsie range, or Campsie Fells, as they are commonly called, is understood to be derived from the remains of certain old forts or encampments on the southern slope of these hills, near their centre; by some supposed to be of Roman origin, but, from the innumerable Celtic designations around them, unquestionably either of native Caledonian construction, or latterly of Caledonian occupation. A fine double specimen of these is still to be found a little west from Kilsyth underlying the Bin, not far from the spot already allocated on the testimony of the text and confirmed by actual survey, as the probable head-quarters of Fingal, still known as Tomfin—that is, Fingal's mount, or the Giant's mount, as the people of the district understand it. Both of these stations, indeed, may have been occupied by Fingal, or one by Carul, and the other by Fingal. According to Gordon in his *Itinerarium*, however, Tomfin seems to have been one of those Forts of Observation erected by Agricola at intervals between the friths, long before the Wall itself was constructed—of which, between Colzium and the Carron, inclusive, he specifies and describes not fewer than thirteen—Bankier, beyond Tomfin, being one of the most perfect and conspicuous. On this supposition, which seems reasonable enough, Fingal's father or grandfather must have driven the Romans back from the Campsie range, as Comhal boasts they did, and so secured possession both of this and of their other forts, as a line of defence against themselves; to which the tradition of the people that they were so occupied by the Fiuns, or Fair-haired Giants, and not by the Romans, corresponds. This long doubtful problem, then, both as to the origin of these forts and their compulsory evacuation by "the kings of the world," when and how, may be considered a settled point in the history of the region. Their final loss to the invaders must have occurred between the end of the first and the beginning of the third century; and therefore, although really built by Agricola, they would scarcely ever be called by his name. But at whatever date their present designation was conferred, it is certain that between the two points now in question—one at Kilsyth, the other a little east of it—was the rendezvous of Fingal and his followers in the campaigns of the Carron; and that from the commencement of the third century at least, the Romans never set foot unchallenged beyond the Kelvin or the Crona.

How Fingal, as generalissimo, assembled his forces there, or by what routes they travelled thither from the distant north; and how far they occasionally penetrated southward, in pursuit of retreating foes, are now questions of so much additional interest as to demand separate investigation. But in the meantime, if a reader, with the text of Ossian alone to direct him, may traverse the Island from Arran to the Forth, and set his foot on every specified point with more certainty than any guide-book for the line could guarantee;—it is reasonable to ask why a persistent charge of forgery and fable should be made against a history like this, which invests the very fields with new sense, and impregnates the soil with life and miracles?

VIEW FROM FINGLEN.

## CHAPTER IV.

#### FINGAL AND HIS PEOPLE IN THE LAND OF THE STRANGERS—
#### ROUTES AND BOUNDARIES.

I. ROUTES.—1. Fingal's ordinary, if not his invariable route by sea, touching at Arran, to Ireland and the Solway, was Loch-Fyne—so called since his day, as we have already explained, Part Second, Chapter I., in commemoration of the fact; but his route inland to the banks of the Carron, from Morven or Glencoe, might be varied. Two routes from Glencoe were possible, and they seem both to bear traces of his footsteps. The first of these, indeed, was a route apparently marked out by his predecessors and forefathers—Trenmor, Trathal, and Comhal. "Often did we pass over Carun to the land of the strangers," says Clessammor, in *Carthon*, speaking of those days; from which it is obvious that these remotest Celtic warriors, to avoid crossing the Forth, and the perhaps worse impediment of penetrating the Caledonian forest which stretched nearly across the Island, and in which we are aware so many Romans perished—must have marched from the head of Glencoe by the head of Loch-Tay, down the strath of Balquidder and up the valley of the Endrick, to the head of Carron Water on Campsie-muir, and so down the banks of that stream, crossing over at their leisure to the Crona. Fingal himself, in the fourth generation, seems to have followed their track; for the pass at the head of Loch-Tay is called Finlarig, or Fingal's pass, to the present hour; and the reader, on turning to a survey, will find, with as much astonishment perhaps as the present writer himself did, that along the route thus imagined, beginning from Glencoe, we come successively to Auch-*Fin*-der, to *Fin*-larig, to Glen-*Fin*-glass, to *Fin*-tray, to *Fin*-nich, and to *Fin*-nich-haugh—a grassy plain among the moors on the very banks of the Carron, but across the stream—where there is still a passage, and within an hour or two's march over Ardven to the Crona at Tom-*fin*.

2. The other route might be by Tyndrum from Glencoe, southward by the banks of Loch-Lomond, round the corner of the Strathblane range by the nearest opening, and so up the valley of the Blane Water first, and then of the Kelvin or *Col-amhain*, to Kilsyth; on which route we find, in the same unexpected manner, Glen-*fin* at the head of Loch-Lomond, Dum-*fin* as a landmark within sight of it, with many an intervening ford and field bearing Fingal's name; then *Fin*-glen, the passage or retreat already indicated at the western extremity of the Campsie range, where reserves would concentrate; and then, a little to the east

of it, Tar-*fin*, by the base of the range, but commanding the valley of the Kelvin, and within two hours' march of Tom-*fin* on the Crona. It is possible, indeed, there may have been even a third route from Morven, if not from Glencoe, partly by sea and partly by land; through Loch-*Fyn*, in the first place, to Dumbuck on the Clyde by sea; thence by *Fyn*-loch on Dumbarton-muir, again up the valley of the Blane to Dum-*fin*, the unmistakeable landmark; thence by *Fin*-glen and Tar-*fin* as before, at the foot of the Campsie range, and so onward to the invariable rendezvous at the source of the Crona.

Such routes were all possible or certain, and the reader will observe that, in proportion as they converge, the name of Fingal multiplies. In the valley of the Endrick, indeed, and along the Campsie range, we meet local designations at every step in which that well-known syllable occurs, as in *Fin*-land, *Fin*-nich, *Fin*-ary, *Fin*-glen, Dum-*fin*, and Tar-*fin*, besides the *Fin*-nich or *Fin's*-haugh on the Carron, and Tom-*fin* where the converging routes from Morven or Glencoe, by sea or land, seem to terminate. Tomfin, or Fingal's mount, as we have already explained, was the highest convenient point of rendezvous or observation facing the Roman Wall, between the Forth and Clyde, where such convergence therefore might reasonably be expected; and we have now only farther to note, that allowing for the loss of time in fording rivers and following glens or penetrating forests, it would be about three days' journey, at the rate of thirty miles a day, from the foot of Glencoe, or from the adjacent shores of Morven; a calculation, by which not only the truthfulness of the incidental statement as to distance, incomprehensible to MacPherson, in the *War of Caros*, is confirmed —"*Three* days" Hidallan, banished in disgrace by Fingal from the camp at Crona, "strayed unseen, before he came to the mossy halls of his fathers at Balva;" but also the fact, that the valley of the Cona from which these expeditions started must have been identical with Glencoe, and that Selma, the chief residence of Fingal, was in the land of the modern Morven.

3. As to Balva itself, although of little consequence otherwise than as a basis for measurement, nothing with much certainty is ever likely to be known. But the reader will find delineated in any good old county atlas, a small stream in a little valley called the Auld-Ba, which by obvious transposition is the Bal-va, about three miles north-east of Glencoe, the nearest approximation possible both to name and to locality—" His name remains on the rocks of Cona, and I have often seen the streams of his hills." With respect to some other names on the routes represented, the most natural account of their application to the points in succession where they occur can be afforded by etymology also, without difficulty or force. Thus Finlarig, or Fingal's pass, at the head of Loch-Tay, is a point maintained, by jealous and invariable tradition, as Fingal's route from the

north. Glenfin-glass, in like manner, or the Glen of the Fair-haired man—that is, Fingal—on the western skirts of the great Caledonian forest, is the pass by which that forest would be penetrated in his day. But no march, however orderly, could be effected through such a forest without the straggling of his followers, and Fintry, more accurately Fintray, or Fin's gathering place, on the other side, would be the point at which they re-assembled; whilst Fin-nich, or Fin's washing place, must have been the ford by which they crossed the Carron, of which, more hereafter. On other occasions, when more to the westward by the banks of Loch-Lomond, they might either march in detachments by Killearn to the Finglen, or round the range of Strathblane by Dumfin, as already explained. But if that hill was a favourite landmark of Fingal's, it would soon acquire his name: and by this very route, on one occasion, it is almost demonstrably certain that both Fingal and Ossian themselves, within a few days of each other, must have travelled between Crona and Glencoe. Fingal had been victorious, as we have seen, at Crona; he "had scattered his foes; he had rolled away the strangers, like a troubled sea;" and Ossian was sent to signalise the victory, by raising a stone in commemoration of that triumph on the spot. This must have been immediately thereafter, for "the blood of Fingal's foes hung curdled in the ooze" of the stream. He came up the Col-amon and down the Crona, to perform this ceremony; and so must have reached that valley, either by Finglen or by Dumfin. But he was still a youth, and seems never to have been in the neighbourhood before; for although accompanied by his friend Toscar of Lutha, and preceded by shield-bearers and bards, he came obediently "beneath the voice of the king," and so "moved to the streams of Crona"—that is, he came not only by the authority of the king, but according to his direction for the route; which must, therefore, have been by Dumfin, the recognised landmark from Loch-Lomond. By the same route, most likely, he would also return, although we are not so informed; and the probability is, that by whatever route circumstances might induce them to march on Crona, it was always by this lower route both the chiefs and the people returned, as being the levelest and pleasantest of the three. The situation of *Tar* or Tor-*fin*—some fortified seat of Justice on the line, similar to those in Arran, where affairs might be administered, and where Fingal therefore might halt—about half-way between Kilsyth and Dumfin, is in corroboration of this idea. Fin itself, through all these local designations, indeed, imports much more in Stirlingshire than a mere nominal affix. It is, in fact, a mistranslated descriptive epithet, giving an idea of the man as a giant, or of his people as resembling himself, as well as of his name as an individual; and is so explained in Appendix to Nimmo's History of Stirlingshire by the Editor of that work, Rev. William MacGregor Stirling, in 1817, without the slightest reference to Fingal. According to his authority, which may therefore be deemed impartial, every local name of which Fin is a component part, and many in which it is corrupted to *Funn* or *Fann*, has the oldest traditional reference to the giants who formerly invaded the region, in the same way as the giants' graves in Arran are traditionally referred to the same people; thus indicating the belief of the populace both in Stirlingshire and in the Islands of the Clyde, that Fingal and his followers were men of supernatural strength and stature. But Fin, or Fiun, means the fair or the fair-haired man, and not the giant, although Fingal himself, the son of Comhal, and all his race, are described as giants. "Was he white as the snow of Ardven?" says Comala, speaking on the very spot—"Blooming as the bow of the shower? Was his hair like the mist of the hill, soft and curling in the day of the sun? Was he like the thunder of heaven in battle? Fleet as the roe of the desart?" In Arran, where the Gaelig language is still spoken in purity, such details, both of name and of personal characteristics, are of course more accurately preserved; but the impression produced by these warlike strangers in Stirlingshire, still traceable within the last hundred years in the recollection of the natives who know nothing of Gaelig, but on the contrary have utterly disused or corrupted it, is in such perfect correspondence with the text of Ossian who records their visits to that region, as friends and allies or royal generalissimos in war, for more than five generations together, including a period of fully 250 years beyond the range of common history, that no stronger circumstantial evidence on the subject could be desired. According to him, they were tall, stately, and fair, and they were the people of Fin or Fiun; according to the traditions of the district, they were giants, and every spot they once occupied or visited retains the name of Fiun, or of Fin.

It must be almost needless to say that such facts and coincidences were utterly unknown to MacPherson, and it would be superfluous to add a word to the sum of such evidence, echoed by the moors and mountains, through centuries of neglect and unbelief, to the truth of these wonderful records. Whether local traditions elsewhere—as well as at Finlarig, Finglen, and Dumfin, and the whole surrounding neighbourhood, where they are distinct—may concur to support this testimony, has not been ascertained; but it is not of essential consequence. Such an accumulation and coincidence of names alone, still adhering to the soil, along the routes in question; accumulating and coinciding on these routes precisely where they should accumulate and coincide, from west and from northwest and from north, is beyond the obstinacy of average unbelief to question, or the trick of fancy to invent. It might be the basis, in fact, for an independent history of the campaigns of that era, which it might be worth any antiquarian's while to investigate and extend; and is proof at least, to almost mathematical certainty, that on these very routes, hitherto untraced and unimagined, Fingal travelled. If every village on the line had been a finger-post, it could hardly have been clearer; the testimony of the rocks themselves, if they could speak, would not be more convincing.

II. BOUNDARIES.—With such tracks, then, like the Broad Arrows in an Ordnance Survey, to guide us, and which will multiply as we go; with a point of convergence so distinct as Tomfin, and a pass like that of Castlecary opposite— where the Roman forces were chiefly concentrated, and against which, therefore, the attacks of the Caledonians were most frequently directed—as a new point of departure before us; and with the Clyde itself, as a great highway of traffic or retreat, beyond us; we must now prosecute our researches southward, and ascertain, if possible, both the extent and the direction of these military expeditions from the north into the Land of the Strangers.

1. In the *War of Caros*, it may be remembered, the Roman usurper is represented as having been driven up the Frith of Forth in a storm to Larbert, where "the ghost of night rolled the wave to his ship;" and it is worth observing, as a curious coincidence at least, that in *Comala* the defeat of Caracul by Fingal is accompanied also by a storm, with thunder and lightning—" The thunder rolls on the hill: the lightning flies on wings of fire; but they frighten not Comala!" Caracul's flight on that occasion would be to southward of the Wall, through Castlecary-glen, or by the Roman road on Fannyside-muir, and between the two lochs there, in the direction either of Slamannan or the Monklands south-eastward, or of Hogganfield and Rutherglen south-westward;—in which retreat, however, Fingal does not seem to have pursued him far, for the king of Morven returns in the evening, up the banks of the Crona, to where Comala dies. On subsequent occasions, he or his people must certainly have penetrated much farther south, as we shall immediately see; but in the meantime, if the "gathered heap," where Caros was defeated, was some military station on the Roman road at Larbert, what of the Roman Wall through which Caracul, more than seventy years before that, fled? Was an object of such importance in the region overlooked by Ossian? or has MacPherson forgot to introduce it? MacPherson, in the first instance, mistook the station for the Wall, as we have seen; and in the second, did not distinguish the Wall when it was referred to. Only once, however, is such reference by Ossian made, and that incidentally, not in the *War of Caros* but in the poem of *Carthon;* and MacPherson, bewildered on the one hand already by his own misapprehension about the station, may perhaps be excused for not being able to recognise the Wall, or the forts which were the foundation of it, when they were really alluded to, on the other. In either case, he was guiltless of forgery, and as innocent of guile as a schoolboy in a corner.

2. The reference in question to the line of Wall is brief and simple, indirect and almost obscure in its simplicity, and therefore beyond suspicion by the most scrupulous sceptic; yet clear and suggestive enough when seen, even for a moment, in its proper light. It occurs thus in *Carthon*—" Ye have fled over your fields, ye sons of the distant land! The king of the world sits in his hall, and hears of his people's flight. He lifts his red eye of pride, and takes his father's sword!" Again; "Often did we pass over Carun to the land of the strangers: our swords returned, not unstained with blood; nor did the kings of the world rejoice." To understand which clearly, the reader must remember that both in *Carthon*, and elsewhere incidentally, two distinct classes of enemies are specified by Ossian as in Scotland—first, the Romans or "kings of the world," who are called also the "sons of the distant land," and are easily identified by the "wings of their pride," or the eagle on their standards; and second, "the strangers," who were the people of hostile British tribes under protection of the Romans, or occupying the territory south of their Wall. This distinction MacPherson himself correctly recognises. In the above quotations, therefore, we have (1.) an exact allusion to Roman forces driven by Fingal within their own line of defence—" Ye have fled over *your* fields, ye sons of the distant land;" and (2.) a general allusion to previous victories of the same sort, by Comhal and his friends, before Fingal was born, when the Romans had a footing still farther north.

In the case of Fingal's own forays, much booty was brought back in the shape of luxuries, and a thousand tapers, part of the spoil on more than one occasion—compare *Carthon* and *Carric-Thura*, at the commencement respectively of both poems—were lighted, to celebrate his return to Selma. But in every case, the "kings of the world" are represented as hugely mortified at their repulse; and at the news of Fingal's victory in particular, as recounted in *Carthon*, "the king of the world" himself "sits in his hall, and hears of his people's flight" with rage—" he lifts his red eye of pride, and takes his father's sword." These victories, it is obvious, both by Fingal and his forefathers—by Comhal his father, in particular—were obtained south of the Carron, and the chase of the fugitives must have extended far beyond the valley of the Crona southward—most probably by Castlecary-glen, either to the neighbourhood of Hamilton and Lanark on the one hand, or of Blantyre and Rutherglen, on the other; on which route we find a station to this day called Cuil-hill or Coul-hill, that is, Comhal's hill—where some encampment of his before traversing the Clyde, up or down, on his way to the siege of Balclutha, must have been held. On this supposition, we have reliable trace of Fingal on the same route—

For " I have seen the walls of Balclutha," he says, " but they were desolate. The fire had resounded in the halls, and the voice of the people is heard no more. The stream of Clutha was removed from its place, by the fall of the walls. The thistle shook, there, its lonely head: the moss whistled in the wind. The fox looked out from the windows, the rank grass of the wall waved round his head," &c.

All which ruin, we learn from the same poem of *Carthon*, was his father's work three years, or thereby, after Clessammor's visit to Balclutha and the birth of Carthon there " in the days of peace"—ruin not altogether unprovoked, perhaps, by some unkindness in the meantime to his relative Clessammor. Besides which specific evidence of Fingal's reconnoitering in the valley of the Clyde beyond the Wall, we have clear enough trace of him on the intermediate moorland wastes, expressly spoken of as "heaths," about Cumbernauld, between Castlecary and the Clyde going southward; where his name is still preserved at the Fan-ny-side or Fin-lochs—which is but a corruption of *Fin-nich-seid*, or Fingal's washing place-with a grassy turf-between; a name corresponding precisely to the relative situation of these lochs, which are separated from each other only by a grassy ridge, on which a rude turnpike near the old Roman road, as the only passage through the moor, still runs—so that, in pursuit of the Romans, Fingal must of necessity have passed this way, and on return might very naturally refresh himself there. In connection with which, it is worth observing that Fan-ny-side or Fin-nich-side, on the south, corresponds in position very much to Fin-nich-haugh on the north of the Wall, which was undoubtedly the old ford or washing place of Fingal on the Carron; whilst *Fin* and *Fan*, the first and characteristic syllables of these words respectively, are interchanged in Blaeu's atlas, as if the syllable itself was the same, or its spelling was indifferent. It is also equally, and for our present purpose still more worth observing, that due south from Fan-ny-side we have Car-fin—that is, Castle-Fin—near Bothwell on the Clyde; to which Fingal on some occasion may have penetrated by this route, as the limit of his raid; and which certainly, on more than one occasion by another route, he must have reached and occupied, and thence returned.

3. But to resume our present argument on the existence of the Wall as known to Ossian, and its Halls or fortifications as alluded to by him—it should be distinctly borne in mind that the Fin-lochs and other localities above named, from Castlecary to Balclutha—wherever that might be—were within the ascertained boundary of the Wall, and in "fields" which are expressly described as in subjection to "the kings of the world." But these kings of the world could maintain no such dominion there without some line of defence, by forts like those of Agricola, or a wall like the Wall of Antonine. The strongest wall they could build, indeed, behind marshes and streams like those of the Kelvin and Bonny Water, proved ultimately ineffectual; and it is notorious as a matter of history,

that, in consequence of such incursions and barbaric victories as those ascribed to Fingal and his father, they were forced at last to abandon that wall, and retire behind their original rampart from Tyne to Solway. Ossian's text alone, although no wall is mentioned, seems to indicate the gradual repulse of the common enemy beyond some such special limit. Nay, the very character, progress, and extent of that limit, from generation to generation, may be ascertained from the style of his narrative. In Trenmor's day, it is obvious from the quotation already made (p. 191) that "the strangers," or provincial Britons, had no such defence to rely upon. They committed themselves openly to the field in concert at Crona, between Myot Hill and the Carron—where, once at least, they were signally defeated after partial success. But no mention is made of "the kings of the world" on that occasion, or of any Wall or HALL of theirs, to support the invaders. The probability, therefore, is, that Agricola was but commencing his fortifications at that date, and that preparations to draw a barrier across the isthmus were not in progress. In the days of Comhal, his son and successor, the aspect of affairs had changed. Comhal had to encounter "the kings of the world" as formidable enemies in possession, and permanently present on the same ground; who certainly would not be there without camps and entrenchments to maintain them. In Fingal's days these camps had been converted into Halls or palaces, fit for the accommodation of kings or their lieutenants, and were actually so tenanted. The most conspicuous fort on the whole line, both then and since, was in fact Castlecary—estimated by rough measurement at about 600 ft. square, with external rampart, ditch, wall proper, raised military causeway inside, and huge embankments round; was furnished, as we know, with costly ornaments, decorated with sculptures, supplied with baths, conduits, and other luxurious appliances suitable for the service of a Proconsul, or of an Emperor himself in war; and, compared with the rude establishment of Fingal, might well be called the Hall or palace of a king. Another similar fort, a little to the east of it, is still known by the name of Rough-Castle; a third seems to be indicated by Palacerig near Fannyside, at the old Roman road there—where, if our previous conjectures be correct, Fingal in passing may have seen "the king of the world in his hall," furious at the flight of his people; and a fourth to the west, on the banks of the Kelvin close to the Roman road at Cadder, retained the very name of Palace till within the last few years. In a map of Glasgow and neighbourhood, 1795, it is so described, although the title has since been superseded by the more prosaic designation of Crofthead. These forts were types and specimens of what Ossian recognised as Halls; and were erected at intervals along their line of defence by the Romans, for the accommodation of the emperors or their lieutenants on military survey—designed originally by Agricola, but maintained afterwards in connection with the Wall. On some occasions, it would appear, victory was achieved over lieutenants only, whilst the "King" himself so called was in the fort; but from what we find recorded in *Comala*, it is certain also that Caracalla, who is expressly designated in that poem "the son of the king of the world"—being, in fact, his father's deputy and immediate heir, in command of the imperial legions at Castlecary—was ignominiously defeated and put to utter rout by Fingal on the Carron, opposite that fort :—" Raise, ye bards of the song, the wars of the streamy Carun. Caracul has fled from mine arms along the fields of his pride. He sets far distant like a meteor that encloses a spirit of night, when the winds drive it over the heath, and the dark woods are gleaming around."

4. But fortifications like these, we may conclude, were not without connecting ramparts, roads, and towers, even before the Wall itself was built; and accordingly we find, that even in Fingal's youth old Carul does not march to the Clyde, but takes his canoe by the Kelvin; Ossian himself, in succeeding years, when on expeditions of relief to people on the Tweed, keeps the frith from Morven; and every step of Fingal's routes, from Fyn-loch on Dumbarton-muir to Finnich on the Carron—except in the two solitary cases already alluded to, when in pursuit of his enemies by Castlecary-glen—are to the north of the finished rampart. They must sail, in short, because they can no longer march, and they do sail, as we shall find, along all the western coast from the Clyde to the Solway, penetrating inland; or they must march on the safe side of the boundary. Ossian's pride will not allow him to mention this; but the fact is obvious—his only consolation being, that he himself and his father's house, though they were the last of men, had always been the friends of the fallen, and themselves unconquered. For his son, was reserved apparently the honour of striking the latest blow against the hated invader—at least we have no later record; on which occasion Caros, or Carausius, was no longer *behind* the Wall, but on the coast of the frith *before* it, approaching with a fleet and supplies for its defence or reparation. To which general outline, so indefinite as to escape observation at first among the details of poetry, but so clear and consistent, when thus traced, as to be indisputable, all facts hitherto ascertained from the page of unpoetic history, correspond; and with so much poetic light reflected on them, as to be almost of ten-fold interest. Thus, for example, in addition to what has been already stated, we learn from general history (1.) that there were occasional intervals of peace, and doubtful terms of mutual forbearance between the Romans and the Northern Britons or Caledonians, from the time of Agricola downwards: and from Ossian we learn incidentally how such intervals of peace were sometimes occupied by the native tribes. " ' It was in the days of peace,' " replied the

great Clessammor, 'I came in my bounding ship to Balclutha's walls of towers'"
—that was either to the neighbourhood of Dunglass, where the last of Agricola's
forts to westward had been built, and which, therefore, "in the days of peace,"
might be approached with safety; or more probably, as we shall by and by see,
to the neighbourhood of Rutherglen near the Roman road there, but much farther from the Roman Wall, and therefore more completely in the "land of the
strangers." "'Three days I remained in Reuthámir's halls, and saw that beam
of light, his daughter'"—on which followed a romance of war and sorrow—the
subsequent destruction of Balclutha, the ruin of Reuthámir's race, and the death
of Clessammor's son by Clessammor's own hand unwittingly; all as recorded
in *Carthon*, and incidentally explained to the reader—Part First, Chapter IV.
(2.) We learn from credible and hitherto unquestioned history, that there were
at least three humiliating treaties of peace assented to by the Romans with Caledonians beyond the Wall, at Dunipace or Larbert—the first by Severus in 210
A.D., when he attempted to regain the Wall; the second by Caracalla, his son
and ultimate successor, shortly afterwards, probably in 211 A.D., when he was
driven back from the Wall; and the third by Carausius in 286 A.D., about the
time when he came to repair the Wall: and we learn from Ossian incidentally
that the second of these treaties must have been compelled by the success of
Fingal, then a youth of seventeen, just returned from an expedition to Norway
at the crisis of Caracalla's invasion, and accompanied by an Orkney princess, his
betrothed wife Comala, to the neighbourhood of the field; and that the scene
of Caracalla's defeat, when "he fled along the fields of his pride," was on the
precise spot, between the Carron and the Bonny Water, assigned to that treaty
in Roman Annals—Fingal's camp on the occasion, as we have shown, being a
little north-east of Kilsyth. And (3.) we learn farther from history, as already
intimated, that Carausius, shortly before the date of the third treaty, came to
Britain with a fleet for the reparation of the Wall of Antonine: and from Ossian
we learn incidentally that this fleet of his was grounded in the Carron, that his
head-quarters in consequence were at Larbert, that he was surprised and signally defeated there next morning by Oscar, whose head-quarters were about
the Haggs; and, what is more to the purpose perhaps, that Oscar, heathen and
barbarian as he was, spent the night before battle in devout communion with the
spirits of his fathers—of Comhal who had triumphed there before, and of Trenmor who had been victorious at Myot. In the treaty itself which followed this
defeat Oscar personally could hardly have had a share, for he fell by treachery
in Ireland, within a year at most, after his victory "at the stream of resounding
Carun."—Compare *War of Caros* and *Temora*, B. 1.

Such coincidences as these, unsuspected hitherto alike by critic, antiquarian, and translator, between the details of history and the text of Ossian, in relation to events and localities common to both, require no commentary to enforce them. Roman historians may be good, but without Ossian they are not perfect. Our picture of the country, then, both north and south of the Wall, as reproduced from this divine barbaric writer, and vouched for by the barest annals of the time, is complete. The Wall itself, as we see, did not exist in Trenmor's day, and the people to the north of its line were independent tribes of Piks, Caledonians, or Celts, each with its petty king; and Trenmor himself, at Myot hill, was their first elected royal generalissimo. In Fingal's father's day, the forts of Agricola had been built, or some line of defence established by the Romans; in spite of which the northern tribes made incursions southward with Comhal at their head, "Scotch wanderer on the heath," and defeated the Romans within their own entrenchments. In Fingal's day the Wall had been finished, and he must hazard the fate of war before he crosses it. Almost all his warlike operations by land, therefore, are to the north, or entirely to the south-west, of it. In Ossian's day the same, or similar, conditions prevail; in Oscar's day, Ossian being still alive to chronicle proceedings, the Wall is to be repaired, and Carausius with his fleet in the Carron, with horses, men, and stores for the purpose, is repelled, and with a repulse so signal that the fame of it in a twelvemonth is spread abroad in Ullin—during all which eventful period, of not less than 250 years, the house of Trenmor was supreme as royal generalissimos in Scotland.

Of the facts thus so intimately connected with the Ardven of Stirlingshire, and even of the scenes of their occurrence, MacPherson, as we have seen, was almost absolutely ignorant. Yet the region was full of them. One can hardly touch a point on that range, or cross a brook that flows from it, without awakening the spirits of the dead; and we must listen, whether we please or not, to the voice of their rehearsals. Fortunate it was for MacPherson, we again repeat, that he knew nothing of it—that he could found no theory upon it; that he could offer no explanation of it; nay, that in his very attempts at explanation he turned it upside down, and that in his chronological calculations based upon it he contradicted himself, in the age of Fingal alone and all that depended on it, by nearly half a century—Part Second, Chap. IV. Had it been otherwise—had his idea of facts, dates, and localities, coincided with reality, every word of the *War of Caros* and of *Comala* and of *Colna-dona* would have been premeditated imposture and a double lie in the estimation of objectors. These poems, as regards Scotland, may now be verified beyond contradiction, to their minutest syllable, and must henceforth be accepted as amongst the most ancient and interesting documents in the history of Great Britain. There Carausius fled before the boy Oscar; there Caracalla was defeated by Fingal; and there, at still remoter dates, the allies of Agricola were defied under the standard of Trenmor at Myot—" Often did we pass over Carun to the land of the strangers: our swords returned, not unstained with blood; nor did the kings of the world rejoice"—and a poet was then singing in the intervals of battle, with a soul beyond the patronage of Augustus, and with gifts of his own beyond the genius of Virgil. What Gibbon sighed to believe, " that Fingal lived and that Ossian sung," becomes thus an historical reality; for however like a dream, nothing can be more certain than that we are in the presence of the Romans with Fingal and his people in the pages of Ossian; that we witness the discomfiture of these Masters of the World on the banks of the Carron by real men, who have hitherto been looked upon as fabulous; and that we have minute points detailed in their occupation of North Britain with a picturesque fidelity equal to that of Homer, and beyond all rivalry or competition by anything known in the prosaic annals of our history. Tacitus and Cæsar, as chroniclers, retire alike discomfitted by the voice of Ossian, as the soldiers and tyrants of their race did, in the years of their declining empire, before the sword of Fingal.

But all this, it may be said, has been invalidated, or at least discredited, by the magniloquent exaggerations of the poet himself. Who, then, supplied gratuitous oratory for the heroes of Livy and Cæsar? and put splendid periods he never spoke, but only should have spoken, into the mouth of Galgacus? Yet Livy, Cæsar, and Tacitus, with ten times the exaggeration of Ossian in this respect, are esteemed reputable and reliable historians. " Let us not judge according to the outward appearance; let us judge righteous judgment." Or is it possible after all, that the eloquence of the Caledonians was not exaggerated by Tacitus, and that Ossian himself had a rival and a model, through " his own dim years," in the inspired patriot of the Grampians? The Bards had not forgotten *him* in the days of Trenmor, and Ossian only emulated his fame. There was, in fact, a tradition in MacPherson's day, that the Colgach of Ossian referred to in *Temora* was the Galgacus of Tacitus; and although MacPherson did not entirely believe in it, it seems to have been one of the many shrewd guesses of antiquity in which there was a foundation of truth. Colgach at least was Vergobret, or petty sovereign of the Caledonians, at the date in question, and might very well have been commander at the Grampians in the struggle of his tribes against Agricola; on which supposition, the student may find both amusement and instruction in comparing the imaginary declamation put into his mouth by Tacitus with the exhortations before battle, by Fingal or Cuthullin, in the text of Ossian.

But the Clyde above Dumbarton, and the " Land of the Strangers" beyond the Clyde, require still to be investigated.

## CHAPTER V.

**FINGAL AND HIS PEOPLE IN THE LAND OF THE STRANGERS (CONTINUED)—RUTHERGLEN, BALCLUTHA, AND THE CLYDE.**

I. AT an earlier stage of our inquiries—Part First, Chapter IV.—we had occasion incidentally to touch on the probable whereabouts of Balclutha, and suggested hypothetically that it might be either on the hill-side above Dunglass, close by the river, then a frith with a current there on the north shore; or that it might be higher up the stream, as high, indeed, as Rutherglen. According to MacPherson himself, Balclutha was " probably the Alcluth of Bede "—some fortress, that is, near Dumbarton, if not Dumbarton itself; a conjecture which Clerk seems to adopt; but protects Ossian from any misconstruction, by reminding the reader that " the genuineness of his poems depends in no degree on the system of chronology or topography adopted by MacPherson." This and much more, as our readers are aware, we have had occasion, in the course of our present investigations, fully to verify; and although we were content at the moment to assume MacPherson's theory in this case as possibly correct, knowing nothing then to the contrary, and having even strong reasons in support of it; yet on reflection, it seems to deserve more careful notice, and reconsideration from other and different points of view.

1. Laing, it appears, in the first place, discredits the truth of Ossian entirely on the very uncertainty connected with this name; alleging that there could be no such place as Balclutha at all, because Ptolemy does not mention it. After what our readers have already seen in the way of geographical revelations beyond the reach of Ptolemy, they may perhaps be inclined to smile at such an argument founded on Balclutha, and to look a little more carefully round before either denying the existence of the place, or doubting the reliability of Ossian in connection with it. Ptolemy, in short, was not omniscient, nor was Laing by any means infallible. Our own reason at first for suggesting a choice of sites, so distant from each other as Dunglass and Rutherglen, for this important stronghold—which, if we could fix it, would mark the frontier capital of an old British kingdom—is that between Dunglass or Dumbuck and Rutherglen, a distance of nearly 15 miles, no other point now known to us on the whole course of the Clyde presents any features at all corresponding to those distinctly assigned to the position of Balclutha in the text. (1.) It was in " the land of the strangers;" (2.) it was under some local ridge; (3.) it was close by the stream of the river;

and yet (4.) not far from the sea. Three of these conditions—2, 3, 4—would be sufficiently fulfilled by any fortress in position on the hill-side of Dumbuck— it would be under the ridge, close by the stream, and not far from the sea; but the first would not be fulfilled, for a fortress at that point, or within several miles of it, would not be in the land of the strangers properly so called; it would be on the very line of the Roman Wall, in fact, and not elsewhere. In proportion as we ascend the river, the land of the strangers would of course be neared; but two other conditions would fail—the local ridge and the stream of the Clyde would both be awanting, until we reached Rutherglen, when all the conditions above specified would be fully implemented; more especially the first, which requires Balclutha to be identified, as we have said, with some fortress in " the land of the strangers." In pursuing which track, it is of importance to remember that Carthon itself is a name which carries us up the Frith of Clyde far beyond Dumbarton; and when we reflect that Comhal, who destroyed Balclutha in one of his raids from Castlecary to the Clyde, must have followed the Roman road first to Cuil-hill and then to Rutherglen; and that Fingal himself, twenty years or thereby afterwards, on the same or on a parallel track, saw the ruins of Balclutha in the stream, which " was removed from its place" by their fall; we may admit, perhaps, that both Ptolemy and MacPherson were mistaken, as well as Mr. Laing, and that the scene of Carthon's birth and of the ruin of his father's palace was at Rutherglen or Cathcart after all.

2. Having reached this point, however, many other conditions—more minute than those already specified, but of equal importance in detail—have to be considered, before we can look with certainty to any ground in the neighbourhood for the site in question. But in support of our position thus far, the following topographical discoveries may be adduced, as both pertinent and reliable:—(1.) That the Roman road, or Watling street,* has been traced from near Longtown in Cumberland, by Lockerby and Closeburn in Dumfriesshire, and so onwards by Errickstane, through Lanarkshire, to Maulsmyre or Millksmyre near Castlemillk; whence doubtless it proceeded north by Rutherglen to the Clyde, and so by Hogganfield, as represented in our map, to Kirkintilloch on the one hand and to Cadder on the other—both stations being on the line of the Wall. The track by Cuil-hill, on which we suppose Comhal to have marched, would be a little farther to the east, but in a directer line to Castlecary. (2.) That according to Ure, 1793, mounds, tumuli, cairns, and cists, with many interesting and valuable reliques of antiquity had been found in the whole surrounding region—

---

* So called "from one *Vitellianus*, supposed to have superintended the direction of it, the Britains calling Vitellianus, in their language *Guetalin*."—Cambden's *Britannia*, Vol. I., p. 47; or Ure's History of Rutherglen, p. 133, from which the present reference is quoted.

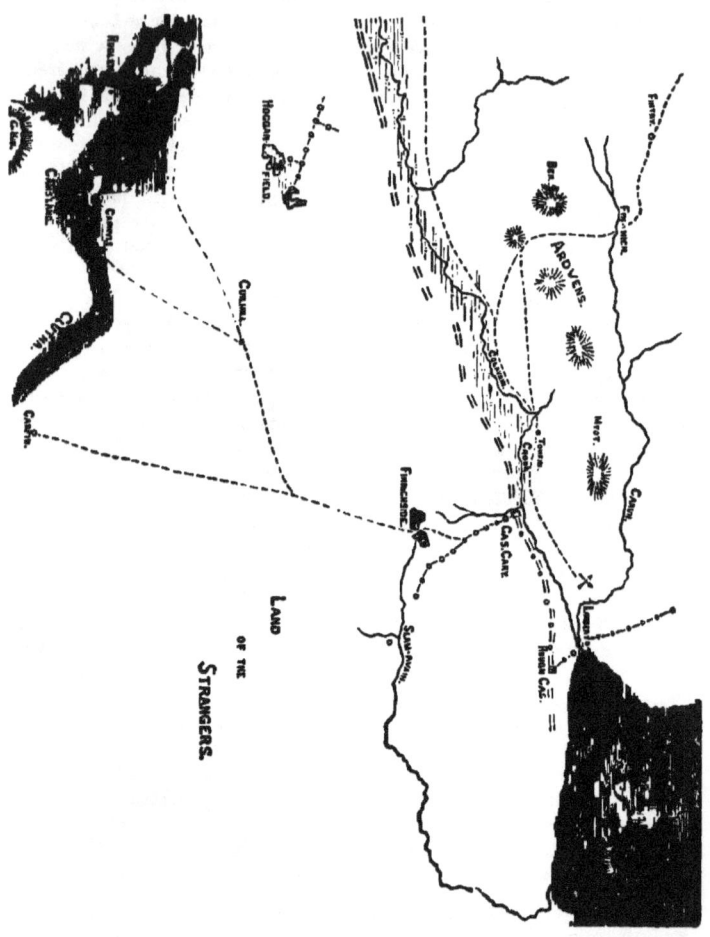

in particular at Polmadie, Gallowflath, Maulsmyre, and on Cathkin Braes near Castlemillk. Those at Gallowflath and Castlemillk were especially noteworthy, both from their size and from the number of urns and cists discovered in them. The tumulus at Castlemillk, which was on the Cathkin ridge there, " was intersected nearly in the middle by a stratum of burnt earth, about a foot in thickness. . . . In the bottom of the cairn, and exactly in the centre of the area which it occupied, was a *coffin* or *chest*, of large flags. It was about 4 feet every way; and a very large stone that required the strength of six or eight men to remove, was placed over it for a covering or lid. A small quantity of earth was all the treasure it contained. Close to it, however, was a considerable number of small bones, mostly fragments. Among them was a tooth quite empty within; but the enamel was entire. The want of the osseous substance affords proof that it was the tooth of a child."—*History of Rutherglen*, pp. 217-219. Although this remarkable ruin is described only as a tumulus or cairn, " about 18 feet in height and 120 in diameter," it was nevertheless surrounded " with a narrow ditch; and a small dyke of earth;" and had doubtless, therefore, been the residence, as well as the untimely burying-place by conflagration, of some chieftain's family. Besides, if it was 18 feet high after such a catastrophe and the lapse of seventeen hundred years, it might have been twice as high at least, before its destruction occurred; and when we consider its position on the ridge of a hill— the most remarkable ridge in all that region of the Clyde—it is hardly possible to read such a description as this of Ure's, without recalling Carthon's words on the overthrow of his own birth-place.

"Have I not seen the fallen Balclutha? and shall I feast with Comhal's son? Comhal! who threw his fire in the midst of my father's hall! I was young, and knew not the cause why the virgins wept. The columns of smoke pleased mine eye, when they rose above my walls; I often looked back with gladness, when my friends fled along the hill. But when the years of my youth came on, I beheld the moss of my fallen walls: my sigh arose with the morning, and my tears descended with night. Shall I not fight, I said to my soul, against the children of my foes? And I will fight, O Bard: I feel the strength of my soul."—*Carthon*.

The stratum of burnt earth about a foot in thickness, the small bones, the child's empty tooth, and the scene of desolation on Cathkin Braes are all here reproduced and associated almost with the very spot in question. When we learn farther that " this aged monument afforded materials, these many years past, for building dykes in the neighbourhood," we are reminded again of Fingal's words—

"I have seen the walls of Balclutha, but they were desolate. The fire had resounded in the halls; and the voice of the people is no more. The stream of Clutha was removed from its place, by the fall of the walls. The thistle shook

there its lonely head; the moss whistled to the wind. The fox looked out from the windows, the rank grass of the wall waved round his head"—
and can hardly help concluding that this so-called "monument" at Cathkin was some stronghold after all, converted into a cairn among its own ruins and in memory of its frightful desolation. If the Clyde, or any "stream of the Clyde," ever flowed near enough the foot of Cathkin ridge to receive the larger fragments of ruined masonry as they fell; and if any such rude blocks have been found embedded in the marshes below, we may be almost as sure as we can well hope to be, that this burnt-out heap was either Balclutha itself, or some sister-fortress on the Clyde, that had shared a similar fate from the hand of Comhal or his followers. These are points which of course require to be settled, by a minuter survey, perhaps, than it may now be possible to make; but it should be observed in passing, that it was from this identical ruin, before it was finally demolished, Queen Mary surveyed the field of Langside—beyond which it "commanded also a distinct prospect of the tract of Clyde from near Hamilton to Dumbarton;" so that the young king of Balclutha, if he ever either dwelt or stood here, must have been familiar enough with the frith, and even with the peaks of Dumbarton themselves, as landmarks in the distance for his own navigation westward. About its great antiquity, we have only farther to remark in conclusion, that according to Ure himself, the date of its erection "was in all probability prior to the introduction of Christianity;" and we are thus carried back without difficulty to the days of Trenmor, or at least of Comhal, when the catastrophe of its destruction by fire, if it was indeed the dwelling of Reuthámir, was accomplished.

(3.) Almost all the names on the rising ground about Rutherglen, as already explained, are Gaelic. Thus we have Cambuslang, or the ship's bay, on one side; Langside, or the ship's grassy resting-place, on the other; and Rutherglen itself, or the point of the west valley, between them. We have Gallowflath also, or the hiding-place of the hero, implying troublous times long ago, in that neighbourhood—at which a remarkable tumulus, containing an extraordinary subterranean passage and a number of rare and valuable reliques, of which more hereafter, was opened in Ure's day. We have also Cathkin, otherwise Carth-caen, the headland range of battle, or the castle of the headland range, above it— whereabouts the ruin already described was found; and Maolsmeur, otherwise Millksmyre, now Mallsmire, the low bald brow of the marsh, or the low-lying marsh, or the fork, or the servile stream of the river, between the Cart and the Clyde, below it. But there is a certain class of names in Ossian, as we have also seen, which carry us up irresistibly, both by sound and by historical association, to this very neighbourhood, and which we seek in vain to localise anywhere else—such as Carthon, Cathmol, and Cathlin; to which Crathmo and

Reuthámir have now to be added—Crathmo the name of some low ridge a little beyond or about Balclutha, and Reuthámir the name of Balclutha's aged king, the grandfather of Carthon; both which names are included by him affectionately in his dying breath—

"'King of Morven,' Carthon said, 'I fall in the midst of my course. A foreign tomb receives, in youth, the last of Reuthámir's race. Darkness dwells in Balclutha; and the shadows of grief in Crathmo.'"

3. Crath, Carth, or Cath, Kin or Caen, Maol or Mol, and Reuth, are therefore the roots or significant syllables we have now to combine, in order to unravel the etymology of the district and connect it inseparably with the text of Ossian. Two of these, as in Cathkin, are already combined; a third, by the transposition or dropping of a single letter, gives Cart, and by combination with the second, will give Cath-cart—with which Ossian, however, for the present has no obvious connection; but Cath-maol, or Cath-mol, brings his text to our tongues immediately; and by restoring Carth to Crath again, and softening Maol to Mao' or Mo, we have Crathmo—that is, the lower ridge of the Carth—which also should be in the neighbourhood of Maulsmyre on some still lower fork of the river, and in the very shadow of some adjoining hill with the setting sun behind it. All this, the reader must observe, is but an inference from the text in the meantime; but a very rapid survey of the ground, to the south and west of Rutherglen, will confirm its truthfulness to the letter.

(1.) In Blaeu's atlas, 1663, we find Cathkin abbreviated to Carth—which gives us the root of all the compounds in Ossian now in question. (2.) From a local map, 1795, and from natives of the district living, we find that Millk (not Milk, although commonly now so spelt, as in Castlemilk and Milksmyre) is but a corruption of Maol or Maul, signifying a low, more correctly an inferior, or subjacent range; thus traced by the people themselves unconsciously to a period long before their own occupation of the soil, from *Milk* to *Millk* or *Mulk*, thence to *Mill* or *Mull* or *Mall*, and so to *Maul* or *Maol*, as if to the very lips of Ossian—varieties of pronunciation still commonly preserved in the dialect of the district.* (3.) The Roman road, as we have seen, was traceable in Ure's, or at least in Cambden's day, from Errickstane near Moffat, and from beyond

* The writer does not forget that Rutherglen mill appears, on the old map in question, at Bankhead between Rutherglen and Castlemilk (*sic*). But that does not at all interfere with the derivation of Castlemilk and Millksmyre as now given in the text, and in conformity with Ure in his *History*. It is worth observing, however, that Bankhead, on its rocky perch at the old mill-dam there, seems as likely to indicate the site of a British Caer or a Roman Castellum as any other point in the neighbourhood; and the ruins of a fortification, if precipitated thence, would certainly remove what was once a deep-flowing "stream of the Clutha from its place, by their fall."

that, to Maulsmyre or Millksmyre on Castlemillk estate, at Rutherglen—which places, as the reader will observe, are inseparably connected not only by name but in position; and at one of them, doubtless, as a point of defence and rendezvous before crossing the Clyde, there would be some fort or castle on the Roman line. But *Castellum* in Latin is equivalent to *Caer* in Gaelig, and thus from the Romans we have Castle-maol, or Castle-millk, on the one hand; and from the Celts we have Caer-ath-maol, contracted Carth-mol, and softened as in Ossian to Carthmo or Crathmo, on the other, both signifying the Castle of the Low ridge—the points so designated being identical. Again, the same root combined with Caen, now ken or kin, the high ridge, gives us Carthkin as in Blaeu, or Cathkin as in the speech of the people; and these two names distinguish precisely the relative positions of the two places—the one being the Fort of the Low ridge, the other the Fort of the High ridge, as a moment's glance at Castlemillk and Cathkin will explain and determine. (4.) The frith of Clyde, as a matter of geological certainty, must not only have flowed up to the very threshold of Castlemillk, spreading eastward in the hollow; but must also have received a considerable tributary there, flowing down between adjacent ridges from the south; and the ruins of any fortification on the verge of it must of necessity have rolled into the tide. (5.) By far the most conspicuous aerial feature in the landscape at this point is the long equal shadow, like an eyelid, projected by the setting sun from the Cathkin ridge above on the level land at Castlemillk below—so beautifully and intensely suggestive, that the spectator must be devoid of sense as well as of imagination who does not observe it; and more ignorant of Ossian than the reader of these pages is supposed to be, if he does not involuntarily exclaim "the shadows of grief at Crathmo!" when he sees it. (6.) And finally, looking north-west towards Glasgow, down the valley or glen, once a branch of the frith, now the bed of Polmadie Burn, Maulsmyre or Millksmyre, the ridge of that low-lying marsh, is discernible; which would make a fork with the Clyde, as its name also implies, when the river as a fiord penetrated eastward, from Polmadie to Gallowflath, behind Rutherglen; but which in the course of centuries, by the natural process of absorption, drainage, and decay, has been first a marish, then a mire, and is now the course of a paltry rivulet, designated expressly in our most recent surveys, "Mall's-mire-burn"— a combination of syllables which accurately represents its history. Thus every point in the landscape, as well as every link in etymological connection, between Cathkin, Castlemillk, and Crathmo is established; all relating to which, the reader will remember, is supposed to have been the work of a man who, like the rest of us, in his innocence put Balclutha on the Clyde at Dumbarton, and Crathmo in the "Land of the Strangers," nowhere! Whether Balclutha, therefore, was at Rutherglen or Gallowflath—on the stream of the Clyde itself, or only on some low-winding servile tributary—Crathmo would still be in the neighbourhood, as between these points, and almost equidistant from both. With Cathmol of Clutha himself, "by the winding of his own dark streams," we are not now immediately concerned. His residence must have been somewhere in the marshy hollows, of which there are still not a few, about Maulsmyre, and therefore not far from Crathmo; but we have no recognisable bearing, beyond "the rushy desart" spoken of by his daughter Cathlin, to guide us, and may abandon the search as hopeless. Within a mile or two of Rutherglen, south-east or west, it certainly was. Reuthámir, on the other hand, is a much more significant designation, more easily and distinctly traceable; and as the name of Balclutha's ruined king, it should be localised and fixed along with that of his capital, if our means of identification at this distant date will permit it.

II. In prosecuting this etymological inquiry, then, we may remind the reader —1. That *Reuth*, *Ruth*, or *Rudh*—the root syllable alike of Rutherglen and Reuthámir—means descriptively a point running into the sea. By softening and contraction, a process so familiar among all words of the sort as to require no farther reference, it becomes Ru; hence Ru'glen for Rutherglen, Ruhmar for Ruthámir, and the Row—a point opposite Roseneath in Dumbartonshire, which almost divides the Gareloch into two by the prominence of its projection seaward. But *Rudha*, the primitive and perhaps the correct form, spelt *Reuda* by Bede, is identified by Ure, on Buchanan's authority, with Reuther the name of a man, king of the Dalreudini, 213 B.C.; who, after "various changes of war, . . . . retired to the mountainous country of Argyle, where he remained in peace for several years. Finding at length that his forces, now greatly increased, were inflamed with the love of war, he left his retirements, and by many successful attacks on the Britons regained the ancient boundaries of his kingdom." This Reuther's race, it should also appear from the same authority, remained at Rutherglen for many centuries after it was thus reconquered; and it was from the fifth of that name in genealogical descent from Fergus I., that this ancient capital of the Strath-Clyde Britons received its present designation.

2. Again, as Ure is careful to point out, in support of his etymologies, *Dal* prefixed to Reuda is the same as *Glen* affixed to Reuther; and thus Dalreuda— whence Dalreudini, the Latinised name of the old Scots, or "strangers," who dwelt south of the Clyde—is synonymous with Rutherglen; the name of the place, according to this authority, and the name also of the people being compounded alike of two terms, one of which was the name of a man and the other of the region—a strath or valley—where the capital of his kingdom was situated. Bede, Buchanan, and Ure, it may be observed, know nothing of Gaelig beyond

the Dal and the Glen which represent this region—Reuther, or Reuda, as they understand it, being the name exclusively of the king; but Ruth or Rudha, notwithstanding, is certainly a point, and Ruth-er is the west-point, running into the sea. We have thus unexpectedly two derivations of the name—one purely local and descriptive, the other partly personal and proper; one founded on geography, the other on tradition; yet both confirming the narrative of Ossian, and one all but literally confirming the very letter of his text.

3. The root of Rutherglen and Reuthámir having been thus doubly determined, in favour of our theory as to the connection of both with Balclutha and its king, the two remaining syllables of each, *erglen* and *amir*, require some investigation also, that the names themselves of which they are important parts may be identified conclusively as now one and the same. *Erglen*, as we have already seen, on the clearest principles of etymology, means the west valley; and so Ruth-er-glen must mean the point of the west valley, running into the Clyde. But *amar* itself means the trough or channel of a river; or by separation of the syllables, and the slightest change of orthography thus—*am-iar* (on which, however, we do not insist, although quite permissible)—it would mean also the west; and so Ruthámir would mean the point in the channel, and Rutham-ir the point of the west; that is west-point, or point in the channel, omitting valley, as the reader himself may incline. That Balclutha was so situated in relation to the Clyde is certain, for Fingal saw its ruins in "the stream;" that it was to the westward of his ordinary bearings in that region is also certain, for he marched through "the land of the strangers" from Castlecary or Cuil-hill on the east towards it; and that Reuthámir might have had some fortress there, although not certain, is probable—for he was the man of the point, the man of west-point, and the man of west-point in the stream, by a triple or quadruple play on his own personal appellation. That he might have had another fortress also, on the banks of the Cart, which would then be a rapid tributary of the Clyde, is by no means impossible; and these two—the one at Rutherglen, the other at Castlemilk or Cathcart—would be both on the verge of the frith, both below mountain ridges, and both on the western frontiers of his kingdom: both would afford a "prospect of the Clyde from near Hamilton to Dumbarton," no other point whatever intervening; and thus one, or either, or both of them might with the greatest propriety be called Balclutha, or the Town of the Clyde, before Dumbarton or Dunbriton itself was in existence.

4. It would be very difficult, if not impossible, to produce any arguments half so conclusive in favour of Dunglass as identical with Balclutha; and it is almost needless to observe that details like these were all a mystery to MacPherson, and an impossible dream to Ptolemy. The only objections which can be urged against

the theory are (1.) that the Balclutha of Ossian seems closer on the Clyde, and more immediately under some mountain range, as Dunglass undoubtedly is, than any point we have suggested above it; to which, however, it may be replied, that if we knew precisely the very site of such a fortress at Cathcart, Castlemilk, or Rutherglen when the Clyde was a fiord there, not only would that difficulty disappear, but more unequivocal proof of its identity with Balclutha would be obtained. (2.) That if Comhal pursued the Romans or their allies from Castlecary by Cuil-hill to Carmyle, for example—how did he cross the river thence to Rutherglen? To which also it may be replied, how did the Romans cross? By ships or rafts, undoubtedly, which were common enough on its waters there, as the reader has already been informed. The bight or bay of Cambuslang, in fact, was then the harbour of the frith, as its very name implies; and might often be as much crowded with the primitive craft of the river as Bowling Bay now is with disabled steamers, or Gourock Bay with yachts and pleasure boats for hire. But in proportion as the frith receded, trade would recede also; and ships of a sort that once sheltered in Cambuslang, would be reduced at last to the necessity of mooring at Rutherglen. Rutherglen itself, indeed, although more exposed, was a seaport long after the date in question, as the records of the place and common seal of the Burgh to this hour attest. The gradual subsidence of the frith is thus chronicled, so to speak, by the very changes on its margin; and so late as the end of last century we find express verification of the fact.

"To the Charters of the Corporation," says Ure, "are suspended seals, containing impressions of the Town Coat-of-Arms. It consists of the Virgin and Babe, attended by two priests, holding up thistles in their hands. On the reverse is a ship with two mariners on board. . . . The ship represents the River Clyde, which is navigable up to the town. . . . It is highly probable that Rutherglen, at that time, was the only town of mercantile importance in the strath of Clyde; and that to it any trade that might be in the river chiefly belonged. That the channel of the Clyde was then naturally much deeper than at present, we have no reason to doubt, when we reflect that many million cartloads of mud and sand have since been thrown into it from the land. Trading vessels, therefore, which at that period were of small construction, might be carried with ease up to the town. We are sure, however, that till of late, gaberts of considerable burden sailed almost every day from the quay of Rutherglen to Greenock, &c. . . . The ship, therefore, with propriety constituted a principal part of the coat-of-arms. On the old seal, which is long ago lost, the human figures were ill executed, but the form of the ship was somewhat uncommon. It resembled the *navis antiqua* of the ancients, and is known by the name of the Herald's ship, because it was introduced by heralds into the blazoning of coats-of-arms. It is hoped that the draught of the impression will not be unacceptable to the curious."—*History of Rutherglen*, p. 79.

For an opportunity of consulting Ure, and of making a correct representation of this curious relique from his pages, we are indebted to the polite attention of our old friend and school-fellow, Mr. William Denholm, Rutherglen.

In the modern seal, as our readers may satisfy themselves, the ship occupies a very subordinate position in the background, and its mariners have disappeared. In other words, when the arms of the Burgh were revised, the trade which was once at Cambuslang and came afterwards to Rutherglen, as the river fell, had already begun to accumulate at Glasgow; and but for the incessant application of scientific means, it would long ago have left that city also. The possibility of yet intercepting it from Glasgow, and of reducing the Clyde, as it still ebbs away, to the rank of a mere canal, or even of blocking it up altogether, is now obvious to Greenock; and nothing but the most energetic measures, both legislative and scientific, will prevent it. At all events, the frith being thus freely frequented by ships or canoes at Cambuslang and Rutherglen, so early as the commencement of the Christian era, not only might the Romans pass the river in their flight by such means, but Comhal also, with ease, might follow them; Calthon and Colmal, in their journey from the Tweed at a later date, as we have seen—Part First, Chapter IV.—might with still greater ease find some "dark-bosomed ship" to waft them, in their extremity of distress and haste, from Bothwell, or even from Hamilton, to Loch-Fyne; and finally, Carthon might equip himself with a fleet, as he probably did, at Rutherglen, as well as he could have done at Bowling—where both transports and sailing-ships, with weapons of war attached, were to be found, as actual discovery has assured us.

5. By way of supplementary evidence in support of the position thus assumed for Balclutha so high upon the frith, we may remind the reader that Fingal himself passed in sight of it, if not close by it, either when in pursuit of the Romans

on the route from Castlecary to Carmyle; or, which is equally probable, on his return down the valley of the Clyde to Rutherglen, from his pursuit of them beyond Lanark—as Carfin to the east, already mentioned, on the line to Lanark, where he would cross the Clyde, seems to indicate :—and that he had obtained much fame by such exploits in that region is certain, from the mere allusion of Carthon to the fact—

" ' Art thou that king so far renowned?' replied the carborne Carthon. ' Art thou that light of death, that frightens the kings of the world?'"

The sense of these words, which we print thus separately, as indicating the direction and extent of Fingal's warlike operations between Castlecary and the Clyde, is worth a thousand arguments on the subject; and their authenticity is indisputable. No impostor, by any chance, could have put language so suitable in the mouth of an imaginary speaker, whose own whereabouts was confessedly unknown; but a prince who lived actually at Rutherglen, and who knew all that had occurred for a lifetime between that and Lanark, might employ them in casual compliment, as he does, with the utmost propriety.

As for Clessammor, as we also know, he drifted up the frith towards it, and was driven again by an east wind, a few days afterwards, away from it. But his rival in Moina's love was "the son of a stranger," who must therefore have come from the east or south-east; for he has heard of Comhal's ravages there, and challenges Clessammor, as Comhal's friend, to defend himself as an enemy and intruder. He is spoken of, also, as a "son of the winding Clutha"—that is, as a native of its upper reaches above Hamilton, before the stream had developed into the fiord. But it is certainly more reasonable that a youth, in these circumstances, should visit on foot a neighbouring princess in her father's halls at Rutherglen, than in a fortress at Dunglass on the very verge of the Roman Wall, and with a sea between him and her, even in "the days of peace." The writer has thus reasoned himself unexpectedly into the clearest conviction on the subject, but leaves the argument on both sides, frankly advanced, for his readers' satisfaction. Assuming, however, as he now must do, that Balclutha was somewhere on the Clyde about Rutherglen, Castlemilk, or Cathcart, *Carthon*, as a poem, will fall to be assigned, in the origin of its story, to Lanarkshire; and all the first movements of its actors to the Land of the Strangers between Bothwell and Langside, along the range of the Cathkin hills, and by the frith of the Clyde itself in face of Glasgow—when the Rottenrow was a ridge of boulders, when Stobcross was submerged in westerly gales, when from the Gallowgate to Ladywell was a gulf, and when the Fleshers' Haugh was a sea.

III. By carrying our researches still southward and westward in this "land of the strangers" beyond the Clyde, we should doubtless find traces of Fingal or his people in Renfrewshire and Ayrshire, if we had but a landmark or two in some poem to guide us. Besides *Carthon*, however, already analysed, *Cathlin of Clutha* is the only narrative which undoubtedly refers to that side of the river, and seems to conduct us from beyond Rutherglen, by Langside and Paisley, to the frith; but as we have already said, there are no bearings in the poem sufficiently explicit to determine localities, and conjecture in such a field without them would be waste of time. For the same reason, all hope of identifying Balteutha may be abandoned, although it is demonstrable from *Calthon and Colmal* that Dunlathmo was a freebooter on the Border who made occasional forays northward, and carried off both plunder and prisoners from the valley of the Clyde—most probably from about Hamilton or Lanark—to some fortress of his own on the Tweed; and that the name of Fingal was protection, or at least a terror there—a fact which incidentally corroborates all that has hitherto been advanced as to the extent and direction of his southern expeditions inland, from Inis-huna, through Galloway and Dumfriesshire.

Whether Cowal in Argyllshire, on one side of the frith, and Kyle or Coil in Ayrshire, on the other—which are but variations of Comhal, Coul or Cuil—have any connection with Fingal's father, so celebrated for his raids as the wandering Scot who devastated the land of the strangers from Carron to the Clyde, and kept those allies of the Romans, if not the Romans themselves, in dread, is perhaps doubtful; and we shall found no argument whatever on the supposition. Coilsfield—associated so intimately with the early life of Burns, and in the neighbourhood of Torbolton, which must have been similar in all respects to the Tors in Arran—was so called unquestionably from some ancient Caledonian or Pictish king interred there; and Burns's own admiration of Ossian may not have been without some secret connecting link in that direction—

> There, where a sceptr'd Pictish shade
> Stalk'd round his ashes lowly laid,
> I mark'd a martial race, pourtray'd
>   In colours strong;
> Bold, soldier-featur'd, undismay'd
>   They strode along.   *Vision:* Duan First.

But as we have no allusion now extant in Ossian himself to guide us, we must forego all mere conjecture on the subject as comparatively worthless.

The only feasible, and not altogether improbable conjecture is, that Comhal fell in conflict with Morni, on the moorland wastes between the Ayr and the Cree; which is, in fact, the country of the MacMorrans, and in which more than one monument in the shape of "standing stones," and lochs with the name of Fingal are to be found, attesting the presence or the passage of the kings of Morven through the district. In connection with which, we are reminded by a note to Mr. Jerram's scholarly translation of *Gaul* in the *Sean Dana*, recently published, that Barbour in his *Bruce* refers to Gaul, the son of Morni, as Gow MacMorn—the very name associated to the present hour with the country in question, as readers also of *Guy Mannering* may remember. On this supposition, old Morni must have removed to the north, after Fingal subdued his tribe; for we find him latterly on the banks of the Strumon, as an ally of Fingal's at Selma. This is, no doubt, a difficulty in the way; for why should he be called " King of Strumon," who was never a king there?—unless, indeed, it was by mere courtesy, to soothe his wounded pride after total discomfiture. But there is another difficulty. Morni is spoken of in a certain fragment, as the " son of Colgach;" and Colgach has been all but identified with Galgacus. If that were the case, then Morni's realm should have been north of the Carron, and not far from the Grampians. On the other hand, it is not impossible that, after his father's final overthrow, he may have removed from that region and established himself elsewhere. We are expressly informed, indeed, by a note to *Temora*, B. III., that he made a grand reconnoitering expedition, shortly after, to the Clyde, which is thus alluded to in the text of that poem—

" Who rises from his car, on Clutha? The hills are troubled before the king! The dark woods echo round, and lighten at his steel. See him amidst the foe, like Colgach's sportful ghost; when he scatters the clouds and rides the eddying winds! It is Morni of the bounding steeds! Be like thy father, Gaul!"

It is beyond dispute, however, that both Fingal, Ossian, and Oscar, with their people, visited and fought, as allies or avengers, on the Wigtownshire coast from Culhorn or Caldarnu to the Whithorn promontory on the shores of the Solway, if not beyond it; and the name of Fin or Fiun, attached to more than one locality inland there, looks like a trace of their wanderings. It is worth while also to observe, in passing, that monumental stones, similar to those in Arran and elsewhere traceable to their era, are to be found still standing in the valley of the Girvan opposite Killochan, at a considerable distance from the sea; and that men so well acquainted with every creek on the frith should not have sailed up the fiord of the Girvan, seems most unlikely, more especially when we remember that there is a Knoc-Oisshen or Knoc-Usshon at the mouth of it, and that Ailsa Craig, or the Lonely Isle, their beacon of the frith, is visible from the valley for many miles inland. The Highlanders of Arran and Cantyre, in fact, are still looked upon by the people of Girvan as a sort of traditional invaders.

As to Renfrewshire and Buteshire, the presence of Fingal or his followers there, although only to be inferred as a probability from the text of Ossian, is demonstrable as a fact, on other evidence. The natural marine canal from Bishopton to Ardrossan, as we have already seen, was certainly one of their tracks in navigating the frith, and in all probability the very track on which old Carul pursued Duthmocarglos from Kelvin to the Kyles. The larger Cumbrae, also, must have been often frequented by them; and Fintry bay on that island, where several stone cists similar to those in Arran have recently been discovered about a hundred feet up from the shore, was in all likelihood, as its name implies, the scene of their rendezvous from Arran or Loch-Fyne in expeditions to the mainland opposite. A little farther north, accordingly, on the Renfrewshire coast near Innerkip, we find a Finnich and a Finnich-bog, that is, the washing-place of Fingal or his followers, as formerly explained; and more inland in the same county, we have the names of Fingart and Fingalton recognisable to this day—the latter of these, a little south of Barrhead, being in a direct line along the then verge of the frith, from Finnich to Rutherglen. In all these links, etymology alone must be our guide; but when we find a Fintry or Fintray, and a Finnich, and a Finnich-side, between Stirlingshire and the Clyde on one hand, on a route unquestionably followed by Fingal; and a Fintry bay, a Finnich, and a Finnich bog in corresponding succession, with a Fingart and a Fingalton beyond, between Buteshire and the Clyde on the other, the coincidence is so strong as to be all but convincing. And the fact itself, that after these long marches or voyages to places of rendezvous, inland or island, there was a Finnich or washing-place in lake or river, so far from being strange, was in perfect consonance with the habits of the people in such expeditions; and corresponds so exactly to the record of the Irish chroniclers that there can be no reasonable doubt of its certainty.

"And the warriors moved towards the south, and when we came to the waters of *Buidaman* [the Boyne Water, apparently], we washed ourselves therein. And we passed through *Gaelen:* the men of that region were amazed, they thought not of our coming."—*Chronicles of Eri*, Vol. II., p. 73.

In collating which singular statement, as a matter of fact, with our remarks on this subject in the preceding chapter, the reader is requested to observe that the statement was not discovered till long after such places as Finnich, and Fanny-side, or Finnich-side, had been found and noted by us in the track of Fingal. In marching from Innerkip to Fingalton next, on their way to Rutherglen, the route of Fingal's men would be by the Calder-Water down to Loch-Winnoch, where the marine canal above referred to would of course interrupt their progress; and it may be said, that this would be too formidable an obstacle for invaders who had left their shipping behind them on the coast. But canoes have been found in Kilbirnie-Loch, similar in most respects to those discovered lately on the Clyde at Bowling; so that not only is the means of their passage at this point accounted for, but the continuity of the frith from Bishopton to Ardrossan, in such breadth as to require canoes for transit, is established also.

It is curious, in connection with all this, to observe that two of Morni's sons—brothers to Gaul—fell in battle, apparently on the same ground, against "Coldaronnan, a chief of Clutha;" as if they were still contesting, with the help of Fingal, after their father's death, the supremacy of that region. But this name Coldaronnan is certainly nothing more than a variation of *Caldar-annan*—that is, the Calder-Water; and there are three notable Calders in the district—one flowing from the neighbourhood of Shotts, by Wishaw, to the Clyde at Orbiston; another from beyond Kilbride, by Blantyre, to the Clyde at Uddingston; and the third, in an opposite direction, on the confines of Renfrewshire and Ayrshire, from the south-east of Innerkip and Kelly into Loch-Winnoch. Between these distant limits, therefore, or adjacent to one of them, this chief of the Coldarannans, or Calder-waters, might dominate, and would be a powerful "chief of Clutha" besides. To assist the sons of Morni, now tributaries of his own, in asserting their ascendency in this disputed tract, Fingal may have made more than one expedition to the southern shores of the frith; and in so doing from the west, must have traversed the whole region within the above bounds. The reader has already the clearest evidence of his route, by one of these very Calders, from Innerkip to Rutherglen, along the margin of the frith; and that many a desperate conflict has happened in this land of the strangers, between themselves and their Celtic invaders, is equally certain. The surface of the intermediate country everywhere bristles with old entrenchments, and has been literally strewn with mounds, tumuli, cairns, cists, and urns, precisely similar to those at Gallowflath and Cathkin; most of which, however, have either been emptied of their contents or levelled with the soil in the progress of the plough. The whole region, in fact, from the coast at Innerkip to the Roman road at Maulsmyre and beyond it, has been the theatre of such forgotten campaigns—forgotten by all but Ossian, in his sorrowful glimpses at Balclutha and the ruined strongholds of the Clyde. Laing has been pleased to characterise the entire episode of Coldaronnan as one of the last and most impudent forgeries of MacPherson; but at the present stage of our inquiries, the reader must be sufficiently aware that the details now adduced in evidence of its reality were as little known to MacPherson as they were to Ptolemy, or to Laing himself. Some interesting facts, connected with the geology and with the antiquities of this district, will be found stated in the Appendix, in a Note to Part First, under the head of Paisley.

IV. To much of this it may perhaps be objected, that we are associating the name of Fingal with every corner of the Lowlands as intimately as with Arran and Ireland; but it must be remembered that Fingal was known and feared far beyond the limits of his native country, as well as beyond the moors of Morven. His presence was as familiar in fact, and his achievements as common, among the

Orkneys and on the coasts of Norway, if not beyond both, as in the valleys of
Ullin or on the Frith of Clyde. "His fame came," says Sulmalla, "like the
sound of winds, to Cluba's woody vale,"—that is, to the very extremity of the
south-western mainland. His real character, in short, was as far removed from
the vulgar idea entertained of him, as the character of a great hero is from that
of a gigantic homicide. He was an experienced traveller, a wise king, a skilful
generalissimo, a patriotic soldier, a generous man, and an accomplished physician.
To whatever scholarship or science besides was then attainable, as in music and
poetry, he must also have had claims; and seems to have been a more liberal
and discerning patron of such arts than many civilised potentates of far higher
pretensions. It was to this varied culture and experience, and to the necessity
he was under of associating with men of all nations and of all ranks—from
"kings of the world" and Celtic neighbours, to sea kings and savages—that
much of the dignity, freedom, and courtesy of his bearing is no doubt to be
attributed. But being such as he was, and everywhere appealed to for help and
protection by the oppressed or the unfortunate, against private wrong or the
enemies of his country, it should not seem wonderful that he traversed all its
most important, or even dangerous and desolate tracks, in fulfilment of his royal
mission; or that having so traversed them, his name, as that of the most distinguished celebrity of his age, should adhere to his very footsteps. Besides which
general consideration, we must remind the reader that in these local notices of
his presence in Ayrshire, or in the south, we have been guided in almost every
instance by the letter of the text; and where that could not be quoted, we refer
only to the testimony of the soil as the next most reliable authority. Where
the text and the soil concur about his presence, there can be no reasonable doubt
of it; where only the soil itself can testify to the passage of such a man on its
surface, there is still probability in its mute tradition that he was there.

In reviewing a character and a career like this, one is insensibly reminded of
Charlemagne. There are, indeed, many specific points of resemblance, as well
as of general outline, between them; and it is only because the one has hitherto
been looked upon as fabulous, while the other is known to have been veritably
historic, that the parallel is not now insisted on. Fingal seems to have passed
away, Charlemagne practically survives; and the world will neither listen to,
nor believe more on the subject. Yet the influence of Fingal, in his day, was
as real as was Charlemagne's, and more beneficent; his moral character infinitely
purer and higher; and if the scene of his patriotic achievements was more limited
—as much less, indeed, as Scotland and Ireland together are less than all central
Europe—his adversaries were incomparably greater. He had the Romans themselves with British allies, on the one hand, to face on the Crona; Norwegian sea

kings and united Irish, on the other, in Ullin; Charlemagne had but the savage hordes of Germany, with thousands upon thousands of disciplined chivalry to meet them. Fingal had the Druids to oppose, Charlemagne had the Church to support him; Fingal was but generalissimo of conflicting tribes, Charlemagne was the anointed successor of the Cæsars. As a curious coincidence, still farther to Fingal's advantage, it should also be mentioned, that whereas Charlemagne, aged 30, at the commencement of his German wars, destroyed the Herman-Saul, a mysterious pillar-like idol on the castellated rock of Lhresburg; Fingal, aged only 17, at the beginning of his Norwegian wars, encountered and dislodged, from its rocky altar-seat in Hoy, the electric spirit of Scandinavian Loda himself, and sent it shrieking in dismay along the winds. These are points which might be insisted on in detail, with perfect propriety; but the chief superiority of Fingal is in his moral nature. Heathen as he was, he was a model of purity in comparison with the most Christian Charlemagne. Thrice married, no wife of his, as Charlemagne's were, was brutally divorced to make way for another; revered and submitted to with awe, as the first of mortal men, no child or friend of his was ever prompted, in revenge for cruelty, to attempt his assassination. The weak, inspired by the instinct of confidence, fled to him everywhere for protection; the base and guilty alone trembled at his approach:—in all which he differs as much from the real Charlemagne of European history, as from the fictitious fools and monsters of Irish mediæval romance. He appears, in short, among the desert scenes and savage tribes of Scotland, and on the verge of Roman civilisation, like a meteor rising from the soil, and transferred to the clouds with obsequies of music. Yet according to our most sagacious critics, this embodiment of heroism, generosity, and devotion—whose shadow may still be traced along the banks of the Clyde and by the shores of the Solway; and whose victories are chronicled to this hour, among the streams of the Carron and Six-mile-water—was the creature of a boy-schoolmaster's brain too richly imbued, they know not how, with the genius of falsehood and forgery.

But now leaving the Land of the Strangers, and returning again, by the Wall or by the Roman road, to the Kelvin and the Crona, and looking northward beyond them, we shall by and by be able to establish a romantic relationship between Stirlingshire and the Orkneys—in which direction also, the spirit of Loda beckons us. For the present, we shall content ourselves with observing that Castlecary, a designation which has hitherto puzzled all antiquarians, seems to be nothing more than the corruption of Castle-Carul, by dropping the l and softening the u into y—changes which are the commonest in every language, and which may be easily exemplified in other names, as in Gartcow and Garchew, both from Gart-cul, in the same neighbourhood. Old Carul who lived at Col-am or Colzam, a little to the west, as we know, was a petty sovereign there, sometimes at feud with Fingal and sometimes with the Romans; but his territory, if he had any at all, must have included Castlecary to the south-east. If so, on account of its importance, that would be his residence; and when he was deprived of this stronghold by the Romans for the building of their Wall, and forced to retire beyond the Crona to the fortifications of Col-am, nothing could be more natural than that his name at least should remain associated, in the mouths of the people, with the place where his court between the friths had formerly been held. No other derivation, with which we are acquainted, seems half so reasonable; and it is perhaps only because Ossian was not known, or his geographical allusions understood or relied on, that the origin of the name as now explained has never before been suggested.

CANOES (two varieties) and WAR CLUB, found at Bowling.
Compare also p. xii. Appendix.

**END OF PART FOURTH.**

# Part Fifth.

# CRITICAL AND STATISTICAL:

WITH

## TWO ROMANCES,

AND

# OSCAR IN ICELAND.

# CONTENTS.

## SECTION FIRST.

                                                                                                                                    PAGE
CHAPTER I.—MacPherson and the Text—Laing's argument finally disposed of—Various editions of Ossianic Fragments—Proofs of honesty in arranging them—Connecting links not seen—Aerial Phenomena misinterpreted—Cloudland of the Clyde, ... ... ... ... ... ... ... ... ... ... 259

CHAPTER II.—MacPherson and the Text (continued):—*Berrathon* and *Croma*—Their relation not perceived by him—Date of their composition in Arran—Interesting details in history of Ossian connected with them—Birth of Fillan in King's Cove—Compare Part Second, Chapter III., ... ... ... ... ... 274

CHAPTER III.—*Conlath and Cuthona*—a Romance of the Clyde—Proof of MacPherson's integrity in reading the Text—Scene of Romance, from Arran by Cantyre to Sanda, determined, ... ... ... ... ... 283

## SECTION SECOND.

CHAPTER IV.—Old-World Miscellaneous Statistics compared with New—Geography—Warlike Equipments and Usages—Habits, Customs, Arts—Superstitions—with Parallels from Modern Life and Science, ... 293

CHAPTER V.—Philosophical Statistics—Navigation—Geology—Electricity—Fabrication of Weapons—Knowledge of the Metals—Gold, rare and beautiful; manufactured in, and obtained from the Land of the Strangers—Carriage of Materials—Modes of Building—Knowledge of Medicine, ... ... ... ... 299

CHAPTER VI.—Romance of *Carric-thura*—or, a Glance at the Orkneys—Origin of Name—Laing mistaken—Voyage from Morven—Geographical Bearings—Landmarks and Localities—Inis-tore identical with Hoy—Carric-thura identical with Thurwo—Original Aspect of the Orkneys—Electric Storms, and other Indications of approaching Volcanic Ruptures, ... ... ... ... ... ... ... ... 311

CHAPTER VII.—*War of Inis-thona*—Inis-thona identified with Iceland—Oscar's Voyage—Fountain of Mossy stones—His victory at Lano, now Thingvalla—Sovereignty of Denmark there at that date—No Eruption of Mount Hekla as yet—Connection of that Volcano with Subterranean range from Ireland by West of Scotland and the Orkneys—Lapps and Finns, did Ossian know them? ... ... ... ... ... 325

CHAPTER VIII.—Religious Faiths—Funeral Rites, &c., Origin of these, (?) from the East—Fire and Serpent Worship—Varieties of Sepulture, where and of whom—Turriff and the Farne Isles, ... ... ... ... 339

CHAPTER IX.—Altars and Tombstones—The Mode of their Construction—Various Examples—"Auld Wives' Lifts" at Baldernock—Indian and other Cairns—Circles, Monoliths, and Tombs in Arran—Their fine adaptation to the Scenery—Address to Goatfell, ... ... ... ... ... ... ... ... 349

## ILLUSTRATIONS.

ISLE DEVRAR, in Campbeltown Loch, ... ... ... ... ... 289
SANDA ISLE, Ireland in the Distance, ... ... ... ... ... 288
SOLID TORQUE, or Ring Money, ... ... ... ... ... 310
DWARFIE STONE (from Barry's Orkney), ... ... ... ... 316
AULD WIVES' LIFTS, (from Ure's Rutherglen), ... ... ... ... 351
PANDOO INDIAN CAIRN (from Maria Graham's India), ... ... ... 351

# CRITICAL AND STATISTICAL.

## SECTION FIRST.

### CHAPTER I.

#### MACPHERSON AND THE TEXT.

I. THE commencement of our concluding Part, and the beginning of the first chapter, is now the proper place, perhaps, to dispose finally of Mr. Laing and his celebrated argument of plagiarism against the translator of Ossian. 1. Besides an elaborate dissertation on this subject, affixed to the second volume of his own *History of Scotland*, remarkable for its boldness and much esteemed at the time for its critical ingenuity; in which, from eight different points of view, supposed by him to be quite unassailable, he endeavours to demonstrate, step by step, the systematic imposture of MacPherson; Mr. Laing compiled a series of parallel passages from various authors, ancient and modern, to identify the sources from which the imposture was drawn, and published it afterwards, in the shape of Notes to an edition of MacPherson's works already referred to. By an analysis in our Appendix, drawn carefully up for the reader's satisfaction and amusement, it will be seen that Mr. Laing has thus accumulated not fewer than 966 instances of alleged quotation from 88 different authors, in the so-called works of Ossian; on which he rests the dogmatic conclusion that the works themselves were a forgery. That parallel passages, words or phrases, to that number have been found, after immense critical research, is undeniable; and as they extend over a long list of authors, from the Bible to an Irish Ballad, from Psalms to the *Flowers of the Forest*, from the *Iliad* to the *Rape of the Lock*, and from *Paradise Lost* to Mason's *Elfrida*—they would imply the same extent of reading on the translator's part before they were acquired, systematised, and employed. Mr. Laing, in point of fact, must have begun this research not much later than 1790, for the first instalment of his discoveries appeared at the end of his History in 1800; and he must have continued them for four years or thereby afterwards, for they were not published entire, as we have seen, until 1805—thus including a period of fifteen years at least; having himself in the meantime attained the mature age of 43, with all the advantages of wealth, ease, and the Advocates' Library in Edinburgh, to assist him. MacPherson, on the other hand, in certain poverty, must have commenced the same sort of work by stealth at the age of 20 or 21; must have carried it on in secret, accumulated all the quotations alleged in his unaided memory; adapted, diversified, and wrought them out into two grand and twenty minor epic poems, first in English then in Gaelig; and finally prepared them, with Notes of his own and innumerable traditions, for the Press, before he concluded his 25th year—that is, in less than five years altogether.

With a presumption so serious against his own view on the face of it, it seems unaccountable that Mr. Laing, if he was conducting this investigation on any reasonable principles—and not merely to display his own learning, or to propitiate the frequenters of Parliament House and the founders of the *Edinburgh Review*—did not reflect (1.) That men like Moses, Homer, David, Milton, and Ossian, who were all poets of nature, must have had innumerable ideas in common suggested by nature, and which therefore could not be otherwise expressed than in the same or similar language. MacPherson himself points out not fewer than 118 of these—from the Bible, from Homer, from Milton, and others; being apparently ignorant of the rest. (2.) That in rendering any one, or all of these authors into another tongue, the resemblance between them severally would be increased; and what may be called a unity of speech, as well as of idea, would be the natural result in the hands of any translator. (3.) That in doing justice to an original like Ossian, a translator of taste, which MacPherson unquestionably was, would of necessity select both the best and most elegant, as well as the most literal terms he could find, from reading or otherwise; by which the original similarity of ideas would be strengthened—a process of accommodation which no impostor in his senses, who had the field free from the beginning, would ever have adopted. (4.) That an immense proportion of such coincident phrases on ordinary topics might be purely accidental. How many such expressions are in use every day, by the inhabitants of every city, unconsciously and inevitably; and men by hundreds speak both prose and poetry on all sorts of subjects, in identical terms of their own, without being aware of it. In spite of these natural explanations, however, Mr. Laing chooses to maintain that a youth like MacPherson, in the space of five brief years, out of these 966 miscellaneous quotations of phrases, words, and often mere syllables—which it must have taken Mr. Laing himself, at his leisure, not less than fifteen years to collect—concocted, on the foundation of absurd Irish Ballads, a series of dramatic and descriptive poems hitherto unrivalled in the language—to say nothing of the obvious fact, that in these alleged fabrications, the finest and most characteristic passages are without any alleged parallels. It is difficult to say whether the compliment to his genius implied in such a charge of forgery against the youth who was the subject of it, or the folly of the man who could deliberately imagine and propound it, in two elaborate volumes, is the more outrageous. It is only a little more pitiful to hear another, like Wordsworth, accepting such a theory, and apostrophising MacPherson with a contemptuous " All-hail!" as the " sire of Ossian."—" As the translators of the Bible," says he, "and Shakespeare, and Milton, and Pope could not be indebted to MacPherson, it follows that he must owe his fine feathers to them." But if similarity of style alone were any proof of such a forgery, one might as well affirm now, in 1874, that the speeches of Fingal had been copied from that royal oration of Pharaoh Rameses III. to the princes of Egypt three thousand years ago, translated but yesterday from a scroll of papyrus in the British Museum; with this difference only, that MacPherson's work as an imitator was infinitely better done.

2. But at the other point of view from which we are now able to consider it, its falsehood, as well as its folly, becomes apparent. The poems in question, alleged so to have been concocted, are not only dramatic and generally descriptive, but historical, minutely topographical, and even statistical; extending over a period of nearly three centuries, and representing both scenes, individual objects in nature, and countries which should all be recognisable—which were nevertheless not only unknown, but undreamt of by the youth who was alleged to have been guilty of the fraud. Is it possible, then, that the countries so spoken of can still be distinguished and defined, that the scenes represented can be identified, the objects so described pointed out, and the accidents detailed verified—the sole means of such verification being his own unconscious phraseology, and yet the work from which all this intelligence is obtained, at the distance of more than a hundred years, should have been a fabrication? Without the use of such terms and figures as Mr. Laing himself objects to, and parades in his list of plagiarisms as proofs of the grossest fraud, such discoveries as we have just recorded would have been impossible. If the sun, for example, had not been shining from the east on Fingal and from the northwest on Cuthullin, the course of the Lubar would have been a mystery; if the full moon had not been setting in a cloud, as we shall see, Carric-thura in the Orkneys would have been undistinguishable—Mr. Laing, himself a native of the neighbourhood, did not even dream of that; if lines from the west and north had not converged on Malvina's grave, Tor-lutha would never have been identified; and if Comala had not been sitting by a rugged ravine, with her face to the south-east on the brink of an oozy torrent, the rock where she died would never have been seen, "the place of renown," with its stones of victory, would

never have been discovered, nor the defeat of Caracalla determined:—and so, in innumerable other instances: yet all these, according to Mr. Laing, were scratch quotations from Homer and the Song of Solomon! Poor Comala, panic-stricken on the banks of the Crona, is actually converted by him into the Spouse coquetting with the King among the rocks of Sion. If Fingal, forsooth, had not been acquainted with Solomon, he could never have addressed her as he did —" Look from thy rocks, my love; and let me hear the voice of Comala!" Alas for the Bonny Water, and its silent refutation of all this fine theory!

Mr. Laing's own learned ignorance of the facts now thus in question is not the least amusing part of his appearance, as the collector of plagiarisms and the demolisher of texts. He spends five full pages, large and small type, octavo, of his dissertation, to instruct the reader that Malvina's dream, both in English and Gaelig, is a philological absurdity, and must therefore have been an editorial lie; and does not know that every syllable of it may be confirmed, and most exquisitely illustrated, by a morning's walk on the west coast of Arran, not less than 70 miles distant from the spot where both he and MacPherson imagined it was seen. He spends nearly two pages more to show that Larthon's dream, in like manner, is a grammatical imposture; but has no idea that the cave where it occurred can be identified at Ardglass, 140 miles nearer home than where his youthful impostor had located it. And finally, to quote his own words—with their conspicuous *italicised* insinuation of mercenary fraud:—

" The Temora was afterwards *translated* or extended to eight books, at lord Bute's desire, and published with additional poems, without a second expedition to the highlands; but Moi-lena, in King's county, and the palace of Temora, at Tara in Meath, were transferred to Ulster, by another fatal mistake, like Carric-thura and Balclutha, which destroys the authenticity of the whole poem."

It is wonderful, indeed, that a " second expedition to the highlands" could be safely dispensed with, in preparation for this lie: but Moi-lena, we have seen, *is* in Ulster and not in King's county; Temora was in Antrim, and not in Meath; Carric-thura, we shall see, was not on the coast of Caithness, but in one of the Orkneys—within no great distance, less than 20 miles, of Mr. Laing's own door; and Balclutha was not at Dumbarton, but at Rutherglen! The fatal mistake, for Mr. Laing's credit, was in Mr. Laing's own arrogance; the fortunate mistake, for MacPherson's credit, was in MacPherson's innocent misapprehension; the truth alone was in Ossian, whose text also had been faithfully translated; and the authenticity of the poems, thus loftily challenged, has been more indisputably confirmed than ever. We thus take farewell of Mr. Laing, not ungratefully by any means, or without due appreciation of his learning. His courage and hostility, on unknown ground, have been as amusing as Don Quixote's at the Wind-mills; and his infallible philological conclusions, and portentous list of plagiarisms, like a dream that perisheth. But to proceed——

II. Having concluded our geographical researches, as far as we are at present able to pursue them with certainty in Scotland and Ireland, and having accumulated in the course of these an amount of evidence, both for the authenticity of Ossian and for the historical truth of his narratives, which seems irresistible, it remains only farther in the way of argument to consider how far MacPherson's translation is reliable in respect to separate poems and minor details. This aspect of the controversy has hitherto been looked upon as most important, inasmuch as tampering with the text was supposed to be the translator's failing, even by those who were agreed to acquit him of the more serious crime of forgery. After the minute historical and geographical proofs of accuracy, however, even where error might well have been expected and excused in the translator of fragmentary works so old, and to himself so indistinct, the reader will not perhaps be disposed to regard the question of editorial exactness in words and letters of such vital moment as hitherto. But it is a matter of importance, notwithstanding, that MacPherson's integrity in this, as in other respects, should be established, that the public may be satisfied not only of the authenticity of Ossian, but of the general reliability of the text of Ossian as represented by him; and it should be matter of congratulation to all interested in the subject, that the minutest investigation we can prosecute in this department results in his complete vindication from every suspicion of dishonesty. Whether the text on which he relied was the truest text to be found, is another question, and one which we do not feel ourselves at present competent to determine. But no truer text, so far as we are aware, has yet been produced; whilst obvious errors and deficiencies may be shown in editions which purport to be purer than his. It is with his own editorial fidelity in the treatment of the text as he found it, we are now concerned, or with his discretion in selecting the truest version from among several before him at the time; and in this, which is the sole remaining question to be discussed, we shall find the clearest proof both of great sagacity and of unimpeachable integrity.

The most convenient method of prosecuting this inquiry may be to consider first his own original arrangement of the poems as they came to hand, with the various minute links of association and other characteristics by which they are connected, often apparently without his observation; and then to select an instance or two in which fraud or tampering might easily have been effected, yet has not been even so much as thought of. Many beautiful incidents, it may be observed in passing, will occur to notice in the course of this investigation; and one romance at least of the sublimest tragedy, hitherto inexplicable, will require to be illustrated, so that the reader may have additional inducements to follow it attentively to the end. Proceeding then on this principle, we may classify the results of our general critical review, as under.

1. Several poems included by MacPherson, as among the number of Ossian's works, have been omitted from authorised Gaelig editions published since his day, as being either presumably not known or not recoverable as Ossian's from any independent source. Among the rest, is the poem of *Berrathon*. But *Berrathon*, if MacPherson had understood it correctly, afforded the most conclusive evidence imaginable of his own honesty. The original, therefore, if it was ever in his hands, could not have been destroyed by him intentionally; nor does he even turn the translation, as published by him, to his own account as a translator. In every view of the matter, therefore, he must have been absolutely innocent as regards that poem—which, as we have already shown, is the key to the whole argument in his favour.

2. He had no idea that *Croma* was composed at the same place as *Berrathon*, probably but a few days before it, and both within a few weeks or months of Ossian's own decease. This fact, so obvious on the face of them, was as dark to MacPherson as if these poems had never seen the light, either by his own or any other agency; an oversight the more remarkable inasmuch as, although the poems appeared originally in their natural sequence—*Croma* first and *Berrathon* immediately after, at the end of his first volume in 1762—they were afterwards separated by a great interval, as if they had no historical or biographical connection whatever.

3. Only part of *Temora*—the introduction—was originally published in 1762, in which the scene of action is called Lena. The year following, the whole was published as a perfect poem, in which the same scene is called Moi-Lena, apparently on some new and better authority than he had before, for in one case the word is omitted entirely; in which editorial emendations, however, he could have nothing but the text and his own judgment to guide him, as his want of acquaintance with the subject in other respects proves. In two instances alone, where the substitution of one word for the other has been made, the present writer is of opinion that the original reading of Lena is still to be preferred; but in every other instance MacPherson's verdict now, at the distance of a hundred and ten years, has been ratified by fact. The word Lena occurs only twice throughout the remainder of the poem, and in such peculiar apposition to Moi-Lena as clearly to imply that the terms were distinct, and restricted in their application to distinguishable parts of the valley. In *Fingal*, on the other hand, it is uniformly Lena, never Moi-Lena; and if any change of the term had been unwarrantably introduced by the translator in that poem, it might have involved

the geography of the entire epic in confusion. Lena, in fact, as we have seen, was but the entrance to the valley of the Lubar; Moi-Lena was the valley itself, expanding wider and wider westward. In Lena, the campaign of *Fingal* was fought; in Moi-Lena chiefly, the campaign of *Temora*. MacPherson himself never clearly understood this; but his fidelity to the text, even among conflicting editions, enables us to prove it; whereas any impostor, ignorant, as he manifestly was, of the facts of the case, would have harmonised the terms in both poems, or assigned same imaginary reason for their difference. MacPherson does neither; and the whole case, as affecting his integrity in the handling of two such important manuscripts, is perhaps altogether unparalleled in the annals of unintentional and unconscious self-justification.

4. The arrangement of *Temora* itself in Books was made avowedly and entirely by himself from fragments, which came to hand in confusion as they were discovered. This has been so admirably done as to leave no doubt of its perfect accuracy, yet with such obvious ignorance of the scene described as to preclude the very idea of forgery. In this re-arrangement, the harmonising of names— not only of Lena and of Moi-Lena, as already pointed out, but of many others— could have been easily accomplished, if the translator had been actuated by any considerations other than those of simple adherence to the text. Indeed the multiplication of the same or of similar names, as we shall by and by see, to the almost inextricable confusion of certain narratives on first reading—unnecessary, and therefore incredible on the part of any forger, is a source of perplexity that might have been avoided with the greatest ease in the re-arrangement and revision of the various poems in which they occur, if external harmony and perspicuity alone had been aimed at. Real harmony and perspicuity may indeed be attained, by much critical research and elaborate critical collation; but in works of pure fiction, which were gradually growing in the hands of an impostor to a perfect whole, such superficial obscurity was a blemish. The obscurity, as it stands, when fully explained, enables us to establish the clearest harmony; but MacPherson takes no special pains to do this—in some important cases, does not even attempt it; and nothing but historical accuracy in Ossian on the one hand, and the most scrupulous fidelity in his translator on the other, could justify the bewildering reiteration complained of.

5. We have already seen how many of the poems in MacPherson's collection are connected together by descriptive and historical associations. *Fingal* and *Temora*, for example, are independent epics, which nevertheless can hardly be separated; *Darthula* and the *Death of Cuthullin* are intermediate narratives, which illuminate the background westward; *Cathlin of Clutha* and *Sulmalla of Lumon* episodical narratives, which carry us beyond the background eastward, and cast

a reflected light from Ireland, through the Solway Frith, to Norway; *Colna-dona*, the *War of Caros*, *Cathloda*, *Carric-thura*, and even *Comala*, more remotely connected, interweave the annals of Stirlingshire and central Caledonia with the Clyde, with Ireland, with the Orkneys, and again with Norway, besides bringing us by the most explicit narrative face to face with Rome. *Berrathon* and *Croma* are inseparable links, which unite Arran, Ireland, Cantyre, and Zetland; whilst *Conlath and Cuthona*, by a single word incidentally occurring—Lano, the name of a pestilential lake in Lochlin—unites three generations, and transports us from Glencoe to Sanda, from Sanda to Ireland, twice from Ireland to Norway, and back once more to the shores of Morven: and these all, sometimes by substantial narrative; sometimes by the thread of a mere syllable, are dovetailed or interwoven with the most important histories. The same sort of relationship might easily be traced among other pieces in the collection, if necessary; but the point more immediately deserving our attention is, that these poems were neither published nor arranged by MacPherson so as to illustrate their historical sequence. They appeared first in disorder, as regarded their subjects, and they remained in disorder as regarded their dates; where natural order was accidentally observed at the beginning, it was ultimately violated on revision; and, in the final edition of 1773, everything was thrown once more into chronological chaos. For this extraordinary process of detail among pieces intended to have a sequence, which really had many perceptible links of association, and might have been made to present not only a rude, but often subtle coherence, with very little editorial care in the hands of a man to whose fertile imagination they all owed their very existence, no explanation, not even an apology can be offered in excuse. No fabricator who knew the links beforehand would have allowed them thus to be lost sight of; no man who had even received all the materials of an original work at once, however much in disorder, would have suffered them to leave his hands so disorganised. No other reason, in short, can be assigned for such a system of publication or adjustment, but that the fragments were translated and given to the world as he found them, by MacPherson; and that some of the finer links of association, as between *Berrathon* and *Croma* and *Colna-dona*, were never discovered by him as long as he lived. This verdict, we are certain, will commend itself to any jury of intelligent critics who investigate the premises; and implies no worse reflection on the translator himself than a want of perceptive faculty, acute enough to distinguish the subtler traces of relationship in a mass of fragmentary materials thrown confusedly and unexpectedly on his hands. That he could have been the fabricator of these materials as they now stand, disjointed and yet perceptibly related by the slenderest fibres, many of them beyond his knowledge, is a moral, or rather a metaphysical impossibility on which no experienced student of human nature will bestow a second thought.

6. But among these links there is one beautiful pervading influence, which seems to attract every idea to itself like a magnet, and to fuse all fragments into one like electricity. This influence is the magic of Malvina's filial love, which seems to have been at once the solace and source of inspiration to her adoptive father. Her name, or direct reference to herself, as his daughter-in-law and companion, assistant with the harp and affectionate listener to his tales and praises of Oscar, occurs in so many separate poems, with dedications and apostrophes and appeals to her, and with allusions to her family in so many more, besides the poem which commemorates her death—that she may be called, without the vulgarity of exaggeration or the emptiness of fiction, the muse of Ossian. Of the poems with which she is thus intimately connected, three at least, if not more, are themselves connected with other poems to which they are historical supplements—so that on the whole, there is this literal identification of her name, or of her family with considerably more than two-thirds in extent of the reputed works of Ossian, and these historically by far the most important of them all. Can any one then, with the slightest claim to critical impartiality or discernment, believe that a personage whose birth, life, love, habits, history, comings and goings, disappointments, sorrows, death and burial—whose very existence, in fact, was absolutely in his own hands, could have been so identified accidentally, incidentally, episodically, historically, geographically, and poetically with the legendary lore of a whole epoch by any impostor who knew nothing, after all, about where she was born, or where she lived, or where she died, as represented in his own fable? more especially when the change of a single word, as we have seen, would have harmonised the whole with his own absurd theory on the subject, and effectually concealed his ignorance? Such critical credulity, if it can longer exist, must be the credulity of the fatuous.

But all this, it may still be reiterated, is no answer to the charge of occasionally falsifying the text in points which are beyond our own observation. For what is beyond our observation in any word or letter, it is also beyond our power, of course, to vouch; but when no tampering can be seen where the best opportunities and strongest inducements to tamper are obvious, it comes then to be the burden of those who reiterate this charge, to specify the suspected points and to prove their falsification. We have already shown by innumerable instances that, in all human probability, such a charge in any case is groundless; and with respect to cases unknown or conjectural, we shall content ourselves once for all with a parallel from modern art which, as regards fidelity of transcription, translation, and general editorial supervision, seems to be unanswerable. In Rogers' Century of Prints from the Great Masters, London, 1778, we find by the text that Domenichino in love represented his mistress as a handsome youth in cavalier's attire alarmed at the approach of a furious horse, in his grand painting of the Emperor Otho III.'s visit to St. Nil, of which all the details in colour and costume are given. Having beside us also a volume of engravings in outline, from older and larger prints of the works of Domenichino exquisitely done, and published at Paris, 1813, we turn this volume over, as a matter of curiosity, in search of the lady cavalier. In the centre of the picture referred to, we find the figure in question distinctly recognisable to the minutest particular of costume, colour of course excepted—and recognisable not only as the figure described, but as the figure of a woman in disguise. This being so, would any one, in the mere wantonness of scepticism and without proof, be justified in maintaining or even suggesting that the other figures, done all with the same care, were falsely done? If not, how much less would he be justified in asserting that the whole engraving was a forgery; and least of all, that the painting itself in Domenichino's name was an imposture, got up in the meantime, between the first and second engravings, to support the romantic story? Not having seen the original, any unprejudiced reader or student of the subject would certainly rather accept the whole engraving as honest, and every other detail as substantially true. But for Domenichino the painter, put Ossian the poet; for the lady in disguise, Malvina the huntress; for the principal figures St. Nil and the Emperor, put Fingal, Swaran, Cuthullin, Oscar, and the rest; for the engraver of 1813, MacPherson; for Rogers or his authority, the reciters and rehearsers of Gaelig traditions—and the parallel with all its logical consequences is complete; with this addition to its force, that whereas the engraver most probably knew the story of the lady's portrait beforehand and might give it more effect in the delineation if so disposed, MacPherson knew nothing of Malvina's.

When thus verified and grouped, on ordinary principles of time and place, the poems of Ossian resemble a forest, perhaps, more than a picture—a forest of trees planted all by the same hand although not always on the same ground, but growing all from their own historic roots independently, wreathed with tradition and branching to the top; where their boughs and minutest tendrils, each inscribed with the name of some hero or heroine, are interwoven in one gorgeous head of foliage, swaying to the tempest or glittering in the sun. Gaps among them by accident, or the hand of time—none of them, apparently, wilfully made—are no doubt obvious, which can never be repaired; yet, intertwined and supporting each other thus, they overarch seas, and stretch along mountain ridges, and clothe the intervening valleys with the texture of song, till the whole western coast of Europe, from Ireland by the Orkneys to the shores of the Baltic, has been enriched and beautified by their growth. The epics of *Fingal* and *Temora*, in fact, springing clear from the soil of Ullin, interweave their arms with the oaks of Norway; and the *War of Caros*, beyond floods and ramparts, telegraphs a defeat to Rome. Rivers in the meantime, now dwindled to rills, and friths subsiding into rivers, are seen gliding by their roots, and the sites of towns and cities resplendent in modern civilisation may be pointed out with precision among these very waters; the tombs of the mighty are still traceable on their skirts, or distinguishable through their vistas; the spirits of departed kings and heroes, like meteors of the night, illuminate their deepest gloom; and the "darkbrown years" of twenty centuries encircle all. Too much of this, it may be objected, is sorrowful, monotonous, or dark; but it must be remembered on the other hand, that every trunk of that forest sprung from soil that had been actually steeped in blood—by no fault of the poet's, and that every legend interwoven with its growth was the record of some real misfortune: yet not the smallest stem we see there but has its roots in the rim of life, or the slightest leaf that twinkles in the mass but is gilded with the light of poetry, or moistened with the dew of love. It is all genuine; and if sad, it is also sublime: but its sadness and sublimity alike are of the universe it represents—of a generation that was fighting itself for honour to death, and of a people that were being hastened by their own very generosity to decay.

Such is the idea presented to us now by MacPherson's collection of these wonderful productions, although never adequately realised or expressed by him. With all his faculty as a translator, which was admirable, he could not re-arrange that magnificent fall of timber as it once stood, or interpret its relation to the globe. Many a beautiful link, no doubt, beyond what was patent on the surface, he supplied, and many a situation he boldly conjectured; but as it grew up, tree by tree once more, under his own eye, he got bewildered among its intricacies and incredulous about its bearings; transposed or transplanted masses of it, till he had well nigh destroyed its identity; groped assiduously for its roots, at the distance of hundreds of miles from where they were actually fixed, and found himself occasionally suspended, like Absalom, inadvertently or unconsciously, among its branches—where his adversaries, if they could, would have thrust at him till he died. To suspect him, therefore, of forgery in its reproduction is worse than critical injustice; it is morally and logically preposterous.

II. Before quitting this subject in its general bearings, and by way of extending our idea both of the fidelity of Ossian to nature, and of the fidelity of MacPherson to the text even when he did not realise its ulterior relations—as to scenery, for example, and situation; we may glance for a moment at a certain pervading feature in most of Ossian's descriptions, which MacPherson in the circumstances could not fully understand, but which he has neither exaggerated nor diminished, we may verily believe, to the extent of a letter. What we refer to is the prevalence of aerial aspects, and their relation to the earth, so remarkable in all the reflections, descriptions, and similes of the poet, and in what may be be called his religious or speculative philosophy as founded on these. That such allusions might be common enough in the speech of any man like Ossian, as they are also in the speech of Homer—to whom external nature, above and below, was the source and theme of perpetual inspiration; and that they would be quite intelligible, therefore, to a man like MacPherson, who was capable of translating Ossian so well, although he failed on Homer, is of course admitted. But it will be found on examination, that there is a natural congruity and significance in the order of these allusions of which MacPherson was not aware, and which it would have been morally impossible for him to see without noting it; yet nothing has been done by him, in his general rendering, to destroy that effect, so that others should not be able to realise it. This will be more apparent in detail—

1. The cloud scenery of the Clyde from Cantyre to Dumbarton and Ben-Lomond, over the peaks of Arran and the peninsulas of the frith—both for variety of form, from mountain masses to the faintest flakes of ghost-like vapours; and for colour, from dazzling silver to the richest purple or the glowing red, with simultaneous contrasts of the saddest grey, deepening in an hour to frowning black—is unsurpassed for beauty in the whole Island, perhaps on all the western coasts of Europe. Such beauty, indeed, as Ossian saw it, and before steamboat emanations and the veil of smoke from manufacturing cities had obscured it, must have been often transcendental. In this cloudland Ossian wandered as in a celestial paradise of his own, and tabernacled his progenitors there in glory, with their robes of mist and meteor ensigns, in palaces of air— all which MacPherson might very well understand and appreciate. But it must not be forgotten that the fragments of these atmospheric landscapes, broken and drifted by the storms from the south-west, are accumulated again, although with fewer fantastic shapes, along the interior ridges of the Kilpatrick and the Campsie hills; which they shroud occasionally from view altogether, or seem to elevate nearer to heaven, with softer outlines accommodated to their forms. These aerial aspects too, of the country between the friths, Ossian had studied from the banks of the Kelvin and the Crona, with the eye of a meditative man; and had peopled the Ardven of Stirlingshire thus with the ghosts of heroes who defied the Romans, and still hovered on the heights from midnight till dawn to watch the struggles of their children against the common enemy, or to scatter the invaders of their solitude with shafts of fire. All this, so true to nature, and in such absolute conformity with facts, was inexplicable to MacPherson,

who knew not even the very region where such sights were to be seen, much less the connection of such sights with the uttermost range of the poet's observation; who, in accordance with the plainest principles of meteorology, brought witnesses to the conflicts of the Carron on troops of clouds careering "like the steeds of the stranger," over seas and lakes and forests, from Cromla and Goatfell, or from Morven and Glencoe, as directly and truly and swiftly, as the drift from the Atlantic could carry them.

His descriptions of, or descriptive allusions to the air currents of the Orkneys, and their perplexing or dangerous effects on navigation there, as the work only of some dæmonic power in the atmosphere, are equally true; and in the guesses they imply, at the cause of such phenomena, are almost philosophic. It was not the ghosts of his fathers who presided in, or cared to inhabit those heavens; but the malignant spirit of Loda, with which his fathers were at perpetual war, and dared to dislodge from the cloud with magic sword. All which, in like manner, MacPherson so sadly misunderstands, yet does not tarnish the splendour of the figures by the wilful mistranslation of a syllable. How little these representations of Ossian founded on his observation of meteoric phenomena, and his deep religious faith of another world, have been understood or appreciated by others as well as MacPherson, is obvious from the very ridicule and discredit attached to them. Emerson sees a pair of expanded wings in the clouds with a circular cloud between them, which in his opinion wants only two eyes and a mouth to convert the whole into what mediæval artists represent as an angel, and he is called a philosopher in imagination justly. Ossian sees in clouds giants, ghosts, heroes, dogs and horses—the disembodied spirits of his fathers, with their retinue in the chase; or seated forms, with lambent meteoric light between them—his fathers in council, with attendant ministers of fire to illuminate their airy hall and discharge their behests to the lower world; or stooping forms—his fathers in glory, bending from the clouds to receive their offspring again to heaven; or fleeting forms, with prophetic rustle in their dissolving wings: and he is scouted as a dull melancholic dreamer, who can fancy no more comfortable paradise than a wreath of mist; or MacPherson, for honestly translating him, although he does not understand one-half of this philosophy any more than others, is condemned as an impostor. Our critics thus contradict and amuse themselves; but Ossian's embodiments remain, and the cloudland of the Clyde reproduces them.

2. One other feature only we shall note, which by its frequent occurrence may be said to be almost a peculiarity in Ossian as an observer of nature, and by which his absolute fidelity to sense, and his faculty of perception also, as chief among natural poets, are equally distinguished—the moral reference he so often makes to the effects of sunshine and shade on the face of the landscape. Such effects,

changeful and varied, and almost like revelations or new-creative actions in the soil itself—brightening, darkening, and moving, obliterating and restoring the everlasting hills—are possible only through a clouded sky continually agitated by conflicting currents, and on a surface of corresponding inequality; where light and shade thus irregularly passing reveal depths that would be otherwise unseen, and give prominence to subordinate outlines that, in the uniform glare of an unclouded sky, would be lost on the common horizon. The very plain itself, by these atmospheric transitions, seems to be converted into a magic canvass, but it is only from some neighbouring height that the full effect of their transforming influence can be realised. Let any one who doubts this survey the plain from Abbey Craig or Stirling Castle up the valley of the Forth, on a day of mingled clouds in motion and of average sunshine between—much more of brilliant sunshine, and he will be more than satisfied of the correctness of these observations. But Scotland at large, and more especially on the west coast—to which Ossian's descriptions chiefly apply, is not only remarkable for such phenomena, but is celebrated over the world for their richness and variety; for the double landscape beauty, so to speak, terrestrial and aerial, which is created by them, combined. The Island, indeed, may be said to be renewed by these every day of the year; to be lost and restored again, in the flight of a few hours; or to be reproduced and multiplied, the same and yet another, by every passing cloud and every glimpse of sunshine. It was to this endless transformation of the surface, to these fleeting and yet ceaseless effects of light and shade; to the rise, the progress, and the decay of every passing cloud—whence, whither, and how; and to the very shade-creating action of the wind itself on the long pliant grass, which must then have been luxuriant, and only half depastured in the valleys —" as the wave passes over the field;" to these, and to their moral influence on the thoughtful observer, Ossian was so instinctively and so minutely alive, that without any other evidence to guide us than his glance at earth and heaven, we may be absolutely assured not only that he lived in Scotland but on the west coast of Scotland, and that his poems were all inspired and spoken there. Of other lands, with their characteristic peculiarities—as of Norway and its snows, or Ullin with its green vales and marshy lakes; and even of their woodland deer —their boars, their spotted bulls, and their bounding horses—he was equally observant; but in the Western Highlands of Scotland he must have lived, and through the intermediate vistas of its cloudland he had the purest light of inspiration. If a heaven was pre-supposed by him at all, it was behind those mystical battlements of vapour; and if human life was to be allegorised, or human history repeated, it was in the wave of sunshine and of shade—always the same, and always different—that swept, without any abiding trace, along his native valleys; and God himself for him was but the presiding, yet invisible spirit or principle of change, that renewed and regulated all.

It would be incorrect, of course, as well as ungenerous, to say that MacPherson was insensible to all this, or that he did not understand it; but he failed to observe the intimate dependence even of its sublimest parts on the simplest meteorological facts in nature, which gave precision and reality to the whole; which converted such dreams and reveries into a chart of the local sky. He never traced the motion of the cloud with a spirit in its bosom, nor turned his cheek, as the blind man would, to catch the current of the breeze which sighed in its passage over the grave of the departed. These came and went whithersoever they listed, without any observation of his about their origin or errand. He saw nothing in any simile, like a point of the compass, to guide him; and nothing in any shadow, beyond the mere darkening of the sun. He took no note of the phases of the moon, of her rising or her setting, to indicate localities; or of her place in the sky, as Ossian did, to connect distant scenes. Hence Comala's rock on the Crona, and Carric-thura, where she was born, in the Orkneys, have no meteoric relation, so to speak, in his eyes; yet the half moon or thereby of Crona, which lifted her soul when she died, becomes the full moon of Carric-thura a few days afterwards, where, years before, she had been born. Hence also, Malvina's grave, and Oscar's tomb, and Fillan's birth-place, and it may be a hundred scenes besides, which can now be identified, remained absolutely unknown to him; yet, as we have already observed, and must once again reiterate, the change or omission of a single syllable in one of those allusions would have prevented their discovery for ever. But the details of this investigation, as the reader has been informed, will require the selection of one or more prominent cases, in which the scrupulous fidelity of the translator in all these respects may be demonstrated, fully to illustrate and prove them. Many such cases might indeed be easily produced; we shall confine ourselves, however, to the minute examination of two only.

## CHAPTER II.

#### MACPHERSON AND THE TEXT CONTINUED.

##### BERRATHON AND CROMA—CONNECTED POEMS.

1. *Berrathon*, otherwise called Ossian's Dying Hymn, with its philosophy, its geography, and its facts, we have already ascertained to be entirely beyond MacPherson, not only in its authorship, but in the very idea of it. From being some doubtful document in a printer's hand, or a groundwork of forgery in an editor's, it turns out to be the embodiment of a sublime philosophic faith, and a geographical memorial in which the science of the age is concerned—with which, therefore, neither printer, nor editor, nor translator from henceforth should be permitted, without evidence of authority, to intermeddle. By whom, then, was this magnificent effusion written, or rather first conceived, and how has it been transmitted to us? That MacPherson himself received it in the north, and knew nothing more of it whatever, need hardly be repeated, for it is obvious, undisputed and indisputable. How, then, did it reach the north, or by whom was it conveyed thither—without note, comment, or tradition to explain it?

1. In Mr. Bannatyne's letter, already quoted—Part Second, Chap. II.—we find, on second reading, a floating tradition mentioned to the effect that Malvina's death occurred when she was travelling with her father southward at the head of his army, probably on its way to Ireland. There is nothing in the poem itself to countenance this part of the tradition, nor is it very easy to believe it. Ossian, indeed, old, blind, and infirm, might have had a small following, the remnant of his father's troops, to escort him, or which he might have been marshalling on their route to Ireland, when he died at Clachaig. This certainly is quite possible, but it would be the uttermost. The tradition, however, is not without its value and significance, for it proves the frequent march of armed men from Morven through Arran on their way to Ulster; and it confirms this other fact, already mentioned, that this visit of Malvina, on which she died, must have been her second return from the north to the place of her nativity at Lutha. But if there was no great warlike following with Ossian, there was at least a personal attendant, the son of one of Fingal's bards, himself a singer and a harper, who officiated both as his guide and as his assistant, with occasional interludes of music in his hours of poetic inspiration. To this youth, almost in the very words of Milton's Samson to the Philistine lad who leads him—

"A little onward lend thy guiding hand,
To these dark steps, a little farther on;"

the aged Seer, in his own blindness, though not a prisoner like Samson, says—

"Lead, Son of Alpin, lead the aged to his woods. The winds begin to rise: the dark wave of the lake resounds. Bends there not a tree from Mora, with its branches bare? It bends, Son of Alpin, in the rustling blast. My harp hangs on a blasted branch. The sound of its strings is mournful. Does the wind touch thee, O harp! or is it some passing ghost? It is the hand of Malvina! But bring me the harp, Son of Alpin; another song shall rise. My soul shall depart in the sound; my fathers shall hear it in their airy hall. Their dim faces shall hang with joy from their clouds, and their hands receive their son. . . . . Strike the harp and raise the song: be near, with all your wings, ye winds. Bear the mournful sound away to Fingal's airy hall. Bear it to Fingal's hall, that he may hear the voice of his son; the voice of him that praised the mighty. The blast of north opens thy gates, O King, and I behold thee sitting on mist, dimly gleaming in all thy arms," &c.

By this youth, then, undoubtedly, who waited on Ossian, as a page might wait on David, or as Elisha, though older, might wait on Elijah—by him, thus solemnly charged in the very hearing of the winds, was the Dying Hymn first set to music from Ossian's lips, and rehearsed as his final composition, and carried home to the north in sorrow, as his last poetical bequest to his fellow-countrymen there. Such, to any unprejudiced reader, would be the natural and satisfactory explanation of it; yet objectors may be found to urge that this youthful bard himself, this musical amanuensis, so to speak, was the author of that hymn, and rehearsed it in compliment to his master's fame as his. To which we reply he could not, for many reasons, both intellectual and moral. (1.) The hymn itself embodies a long narrative, equally sublime, of events of which the lad could know nothing, and which he could never of himself have described, including many foreign names and a minute account of foreign scenes and foreign transactions. (2.) The ideas, as testified by the above quotation, are those of old age, and of melancholy, yet triumphant resignation; not of youth personating old age, or of false, pretentious ambition. (3.) There was no credit to be obtained for himself by ascribing to his master what was really his own: (4.) and finally, there would be infinitely too much reverence in the soul of any youth, so trained and honoured as this son of Alpin seems to have been, to dream of such a forgery, which neither self-interest nor experience could justify. One might as soon affirm that some ambitious son of the Prophets was the author of David's lament for Saul and Jonathan, or of his passionate outburst on the death of Absalom his son; that Walter Scott, at sixteen or at twenty-six, would or could have forged a lyric like "O wert thou in the cauld blast," in Burns's name; or that Milton's daughters were the authors of *Paradise Lost* because they transcribed that poem. Every inducement, in fact, was on the other side for this son of Alpin, with a hymn like *Berrathon* in his possession, to report it as his own, if he dared. But granting, by the merest gratuity of supposition, it had been all as such objectors insist, the antiquity of the Hymn itself would be as high as ever, and the previous fame of Ossian as great as ever; for if he was not already universally known as the greatest poet of his age and country, the ascription of such a work to his authorship would have been an absurdity; and for a youth that had been only his servant to have attempted to palm anything else than Ossian's own as his on those who had heard him speak and sing, would have been worse than absurdity—it would have been social and professional perdition to the impostor. Why, then, should not this work be ascribed to Ossian as tradition ascribes it, and as the Son of Alpin himself, according to this very hypothesis, is supposed to have done?

2. But again, we may be told that the men of Arran themselves, having such traditions floating among them as we see and hear, might have embodied them thus in some lyric effusion of their own as Ossian's, and got it ultimately reported to the world as his. In reply to which the following obvious inquiries must also be disposed of:—(1.) At what date was this gratuitous ovation to Ossian's memory made, and how did it travel to the north? (2.) If at a much later date, how is it that the name of Arran itself, where it must have been written in honour of the man who died there, does not appear in the poem from beginning to end? (3.) How is it that every other name which does appear has now been so completely obliterated in Arran that the true scene of the poem, till pointed out only a few months ago by the present writer, was unknown; unsuspected even, or only guessed at by MacPherson himself, as some unrecognisable locality in Morven? Nay, that the very inhabitants knew nothing of Lutha, or of Tor-lutha, or of Ronan's Cave, or dreamt of the Lake in Shisken that has now vanished from their island, as the spot where Ossian sat and sang in the very poem they may, by supposition, have forged in honour of his memory? (4.) Why did no tradition connected with such a subject, and that should have been embodied by men upon the spot who were writing in Ossian's name, accompany the poem to explain the loss of those ancient designations, and to tell us where Tor-lutha stood? In a word, how did MacPherson, beyond Lochaber and Glencoe, or in Harris, or in Skye, or by Loch-Ness, receive a poem coined in Arran, blank and bare, with not so much as a vestige of traditional clothing about it to guide him to its origin?

3. In the assured conviction that no reasonable attempt to reply to such inquiries will ever be made, we shall dismiss this topic for the present with the last hypothesis of editorial dishonesty imaginable—viz., that the bulk of the

poem may be genuine, but that MacPherson improved it for the Press, or got others to improve it for him, and make it sublime or beautiful according to their fashion or their fancy—in short, that it is not Ossian's. Then it must be obvious on the face of it, that to intermeddle thus with a fragment which was not only historical but geographical, and of which the scene was confessedly unknown to the alleged impostors, was at the inevitable risk of destroying, by the change of a single word, all trace of its whereabouts; but the longer the poem is looked at, and the more all points are collated, the clearer its locality becomes, and the more perfect its poetical, historical, and philosophical harmony. There could have been no intermeddling, therefore, to any appreciable extent, with the phraseology or fabric of such a poem—nay, that not even a syllable of it has been wilfully changed may now be demonstrated beyond doubt. Such change, it is admitted, could only have been for rhetorical effect, no other object being to be gained. Now, the only objectionable phrase in the whole poem, and which occurs in the quotation above given, is " The blast of north." The idea it conveys is unpleasant in the circumstances, and the expression itself is abrupt and elliptical—far from euphuistic or harmonious, to say the least of it. Not one editor or translator in twenty but would have altered it, and no catch-penny impostor in the world would have introduced it; yet it stands there to the last untouched, as if some magic consideration had preserved it; and now, upon examination, has a far deeper significance than MacPherson ever imagined—a significance overturning entirely the only idea he could hazard as to the scene of the poem in which it occurs. By a note to the poem itself, as we have seen, 1762, he gives up the locality in despair. " It is impossible," he says, " at this distance of time, to ascertain where the scene here described lies. Tradition is silent on that head, and there is nothing in the poem from which a conjecture can be drawn." In another note to another poem—*Temora*, B. VI., 1763—he seems to venture a guess, but without any support from text or tradition, that " Lutha was the name of a valley in Morven, in the days of Ossian"—a self-contradiction too palpable to be either explained or excused. Ossian complains of being far distant, but such a locality would have brought him to the very door; besides, no north wind from Glencoe could ever reach that unknown valley, much less could " the blast of north," sweeping high over Glencoe, that " opened the gates" of heaven, as he says, and made a path for itself down valley and loch, beyond the range of Morven. This impossibility, indeed, might well occur to MacPherson, and would certainly confuse all his ideas of geography, if it did; but it did not confuse his conscience or affect his honesty. If there was one word disagreeable or inconvenient for him in the whole poem, it was this— therefore he could not have introduced it; and nothing was easier than to modify or change it. But by changing that word or extending the phrase by a syllable, the geography of the whole unknown scene might also have been changed beyond all hope of future identification. It was that word, in fact, which determined the position of Malvina's grave, although he knew it not; yet he conscientiously abstains from touching it; and so " the blast of north," with all its abruptness and apparent incomprehensibility, remains to bear witness against his penetration but in support of his fidelity, to the present moment. He has been faithful in little, where he might have been false with impunity in much; he has been scrupulous in trifles to his own disadvantage as a scholar, where he might have been reckless beyond measure without the possibility of detection; and it would be contrary to every canon of criticism and common sense to accuse him of dishonesty in higher matters. Of which, more hereafter.

4. In conclusion, however, it may still be alleged that he might tamper a little with the figures and ornaments, if not with the descriptive phraseology of the piece; but that was equally impossible, for it is in these very figures, and in some of these ornaments, that its sublimest sense is found—a sense which Mac-Pherson did not understand, and has not been able to obliterate with all these alleged interpolations. There is, indeed, one grand figure near the close—the succession of generations among men, as among leaves of the forest; to which, by a note, he points out the well-known parallel in Homer, which Pope's translation had recently made familiar to the world, and which, therefore, he might have been suspected of quoting into Gaelig or English. But there are other parallels as obvious—with David and with Milton—which he does not point out, and does not even seem to see. Laing indeed saw them, after his own fashion, and commented on them accordingly, as impostures; but we know what his acquaintance with the whole subject amounted to, and the value of his opinion—

" The thistle is there on its rock, and shakes its beard to the wind. The flower hangs its heavy head, waving at times to the gale. Why dost thou wake me, O gale, it seems to say, I am covered with the drops of heaven? The time of my fading is near, and the blast that shall scatter my leaves. To-morrow shall the traveller come; he that saw me in my beauty shall come; his eyes will search the field, but they will not find me! So shall they search in vain for the voice of Cona, after it has failed in the field."—" As for man, his days are as grass; as a flower of the field so he flourisheth: for the wind passeth over it, and it is gone; and the place thereof shall know it no more."—Ps. ciii. 15, 16.

Again, says Larthmor in the same poem, lamenting the death of his rebellious son in circumstances, except the oak, very similar to those of Absalom's:—

" Ye are silent, ye sons of Berrathon, is the king of heroes low? My heart melts for thee, O Uthal; though thy hand was against thy father. O that I had remained in the cave! that my son had dwelt in Finthormo! I might have heard the tread of his feet when he went to the chase of the boar; I might have heard his voice on the blast of my cave. Then would my soul be glad: but now darkness dwells in my halls!"—" And the king said unto Cushi, is the young man Absalom safe? And Cushi answered, The enemies of my lord the king, and all that rise against thee to do thee hurt, be as that young man is. And the king was much moved, and went up to the chamber over the gate, and wept; and as he went, thus he said, O my son Absalom! my son, my son Absalom! would God I had died for thee, O Absalom, my son, my son!"— 2 Sam. xviii. 32, 33.

There is no occasion, in present circumstances, to read homilies on the question of inspiration, natural or divine; but these are splendid parallels, to say the least of them; and it will be difficult, we should think, to convince any honest reader that the passages quoted are not all equally genuine. Yet, whilst modern sceptics—whose sole function in this world seems to be to go about seeking what they may outrage or devour—are staring with all their eyes to distinguish between them, to say which is Ossian and which was David, and to damn them both; MacPherson, who knew his Bible as well as another, and certainly knew Homer well enough to mark an occasional parallel in him, seems never to have noticed these, or at all events is absolutely silent in regard to them. A bold and gifted forger, indeed, was this, or an honourable and an honest man!

We seem entitled to maintain, then, not only that Ossian's Dying Hymn was his own composition, and that its date was beyond the date of all mediæval history in Arran—beyond the date, even, at which Arran itself was a name among the islands of the Clyde; but that the text of that poem, as it now stands, in all essential particulars, even to the number of its syllables, is precisely as MacPherson found it. If it had not, indeed, grown thus out of the very soil beyond all human knowledge, and if every word and look and step of the speaker —from the tomb by the shore between the rock and the river still standing, to the tree in the wood but lately fallen; by the margin of the lake now drained; beyond the castle mound, dark and silent in its sorrow then, and yet visible in ruins—could not be traced and heard as distinctly, one may say, as the wires of the telegraph or the beat of an electric clock through centuries, a sceptic might still be allowed to question it. But with all this obvious, with the most important and only objectionable syllable in its narrative untouched and verified, and with every other claim to authorship on earth removed, the man who will persist in denying that it was Ossian's, or that Ossian rehearsed it thus in Arran, must be left to the indulgence of his scepticism without further serious reply. But the critical accuracy of this poem, as we have seen, is but the first link in an argument of the same kind, that will conduct us, with almost as much certainty as geographical analysis, through the entire collection of his works as reproduced by MacPherson.

II. 1. Closely connected with *Berrathon*, for example, is the minor narrative of *Croma*; in the introduction to which, as in the introduction to *Berrathon*, the scene of Malvina's death and burial is described, the very programme of sorrow is rehearsed, and the performers at the ceremony are specified—Malvina herself, by prophetic anticipation, recounting all. The spot on which this occurs is the same on which her own burial occurs in *Berrathon;* the same chief actors in the scene are assembled—Ossian, herself, and the virgins; the same hall, where she spent her youth, is to be darkened with sorrow for her departure; and the same lake is to be ruffled with the mountain breeze, at which she sits and mourns for the death of Oscar. Lutha, which now murmurs beside her, will be sad when she departs; Ossian will lament, and the virgins will grieve; but Oscar, who sleeps at Moruth, beckons her, and the airy halls of Fingal and her father, will open in the clouds to receive her home:—all this so specifically noted, as the reader may remember, that the very rays of sunlight, and the aspect of the clouds, and the breath of the breeze from the desart, may be identified with the atmospheric and meteoric phenomena in the Vale of Shisken. These points of impending grief, moreover, must have been recited by Ossian, all in *Croma*, but a few weeks, perhaps only a few days, before the events recorded in the introduction to *Berrathon* occurred; all which, notwithstanding, was so obscure to MacPherson that he not only does not perceive the connection, but in his final edition separates the poems as if they had no connection, and by a mere incidental note in a third poem transfers the whole scene once more, on chance, to the wilds of Morven. " Rushing came Fillan of Moruth "—*Temora*, B. V., 1763—on which he remarks that " Fillan is often called the *Son of Moruth*, from a stream of that name in Morven, near which he was born." In his final edition, however, both this reading is altered to "rushing comes Fillan of Selma," as if the other version of the poem already noticed had been before him, and the note about Fillan's designation of Moruth is withdrawn; but another note, in which Fillan's sword is called the "*cloncath*, or reflected beam of Moruth," remains. These changes, thus frankly made by the translator, without the slightest knowledge on his own part of the locality in question, in the same way as the original note about Lutha itself was withdrawn or altered, on the supposition that they were both somewhere in Morven, must have been entirely due to conscientious editorial revision, and seem to mark the utmost limits of a new reading founded on the collation of a double text. No other motive, indeed, for such a change can be imagined, for the translator made nothing clearer, and was forced in the meantime to obliterate a note.

2. But Moruth, we have already seen, in our analysis of *Croma*—Part Second, Chapter III.—was but another name for the Sliddery-water, within a few miles' distance of Tor-lutha. On the banks of this Moruth Oscar was buried, and according both to the first edition of *Temora* and the tradition of the bards, Fillan his uncle was born or brought up in the neighbourhood. Fingal and his second wife Clatho, therefore, who was the mother of Fillan, must have been for some time on a visit to Arran, or even resident there; and the only retreat where Clatho could be accommodated, on that occasion, was Ronan's Cave, now called King's Cove, the well-known temporary abode of Fingal when traversing the Island. Fillan, as we have also seen, was called the Son of Ronan by the Irish bards, from some tradition of his birth they did not fully understand, but which is now thus clearly intelligible, when the spot where it must have occurred has been identified. Compare Note in Reply to Laing, p. 169.

3. Of the interesting fact thus incidentally established, still farther unconscious evidence from MacPherson himself is forthcoming. In his final conjectures about the locality of Lutha, he suggests, as we have seen, that it might be somewhere in the north about Morven; and the passage he founds upon is again in *Temora*, B. VI. " An eagle he [that is, Fillan] seemed, with sounding wings, calling the wind to his rock, when he sees the coming forth of the roes on Lutha's rushy field"—in which, however, there is not even the shadow of a reason for transferring it to Morven. But if he had known anything about Arran, the sense of that passage, to say nothing of its descriptive beauty, would have been obvious to him in a moment. Not only was Arran famous for the multitude and splendour of its eagles long ago, and for the superabundance of its deer; but there was the Eagles' Cliff—*charraig-nan-iolair*, or the Eagles' Craig, the identical words used by Ossian—recognised to this day as their oldest favourite haunt in the Island. It rises by the verge of Glencloy, in the very neighbourhood of Fingal's hunting grounds, when he halted his armies in Arran, and lodged in the cave of Ronan; and from above it the royal bird, soaring to westward on the wind, could see every roe that issued from the woods of Moruth on the fields of Lutha—that is, from the forests of Sliddery or Glenscordale on the muir of Machrie or the valley of Shisken; where Malvina herself used to hunt, in company with Oscar and Fillan. Nothing, then, can well be more reasonably affirmed, than the fact of Fillan's birth in this very cave on the shores of Arran; and nothing is more probable than that he resided there in his boyhood—possibly under the tutorage of Ronan, who seems to have been some experienced old master of the chase—till his name became identified with the region, and his haunts were as familiar to the people as the eyries of the eagles in Glencloy. All this, however, we must again observe, was darkness to

MacPherson. He did not so much as dream of it; yet not even his own most scrupulous emendations of the text in such ignorance have hidden the fact, or obscured the splendour of Ossian's fraternal compliment to the native—literally, native-born majestic bearing of his younger brother.

The substance of the narrative in *Croma* conducts us apparently to the head of Belfast Lough, perhaps considerably up the channel of the Laggan; but the want of definite landmarks there prevents our identification of the scene. It lay probably between the Laggan and the Bann, or between the Laggan and the verge of Lough Neagh—in which case, Mount Divis would be a prominent feature in the foreground, for much of the intervening country would then be under water. The expedition recorded, of which he himself is the hero, was in Ossian's youth; but the poem was composed or recited in Arran by him in old age, near the close of the third century.

The Author has no wish to attach any undue importance to his own conjecture, as above indicated, that Ronan was Fillan's tutor in the chase; but Irish fable and the circumstances of Fillan's youth, alike, seem to support it. The fact that so many important names from Ossian were reproduced, with absurd contradictions, in Irish mediæval romance, perplexed even Pinkerton himself—who was no believer in either. How did such names come to be known there? and how were they so strangely confounded? The reader has already been informed—Part Third, Chapter III.—although Pinkerton could not understand it. Ossian, for example, in one of these romances, is called the *Son* of Oscar! Fillan, in like manner, is called the son of Ronan, as we have seen, and the foster-son of Fingal. Fillan, in reality, was the son of Fingal; but might well be called the foster-son of Ronan, if he was not only born by accident in the Cave of Ronan, but educated by Ronan to the chase. In point of fact, the sons of the king, like the king himself in his youth, had all some education of the sort; and who more fit to be entrusted with Fillan's education, than the aged hunter in whose rocky retreat he had been nursed or born?

## CHAPTER III.

*CONLATH AND CUTHONA*—A ROMANCE OF THE CLYDE.

In pursuing this subject of verbal coincidences, in poems which seem at first sight to have no other connection, and were not supposed by MacPherson to be connected at all, we come to one of the sublimest, but also the obscurest, in the whole collection—brief, pathetic, and tragical; but hitherto without any historical association to give it permanent interest in the reader's mind. The poem seems to have been regarded by MacPherson, indeed, as a piece of mere isolated tragedy, and the scene of its sorrowful romance geographically beyond all reasonable human conjecture. The connection of *Conlath and Cuthona*, however, with other poems, may be satisfactorily established from MacPherson's own edition, and its scene as a romance of the Clyde identified without difficulty— by both of which discoveries, his integrity as a translator, and his reverence for the text of his original, are made equally conspicuous.

I. Of VERBAL COINCIDENCES, where tampering by a translator was possible; and where emendation by an editor was admissible; and where neither one nor the other has been attempted by MacPherson. In comparing certain poems, of which *Conlath and Cuthona* is one, not supposed by him to have any relation, we find that certain proper names occur, the same or similar, which may be arranged for examination as under—

 1. Conloch, Toscar, Ronan; Ardven, Mora:
 2. Conlath, Toscar, Ma-Ronan; Ardven, Mora:
  *Second Edition* . . . Mora, . . . .

The words thus printed in the first of the two above lines are to be found in *Fingal*, B. II., or in *Berrathon*, and are obviously connected with the same place and family—Malvina's birth-place and Malvina's family. The words in the second line are to be found in *Conlath and Cuthona;* and a very slight change of spelling, as the reader will see, would harmonise them all. Ardven in MacPherson's second edition, as intimated, gives place to Mora in the second line, and Ma-ronan by Clerk is translated Ronan; so that only Conlath and Conloch remain to be adjusted, and it is quite possible that some slight provincialism among early reciters may account for that difference. Clerk, indeed, expressly translates the first of these two words Conloch; but we shall not insist on this, for he changes Conloch itself into Comloch, so that a slight discrepancy, although very slight indeed, remains. In these circumstances, therefore, what we must observe is first, that if MacPherson was guilty of forging the MS., or did even actually copy it out with his own hand, correcting it as he went on, the difference now indicated —which is the only difference—must have been known to him, more especially as the change from Ardven to Mora, in his second edition of the second line, shows that he was attentive to such minutiæ; and second, that by changing *three* letters, (of which a subsequent translator, as we see, has actually changed two) he could not only have cleared from all obscurity the obscurest poem in his collection, but might have harmonised a conflicting passage in the history of the period, and made one dark but sublime tragedy a most affecting supplement to another. This change of three letters, as the reader must see, has never been made, and the obscurity connected with *Conlath and Cuthona* remains till the present moment, so far as we are aware, totally unexplained; nor did MacPherson himself seem to think that any such explanation was either necessary or possible.

II. Of LOCALITIES misunderstood by MacPherson, but identical; and of persons with the same names, but not identical; in the poems now under consideration. A few words on this point, we trust, will suffice to make all clear; but before suggesting these, we shall quote MacPherson's own idea on the subject, that no escape from the inevitable conclusion of his honesty in the matter may remain. " I-thon, or I-thona, island of waves," and scene of *Conlath and Cuthona*, he says, " is one of the uninhabited western isles"—which Clerk, commenting on in his recent translation, thinks " is probably Tiree—by others identified with the far-famed Iona;" which, however, he disputes: and thus all known authority on the question of geographical position is exhausted. The facts of the case then, under the present head of inquiry, seem to be these—

1. There are two Moras—one on the Cromla range in Ulster, as we have seen, and another on Machrie muir in the Island of Arran, which is the Mora where both Conloch and Conlath lived in the poems before us.

2. There are three distinguishable Ardvens—one in Stirlingshire, on the Campsie range, as we have also seen; one unknown, but in the neighbourhood of Selma in Morven, or wherever Selma was; and one near Mora in the Island of Arran, with the geographical position of which we are now more immediately concerned. It was probably identical with Ben-Varrain, a few miles to the north of Mora; which by softening and contraction, or by dropping the prefix alone, would become Varrain, Arrain, or Arran—the ultimate designation of the whole island. Other derivations of this name are, of course, given, but with much contrariety among themselves, and all with this obvious drawback—that not one of them is to be found in Ossian; whereas the derivation now suggested is not only reasonable in itself, but receives a curious incidental confirmation from

Ossian, for "the people" in *Conlath and Cuthona*, according to MacPherson's own rendering, "call it Ardven"—and this, it must be observed, long before the word Arran itself was known, or any theory of Ossian's connection with Arran had been imagined. But however this may be, the Ardven or Ardbhein by Mora, and the Mora by Ardven, were in the Island of Arran; and Mora itself, in the neighbourhood of Tor-lutha, was on Machrie muir. There the towers of Conlath, Cuthona's lover, rose; and there, from "the distant steep which bends over the sea, with aged trees and mossy rocks, the billows rolling at its feet, and on its sides the dwelling of roes"—as obviously Drumadoon or Tor-lutha, as if it had been named—he " looked over the sea"—that is, to the coast of Cantyre across the frith—"for his only love." The "isle of waves" where she and her companions were hunting, and from which she was carried off by Toscar, would then be the Isle Devhar—that is, the "isle between the headlands"—at the entrance of Campbeltown Loch, emphatically an island of waves, or *breakwater* to the bay behind it. The I-thon or I-thona of the poem, however, another "island of waves," to which she was carried captive, half-way between Arran and Ireland, was probably one of the Sanda group, from which the Arran shore would be distinctly visible; the "desart" of the poem would then be Cantyre itself, celebrated till within the last fifty years for its sterility, or the mainland of Sanda as distinguished from the barren islets around it; and the favouring breezes of Ullin in the poem, which were to waft Cuthona back to her lover at Ardven, would be the southerly winds of the channel, the most conspicuous prevailing, and the same which to this day blow right over Sanda from beyond Belfast Lough to Arran.

3. But who were these Toscars, and how related, if at all? The first was Ossian's earliest and most attached friend, the lord of Tor-lutha, and the father of Malvina; the other, in *Conlath and Cuthona*, was a native of Ullin and dwelt on the Cromla range near the Cave of Tura—that is, about half-way between Carrickfergus and Belfast. Their relationship, if any, is more a matter of conjecture. They were cousins most probably, or half-cousins—certainly of the same blood, as the Irish Toscar seems to imply, when he says that Conlath was his friend at Mora, with whom he had feasted as a guest for days. The Ronans or Ma-Ronans, in like manner, were of kindred nationality, but apparently separated by birth. One of them, according to MacPherson, was the brother of Toscar in *Conlath and Cuthona*—therefore a native of Ullin; the other, as we see from *Fingal*, B. II., was the man who frequented the cave at Mora—hence called Ronan's Cave in that poem, now King's Cove—where the daughter of Conloch, as the reader may remember, was accidentally slain; and where Fillan was born, during his father's temporary residence in the Island. But it is just

possible that these two, apparently different men, were one and the same. The Ronan of Cromla, like his brother Toscar, might have been a frequent visitor in Arran, and having chosen that cave as a place of resort would bequeath his name to it among the people. It is certain at all events, beyond doubt, that the Toscar of Ullin had a namesake in Arran older than himself, and was hospitably entertained by Conlath in Arran for friendship's sake. How he repaid that hospitality, and how his return to Ireland was interrupted, the sequel of the poem now in question shows.

It was to harmonise these conflicting details, by changing Conloch into Conlath, or Conlath into Conloch as Clerk does; by adjusting the dates a little, and by determining the localities connected with these and the other names; that would in some degree have relieved the poem of its obscurity, and allowed MacPherson as an impostor, with all the materials of imposition in his own hands, to interweave it at pleasure as an episode in the family history of Fingal; which he not only does not do, but takes special care, without any ostensible object, to give us a separate genealogy of the persons referred to. The Conloch in *Fingal*, B. II., he says, was father to one of the Toscars and grand-father also to Malvina—Note, *Temora*, B. VI.—thus carrying him at least a generation back; the Conlath of *Conlath and Cuthona*, was son to Morni, brother to Gaul, and friend of the other Toscar—yet they both lived as independent chiefs, with names that might be so easily mistaken for one another, at the same place and within the limits of the same generation, if not exactly at the same time; for the one was intimate with Ossian, and the other was a friend of Oscar's—all which information, as the reader must perceive, is entirely gratuitous and serves no immediate purpose whatever. MacPherson does, indeed, go so far, on revision of the text for his final edition, as to change the old name of Ardven, where one of them lived, to Mora. In his first edition, "the people call it Ardven" at Mora; in his last, they "call it Mora" alone: but this only limits the locality with greater precision than before to the neighbourhood of Drumadoon; brings the residence of the one nearer to the residence of the other, in fact; and thus increases the very obscurity complained of in the rest of the poem. In addition to which, it may be observed, that when Conloch, the grand-father of Malvina, was living at Mora, there was another chief also than Conlath living at Ardven; but he was not the father of Conlath, as the reader will see by comparing *Fingal*, B. II., at the end. Thus we have three or four important personages, some of them with names alike, all crowded together at the same spot, unconsciously, it should seem, to the very author of the fable; a circumstance, as we shall by and by see, of great significance in the history of the time, but which there is no attempt to explain or turn to any poetical account in the story.

III. But can this same story of Cuthona, as now geographically represented, be verified? it may be said. To which we reply, the proof is obvious and easy—so obvious, indeed, that but for inveterate prejudice, or habitual disbelief in the truth of the story itself as an incomprehensible fiction, an intelligent reader need only take the trouble to consult an atlas, follow the coast line with his finger from point to point, compute the distances, observe the bearings, and compare the whole with the text of the piece, in its relation to places, winds, and currents; and he will not only no longer have any doubt on the subject, but will begin to realise the amazing accuracy of Ossian's delineations even after the lapse of years, with all the disadvantages of blindness, and in the very poems most strongly characterised by his own peculiar style of dramatic abruptness. To assist the student, however, or as the case may be, the tourist, in such a novel survey; and to demonstrate in words what may be much more satisfactorily ascertained by personal observation, the following details are specified:—

1. Conlath, whose castle is on some hill near Mora on the south-west coast of Arran, which "the people call Ardven," looks over the sea—most probably from Drumadoon or near it, as the point from which the best view could be obtained—for a glimpse of "his only love" Cuthona, returning from the chase on some islet to the west, called Ithona or the "isle of waves," and visible from Arran: but no other island on the coast of Cantyre distinguishable from Arran, or on which the chase, even as by women, could have been pursued, except the Isle Devhar in Campbeltown Loch, is in existence. Devhar, however, is distinctly discernible from Arran, and is not more than 15 miles distant from Drumadoon, south-west by south. Toscar from Ireland, in the meantime, an old friend of Conlath's, as we have just seen, has been feasting in Conlath's halls at Mora. Whether he learns that Cuthona was then abroad with her companions pursuing the chase, and where, we are not informed; but he returns by the coast of Cantyre—which must have been with a northerly wind on his quarter—and carries off Cuthona, as a prize, from this lonely island—

"I lifted up my sails with joy, before the halls of generous Conlath. My course was by the isle of waves, where his love pursued the deer.
'Come to my soul,' I said, 'thou huntress of the isle of waves!' But she spends her time in tears, and thinks of generous Conlath."

On his way to Ireland thence, along the same coast—the only route he could possibly pursue—a storm overtakes him, and he disembarks or is driven ashore with his captive on another island, still apparently in sight of Arran; called also an "island of the waves," but distinguished by that term, as a proper name, being the scene of the tragedy. The relative position of these two islands—both *Ithonas*, or "islands of the wave"—as seen from the neighbourhood of

Drumadoon, where Conlath must have been standing—is accurately represented in the accompanying sketches taken from Fingal's grave, near the spot.

PLI DEVHAR, IN CAMPELTS WN LOCH.

SANDA ISLE—IRELAND IN THE DISTANCE.

2. But no island visible from Arran, half-way to Ireland on the coast of Cantyre, exists or was ever known to exist, except Sanda with its group of islets. Further, however, to make identification certain, we are informed that there was a cave on it, or in it, or near it, with " a stream roaring at its mouth"—in which the ravisher seems to take refuge with his victim. This cave itself, besides, has a designation of its own. It is not called a cave on I-thona, but the Cave of Thona—that is, a sea-cave or " cave of the waves;" so that the stream roaring at its mouth was not a river, but some current of the ocean like a stream. The whole of this scene also, it must be remembered, is described by Ossian from memory, with some dimness, at the distance perhaps of fifty years. We must endeavour, notwithstanding, to identify this locality, for it is of much importance in the geography of the poem. Now the coasts of the frith in the whole of this region are remarkable for caves, and almost every island has more than one of them. In Ailsa Craig, for example, there is a magnificent specimen; on the west coast of Cantyre there is a series of such cavities, celebrated as the residence of eccentric natives who claim a sort of lordship in their limits, and visited by the most distinguished personages as the greatest natural curiosities. On the Island of Rathlin, between Ireland and Cantyre, are caves still more celebrated, in which Robert Bruce for a while took shelter; and on the east side of the same peninsula there is a very large cave right opposite to Sanda, where many

a feudal atrocity has been committed; and in Sanda itself there are most probably similar clefts on the shore. But between Sanda and Cantyre, and therefore at the mouth of the great cave, runs the well-known "stream" of the coast, so strong as to carry ships in full sail back, against the wind; and with an undercurrent so powerful as to cast out upon the beach the sea-ware and tangle of the bottom, in an opposite direction from the current which runs with such violence on the surface. In crossing this stream, an angle of some miles must be taken to reach any given point on the opposite shore; a miscalculation in which would be fatal to the voyage, if not to the craft itself that was so unskilfully navigated among such waters.

3. It was in a cave there, or thereabouts, as we have said, precisely so situated, that the abductor of Cuthona in the storm took refuge. The island they have been driven upon is described as a small island; the breakers seem to surround them where they stand, and the situation thus becomes critical. He relents at Cuthona's supplication, and prays for a gentle gale from Ullin to carry her back to her lover. "Rise, ye gentle breezes of Ullin, and stretch my sails towards Ardven's shores. Cuthona shall rest on Ardven, but the days of Toscar will be sad." In the meantime, however, the outrage has been reported at Ardven by her companions returning from the chase—which proves the close proximity and compactness of all the points in the scene. "There the towers of Mora rise. There Conlath looks over the sea for his only love. The daughters of the chase returned, and he beheld their downcast eyes. Where is the daughter of Rumar? but they answered not!" This silence implied everything. Conlath, in his ship, pursues and overtakes his guilty friend—for the wind, as we have seen, being in his favour; and Toscar with his company having been thrown upon a rock; to come up with them would be the work of a few hours. "He comes along the rolling sea: the death of Toscar is dark on his spear; and a wound is in his side." In short, they fight and fall by mutual wounds, themselves and their followers, together there. But their death is involved in mystery —where precisely, or how, Ossian knows nothing of it—"The vision grows dim on my mind; I behold the chiefs no more." One thing only is certain, that they die; and that Cuthona in her grief, with exquisite devotion, watches them there, till death lays her silent beside them.

"Art thou pale on thy rock, Cuthona, beside the fallen chiefs? Night comes, and day returns, but none appears to raise their tomb. Thou frightenest the screaming fowls away, and thy tears for ever flow. Thou art pale as a watery cloud, that rises from a lake. The sons of the desert came, and they found her dead. They raise a tomb over the heroes; and she rests at the side of Conlath."

Notwithstanding the obscurity of the original dialogue in its dramatic abruptness and occasional involution, there is a speciality of description in these incidental points, when thus arranged and connected, as the reader must observe, that seems to identify the scene as distinctly as any local guide, from the amplest tradition, could fix it. There are, indeed, in our enumeration, three islands with caves to choose between, it may be objected; but there are also obvious conditions to determine that choice. (1.) These I-thons or I-thonas, as described in the poem, and as their name indeed implies, were small islands—mere islands of the waves, around whose shores from almost any point the breakers could be seen—" But we are in dark Ithona, surrounded by the storm. The billows lift their white heads above our rocks; and we tremble amidst the night." By this condition alone, therefore, the Island of Rathlin would be excluded; and the choice would remain between Ailsa Craig and one of the Sanda group. But Ailsa Craig could never be over-topped by the waves—was no mere *ithona* in that sense, and besides, was entirely out of Toscar's route from Cantyre to Ullin. The Sanda group, on the other hand, was fair before him with a north wind, and the natural resting-place of a guilty fugitive—was in fact the rendezvous of pirates; and although the mainland of the group is of considerable size with an admirable harbour, there is one islet at least, adjoining it, rocky and barren enough to be spoken of precisely in the terms of Ossian. (2.) A gentle breeze from Ullin, blowing over this rock, should carry Cuthona back to Ardven: but a breeze from Ullin over Rathlin would have carried her out to the Atlantic, and over Ailsa Craig would have carried her up the frith; whereas the same breeze, as already stated, over Sanda would carry her ship to Ardven in Arran as directly as if it were drawn by a line. And (3.) There is the " roaring," or rushing, of the " stream" at the mouth of the cave, which must supplement all other conditions. This remarkable feature in the scene we have already explained; and have only farther to add, that it was probably by the force of this very current which runs between Sanda and Cantyre that Toscar, a comparative stranger, and overtaken with his captive in a storm, was driven involuntarily on the rock from which escape was found ultimately impossible, instead of on the island, where he would have been comparatively safe. Ossian, indeed, does not expressly indicate this—because he does not know it, possibly never knew it; but it might be the case notwithstanding, and in all probability was so.

IV. Here, then, we have a romance of crime and cruelty, originating in the lawless love of a stranger on the coast of Arran, carried out on the coast of Cantyre, and punished on the rocks of Sanda: and considering all the circumstances of the story as it has now been detailed, which a change of three letters, with a little tact in the use of a name, might have interwoven with the domestic history of Ossian or Fingal; and a better acquaintance with the geographical outlines of his own country might have enabled the translator to assign to its legitimate unquestionable place, among the traditions of the Clyde; but which has been transferred by him, in his confusion of localities, to the utmost bounds of the Scottish Hebrides—we must again demand with the precision of formal inquiry, whether it is conceivable that a man, who did not realise the advantage and propriety of so small a change to produce so fine and true an effect, could have been guilty of fabricating, or mendaciously altering a poem, which even in its critical structure, according to his own version, he so much misunderstood? He was restrained, it may be said, by the authority of some tradition connected with the letter of it: but tradition in the hands of a forger, or even of an unscrupulous editor, has no authority—has no existence. It depends upon himself entirely to be acknowledged or ignored, admitted or denied; and by MacPherson in the present, as in all other cases, it is acknowledged. MacPherson implicitly adheres to it; blunders along in submission to it, if blundering it be; will not alter three letters to get rid of it; reproduces the poem affected by it, with the possible scars of error and obvious clouds of ambiguity on its face, inflicted by it; and leaves succeeding generations of readers and critics to deal both with it and him. Nay, in his indifference or bewilderment—for it is by no means certain which—he transports it all, as we have seen—men, women, rocks, caves, waves and islands, whose place and action are within a radius of 15 miles—from the south-west end of Arran to some imaginary ground in the Atlantic, where there is nothing known on the face of nature corresponding to it. Yet this is the man who has been accused of forgery, of interpolation, of tampering with the text, and of brazen effrontery as an author, by men who say they see, and whose sin, therefore, of arrogant abuse against a conscientious fellow-labourer, remaineth. The only question, then, which survives for the curious to determine, is whether Conloch and Conlath—or Comloch and Conloch, as Clerk has written them—were one and the same, or different men? They were different men undoubtedly, although their names so nearly correspond, and they dwelt as independent chieftains in the same immediate neighbourhood. Their lives, their parentage, their history, and the romance associated with them both, were entirely different. MacPherson, on the authority of his text, and with the consent of tradition, distinctly and deliberately affirms it; and after such an investigation, in which all the possibilities of alteration and imaginary improvement have been canvassed, it would be impertinence either to deny or to doubt it.

One practical conclusion of great historical value, however, results from this inquiry—viz. That Machrie-muir, in Arran, was not only the rendezvous of armies in their southern expeditions, but the favourite residence of the most powerful chiefs of the Celtic confederacy in Fingal's day; and that Tor-lutha itself there, as a military centre, and as a court where the bravest men and most celebrated beauties of the race assembled, and where hospitality was practised without stint or suspicion, was second only to Selma. Here the King with all his retinue, when traversing Arran, resided; here were his favourite hunting grounds in intervals of war; and within sight of this spot he was murdered and interred. His children and grand-children in the meantime, however, had made the most affectionate life-long friendships here with its nobler inhabitants; and one family relationship at least was contracted among them, which seemed to promise the continuance of his race, and which inspired the sublimest effusions of his son. Here certainly Ossian composed or revised many of his poems; here, drawn hither with the cords of Malvina's filial love as with the bands of fate, he occupied the close of his life; he rehearsed his latest stories, he suffered his last bereavement, he sung the requiem of his beloved child, and prepared to resign his own body to the tomb—many of which facts we have already had occasion to prove incidentally in the progress of our inquiry; and their natural sequence now, as the most interesting domestic events in the history of a royal family for two centuries or thereby, becomes quite apparent: yet these are facts which totally escaped the observation, or at least the editorial remark, of the very author by whose alleged dishonesty they were accumulated.

It is with no slight personal satisfaction, we bring the argument founded on this particular poem to a close. All hope of identifying the scene had been abandoned, by MacPherson alike, and by every succeeding commentator and translator. Even Dr. Smith himself, so intimately connected with Campbeltown and a believer in Ossian, knew nothing of it. The mistake of transferring it at first to the Western Islands was doubtless the origin of so much mystery and confusion; but no attempt to rectify this geographical error was ever made. With the details of the poem vividly enough before him, it has been the present writer's good fortune to survey the scene more than once, both from Drumadoon and Fingal's grave, on the coast of Arran; and every new survey has enabled him more distinctly to realise the whole. In a case of such previous obscurity, he is bold enough to believe that the elucidation of the text of this short and difficult piece alone would be sufficient to vindicate MacPherson's fame; but discoveries of high historical importance also, as the reader perceives, have been attained by the investigation of it.

# SECTION SECOND.

## CHAPTER IV.

### OLD-WORLD MISCELLANEOUS STATISTICS COMPARED WITH NEW.

BESIDES the alleged imperfections of the text in Ossian which we have just been discussing, a more serious objection has been founded on what may be called the imperfection of his statistics. As an epic poet, it is said, he should have given us the same sort of details as Homer gives of the customs, manners, arts, intercourse, food, raiment, &c., of the people he describes. Instead of which, it is contended, all is vague, incoherent, rhapsodical; empty declamation, unreliable rehearsal, incredible romance, &c. His people, we are contemptuously told, might go naked, live on the air, dwell under ground, walk on the wind, for anything we know to the contrary; they seem neither to dress nor feed, and could never be real inhabitants of this lower world; yet stalk across the stage like demigods, in panoplies of sounding steel—and so forth. *Fingal* and *Temora*, as epic poems of considerable length, are made specially obnoxious to this sort of ridicule, and therefore, to satisfy himself, the present writer has taken some pains to examine one of these with a view to classify its contents, in reply to this argument. Both *Fingal* and *Temora*, however, it must be observed, although called epic poems, are essentially dramatic, consisting much of dialogue, of rehearsal, and of lyric interlude; and therefore, if Ossian had been greatly more profuse in his details, he might have been subjected by these very critics to still worse misrepresentation: yet from *Fingal* alone, which does not extend to more than 90 pages octavo, the following results, on cursory analysis, appear:—

I. In GEOGRAPHY—already in part anticipated, and immediately to be farther discussed—we find—1. Erin and Alnecma, Ullin and Innisfail; with their lakes, rivers, bays and harbours; mountain ranges, monuments, and caves—localised and distinguished, or correctly alluded to:—and their natural products, as in cattle, in horses, and in dogs, described and specified.

2. Lochlin, a snow-covered region beyond the Orkneys, most probably Norway, or allied to Iceland, certainly some part of Scandinavia; Gormal a wooded region, part of the same, or connected with it; Inistore, or Island of whales, one of the Orkneys; Dunscaich, a fortress in Skye, or Island of the mist; the

"Lonely Isle," supposed by some to be Staffa, but certainly Ailsa Craig—in second edition, spoken of in the plural, as "lonely isles," including Sanda on the coast of Cantyre. The passage from Lochlin to Ireland, as we learn, was by the Orkneys outward; from Morven, on the other hand, it was inward by Arran and the Lonely Isle—a route which may be identified not only by tradition, but by obvious inference from the text.

3. Deer very numerous in Ireland and Arran, wild boars in Lochlin and Gormal; oak, fir, ash, willow-wood, and yew, common.

II. WARLIKE EQUIPMENTS AND USAGES.—1. Navies were of long ships, high-masted, high-shrouded, and full-sailed square; with additional power of oars, plied to the sound of voices. Ships might be hauled up and launched by their crews; but were large enough, some of them, to convey horses and chariots, cattle and dogs, as well as armed men and passengers; are represented as dark, and dark-prowed; their sails as white, as sheets of snow, as low set like the crests of waves, &c. These, therefore, might be either of coarse white canvass, in which case weaving was known; or of white bull hides, in which case tanning was known; whilst their shrouds and tackle, as we find by glancing at another poem, were of flexible thongs or strips of raw leather. The stars of the north, and of other given quarters of the heaven, were recognised as guides.

2. War chariots most artistically fashioned, richly ornamented with thongs, and with studs or gems—" Of polished yew is its beam, and its seat of the smoothest bone: the sides are replenished with spears, and the bottom is the footstool of heroes." Horses with trappings to correspond, elaborate and handsome, " hard-polished bits in a wreath of foam; their thongs, bright-studded with gems, on the stately necks of the steeds"—two to a chariot; the entire equipment, although simple, strongly resembling the Babylonian outfit.

3. Personal equipment, helmets, swords, and mail of polished steel; shields sometimes of steel, sometimes apparently of bronze, sometimes of tanned hide, with bosses; spears of ash or willow-wood, tipped with steel; bows of polished yew, arrows with polished heads, darts and javelins to correspond; and a broad belt to gird the waist and loins. Those who desired to excel in the use of arms were educated at a school established for that purpose in the North of Ireland, called Muri's—the precise signification of which name seems to be a little doubtful to MacPherson. Compare *Chronicles of Eri* in Appendix.

4. Shields, furnished with bosses, were used for giving signals by sound in battle. One of these heard along the whole ridge of Cromla.

5. Horns used (1.) in battle, for charges; (2) for challenge to combat, as afterwards the trumpet was in the lists of chivalry; (3.) for rendezvous, as now the bugle; and (4.) for assembling dogs and men to the chase.

6. Bards, with harps, accompany the troops to battle, to stimulate and cheer, sometimes to rally them; and, as ambassadors of peace, are sent to negotiate.

7. Swords surrendered in token of submission; returned again, in compliment to valour. Prisoners of importance, when taken after resistance, bound.

8. Sons of kings are constantly employed as aides-de-camps.

9. Friendly intercourse, and even convivialities, before, and during, and after battle, between the leaders of opposite sides, common; and the utmost courtesy, as well as the highest magnanimity, displayed between personal antagonists.

10. Dress of Scottish warriors apparently red, or yellowish red, for they are described as ridges of fire on the mountains.

III. HABITS, CUSTOMS, ARTS.—1. Food, chiefly of venison, and other animals of the chase—hence, unquestionably, the strong animal passions and immense vitality of the people. Herds of cattle, numerous and fine; objects of contention to kings, and of special care to princesses—hence milk, butter, cheese, and flesh might be in use. The breed apparently of the old white stock, with black spot on muzzle and tips of ears. Finest specimens much coveted.

2. Feasts of venison for an army, rudely cooked, among heated stones and blazing branches, on the field.

3. Strong liquor, exhilarating and probably intoxicating, served in shells; described elsewhere as "blue water," which sparkled on the gems like wine. From which we may conclude that these gems were of some reddish tint, and that the cups themselves, called shells or in the form of shells, so decorated, were of foreign manufacture; and incidentally, that wine was not unknown, as a luxury used by, or obtained from, the Romans. Compare Chapter following.

4. Songs after war and the chase, in which voices of women join.

5. Skins of animals killed in the chase used for beds.

6. Seats of stone: hall of Fingal ornamented with white pillars—stalactites most probably, or purest specimens of basalt that glittered. Dwellings, during campaigns, often in caves and rocks. Druids, or hermits mentioned, as occupying similar abodes; receiving the homeless there, and comforting the distressed.

7. Dogs chained at gates, and taken with armies on expeditions, and to the field; they compete in swiftness at the chase.

8. Habits of the whale known; its track described. Pursuit of the whale, if not whale-fishing, also known and practised.

9. Wood-cutting by axes; smith work by hammers, anvils, and forges; and most probably the manufacture of weapons, chariots, and harness, known and practised—such articles, at all events, in use, as already noted.

IV. DRESS AND MORALS.—1. Virgin huntresses follow the chase in company; dress nearly up to the throat, arms and ankles bare, hair flowing on neck and shoulders; weapons, bow and arrows. Are often disguised in love adventures. They lament the dead on field of battle, and sing in funeral chorus at the tomb.

2. Are given away by their fathers in marriage, often after mortal conflict among suitors for their hand; sometimes carried off by violence; sometimes, without knowledge of their parents, seem to give away themselves. No special form of marriage ceremony recorded, beyond the giving and taking of the bride.

3. Married women claim the right of divorce at discretion, with equal division of property in herds of cattle at leaving. Violence, abductions, elopements, and murderous retaliations common, in consequence. But strong attachments and fidelity to death, on both sides, are also celebrated.

4. As a rule, love, honour, humanity, courage and forgiveness, or duel to the death, are the only laws which govern their society. Meanness, falsehood, and breach of treaty are universally execrated.

In the whole of which details, we must observe, there is not one word indecent, improper, indelicate—not a syllable of the sort, to be found. One column of newspaper reporting from our modern divorce courts in this Christian civilised Great Britain of ours, now in the nineteenth century, would eclipse all Ossian's narratives of crime together as in pestilential literary midnight.

V. SUPERSTITIONS—Some of which will be hereafter more fully treated of, may for the present be summarised as follows:—

1. Lives of the departed pass into vapour, occupy the clouds, and become spirits. The dead disquieted till their obsequies are performed; but afterwards revisit their friends on earth with revelations, warnings, and help; converse, entreat, and reason with them—as having the deepest interest in their welfare.

2. Spirits thus disembodied fly on clouds, travel on beams of light, on flashes of fire; are transparent, so that stars can be seen through them; rush on the tempest, shriek on the wind, trouble the ocean, contend for possession of a wave, break the woods, terrify the traveller, give music on the hills, listen to their own praises, are propitiated, soothed, &c., by human kindness, courage, or address.

3. Malicious spirits occasion shipwrecks, and sit on the hills to enjoy the catastrophe; may be encountered by mortals with the sword, and driven from their hiding-place in mists—an idea which reminds us very strongly of Vasco di Gama's triumph at the Cape of Good Hope—but implied much more than a mere superstition, as we shall find, on closer examination of the text.

4. Dogs howl on the death of their masters at a distance, as if sensible of their loss, by some instinct, or moral affinity.

5. Interments, of which also more hereafter, solemnly conducted, with emblems of war, of the chase, and of personal dignity, deposited along with the remains; and a " green-headed hill"—that is, a double tumulus, similar to the

one elsewhere described, at Clachaig, as Ossian's grave—was to be raised over those of the most distinguished persons.

6. "Spirit of heaven" and "soul of man" are expressions which occur only once in *Fingal*, and seem to occur nowhere else in the text of Ossian.

7. Some stone, called the "Stone of Power," also the "Stone of Fear," celebrated in the north, was resorted to by the Scandinavians as an oracle, somewhere in the Orkneys—like the "Dwarfie Stone," or the "Stones of Stennis," alluded to and described by the Author of Waverley, in the *Pirate*. Compare Appendix; also Chapter VI., of present Part and Section.

These particulars, which relate alike to Ireland, Scotland, and Norway, have all been gathered by the cursory analysis of a single poem, by no means of great length, as above stated; and they might easily be multiplied to a perfect system of statistical information, by a more careful analysis of other poems—which, in part, we shall attempt in succeeding chapters; but the facts already classified, however briefly, may suffice in the meantime for general illustration; and the value attached to them lies chiefly in the circumstance that they are all incidentally introduced by anecdote, or dialogue, or description, and can only be arranged in a statistical form by careful study and collation of the text. They are neither obtruded, nor dwelt upon, nor systematised there; nor even pointed out by the translator, or apparently thought of by him at all, as parts of a possible system. Notwithstanding their obvious importance, however, they may still be rejected with suspicion, or recognised at the utmost as fragments of some old-world apocrypha unworthy to be admitted in the canon of orthodox modern science. Yet how many wonderful parallels they suggest to modern modes of civilisation after all, particularly in the department of statistics, and by no means to our advantage considering our opportunities and experience. What, for example, has all our knighthood been, celebrated in romance and poetry? Our autumnal manœuvres, sham fights, fancy campaigns, and bivouacings of citizen soldiers, with endless reports in the *Times*, and caricatures in *Punch*, and special correspondence to the *Provincials*? What are all our universal expositions of industries and arts, inaugurated by Princes and adopted by the world? Our cattle shows, and Highland agricultural societies, and periodical exhibitions of dogs and cats, or, incredible as it may sound, of barmaids and babies? Our deer-stalkings, fox-huntings, hare-huntings, battue-shootings, grouse-shootings, and pigeon-matches, in which the gentry and nobles, and even princes of the land, rejoice? What all the talk of Women's Rights associations, and the privilege of divorce, and the due division of property, and independent household government, and political suffrage, and the advantages of medical and anatomical instruction on a footing with gentlemen of the walk? What all our fashionable extravagance of attire, and questionable decencies of theatre and ball-room; the revelations of our divorce courts, and insufferable details publicly recorded there of human moral madness, and social insanity?

In another department, what are all our doctrinal theories of an invisible world, our spirit-rappings and clairvoyances? Our discussions upon " spirits in prison," and our remodelling of Confessions of Faith to accommodate the tenderness of expanding consciences? Our sumptuous funeral processions, our ornamental cemeteries, our gorgeous tombs, our whole undertakers' paraphernalia? One might even go on to ask what are most of our classic studies, our Roman antiquities, our Grecian arts, our relics of Herculaneum and Pompeii and Nineveh? Our Egyptian mythologies, our Hindoo revelations, our Hebrew ordinances in type and shadow? Our geographical surveys and explorations north and south, from the pole to the equator? Our ship-building, railway-running, steam navigation, telegraphic systems, manufactures, and wars? What in short is anything or everything in this modern world of ours after all its progress, if what Ossian tells us, often higher and better, of the world in which our forefathers lived two thousand years ago, is to be scouted unceremoniously as fiction or ridiculed as bombast, without the shadow of evidence that it is either?

But whatever its valuation may be, historically or statistically, such information is still to be had in Ossian—and there lies the pith of the argument—all incidentally, not artificially chronicled there, in the compass of a single poem; hitherto called forgery, in ignorance of its simplest facts, and denounced as imposture by every idle critic who thought himself at liberty to affix his stigma to any manuscript beyond his reading in the library of Apollo. Might not our social science philosophers look back with advantage, to an era when simplicity and honour were the only law? and members of the Education League reflect with benefit that miracles of valour and prodigies of goodness, and even marvels of skill, were achieved by men who had scarcely an alphabet in character, and could neither read nor write? and our clergy even, without the slightest derogation from their claims to reverence, consider what might be done for the salvation of the people by truth, by charity, and by forgiveness alone? Not that police, or education, or doctrinal instruction are of no value—far from it; but that a secret of moral strength, of good government, and of social well-being was known to those who, " having not the law, were a law unto themselves, and shewed the work of the law written in their hearts," which, with all our civilisation and progress, seems to have been irrecoverably lost.

# CHAPTER V

PHILOSOPHICAL STATISTICS—NAVIGATION, GEOLOGY, ELECTRICITY, &C.

By extending our survey, as proposed, to other poems, we may enlarge to almost indefinite limits our acquaintance with the geography, with the science such as it was, and the arts of the period; and may obtain many curious and instructive glimpses, also, into the social life of the old northern world. Thus—

1. From *Temora* alone, for example, by collating it with *Fingal*, we are enabled to determine, as the reader has already seen, the exact position and extent of Ullin itself, with its mountains, lakes, and rivers, as distinguished from the rest of Ireland—that it was co-extensive, in short, with Antrim; and can trace the routes by which the various hordes of immigrants or of invaders on the one hand, and troops of allies on the other, entered it. We can distinguish its principal harbour without difficulty, and note the very approach of vessels to its shores. From *Temora*, *Carric-thura*, *Cathlin of Clutha*, the *War of Inis-thona*, and some others, we learn farther the origin, the progress, and the conditions of navigation from the Solway Frith, by the inland lochs of Argyllshire, among the currents of the Hebrides and Orkneys, and in the fiords or rocky inlets of the Norwegian coast—as far, perhaps, as to the outlying dependencies of Iceland. Ships of single oaks, as we have shown, were first scooped and rigged in the Solway, some centuries before the Christian era, and navigated thence to Ireland, as the nearest inviting shore; the stars were named, noted, and watched with nautical precision and patience, as the true guides of the adventurous seaman in his square-rigged vessel, on all such expeditions; dangerous currents were stemmed, or skilfully avoided; wide and intricate estuaries, like the Clyde, were penetrated far inland, and their intervening or connecting channels were ferried over in canoes; harbours of refuge or rendezvous—that is, sheltered bays on the route, as between Ireland and the North, one or two in Arran, two or more—as Langside, Rutherglen, and Cambuslang—in the Clyde, and one especially at Morven called Carmona's bay—were frequented as regular ports; and the direction of the wind, for these and for other points, was carefully studied in every voyage:—among all which, however, we find no trace of any expedition on the eastern coast of Scotland. The navigation of Fingal and his people, according to Ossian, was confined entirely to their own side of the Island—to the waters of the Clyde, inward; to the Irish channel, the western lochs, and the northern passage by the Orkneys to the shores of Scandinavia, outward. The Romans

are seen once with a fleet in the Frith of Forth, as detailed in the *War of Caros;* but the people of Fingal never—either in the poems now specified, or in any other ascribed to Ossian: a fact which seems to have been quite overlooked by MacPherson, yet when properly considered in relation to other facts, is in perfect harmony with the minutest geographical details everywhere else recorded; and affords the strongest corroborative evidence not only of the authenticity, but of the historical accuracy, of these wonderful narratives.

2. In the course of the same poems, we learn also more fully the true volcanic or mephitic character of certain waters—as of Lake-Lego or Lough-Neagh in Ulster, and Lake-Lano, not yet sufficiently identified, on the Scandinavian coast. The exhalations of both were mischievous; of Lano, in particular, they were fatal: but whether Lano was in Iceland, or whether it was some stagnant basin among the hills of Norway, cannot without farther evidence be determined. If it was one of the caldrons in Iceland, which is by no means improbable, then Lochlin, as an extensive sovereignty, must have included that island; and the inhabitants of Iceland were then to be reckoned as among the Scandinavian peoples of the globe—on friendly, sometimes on hostile terms, with the Celts of Scotland; but entirely distinct in manners, religion, and blood.

3. Following the track of navigation thus suggested, we trace the operation of earthquakes, with much subterranean disturbance, the moving of mountains, the fall of rocks, the frequent and often terrible discharge of electricity, the formation of new water-courses inland and the violent agitation of the sea outward —from Lough-Neagh in Ireland, through Arran and Argyllshire by Glencoe, to the uttermost verge of Caithness and the shattered islands of the Orkney and Zetland groups—that is, by the line of the Caledonian Canal and Loch-Ness to the Moray Frith and the Pentland, as we see them delineated in our atlases at the present moment. Such information, it is true, comes only piecemeal to us from the text, but it is so much more valuable as being thus purely incidental. It would mean nothing of itself, in mere fragments, and would be suspicious if the translator had attempted to systematise it—which he never did, and could not do; but the facts recorded at random, as they are, may still be easily arranged, and their significance then becomes indisputable. The formation of a lake with sulphureous exhalations like Lough-Neagh; the trembling of mountains and the falling of rocks in Ulster; the absolute disappearance of another lake in Arran, which once existed there; the rending of hills and the birth of new torrents in Glencoe, as literally described, from personal observation, by Ossian; and the sudden rise and reflux of the sea, in the Pentland Frith or on the shores of Orkney, as represented in *Carric-thura*, are phenomena which cannot be mistaken; and when surveyed geographically in line, can hardly be misinterpreted. The

great trough of the Caledonian Canal, indeed, might have been in existence before the date assumed in Ossian; but such an earthquake as that which subsequently sunk the whole or great part of Machrie-muir to its present level and emptied the lake behind it, which cleft the Kilpatrick range above Dunglass, at an earlier date perhaps, as with the chisel of a Titan, and tore masses of granite in Ossian's own day from the sides of Cromla and of Glencoe, might well have opened up connecting gorges also between Fort-William and Inverness, and so deepened or widened the magnificent water-course which now almost severs the Island. Certain above all, it plainly is, that the sea line along the coast of Scotland in the meantime has been depressed, or that the coast line itself has been raised from 50 to 100 feet in perpendicular elevation—the data for all which changes, in time and manner, with the minutest pictorial indications of their progress, are to be found without difficulty in the text of Ossian.

4. Coincident with some of the phenomena thus recorded or alluded to, there seem to have been also violent electric storms, as we have said—one in particular, at the same moment apparently as the reflux of the ocean on the coast of Caithness: on which, however, no theory can now be founded, inasmuch as such atmospheric agitations might occur at any time. But the action of certain heroes—Fingal himself, among the rest—in relation to them, as described by the poet, is a matter of the highest interest, and involves a question of scientific knowledge, or of instinctive acquaintance with the mysteries of nature, that looks almost like a miracle. These storms, in the philosophy of that simple age, as we have seen, were all the work of spirits—turbulent or vicious—who had the lightning, as well as the winds and waves, at their disposal; but they were not beyond the control of human strength, or the government of human courage. It was only by the use of certain means, however, that even the bravest or the boldest could dislodge them. They hovered in the low-hung cloud from which the lightning flashed, and it was the well-directed thrust of a blade in some hero's hand alone that expelled them. Here lay a secret of triumph then, like Elijah's at Carmel, that might well be called divine; and a test of courage and skill, in the circumstances, that rivalled the daring of Franklin. It may seem incredible, perhaps, that such things were ever done, but there can be no serious doubt of it; or that the doing of them was on any principle of science, but that is equally certain. Only heroes, indeed, like Fingal, with intellect and courage to correspond, could attempt such deeds; but instances are recorded by Ossian which seem to make their achievement indubitable, and mark the very process of victory over nature, as distinctly as the report of a modern electrician's experiment. The passage in *Carric-thura*, where one of the most remarkable of these exploits is described, is as follows:—

"He [the spirit of the cloud] lifted high his shadowy spear, and bent forward his terrible height. But the king [Fingal] advancing, drew his sword; the blade of dark-brown Luno. The gleaming path of the steel winds through the gloomy ghost. The form fell shapeless into air, like a column of smoke which the staff of the boy disturbs as it rises from the half-extinguished furnace. The spirit of Loda shrieked, as, rolled into himself, he rose on the wind. Inistore shook at the sound. The waves heard it on the deep: they stopped, in their course, with fear: the companions of Fingal started, at once; and took their heavy spears. They missed the king: they rose with rage: all their arms resound. The moon came forth in the east. The king returned in the gleam of his arms: the joy of his youths was great; their souls settled as a sea from a storm. Ullin raised the song of gladness: the hills of Inistore rejoiced. The flame of the oak arose; and the tales of heroes are told," &c.

which is either, as MacPherson considers it, one of the most exaggerated hyperboles of fiction without a meaning, ever employed; or, as seems to us much more probable, it is the figurative description of an electric cloud somehow disarmed, by means in which human instrumentality had a share; with all the concomitants of an earthquake in the war of elements, like that detailed at Sinai or in the 18th Psalm, and the rise of the waters along the coast of Palestine at a later date, as recorded in the 46th Psalm—circumstances which, taken in connection with the tradition that this poem was dedicated to one of the earliest Christian missionaries in Scotland by Ossian, as a vindication of his own faith in the superiority of man to all elemental antagonism, opposed to the missionary's teaching of a Higher Power, have a singular significance. It seems just within the range of possibility, indeed, that Ossian might have heard such Psalms recited by one who was a believer in the inspiration of David. The precise locality where this phenomenon, of whatever kind it was, occurred, can now be as clearly identified as many others have been in the course of our researches, and some attempt to explain the phenomenon itself will in due time be laid before the reader.

Another, somewhat similar and in the same neighbourhood, but a more doubtful case, is alluded to in *Fingal*, B. VI.; where an encounter with ghosts in the circle of Brumo, and their discomfiture by Grumal is described—"they fell by his mighty hand, and Grumal had his fame." A third might be guessed at in B. II. of the same poem, where Cuthullin demands of Connal—"Hast thou inquired where is his cave? the house of the son of the wind? my sword might find that voice, and force his knowledge from him!"—in singular conformity with that superstition of the Zetlanders preserved in the *Pirate*—Chap. XXVIII. —where the Udaller says to Norna—unconscious, apparently, that he is but rehearsing the speech of Cuthullin—"I know, that when the Kempies were wont, long since, to seek the habitations of the gall-dragons and spae-women, they came with their axes on their shoulders, and their good swords drawn in their hands, and compelled the power whom they invoked to listen to and to answer them, ay, were it Odin himself." But a fourth is so minutely detailed in B. III., that all doubt about its real character, as being, in some sense and to some extent, a scientific adventure, is dispelled.

"Cormar was the first of my race," says one of the heroes there. "He sported through the storms of the waves. His black skiff bounded on ocean, and travelled on the wings of the blast. A spirit once embroiled the night: seas swell, and rocks resound. Winds drive along the clouds: the lightning flies on wings of fire. He feared and came to land; then blushed that he feared at all. He rushed again among the waves to find the son of the wind. Three youths guide the bounding bark; he stood with the sword unsheathed. When the low-hung vapour passed, he took it by the curling head, and searched its dark womb with his steel. The son of the wind forsook the air: the moon and stars returned. Such was the boldness of my race; and Calmar is like his fathers. Danger flies from the uplifted sword: they best succeed who dare."

Whether a secret like this, allegorised among the ancients as the theft of fire from heaven by Prometheus, and first acquired by Moses with his rod on Horeb, where the ground itself as well as the atmosphere betrayed it, had been transmitted through ages among the wandering tribes of Europe; or was accidentally discovered by the Celts themselves, in the use of swords and spears with non-conducting handles, brandished against the clouds, may be uncertain; but that electricity was thus extracted from the air by weapons of steel or bronze, with hilts which protected the wearer, is as clearly affirmed as any modern experiment could be in the laboratory of a chemical philosopher: and the more closely we examine this theory, the more reasonable it will appear. Among the list of non-conductors we find dry wood, leather, gems, and amber—which were precisely the sort of materials best known to, and in greatest request among the people of Ossian's time, in the construction of all warlike implements. In point of fact, their chariots so-called, or war-sleighs, were a mass of leather, wood, and stone, as we have seen, by a previous quotation. "Its sides are embossed with stones, and sparkle like the sea round the boat of night. Of polished yew is its beam, and its seat of the smoothest bone. The sides are replenished with spears, and the bottom is the footstool of heroes. . . . A thousand thongs bind the car on high. Hard-polished bits shine in a wreath of foam. Thin thongs, bright-studded with gems, bend on the stately necks of the steeds."— *Fingal*, B. I.—Their shields were often made of leather, as well as of bronze or iron, and were enriched with studs; their spears, in like manner, might be jointed at the head with non-conducting materials; their shafts, at least, would be of the driest and toughest wood; and what is more expressly to the purpose, their swords were hilted with leather and studded on the thongs with gems—of which amber is well known to have been one of the most admired and precious.

"He went and brought the sword, with all its studded thongs: he gave it to his father."—*War of Caros*. "The sword of Artho was in the hand of the king; and he looked with joy on its polished studs."—*Temora*, B. I. "Oscar lifts the sword of Cormalo, and a thousand youths admired its studded thongs." —*War of Inis-thona*.

Weapons thus furnished, it is obvious, would protect the hand from electricity and prevent a shock, as well as the key at the tail of Franklin's kite, or the sheathed rod with which he proposed at first to make the experiment, or as the glass handle now in the grasp of an operator. MacPherson, however, did not perceive this, and makes no use of the idea whatever, although the celebrated achievement of the great American philosopher in drawing lightning from the clouds had been announced to Europe only a few years before the publication of Ossian, and must have been fresh in his mind. No suspicion of forgery, therefore, or even of exaggeration, can attach to his translation here—indeed, he expressly comments on the scene in *Carric-thura* as preposterous. The facts of the case, notwithstanding, as now explained, seem to be unquestionable; and besides indicating the possession of a scientific secret by the Celtic people in the second century, presumed to have been the exclusive triumph of the eighteenth, they demonstrate still farther the knowledge of the metals, and the use of steel or bronze in the fabrication of weapons supposed to have been utterly unknown at that date among the aborigines of Great Britain.

5. Besides this use of steel, however, we have brief incidental allusions to a more precious metal, which glittered like the rays of the sun, and is described as "the gold of the stranger." One of these allusions by comparison we have already glanced at, in our quotation from *Croma*, to identify the position of Oscar's grave; but in two other instances we have the mention of gold direct, as a metal known in manufactured forms. In *Carthon* we find a shield studded with gold, the distinguishing ornament of the hero of that name, who came to Selma from the region of the Clyde, then occupied in part by "the strangers."

"The chief was among them, like the stag in the midst of the herd. His shield is studded with gold, and stately strode the king of spears. He moved towards Selma; his thousands moved behind. 'Go with thy song of peace,' said Fingal: 'Go, Ullin, to the king of swords. Tell him that we are mighty in battle; and that the ghosts of our foes are many. But renowned are they who have feasted in my halls! They shew the arms of my fathers in a foreign land: the sons of the strangers wonder, and bless the friends of Morven's race; for our names have been heard afar; the kings of the world shook in the midst of their people.'"

In *The Battle of Lora*, again, we find an arrow made of gold, with a sparkling shell, as the tokens of peace offered to an enemy—both brought, apparently as trophies of war, from the land also of "the strangers"—

"She [Bosmina, daughter of Fingal] came to the host of Erragon, like a beam of light to a cloud. In her right hand shone an arrow of gold; and in her left a sparkling shell, the sign of Morven's peace." Besides which, ten other "shells studded with gems" are offered—"the blue water trembles on their stars, and seems to be sparkling wine. They gladdened once the kings of the world, in the midst of their echoing halls."

These seem to be the only instances, so far as we can observe, in which gold is distinctly specified as an article of ornament in use—and in both cases, it is clearly traceable as an importation from "the land of the strangers." These strangers, as we have elsewhere shown, were the Britons inhabiting Scotland south of the Clyde, under Roman rule in Ossian's day; but among whom the Phœnicians also, at an earlier date, had been traders, and had in all probability left specimens of the precious metal behind them. Certain it is, that graceful ornaments for the head, neck, and wrists, called torques—made of the finest gold, and in the form of double twisted wires tapering to a clasp at the extremities, supposed to have been worn exclusively by chiefs and men of distinction—have been found not unfrequently, both in the Island of Arran and in the North of Ireland, the very scenes of rendezvous and of campaigns by the people of Fingal. Ornaments of smaller size, but of much greater weight in proportion; also of the finest gold, and same sort of pattern, but closed at the extremities—without clasp or solder—so as to form a complete serpent-ring; have likewise been found—two of them together, so late as 1869, in one of the Hebrides not far distant from Arran. These are supposed by antiquarian authorities to have been used as money; and to have been carried either slung on thongs round the neck, or attached to the dress as ornaments, in the same way as Highlanders are said still to wear silver buttons on their coats to defray charges in a foreign land for sick-bed or funeral. The reader will find at the end of this chapter, and on the cover of the volume, a correct representation of one of these rare and beautiful rings, now in the Author's possession; which will explain, better than any words of his can do, the nature of the ornament, as to shape and size. The weight of the ring so represented exceeds that of two sovereigns, in pure gold. His object at present is simply to remark—(1.) That the colour of the gold corresponds precisely to the reflected light of the sunbeam, as Ossian describes it, being of a rich yellow; and (2.) that such valuable articles—whether torques, arrows, or rings, and by whomsoever manufactured—were the spoils of war to Fingal's people, and foreign objects of interest in the keeping of princes and princesses. If modern antiquarian theories should seem to be at variance with this fact, the theories themselves will require revision; for the testimony of Ossian on the subject—to whom this very gold was a theme of poetic admiration in the hands of his sister—is explicit. It was rare and strange to people of his race, and allusions to it are equally rare in the text of Ossian. Terms in combination with the name of it had not even yet become familiar; and it is a singular fact, indicative of MacPherson's integrity, that the adjective golden, in its figurative sense, occurs only once in the whole of his translation—" Hast thou left thy blue course in heaven, golden-haired son of the sky?"—*Carric-thura*—which would not have been the case had he proceeded, as an impostor might, on the assumption that gold was common, or that figures of speech founded on its currency would be intelligible to the people. There is but one other instance where a similar expression occurs in his first edition—" It bends like a wave near a rock: like the golden mist of the heath."—*Fingal*, B. I. On collation, however, it appears that " golden" in this passage is but an English equivalent for sun-bright, there being no allusion to gold in the original; and in his final edition he substitutes the correct term accordingly—" like the sun-streaked mist of the heath"—a revision that really speaks more, than a volume of argument, in support of his honesty.

As a matter of curiosity, it may be worth notice in passing, that in the list of treasures quoted from, above, as offered to propitiate a stranger and prevent bloodshed, we find enumerated, besides the arrow of gold and the shells studded with gems, " an hundred steeds, the children of the rein; an hundred maids, from distant lands; an hundred hawks with fluttering wing, that fly across the sky; an hundred girdles, to bind high-bosomed women, the friends of the births of heroes, and the cure of the sons of toil"—which has been much objected to, as incredible or extravagant. Some allowance, indeed, must be made for a little poetical license in the mouth of a girl, deputed as an ambassadress to negotiate with an enemy; but it must be remembered, also, that it was not her father's wealth alone, real or imaginary, she tendered in pacification, but the accumulated wealth of the guilty seducer who took refuge at her father's court, and who, therefore, was bound to avert every threatened mischief by surrendering all that belonged to him. In such circumstances, what would have been extravagant or incredible indeed, was excusable and even natural, if not absolutely truthful, in the mouth of a mediator like Bosmina; who might have no great fear after all that her offer would be accepted, or that she would ever be reproached with the want of its fulfilment. In such a view of the matter, the splendid, although perhaps impossible compensation tendered may be explained on the basis of diplomacy alone, without invalidating the honesty of Ossian, or the credit of

MacPherson, to the extent of a letter. Bosmina, as the agent in a hopeless negotiation, is dramatically responsible for the truth or falsehood of her own conditions; neither Ossian nor his translator is compromised at all. But what is of much greater statistical importance, is that the property described, although it might not amount to half the value, must have been accumulated chiefly by successful expeditions to the Roman provinces; and that captives, as well as cattle and other booty, constituted part, and a considerable part, of the spoils of the victors. Socially, there is yet another point of interest—viz., that this is almost the only, if not the sole, instance in which childbirth and its concomitant provisions are referred to by Ossian. Even children, as infants, seem to be forgotten by him. It is only when they have attained the age of youth, in womanhood or manhood, that they are introduced in his descriptions. To glance at the boy with his staff smiting the thistle, or disturbing the column of smoke that rises from the furnace, as a type of innocent indifference to the concerns of mankind, is the nearest approximation he will tolerate to the thought of infancy. Only once, and with the delicacy of Shakespear, is an orphan child, addressing his widowed mother, referred to by him; but this child was the son of a hero, Cuthullin, and himself destined to become a hero—hence the reference.

"Thy spouse is left alone in her youth, the son of thy love is alone. He shall come to Bragéla, and ask her why she weeps. He shall lift his eyes to the wall, and see his father's sword. 'Whose sword is that?' he will say: and the soul of his mother is sad."—*Death of Cuthullin.*

All other human beings must be men or women, before Ossian condescends to notice them—a sort of deficiency in sentiment, which no impostor in the world, desiring to produce an attractive fable, would have had courage to contemplate in himself as possible for a moment.

6. We have glanced already, in our miscellaneous statistics, at the sort of architecture of the period—which seems often to have been but the adaptation of caves to human residence; sometimes the erection of rude fortresses of great strength, with blocks of huge size, as at Tor-lutha; and sometimes the construction of a sort of palaces, of timber intermixed with stones or turf, and furnished with pillars and benches of wood or stone—in the midst of which, as in a spacious hall, the midnight fire of oak at the feasts blazed on a common hearth. These palaces or forts had also gates, as we distinctly learn, often shaded with trees, as at Tura; and guarded sometimes by the dogs of the chase, chained at the entrance to give warning—"Bran does not shake his chain at the gate, glad at the coming of Lamderg."—*Fingal,* B. V. Of regular architecture they were probably ignorant; but the skill or labour with which they must have quarried and transplanted such huge blocks as still remain in the foundations of their

edifices can hardly be over-estimated, as among semi-barbarous tribes, to whom road-making was unknown, and who are supposed to have been destitute of the ordinary implements of masonry. The mode of conveyance for such masses of stone from a distance, through rugged moors and even across intervening rivers, is said to have been by lodging the block among the branches of a felled tree, and then dragging the whole burden forward by the roots of the tree, or by thongs of hide made fast to the trunk of it. This process, as we learn from the Rev. Charles Stewart of Kilmorie, was that actually practised in Arran; and that the stones to build Tor-lutha were quarried at the distance of several miles among the mountains to the north-east, and were transported thus, or in some similar rude fashion, across the Machrie muir to Drumadoon, seems highly probable; for one of them, having slipped from its cradle, remains, it is said, to this day in the bed of the river, a monument of misadventure in the industry of brave and indefatigable people, before railways or even roads were invented— a deficiency of accommodation proved by the very contempt with which the "gathered heap," or causeway of the Romans, at Larbert, is spoken of in the *War of Caros*. But these details of transit themselves, for materials of such magnitude and weight, to say nothing of the felling and scooping out of single trees large enough for ships, implied the use of iron implements like axes, and some knowledge of woodcraft among the people, which might have enabled them, for anything we know to the contrary, to have finished the interiors of their primitive dwellings with something like taste and efficiency. The walls, at least, are invariably described as decorated with arms and warlike accoutrements and musical instruments—such as harps, suspended alternately with spears and shields—the heirlooms of generations, spoils of war or the workmanship of the people, both native and foreign—Fingal's own sword, for example, was of Scandinavian manufacture, by a blacksmith called Luna of Lochlin; so that these walls or partitions must have been of some height and extent, to be thus occupied: and that forests were hewn down to supply timber in some shape, for rafters and pillars in palace-building, or for masts and hulks in shipbuilding, or firewood itself at festivals, is borne out by incidental allusions in the text frequently—

"As stones that bound from rock to rock [possibly in quarrying from heights]; as AXES in echoing woods; as thunder rolls from hill to hill, in dismal broken peals; so blow succeeded to blow, and death to death, from the hand of Oscar and mine."—*Fingal*, B. IV. "When chiefs are strong in battle, then does the song arise! But if their swords are stretched over the feeble; if the blood of the weak has stained their arms; the bard shall forget them in the song, and their tombs shall not be known. The stranger shall come and BUILD there, and remove the heaped-up earth."—*Carric-thura*.

A process which implied the choice of elevated, possibly of romantic sites, and some trouble in excavating foundations; and perhaps a prediction also, literally fulfilled, even where no such reproach could attach to the silent inhabitant— Ossian's own tomb, as we have seen, in spite of all its reputed sanctity as his, having been actually so desecrated for road-making, and in danger of being utterly destroyed but for the spirited interference of a "stranger" tacksman.

7. The only point remaining, under the head of philosophical statistics, worthy of special notice, is the possession of a certain medical skill by individual heroes at the period. This seems to have been chiefly, if not entirely, in the application of herbs to restore exhausted animation, to check the inflammation of open wounds, or actually to close them. Whether such wonderful results were really obtained may be doubtful, but it is certainly in such cases the application of the remedy is recommended, and spoken of as infallible.

"To close the wound is mine," says Fingal: "I have known the herbs of the hills. I seized their fair heads, on high, as they waved by their sacred streams."—*Temora*, B. VIII. "Can the hand of Gaul heal thee, youth of the mournful brow? I have searched for the herbs of the mountains; I have gathered them on the secret banks of their streams. My hand has closed the wound of the valiant, and their eyes have blessed the son of Morni."—*Oithona*.

The mode of collecting these herbs, and presumably of distilling their virtues, the reader will observe, is the same; their *habitat*, as mountain flowers with high-blooming heads, by secret or by sacred streams, is the same; and the application of their juices, to stop the flow of blood or to draw the lips of a wound together, is the same. This is the only point, indeed, on which MacPherson bestows attention, or which he seems to notice as a fact in the category of scientific knowledge in the era. He says tradition ascribed high celebrity to Fingal in connection with it. He does not say the same of Gaul, however, who employs almost the very same words, as we see, on the subject; and this distinction of credit he would never have marked, or even have given occasion to remark— had the passages in which the claim occurs been fabricated by himself on purpose. They would not, indeed, have been so arranged at all, or couched in terms, without reference to one another, so exactly similar. The one hero does not borrow or detract from, or even allude to the other, in his boast; yet it was only Fingal, according to tradition, who was celebrated for acquaintance with this healing power of herbs; and it was he alone, according to farther tradition, who carried a cup of such miraculous elixir with him to the field that he could heal on the spot the wounds received by his friends and followers in battle. This latter tradition, however, as MacPherson admits, is from the Irish bards and chroniclers, whose testimony on this, as well as on many other points, is worse than doubtful, and neither to be confounded with, nor accepted as equivalent to the unsophisticated averments of Ossian; who never actually describes any such cure, but only allows his heroes to promise or predict it, if time and opportunity sufficed to have it wrought. The medicine, therefore, whatever it was, we may certainly conclude, was available only for surface or for flesh wounds; and neither was nor could be applied with success, where injury had approached the vitals—a theory strangely confirmed by the reputed skill of the Zetlanders in the use of such liniments within the last two or three generations, as illustrated in the *Pirate*—Chap. XXXIII.—with a similarity of terms so great, that they might seem to have been originally selected for the purpose :—

"We now find him in the situation of a convalescent—pale, indeed, and feeble, from the loss of much blood, and the effects of a fever which had followed the injury, but so far fortunate, that the weapon, having glanced on the ribs, had only occasioned effusion of blood, without touching any vital part, and was now well-nigh healed; so efficacious were the vulnerary plants and salves with which it had been treated by the sage Norna of Fitful-head."

Scott, we need hardly add, when accumulating such legends among the wilds of Zetland and Orkney, was entirely oblivious of Fingal and of the son of Morni, who had been there before him.

SOLID TORQUE OR RING-MONEY:
Found in Jura, 1869.

## CHAPTER VI.

#### ROMANCE OF *CARRIC-THURA*; OR, A GLANCE AT THE ORKNEYS.

WITH such information as our preceding statistical inquiries afford, we are now in a better position, than we should otherwise have been in, to look beyond the mainland of Scotland northward; which has been our chief reason for postponing a glance at the Orkneys so long. In the Orkneys, however, we shall find equally interesting illustrations of Ossian, and proofs as strong as any we have hitherto adduced of his authenticity. Nay, in these remote Island dependencies, once of Norway, now of Britain, we shall discover the most romantic links of intercourse with the very heart of Scotland, and stepping-stones between the western sea-board of continental Europe and the " uttermost ends of the earth." Here vi-kings from the north took refuge in their piracies, beyond the Thule of the Romans; and here adventurous Scots, in their explorations northward, rested and feasted and intermarried; here forests rose in primeval splendour where no tree now is to be seen, and the wild boar and the deer, long since extirpated, were pursued through their mazes; here earthquakes travelled and electric currents flowed among the precipices, with recorded effects, when no theory of their action, but that of ghostly power, had been invented; and here Pagan rites were observed, and devil worship, with faith in the presence of disembodied spirits, reigned, before cathedrals were built or any form of Christianity had been promulgated. It is to connect all this to some extent with the poetry of Ossian, and to illuminate its progress by quotations from his text that we now resume the thread of our historical investigations, and direct our inquiries for a few minutes to a region thus remote, where dates and occurrences at the commencement of our own era would have been otherwise beyond our reach. To attempt to identify every spot in an archipelago so extensive and intricate, without scientific bearings to guide us, would be hopeless; but to determine which or whereabouts the most conspicuous localities were, and by what sort of route, or through which channels, the fleets of our forefathers sailed or were sometimes driven, will be interesting and possible; and we shall confine our attention, therefore, in the present brief survey, to such investigation exclusively.

That Inis-tore, translated by MacPherson the Island of whales—which others read Inis-torc, the Island of the wild boar—was identical with one of the Orkneys, if not with the entire group; where Fingal found an occasional harbour of refuge, on his expeditions to and from Lochlin; may be accepted in the meantime with as much certainty as that Glen-cona was Glencoe, or that Morvhein was Morven—" As ebbs the resounding sea through the hundred isles of Inistore."—*Fingal*, B. III. And therefore, that Craca, Cuthal, Rotha, and Carricthura were points or places in connection with the Orkneys, is equally certain. If Buchanan's derivation of Kirkwall or Kirkcua, by corruption of Cracua, from Cracoviaca, the Danish designation of that place, be correct, there can be little doubt that the Craca of Ossian was on the north-east shore of the mainland, otherwise Pomona; and the name of Crega which still occurs, as that of a township in the parish of Orphir, in the same neighbourhood, a little south-west of Kirkwall, seems to confirm this supposition. Further, we learn from the story of Grumal—*Fingal*, B. VI.—that the people of Craca " placed him, far from his friends, in the horrid circle of Brumo; where often, they said, the ghosts of the dead howled around the stone of their fear"—from which we may reasonably infer that this place of supernatural torment and trial was in the neighbourhood of Craca, or at least within the jurisdiction of its chief. But no scene in all Orkney corresponds so much to this locality as the celebrated circle of Stennis—for a detailed description of which the reader is referred to the Appendix; and Stennis is not only in the immediate vicinity of Crega, but only a few miles west from Kirkwall. These circumstances together seem to afford the highest presumptive evidence that Craca was identical with Pomona, or the mainland of the Orkney group; yet MacPherson, forgetting alike the well-known derivation by Buchanan and the incident of Grumal's imprisonment as narrated in *Fingal*, and his own interpretation of Inistore, transfers Craca and all that belonged to it to Zetland; whilst Laing, on the supposition that the whole was a forgery, endeavours to trace *Carric-thura* from Carrick, a comparatively modern castle in the Orkneys, back to Thurso or Thura on the coast of Caithness; although he had read the poem first in his youth at his " own house" of Carrick, " with a pleasure to which even the triumphant satisfaction of detecting the imposture was comparatively nothing." A curious coincidence, certainly, and a candid confession! But about the detection of the imposture, we must inquire a little more carefully than he did, overlooking the whole scene so triumphantly, as he seems to have done, in an unconscious manner, from his drawing-room windows.

Besides the general outline which thus includes the group, and brings us incidentally almost to the centre of it, there are a few special outlying points prominent enough, perhaps, to be identified with some approximation to certainty; and which we shall glance at, by and by, in their order. But those which are immediately before us, in the neighbourhood of the mainland, are of so much greater significance in our present inquiry that they must be localised at once, in order to determine our true position in the archipelago. We shall proceed,

## A GLANCE AT THE ORKNEYS.

therefore, on the distinct understanding that we now approach the Orkneys, and shall accurately note every recognisable feature on the chart, systematising what follows, as much as possible, for the sake of perspicuity.

I. GEOGRAPHICAL BEARINGS.—1. There are not fewer than seventy large or distinguishable islands in the Orkney group, of which Hoy and Pomona, or the mainland, are the two largest; and of these Hoy, by ten or fifteen miles, lies nearest to the Caithness coast, and by so much also, therefore, nearer to Morven. But the recognised route to and from Lochlin or Norway, in the navigation of the northern seas, by Fingal and his allies or enemies, was round, that is outside of Inistore. " Scatter thou the sons of Lochlin, and roar thro' the ranks of their pride. Let no vessel of the kingdom of snow bound on the dark-rolling waves of Inistore."—*Fingal*, B. I. " Cut down the foe; let no white sail bound round dark Inistore."—B. IV. Craca, we have just seen, with almost absolute certainty, was identical with Pomona; if Inistore, therefore, was identical with Hoy alone, which seems most probable, the passage thus indicated would be by the Sound of Graemsa, on which island there was an admirable harbour, safe for shipping from whatever point the wind might blow. If Inistore, on the other hand, included Pomona as well as Hoy, then the voyage, for greater sea-room, would be round them both by the wider Sound of Eaglesha—of this, however, we have no proof. But in any case, the Pentland Frith seems to have been avoided, either because the separation of Hoy from the coast of Scotland, " by some convulsion of nature" already referred to, had been so recent that that frith was not sufficiently known, or because the passage was still so dangerous that navigators were afraid to attempt it, if any other could be found.

2. With respect to the Carric-thura voyage in particular, which we have now in view, Fingal's approach to the coast of Inistore where Carric-thura was, and his disembarkation in some natural harbour there, was certainly from the west; so that not only must the island of that name have been nearer to Morven than the rest, but the bulk of the island must have been all to the east of him, and Carric-thura itself, being situated on the island, must have been inland or on the opposite shore; for " Fingal," we are told, " bade his sails to rise, and the winds came rustling from their hills. Inistore rose to sight, and Carric-thura's mossy towers : but the sign of distress was on their top; the green flame edged with smoke. The king of Morven struck his breast: he assumed at once his spear. His darkened brow bends forward to the coast : he looks back to the lagging winds. His hair is disordered on his back : the silence of the king is terrible. Night came down on the sea : Rotha's bay," which was also in Inistore, " received the ship," &c.; but with all this expedition and anxiety, Carric-thura was still comparatively distant. If Carric-thura, then, had been on the

western coast, either of Hoy or of Pomona, Fingal in such extremity, becalmed and depending on his oars, or even on the tidal flow from the Atlantic, might have reached it as his destination direct, as easily as the Bay of Rotha; and he does ultimately, after a night's delay, reach it by ship—" their eyes were turned to the sea: they saw Fingal coming in his strength," &c. Carric-thura, therefore, must have been on the opposite side of Inistore, under " the wan, cold moon in the east"—that is, on the eastern side of Hoy, or the north-east side of Pomona. There seems to be very little doubt, indeed, if any doubt at all, that it was identical with Thurwo, pronounced Thuro—otherwise Thurway, pronounced Thurae—to which the prefix of Carric or Craig makes Carric-thura —a small village or township in a pleasant bay, with a little stream flowing into it, on the east coast of Hoy, as above suggested. Nothing whatever in Pomona can be found corresponding to it; much less, on the coast of Caithness.*

II. LANDMARKS AND LOCALITIES.—1. With respect to " Rotha's bay," however, in which Fingal was becalmed, there is more latitude for conjecture in the meantime—there is even a perplexing alternative which must be carefully considered, before any decision can be arrived at. On first blush, Rotha seems, and after the minutest investigation we have no doubt will also be found to be identical, beyond dispute, with the celebrated promontory of Rora, otherwise called Rora-heid or Braburgh, on the north-west corner of Hoy; immediately under shelter of which is a double harbour or bay of refuge facing south-west, as directly in the line of sail from Morven to the Orkneys as if it had been created to receive voyagers thence. Braburgh is described by Blaeu, and the description is confirmed by others, as a most magnificent natural fortress with a bay on each side—" Close to the Cape of Rora-heid, one sees a fortress the most magnificent and natural, towards the winter sunset, which is impregnable, and which the people of the country call in their tongue Braburgh;" on which, therefore, there must have been a place of strength most anciently, as the name of *burgh* or *burg* implies—which is all in harmony, thus far, with the letter of the text:—" Rotha's bay received the ship [direct from Morven.] A rock bends along the coast with all its echoing wood. . . . . He rose in the midst of his arms, and slowly ascended the hill, to behold the flame of Sarno's tower," to eastward; and Carric-thura, as identical with Thurwo, would then be about seven miles south-east from the position thus assumed on Rora.

But it is farther stated that " On the top [of the hill] is the circle of Loda, and the mossy stone of power. A narrow plain spreads beneath, covered with

---

* It should perhaps be noted, that the bay at the head of which stands Thurwo is called the Ors Hope; which seems to confirm the Reading of Inis-tore, in preference to that of Inis-tore; and goes far to establish our present argument on separate grounds, that Inis-tore was identical with Hoy.

grass and aged trees, which the midnight winds in their wrath had torn from the shaggy rock. The blue course of a stream is there, and the lonely blast of ocean pursues the thistle's beard ;" and in point of fact, once more, everything here described—the narrow plain, the shaggy rock, the blue course of a stream, and the lonely blast of ocean—everything, even to the now deserted " circle of Loda, and the mossy Stone of Power," on the adjacent rocky ridge, is to be found in exact counterpart at Rora. For if the reader can be satisfied that the old fortress or burgh, from which the place derives its name, was originally a circle for idolatrous worship as well as a place of refuge in war—and that it might well have been so, may easily be inferred from Scott's description of such a stronghold as Norna's residence at Fitful-head in the *Pirate*, as a fortress of " circular galleries or concentric rings;" then it has only farther to be added, in literal confirmation of the text, that the Wart or Ward or Watch-hill, surmounted by the Dwarfie Stone, which is also a mossy stone and the well-known Stone of Power so picturesquely described in the same romance, are both in the immediate neighbourhood; as closely adjoining in fact, as they could well be, to Roraheid and the harbour—represented together in the accompanying sketch. And lest the Author of Waverley, in the passage alluded to, might be supposed to exaggerate such a scene for the purposes of fiction, we shall quote the testimony of a geographer whose neutrality in the matter cannot be questioned.—" There are two valleys here," says Blaeu, " the lowest and deepest of all in the Orkneys, which inspire with terror all those who journey there ignorant of the road, whilst they regard their depth; which are more fitted, indeed, to be the abode of evil spirits than of human beings. One may truly say of those who journey in these valleys, 'Woe to the man who is there alone!'"—which seems to be almost a prophetic commentary on the text of Ossian fully a hundred years before it was known: " a blast came from the mountain [for the present, hypothetically, the Ward-hill] and bore on its wings the spirit of Loda. He came to his place of terrors, and he shook his dusky spear. His eyes appear like flames in his dark face, and his voice is like distant thunder"—an electric apparition, doubtless, but in absolute harmony with the scene described. Further, says Blaeu, " we find here in this Isle [of Hoy] on the descent between two mountains [as above], a stone called the Dwarfs', vulgarly the *Dwarfie steene*," which he vaguely estimates at " a dozen feet in length and six in breadth," but which in reality is more than twice that size, as the reader will find detailed in the Appendix; and which we still further learn, from a note to the *Pirate*, is actually *on* the slope of the Ward-hill, and connected by a long series of " barrows or small cairns" opposite " with a very large cairn" on the shore, " where we landed "—and where Fingal most probably, more than sixteen hundred years before, although

Scott did not dream of it, landed also; for these mountains, Blaeu adds, "are so high as to serve for beacons to those who make the voyage of America, or who return thence, and who regulate their course by these:"—much more, therefore, might they be for beacons to voyagers from Morven—the first they could espy, as the text imports; or for points of observation, when reached, to survey the rest of the Orkneys eastward in all possible directions. As if to complete the argument from this point of view, Scott farther adds unconsciously, " this curious monument may therefore have been intended as a temple of some kind to the northern Dii Manes [or Infernal Gods], to which the cairns might direct worshippers:" so that Fingal, as well as the Author of Waverley, guided alike by mountains and by cairns, might both ascend the hill and visit this " place of terrors," at one and the same moment. Surely never was coincidence more perfect, even in the pages of romance! Indeed, although Scott had been a professed believer in Ossian, which he was not, and had intended his allusions to the scenery and traditions of Hoy, both here and elsewhere throughout the *Pirate*, to be in illustration of *Carric-thura* as now interpreted, which is chronologically impossible, his ideas and very words could not have been in more perfect conformity with the text of that poem; to which, however, from beginning to end, he does not make even the shadow of reference—an omission rendered still more remarkable by the fact, that he was then on his way to Morven and the Hebrides, where Ossian could never be forgotten.

2. These arguments, from unpremeditated and unperceived coincidence, the reader may now possibly concede, seem all so entirely conclusive, that the question might be determined without farther inquiry; and our investigation would indeed terminate accordingly, if another spot almost precisely similar was not to be found on the Pomona shore, about twelve miles due northward.

" In the township of Yeskenaby, not far from the boat *noust* (place for boats), are the ruins of a small church, with an enclosure about it like a church-yard; and in several other places, a kirk-green or burying-ground. Between the top of Lingafiold and the Loch of Clumly, are the Stones of Via, which are worthy of the antiquarian's notice, and which are supposed to be a cromlech, or heathen altar. Indeed the figure of that with the head-stone, in the hundred and fiftieth plate in the *Encyclopedia Britannica*, published in 1797, might pass for a representation of this monument before the displacing of its pillars. . . . . It is nearly in the centre of an old circular enclosure 275 paces in circumference, with a small tumulus on the south side of it, which was lately opened, but nothing found in it except a parcel of large stones."—*Statistical Account of Scotland*, 1845.

And, as if to perplex one still more, we find that Yeskenaby-head has not only a harbour, or boat *noust*, as above described, but a little valley to the north intersected by a stream of its own, which flows from the Loch of Clumly, and a burgh on its precipice also, like Rora; so that in almost all points of comparison topographically, our choice is equal—except in the much greater relative distance of Yeskenaby than Rora from the route of Fingal, and the much smaller size of the Yeskenaby cromlech than the Dwarfie-stone at Rora. By the etymological coincidence, however, between Rora and Rotha, which resemble one another almost as closely as could well be imagined, and the fact that both places so called—as well as Thurwo or Carric-thura, are in Hoy or Inistore, we are brought much nearer to a solution of the problem, in favour of Rora. But the circumstance which would be most decisive in the difficulty, and which perhaps alone would settle it, would be the impossibility of observing with any distinctness a beacon-light at Thurwo from such a distance as Yeskenaby. From Rora-heid, through the intervening valleys, it might be possible and easy enough to distinguish both smoke and flame, for the precise distance by measurement for observation does not exceed seven miles; but the nearest line that could be drawn from Yeskenaby to Thurwo, with many an interposing range to obstruct the vision, would be fifteen, which renders it at least improbable.

3. As no experiment, however, is ever likely to be made to determine such a point, we must recur once again to the text for final information on the subject. The fire on Carric-thura towers, when first seen from the ship at sea, is green with a fringe of smoke—that is, it is a green-wood fire kindled in haste for a beacon. "Inistore rose to sight, and Carric-thura's mossy towers: but the sign of distress was on their tops; the green flame edged with smoke." The moon, then seen at the same moment, "rose wan, and cold in the east:" but when Fingal ascends the hill at Rotha, "the flame was dim and distant"—for he was then higher north—"and the moon hid her red face in the east." This must have been about midnight, for "night came down on the sea" before "Rotha's bay received the ship;" since which they had disembarked and feasted, and "sleep had descended on the youths." But the moon which rose, "wan and cold, in the east," would be full moon; and by midnight, although still in the east, her position would be more to southward and comparatively low on the horizon. In the meantime, a partial obscuration occurs and an alteration in the colour of the moon, which implied not only a change in the state of the atmosphere with a sudden accumulation of electricity, most common in the region; but a veer of the wind as in electric storms, which would bring the smoke of the beacon from the horizon between Fingal on Rora and the moon's disk in the east, thus affecting the colour of her light—in which very cloud, partly of smoke, partly of electricity, the spirit of Loda was enshrined. That the aerial changes successively recorded as the night advances, and which would otherwise imply some contradiction in the piece, may be thus accounted for is obvious; and that

the cloud came directly from Carric-thura is also obvious, for the spirit of Loda is represented as speaking out of it, commanding Fingal to be gone, for the siege of Carric-thura and the ruin of Sarno would be accomplished in spite of him—

"Fly to thy land, replied the form: receive the wind and fly. The blasts are in the hollow of my hand: the course of the storm is mine. The king of Sora is my son; he bends at the stone of my power. His battle is around Carric-thura; and he will prevail. Fly to thy land, son of Comhal, or feel my flaming wrath."

That the beacon smoke was connected with this cloud as much as was the electricity, and might even assist in the precipitation of the electric fluid by the sword of Fingal, may be equally inferred from the express terms of description employed—"the form fell shapeless in air, like a column of smoke which the staff of the boy disturbs as it rises from the half-extinguished furnace;" and finally, that Carric-thura from which it came must have been eastward of Rora is also obvious, from the words of Loda to Fingal above quoted—"Fly to thy land, receive the wind and fly"—which from Rora-heid, in the first instance, might well be an east wind, although his return, as afterwards described from Thura and at a more distant point of his voyage, was partly by a north wind—whilst at the same time the wind was also north-west beyond the Orkneys, indicating the great and well-known variableness of the atmospheric currents in that region. "The winds of the north carry the ship of Fingal to Morven's woody land: but the spirit of Loda sat in his cloud, behind the ships of Frothal," which were sailing in an opposite direction.

In the circumstances of obscuration both by smoke and by electric gatherings, as now detailed, between Fingal on Rora and Carric-thura in the south-east, not only would the beacon there show dim and distant behind its own drift, but the moon herself, as seen through the double haze, would be partially darkened; so that with perfect accuracy, as well as with singular poetic propriety, it might be said that she "hid her red face in the east." Yet again, when he comes down from the hill to his people on the shore, after the cloud had been dispelled and the atmosphere cleared, and when his own position also had been changed with respect to Carric-thura and the smoke of its beacon, "the moon came forth in the east, the king returned in the gleam of his arms; [and] the joy of the youths was great:" but no such effects could have been witnessed from Yeskenaby, although at Rora they were absolutely natural. Thus, even to the tint of a moonbeam through a screen of smoke and the lurid haze of electricity; and to the age of the moon itself, which six days before, on the Crona, was rather more than half-moon, but now beyond Carric-thura is full-moon, wan and low and cold in the east; the accuracy of this poem may be relied on, and the position of a beleaguered fort among the Orkneys, hitherto as little known as Tor-lutha on the coast of Arran, may with almost geometrical certainty be determined.

III. But there are other circumstances, it may be objected, which invalidate the truth of the story.  First, it may be said, there are no oaks now, or trees of any kind, in Orkney, with which to kindle either such a fire on the beach or beacon on the walls of a castle; and much less are there forests, as represented, for the chase of the wild boar or the deer—" the boars of his woods are many, and the sound of the chase shall arise;" . . . . " the flame of three oaks arose;" . . . . " the flame of the oak arose;" . . . . " Frothal sits in sadness beneath a tree," &c.: to which it may be replied, (1.) With respect to the light of the beacon, we know that such signals have been in use, time immemorial, among the people of the Orkneys—" that the dispersed inhabitants of the countrey, having thereby notice given them, might conveen for their [mutual] succour"—*Brand;* and we may therefore conclude, that in every fortress the means of kindling such fires, which might be either by drift-wood or brush-wood, would be always kept in store—materials which would certainly produce the very sort of flame described, " the green flame edged with smoke." It is worth while also to observe in passing, here, that Carric-thura, as identified with Thurwo, would not only be very open to attack from Norway or Denmark, but would be also a most suitable position for the display of beacon-lights, being close on the very spot selected in our own day for a Martello tower on that coast. (2.) As to the possibility of finding oak or other wood in growth along the shore, or forests fitted for the chase, the following quotations from neutral and independent authorities, ancient and modern alike, will be found not only evidence in point, but " confirmation strong as holy writ" in support of the minutest details in Ossian. " There are no trees (except at Kirkwall and at Hoy some shrubs) but briers; which happens not so much from the inclemency of the sky or the poverty of the soil, but chiefly from the negligence of the inhabitants; which appears distinctly from the fact, that one digs up in many places the roots of trees."—*Buchanan,* 1582; quoted in *Blaeu* about a century later.

" There is no Forest or Wood in all this country, nor any Trees, except some that are in the Bishop's garden at *Kirkwall,* where there are some ashes, and thorn, and plum-trees. . . . . . Yet it seems there hath been woods growing in this country, for in the mosses they find trees with their branches intire of 20 or 30 foot length."—*Wallace's Orkney,* 1693.  " In our peat mosses roots of large trees are often dug up, and they have also been found in Sandwick bay, where they are generally covered by the ocean.  Hazel nuts, deers' horns, &c., have likewise repeatedly been found imbedded in our peat—and this makes it probable that forests have formerly grown in these islands, where there is nothing now that deserves to be called a tree, except in gardens."—*Statistical Ac-*

*count of Scotland*, 1845. "The highest peak is divided from another eminence, called the Ward-hill, by a long swampy valley full of peat bogs. Upon the slope of this hill, and just where the principal mountain of Hoy opens into a hollow swamp, or corri, lies what is called the Dwarfie-stone."—*Notes to the Pirate*, 1831.

But this valley full of peat bogs, and this hollow swamp at the hill of Hoy, are the very spots where, according to Ossian, the material requisite for the formation of peat was beginning to be deposited by decaying forests in Fingal's day— "On the top is the circle of Loda, and the mossy stone of power. A narrow plain spreads beneath, covered with grass and aged trees, which the midnight winds, in their wrath, had torn from the shaggy rock. The blue course of a stream is there [now choked apparently]; and the lonely blast of ocean pursues the thistle's beard"—the result of which, after the lapse of 1600 years, is a peat bog; and so vivid is the whole of this—the drift, the decay, and the accumulation in the swampy corri—that one might with perfect confidence proceed to disinter these very trees! In point of fact, forests must have grown there and were beginning to fall in Ossian's day; and the want of trees, now admitted and lamented, is not exclusively due to the negligence of the inhabitants, any more than the disappearance of the wild boar and the deer, but to some great revolution both in the climate and in the conditions of the soil, which began at the date of *Carric-thura*—"When the hills of Inis-tore shook at the sound" of the first convulsion, when "the waves heard it on the deep," and when "they stopped in their course with fear"—but of which neither Buchanan nor Blaeu, Brand, Wallace nor MacPherson, nor the Author of Waverley, nor the writers of the Statistical Account of Scotland had the slightest idea; and of which no intelligible or reliable account in the world is to be had, but in the pages of Ossian himself—both here and elsewhere, as we shall by and by see. Surely the ghost of his translator, if cognisant of such evidence, must feel pacified and avenged.*

2. Another point, in the way of objection, to be considered, is the rate of sailing and the mode of navigation employed—Was such a voyage, it may be asked, in the circumstances described, a possibility? to which equally satisfactory replies may be given. (1.) Fingal is represented as having left his own residence of Selma in Morven at the break of day, and to have neared the coast of Inistore at night-fall. "Such was the song of Cronnan, on the night of Selma's joy. But morning rose in the east; the blue waters rolled in light. Fingal bade

---

* "There is a tradition that the district of Deerness in the Island of Pomona was once covered by a splendid forest, abounding with deer; and that in one night it was submerged and laid waste by an inundation of the sea"—a tradition which has been charmingly illustrated by Mr. Archibald Maclaren, in his volume of legendary ballads entitled *The Fairy Family*—Macmillan & Co., 1874—but without any allusion whatever to Ossian or Carric-thura.

his sails to rise, and the winds came rustling from their hills. Inistore rose to sight, and Carric-thura's mossy towers;" .... but "night came down on the sea," and " Rotha's bay," which must therefore have been close before them, for the wind had failed, "received the ship." As we cannot determine with anything like certainty the position of Selma, we must assume that there was sea-room, at starting, for a voyage due north; and computing roughly the distance from the Sound of Tobermory outward to the coast of Hoy at 160 or 180 miles, and the entire time occupied at 18 hours, we shall have an average rate of speed, with a fair wind during the greater part of the voyage, of about ten miles an hour. But the Zetlanders, as represented in the *Pirate*, boast that " with the wind on their quarter they run fifteen knots by the line;" and when we remember that Fingal's ship was a long one, and must have had more sails than one—for *sails* are expressly spoken of—and that the wind, till near Hoy, was in his wake, all difficulty about accomplishing the distance in the time specified disappears. (2.) Again, the navigation from Rora to Carric-thura would be by doubling the headland of Hoy and following the Graemsa Sound round the eastern side of the island—which to Thurwo might imply a route of 15 or 20 miles; but to do this, and to disembark his people on the shore in order of battle, he has from the waning of moonlight in the morning till after sun-rise of the same day—which even without much wind, or with the help of oars and strong currents against the wind for some part of the way, would be more than sufficient. Besides which, we must remember that the change of atmosphere after the thunderstorm, and his own hazardous yet sublime experiment with the lightning of Loda, had renewed the action of the wind in such a manner as might obviate all the imaginary obstacles in question.

3. A third difficulty, however, perhaps even more important than the others, may yet be suggested, as to the credibility of the expedition itself. Fingal, it may be said, is here represented as sailing with a single ship, and therefore with a limited force, from Morven, to raise the siege of a fortress in the Orkneys beleaguered by two Norwegian vi-kings, with little less than a fleet at their command; and by his solitary prowess discomfitting both these leaguerers, and so reducing the siege :—can such an achievement be credited, as an historical matter of fact? or must it be relegated, like much else, to the questionable region of romance? To say that Ossian, in narrating his father's achievements, did not diminish their splendour by prosaic details, is unnecessary; or to say that he did not even exaggerate their glory a little by the splendour of his own poetic diction, is not required :—yet in the present case, so far as the result of the expedition is concerned, there seems to be nothing exaggerated or incredible in the circumstances. (1.) Fingal's ship, we see, must have been of considerable length

and capacity, for it carried more than a single sail. It was probably what the Romans called a "long ship" or galley, although of barbaric build, and might have been fitted with two, or even three masts, with a single sail on each; and the fact, thus incidentally disclosed, is of much antiquarian interest, as regards the naval architecture of the time. But, being thus a "long ship," it would be capacious in proportion, and might accommodate without difficulty, for a voyage of one day, from forty to fifty men close set. (2.) Fingal did not leave Morven on this expedition with any warlike intentions; on the contrary, it was to spend a day or two with Cathulla—Sarno's son apparently—and with an object of a very different kind in view, as we shall immediately perceive.

"Sing on, O bards; to-morrow we lift the sail. My blue course is through the ocean, to Carric-thura's walls; the mossy walls of Sarno, where Comala dwelt. There the noble Cathulla spreads the feast of shells. The boars of his woods are many, and the sound of the chase shall arise."

It was only when he came close to the western shore of the Orkneys that he discovered signs of distress at Carric-thura, and this discovery changed immediately the whole character of his expedition. (3.) Stimulated, as well as surprised, by these signals, he redoubles his exertions to reach Carric-thura with what succour he may, where he finds a superior force undoubtedly on leaguer; but his own personal prowess, and the support of his personal retinue, with the help of the leaguered themselves, are equal to the emergency in which friendship has thus involved him, and he speedily compels the besiegers to accept terms.

"He [that is, Frothal the besieger] went forth with the stream of his people, but they met a rock: Fingal stood unmoved; broken they rolled back from his side. Nor did they roll in safety; the spear of the king pursued their flight. The field is covered with heroes: a rising hill preserved the flying host."

A single combat then takes place between Frothal and Fingal; in which Fingal, with some romantic incidents of generosity, is victorious, and a compromise for raising the siege and restoring amity is effected. All this, however, considering the well-known character of the king and the devotion of his followers, is in perfect harmony with presumable matter of fact; and the result of the expedition as a triumph, strategical and moral, becomes highly probable.

In this investigation we have had a double object: not only to determine the actual scene of an interesting poem, and to identify certain islands of the Orkney group, which seem to have been entirely unknown to MacPherson—who can only guess, and contradict himself in guessing, at their whereabouts; but to give the reader some idea, also, of the birth-place and people of Comala; who, smitten with love, accompanied Fingal in disguise on a former voyage from Inistore, was afterwards affianced as his bride, and died, by the rocks of Crona at Kelvin-head, of apprehension for his safety in battle with the Romans—for this Comala was born at Carric-thura, and her father was old Sarno its " battling chief," and Cathulla, who dispensed hospitalities there in Sarno's name, was in all likelihood her brother. The expedition occurred immediately after Fingal's return, as we have seen, from the " strife of Crona;" and his object, beyond doubt, was to convey the sad intelligence of her death to the friends she had forsaken to follow him. Looking back thus, through the long vista of centuries, we find Stirlingshire and the Orkneys united by an indissoluble link of love and sorrow; and perceive how strongly the domestic and social affections of the people operated, in originating and directing their most hazardous enterprises. For Comala's love, Fingal, in all the glory of a triumph over the Romans, will not rest at Selma a day, till he has explained with his own lips at Carric-thura the secret of her flight, and the disastrous issue of her attachment; whilst Frothal, whom he encounters there, had come thither from Sora in quest of her—the second time apparently, and pretty much with the purpose of a pirate—knowing nothing, in the meantime, of her death. On this second lawless enterprise, he was followed, as seems to have been not uncommon among adventurous women at the time, by a lady who had truer claims on him, and was jealous of Comala's power. Her own name was Utha, and her father's name was Herman—

" ' But, Thubar! I love a maid; she dwells by Thano's stream, the white-bosomed daughter of Herman, Utha with the soft-rolling eyes. She feared the daughter of Inistore, and her soft sighs rose, at my departure. Tell to Utha that I am low; but that my soul delighted in her.' "

Discomfitted and admonished by Fingal, Frothal repents, and Utha returns home with him reconciled; which is only farther worth noticing from the fact, that her parentage recalls us to Germany, and seems to confirm the idea that Sora was in Zealand. The illustrious general of the German forces to whom that strange monument the Herman-Saul, already referred to as having been destroyed by Charlemagne, was erected, might possibly be some ancestor of hers—grandfather or great-grandfather. Her father's name at least, which signifies the Chieftain, is identical with his. In that case, " the blue waters" of the Thano, or of the Tora, where Utha dwelt, would be some branch of the Elbe or the Rhine River—facts which MacPherson not only does not comment upon, but does not seem even to have been cognisant of, any more than Laing.

## CHAPTER VII.

*WAR OF INIS-THONA; OR, OSCAR IN ICELAND.*

AT more than one point, in our previous investigations, we have glanced by inference at Iceland as a region connected with Lochlin, and therefore possibly known to Fingal or his people. There was no evidence, sufficiently conclusive at the moment, to justify more than such inferential allusion; but whilst the preceding pages were in press, a careful collation of the text, and a comparison of known facts with the statements of Ossian in the *War of Inis-thona*, have left very little doubt indeed that Inis-thona itself was any other than Iceland. The importance of this conclusion, if correct, can hardly be over-estimated in the history of civilisation, literature, and science in the northern world; and therefore with some patience, and as much minuteness as possible, on the comparatively narrow and hitherto unsuspected grounds afforded to us, we proceed now to investigate the subject.

I. There are several—*Thons* or—*Thonas*, as our readers may remember, in combination with other terms to distinguish them from each other, in the poems of Ossian. Berra-thon, for example, the subject of a poem so-called written in Arran, was itself some island, with rocky sea-surrounded promontories, on the outside route from Morven to Lochlin, and probably in the Zetland group. It was as likely, therefore—more likely, indeed, for many reasons, both of aspect and position—to have been the mainland there, with its terrible cliffs, Sumburgh and the Fitful-head, so graphically depicted in the *Pirate*, than any other that could be named in all our northern seas. Troma-thon, again, which means the deep-sounding surge of the sea, was another island—small and barren, described also as blue like a shield on the distant waters—and certainly one of the extreme Zetlands, as we shall hereafter see. I-thon and I-thona, as we have just seen, are but diminutive forms of designation for mere islets of the wave, and were identical respectively with the Isles Devhar and Sanda on the coast of Cantyre; but Inis-thona in full, or the Island of the Sea, was a very different place, both in size and situation—to identify which is the object of our present inquiry.

1. As to SIZE. Inis-thona, as some island of importance, worthy to be so called—not part of the mainland anywhere, or near the mainland, but an island of the sea—was large enough to be not only a kingdom for Annir, but to be divided between himself and Cormalo, an independent prince; who dwelt by the Lake of Lano, and who made war on his sovereign. This formidable vassal

is represented as having "ten thousand spears" in his retinue—which may be a poetical exaggeration, of course; but it still indicates the size of the island, which could thus accommodate two kings with their respective armies, and was thus distracted with civil war. Nor was this all. The region around Lano, wherever it was, was large enough in itself also to maintain seven other independent chiefs, besides Cormalo; who are specified by that collective number, although not by name, in Swaran's expedition to Ireland.—*Fingal*, B. IV. Now, no island on the coast of Norway, or near it, could be compared in size to this; nor could the mainland of the Zetland group—Berra-thon, as we presume, with its lofty towers of Finthormo; that is, of Sumburgh, or more probably of the Fitful-head, where such towers were still extant in our own day—afford either space, or the means of subsistence, for such a multitude; besides that it was otherwise removed both by aspect and situation, as we shall see, from comparison with Inis-thona. But Iceland in magnitude, and Iceland alone, corresponds sufficiently; being, in point of fact, much larger than all Scotland, considerably larger than Ireland, and divided, like Ireland, into four distinct provinces; and notwithstanding its present sterile aspect, and the enormous fields of sulphur and lava which now intersect it, maintained, not many generations ago, a population of 100,000 native inhabitants. About its present connection with Denmark, and its former connection with Norway—its discovery and repeopling, in fact, by the Norse in 874; an event which is now being celebrated with royal festivity, as the most remarkable in its history—we need say nothing here, except to show that its original subordination to Lochlin, in the days of Fingal and Starno, was no impossibility: which brings us thus naturally, in the next place, to consider its relationship to that country.

2. As to its feudal DEPENDENCY, or otherwise. The only point on which MacPherson is clearly correct, is that the kingdom of Inis-thona was tributary to Lochlin. He calls it so, in a note, expressly—"Inis-thona, *i.e.*, the *Island of Waves*, was a country of Scandinavia subject to its own king, but depending upon the kingdom of Lochlin." But how such a kingdom, as he himself in his translation describes it, came to be an island on the coast of Norway, he nowhere attempts to explain. His only alternative, in that view, would have been to urge that it was identical with Zealand at the mouth of the Baltic; but so many arguments render that supposition improbable, that he does not even suggest it. His ideas of Scandinavia and its dependencies, indeed, seem to have been quite limitless or indefinite. Where that region called Lochlin, including Gormal and Sora, begun or ended, was a mystery to him. He believed only that the Norwegian coast, with its rocks and islands and snow-covered mountains, included all; and that Inis-thona could be Iceland, any more than it could

be Zealand, never entered his imagination—which we may accept, once for all, as the clearest proof of his editorial integrity.

But to return to the text, by which alone we can be guided, where the translator himself is so obviously at fault—we may infer without much doubt that Inis-thona, as an island, could neither be an integral part of Lochlin, nor even closely adjoining; for in the *War of Inis-thona*, it not only receives no assistance from Lochlin, but the name of Lochlin does not once appear—which, in the circumstances of the case, if Inis-thona had been Zealand, would have been almost inevitable. Yet there must have been some feudal alliance, or political connection between them, for we find men from Lake Lano, as we have said, chiefs and followers, in Swaran's expedition to Ireland. To what this bond might amount, indeed, is not very clear; for the king of Inis-tore, the king of Inis-con, Mudan's chief, and Terman's battling king are specified also in the league, as under the command of Swaran " king of roaring waves," in the same expedition. These names, however, being connected with the north—with the Orkneys or the Zetland Isles—seem to indicate at least that Inis-thona was in the same direction, and therefore necessarily beyond them. But at an earlier date Annir, the then youthful king of Inis-thona, is referred to by Fingal as a rival of his own at the Court of Starno, for the hand of the unfortunate Agandecca—in circumstances, which we elsewhere learn implied that Annir was a sort of tributary, and which did not redound by any means to Annir's own credit as a man. Annir, in fact, as an ally of Starno's, seems to have been a conspirator against Fingal's life at the time; but as his name is omitted in the story—*Fingal*, B. III. —he must have the benefit of doubt in his favour. Fully to elucidate this point, however, a little additional information is required. The reader, then, must observe that there are no fewer than three kings of the name of Annir distinctly recognised in Ossian—(1.) Annir of Lochlin and Gormal, father of Starno and grandfather of Swaran and Agandecca; therefore, two generations beyond Fingal. (2.) Annir of Sora, another Scandinavian, father of Frothal and Erragon. Frothal, who succeeded his father as king in Sora, was the personal antagonist of Fingal at Carric-thura; and Erragon, who succeeded Frothal apparently, was afterwards slain at Glencoe, as recounted in the *Battle of Lora*. Annir their father, who was thus one generation beyond Fingal, died in Fingal's own youth, and " the stone of his fame arose." This Annir, therefore, could not be the king of Inis-thona in Oscar's day, to whom Fingal sent a message of recognition by his grandson; nor could Sora, where Frothal was king, be identical with Inis-thona. That Sora was at some great distance from Morven, and required the aid of the west wind to reach it; and yet was not one of the Orkneys, but even far beyond them, and must therefore have been on the Norwegian coast, and yet not tributary to Lochlin, is all we know. Whether it was on the mainland there, or in the Island of Zealand, is quite uncertain; but it is worth while perhaps, in passing, to observe that there is a district in Zealand called Soroe to this day. (3.) Annir of Inis-thona, the youthful ally of Starno, and the rival of Fingal for Agandecca's hand; therefore also, a co-eval of Fingal's at the time. This Annir survives for two generations longer, like Fingal himself; and is the king of Inis-thona to whom Oscar brings relief, when at war with his own vassal and son-in-law, Cormalo.

These points may be all easily determined by a collation of the text in *Fingal, Carric-thura, Cath-loda,* the *Battle of Lora,* and the *War of Inis-thona:* and that MacPherson, with such facts distinctly recorded in his own translation, should have confounded Lochlin or Scandinavia where the first Annir lived, with Inis-thona where the third lived three generations later—as he seems invariably, without reflection, to do; and should have omitted the name of Annir, king of Inis-thona, altogether, as we see in *Fingal,* and yet make Fingal speak of him in the *War of Inis-thona,* as if he were already known by name to the world—is convincing proof both of his honesty and of his unconsciousness. No such oversight could have occurred, if he had seen the connection of the narratives; for both the omission, and the subsequent mention, are equally natural. The omission, in the first instance, is made not by Fingal, but by a mere rehearser of the story; the mention afterwards is by Fingal incidentally, to whom all the particulars were known, and who therefore might well remember the names; but Fingal, in that recollection, imputes no blame to Annir. It was morally impossible that any impostor could make so beautiful a distinction as this, without himself being aware of it. But the point in question is of still greater value in the present case, to determine the relation of Inis-thona to Lochlin, which MacPherson only in part perceives. Inis-thona, in fact, although tributary to Lochlin, was politically independent and geographically distant; whereas Mac-Pherson, by oversight or implication, not knowing how to distinguish the one from the other, confounds the two. These matters, then, being thus distinctly ascertained, and MacPherson's integrity once more vindicated, we have now to look for Inis-thona outside of Lochlin and beyond the Orkneys, relying, as hitherto, on the authority of the text alone.

3. As to POSITION. Inis-thona was at a great distance from Morven, with no resting-place apparently intervening, from which help could be derived or through which intelligence could be conveyed. Inistore, as we know, was half-way between Morven and Lochlin, and afforded both refuge and hospitality to Fingal and his people on their expeditions thither. It might be half-way also between Morven and Sora, for the kings of Sora more than once, in the charac-

ter of pirates, touched at Inistore and at the neighbouring Island of Craca. One of them, indeed, pursued his victim thence to Morven—compare *Fingal*, B. III., and the siege of Carric-thura, as detailed in the preceding chapter. But Inis-thona is spoken of by Ossian in very different terms, as to distance and direction.

"'Let me fight, O heroes, in the battles of Inis-thona. Distant is the land of my war! Ye shall not hear of Oscar's fall. Some bard may find me there, and give my name to the song. The daughter of the stranger shall see my tomb, and weep over the youth that came from afar. The bard shall say, at the feast, hear the song of Oscar from the distant land!' . . . . They lifted up the sounding sail; the wind whistled through the thongs of their masts. Waves lash the oozy rocks: the strength of ocean roars. My son beheld, from the wave [not from any neighbouring island] the land of groves. He rushed into the echoing bay of Runa; and sent his sword to Annir, king of spears."\*

The character of this voyage, the reader will observe, is artistically veiled, because there was nothing to describe but the action of the winds and waves, and "the strength of ocean"—that is, of the open sea. No intervening spot whatever, to relieve the eye or to occupy the imagination, is to be found; but the same wind, without deviation or interruption, carries the youthful adventurer due north, from Selma's shores with their "oozy rocks," to the bay of Runa. If Inis-thona, then, had been anywhere else than where Iceland is, such a voyage would have been impossible. A glance at the map of Europe, it is hoped, will be sufficient not only to confirm all this, but to illustrate and explain, much better than any words of ours can, the hitherto incomprehensible but most significant text of Ossian in relation to it. The exact length of the voyage also, as well as its character, the reader will observe, is poetically disguised or fore-shortened. No number of days or nights is specified. All we are told is, that it was distant; and that provision was made accordingly, by the equipment of Fingal's own war-ship, as if no opportunity for re-victualling would occur—" Prepare my dark-bosomed ship to carry my hero to Inis-thona." The distance from Morven to the nearest shore on Iceland is, in fact, about 550 miles—a voyage sufficiently great for a youth in the circumstances; and magnified a little in the story, to enhance his valour. It was not greater, indeed, than it would have been to the nearest point of Lochlin—a space that had been frequently traversed by Fingal and others; but it was without any intervening anchorage or harbour ground to rest and refit—which made all the difference in Oscar's expedition.

---

\* It may be almost unnecessary to remark that the word "stranger" in the passage now quoted, and in several others relating to the north, denotes merely a person unknown to, or of a different nationality from, the speaker; and has not necessarily the same peculiar sense as when employed elsewhere to denote the dwellers on the mainland south of the Clyde.

4. As to LOCAL ASPECTS. Inis-thona thus reached, by a run before the wind from Morven, we have now to consider what aspect it presents, and the most prominent features alluded to, inland or on the coast, by Oscar on his return. These may be arranged in their natural order, as follows:—(1.) He " beheld, from the wave, the land of groves"—which implied that there was then wood enough in the valleys, at least, as seen from a distance, to present the appearance of groves. (2.) " He rushed into the echoing bay of Runa"—which, if Inis-thona were Iceland, would be what is now called the bay of Reikum—the largest but one on that side of the island, and in the very track of his ship from Morven. (3.) He sent his sword, as a token, to Annir, king of spears; he was invited to feast in the Halls of Annir at Runa; three days they feasted together, on the fourth his name was announced; on the fifth, or some succeeding day, " they pursued the boars of Runa. Beside the fount of mossy stones, the weary heroes rest," implying some considerable excursion inland; and then the story of old Annir's grief for the loss of his two sons, Argon and Ruro, by the vindictive cruelty of Cormalo, their brother-in-law, is related. The unhappy youths had been assassinated by him in the adjoining wood, and their tomb was by the stream of the fountain; having accomplished which atrocity, Cormalo had carried off their sister to Lano, and was now waging war upon Annir; but Annir frequented the tomb of his sons in the valley—" We found them here, and laid them by this mossy stream. This is the haunt of Annir, when the chase of the hinds is over. I bend like the trunk of an aged oak above them; and my tears for ever flow." We farther learn that the background of the scene at Runa was mountainous, and that the wild boar frequented the forests there. On the supposition again, to which we adhere, as the only geographical possibility in the case, that Runa was at Reikum, and that this hunting ground was in the valley behind it; and reverting more minutely to topographical authorities on the place, we find in the wreck of what the fire and the lava, and the scalding steam and the liquid brimstone have destroyed, as much as we could wish, and more than we could expect, in confirmation of our theory. The mountains still remain there, as a background to the picture, but scorched and blackened by volcanic heat, and strewed with slag instead of being clothed with coppice; in the valley, where the lava has not touched it, the herbage is still beautifully green by the boiling caldrons—" close to this, and in one spot, very near the well itself, the grass grows with great luxuriance;" and what is most remarkable of all—

" ' Towards the upper end of the valley, there was a very curious hole, which attracted much of our attention. It seemed to have served at some former period as the well of a fountain. It was of an irregular form, and from four to five feet in diameter. It was divided into different hollows or cavities at the depth of a few feet, into which we could not see a great way, on account of their direction. A quantity of steam issued from these recesses, which prevented us examining them very closely. .... We could discover no water in any of the cavities; but we found near the place many beautiful petrifactions of leaves and mosses. They were formed with extreme delicacy, but were brittle, and would not bear much handling; their substance seemed chiefly argillaceous.'"—*Mackenzie's Travels in Iceland*—quotation from Sir John Stanley's *Letter*, &c.

Here, then, almost beyond a doubt—by this old "fount of the mossy stones," now dried and emptied by volcanic heat, at the head of this once verdant valley, sat Oscar and Annir, when wearied by the chase; the old man rehearsing the story of his grief, and the youth vowing vengeance on the aggressor—nearly sixteen hundred years ago. Although leaves and mosses had been petrified on purpose at the moment, they could not have borne more convincing testimony to the truth of his romantic enterprise! Little did MacPherson know, and quite as little did the present writer know, at the commencement of this chapter, that such corroboration of the text was in store for him—for this was not one of the "known facts" referred to there, which included only the general geographical bearings and more prominent features of the region. No such minute identification, indeed, was ever dreamt of: but the reading of the text was plain, and the corroboration, as a matter of course, followed. In point of fact, he had put his finger on the very spot at the Reikum springs in Mackenzie's map, before Mackenzie's own letterpress was consulted—when, at pages 264-5, the above description, quoted by the unconscious Baronet himself from Sir John Stanley's report in the Transactions of the Royal Society of Edinburgh, was discovered. Yet it was not altogether a matter of course, and, in the peculiar circumstances of the case, might well have been otherwise; nor would the want of such evidence have destroyed the argument. For although the well was there with its mossy brink, the petrifactions might not have been made, or might not have been preserved, or might not have been noticed; but thanks to the consolidating touch of mineral agents, and to the discriminating labours of sharp scientific explorers, these fragile witnesses have actually been found and sworn in their natural order, and the import of their testimony cannot now be invalidated. This proof indeed, so unexpected, unique and wonderful, might almost suffice to conclude the argument; if the text of the story itself, demanding farther investigation in its own right, so to speak, did not beckon us forward.

(4.) Having heard the recital of Annir's double bereavement, in the loss of his sons and the abduction of his daughter by their murderer; and fired with indignation at Cormalo's atrocities, Oscar resolves to encounter him at Lano, and put an end to his career: at which point, it is of immediate importance to observe that the celebrated lake, called Lake-Lano; from which clouds and vapour breathing death—worse, apparently, than those of Lake-Lego, though undoubtedly of the same kind—were constantly emanating, and covering the land, lay not in Scandinavia at all, as MacPherson persists in affirming, but in Inis-thona itself, and at no great distance from Runa. Runa being on the coast, therefore, Lano was of necessity inland; and the habitable region around it, notwithstanding its pestilential exhalations, must have been very extensive, for Cormalo, as we know, could assemble ten thousand spears, and maintained an independent jurisdiction. Whether the " seven chiefs" in Swaran's expedition were included in this array, is uncertain; but they were certainly chiefs at Lano, and the district partitioned among so many could have been of no limited dimensions. The lake itself is like Lego, dismal and dark-rolling; " the children of the lake" convene for war, but retreat "to their secret vales," when defeated; the lake is distant from Runa, or rather from " the fount of mossy stones," some half day's journey at least; and the ground intervening is a " desert" or wilderness.

" ' O Ronnan,' said the rising Oscar, ' Ogar, king of spears ! call my heroes to my side, the sons of streamy Morven. To-day we go to Lano's water, that sends forth the cloud of death. Cormalo will not long rejoice: death is often at the point of our swords.' They came over the desert like stormy clouds, when the winds roll them over the heath: their edges are tinged with lightning: and the echoing groves foresee the storm. The horn of Oscar's battle was heard; and Lano shook in all its waves. The children of the lake convened around the sounding shield of Cormalo. Oscar fought, as he was wont in battle. Cormalo fell beneath his sword; and the sons of the dismal Lano fled to their secret vales. Oscar brought the daughter of Inis-thona to Annir's echoing halls. The face of age was bright with joy; he blessed the king of swords."\*

To determine this remarkable region then, with the " fount of mossy stones" at the head of Reikum valley for a starting-point, we have but to march for half a day's journey or thereby north-eastward, into the centre of the island; and before we have proceeded over many miles, we shall find all that is required, even in the altered circumstances of the country, to justify our expedition.

---

\* It might be a curious antiquarian speculation, whether such tributary kings as Annir, and generals in war for the time, received this title as commanders, in proportion to their contingent in the field. There are numerous instances in which the same rank is ascribed to men who were not otherwise kings, than as the leaders of a force in battle. Oscar, for example, is here called the " king of swords," in allusion to his present expedition, as Annir above is called " king of spears," and Ogar, in this very quotation, Fingal himself is called oftener, perhaps, " king of men," or the " first of men"—being generalissimo of the Caledonian confederacy, as Agamemnon was of the Greek—than king of Morven, which was but a local title. We found nothing more on the fact, than as it illustrates incidentally the true rank and relationship in war, of these feudatory princes.

"Our ride [from Mossfell, north-west of Reikum] was now dreary and tiresome, though the path was good. We halted to refresh the horses on a small spot where there was a little grass, the principal covering of the soil being dwarf willows. Near Thingvalla we entered a deep and frightful fissure, called Almannagian. This has been formed, with many others of smaller dimensions, and another large one which runs parallel to it at a considerable distance, by the sinking of the ground during some of those terrible convulsions which have shaken Iceland to its foundations. The whole rock bears marks of having been affected by fire. . . . . We got out of the hollow by a narrow path, and after crossing a small stream that runs into the lake, we arrived at the place of Thingvalla, which is about twenty-six miles distant from Reikiavik [about ten from the valley of Reikum, or less than a day's journey from the fountain at the head of it.] . . . . The scenery about Thingvalla is romantic, but the want of wood, and the effects of subterraneous heat, combine to give an impression of dreariness. The lake is a fine sheet of water, reckoned to be about ten miles long, and from three to seven in breadth. There are two pretty large islands in the lake, called Sandey and Nesey, composed entirely of volcanic matter. The mountains at the south end are very picturesque, and the vapour ascending from hot springs on their sides contributes to the solemnity of the scene, which has been created by the most dreadful commotion, and the destruction of a country that may once have been beautiful and fertile. Near this place was the building where the courts of justice were held formerly. . . . . . . . Why Thingvalla was originally chosen as the seat of justice, does not appear; . . . . . . . . few remains are left to mark a spot so famous in the history of Iceland. The only building was a small wooden house in which the consultations were held, and sentence pronounced by the Stiftamtmand or Governor. The magistrates and people, assembled on the occasion, lived in tents. Those culprits who were condemned to die were beheaded on a small island in the river Oxer-aa, which here flows into the lake. The females were drowned in a pool below the lava, a little farther up the valley. . . . . . The road [to mount Hekla] lies along the north end, and part of the east side of the lake, where there is a considerable tract of stunted birch, and willow trees. The depth of the lake is said to be very great, a line of a hundred fathoms having been sunk without bottom. After many turnings, and crossing some bogs, we came to a low hill, round which we passed, and having got safe over another bog, which seemed to be fully as hazardous as any we had formerly attempted, we reached the bank of a large river called the Bruer-aa, which takes its rise from the Apa Vatn. This lake receives the waters of the surrounding bogs; and near it, in different places, we saw vapours ascending from hot springs," &c. —*Mackenzie's Iceland*, pp. 209-11.

Here, again, in the very region indicated and at the distance alleged—that is, within ten miles direct from the fountain, and not more than twenty by a circuit, through moors and mosses—we have more than one lake, but one in particular, with every characteristic of Lake-Lano. (1.) A surrounding country, which, before it was destroyed by fire and rent by earthquakes, must have been fertile enough to maintain a large population, with woods, of the very sort described by Ossian, still traceable on its surface. (2.) An explanation of the dismal clouds which constantly issued from its waters, before the volcanic heat which thus affected them and threw off those deadly vapours, had found a natural vent for itself in the crevices of the adjoining mountains. And (3.) a sufficient reason for the Thingval, or Supreme Court of the Island, having been originally fixed in that neighbourhood, which seemed so inexplicable to Sir George Mackenzie. It had been the most fertile region in the Island, in fact, and the head-quarters of an old principality; to which the natives, by a sort of traditional instinct, clung, without being able to account for their own prepossession—an instinct which seems to be again reviving, in the selection of Thingvalla as the principal scene of approaching national festivities in 1874. Here, at all events, unquestionably Cormalo dwelt; and partially protected by intervening morasses and pestilential bogs, maintained among the woods and valleys his army of "ten thousand spears." Whether culprits in his day were beheaded on that island in the Oxer-aa, or women were drowned under the lava, is no doubt uncertain. If no lava yet existed there, such mode of punishment was of course impossible; but that he himself was a savage assassin of the Berserker type, for which that region was long after notorious, is manifest from what Ossian records; and that he was slain there in expiation of his crimes, and the guilty partner of his unnatural rebellion brought home again to her father by Oscar, is almost as certain as any corresponding facts in history can be. The fall of Macbeth, and the guilt of his countess, are not more certain.

II. On the present, however, as on former occasions, there may be difficulties and objections worthy of consideration, and these accordingly must be looked at and replied to. 1. If the lake was so pestilential, it may be objected, how could so large a population survive in its immediate neighbourhood? To which it may be answered—(1.) That the fact is recognised repeatedly in Ossian, both by author and translator, and would not have been introduced if it had not been well known, or had seemed incredible to either. (2.) That it was not more wonderful than that a large population should have survived at Lake-Lego, at Lake-Avernus, or Lake-Quilotoa. And (3.) that in point of fact, although such exhalations might be fatal to delicate children or to infirm adults, or to cattle which carried their heads closer to the ground, those who survived the injurious effects were really stronger in proportion than their neighbours; as is known to be the case among the marshes of Iceland still, and to have been the case in similar localities elsewhere in the world. The atmosphere of the Dog Cave at Herculaneum, for example, near Lake-Agnano in Italy, was fatal to any quadruped with its head near the ground, although men, walking erect, were exempt from its influence; but if the traveller lay down to rest, he never rose again—in consequence of which danger, it was ultimately closed: and in a certain parish of Ayrshire the adult population are, or were, proverbially taller and stronger than the people of the adjoining districts, although there was more mortality among children in proportion, attributable solely to the injurious exhalations of the valley.

2. From the same point of view, it may also be inquired how a population, so numerous and strong in Ossian's day, 250 A.D., had almost entirely disappeared when the Island was discovered by the Norse in 874? To which, in like manner, it may again be replied that the Island, in that very interval, had in all probability become the scene of such devastation by volcanic fire as would more than account for the disappearance, in a great measure at least, of its original population. In Ossian's day, it must have been clothed with verdure, and was shrouded with forests. When the Norse discovered it, it was comparatively a barren waste, and has since been torn to pieces by earthquakes, scorched by fire, overrun with lava, encrusted with sulphur, drenched in steam—yet traces of its original beauty remain in petrified mosses by the empty fountains, and notwithstanding such frightful ravages, it has been known to maintain 100,000 inhabitants. In Falconer's *Geography*, so late as the middle of the 17th century, the soil on the south side of the Island is described as " reasonably fertile, and affording pasture for Horses, Cows, Oxen, and other Cattel. . . . . . . In the Woods are White Bears, Foxes, Hares, and other game; of whose skins the inhabitants make their cloaths. . . . . Such shoals of ice with melted snows come down from the mountains that frequently trees and cattle are carried away. . . . . The houses are built of wood, and covered with the bark of trees, skins or turfs," &c. . . . Circumstances which imply, at that date, the continued growth of forests in the very neighbourhood visited by Oscar. Much of this also has no doubt since been destroyed by the eruptions of subsequent years. Why, then, before such terrible calamities were known, and when nothing but the sulphur-clouds of Lano were yet visible, might not a population such as Ossian describes, strong and numerous, although savage and implacable, have been supported by the cattle on its pastures or by the wild deer and boar in its forests? What the sufferings of the unhappy people were, when the exterminating fire reached them, or when the subsequent famine thinned their tribes, we have no record in Ossian or elsewhere, and need not now conjecture. Herculaneum and Pompeii were submerged in a night by ashes; the original inhabitants of Iceland, by thousands, might be engulphed alive.

3. If Oscar's expedition was from Reikum to Thingvalla, or anywhere in that neighbourhood, he might have seen or heard something of Mount Hekla— why, then, it may be said, was such a remarkable object as a volcano in action

forgotten in the poem? To which also, it may be replied—(1.) That the omission of such reference is another clear proof of MacPherson's innocence alike, and of his ignorance, in the matter. If MacPherson had been either an impostor as alleged, or even guilty of tampering with the text, on the one hand, having Iceland in view; or had had the slightest idea, on the other, that Inis-thona was identical with Iceland, some notice of Mount Hekla would have been introduced beyond doubt in the narrative, or a note would have been added at the close to explain the omission. On the contrary, all that MacPherson could discern in the various and repeated allusions to Lake-Lano was, that it "was a lake of Scandinavia!" He did not even imagine where Inis-thona was. (2.) Our argument from the beginning has been, that Oscar was not necessarily within sight of the volcano—his track being by the heath between Reikum and Thingvalla, fully 30 miles from Mount Hekla. And (3.), which is of much greater importance in every point of view, both scientific and historical—that Hekla had not yet opened as an active volcano, but was only accumulating its resources for an eruption at some later date. The subterranean fires, indeed, were already kindled, and the mephitic vapours were beginning to be exhaled; but the fields of Iceland had not yet been scorched with lava, or its forests smothered in flames. This was in the middle, or towards the end of the 3rd century; when the spirit of Loda was still dormant in the northern sea, or only shrieking on the cliffs of Inistore. But symptoms of his awakening were beginning to be seen and felt, both north and south, at the date in question. Earthquakes had been felt in Ullin, and thunder heard in the ground; rocks had fallen from Cromla, deadly vapours were being exhaled from Lake-Lego, and green-vallied Erin trembled from sea to sea. Lightning, in the meantime, accumulates, the sea rises in terror, and the cliffs quiver at Inistore; and Lano, with its sable surge, beyond them all, breathes death or disease on Inis-thona. Thus, after his own poetic fashion, or according to the reports of his people, are such significant phenomena chronicled by Ossian. In plain terms, or in more scientific phraseology—which some of our readers may possibly prefer—we have thus, looking back, two similar lakes with mephitic exhalations, one in the North of Ireland and the other in Iceland, at opposite extremes of the volcanic drift; with an almost unbroken series of volcanic ruptures in the land between them, and violent abnormal agitations of the sea where the land terminates, distinctly recorded at intervening dates: and although no eruption of Mount Hekla at the time has been mentioned, the facts thus ascertained seem to indicate very plainly, not only that some great eruption was in progress, such as afterwards shook Iceland to its foundations and opened its miraculous springs; but that the volcanic current underneath, which at last found vent in Hekla, had its course from the North of

Ireland, along the west coast of Scotland, through the Orkneys, and then under the ocean, till it exhausted its force by an explosion in Iceland, as the terminus of its range: and finally, that all this was partially manifest in progress, with many unmistakeable symptoms in the 3rd century, although probably not completed till the beginning of the 4th; and the supposed first eruption of Hekla in 1004 A.D., was only the second or third after all. Does the reader, then, imagine that if James MacPherson, with his acknowledged astuteness and sagacity, ever had the slightest glimpse of this, he would not have announced it; or that this not being announced, and yet so manifestly contained in that poem, the *War of Inis-thona* could by human possibility be an imposture? It must seem strange, after evidence like this, that a fragment so wonderful should not be included in the Gaelig editions of Ossian since MacPherson's day; and amusing, although not strange, that Laing, with his customary complacence, should identify Inisthona itself with Inis-owen at the mouth of Lough-Foyle—where nothing is found to correspond, but which he coolly asserts was adopted and transformed by MacPherson, into a pleasant sounding name for a new fable!

4. But finally, in the way of objection, it may be urged that Iceland was not known at all till discovered by the Norse in 874, and was so called by its discoverer, from the enormous fields of ice by which it was everywhere overspread. This is no doubt the Norwegian account of its discovery and designation, and may be true so far as the knowledge of that adventurous people is concerned. The millennium of its discovery by them, in fact, is now being celebrated with solemn festival on the Island, and by a state visit of the king of Denmark this very month of August, and whilst these pages are in press, to that outlying dependency of his crown. But it is an equally certain tradition that monuments of Irish occupation long before that—so early, indeed, as the 5th century—have been identified along its southern shores, in the shape of crosses, &c.: which, considering the correspondence between the king of Morven and the feudatory kings of the Island in the 3rd century, is by no means an improbable fact. If Fingal, Ossian, and Oscar already knew the way to Iceland, either as friends or foes, why should not their allies or successors—in a certain sense, their kinsmen or descendants—from the shores of Ulster, with missionary objects in view, in the days of Columba, have followed their track? But the kings of Inis-thona, in Fingal's day, were also tributaries to Lochlin; that is, the kings of Iceland were tributaries to Norway: so that the Norse or the Danes, as discoverers of the Island, have still a prior claim to its sovereignty; and the king of Denmark at this moment, in celebrating the origin of his title in 874, is unconsciously confirming a much older right, which may now be traced, without doubt, to the beginning of the 2nd century, and may possibly extend to the very commence-

ment of the Christian era. As for the origin of the name, and without disputing the correctness of its modern derivation, it is proper also to observe that the name itself is spelled indifferently in our older geographical authorities Isle-land, Ise-land, Is-land—which re-appears in the adjective Is-landic—and Eis-land; which, besides meaning the Land of Ice, means also the Land of the Sea; and which, as our readers will now easily perceive, is but a mixed translation into Celtic and Teutonic of INIS-THONA.

III. Whether Ossian knew much, or anything, of the regions still farther north, now distinguished by the names of Lappland and Finnland, or had ever encountered their adventurous inhabitants at sea, would be an interesting question also, in conclusion of our present researches; on which, however, only the light of conjecture can be obtained. There seems to be no direct reference to those countries or peoples in his text; but it is notorious that the Finns and Lapplanders used to make voyages of incredible extent in their canoes—that they did, in fact, within recent generations, make periodical visits to the Zetlands and Orkneys, for fishing or other purposes, and would " flee away so swiftly" when pursued, as Wallace in his curious history informs us, that to capture them was as difficult as to seize a bird. On such occasions, therefore, it is quite possible that Ossian may have seen them, although his own expeditions did not extend to their coasts; and the frequent contemptuous allusions to " the race of little men," and their probable supremacy in Scotland at some future day as the last disgrace that could overtake his country, which in melancholy moods he indulged in, may have been suggested to him, or even vividly impressed on his mind, by the accidental notice of such nimble dwarfs on the ocean, so entirely different in all respects from his own gigantic people. There might be inferior tribes in the Highlands as compared with the descendants of Trenmor, doubtless, to whom he directly referred; but no other " race of little men" known to us, anywhere existing in Scotland or the Isles, could have been objects of such scorn to a man so pre-eminently noble. On the other hand, by a kind of voluntary exaggeration, to think of Lapps in the palace at Morven, or of Finnmen as the lords of Glencoe, would be humiliation worse than death.

This very apprehension, however, which haunted him in his declining years, that some inferior race would occupy his own much-loved territory, may have been due to the fact that he had occasionally seen such people, and looked on them with a kind of superstitious dread as some abnormal types of humanity— whose mysterious presence, from time to time, on the shores of Scotland might portend the ultimate degradation and ruin of his country.

## CHAPTER VIII.

#### RELIGIOUS FAITHS—FUNERAL RITES, &c.

I. 1. The great principles of organic existence, according to the Mosaic philosophy, were the spirit, the water, and the blood; represented ultimately in man, most perfectly in Him who was the Son of Man, and by Him or in His Gospel embodied for the redemption of the world—" And there are three that bear witness in earth, the spirit, and the water, and the blood: and these three agree in one."—1 John v. 8. Two of these elements at least were known to our forefathers, before the promulgation of Christianity; were accepted by them as ultimate essences into which organisation was resolvable, and taught to the people through their successive generations, both by speech and song, as fundamental ideas in their common faith—the water and the spirit, the moisture and the atmosphere, the vapour and the breath, the mist and the wind of heaven. Men, co-existing of these elements, and sustained by them in union, lived; losing one or both, they died, and were resolved again into their separate constituent parts—the soul, or breath, or spirit, ascending on high, and the body, unless otherwise preserved, dissolving in moisture. In the case of those who had been highly distinguished on earth, by deeds of generosity, courage, or strength, the spirit drew the moisture with it, and shaped for itself a cloudy frame, in which it lived and moved and had its being in the sky; or floated on the surface of the earth, or re-visited the scenes of its former greatness and the companions of its mortal pilgrimage, with gifts of intelligence and foreknowledge amounting to prophecy, for their advantage, superadded. In the case of others, less noble or distinguished, such immortality was perhaps tacitly ignored, as unattainable; and in the case of the mean, the vicious, or the grovelling, no ascension of the soul was even tolerated; but the spirit, lodged in low damp marshes, was shut up like pestilential vapour in caves or chinks of the earth, from which, according to its nature, it shot forth the darts of disease; or it was driven along the valley and the face of stagnate streams, as a trivial gas, or sunk as a leaden exhalation incapable of rising to the heavens. This doctrine, in both its aspects, is constantly represented in Ossian as the recognised popular faith of his age, and as having been the faith of his people for generations.

" His soul is great; his arm is strong; his battles are full of fame. But the little soul is a vapour that hovers round the marshy lake: it never rises on the green hill, lest the winds should meet it there; its dwelling is in the cave, it sends forth the dart of death."—*Temora*, B. I.

A contrast in all respects to the apotheosis of the hero, as elsewhere described—

"Let his robe of mist be near; his spear that is formed of a cloud. Place an half-extinguished meteor by his side, in the form of the hero's sword. And oh! let his countenance be lovely, that his friends may delight in his presence. 'Bend from your clouds,' I said, 'ghosts of my fathers, bend.'"—*Dar-thula.*

2. The third principle of earthly witness-bearing, or the blood, is not recognisable as an element of public faith at the period in question; but in place of blood, the extraneous element of fire was substituted, and introduced, as it were, to be a purifying agent for the happiness and perfection, or for the highest glory of the most illustrious or beloved dead. By the action of fire, the spirit was more perfectly liberated from the corruption of the body than it otherwise could be; or rather, the corruption of the body was anticipated and prevented from contaminating the spirit, which then rose in purity and satisfaction from the burning remains, to take its place in the loftiest region of immortal consecration as a beam of light, as a spark of fire, as a happy meteor escaped from earth and restored again to heaven. This doctrine, essentially religious in itself, as well as sublime and beautiful, taught apparently by the Druids and supported by the chiefs and bards, may have been of purely native origin; but its resemblance to the teaching of the Bible is obvious, and it is neither unphilosophical nor improper to trace this analogy to its limits.

The origin of all men, according to the Druids, was by the action of solar heat on the surface of their parent planet; and various races of men were thus created, according to the nature of the soil. Hence fire-worship originated in the east, and hence offerings by fire, often human sacrifices, to Baal or the sun, as the author of their existence, were thought appropriate among the people under that superstition; which gradually spread by the emigration of the Canaanites and Phœnicians westward—compare Appendix—till it became the established religion of Spain, of Great Britain, and Ireland; and in these countries was administered with some authority and pomp by an immense hierarchy of Druids, under whose auspices, there is too much reason to fear that human sacrifices occurred in the British Isles as well as on the coasts of Africa, and that our forefathers sent their sons and daughters through the fire to Molech, as well as the Idolaters of Canaan. The process of burial, as represented in Ossian, is not, of course, in any proper sense, a sacrifice; yet in connection with a rite so popular and common, and which might easily be mistaken for a sacrifice, it is proper to observe that the earliest sacrifices recorded among men, Druidical or other, were presumably by fire; and it is remarkable that the most acceptable of the typical sacrifices so made was that by which the remains of animal organisation were purified by burning—" and the Lord had respect unto Abel and to his offering."

Farther, the sacrifices of the patriarchal era and of the Temple which followed, were by an elaborate process of combustion, and every sacrifice from that day forward among the Holy People was salted with fire. If, therefore, human sacrifices, so obviously contemplated in the offering of Isaac and for ever abolished in his release, were at any time practised by the Druids in Western Europe, the substitution of a body to be consumed on the funeral pyre for a living victim to be sacrificed on the altar, would be a natural and blessed change. Besides which, in a moral point of view, salvation itself in Christ's dispensation is said to be as by fire; nay, "there standeth one among you whom ye know not"—a phrase divinely suggestive of the unrecognised presence of that Teacher always among Jews and Gentiles, Barbarians, Scythians, bond and free—" who shall baptize you with the Holy Ghost and with fire;" and finally, even in its physical sense, the world is said to be "reserved unto fire against the day of judgment," for ultimate purification of its elements, " and perdition of ungodly men"—an idea which was far from being forgotten by these heathen at the burning of their dead. There was even some correspondence in this theory of life and immortality to the latent laws and relationships of the world. The souls of the good and great, like a breath from heaven, return thither on high; the souls of the mean and vicious, like pestilential vapours, cling to and curse the earth from which they issue; but the principle of fire, like some divine meteoric agency traversing the whole, purifies and reconstitutes them all. Nor must we forget, whilst thus accumulating parallels, that other nations besides the Celts of Europe or Great Britain adopted the same process of burial by fire, and even of voluntary incremation, as the Greeks, Carthaginians, Canaanites, and other Asiatic tribes. Whether the doctrine, therefore, as taught by the Druids, and popularised by men like Ossian in their public hymns, was of directly inspired origin, borrowed from and connected with the earliest worship of the True God; or was only a system of typical ideas, elaborated from a study of nature and embodied in mystical rites, accepted and preserved by the people themselves from time immemorial; it had nevertheless a fixed and undeniable relationship to the profoundest realities in the universe, and was undoubtedly but a part, however dark, of that sublime comprehensive faith in which the souls of all men shall at last rejoice, and by which they shall be transformed into a truer likeness of the Deity. If to all this we could eke on, by any reference in Ossian, the mystery of serpent-worship, so clearly proved by Mr. Phené, in his recent most interesting investigations, to have been once practised in Scotland, in sight of Bencruachan, and most probably also in Arran—we might then with certainty identify the Druids and the Celts of Trenmor's tribe with the very earliest inhabitants of North Britain, and even trace their advent thither from the plains of Hindostan; but no such reference appears. Ossian was indeed acquainted by observation with the superstitions of Scandinavia, and had been a witness of religious rites in honour of their gods at the circles of Brumo and Loda, whatever deities these might be; but, as MacPherson correctly notes, he looked on with indifference or contempt, and defied their machinations with the sword. All such local gods, to him, were objects of ridicule. He recognised the Deity, if he could be said to recognise him at all, as an omnipresent vital essence, everywhere diffused in the world, or concentrated for a lifetime in heroes. He himself, his kindred and his forefathers, and the human race at large, were dependent solely on the atmosphere; their souls were identified with the air, heaven was their natural home, earth their temporary residence, and fire the element of purification, or the bright path to immortality for them, when the hour of dissolution came.

3. Whether Trenmor and his people brought a faith like this with them by tradition from the confines of Paradise, or borrowed it from Zoroaster as they journeyed from the east,\* or copied the practice only from the Greeks when they buried their dead on the plains of Troy or among the mountains of Thrace, may be matter of conjecture; and whether the Druids were but worshippers of Baal, as their Baaltein fires, long kindled periodically in Scotland, implied, or superstitious devotees and unconscious servants of the Most High, we who enjoy purer light, and worship Him who is the Father of lights as well as a consuming fire, need concern ourselves little to prove. But it is pleasant to reflect that, in this same country of ours, the foundation of such a faith was held as the last consolation of gifted souls in surrounding darkness, and taught to the people by songs and signs as a hope of glory hereafter. Purification by fire for body and soul, and assimilation thereby to the purest essence of the universe, were the fundamental ideas of their creed; and however they may have been introduced, these were articles of faith most devoutly cherished and solemnly acted upon, wherever circumstances would permit, by the people high and low, of Ossian's day and kindred; and were by him celebrated as the infallible means of the highest and most acceptable apotheosis. The incremation of Malvina's remains, on the principle of transmutation and escape from dark perishable clay to luminous and immortal ether, misunderstood by MacPherson but so clearly indicated in the text as already quoted—Part II., Chap. II.—is a beautiful illustration of this; and the well-known practice of burning the dead generally, wherever that was possible, is proof of it. Whether the same, or even a similar process was uni-

---

\* Unconsciously confirmed by Pinkerton, who derives the name of Drust, an early Pickish king, from the Persian for *sincerity*, and associates it with *Zerdust*, the Persian name of Zoroaster—philosopher, reformer, and king.—*History of Scotland*, Vol. I., 285.

formly adopted in the burial of the common people, more especially of those who might fall by hundreds in battle, is uncertain. If so, then the burning of their remains must have been by immense conflagrations in the mass, which, although very unlikely, is not impossible; or if that could not be conveniently accomplished, as very often it might not, then the singing of a requiem in their praise to console their spirits for the want of that honour, and to reconcile them to their comparatively unhappy fate, was substituted as the only available compensation—an act of love and gratitude, or of justice to them, which seems always to have been sufficient to gratify and soothe them.

" Faint glimmers the moon on Moi-lena, through the broad-headed groves of the hill: raise stones, beneath its beams, to all the fallen in war. Though no chiefs were they, yet their hands were strong in fight. They were my rock in danger; the mountain from which I spread my eagle wings. Thence am I renowned: Carril, forget not the low. Loud at once, from the hundred bards, rose the song of the tomb," &c.—*Temora*, B. III. " Let not the fallen be forgot, they were mighty in the field. Let Carril pour his song, that the kings may rejoice in their mist."—*Ibid*. B. VIII.

In the above ceremonies, however—either the application of fire to purify and liberate the soul, or the chanting of the hymn of praise to console it—the presence of the Druid or Fire-worshipping priest was not necessary. The relatives, the people, and the bards together were the only, or at least the most frequent performers. At great public celebrations, by sacrifice or otherwise, the priests as a matter of course, by right or privilege, might officiate or preside; but their assistance at funereal rites seems nowhere to have been required or incumbent. In the cases above quoted from *Temora*, for example, a Druid, or dweller in the cave, though residing in the immediate neighbourhood, does not intrude, and does not seem to have been invited even to join in the obsequies. This might either be in consequence of their declining influence and authority, or because the Scots were then, as they still are, in religion and politics, a democratic people. The interment of the dead, however, was not the less solemn or sacred on that account; and although reverence for the priest may have returned with Christianity, reverence for the dead has not diminished, at least among the Celtic population in their native homes. In Arran, so intimately associated with the history of the entire Ossianic era, this sentiment survives to the present day, like some hereditary instinct of the people. So strong, indeed, is this feeling of awe in the presence of death among the natives of that Island that not only the immediate relatives of the deceased, but the population of a whole district, young and old, will cease from their ordinary avocations, as if for an act of public worship, whilst the body lies in shroud awaiting sepulture; and friends of the remotest relationship will assemble to assist at the funeral, from a distance, it may be in some cases, of twenty miles around the spot of interment.

II. 1. The modes of burial, as detailed by Ossian, were four-fold, and varied according to the rank, the services, and the estimation of the deceased. The commonest, of necessity, was a simple grave with turf and head-stone, for the undistinguished mortal who perished like his neighbours, without any deed of renown. The next was by several monumental stones, two or more, at head and foot or sides of the body, in standing commemoration of a hasty burial, however distinguished the dead might be—as Ryno's in Ireland, and Oscar's and Fingal's in Arran  A third was by the erection of a cairn or mound, enclosing in its topmost layer the small stone cist or coffin, with the ashes of the dead collected and placed there after burning, as in Cuthullin's tomb in Ireland by the borders of Lough-Neagh, or in Ossian's own tomb at Clachaig—the most honourable sepulture of all; in which hundreds of voluntary labourers, with bards and military chiefs in attendance, would be employed at a time, as on one of the occasions now referred to, we are expressly informed was the case.

"We came to Lego's mournful banks: we found his rising tomb [Cuthullin's]. His companions in battle are there; his bards of many songs. Three days we mourned over the hero: on the fourth, I struck the shield of Caithbat: the heroes gathered around with joy, and shook their beamy spears."—*Dar-thula*.

The fourth was by placing the ashes in an urn under a slab or tombstone on supporters, a compliment reserved most probably for women of rank or distinction, as Malvina's tomb and others of a similar description in Arran seem conspicuously to indicate; in which cases also a choir of girls, with harps and hymns, may have assisted at the ceremony.  "The maids are departed to their place; and thou alone, O breeze, mournest there."—*Berrathon*.

2. In each or all of these modes of sepulture, burning might precede the burial, as circumstances would allow; and articles of value pertaining to the deceased, as beads, rings, a stag's horn by way of distinction, or some weapon of war might be deposited along with the remains, but not necessarily. Special interments of love, sympathy, romance, and honour, are also recorded; in which lovers, for example, were laid together in the same tomb—as Conlath and Cuthona in the poem of that name; Connal and Crimora, in *Carric-thura*, and Comal and Galvina—*Fingal*, B. II.; rivals were put side by side, with the object of their jealousy near them, as Lamderg, Ullin, and Gelchossa—*Ibid.* B. V.; and heroes interred, as Orla and Ryno were, near other heroes who had fallen before them, whose graves were all marked with trees planted suggestively, or with stones expressive of the circumstances—*Ibid.* B. V.; or with special romantic and poetical adjuncts, as at the temporary resting-place of Fillan.

"Ossian, give me that broken shield: these feathers that are rolled in the wind. Place them near to Fillan, that less of his fame may fall. . . . Lay me in that hollow rock: raise no stone above; lest one should ask about my fame. I am fallen in the first of my fields; fallen without renown. Let thy voice alone send joy to my flying soul. Why should the feeble know where dwells the lost beam of Clatho."—*Temora*, B. VI.

The warrior, as we have seen, who was bloody and remorseless in fight, had his victims entombed around him, like Foldath—*Ibid.* B. V.; and where the warrior who was also a hunter reposed, his dog was laid beside him on the left, as if waiting to attend his summons on fields of air beyond the verge of earth —like Oscar's at Glenree, and like Cuthullin's by Lake-Lego.

"By the dark-rolling waves of Lego they raised the hero's tomb. Luath at a distance lies, the companion of Cuthullin, at the chase."—*Death of Cuthullin.*

Love, honour, and veneration, it may be said, were the prevailing sentiments in all such ceremonies. To dig a grave, or to raise a tomb, without some sort of ennobling sympathy, seems to have been an impossibility. Death extinguished all resentment; failure was covered by generous apologies, and the fall of the worst enemy ensured forgiveness of his crimes. Hundreds of victorious people would assemble willingly to raise the tomb of their vanquished oppressor in mere sympathy to his soul, and to refuse such consolation was esteemed the most contemptible cruelty. Where love and affection on the other hand, as was of course most commonly the case, presided at the obsequies and inspired the mourners, no sacrifice of labour, no patience or toil, was ever grudged in honour of the departed; and one touching instance of filial affection in such a case is recorded by Ossian, rarely if ever equalled in the annals of war—in which a youth of eighteen, left alone in the enemy's territory with his father's corpse, began its interment single-handed in the desert, fed himself on the venison he could kill in the meantime with his bow, and slept seven successive nights with his head on the rising turf, till "at length the steps of Colgan came, the Bard of high Temora: Duth-caron received his fame, and brightened as he rose on the wind."—*Temora*, B. III. This youth's name was Connal, himself the coeval and long the contemporary of Fingal; and his father, Duth-caron, had been the grey-headed preceptor in archery of the future king of Morven.

3. Being informed as we now are, by the most conclusive proofs, of the genuineness of such memorials, not only as monuments of the dead, but as landmarks in history, and types or traces of our oldest civilisation and religion, it might be matter of regret to many of us, and even of reproach hereafter, if they were allowed to decay unrecognised, or to be violated without reasonable apology. To identify and preserve them everywhere, should be esteemed a privilege and

a duty; and that many of the tombs described in Ossian, and scattered on the track of his expeditions, now traceable as distinctly as the march of a modern army, both in Scotland and in Ireland, might so be discovered and identified, is as certain as that the tombs in Arran already described and represented in this volume belong to the remains of those whose names by tradition adhere to them. In particular, it is now suggested, from the evidence which has been accumulating in the course of our inquiries—(1.) That in Ireland the joint tomb of Lamderg, Ullin and Gelchosa, with the adjoining tomb of Orla and Ryno, might be identified on the northern slope of the Carrickfergus range, between the upper and lower Carneals (Ossian's Cormul) and Lake Mourne on the mountains there—there, or in that immediate neighbourhood; and Cuthullin's tomb, certainly a mound, on the banks of Lough-Neagh, about Antrim Bay, or towards the valley of the Lower Bann, north-westward. (2.) That in Scotland, the joint tomb of Comal and Galvina may yet be identified, if it has not already been explored by antiquaries unconscious of its site, somewhere on the shore and most probably to the north, of King's Cove in Arran; and (3.) that Comala's grave—the Orkney princess and the betrothed of Fingal—although not formally described, may still be discoverable by the verge, or in the shadow, of some rocky bank at the head of Bonny Water in Stirlingshire. "Rise, Comala, from thy rocks: daughter of Sarno, rise in tears." But she will not rise. "There Comala sits forlorn;" and afterwards, of apprehension, she dies there, as we have seen; and there she seems to have been interred—" Meteors roll around the maid, and moonbeams lift her soul."—The Author has endeavoured both by inquiry, and by personal search in the neighbourhood, to obtain some traces of this interesting sepulture, but hitherto without success. The bank in question, opposite Orchard Mill, has long ago been cleared for agricultural purposes, but no discovery of the sort at that time has been recorded. Anything whatever in the shape of an urn, or of a cist, or of female human remains of a distant date, hereafter disclosed, between the high road there, or thereabouts, and the base ot Tomfin, should be carefully noted; for such a discovery would be little less than the sign manual of Ossian to the authorship of *Comala*.

Other places of interment might also be suggested, not quite so easily defined, although they might be stumbled on by accident, with much certainty. In the neighbourhood of Turriff, supposed by some to have been the scene of an Ossianic poem, a discovery was made about a twelvemonth ago, and whilst these pages were in preparation for the press—by which the resting-place of some hero, precisely similar to Ossian's own, although perhaps a little ruder, has been identified. It is described in the local papers, with astonishment as usual at the unknown mode of transporting and placing such huge blocks, as follows:—

"STONE CIST DISCOVERED ON THE FARM OF SLAP, TURRIFF.—While the contractors were digging sand for new buildings at Slackadale, they came upon stones which, on close examination, were found to be a cist, constructed of five large stones—four set on their edges, so as to form an oblong internal area of 3 feet by 2, the fifth a large block on the top, leaving a height from the floor of about 20 or 22 inches—the whole packed up with a few outlying boulders, not unlike an old-fashioned stone drain, shut up at both ends. The large stones were all of the sandstone conglomerate, such as can be got here and there on the farm, not far from the surface, although not near the field in which this has been found. Such huge blocks could not have been very easily got to the place, yet very little if any labour seems to have been expended in squaring or dressing, save perhaps a little flattening on the inner surface. One could not tell which was the head or foot of the cist, but it stands nearly east and west. The bottom had no paving, and was nearly five feet from the present surface, but, being on a slightly rolling eminence where houses stood some thirty years ago, and now all levelled away, it might at one time have been considerably deeper. On careful search being made in the interior, a few fragments of flint, such as arrow points were wont to be manufactured from, were found, but no perfect arrow points. With the exception of a little blackened sand, and what was thought to be the slightest trace of calcined bone, no other organic remains could be found."—*Glasgow Herald*, July 4, 1873.

The poem in question is *Oithona*, in which and in *Lathmon*—to which it is a sequel—references to Dunlathmon a fortress, and to Duvranna a river, both certainly on the north-east coast of Scotland, occur, so explicit as to justify the opinion entertained by MacPherson himself, and adopted by recent local writers, that the scene described was really in the neighbourhood of Turriff. The points relied on are (1.) that the Duvran or Dovran is still the name of a well-known river there; and (2.) that Dunlathmon, as represented in Ossian, corresponds precisely to a fortress on its banks; for farther particulars of which the reader may consult the Statistical Account of Scotland, 1845, under the head of Turriff; and to which it may be added, from the text of *Oithona*, (3.) that Dunlathmon, like Turriff where its limits touch the coast, is about three days' sail from the outlying rocks of the Zetland or Faroe Isles, to which the catastrophe of the poem is transferred—" On the third day arose Tromàthon, like a blue shield in the midst of the sea." Nothing else remains to identify the region, but nothing more is required; nor is any special interment at the place recorded in the poem, although many a hero, as we learn incidentally, must have fallen at the walls of Dunlathmon. Whether the tomb now discovered has been the resting-place of old Nuäth, father of Lathmon himself and of the hapless Oithona, must remain matter of conjecture most probably for ever; but as another link in the accumulating chain of evidence to verify and localise the poems of Ossian, this discovery is of no slight importance. Besides which, it explains (1.) the extent of

Fingal's fame, and indirectly of his authority, throughout the mainland of Scotland eastward; (2.) the possibility of Morven being invaded in his absence, as recorded in *Lathmon*, by adventurous Caledonians from beyond Lochaber and Strathspey; (3.) and chiefly, the generosity of his own administration as royal generalissimo, and the amicable spirit, as well as the dignified tone of all his negotiations with independent princes beyond his own frontiers.

"'Son of Nuäth,' he said, 'why dost thou search for fame in Morven? We are not of the race of the feeble; nor do our swords gleam over the weak. When did we come to Dunlathmon, with the sound of war? Fingal does not delight in battle, though his arm is strong. . . . . Lathmon! retire to thy place. Turn thy battles to other lands. The race of Morven are renowned, and their foes are the sons of the unhappy.'"—*Lathmon*.

To students of Scottish history, these facts, thus recently and accidentally established, are of the utmost significance; but their bearing will be best understood by a careful examination of the poems themselves, from which they are now briefly collected—to which, however, the limits of our present work prevent us from adverting farther, in the way either of criticism or of illustration.

We have only space to observe, and we do it with pleasure, that Mr. Clerk, in his recent translation, has identified in his own neighbourhood, both by name, aspect, and actual tradition, three or four scenes hitherto doubtful, connected with the minor poems of Ossian. The Lora, for example, he identifies with the Connal near Oban; the two names Usnoth and Nathos in *Darthula*, with the Island of Usnoth and the wood of Nathos, in or near Loch-Etive, and "Darthula's sunny spot" with a hill at the head of that lake. Farther, he states that Selma, by tradition, is identical with Dun Mac Uisneach [? Ard-Mucknish], between Loch-Creran and Loch-Etive on the shore, about two miles distant from the Lora—which is by no means improbable: Compare pp. 198, 227, 305. He thinks it "possible that more careful research would enable us to recognise other Ossianic scenes," but maintains "that the reality of special battles described, whether with Caracul or Swaran, cannot be proved"—a sort of infidelity, we hope, which will by and by be shaken. He quotes also, from Dr. Smith, the identification of Innis-Erath on Loch-Awe with the scene of Daura's melancholy death in the *Songs of Selma;* which, on the supposition that Loch-Awe was then an arm of the sea, as it probably was, we are willing to concede; and thus not only our own theory of sea-levels on the western coast will be established, but almost every geographical position worth inquiring about in Ossian will have been determined.

## CHAPTER IX.

### ALTARS, MONOLITHS, AND TOMBSTONES.

As a natural supplement to our preceding remarks, and in conclusion of our present investigations, we shall now devote a few pages of inquiry as to the erection of the monumental and other similar remains still extant in Scotland and Ireland, some of which have come already under our notice from other points of view. The origin of these monuments, in some instances, is doubtful, their uses even may be questioned, and their date is uncertain; but their construction, above all, is wonderful. In other instances, as regards the tombs in Arran for example, after the discoveries already verified and recorded, there can no longer be either doubt or difficulty. That they belong to the second or third century of the Christian era has now been demonstrated, and that they must have been erected by the Celtic population of that era, inhabiting or passing through the regions where they are found, is as certain as that St. Paul's Cathedral was the work of Sir Christopher Wren. In arriving at these conclusions, what was only tradition at first has been converted into history; but without tradition to assist us, we should not have been able to attain to them. The mode of mechanical procedure in the construction of such monuments, however, is still a mystery, and we must be content to follow tradition a little farther on its own track, if we hope to obtain any solution of that.

In attempting to elucidate this subject, whilst it was yet totally obscure as matter of history, the present writer addressed a letter, in pursuance of certain others already quoted, to the local paper in which they appeared; from which the following extracts may now be made. That letter, however, which is dated September 11, 1871, contained some preliminary remarks on the value of tradition as a guide to historical investigation, which seem still so much to the purpose in our present inquiry, and to have been so fully borne out by all our intermediate researches, that it may be proper in the first place to reproduce these entire:—

ELMGROVE PLACE, *Sept.* 11, 1871.

SIR,—The longer we reflect on the authority of tradition, the more we shall be inclined in its favour; and the more carefully we apply it in solution of existing problems both in history and science, the more we shall realise its value. To neglect or despise it, I am persuaded, is to neglect one of the most important sources of historic knowledge in the world. Man spoke before he wrote, and sang before he printed ; and his collective memory goes far beyond the date of chronicles, with as much accuracy and with far more meaning in it than many a Parliamentary record. To tell the right tradition from the wrong, and to separate fable entirely from fact, may sometimes be difficult or even impossible, where facts were so surprising that their very simplest narration would seem a fable. But neither facts nor fables are to be discredited, till their inmost signification is ascertained. One most remarkable, incontrovertible, and solemn fact, for example, is the existence of stone altars in this country, composed of such enormous blocks as to baffle all attempts to account for their erection, except by giants or magicians, or by mechanicians, in all their rudeness, infinitely superior to ourselves. But we deny the existence of giants, we scout the thought of magicians, and we coolly converse of our predecessors on the soil as ignerant barbarians, little better or wiser than the brutes. How, then, or by whom, were these monuments erected with such ease and skill as to defy discovery? It will not do, with facts like these before us, to talk of the ignorance of bygone generations, or to deny their strength. It is to no purpose either to say they had a knowledge of mechanics superior to our own, but now lost; that is no explanation. The mystery must be honestly solved, or our pragmatic contempt and idle talk about savagery must be abandoned.

These remarks are then subsequently illustrated in the letter, as follows :—

To take a solitary instance at our own door :—There is an altar composed of three huge blocks of stone within an earthen circle, called " The three auld wives' lifts," on Craigmaddie Moor, in Baldernock parish. Everybody, of course, knows that three auld wives, by day or night, never lifted such burdens, much less by their apron strings ; but that very tradition is a confession of our ignorance, a fable to account for what we cannot understand. A similar magnificent altar is to be found in a corresponding circle in the North of Ireland, still carefully preserved, but no reasonable account of its erection that I am aware of has ever been given. The question is not now by whom—Druids or Scandinavians, or ancient Caledonians, or Picts, or Fingalians—these monuments were built, but how? Men who smile at Ossian and Fingal, or the people they represent, as impossible, have no right to be heard in the meantime. They must renounce their contempt before they argue, and learn to talk soberly. There lie the tombstones, there swing the rocking-stones, there stand the monoliths and altars; how did imaginary beings or savage mortals raise these? The largest and uppermost of the auld wives' lifts, according to Ure (who seems accurately to have measured them,) " is about 18 feet in length, by 11 in breadth, and 7 in depth," and the two underlying blocks, of prismatic shape, which support this are scarcely less each. But these have been piled together, in the middle of a

THREE AULD WIVES' LIFTS.

PANDOO INDIAN CAIRN.

barren, mossy moor, not only artistically as an altar, but geometrically or astronomically, as a monument, east and west, north and south, at a date beyond all our historic acquaintance with antiquity. Will the artizans of Glasgow, then, or the peasantry of Dumbartonshire and Stirlingshire, with the gentry and clergy (whose influence, in some respects, may represent that of the Druids,) at their head, undertake to remove and replace these fragments, without the assistance of any known implement of wood or iron, without crane or tackle, without theodolite or compass? If so, let them proceed, or at least explain to us how it could be done, and they will do more for the progress of civilisation than all the political or trades-union meetings, or politico-religious gatherings, or British Associations, that have been convened in this country for a generation. I am in earnest, you observe, sir, for facts inspire me, and the necessity of the proof is great. I might hazard a guess, indeed, of my own; but a guess for the present, and no more, it must be. Such altars of the size are very rare, and the two most remarkable—one in Baldernock, and the other in the North of Ireland—are in hollows. Is it not possible, then, that the two supporting stones were originally, by search or accident, discovered deeply imbedded where they stand; that the third from the adjoining level, was rolled and adjusted above them; and that, when the work was finished, the surrounding earth was removed and formed into an amphitheatre for worship? But even this suggestion leaves a world of mechanical appliance unexplained, and we are almost as much in the dark as ever. The building of the Pyramids, I may be told, was as difficult and mysterious. Undoubtedly it was; and even more so, considering their enormous height. But the Egyptians were admittedly the most scientific race of mortals in the world, and our poor old Druids, in their caves and groves, were benighted savages—there lies the difference and the difficulty. What corresponds to these remains in Britain, however, and to similar remains in France and Ireland, most nearly, both in figure, size, and circumstance, are the old Indian cairns and monoliths, whose resemblance to them, indeed, is so great as to have suggested to many antiquarians a common origin for them all, and whose erection—because it could not be otherwise explained—was attributed, not to old women certainly, but to the five sons of Pandoo, equally fabulous, who lost their father's kingdom in gambling, and were doomed to twelve years' penance and labour long ago, in the mountains and forests of Hindostan, to propitiate the deities and regain it.

Along with these remarkable works, it is now obvious that the rocking-stone of Cromla in Ullin, known to Ossian as a landmark there, and still extant in the Isle Maghee; and that yet more wonderful monument, the mystic-stone or circle of Brumo at Stennis, where Grumal fought with ghosts, and which antiquarians admit to be second only to Stonehenge in Britain; or that other at which Fingal dislodged the electric spirit of Loda, most probably in Hoy—and to which so strange a parallel occurs in the *Pirate*, as we have seen, both as to situation, superstitious associations and atmospheric accompaniments, in the Legend of the "Dwarfie Stone"—may all be classed. Without apparently being conscious of the fact, but guided solely by the traditions of the country, as we have already observed, Scott in his description of that Stone, and of the thunderstorm which passed over it on the occasion of Norna's visit, and the electric flash which both paralysed and inspired her there, has produced as perfect a parallel, indeed, to the narrative in *Carric-thura* as if he had been founding on the text of Ossian or the translation of MacPherson throughout. That the stone in question has been hollowed within for human residence, or for the accommodation of the demongod, as Scott in fact supposes—again unconsciously—is no argument against its being identical with the sanctuary of Loda, but rather, indeed, confirms that view. The point now chiefly to be observed, however, is that the existence of such a monument as the Dwarfie Stone, of unknown antiquity and workmanship, in the same region as the Stone of Loda, where revelations were supposed to be vouchsafed by electricity, or by some spirit which had power in the air, is confirmatory at least not only of our own theory on that subject already advanced, but of the general hypothesis that such reliques of heathen fire-worship were both extant in Ossian's day, and in some sense familiar to him, with whatever contempt he might treat the terrors connected with them as the sanctuaries of demons. There they still are, as inscrutable as ever in their origin, and with the same traditions of supernatural power associated with them now by the most gifted writer of romance in the nineteenth century, as then, according to the faith of heathens, narrated and ridiculed by the greatest epic poet of the third.

But it is with tombstones, or stones of covenant—to revert once more to our original theme—and not with altars or sanctuaries we have now, in our concluding pages, more particularly to do; and we shall select those only already known to us, in connection with the text of Ossian, as the subjects of our present remarks. Such monuments in Ireland, although they must be numerous, have not yet been identified, and therefore can neither be measured nor described; even Fingal's grave in Arran must be excluded from survey as a proof of art, because the immense blocks which define it may have been discovered in position as they stand. It is only from such as are obviously artificial we can draw any inference at all, as to the strength or skill of the people who constructed them; and these, so far as our acquaintance with Ossian conducts us, are the tombs respectively of Ossian himself, Oscar, and Malvina, and the grand monolith on Machriemuir, otherwise called the "Stone of Mora."

The tombstone at Clachaig on Ossian's grave is not, indeed, to be compared in size or weight with the "Auld wife's lift" at Baldernock; yet, as described, it is still a stone of some magnitude, and considering its position on so small a foundation as an open cist on the top of a mound of loose earth and boulders, the strength or skill implied in its elevation must have been far from despicable. Even to raise it on edge, would be difficult; but to quarry it from the shore at a distance, to transport it thence, over creek and river, by floats or on some branchy cradle, and then to lift and lay it in place without damaging the framework of the coffin it covered, which is as secure as the day it was built—is the sort of work in question. In Oscar's tomb the art is much ruder, but some of the stones are much larger, and the site is infinitely more difficult. The headstone, for example, now deeply imbedded in the soil, and therefore not easily measured, must be a solid mass of triangular shape not less than $3\frac{1}{2}$ tons burden; and the difficulty of conveying this from the distance of a mile or two at least, up a steep hill-side, and across precipitous ravines, or by a deep river, would be a sort of task at which even modern mechanicians, with trucks and railways to assist them, would draw breath for a little. Yet there was no other line on which it could be moved, and no nearer quarry from which it could be cut by those savage labourers, imaginable. At Malvina's grave we must pause again for a moment, to consider both the mode of its construction and the materials of which it is composed. The burial, we have seen, was by incremation and the deposit of the ashes in an urn : which again was covered by a tombstone resting on smaller blocks, and finished with an upright pillar or monolith, to signalise the spot. But the incremation must have taken place on the tombstone itself, from which, as from a funeral hearth, the ashes would then be gathered and deposited in the urn; and when the urn had been consigned to its place in the grave, the stone would then be lifted as a level load and laid gently on the supports above it. This idea is suggested by the look of waste, as from fire, in the very centre of the tombstone—represented, as the reader will find, by a few rough touches of the graver in our woodcut—p. 83. But the stone itself so marked on its surface, and measured as accurately as its peculiar form will admit, must be fully $2\frac{1}{2}$ tons weight; and could not have been obtained, but by accident, within less than several miles of the spot. An ineffectual attempt, indeed, to transport a still larger one bearing evident marks of the hammer on its edges, from the adjoining hillside, seems to have been made and abandoned. The reader must therefore account for its discovery, conveyance, and dead lift elevation to its present site over the funeral urn, on whatever principles of strength or skill may seem most natural.

The principal monolith on Machrie-muir, however, just visible from Drumadoon, is of so much greater dimensions, and the difficulty of placing it in an upright position must also have been so much greater, that its existence as a land-mark there, from before Ossian's era to the present moment, throws all question of mechanical contrivance or of human strength in the other cases into the shade. The stone in question, according to Pennant in 1772, was 15 feet above ground and 11 feet in circumference; according to Dr. Bryce in 1872, it seems to have been only 14 feet high, which implies an increase of the surface soil of about 12 inches, in the interval of a hundred years exactly. According to the same authority, it measures 3 to 4 feet broad and 11 to 22 inches thick —that is, on average, about 11 feet in circumference—which confirms precisely the computation of Pennant. If we allow 3 feet underground for a foundation, which seems extremely moderate, then the whole perpendicular mass cannot be much less, and may be a good deal more, than 18 or 20 feet, by $3\frac{1}{2}$ broad, and 16 inches over all in thickness; which at the average weight of sandstone will give about $6\frac{1}{2}$ tons. This immense mass, like several others surrounding it— which are not quite so large, however—must have been quarried, according to Dr. Bryce, from the "cliffs towards Auchincar. . The intervening country is rough and difficult; yet there does not appear to us any other conclusion possible," says the Doctor, "than that this is the origin whence they have come." In which we have no doubt Dr. Bryce is correct; but this admission does not explain the means or method of their transport. Dr. Bryce farther admits that "all of them have plainly undergone a certain amount of coarse dressing—but with what tools it is impossible to say."—*Bryce's Arran*, p. 212. Here then, we have new problems to encounter, both as to the instruments of labour and the means of locomotion, as well as to the amount of mechanical skill and physical appliances to erect and "stablish" such monuments at Machrie, or such others as those at Stennis, Baldernock, or Stonehenge—on some of which there are also traces of the chiselling iron. The difficulty would be still farther increased if we accepted Dr. Bryce's computation of weight for the stones at Machrie, which much exceeds our own; but adhering even to the lowest computation as above, it is sufficiently perplexing to account for the quarrying and carriage of a stone six or seven tons' weight, over mosses, ravines, and rivulets, for a distance of several miles, and its secure plantation upright in the centre of an open moor. For ourselves, we have no other theory in the matter to propound than that already advanced in the letter above quoted from, to which we must, with a few verbal adaptations, again recur. Was it Demonology and witchcraft? or strength and sagacity? Strength and sagacity doubtless; strength and sagacity then, without the slightest derogation from science and philosophy now. But strength and sagacity how applied or obtained? The greatest number of men, for example, that could actually get hold of such a stone as that which now stands over Oscar's grave would be about 18, and the weight each man would have to lift would be 4 cwt. By the use of handspikes the number of men might be increased to 30, and their individual burden reduced to 2 cwt. But the ordinary dead lift for men of the present day is only 1 cwt.; for stronger men, perhaps a little more. Twenty tons weight in the shape of a ship's mast has been borne and carried by two rows of coolies in India, with straps and bamboo bearers on their heads and shoulders, leaning close on one another as they went, to equalise the burden; but in the case of a square block, like a tombstone, no such distribution could be made; and if men were then of greater stature than they now are, of which there is the clearest evidence in the size of their bones discovered, then only two-thirds of the number above supposed would be admitted to the work, and their respective burden correspondingly increased. In short, we are driven to the conclusion that strength in the individual men who accomplished such feats was far superior to our own, and that their sagacity in thoughtful adaptation of the simplest external advantages to the object in view was little, if at all, inferior to our finest science. Four men, then, I do not much hesitate to believe, had the physical energy of nearly a dozen now, and that energy was directed and stimulated by the shrewdest perception and the necessities of the moment. Such stones, "daughters of the rock," as Ossian calls them, if not found detached, must have been quarried with skill, pains, and patience, possibly at the lowest tide, and in Arran at least would be floated up by water carriage, in the estuaries or rivers, to the utmost verge. Their progress thence might be by dragging on a cradle of branches, as already explained,—p. 308, or by continued leverage, and rolling or turning; and their lifting and laying on the spot, as of the grave in question, would be by united individual strength alone, or in an upright position, as at Machrie, by slow and careful wedging, or prizing and blocking from the outer end, on the verge of the pit or hole prepared to receive them. Besides all which, the quarrying, chiselling, and sometimes boring, with what sort of tools (as Dr. Bryce inquires) must be accounted for. That is an additional difficulty, doubtless; and it remains to be explained by those alone who deny the use of iron in Ossian's day. There lie the stones, quarried, squared, and chiselled; those who quarrel about the process must provide the tools.

The only new suggestion it occurs to us to make with respect to the fixing of such a column as that on Machrie-muir upright, is in connection with the fact that that pillar, and perhaps some others, were placed originally in the centre of woods. At Machrie, as we have seen, this was certainly the case; and the woods there being of magnificent oaks with spreading branches, it is reasonable to suppose that, by the use of long leather ropes or thongs of raw hide fastened to one end of the stone, people sitting on the branches, or passing such ropes over the bight of the branches and pulling by hundreds from a distance beyond, so as to lessen the friction, might raise, or materially assist in raising so large a block to an upright position. The same sort of process might have been adopted at Malvina's grave with comparative ease, by swinging the tombstone in leather slings, because the slab, although large, is of much less weight than the monolith, and we know from the text of Ossian that oaks overhung the spot. At Oscar's grave it might have been different, for both the shape and position of the headstone there might render such an application of skill impossible; but however this might be, there was a fine adaptation of mechanical science in all these supposed rude efforts—and still more wonderful, if we do not suppose them—which must astonish the sceptic, who questions the knowledge of blocks and pulleys or the use of levers and inclined planes among our savage Celtic ancestors. But to proceed with the quotation of our letter:—

The individual strength implied and the time consumed have still to be verified and measured. If the strength, as we suppose, in the first place, was great—much greater than our own—the time required for such operations would be comparatively short, and that the strength was great and the time allowed comparatively short is demonstrable. Instances of individual strength sufficient for the purpose, such as tearing an oak from the mountain's side to kindle a watch-fire, incidentally mentioned by Ossian, are frequent; and the rapidity with which such monuments had sometimes to be raised, as a mere matter of course that could excite no wonder, is testified everywhere. As regards one interment at least, that of Ryno—his own youngest brother, who fell in Ireland, and whose grave, as minutely specified, may very possibly be discovered yet—we learn from Ossian's own text that the obsequies, the dirge, and the laying of the tombstone to cover two were all completed before nightfall of the day on which the death took place. For raising such a monolith as that at Machrie, some additional time undoubtedly would be required, yet not extravagant.

But Ossian, it may be said, imagined all these feats of strength and patience. What then? If so imagine them he did—which is denied—his imagination did not transcend, did not even equal, the indubitable deeds of his kindred on the barren moor or rocky beach before us. Nay, the fact is, that but a few generations ago men lived in Arran and in Orkney—where such monuments more particularly abound—who could almost have done these things. Stories of their individual strength and prowess in both these regions are narrated yet, at which most of our modern athletes would be amazed, and at which ordinary mortals would smile as incredible; yet these were among the "little men" whose prospective advent Ossian deplored! But, with all this rude magnificence of strength in himself and his contemporaries, there was wisdom and poetry and tenderness of sentiment inimitable. Why, then, in spite of Gibbon's doubt, should not men like Fingal have lived and fought, or men like Ossian lived and sung? Greater miracles, to be sure, in stone and iron, by steam and rail, are every day done than were imagined then ; but in proportion to these mechanical supplements our individual strength has dwindled. Greater achievements by pen and press are every hour in progress, too, than the united cunning of ancestors so remote could ever rival, but our individual gifts of light and love, of courage and capacity, have perhaps been impaired. Reporters could transcribe an epic poem now, and the operator at a telegraph could transmit it to the ends of the earth, faster than Ossian could have chaunted it ; but the eloquent untutored tongue that first pronounced and rehearsed it, and the lofty brain that conceived it, are gone together, and no effort of imitation on earth will ever restore or replace them.

Such then, to finish where we first began, are the monuments best known in Arran. There are others, no doubt, which have an interest of their own, but their connection with Ossian, or any of his people, is for the present uncertain. There is such harmony of character in them all, however, both among themselves and with the surrounding scenery, that it would be impossible to conceive anything in more perfect keeping with nature. It seems indeed as if the monoliths, graves, and sepulchres of Arran were as much a part of the Island as its rocks, and caves, and mountains ; and it is almost impossible not to fancy, that the people who constructed or approved of them were inspired by nature to finish the detail of her outlines, and modelled their own memorials of departed greatness on the monumental works of the unknown God around them. Thus Ossian's tomb, like a miniature on the verdant plain, confronts the lonely pyramid of Ailsa from the shore ; the solid blocks of Fingal's grave seem literally to grow out of the very hillside to which they are affixed ; Malvina's cromlech with its headstone is but a lowly type of Drumadoon, in the shelter of which it stands ; and Oscar's monument, in the arrangement of its unwieldy slabs, is an indifferent copy of Goatfell—whose peak must have been familiar to every eye among the people as the unmistakable landmark of all their homeward voyages, both from the inland navigation of the Clyde and the more distant or dangerous waters of the Irish Sea. It would be unphilosophical, of course, to urge an idea like this beyond the limit of suggestion ; but it would be equally unphilosophical to reject it. There is a harmony in all things, the result of inevitable law ; and such harmony is no where more apparent than in the construction of such monuments among the wilds of Arran. That they have at least a resemblance to, and must have been suggested by, the slabs and solitary blocks on the shore from which their materials are borrowed, if not to the mountains themselves among which they stand, is as certain as any parallel between nature and art can be; and if such hints were once adopted by the imagination of the people, it would be difficult to say how far they might not be carried. To "look around" here, as well as in St. Paul's, is at all events admissible; and to guess at the character of the untutored architects, who had only rocks and rivers and mountain-ridges to instruct them in what was suitable or sublime, from the character of the works they have left behind them, setting their seal on the soil, is part of the great moral lesson suggested naturally by the whole. Certain it is, that any other sort of monuments, however magnificent, would be out of place in Arran; and although its aboriginal inhabitants could know nothing of the works of Greece and Rome, the poetry of their own constitution kept them close in their modest efforts to the loftiest types in nature; and if they could not rival, they at least followed them, in simplicity and strength.

## TO GOATFELL, ARRAN:
### ON FIRST SEEING IT FROM THE SHORE.
#### [AT BRODICK.]

Born of earthquakes, lonely giant,
    Sphinx and eagle couched on high;
Dumb, defiant, self-reliant,
    Breast on earth and beak in sky:

Built in chaos, burnt-out beacon,
    Long extinguished, dark, and bare,
Ere life's friendly ray could break on
    Shelvy shore or islet fair:

Dwarf to Atlas, child to Etna,
    Stepping-stone to huge Mont Blanc;
Cairn to cloudy Chimborazo,
    Higher glories round thee hang!

Baal-tein hearth, for friend and foeman;
    Warden of the mazy Clyde;
In thy shadow, Celt and Roman,
    Proudly galley'd, swept the tide!

Scottish Sinai, God's out-rider,
  When he wields his lightning wand;
From thy flanks, a king and spider
  Taught, and saved, and ruled the land!

Smoking void and planet rending,
  Island rise and ocean fall,
Frith unfolding, field extending—
  Thou has seen or felt them all.

Armies routed, navies flouted,
  Tyrants fallen. people free;
Cities built and empires clouted,
  Like the world, are known to thee.

Science shining, love enshrining.
  Truth and patience conquering hell;
Miracles beyond divining,
  Could'st thou speak, thy tongue would tell.

Rest awhile, the nations gather,
  Sick of folly, lies, and sin,
To kneel to the eternal Father—
  Then the kingdom shall begin!

Rest awhile, some late convulsion,
  Time enough shall shake thy bed:
Rest awhile, at Death's expulsion,
  Living green shall clothe thy head!

P. H. W.

Lagg Cottage, June 20, 1871.
    [Stanza 4th since added.]

# APPENDIX.

In consulting this Appendix, the reader will find the miscellaneous information contained in it arranged as far as possible according to the progress of the Work; but as the same particulars have occasionally a more extended reference than to the point immediately in question, a little care may be required in noting them. A certain amount of interest, however, it is hoped, antiquarian or scientific, will be found attached to most of them, beyond their bearing on the text, which may compensate for their separate study.

### PART FIRST: CHAPTER III: P. 20.

POST-TERTIARY DEPOSITS IN THE VALLEY OF THE CLYDE.—At a meeting of the Geological Society of Glasgow, April 3, 1873, Mr. James Thomson, F.G.S., Vice-President, in the chair, we find by newspaper report, April 5, that among other interesting matters introduced—

Mr. JOHN KIRSOP exhibited a large bone, apparently the thigh-bone or *femur* of an animal belonging to the genus *Rhinoceros*, which had been dredged from the bed of the Clyde near Erskine Ferry. It was found embedded in the clay at the bottom of the river, about fourteen feet under low-water spring tides. The species had not yet been fully determined, but it probably belonged to the *Rhinoceros tichorinus*, a bulky post-glacial mammal, whose remains chiefly occur in quaternary cave-deposits and valley gravels. They are also found in the lower brick-earths of the Thames valley; but this would be the first instance, if it were so identified, of such remains having been discovered in Scottish deposits. The specimen now brought forward was therefore of considerable interest, and would be submitted to competent authorities to have the species more accurately determined.

#### POST-TERTIARY CLAYS.

Mr. DAVID ROBERTSON, F.G.S., read some further notes on the post-tertiary fossiliferous beds of the West of Scotland. He first alluded to the brick-clays at Jordanhill, about a mile to the north-west of Partick, and 145 feet above the present sea-level. The clay here is wrought to a depth of from 12 to 20 feet, in some places rather more. One point of interest in examining the clays of this locality is the position in which the shells of the common mussel (*Mytilus edulis*) are found. This mollusc is commonly thought to have its zone or position near the surface, and to lie above the post-pliocene Arctic shells in the clays of the Clyde district. This no doubt is frequently the case, but it also occurs at greater depths, and overlaid by Arctic shells. At Muirhouse brickfield, the mussel is found 19 feet below the surface, and at Stobcross 24 feet. Here it is found at a depth of 14 feet, while at a little distance in the same field Arctic shells occur within six feet of the surface.

In the Whiteinch railway cutting at a short distance, mussels are obtained from about nine feet below the surface, and immediately overlying them Arctic shells are found (*Tellina calcarea*), some with the valves together. At Paisley also, this shell occurs at a depth of 12 feet, and overlaid by well-known Arctic shells, leaving no doubt that the mussel lived in common, or throughout the same period, with the ordinary Arctic species or mollusca in our Clyde beds. Another circumstance to be noted is that in one part near the upper end of the workings, beneath a bed containing Arctic shells, the clay is crowded with nodules, mostly of small sizes and various shapes, but chiefly flattened spheres, perfectly smooth with the exception of occasional small pebbles enclosed during formation. Similar concretions are met with in other clay-fields, but it is unusual to find them in such profusion within the same narrow limits. Another feature of interest in the clays of this neighbourhood is the presence of portions of oak trees, some of considerable magnitude. Such pieces of oak, it is well known, are abundant in the peat of every district, but he was not aware of their having been

## APPENDIX

previously found associated with Arctic shells in the clays of any part of the country. The clay at Jordanhill is not rich in shells or other animal remains, and such as do occur are generally not well preserved, but this arises more from decomposition than from fracture or abrasion. At the north end of the works they are chiefly confined to a narrow band, of two or three feet in thickness. Overlying this is a thin layer containing very small littoral shells, such as *Littorina littorea, Littorina rudis*, and young mussels. Similar littoral beds occur in the neighbourhood of Paisley; but though the species are exactly similar, it is obvious they could not be strictly contemporaneous with those in the bed now referred to, as at the time it was formed the district round Paisley would be deep under water. Mr. Robertson then described the cuttings at the Maryhill Gas Works and Stobcross Railway, giving particulars of the beds exposed, especially in the latter, where interesting sections of boulder clay, gravel, sand, and laminated clay have been laid open during the excavations now in progress. The animal remains are chiefly obtained from a deep bank of clay near the east end, and though not numerous, are sufficient to show the truly marine character of the deposit. Brackish water *Ostracoda*, however, are found in the muddy sand of the excavations for the Stobcross new docks. He proceeded to describe an interesting section of clays at Dipple, near Girvan, where he had found three distinct series of organic remains—fresh water, brackish, and marine in descending order. He concluded by giving a few notes on other sections near Stranraer and along the coast of the Mull of Galloway, and exhibited a large and beautifully arranged collection of the shells and other organisms from the beds referred to.

The CHAIRMAN expressed his sense of the great value of Mr. Robertson's minute and painstaking observations in these post-tertiary deposits. He was convinced a basis was being laid in them for an accurate knowledge of the life of the period represented by these clays, in the only way in which it could be arrived at; and all taking an interest in the subject were indebted to Mr. Robertson for his persevering labours in this department of geology. —*Glasgow Herald.*

As the above report was neither read nor published until more than ten months after the passage in the text referring to the same subject had been written, and therefore could not be known to the writer, the general concurrence so obvious and remarkable between them seems to be highly confirmatory of both; and although no precise dates are assigned in the report below a certain geological epoch, for the deposits alleged, its independent testimony to the same facts renders the truth of such facts, as a groundwork of argument, indisputable. To indicate the extent and character of recent changes on the banks and channel of the Clyde, the following extract from the Rivers Pollution Report may be quoted, from same paper, August 16, 1873:—

### RIVERS POLLUTION—CLYDE.

The Rivers Pollution Commission have just issued the second volume of their evidence, which includes that taken on the basin of the Clyde and of the Kelvin, and the other Scotch rivers.

Lord Blantyre makes the following statement on the pollution of the river:—

My property extends for five miles along the south bank of Clyde from "West Ferry," opposite to Dumbarton Castle, towards Glasgow, and for two miles along the north bank from Bowling Bay towards Glasgow. Throughout this extent, except for a space of less than a mile opposite the mansion house, the Clyde Trustees long ago formed jetties, or groins, and longitudinal walls in the river, intending that by silting and laying the sand dredged from the channel behind the walls, the land should be brought forward, and a beneficial scour produced, which would carry all suspended matters seawards. They have within these few years abandoned this part of their scheme in favour of taking the sand dredged in steam hopper barges out to sea, which, they allege, is cheaper than depositing it behind the walls, and wheeling it up so as to form land. And this plan may be cheaper than hand labour, and yet dearer than if they employed steam to deposit the dredgings on the land, either as at Suez Canal or in other ways now adopted for like purposes. In this way they lose the advantage to the navigation of a perfect scour, the cheapest way in the end of carrying matter to sea, and they inflict upon my property and its inhabitants and neighbours *a large extent of artificially formed marshes*, which, since the pollution of the river, reek with fetid odours, as the spaces between the land and the longitudinal walls form catch-pits for the deposit of sewerage mud; as may be seen by the difference between the state of the shore (clean sand) in front of Erskine Park, where there are no dykes, and at the other points where they have been placed. . . . Salmon-trout, flounders, and sperling, which used to be netted here in quantities in my younger days, *with only an occasional eel*, have disappeared, and the river teems with eels and nothing else, though even these are said to be affected by the chemical sewage, and to

# APPENDIX.

die easily when removed from the water. All net fishing is abandoned as disgusting and profitless. Cattle standing in the river to escape flies seem to abstain from drinking it, but I always fear injury to the live stock from the polluted river, and it cannot be as serviceable to them as the natural river was. These polluted marshes are extensive enough to affect Glasgow, as the prevailing winds will carry the effluvia towards the town; but, apart from Glasgow, there is population enough in my immediate neighbourhood to make it highly desirable that at least the pollutions from Glasgow, Paisley, and other towns should not be added to the mud which the Clyde Trustees' walls cause to be deposited upon from five to six miles out of seven miles of river banks belonging to this property.

As regards the level of the Forth at the periods in question—Part Fourth, Chapter II.—the following newspaper scraps, one of an earlier the other of a later date, are also worth preservation:—

GRANGEMOUTH – OLD ANCHOR FOUND.—When deepening a ditch on the Heuck farm on Friday, the labourers employed by the Grangemouth Coal Company came upon a small anchor or kedge deeply embedded in the old silt. It is of an old-fashioned shape in the flukes, with an oak stock, still comparatively sound. The iron work appears much more corroded, being eaten in to a depth of from half an inch to an inch. The field in which it was found was taken in from the "slyke" about 90 years ago by Mr. Mitchell, then tenant of the Heuck farm, which is on the estate of the Earl of Zetland. The old course of the river Carron ran through it before the present cut was made, on the construction of the Forth and Clyde Canal, and it is more than probable that the anchor now brought to light belonged to some of the small Carronshore craft of old days, and was left *in situ* at least a hundred years ago, and has had crops growing over it for the last sixty. – *Glasgow Herald, July* 7, 1873.

INTERESTING DISCOVERY.—Our Bridge of Allan correspondent writes:—It has always been thought probable that the Carse of Stirling was at some remote period the bed of the sea. This conjecture has been confirmed by the discovery of innumerable shells, chiefly oyster shells, which were turned up by the workmen employed in the new drainage work, at a slight elevation above the Allan. The vast number, the depth and situation in which they were found, exclude the idea that they consist of refuse thrown out.—*Ibid. Oct.* 16, 1872.

Similar shells, of which some beautiful specimens are in the author's possession, have since been found (June, 1874) in digging a well at Cornton Vale, half way between the old high road and the Forth, at a depth of 15 feet, and on the margin of a marshy ravine there running down to the river. At this depth, they would be on a level with the bed of the river, exactly at a point where innumerable shells of a larger type are still seen lying at the bottom. On the other side, nearly opposite, iron rings are said to have been found inserted on the face of Craigforth, for the mooring of vessels—probably Roman, when the whole strath between must have been a sea, and when the Allan and the Teith, as rivers in the neighbourhood, would be totally unrecognisable. All further question, therefore, about the levels of the Forth and Carron in Ossian's day, or possibly even much later, may be dismissed.

It may be interesting, in conclusion of this subject, and by way of ascertaining the probable date and cause of such a remarkable change in the levels of the Clyde, to notice (1.) that the whole region around Paisley is but an undulating plain, supported at considerable depth by an immense moss and a stratum of flowing sea-sand. Where the surface dips towards the Cart, no building of any height can long retain its own perpendicular; certain streets in the neighbourhood vibrate on the rapid passage of ordinary vehicles; and by boring for a different purpose, at given points both in the town and neighbourhood, to a depth of 300 feet, sea-water has been unexpectedly, and rather too easily obtained, excellent fresh water being found at the same points, nearer the surface. (2.) In the line of Loch-Winnoch and Kilbirnie, at the Saltcoats end of the drift, a "trouble" has been touched in the coal mines there, full of small coal or cinders, as if calcined by volcanic heat; and another of the same sort, farther south, in the muir at Irvine. The first of these breaks, 25 fathoms or thereby down, has been estimated at about 40 feet in depth, which would nearly equalise the intervening level with the sea. (3.) The waters of Kilbirnie-Loch were gradually disappearing, to such an extent, that the proprietor of the soil adjoining, to whom also the lordship of the lake belongs—Lord Glasgow—had to mark their decrease and show their original level by " march stones," in order to maintain his rights, although the decrease has since been checked, by the immense deposit of slag from the Glengarnock iron-works, at the south-west end of the loch. That there is some subterranean cavity, therefore, through which these waters were disappearing, is evident; and that some still deeper trough may be traced, through which the tide flows underground among sea-sand to Paisley, is indisputable. For the knowledge of these significant facts the Author is indebted to his obliging friends, Mr. David Semple, the accomplished antiquarian, and Mr. William M'Intyre, Jun., of the Paper Works, Paisley. He may farther add, on the authority of a correspondent intimately acquainted with the country, Mr. William Connell, Pollokshields—that in one of the pits on Irvine-muir the Garnock-water some years ago found an entrance from above, through an unsuspected rent in the superior strata, sufficient to affect its own course to the sea and to drown out the workings—in point of fact, it went down like a whirlpool, and sucked its channel dry. Also, that a pit having been formerly sunk a few miles to the north-east, near Loch-Libo, the waters of that lake rushed in with such violence that the miners had difficulty in escaping with their lives, and the pit has ever since remained unworkable. This would indicate a sort of branch-drift, from the coast at Irvine through the hollow, by Neilston and Barrhead, to Glasgow; so that the whole triangular region between Irvine, Dunglass, and Glasgow, must have been honey-combed or tunnelled in two directions at least by some volcanic current, at a depth from 150 to 300 feet. But in following out the drift which these unquestionable phenomena indicate, from Irvine by Kilwinning northward, it will be found that the line of this volcanic rupture would strike the Clyde at Bowling, where a cleft in the Kilpatrick hills, of corresponding depth, appears; and by tracing it southward to the Solway, it would touch on Loch-Trool, which is obviously of volcanic creation, and in the immediate neighbourhood of which there is another Loch-Winnoch. Upon the whole, therefore, it seems probable that these were all but points in the line of some earthquake, by no means remote, elevating and depressing alternately the intermediate surface between the Solway and the Clyde; and parallel with another line from the north of Ireland, by the Island of Arran, through Argyllshire, to Inverness and the Orkneys. Compare Part Fifth, Chapters V. and VII., with Notes upon, *infra.* In fact, all that is now required to convert this probability into certainty is the testimony of a contemporaneous historian, which we find reproduced by an authority who little suspected its direct bearing on the present controversy.

" Towards the sea," says Herodian, " most parts of Britain are full of marshes, through which the barbarians are accustomed to swim or wade, disregarding the mud as they are almost naked; . . . armed only with a narrow shield and lance, with a sword depending from their naked bodies; but without helmet or mail, which they deem are an impediment in crossing their marshes, whose vapours perpetually obscure the sky."—Quoted by Laing in *Dissertation,* &c.

## APPENDIX.

But the marshes here spoken of were those between the Walls, in the Land of the Strangers—that is, of the Clyde and the Solway, of the Irvine and the Ayr; and the vapours arising from these, which " perpetually obscured the sky," must have been generated, like those of Loch-Lego, by subterranean heat. No other cause could account for them. The low lands of Renfrewshire and Ayrshire, therefore, about this date—end of the third, and commencement of the fourth century—were just beginning to emerge from the sea, and the Frith of Clyde to recede in proportion; and the reader who chooses again to recur to what has already been said on the subject, and to collate the poems—such as *Carthon, Calthon and Colmal, Colna-dona*, and some others—which describe the locomotion of the people in that region about the period, will see how closely the text, unknown to MacPherson, corresponds with these now ascertained geographical realities.

### PART FIRST. CHAPTER IV. P. 39.

OSSIAN AND THE CLYDE—LETTER BY "SAXO."

*To the Editor of The Glasgow Herald.*

SIR,—Your Celtic readers must be greatly obliged to the Rev. Dr. Hately Waddell for his new arguments in favour of the authenticity of Ossian, and are no doubt waiting, as I am, with much interest for the further elucidation of them, as promised. Dr. Waddell believes in Ossian by *instinct*, much in the same way as he believes in the authenticity of the Gospels, whatever Strauss or Renan may urge to the contrary. The "Sermon on the Mount" and the "Lord's Prayer" are beyond our reach. Nobody could have written or imagined them since the time of the founder of Christianity. Like all "true words of God, they take the universe in." In like manner nobody, during the last thousand or fifteen hundred years, could have written the Ossianic poems. The internal evidence of their antiquity is so apparent that the reader must be as the owl at mid-day who can seriously doubt them. They also, in their small way, take the universe in. This is not the "higher critical analysis," but it is infinitely more simple and easy. Belief by instinct gets rid of a hundred difficulties at which reason would stumble; but then instinct, Dr. Waddell tells us, is the surer guide. It is better to be led by the nose than to use one's own eyes. Of course, when a man tells you he believes by instinct, there is an end of all controversy. But if one has not got the same instinct, what then? He must in default turn either to the higher or lower critical analysis, according to his faculty. I confess that I am rather suspicious of instinctive acquiescence in cases of this kind. Whether Fingal lived and Ossian sang a thousand or fifteen hundred years ago is a question which perhaps cannot be absolutely determined by criticism; far less can it be determined, according to my mind, by the intuitions of Dr. Hately Waddell. I remember, during the Sandyford murder agitation, a Glasgow clergyman publicly declared that the celebrated statement of Mrs.¹ M'Lachlan was founded upon as good internal evidence as the Four Gospels. It was impossible that such a declaration could have been concocted in the brain of a poor illiterate woman. He believed in the statement by instinct; and yet it turned out to be only a well-woven tissue of falsehood. I would not say that about Ossian; but may, perhaps, be allowed to ask whether Dr. Waddell's reference to the character of the poems does not prove too much. If they represent a primitive condition of society altogether different from the Highlands in the time of Macpherson, they also represent a state of society altogether different from what we know of other primitive races all over the world. There is a little too much of the noble savage in them; and the noble savage, so far as modern observation goes, is an invention of civilised life. As for the "pure morality, the child-like tenderness and pathos, the lofty unequivocal humanity," the fact that all these are found in the poems has been a long-standing argument that the poems themselves are of far later date than the times they represent. The poems show the higher Christian virtues operating among a race of half-naked tribes, continually at war with each other, stealing each other's wives and cattle, and living a life of "sturt and strife;" and, for my part, I would rather trust the instinct of Dr Johnson, when he refused to believe such an incongruity, than that of Dr. Waddell.

But this is not all. Dr Waddell, for the benefit of those who go by reason and not by instinct, produces evidence of a plainer sort—addressed to those who are of weaker capacity. He finds that the Clyde is referred to in four of the Ossianic poems, and referred to as a navigable river! Who in Glasgow or Greenock can doubt the authenticity of Ossian after this? Clessammor, in his bounding ship, was driven by a storm into the firth, and had to take refuge at Balclutha, which Dr. Waddell, by an off-hand topographical criticism, identifies

as Dumbarton or Dunglass; and he further shows that the "bounding ship" was probably only a canoe, that canoes were built at Bowling, and, further, that about two years ago specimens of the old craft were disinterred at that nearest watering-place on the Clyde. This, according to Dr. Waddell, ought to satisfy every reasonable man as to the authenticity of Ossian, Clessammor's voyage, and the story of his bride. Upon the whole, I would as soon trust Dr. Waddell's belief by instinct as his arguments through the exercise of the critical faculty. His reasoning put into the syllogistic form stands thus:—Ossian mentions bounding ships or canoes; old canoes have been found on the Clyde; therefore, the Ossianic poems are authentic. Did it never occur to Dr. Waddell that all savage tribes, no matter how degraded, who lived near the sea or by inland lakes, have used canoes? Canoes, according to the best authorities on the condition of primitive man, seem to have been among the very earliest inventions. It would have been strange, indeed, had no buried boats been found in the Clyde; but what these have to do with Ossian's authenticity nobody but one who believes by instinct can possibly surmise. Some of these buried boats were discovered, I believe, in Macpherson's day. Two of them were built of planks, with prows like the beak of an antique galley—perhaps they were the bridal boats of Cles-ammor: and another had a cork plug in the bottom, which could only have come, as Mr. Geikie says, from the latitudes of Spain, Southern France, or Italy. We have never heard of cork trees growing in the Western Highlands. Another of the boats contained a "polished celt," not an Ossianic Highlander, but an axe of greenstone, proving that the ancient boatbuilder of the Clyde was unacquainted with the metals when it was sunk. But Dr. Waddell has further evidence on the question, and I wait patiently for it.—
I am, &c.,
SAXO.
*Glasgow Herald*, March 28, 1871.

PART SECOND: CHAPTER I: P 56

TOMB OF OSSIAN—SIMILAR REMAINS.

DISCOVERY OF ANTIQUITIES IN BUTE.

During the present week, as some people were digging potatoes on the farm of Barone Park, in a field fronting the milldam, some more antiquities were turned up by a large grubber which was set to work to prepare for another crop. The first discovery brought to light was a large flat stone, about three feet long, which, on examination, was considered to be the covering of what seemed an ancient coffin. Some of the workers rashly put their grapes into the rude stone cist, when an urn or basin was unfortunately broken to pieces. The urn contained a large number of pointed arrow heads, composed of flint and glittering felspar. Besides this, a calcined lime substance was found, which may possibly be the remains of some ancient warrior burned to the "ashes of the urn." A small ivory tusk was also found in the cist. The fragments of the urn were carefully collected, on the tenant of the farm (Mr. Archibald Muir) being made aware of the discovery. The urn was formed of fine clay, and seemed to be elaborately ornamented externally. The position of this ancient burial spot is on a little knoll at the foot of the field, and nearly opposite the Rothesay Churchyard.—*Glasgow Herald*, August 3rd, 1872.

ANCIENT TOMBS IN CUMBRAE.

Millport, 13th August, 1873.

SIR,—Not a few of your readers, in their walks at this popular watering-place, but will remember Fintry Bay. A more lovely and picturesque spot it would be difficult to find at the coast—so, it seems, thought our ancestors, at least, to repose their dead bodies in. To-day, as the workers on the new road were removing the *debris*, they came on three ancient stone graves or cists. I was present when one of them was uncovered. They are within a few feet of each other, within a stone-cast of the wall, and 115 feet from the ordinary high-water mark. The westmost is 3 feet long, 2 feet 2 inches broad, and 2 feet deep, compactly formed of red sandstone slabs, the material of which they are all made. Its direction is N.E. and S.W. The middle grave is smaller, being 1 foot 10 inches long, 1 foot 3 inches broad, by 1 foot 7 inches deep, and lies N. and S. It was covered by a thick, heavy slab, measuring 4 feet by 3. These two graves are on the same level, and were covered by a sandy soil and small shingly boulders to the depth of 4 feet. The remaining one, a little to the east, is finished evidently with great care. There are neat, well-fitted corner pieces, so adjusted as to prevent any wet from getting in. It is on a higher elevation than the other two, and was covered by about two feet of soil above the thick slab which covered it. It lies due N. and S. There was nothing found in any of the three to offer any clue as to their age. The earth in one of them was of a darkish ashen hue, contrasting with the reddish colour of the rest —evidently the *debris* of the red sandstone which prevails in the locality. The knoll or mound, before the road was cut through, had a pleasant green appearance, and probably contains more of these interesting remains. Their form strictly resembles those exhumed in the north end of the island a few years ago. Having seen them both

when newly opened, I have no hesitation in referring them to the same people. The Fint'y Bay ones seem muc older, from the much greater depth of earth that covers them. Those at Portray Bay contained an urn in a good state of preservation; but these none. It is difficult to speak confidently as to the period when or persons who were buried here. The practice of burning the dead did not obtain among Christians. The graves are evidently older than the Battle of Largs. Are they remains of the Cymbri, the ancient British, who left a trace of their history in the name of the island—Combrae? Perhaps some of our antiquarian friends may be able to determine. Altogether, the scene of these archæological remains impresses us that, whoever were their authors, they were not destitute of a taste for the sublime and beautiful. The Arran hills to the west, with their serried heights; the lovely low lying Bute in front; while to the north rise in mingled majesty the Arrochar and Benlomond ranges—attest their love to nature in her grandest forms.—I am, &c.,  A. M.
*Glasgow Herald*, August 16.

Compare also Part Fourth, Chapter V., p. 252.

### PART SECOND: CHAPTER IV: P. 93

### MEN OF GIGANTIC SIZE.

Besides the gigantic human remains found in Arran, as described in Headrick, we find traces of a similar race on the shores of the Solway. A correspondent of the *Glasgow Herald*, December 19, 1872, writes:—

"That the stern Novantes did not tamely stand by and allow their territory to be possessed by a foreign though civilised aggressor, we appeal to the standing-stones and other antiquities that exist in the neighbourhood of Whithorn. Some of these at least must denote the site of primitive British strengths, and others may be commemorative of resolute struggles between the Romans and the Celtic ab rigines of the district. Evidences are not wanting to prove that the farm of the Catyans, adjoining the Roman encampment, which we lately described, must, in these far-off times, have been the scene of a bloody battle. . . . . And, indeed, the precincts of these farms seem to have been in days of yore the arena of many sanguinary contests. On a portion of the Tonderghie estate —in which the last-mentioned farm is—detached parts of a human skeleton, consisting of a massive skull and the leg-bones of a man, apparently of gigantic proportions, were, about a year ago, exhumed by some ditchers while draining a piece of wet bog land. . . . . The peninsular rocky promontory, called the "Cairn," at the Isle of Whithorn, also presents a rich field of research for the archæologist, and, we are sure, if duly probed, would yield signal acquisitions to antiquarian science." Compare Part Third, Chapter VI.

Among the Orkneys, at the opposite extremity of the Island, but equally within the range of Ossianic narrative, both as to time and place, discoveries of the same sort are recorded.—According to Brand, gigantic men inhabited these islands. Great bones, compared in size to those of a horse, backbone and thigh, have been found in Sanda; and one giant, in later days there, "was of so tall a stature that he could have stood upon the ground and put the copstone upon the chappel [of Clet.]; which no man now living by far could do."

Another of these giants, as remarkable apparently for strength as for stature "died not long since [1701], whom, for his height, they commonly called the *meikle man of Wa'es.*" Compare also Part Fifth, Chapter IX., pp. 350-7.

### PART THIRD: CHAPTERS III V: Pp. 125, 150, 167. &c.

### ROMANCE OF DERMOT AND GRANIA. P. 129.

To satisfy himself of the true character of such compositions, the Author devoted a few spare shillings and some time, to the purchase and perusal of *Diarmuid agus Grainne* (Dermot and Grania), which constitutes Vol. III. of the Ossianic Society's Translations, for the year 1855, printed at Dublin under their direction, and published there by O'Daly, 1857. The Translation itself, edited by Standish Hayes O'Grady, Esq., the President, is handsomely done, with the original Irish on the opposite page, and many useful notes, explanatory of allusions in the text, subjoined; but the only feeling excited by the perusal of the romance itself, so called, was one of surprise that a Society including in its membership and council so many reverend, learned, and influential gentlemen, should have bestowed the expense and labour requisite for the publication in English of so much very incoherent, incredible, outrageous, and often indecent rubbish; to which the histories of "Tom Thumb" or "Jack the Giant Killer," avowedly intended for the nursery, are really far superior in pith and humour. There was indeed another feeling of disgust and astonishment, that such miserable literary brigandage of the middle ages should be received by intelligent Irishmen as the work of Ossian, to compare it with which for a moment is an insult to Ossian, and to accept it for the original of which, is imbecility. The solitary sort of interest attached to it, is in the obvious fact that it must have been concocted for the lowest mob audience by some prolix impostor, from the dimmest acquaintance with one or two remote distorted traditions, obtained, as we have shown, from the natives of Ulster; in which the names of Fingal, Ossian, Oscar, and Roscrana, as chief actors in connection with Dermot, are mixed up with those of the Fenians or Irish Militia—Fingal, in the meantime, however, being transformed into a bloodthirsty besotted monster, Roscrana into a shameless trolloping quean, and Ossian into a fool! And the only additional evidence it affords of the authenticity of Ossian, as an abused authority in Ireland, is (1.) that "the King of the World" is introduced; "but who he was," says Standish Hayes O'Grady, Esq., "it is impossible to say. The title appears to be vaguely applied to some fictitious Continental potentate." In plain terms, as Mr. O'Grady might have known, the title was borrowed by tradition from the genuine Ossian, and introduced at random for any purpose, but without any idea that it was originally applied by him to the Imperial representatives of Rome. (2.) That the "three Kings of Innis Thuile" are also introduced, "by which," says O'Grady, "the writer probably means Iceland." The word *Innis-Thuile*, which means "the Island of the Flood or Ocean," is in fact identical with *Innis-Thona*, and may therefore very well have been applied to Iceland. In Ossian's day, as we have seen,—Part Fifth, Chap. VII.,—there were at least two kings in Innis-Thona; and the king of Lochlin, as supreme, might be the third. Whether the addition of these personages to the story has been made by corruption from the text of Ossian, our readers may determine for themselves; but this allusion to Iceland and its kings by the Irish romancers of the middle ages, is proof at least that that Island was somehow known to them before its colonisation by the Danes.

PART FOURTH; CHAPTERS II. III: PP. 202 TO 215

### KELVIN AND BONNY WATER

We learn from Mr. Graham of Auchencloch, proprietor also of Orchard Mill, that the Kelvin, besides being reduced for the Reservoir and Canal, suffers another reduction still higher up—having its waters laid under contribution to the Bonny, by feudal right, for the supply of the Milldam at Orchard. The Bonny Water is, therefore, by so much indebted to the Kelvin for a considerable share of its present stream; and it is only when there is a redundancy of water at Orchard, that the surplus is restored again to the Kelvin by a sluice at Banton. In wet or wintry weather, however, Mr. Graham explains that the Bonny Water comes down in such torrents of its own, that to attempt to cross it in the glen at Orchard would be at the peril of destruction to man or beast. Long ago, therefore, when the natural course of these rivers was not interfered with, but each had its proper supply—the one descending to the east and the other to the west from the same point, in full flood, "white from the hill, with the rocks and their hundred groves"—they would be equally dangerous and picturesque. "Far be my foot from Crona; death is tumbling there!" We farther learn from the same obliging authority, not only that the old course of the rivers in the marsh below, as described in the chapters above quoted, is strictly correct; but that there is even a remote tradition, that the opposite friths approached, if they did not intermingle, about Kelvinhead; and that the site of a quay can be pointed out in that neighbourhood, where small ships or canoes long ago had been actually moored. If this tradition be exact, or anything like it—which we see no reason to doubt—our argument in the text is confirmed beyond farther discussion; and the very creek where old Carul of Colamon entered his barge, on that voyage of his down the Kelvin to the Clyde, which carried him unexpectedly to Selma, may be identified.

PART FOURTH: CHAPTER V: P. 238.

### PTOLEMAIC GEOGRAPHY.

"Ptolemy, in short, was not omniscient, nor was Laing by any means infallible."

The late illustrious traveller, Dr. Livingstone, commenting on the Ptolemaic Geography, writes thus to the present author, under date South Central Africa, December, 1872 :—

"Ptolemy having flourished as a geographer in the second of our era, I suspect that Portuguese, Dutch, and English were not doing much in the map line sixteen hundred years ago; but much later in the ages they tried to make up for former laziness, and it seems that the map of Ptolemy [for Africa] had the misfortune to be the groundwork on which they ran riot in improvements. This went on till Gerard Mercator collected as many of these lively ebullitions of geographical zeal as he could find, carefully collated them, and conscientiously expurgated all spurious matter. He did a great service to Ptolemaic geography, and imposed a check on the producers of old maps, whose emendations generally rested on 'travels at home and voyages by the fireside.' Mercator could not thus correct the old worthy himself, because his authorities had disappeared, and but few copies of his own work survived the lapse of time. There is reason to believe that Ptolemy, too, departed from earlier authorities, who derived their knowledge from visitors to this very region," &c.

Whether Mercator's revision was any real improvement on the genuine Ptolemy—of whom thirteen or fourteen editions, with obvious errors, may still be found; or what authority Mercator himself had for the alterations he published, as regards the interior of Africa, is not alleged in the above passage, and cannot perhaps be very satisfactorily shown, seeing he himself was not a traveller, but only a student of geography at home. As regards Scotland, however, he made the curious mistake of turning the whole of that part of Great Britain eastward at right angles to the south, so that the headlands of Caithness would abutt on the shores of Norway! His outline of the coast, both east and west, is also very rude and indefinite; but the Frith of Clyde appears, in proportion, much larger than it now does; and expands apparently, as a fiord, as far south-east as

## APPENDIX.

Hamilton. In this respect, and to this extent, therefore, Ptolemy was not so far wrong as he might be supposed to be. But he neither places, nor even mentions Alcluth, much less Dumbarton—the best negative evidence that no such fortification, or stronghold, was then known to the Romans. Laing, in fact, inspired by this very omission, seems to have doubted the existence of Dumbarton

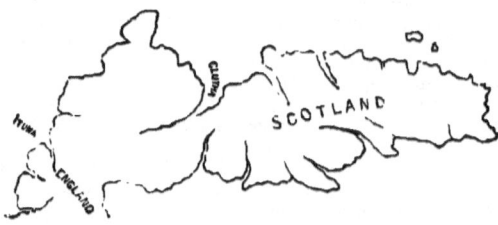

SKETCH MAP OF SCOTLAND, ACCORDING TO PTOLEMY.

itself at the commencement of the Christian era; and so, contounding Balclutha with Dumbarton, denies the authenticity of Ossian. As to the existence of Dumbarton, we entirely concur with him, although for very different reasons. In short, he had no idea of the actual levels of the Clyde, or that the vale of Leven, at the date in question, was an arm of the sea.

### PART FOURTH: CHAPTER V: P. 248.

#### LEGEND OF THE BURGH SEAL OF RUTHERGLEN.

| SIGILLVM COMVNITATIS: VILLÆ DE: RVGLEN. | = | NAVIS: NAVTA: MARIA X SIGNANT: ISTA: TRIA: RATA: |
|---|---|---|
| SEAL OF THE COMMONWEAL: OF THE TOWN OF: RUGLEN: | = | THE SHIP: THE SAILOR: AND MARY X THESE THREE MARK WITHOUT VARY: DECREETS THEREIN: |

### PART FOURTH: CHAPTER V: P. 250.

#### COWAL—KYLE OR COIL—FINGAL'S BIRTH-PLACE?

It is some confirmation of our view in the text, that Cowal at least derives its name from Comhal, to find traces of Fingal's own presence in that region. Finart on Loch-Striven, Fin-trakin on the Holy-Loch, and Glen-Fyne, which divides the tongue of the peninsula from north to south, are indications as clear as could well be looked for that the King of Morven and his people have been there, although no reference to the fact is yet traceable in Ossian. And on the other hand, if we are right in supposing that Kyle or Coil also received its name from Comhal, and that Comhal himself was slain in battle on the moors of Ayrshire between the Girvan and the Cree, then we have a sort of clew to the birth-place of Fingal besides; for according to uniform tradition and his own express words, he was not only "born in the midst of battles," but on the very day on which his father fell. If his mother Morna, therefore, had accompanied her husband Comhal to the campaign in question—which was quite in conformity with the customs of the time—Fingal's birth must have happened somewhere on the borders of Carrick and Kyle. This conjecture as to the locality is by no means improbable, and the circumstance itself goes far to explain both Fingal's intimate acquaintance with that country, and his frequent expeditions to the neighbourhood —notably his first expedition, when he could not have been more than 16 years of age, to avenge his father's death by the subjugation of the Mornis.

PART FOURTH; CHAPTER V; P. 252, &c.

### CANOES, WHERE FOUND.

In the process of dredging the river, near Bowling or Dunglass on the Clyde, two old canoes were dislodged from the silting there, in the summer of 1868. A correct representation of these our readers have already seen at page 256; and we have only now further to specify their dimensions and conditions. The largest, scooped from the trunk of a solid oak, and rudely fashioned with a sort of snout for prow and a perpendicular stern, measures 20 ft. long in the hull, with 15 inches additional for the prow alluded to, by 9 ft. in circumference at one end, and 10 at the other; but the roots of the small branches where lopped off, and other excrescences along the trunk of the tree, still projecting, give slight variations here and there in round measurement. This rather cumbrous and ungainly craft seems to have been used for a sort of transport or luggage boat, for the snout in front has a perforation through it, to which a rope or thong might be attached. The smaller one, made also by scooping, but from a divided oak, measures 12 ft. long, and about 3 across at the broadest. It has notches for a bench, and spurs for a foot-board to the rower. It was therefore propelled by oars, and might have been used either as a skiff for crossing the shallows, or as a tug-boat for dragging the larger one across. They seem both to have had plug-holes in the floor for baling—the larger having three, the smaller two, such openings. At the time the sketch for this volume was taken, they were both much "clung," even rent and twisted, with exposure to the air, although carefully covered in a thick shed, and had thus lost a good deal of their original "line." But we have been expressly assured, not only that they were compact and shapely, as far as such wrecks could be, when taken out of the water; but that sculptures, in the form of strange LETTERS, were distinctly visible on their sides. In one of them was also found a war-club, or weapon with a heavy head sharpened to an edge on one side, of formidable weight and aspect, correctly delineated (on a larger scale than the canoes) in our engraving.*

---

* We regret to learn that since our sketch of the canoes at Bowling was taken, the shed in which they were kept has been broken into, and much damage done. Among other outrages, the war-club, which when entire measured somewhere about 2 ft. 6 in., has been broken or destroyed.

SOLID OAK CANOE, FOUND, JULY 1874, IN LOCH-ARTHUR, KIRKCUDBRIGHTSHIRE.

For a sketch of this interesting relique we are indebted to Dr. T. B. Grierson of Thornhill. The ship measured 45½ feet in length, by 4½ in breadth at the stern, therefore about 2½ deep; and had places for 7 pairs of oars. It might without overcrowding accommodate about 50 men. The stern had been finished by a piece of wood fitted in athwart, so that the magnificent tree of which the ship is made was probably hollowed by decay, and was scooped out from the root upwards where it fell—the first great branch or bend being converted, with admirable taste, into a prow. At the date of its construction, the Nith would be a fiord to Dalswinton, and Loch-Arthur, between that and the Solway, would be in connection with the sea. Our readers therefore, with such a specimen of naval architecture before them, can have no difficulty in understanding either what a "dark bosomed," lofty prowed, ship was, or how voyages in such ships could be made from the Solway and the Clyde to Ireland, from Morven to the Orkneys and Norway, or from Morven to Iceland itself. We regret the notice of this wonderful "find" did not reach us at an earlier date, that it might have been introduced at its proper place in the text. Loch-Arthur is on the estate of Lotus, the property of Mrs. Hyslop; by whom the canoe was placed at Dr. Grierson's disposal. Dr Grierson transferred it unreservedly to the Society of Antiquaries of Scotland; by whose orders, we believe, it has been divided, and the front half removed for exhibition, to their National Museum at Edinburgh.

# APPENDIX.

From memoranda courteously supplied to us by R. W. Cochrane Patrick, Esq., of Ladyland, we learn by the report of Mr. Hislop quoted there, that a canoe, similar to one of the above, was discovered by him among the mud near a small artificial island, now half submerged, at the S.W. end of Kilbirnie Loch—

"It was hollowed out of a single tree, and was about 18 feet in length, 3 feet in breadth, and close on 2 feet in depth. It was broadest at the stern, which was square, and tapered towards the bow; and was entire, with the exception of about 2 feet broken off the narrowest end. There were indications that a hole in the bottom had been mended, and some wooden pins were in it which may have been used for that purpose, or for fixing at the side what is described to me as a sort of bracket. In the mud which filled the hollow of the canoe the [following] bronze articles were found [viz., a Lion-shaped Ewer and three-legged Pot] and also a thin plate or piece of metal which cannot now be recovered. . . . . . . It is difficult to account for these articles, which apparently belong to a comparatively late period, being found in a canoe which was evidently of a much earlier age. It is possible that the connection was merely accidental, and that the articles, which are of considerable weight, when they sank, buried themselves in the canoe already resting at the bottom. Or, on the other hand, it may be, that the canoe, though made and belonging originally to a very primitive period, continued in use down to the later one, and was lost with the articles in it; a theory which, I am somewhat inclined to think, is the more probable."

It is chiefly, however, to the fact that a vessel of this kind should have been found in an inland lake which once communicated with the sea, and at no great distance from the spot where others similar have since been found—viz., at Bowling—in the track of the Frith itself, that we are now directing attention. When these primitive galleys were used, there was either regular traffic in ships of the sort between the coast at Ardrossan and the ridge at Dunglass; or the adjoining lakes of Loch-Winnoch and Kilbirnie constituted so great a body of water, that some means of navigation, to cross them at least, was imperative; and it is quite possible that the bronze reliques above referred to were actual trophies captured by our forefathers from Romans south of the Wall.

It is proper to mention that the artificial island near which this canoe was found has been described by a Correspondent in the *Ayrshire Weekly News*, June 6, 1874, as in fact an old Lake Dwelling, composed of not fewer than five strata—including uppermost one of stones, then lower one of brushwood compressed, and finally one of logs or trunks of trees, not only dressed apparently with an axe, but mortised and checked, with wooden pins in the tenons, resting on the mud; the whole having once had communication with the shore of the lake by a steep narrow causeway, but now all upheaved and dislocated by the pressure of slag from the adjacent furnaces. However this may be as regards the island in question, it is certain there was a canoe attached to it also, and that similar canoes have been discovered deeply imbedded, both in one of the lower streets in Glasgow and also in Duke Street much higher up, near where the Molendinar Burn crosses that thoroughfare, in the same city. The Molendinar, therefore, though now little better than a common sewer, must have been a considerable branch of the upper frith at the date in question; when Loch-Winnoch and Loch-Tanker, otherwise Loch-Tancu, now Kilbirnie-Loch, made a navigable link between the frith itself and the sea.

On the other side of the Island, in like manner, we find that besides the canoe on the banks of the Carron—p. 200—a similar craft of very ancient construction, although more recently repaired and apparently in still later use, has just been discovered on the banks of the Forth—

# APPENDIX.

CANOE FOUND IN THE FORTH AT STIRLING.—Yesterday afternoon, writes our correspondent, a boat which had been discovered embedded in the mud and gravel of the river some days before, near Cambuskenneth Abbey Ferry, was towed ashore by Mr. M'Lean, Master of Works, and a large staff of men. The boat, which seems to have been 20 feet long by 3 feet wide, is cut from one piece of solid oak trunk, and it appears to be of great antiquity. Tradition has it that a boat coming from a "feast" at the Abbey in 1529 with 50 persons aboard was, in consequence of overloading, capsized, and this relic is supposed to be the boat in question. It certainly bears the marks of great antiquity, but undoubtedly has been used in later times, as it bore traces of patching, and iron nails of a make common about 1650 or 1700 were found in one of these. Considerable interest has been excited in the district by the discovery, and many antiquaries have inspected this interesting treasure trove. There are no marks of beauty or comeliness about it to any but the antiquary, and no doubt in due time some member of that society will favour the world with an accurate description of the canoe, which undoubtedly dates from the Roman occupation of Caledonia. In the meantime, the canoe is to be cleaned and preserved, and placed in the Smith Institute, Stirling.—*Glasgow Herald*, May 14, 1874.

And finally, to go beyond the limits of our own shores, to where such galleys are said to have been fashioned long ago in perfection, we find the—

DISCOVERY OF AN ANCIENT VESSEL IN NORWAY.—An important discovery of archæological interest has been recently made in Norway. A tumulus, a few miles to the north of Frederickstadt, has been explored, and embedded in a sort of stratum of firm clay at its base, has been found the hull of a vessel, made completely of oak, and evidently of great age. Both ends taper, so that it is difficult to tell the bows from the stern; the vessel, moreover, is rather "squat" and low in the water. The length of the keel is about 44 feet, and the breadth of beam about 13 feet. Various circumstances combine to prove that it must have been a war vessel for coast use; it was propelled by oars and sails, and there are traces of elaborate carving about the sides. In accordance with an ancient practice in Sweden and Norway, allusion to which is made in some of the Sagas, the vessel was brought hither to cover the remains of its captain, fragments of whose dress, horse accoutrements and harness have been discovered. This vessel evidently dates from the time of the old Vikings, and the Society of Antiquaries at Christiania, with a due regard for its historical and archæological value, have caused the entire lot to be conveyed to Christiania with a view to its being set up within the precincts of the University.—*Academy*, March, 1874.

## PART FIFTH: CHAPTER I: P. 259.

### PLAGIARISMS ALLEGED BY LAING.

The reader will find the number and variety of alleged plagiarisms in Ossian, arranged with as much accuracy as possible, in the subjoined classified list:—

PRINCIPAL AUTHORS.

| Authors. | Parallels. | Authors. | Parallels. |
|---|---|---|---|
| Bible—Miscellaneous, [Books, 23] | 45 | Virgil's Æneid, | 44 |
| Song of Solomon, | 34 | Georgics, | 11 |
| Psalms, | 22 | | 55 |
| Job, | 18 | Homer's Iliad, | 50 |
| Isaiah, | 18 | Odyssey, | 2 |
| 1 and 2 Samuel, | 13 | | 52 |
| Apocrypha, | 4 | Dryden's Virgil, Æneid, &c., | 31 |
| | 154 | Works, | 4 |
| Pope's Iliad, | 98 | | 35 |
| Odyssey, | 20 | Gray's Elegy, Bards, &c., | 25 |
| Works, Windsor Forest, &c., | 33 | Shakespear, | 24 |
| | 151 | Young's Night Thoughts, &c., | 17 |
| Milton's Paradise Lost, | 102 | Irish Ballads, [several editions] | 16 |
| " Regained, | 8 | Pinkerton's Hardyknute, | 12 |
| " Works, | 13 | Mason's Dramatic Works, | 10 |
| | 123 | Addison's Works, | 7 |
| MacPherson's own Works, | 115 | Mallet's Works, | 6 |
| Thomson's Seasons, &c., | 75 | Home's Dramatic Works, | 5 |

# APPENDIX.

### MISCELLANEOUS CLASSIC AUTHORS.

| Authors. | Parallels. | Authors. | Parallels. |
|---|---|---|---|
| Horace, | 4 | Tyrtaeus, | 2 |
| Apollonius Rhodius, | 3 | Catullus, | 1 |
| Ovid, | 3 | Mimnermus, | 1 |
| Theocritus, | 2 | Livy, | 1 |
| Tibullus (Hamond's), | 2 | Sallust, | 1 |

### MISCELLANEOUS ENGLISH AUTHORS.

| Authors. | Parallels. | Authors. | Parallels. |
|---|---|---|---|
| Swift's Works, | 4 | Tate and Brady's Psalms, | 2 |
| Collins's Works, | 4 | Congreve, | 1 |
| Warton's Essays, | 3 | Harte's Gustavus, | 1 |
| Martin's Western Isles, | 3 | Glover, | 1 |

### MISCELLANEOUS SCOTCH AUTHORS.

| Authors. | Parallels. | Authors. | Parallels. |
|---|---|---|---|
| "Braes of Yarrow," | 7 | Blair's Grave, | 2 |
| Jerome Stone, | 4 | Scots Magazine, | 2 |
| "Chevy Chase," | 3 | "Flowers of the Forest," | 1 |
| Old Songs, | 3 | Gavin Douglas, | 1 |
| Buchanan's Psalms, | 3 | Wilkie's Epigoniad, | 1 |

### HISTORICAL AND MYTHICAL.

| Authors. | Parallels. | Authors. | Parallels. |
|---|---|---|---|
| Toland's History of Druids, | 9 | Regner's Lodbrog, | 4 |
| Keating's History of Ireland, | 3 | Percy's Runic Poems, | 2 |

The total being, of alleged parallels 966, and of Authors said to be quoted 88; from which miscellaneous aggregate of "phrases, words, and often mere syllables," with an imperfect foundation in some absurd or puerile Irish ballads, MacPherson is supposed to have concocted and written the entire series of Ossianic poems, epic and dramatic, before the age of 25! Surely never was an idea suggested by an accomplished critic, more unworthy of his own reputation. But to mitigate our censure for a moment—the whole reminds one laughably of that industrious architectural sparrow apostrophised by Miss Taylor in her *Nursery Rhymes.* We quote from memory :—

> Hop about, pretty sparrow, and pick up the hay,
> And the wool and the twigs and the moss :
> I'm sure I'll stand far enough out of your way—
> Don't fly from the window so cross.
>
> . . . . . .
>
> Now come, pretty sparrow,—pray do let us see
> How you build such a beautiful house :
> And I'll sit at the foot of the jennetting tree,
> Whilst you twitter a song in the boughs !

The only difference being, that what the sparrow does according to instinct and with suitable materials, MacPherson was supposed to do according to Laing, and with really no materials at all ; the folly of the supposition being made still more apparent by the fact already stated—that MacPherson himself pointed out not fewer than 118 obvious parallels in his own first editions, which he was under no obligation to point out, and which, if he had been an impostor, he might easily have avoided. These, so far as we have observed, are as follows :—

## APPENDIX.

### NATURAL PARALLELS.

| Authors. | Parallels. | Authors. | Parallels. |
|---|---|---|---|
| Homer's Iliad, | 27 | Milton, | 19 |
| Odyssey, | 2 | Bible, | 14 |
| Pope's Translations of, | 19 | Miscellaneous, | 3 |
| | 48 | | |
| Virgil's Æneid, | 20 | Total Natural Parallels pointed out by | |
| Dryden's Translation of, | 14 | MacPherson in his own text | 118 |
| | 34 | | |

Our readers, we trust, are now satisfied on the subject of Mr. Laing's researches, and on the value of his theory about alleged plagiarisms in the Poems of Ossian.

### PART FIFTH: CHAPTER IV: P. 295.

#### VARIETIES OF FOOD STILL IN USE

To illustrate in some degree how our ancestors in Ossian's day may have lived, in strict conformity with the letter of his text, the following quotations from contemporaneous sources in our own day may suffice :—

ARCHÆOLOGY OF THE LEWS. . . . . Almost every kind of shellfish is willingly received, and limpets are eaten in great quantities by the poor when they run out of better food. They are understood to be very strong and sustaining food, but the intestine, which they declare to be injurious, is always drawn out before eating. Cockles boiled in milk, cockle soup, pickled cockles, are all held by connoisseurs to be super-excellent when well managed. Sufficient may be had in Stornoway for a few halfpence to form a most delicious repast. Clams are always heartily welcome, and, besides their edible properties, the shells are in general use—the convex as a butter scoop, the flat being relegated to the milk basin as a creamer. The sea, the sea, the generous sea, has not yet done its best for the native gastronomy. Sea birds, sea fish, shellfish—these are not all. Besides dulse, so well-known on the mainland, they peel and eat the fresh stalks of the tangle. It tasted to us like a hard turnip, but is much liked among them, and is doubtless beneficial medicinally as an adjunct to their diet. Then there is a dark ware called here "Slochgan," that they boil with butter, and which meets with approbation even among civilised diners. These latter, however, are more partial to carageen, found in quantity on some parts of the coast, and in common use among the educated inhabitants as a pudding. This ware—the Irish moss of commerce—when gathered, is carefully washed, and then bleached for some days in the sun and rain until perfectly white, when it is dried for use. The dried plants when carefully picked so as to be free of impurity, are boiled with milk, and form a pleasant and well-known dish. — *Glasgow Herald*, April 15, 1873.

THE CLAM AS USED IN AMERICA — The *Echo's* correspondent writing on the recent Greeley "Clam-bake," gives an account of that interesting mollusc :—*Mya arenaria!* I dont suppose many of your readers are personally acquainted with this sea-side resident, or have even heard the name before; but here it is an old friend greatly sought after at this season of the year, and just now also filling an important *role* in politics. Our *Mya* is, after all, only the soft shell clam so common on the New England coast, and so abundant even in the days of the Pilgrim Fathers, that in those pinching times some of the Elders lived solely on them for months, thanking God that they could "suck of the abundance of the seas and of the treasures hid in the sands." The little colony has since then become a great nation, but the clam is still esteemed, if not as a necessary of life, at least as one of its luxuries, especially when combined with the holiday trip to the coast and the popular clam-bake. I think the clam worthy of Mr. Buckland's attention; and if it could only be naturalised on English soil, I fancy it would prove a much more valuable article of diet for the poorer classes than the cockle (which, by the way, is unknown here, or at any rate is never seen in New York markets), and be at the same time a grateful addition to the tables of the rich.

In a fragment ascribed to Ossian's Era, *Highland Society Report*, "fish and venison and the choice of the chase prepared," are mentioned by Darthula as delicacies to be found in Glen-Laith, Glen-Masain, and Glendaruel. These are all in the district of COWAL; and this allusion to them there is the strongest confirmation of our own view as to Comhal's connection with that region. See p. x.

# APPENDIX.

## PART FIFTH: CHAPTERS IV. V: Pp. 294-301.

### WEAPONS OF NON-CONDUCTING MATERIALS.

ANCIENT BATTLE AXE.—A perfect specimen of an ancient battle axe was found the other day on the farm of Barrachan, Wigtownshire. The axe is of copper, and measures 6 inches from back to front, and 3½ inches across the face, and 1⅞ inches across the back, and has been attached to a shaft by thongs of hide or green withes. The same gentleman, Mr. John Vance, found a stone axe a few years ago in the same place. The present one is of apparently a different date. It is quite possible that some warrior of the bypast times may have found a last resting-place somewhere in the above locality.—*Glasgow Herald*, October 20, 1873.

THE SWORD OF HAQUIN.—"The Cathedral [of Anslo, or Obslo, called also Christiania,] is dedicated to St. Alward; and in it is shown the sword of Haquin, one of their ancient kings, the hilt whereof is of crystal, and is a notable curiosity for art, as well as antiquity."—*Falconer's Geography*—under head of *Norway*. The Haquin here referred to is Haquin I., 1232; but the manufacture and application of such a material as crystal, in the fabrication of a sword, must have been of a much remoter date—its use at least for that purpose, immediately after invention, would be most unlikely.

## PART FIFTH: CHAPTER VI: Pp. 312, 315, &c.

### STONES OF STENNIS—DWARFIE STONE—YESKENABY &c.

"At the Loch of Stennis in the mainland, where the Loch is narrowest, on both east and west side, there is a ditch, within which there is a circle of large and high stones erected; the larger mound is on the west side above 100 paces diameter. The stones, set about in form of a circle within a large ditch, are not all of a like quantity and size, tho' some of them, I think, are upwards of 20 foot high above ground, 4 or 5 foot broad, and a foot or two thick. . . . . On the other side of the Loch, over which we pass by a bridge laid with stones after the manner of a street, the Loch there being shallow—are two stones standing, of a like bigness with the rest, whereof one hath a round hole in the midst of it; at a little distance from which stone there is another ditch, about half a mile from the former, but of a far less circumference, within which also there are some stones standing, something bigger . . . . in form of a semicircle . . . . opening to the east. Both at the east and west end of the bigger round are two green mounts, which appear to be artificial; in one of which mounts were found, saith Mr. Wallace, 9 fibulae of silver, round, but with an opening like a horse-shoe. It is most probably thought that these were high places in times of Pagan idolatry, whereon sacrifices were offered; and that the two artificial mounts of earth served for the same purpose, or were the places where the ashes of the sacrifices were cast."—Pp. 44-5. Boethius indeed expressly says that these circles were called the ancient Temples of the Gods—*Prisca Deorum Phana*. To which Brand, from whom we thus quote, adds—"Many of the countrey do say, that in the larger Round the Sun, and in the lesser the Moon was worshipped by the old Pagan inhabitants of these isles." The reader who is acquainted with Arran will require nothing to remind him of the similarity between these circles and those on Machrie-muir, which were also originally on the verge of a loch, and which are all, by tradition, identified with the temporary residence of Fingal, both in his warlike expeditions and in his occasional administration of justice. Compare p. 49.

THE DWARFIE STONE.—"This stone, which lies to the south-east of the W'arthill, on the brink of a valley, is a sand or freestone of the same nature with those on the rock above it, from which it seems to have been broken off, either by the hand of man or its own gravity, and tumbled to its present site, where it has been afterwards hollowed out with an instrument, into the whimsical form which it now bears. Its greatest length is 32 feet, its breadth 17, its thickness above the surface of the earth not less than 7½ feet; and the inside of it is divided into three apartments, in one of which is something like a bed, 5 feet 8 inches long by 2 broad; the other is a sort of small room: and between them there is a space that seems to have been intended for a fire-place, as there is a hole cut in the roof, or upper part of the stone, for the smoke perhaps to issue through. To give it still more the resemblance of a dwelling, a stone of the same nature, and nearly of the same shape, has been rolled down, and placed in such a way as to serve the purpose of a door to the entrance of the other. Tradition and some authors affirm it to have been the habitation of a giant and his consort, from which they occasionally issued forth for depredation." . . . . *Barry's Orkney Islands*.

CROMLECH OF YESKENABY, OR STONES OF VIA.—Dimensions. "The Slab of Via is 1 foot thick, 5 feet 10 long, and 4 feet 9 broad. The four pillars under it are each about 3 feet long, and the headstone 3 feet 9 by 2 feet 9 on the surface, and 1 foot 4 thick."—Note to Article on Yeskenaby in *Statist. Account of Scotland*, 1845. By the above admeasurements, the reader will perceive that the entire structure so represented is not to be compared with the Dwarfie Stone; and that the slab and headstone respectively are not so large as those of Malvina's grave at Drumadoon, which certainly could not be an object of terror in any way whatever to a man like Fingal.

### PART FIFTH: CHAPTER VI. P. 318.

#### CHANGE OF COLOUR IN THE MOON AT CARRIC-THURA.

"In the meantime, a partial obscuration occurs and a change in the colour of the moon, which implied not only a change in the state of the atmosphere," &c.

To assure himself on this point, as far as circumstances would permit, the Author took the opportunity, for several evenings, about midsummer of the present year—long after the above passage was written, to observe the aspect of the moon—first as half or three-quarter moon, over Castlecary, and then as full moon on the Frith of Forth, between Stirling Castle and the Abbey Craig; the point of observation being Cornton Cottage, near Bridge of Allan, which is almost in the meridian of Roraheid, and from which, therefore, the planet should present the same, or a very similar aspect. As half moon and three-quarter, it appeared over Castlecary, clear and bright, with beamy lustre in the open sky; as full moon or nearly so, waxing and waning, a few nights afterwards, it rose once "cold and wan" over the Frith, when the horizon in that direction was clear; but when the mists of the river at Cambus-Kenneth, and the smoke and steam of trains at the Stirling railway station intervened, which was most frequently the case, its colour changed to a reddish hue; and on one occasion, as Ossian says, there was even the "hiding of her red face in the east" altogether; nor was it ever till she had surmounted this atmospheric barrier of smoke and mist, that she came forth in proper splendour, north of Stirling Castle. The correspondence of these facts with the phenomena recorded in *Carric-thura* is so precise, that in the circumstances of the case the confirmation may be accepted as conclusive. Transfer names and conditions from north to south, or *vice versa* —for Roraheid read Cornton or Keir, for Sarno's tower read the railway station at Stirling, for "the green flame edged with smoke" read smoke and steam and lurid mist together, which would very nearly resemble it—and all the effects of varying colour in the moon, with temporary obscuration, may be realised any suitable midsummer night at the proper season. When the flame of the passing engine looks "dim and distant"—that is, when the intervening smoke and mist are strong, "the moon will hide her red face in the east;" but when the smoke dies away, or the mist dissolves, or the moon has had time to surmount them, she will "come forth again in the east"—that is, higher in the east, or more to the south-east, as certainly as she once did hundreds of years ago, and would still do, in corresponding circumstances at Carric-thura, to any one watching her aspect there from Roraheid. What the effect produced by electric conditions in the atmosphere, in addition to those above stated, might be, the writer had not an opportunity of judging; but he may state in passing, that no better point for watching the cloud-drifts on their way, along the Ardvens of Stirlingshire, from the Clyde to the Forth, could be desired, than at Cornton or Bridge of Allan.

# APPENDIX.

### PART FIFTH: CHAPTER VI: P. 324.

#### WHAT WAS THE HERMAN SAUL?

HERMAN SAUL; OTHERWISE, ERMEN SEWL.—"Could we rest on the testimony of Verstegan, the name might seem allied to that of H*rmes* [Mercury.] But, under this designation, they perhaps commemorated their illustrious and beloved General *Herman*, or Arminius ‡ . . . . ‡ *Note*. I find that the conjecture thrown out in the text, is confirmed by the judgment of Schedius; 'This pillar,' he says, 'anciently called *Herman's Saul*, was erected in honour of Harminius, the General of the Cheruschi, not less intrepid in war than sage in council, who defeated the Romans with great slaughter.'" *Jamieson's Hermes Scythicus*.

Ermen Sewl, we may remark, means the Pillar of the Poor—which seems to have no proper sense, in the circumstances. Herman Saul, on the other hand, means the Monument of Herman—which has sense enough, in relation to the object, every way.

### PART FIFTH: CHAPTER VII: P. 336.

#### VOLCANIC RANGE FROM IRELAND TO ICELAND.

OLD VOLCANOES IN SCOTLAND.

An additional interest was added to the scenery of North Wales when Professor Ramsay communicated to the Alpine Club a paper on the traces of the old glaciers which had formerly travelled along its valleys, and now Mr. J. W. Judd throws a fresh light on the physical features of another district equally in favour with tourists. But while Professor Ramsay dealt with frost, Mr. Judd deals with fire. In the course of a long paper, showing both care and great caution, read before the London Geological Society last night, he gave the evidence of the former existence of five volcanoes on the west coast of Scotland. The islands of Mull and of Skye each possessed a volcano of far greater bulk than Etna; and Ardnamurchan, Rum, and St. Kilda also had volcanoes of scarcely inferior dimensions. The extent of the lava flows has been traced, and the felspathic lavas appear not to have extended beyond 10 miles from the volcanic vent, while the basaltic lavas reached to distances of 50 or 60 miles, or more. The district was at the time a continuous one, the breaking up into islands being the result of subsequent geological changes. The whole ground surface has been so thoroughly changed by many denuding agencies that only the most laborious geological research, such as Mr. Judd has bestowed, could have unravelled the history of the changes, and arrived at the most interesting results which have rewarded his work. With the clue he affords, others will be able to see the meaning of much they would otherwise overlook, and with the "scientific use of the imagination" picture to themselves the district convulsed by eruptions and covered at times with heated lava. Mr. Judd connects the volcanoes with the Great Tier, which at the same time extended through Greenland, Iceland, the Faroe Islands, the Hebrides, Ireland, Central France, the Iberian Peninsula, the Azores, Madeira, Canaries, Cape de Verde Islands, Ascension, St. Helena, and Tristan d'Acunha, and which constituted, as shown by the recent soundings of Her Majesty's ship Challenger, a mountain range comparable in its extent, elevation, and volcanic character with the Andes of South America.—*Glasgow Herald*, January 22, 1874.

By the help of Ossian's text alone, as the reader has seen, it was possible, before such discoveries were announced at all, and without any use of imagination, to determine more than half of what has since been ascertained, as regards Ireland, Scotland, and Iceland. The rest affords the clearest confirmation of our whole theory on the subject. In addition to which, we may state, on the authority of those acquainted with that neighbourhood, that to the north-west of Killin, and on the confines of Perthshire, there is a mountain whose local designation in Gaelig signifies the "hill of the hot stones;" thus indicating not only that, on the track we have assigned to these volcanic eruptions, such traces of their action may still be found; but that these have been comparatively so recent as to be commemorated in the very language of the natives.

PART FIFTH: CHAPTER VII: P. 337.

## THE KING OF DENMARK IN ICELAND,
### AND
## PUBLIC REJOICINGS WHERE OSCAR ONCE STOOD.

Among the many strange, almost romantic coincidences which have been detailed in the course of our researches, nothing stranger or more romantic has been noticed than the recent visit of His Majesty the King of Denmark to the outlying dependency of his crown, in Iceland; and this visit itself has been rendered all the more remarkable by the fact, that the most interesting ceremonies connected with His Majesty's reception there took place on the very ground where Oscar, so many centuries ago, quelled a native rebellion, and that the ringing farewell to his Majesty was given among the very cliffs, and almost on the very pathway by which Oscar must have marched against the rebels at Lano. If these lines should ever meet the King of Denmark's eye, the allusion, it is hoped, may not be unacceptable to His Majesty.

ROYAL DANISH EXPEDITION TO ICELAND.

Reykjavik, August 9.

His Majesty the King of Denmark and suite arrived in Reykjavik on Thursday, July 30, and were received with a royal salute from the Swedish, Norwegian, German, and French men-of-war in the harbour, all of which, with the exception of the latter, were despatched specially to represent their respective Governments on the occasion. His Majesty landed at 2 P.M., amidst enthusiastic cheering from the populace, and was received on the pier by the Governor, who presented an address of welcome. After the introduction of the members of the Corporation and the other public bodies of Reykjavik, His Majesty, accompanied by the Governor and the Mayor, proceeded to the Governor's residence, which had been fitted up for His Majesty's reception, amidst the prolonged cheers of the people. In the evening the King was serenaded by a choir of amateur native singers, and entertained with the original national melodies. On Friday His Majesty took an excursion on foot in the forenoon, and in the afternoon rode to the neighbouring hamlet (Hafnarfjord), and returned in the evening. On Saturday, August 1, the date on which the new Constitution came into force, the King held a public reception in the morning, and the new Minister for Iceland held a reception in the afternoon. The following day (Sunday) a grand ceremony took place in the cathedral, which was handsomely decorated and bedecked with native flowers. Hymns, expressly composed for the occasion, were effectively sung by the choir. The sermon was preached by the Bishop of Iceland. In the afternoon there was a procession to Oskjnklid, where an open *fete* was held to commemorate the millennial anniversary of the colonisation of Iceland by the Norsemen. In the evening the King honoured the *fete* with his presence, remaining for about two hours. Songs of welcome were sung for the representatives of foreign nations who had honoured Iceland with their presence, and extemporary addresses were delivered in honour of Denmark, Norway, Sweden, and America. The King was everywhere received with enthusiasm. On the 3rd August the King rode to Thingvalla, where His Majesty slept the following night, and proceeded thence to the Geysers. His Majesty returned to Thingvalla on the 6th August, and received the welcome of the representatives of the various electoral districts, and a very enthusiastic crowd of over 3000 people, all living in temporary canvas tents, studded over the plains of Thingvalla, which presented a singularly picturesque appearance. At 10 A.M. the following morning His Majesty received a loyal address from the people. After this various addresses from foreign learned bodies were handed to the Committee of Arrangements in the presence of the King and people. At 11 o'clock a state breakfast was served, and toasts were drunk in honour of the King and Queen of Denmark and the Danish dynasty, the last of which made a strong and favourable impression upon the King and his followers. At 1 P.M. His Majesty started on the return journey for Reykjavik, and was accompanied through the great rest—the Almannagja—by an immense crowd, which gave His Majesty a ringing farewell cheer, which re-echoed along the stupendous walls of the precipices of the rest. The King expressed the highest satisfaction at his reception throughout. His Majesty embarked to-day at Reykjavik for Edim, where the royal party expect to arrive on Saturday, August 15, or the following day. — Maclean's *Telegraph Agency*, in *Glasgow Herald*, August 15, 1874.

# APPENDIX.

### PART FIFTH; CHAPTER VII: P. 338.

#### POSSIBILITY OF ACQUAINTANCE WITH THE FINNS.

RACE OF LITTLE MEN.—"Sometime about this country are seen these men which are called Finnmen. In the year 1682, one was seen sometime rowing up and down in his little boat at the south end of Eda. Most of the people flocked to see him, and when they adventured to put out a boat with men to see if they could apprehend him, he presently fled away most swiftly. And in the year 1684, another was seen from Westra, and for a while after they got few or no fishes, for they have this remark here, that these Finnmen drive away the fishes from the place to which they come. These Finnmen seem to be some of those people that dwell about the *Fretum Davis* (Davis' Straits), a full account of whom may be seen in the Natural and Moral History of the Antilles, chap. 18. One of their boats sent from Orkney to Edinburgh is to be seen in the Physicians' Hall, with the oar and the dart he makes use of for killing fish."—*Wallace.* Ossian, when in the north, may have seen such men.

### PART FIFTH: CHAPTER VIII: P. 342.

#### BURNING OF THE DEAD.

It is impossible for the reader of to-day, in concluding the perusal of this chapter, not to remember that the process of burial by incremation is now being publicly discussed, with a view to revival, both in Great Britain and on the Continent; that a Company for that purpose has even been advertised in London, and that a prize has been offered at Bremen for the best plans and models of apparatus for conducting the process in a becoming manner. In America, the idea has made still greater progress. According to one programme there, "the subject is to be lowered through an altar, and returned in ashes suitable for the urn, in exactly an hour and a half. The work is to be done by machinery, including hot air blast, no mortal hand touching the remains—total cost, 8 dols." The authorities, also, at Vienna, who have adopted the system, "reckon on making a great saving, as well as a considerable benefit to the public health." &c., &c. But with how entirely different moral sentiments, to say nothing of religious faith, the whole theory is advocated, from those which inspired our heathen forefathers in the burning of their dead, is very manifest. At the commencement of the Christian era, both in Scotland and in Germany, the bodies only of the most gifted and honoured among them were so consumed, that their spirits might enjoy a purer immortality:

"No show in their obsequies;" says Tacitus—"they care only that the bodies of their distinguished men should be burned with special wood. The funeral pile they load with neither garments nor perfumes. His own arms for each, and occasionally his horse, is consigned to the blaze. Turf crowns [or builds up] the sepulchre; but the difficult and laborious honour of monuments, as being oppressive to the dead, they despise. Groans and tears quickly, grief and sorrow slowly, they lay aside. In women it is thought honourable to bewail the dead, in men to remember them."—C. Taciti, *Germaniae,* &c., Cap. xxvii.

For "horse," in the above expressive summary, read "dog"—and the words might almost be attributed to Ossian. Thus was it with our forefathers, both Celtic and Saxon, in the first and second centuries of our common era; but in the latter part, now, of the nineteenth century, when science has begun to supersede both faith and poetry, the proposal is to consume the remains of paupers first, and of those who may follow next, on principles of economy and ventilation.

xxii                    APPENDIX.

## Dynasty of Morven.

FROM THE EAST?

TRENMOR,
By
INIBICA, of Lochlin,

|—————————————————————|
TRATHAL,                        CONAR.
By                              See Ullin.
SULINCORMA,

|—————————————|
COLGAR,         COMHAL,
Slain           By
in              MORNA,
Youth.

FINGAL,

By ROSCRANA, 1st,              By CLATHO, 2nd,

| | | | | |
|---|---|---|---|---|
| OSSIAN, | FERGUS, | FILLAN, | RYNO, | BOSMINA, |
| By | According | Slain | Slain | Princess. |
| EVIRALLIN, | to tradition, | in | in | |
| | Ancestor | Youth. | Youth. | |
| OSCAR, | of | | | |
| Slain in Youth, | Scottish Kings. | | | |
| Betrothed to | Hence Fergus II. | | | |
| MALVINA. | from him. | | | |
| Ossian Survives. | | | | |

# Dynasty of Ullin.

FROM SCOTLAND.

CONAR,
Son of TRENMOR.

CORMAC I.
Called CORMAC MACCONAR.

CAIRBAR,
Called CAIRBAR MACCORMAC.

ROSCRANA,
Wife to Fingal.

By BOSGALA, 1st,

By BELTANNO, 2nd,

ARTHO.

CORMAC II.
Assassinated
by
Cairbar of Atha.

FERADARTHO,
Succeeds Cormac II.

[For particulars in this and the following Table, consult Part Third, Chapter V.]

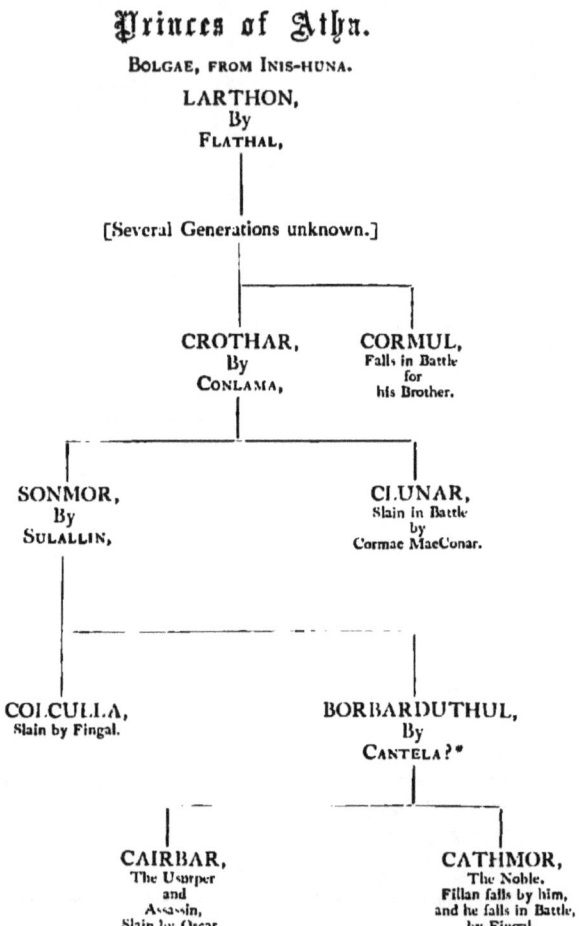

### Princes of Atha.

**BOLGAE, FROM INIS-HUNA.**

LARTHON,
By
FLATHAL,

[Several Generations unknown.]

CROTHAR,     CORMUL,
By           Falls in Battle
CONLAMA,     for
             his Brother.

SONMOR,      CLUNAR,
By           Slain in Battle
SULALLIN,    by
             Cormac MacConar.

COLCULLA,    BORBARDUTHUL,
Slain by Fingal.   By
             CANTELA?*

CAIRBAR,     CATHMOR,
The Usurper  The Noble.
and          Fillan falls by him,
Assassin,    and he falls in Battle,
Slain by Oscar.    by Fingal.

\* It is open to question, whether *Cantela*, which means the Head of the people, was only a title of Borbarduthul or the name of his wife. We incline to the latter opinion.

# Chronicles of Eri:
## BEING
## A SUPPLEMENT TO PART THIRD.

### PRE-HISTORIC IRISH ANNALS—NOT MILESIAN.

The early history of the Irish, according to the Chronicles of Eri, published by The O'Connor in 1822; since then forgotten or treated with contempt as an imposture, but now capable of verification in all substantial respects; may be summarised briefly as follows. The entire work consists of two parts—the first detailing the origin and progress of the people westward till their settlement in Spain, called the Chronicles of Gaelag; the second recounting their emigration thence to Ireland, and their occupation of that country, called the Chronicles of Eri. This second part brings the narrative down to the commencement of the Christian era; and another series from like original documents was promised, to complete the history from that time till the beginning of the nineteenth century; but if it ever appeared, which seems doubtful, the present writer has never had the good fortune to meet with it. The only authentic supplement to this "strange eventful history" known to him, as contra-distinguished from the tales of the Sennachies and the *Annals of the "Four Masters,"* already quoted from and referred to in the text, are the epics of Ossian; which include substantially all that is known, or worth knowing, of the North of Ireland, from the commencement of the Christian era till the end of the third century.

## Chronicles of Gaelag.

1. Origin of mankind traced, by philosophers of Eri, to the action of sun-heat on the soil; hence the worship of Baal or the Sun universal among them, and periods of time computed by them from revolutions of the sun, or his passage through the House of Baal.

2. The GAAL-SCIOT-IBER, of Scythian descent, were settled first under Absal in *Magh-team-ar*—that is, the plain of Shinar in Mesopotamia—between the rivers *Tethgris* and *Affreidgeis*; with kings of their own by popular election, and a priesthood of Baal, chief ministers. Lived in tents, and paid no tribute.

3. Are swept off by an irruption of the EISSOIR, or Assyrians, from the East; who came, under some warlike leader, "like a swarm of locusts or clouds of burning sands, yea even as a torrent of mighty waters that overwhelmeth all things. . . . . And Ardfear, chief of the race, and all the heads of the people who stood in presence of the chief, dwelling round about the tents of Ardfear, escaped from the edge of the sword of EISSOIR. And Ardfear floated on the bosom of Blessed *Affreidgeis*, and the waters bare up his little skiff, till he lighted on the plain of *Ardminn*. And all that went forth from *Magh-team-ar* dwelled in *Ardminn*, and Ardfear ruled that land as aforetime, but in person." This occurred at a date corresponding within a 100 years, or thereby, to that of the Flood; being computed by them as 2246 to 2248 B.C., instead of 2348, according to our chronology.

4. Ardfear dies, and is canonized by the name of NAOI, or Man of the Ship, the chosen of Baal; and is succeeded by his son IAT-FOTH, equivalent to Japheth, 2215 B.C. of their computation; who, in due time, is succeeded by OG his youngest son, at popular election, being a favourite with the people; in whose reign his own eldest brother, IAT-BAN or Javan, the natural heir, and OG-Y-GES—so-called from his first drafting off the population—lead a colony westward, to preserve peace at home.—*Circa*, 2147 B.C.

## APPENDIX

5. To Og, at an interval, succeeds Dorea, who makes his brother Glas regent over *Tu-bhal*, calling it IA-ER—hence Asiatic Iberia of the Romans; in which days another colony goes northwards, passing over the summits of *Gaba-Casan*, or the Smith's path—still the Caucasus; and pitch their tents beyond it, "calling the lands of their dwelling *Iath-Sciot*," or the field of the arrow—which by transposition, *Sciot-Iath*, is now Scythia—"in the memory of our race." 1952 B.C.

6. Tribute begins to be imposed on the children of Iber by their kings, 1935 B.C.; which causes disturbance and revolt, and ultimate emigration. The first demand of this sort was made by Lonrac of Ardmionn, head of the race; to whom the following reply from File, then chief of Iber, was returned by "the mouth of the messengers," and was ever afterwards quoted by the people as a precedent against taxation—

"The men of *Iber* will no tribute pay:
"Should *Lonrac* hither come,
"The way is far, and perhaps—"
"So Lonrac abided in Ardmionn."

7. After a long blank of nearly 400 years in the register, Dalre succeeds to the chieftainship or principality of Iber, now independent, *circa* 1516 B.C., of their own computation; and "in these days the GAAL filled all the lands between *Eis-amhan* [that is, the Euxine—now the Black Sea], and *Ericcann* [that is, the Hyrcanean, or Caspian Sea, of the Romans]; and they excelled all people in the use of the bow. And they extended their borders behind them [that is, westward] and southward; and they became expert in working in the bowels of the earth, and forging of swords, and forming vessels of brass. And they moved on the waters of *Ericcann* with the works of their hands, [that is, they traded in their own ships, with hardware goods, on the Caspian] and their brethren of Ardmionn opened their arms to them, and hindered them not to pass through the land, whither they listed. And the Gaal of Iber increased, and they spread themselves northward over the bosoms of *Ailb-bin* [that is the Highlands] of the region, hence Albania] and dwelt in that land."

8. Cealag, by help of a drunken rabble, "mad with strong drink," and "seduced by him to rise up against the chiefs," having been proclaimed head chieftain or king in Iber, 1494- his brother Calma —'head-pacificator,' so to say, of the crisis, and adored by the people—volunteers to retire and go. He leaves accordingly in 1493 B.C., with 729 men and some women, and is followed next year by his brother Ro'nard, with 81 men and 9 women. They reassemble with acclamations at *Sgadan*, and enter that city, "queen of ships," together—*Sgadan of Aoimagh*, that is Zidon or Sydon, literally herringtown, or great fishing-port, of Hamath by the sea: where they make inquiry for their brethren, former emigrants to the shores of the Mediterranean, and agree to pay for a passage in ships of Zidon to rejoin them. "And whilst the Gaal tarried in Sgadan, NARGAL [the king] took delight in listening to the tales of other times from the lips of Feitam, the words of whose mouth were sweet [from which it would appear that the language of the two peoples was the same]. And fain would he have had him abide in *Sgadan*, that he might be taught to set down his words on tables to endure for ever. But Feitam would not be persuaded; howbeit, he promised to return, if it so pleased Calma, and the way exceeded not the time of one moon." Thus, with "the hand of friendship and kindred" given and received, they take their departure by ship from Zidon, "and are carried towards the strength of Baal [that is, south]; and when they thought to have entered that land [Egypt], lo! the ships moved as the sun was agoing, nor changed their course, till they passed through the flood gates [of Gibraltar] that divide the world of water from the world of land. And the land of *Eis-feine* [that is, of Hispania proper, or southern Spain] was close on their right; after a while, they changed their course, steering towards the fingers of Baal, and on the ninth day afterwards, at mid-day, they entered this land by the streams of the great water thereof" —that is, the *Duor*, by transposition the Duro. Here, after due inquiry, they find their brethren in the neighbourhood, and fraternise; and call the land on which they settle GAELAG, now Gallicia, north of EIS-FEINE-IATH, or Hispania proper, aforesaid; where (that is, in Eis-feine) both the natives and their own brethren were engaged as miners and smelters, and paid tribute to Nargal of Zidon by the output of so much metal yearly, most probably from the very mines wrought or reopened by the Tharsus copper mining company of Glasgow, at the present day. Here Calma dies, and Ro'nard succeeds him, 1477 B.C.; who is followed by his nephew Dull, 1460. This prince, who seems to have reigned for 31 years, dies in 1429, of the plague—some terrible epidemic then raging; from which Enar, a child, hidden in a cave and protected by the burning of sea-weed, escapes alone of the royal house of Calma. A regency in the meantime is appointed, till Enar arrives at age; who succeeds --? as in 1429 B.C., and reigns for 35 years.

9. From this date, a blank with regencies occurs, till EOLUS, the philosopher and lawgiver of his people, appears; who is elected to the throne in room of his father Enar, and in preference to his own elder brother Dalta, 1368 B.C. Before this election, he had visited Zidon, as a student; had penetrated Palestine, acquired the use of letters, engrossed the chronicles of his race from tradition, with dates computed from the revolutions of the sun; and above all, had brought back with him from Palestine the substance of the Moral Law, and certain Jewish traditions, corrupted by the degenerate Israelites of the region—compare Judges ii. and v. 14, for time and place. "It was his wish to go even unto *Magh-Sean-ar*, the abode of our great fathers, but the difficulties were greater than his desire." He resigns, 1359 B.C., in favour of his

# APPENDIX.                                                  xxvii

brother Dalta as regent, and devotes himself to study; establishes schools under Phœnician teachers, or *Olams*, who officiated also as Secretaries or public Historians — as already explained in the text; negotiates treaties of commerce with Zidon on behalf of his people, with resolute protest against payment of tribute, in the old traditional equivocating phrase, and so dies.

It is to the pen of this truly great man, genius at once and lawgiver, as the reader must perceive; who was contemporaneous in his youth with Joshua, and seems to have visited Palestine shortly after that hero's death, that we are indebted for the original of the present strange, and strangely neglected history. "I am that *Eolus*," says he, "the son of *Enar*, the son of *Airt*, of the race of *Calma*, from *Ardfear*, who write down these words for the instruction of those that now be, and of those who are yet to come." And notwithstanding a few obvious discrepancies in dates and details, very easily accounted for in the circumstances; and certain corruptions inseparable from the prejudices of his race—of which, more hereafter; its manifest simplicity and consistency, and its remarkable correspondence in many important particulars of etymology as well as of fact, with all acknowledged history both sacred and profane, should give it a much higher place than has yet been assigned to it, as a subject of study in the annals of the world, to confirm or explain what has hitherto been doubtful or mysterious.

But to resume our Summary again, in detail—

10. Eolus being dead, Don, his son—a great shipbuilder, trader, and speculator—succeeds, 1335 B.C., still of their own era. During his long reign, writing of the Chronicles ill attended to—hence blanks and possible errors in succeeding dates; but covenants for mining in Spain, for sea privilege within certain limits on the Mediterranean, and for commerce generally, after much diplomacy to evade payment of tribute, made and confirmed with Ramah of Zidon. Having lived 93 years, and reigned 67, this venerable and enterprising son of Iber dies, and is succeeded by Lugad, his grandson, —a sage and astronomer; who goes to Edom, attended by certain of his Olams, to study wisdom there, as his distinguished ancestor had done before him; but dies of a pestilence which prevailed in that land at the time—much to the grief of the nation, and possible detriment of science.

11. He is succeeded, first by his brother Ceanmor, 1257; and then by his own youngest son, Cean-ard, 1240, B.C.; whose brother Eochaid revolts, and settles beyond the *Bearnas*, still the Pyrenees, calling the land *Eachaidtan*, hence Aquitania of the Romans. During greater part of this reign, so terrible a famine prevails, that half the people perish; and Mareah, who succeeds 1220 B.C. finds the country desolate. He himself is killed, in 1204, by a fall from his horse, when hunting.

12. During the eight succeeding reigns—from 1204 B.C., to 1066—music, poetry, and romance are exclusively cultivated—which seems to have been the foundation of these arts in Spain. For the study of music alone, many youths were sent to Hamath, in the days of Cuir, 1204 to 1185, "to get knowledge in touching the strings of the harp." By and by, idleness, degeneracy, and disorder succeed; the reading of the Chronicles, and the publication of what science was then known, are not only neglected but obstreperously forbidden; and the priests of Baal regain ascendency. They now elect a high priest of their own, they dictate to the kings, and they trample on the people; till ignorance, despotism and degradation universally prevail. In addition to all which, at the end of the last reign, *circa* 1047 or 1046 B.C., came strangers from the land of Hamath, who told of troubles and afflictions there; with whom also was "a knowledge of sweet melody, music and the dance. Are not Coraheines amongst their brethren? Wonderful to behold are they!" But "deceit and treachery are in the men of Hamath; full of falsehood are the folk of the south country: yet we have not forsaken them now that they are beset with adversities, far from the voice of their kindred." The year next following, Og, then reigning, "ceased — lamented by the priests, and by the priests only."

The reader will find by a comparison of dates and circumstances, that these strangers from Hamath must have been fugitives from the wars of David, which ranged from 1048 to 1040 B.C.—2 Sam. v., and 1 Chron. xiv; and moreover, that the dates of the history now before us correspond at this point precisely with those of Bible chronology, as the Translator himself observes. But the Chronicle has thus lost 100 years by its own computation since the date of the

# APPENDIX

Flood, which the Translator does not observe. Its calculations again deviate as much the other way, in the course of succeeding centuries, still without his perceiving it. All idea, therefore, of an attempt on his part to assimilate such dates for a purpose, or in any other way to interfere with the text, must be abandoned by the most scrupulous objector. How such errors might occur in the original we can easily conjecture, knowing as we do, to some extent, the history of its composition; but the Translator at least, like MacPherson, by such unconscious variations, is self-acquitted of all guilt or blame. But to proceed—

13. At this crisis—1045 B.C.—Ardfear, first of that name since the Flood, having been chosen king, an exciting struggle for supreme administrative power, and the possession of royal favour, takes place between the *Olams* or Teachers, on the one hand, and the *Cruimtears* or Priests, on the other. In the progress of which, the substance of the Moral Law is again strangely quoted, and a story rehearsed to the disadvantage of the Priests, being evidently a corrupt tradition of the life and death of Moses. In the end, the Teachers prevail; and the place, power, and privileges of the Priests are limited and defined by royal edict. Provision is also made by the King for preservation of the public records in his own tent, lest the Priests should destroy them. One special duty of the Priests from this date was to keep watchfires burning on all the headlands of *Gaelag* and *Gran-Iber*—that is, of Gallicia and Cantabria in northern Spain, from the frontiers of modern Portugal along the Bay of Biscay—" to guide the seaman through the darkness of the night. In all, nine times nine priests throughout the land," for such and similar service. Traces of this wise and beneficent institution may still be found along the western coasts of Europe, even up the Frith of Clyde to Largs. On the coast of Spain, as now intimated, they were so numerous that the region was called from them *Breo-eeann*, or the Fire Headlands—corrupted to Brigantia by the Romans. "Now did multitudes from the land of Hamath pour into *Eis-feine*, and ships did pass *Breo-eeann*, and keep their course due on, turning neither to this side, nor to that"—on their way to BREOTAN, distinguished in like manner by similar watchfires, hence called Britain. "And divers of the Gaal do enter into ships of Feine, and do move towards the fingers of Baal, to the strange land, and they have abided therein. And the merchants do bring store of precious things, hidden till now in the caverns of the earth. And when Ardfear had ruled for the course of fourteen rings [that is, till 1031 B.C.], the waters of the mighty sea deluged the extremity of *Breotan*, and tore a passage thro' and thro', leaving many fragments in the midst of the waters separated from the land, and many were they who perished in the depths. Alas!"

We quote this remarkable passage entire, referring so clearly as it does to the separation of the Scilly Isles from the coast of Cornwall, by some earthquake of which there is no other distinct record in the world; but which is nevertheless in perfect accordance with geological fact—compare Lyell's *Geology*, Vol. I., p. 419, and is moreover confirmed by the traditions of the country. The Isles themselves, according to our Translator, are so called from *Scaolead*, pronounced *Scilly*, " separated or torn asunder."

14. In the reign of Bille, prince of *Breo-eeann*, from 1030 to 1025 B.C., the first exploratory voyage to *Breotan*, occupied as yet by Phœnician merchants and miners, is made by Ith his son, to investigate complaints of forced detention in the mines of *Dunmianac* in Cornwall, by the emigrants already referred to there. On which occasion, he is "driven by the winds and waves towards the sun's going, beyond *Breotan*, upon another foreign land," where the men "fled from his presence, as the deer fleeth before the hunter;" the news of which discovery excites the profoundest interest on his return, long looked for. In the end of this reign dies Feilimid, Ard-Olam, "the wisest of all the wise men of *Gaelag*," and Ordac was chosen in his place.

15. Bille succeeded by his son Eocaid, 1025 B.C. Priests, in revenge for their discomfiture, stir up disaffection and civil war between the children of Iber and their brethren—that is, between the north and south; quelled by Eocaid, who is carried home shoulder-high on the shields of the chiefs, with shouts of acclamation. Attempts by Phœnicians of southern Spain to steal the ships of Gaelag frustrated, and war damages for insurrection exacted; also emigrants in Cornwall liberated by negotiation. In the 18th of Eocaid, a tremendous invasion from the south-east under SRU—supposed by Translator to be *Sesostris*—comparable to another Flood. Eocaid, with three of his sons, and a multitude of the people perish resisting it—"what can fire do against water?" This memorable event occurred at *Samur*, now Samora, on the plains of the Duro; and these are certainly the first great Peninsular wars, civil and foreign, on any record. Sru retires

by the Pyrenees, sweeping the country before him; Eocaid's body, and those of his three sons slain in battle, are recovered and interred with profound solemnity; but so great is the gloom occasioned by this catastrophe, that the people for a while neglect to appoint any successor. Eocaid, according to our Translator, is the Go-lam of the bards, and "also the Milesius of Latinity writers of the 15th century, from whom we Irish are ignorantly and absurdly called Milesians."

16. After some discussion, Mataead, eldest surviving son of Eocaid, succeeds him, 1008 B.C., of their own era; in whose reign, to add to the calamities of their condition, a famine by drought follows; the particulars of which, as detailed, correspond so exactly to those of the famine in Elijah's day, that although the dates differ, as already explained, by miscalculation to the extent of a century, there can be no reasonable doubt that the events recorded are the same; and this dreadful visitation was felt in its full severity along the whole coast of the Mediterranean, from Spain to Palestine. "As tho' Sru had not brought enough affliction over the children of Iber, Baal now grew terrible; his wrath was kindled, he sent his fire thro' the land; the earth was scorched, the herbs were consumed, men and cattle perished—nor rain, nor yet dew came on the ground." Compare 1 Kings, xvii. 1 : xviii. 5. Under which visitation, the King, the people, and the priests, precisely as in Ahab's day, are assembled in consternation to consult. The Priests recommend that Baal should "be invoked to cease from his wrath"—on the principle of their brethren in Canaan, as if by natural instinct, "O Baal, hear us!"—a proposal which is treated with contempt alike by princes and people. But nothing can avert the calamity:

the famine increases; depopulation follows; the very beasts of the field are cut off. Emigration to the foreign land beyond Breotan is suggested, as the only means of saving a remnant alive; and preparations are accordingly made under the guidance of Ith, who had accidentally discovered it, for departure to that romantic Isle. The first exploratory voyage is a failure; Ith himself on landing is wounded, is carried to his ship, and dies. The people at home, on the return of the expedition, swear by the sun, moon, and stars, to avenge his death; and prepare for universal emigration — "those who had escaped the captivity of Sru, and the wrath of Baal, taking their departure from *Gael-ag* perhaps for ever, having sojourned here four hundred and four score and four rings [that is, 484 years] precisely":—which, according to their own calculation, should be 1006; whereas according to Scripture chronology, it was probably but 906, B.C. —the concluding year of the great drought in Palestine. In sight of land, they suffered the loss of 12 ships and many people in a dreadful storm from the S.W.; attributed to the anger of Baal, by re-action after the fury of his heat. Among those who perished was Cier, otherwise Daire — he who brought his father's body off from the field of Samur, and was in consequence the idol of the race. His own body was recovered from the waves, and interred under a cairn on a rocky island, still called *Fearmor* or the great man's tomb — at the mouth of Lough Kenmare, on the S.W. corner of Ireland. Another hero, Colba, driven up the channel, was lost at the mouth of the Boyne; which still retained his name, by tradition, at the beginning of this century, as *Imbar Colba*. Distances of separation so great indicate what the hurricane must have been.

It is almost unnecessary to observe that this storm, following so closely as it did upon the drought—being in fact the natural meteoric sequence to it—corresponds exactly to "the sound of abundance of rain," preceded by the "little cloud out of the sea, like a man's hand"—after which "the heaven was black with clouds and wind, and there was a great rain"—in the day of Elijah's triumph. 1 Kings, xviii. 41, &c. The hurricane seems to have travelled up the Mediterranean, dispensing moisture to the burnt-up lands, and finally expending its force in a deluge on Palestine; of which circumstance, forewarned by divine intelligence or by his own actual electrical affinities, the prophet took advantage to confound the worshippers of Baal, and to teach a lesson of reverence to Ahab. This must be obvious, we think, even to the most sceptical reader, and need not be farther insisted on. But it is proper thus to identify the facts, notwithstanding the apparent difference of their dates, and thereby at once to correct and verify the chronicle; for these remarkable coincidences, so indubitable in themselves, are unnoticed by the Translator, much more were they unknown to the writer of the original, and therefore the events recorded could not in any way have been borrowed from Scripture history; nor could Scripture history, which is limited in this case to Palestine, have been borrowed from them. This mutual independence of the records, which agree so plainly about facts, is the strongest confirmation of their respective integrity; and as the very dates, in which alone they differ, may hereafter be reconciled by more accurate chronology, the clearest evidence may thus be obtained of the historical truth of both.

Up to the date of this emigration, the strange and important annals now under consideration are called the Chronicles of Gaelag, although they include much more, as the reader has seen, than what relates to Gallicia; but from the date of emigration onwards they are called the Chronicles of Eri, and refer exclusively to the history of the race in that celebrated Island. Of these however, from the multiplicity of minor details and the prolixity of narration, it will be impossible to give anything more than the most general outline. The style of record, sometimes apparently by an inferior hand, is more diffuse than formerly—although with many characteristic touches, and the events recorded of less consequence in the history of the world; among which, therefore, we must be content to touch only on those which bear directly on the subject of our present inquiry.

## Chronicles of Eri.

1. The emigrants disembark, apparently in Belfast Lough, 1006 B.C. of their own reckoning; find the land in possession of a tribe called Danan armed with clubs, with a crowd of aboriginal serfs called Cloden under them, and a shipwrecked crew of their own kindred. After some skirmishing and negotiation, in which the serfs desert and join them, and their kinsmen officiate as interpreters with the Danan, the Danan agree to retire beyond the old river *Sranamhan* or Shannon, to a region called *Oldanmacht*, and leave the rest of the Island to the new comers. The spot where this treaty is concluded is marked with a large stone—"And Maread said 'Let this place be called *Magmartiomnas;*' and all said 'yea!'" and the place so called, it is said, may be identified by the same name, till this hour.

2. The land is then surveyed, and discovered to be an *Eirland*, or Island; and by its new possessors is called En-i—that is, the Island of Er—hence Erin. The portion acquired by treaty, that is, all to the east of the Shannon, is then subdivided into three parts according to their principal tribes,—corresponding precisely to the modern divisions of Ulster, Leinster, and Munster—with a chief to rule over each, Iaen for Munster, Iolar for Leinster, and En, a boy, son of Cier, under tutorage, for Ulster; with some subordinate principalities—the title of *Erimion*, corrupted by degrees to Herimon, being the highest regal distinction as yet among the race.

3. For this supreme, often nominal rank, fierce contentions ensue between the central kingdom and the south, with consequent confusion and obscurity there for upwards of 300 years. The north, on the other hand, under Er and his successors, men of wisdom and peace, enjoys much prosperity, the law and records being carefully observed, and frequently read to the people. Er dies 931 B.C. and is solemnly interred, the region being called ULLAD, or the Burying Place—afterwards Ullin, now Ulster—in memory of his sepulture.

4. About the same date, a search for metals in the south is proposed by the Phoenicians, with an offer of 5 per cent. produce and all expenses paid, but declined; image worship introduced, and pillars set up to the sun, moon, and stars, by the king at the instigation of the priests, who wish to found an oracle in the name of Baal, whose exclusive representatives they claim to be. Many of the people are disgusted; the king repents and sides with the people, and is found dead in his tent; the priests are accused of his murder, and the high priest is slain by the mob.

5. A king of Ullad, Sobairce, for first time made Erimion, and first castle in Erin—on the rock at Carrick-Fergus—built by him, hence called Dun-Sobairce. Another by his twin brother Ciermna, as regent in the south, is built near Cork or Limerick, called in honour of him Dun-Ciermna—the population everywhere else, both princes and people, dwell in tents. "Ways are now making through the land—the Gael increase—cattle abound—the *Olam* are heard—knowledge is in respect. . . . . Ullad is as the infant reposing on the breast of the mother." These excellent rulers die within a few days of each other—Ciermna for grief at the loss of Sobairce—and are entombed under cairns on the shore, 854 B.C., of native reckoning.

6. Three schools, or *Mur-Olam*, for the study of the law and the writing of the records, established at Drumerit, Drummor, and Dun-Sobairce, in Ullad, by Eolus, second of that name; also nine raths or booths for the entertainment of travellers—790.

# APPENDIX. xxxi

This prince, one of the wisest of his race since Eolus his great progenitor, dies 768 B.C., universally lamented.

7. Although roads, as above stated, had been made, no bridges as yet existed. Rivers are still crossed on stepping-stones at fords, or on rafts and rude ferry-boats in deeper water; and it is worthy of note in passing, that armies on march to battle wash in fording the rivers—" the warriors moved towards the south, and when we came to the waters of *Buidaman* we washed ourselves therein," already referred to, p. 252 of the text. Such modes of transit were obviously dangerous; and in 796 Mumo of the southern kingdom, was drowned in crossing the Suire, "being flung from his horse in passing over *on the hurdles* on the water." That kingdom, now Munster, was called MUMAIN in honour of him, a fact to be noted hereafter in connection with the cave of Moma, in text of Ossian. In 726, Seadna of Ullad was also drowned, but from a different cause, having attempted an exploratory voyage on Belfast Lough without sufficient skill in navigation. Small craft, however, are built, and used on the lakes; but ships for emigration are strictly prohibited: no man shall quit the Island. In the meantime Eunda, son and successor to Mumo, attempts mining operations in the south-west, and "passeth all his days in searching into the bowels of the earth, in the mountains at the extremity of *Eri*, that look over the world of waters"—that is, between Bantry Bay and the river Kenmare, where "abundance of ore of divers kinds" may still be found. This is the earliest effort of the sort on record in the annals of Ireland.

8. In 699 B.C., still of their own reckoning, a great political revolution is inaugurated by Eocaid of Ullad, for the union of the kingdoms, with a code of common laws and a new supreme Head, called ARDRI—to be elected by suffrage of the Assembly for life. Eocaid himself is first chosen to that high dignity, and is crowned, with asion and mantle, on *Lia-fail*, or stone of destiny—about which, is some very apocryphal legend—introduced as an old-world story, but not authenticated, in the Chronicles. Place of Election, hence called the TOHRAOH, or *Tarah*, is in centre of Erin; Hall of Assembly adjacent, built of timber, is called *Teacmor* or *Tighmor*, the great house; to which another hall or college for the Olams, called *Mur-Olamain*, with provision for the teachers and pupils, is added. Triennial, afterwards quadrennial Assemblies, and a representative House agreed upon; revision of laws takes place, and several of the Ten Commandments, with some discussion about their origin—natural or divine? are selected to remain; trial by jury, and punishment by exact retribution, with burial alive for murder, ordained. The Danan are finally admitted to seats in this Assembly, and much harmony for a while prevails; with periodical festivities in excess—of eating, drinking, dancing, and singing—to propitiate all parties, which seems to be the chief business transacted.

9. Eocaid dies 663, having been successively King of Ullad, Ardri of Erin, and Olam Fodla or chief of the philosophers in his reign; but by some agreement on oath in honour of him, his successors on the throne of Ullad continue also to be elected Ardris for nearly a hundred years thereafter, when it passes to Siorna, an aged prince of the south; by whose immediate successor, Roiteactac, carpentry, metallurgy in iron and brass, and weaving "of stuff from the weeds of the earth" are patronised and improved, and a new sort of car for three horses abreast invented. He dies from a wound in his left eye by a spark of hot iron from a forge he was inspecting, in 551. The cars invented by him are introduced in Ullad about 20 years afterwards; and at the same time, hydraulics are first applied by his son and successor Airt, who "caused water to flow, where before his time it was not; he maketh courses for the waters and confineth them, raising them, wonderful to behold. His tents he encompasseth with piles of earth; and what though they do stand above the waters as they flowed afore, he doth lead the waters to his very *rath*. This I Allo say, for I did see the thing in *Mumain*." This gifted royal mechanic dies 529 B.C.

During the long period of 474 years now elapsed since their settlement on the Island, the people of the north, under the teaching of the Olams and by their account, have been models of intelligence, sobriety, and forbearance; in which estimate of their own influence by the Olams there is perhaps some exaggeration from self-complacency. The levity, dissipation, insincerity, and superstition of the south, where the priest and the dancing-master are alternately supreme, are reported by the same authorities to be incurable; in which also there may be some exaggeration, from malevolence. It is obvious indeed, from the facts now quoted on record, that the princes of the south were men of great scientific genius and enterprise; and that the north fully availed itself of their mechanical contributions to the common good. The men of the north, on the other hand, excelled by far in the cultivation of letters and philosophy—were, in fact, the only scholars of their age in western Europe; they were distinguished also as agriculturists, for the rearing of cattle, sheep and goats, and for the breeding of horses and dogs; which were confessedly the finest in the Island, and of which many splendid specimens were from time to time presented to chiefs of the south, to keep them in reasonable humour, without any corresponding gifts we read of being received in return. The natural dispositions of the two kindred tribes, in short, were essentially different; and it must be admitted with sorrow that the south from the first had a tendency to superstition not yet eradicated, a genius for conspiracy not yet extinct, and a proneness to revenge for imaginary wrongs still prevalent. The scene of these conspiracies seems to have been most frequently in the wilds of Mumain, and the crown of Erin, as usual, was the object of such mischievous ambition. The redeeming feature of all, both north and south, in this brief retrospect of centuries, is the unbounded hospitality which everywhere prevails, associated with the love of poetry and the cultivation of music, especially on the harp; on which the highest proficiency is attained, by the bards and minstrels of the whole Island.

Before resuming our epitome, it may be interesting for geologists to learn that in 507 B.C. an avalanche of rock, which removed the entire shoulder of a mountain in Ulster called Ronard, accompanied with tremendous rain, occurred during the night and spread itself in ruin over the plain, destroying three tents with their inhabitants in its progress. The falling mass was so separated in its descent, that no portion of it remained together large enough to deserve a name. The note of this phenomenon was made at the special request of Fioun, son of Cairbre, in whose reign it had occurred without being recorded at the time, and it stands as a postscript to the annals of that reign; but if this hill, wanting its shoulder, could now be identified, or fragments of the ruin traced, it would be much in the way of evidence to prove other things of more importance in the history of the world.

10. In 511 B.C., a company of youths in a small ship from Britain, in search of a lost sister, driven into Belfast-Lough, are hospitably entertained by Cairbre, and sent home with supplies for the voyage. These were kindred from Breocean in Gaelag, whose people had emigrated long before as miners to Cornwall, and thence escaped to the coast of Lancashire. In 503, that being the fourth year of Fioun II., an embassy from Lancashire, encouraged by their report, arrives at Dun-Nobairce for help against the Britons. The chiefs of this embassy with swords slung upon their backs, and shields; their attendants, spears and axes. Fioun is prohibited from leaving the Island, but dismisses them with friendly assurances and good advices. According to their report, the Gael of Breocean had spread inwards from the coast in scattered companies, along the Irwell and the Mersey, into Yorkshire, Durham, and neighbouring counties; "where we recognise them," says the Translator, "as the 'Brigantes' of the Romans."

11. Supreme power has again returned to the north, but war with the south is apprehended. Mumain and Laigean colleague, and frightful outrages follow. Ullad and Oldanmact combine against them, and the crown at last reverts to Ullad on the head of Fioun III., the Long-handed.

During this unsettled period, however, it is worthy of note (1.) that silver was found in the south by Eunda of Mumain; and that an enormous deer, probably some elk, was shot by him with a single arrow—471 B.C.—still borne as an achievement on the arms of the MacArthys. (2.) That Lugad, his successor, was lost in a snow-storm "the like unto which had not been seen aforetime, by the eye of one that lived: and the passages were stopped up, and Lugad perished; and many perished with the king in the mountains of Iber."

12. The title of Ardri again reverts to the south in the person of Lugad's brother, Eocaid of Mumain, who circumnavigates the Island. Peace begins to be restored in 402; and sovereignty returns to the north, 380. Some disgraceful pandering of the High Priest, by means of his daughter, to obtain favour of the King, is here recorded. Now insurrection arises in the south; and the Ardri is slain in a dreadful battle on the banks of the Shannon. The throne is usurped by Duac of Laigean, and wrested from him by his confederate, Lugad II., of Mumain, 340 B.C.: whose own title again is dis-

# APPENDIX. xxxiii

allowed by Ullad and Oldanmact. He invades Ullad with a great force, but is defeated and slain at Dundalk. The array of battle on this memorable occasion may be quoted as a specimen of military order and equipment at the time. "And the host of Ullad moved as Seadna taught; those who fought on their feet were not mixed with those who fought on horses; nor did the slingers mix with the archers, nor were those who used the sword with either." Ullad lost only 4 killed, and 23 wounded, who were carried home "on the cars of war." This decisive action was fought 336 B.C., of Irish reckoning; and Aod of Ullad, the conqueror, was chosen Ardri.

13. Aod, in the meantime, had married Maca, daughter of Magn of Oldanmact. He died, by accident, slipping his foot on the ferry-boat at Redwater when assisting his queen to disembark, and was buried under a mound near what is now called Ardmagh, 324. He left a daughter by this queen, called also Maca, who remained with her mother there. Magn, father of the queen, died shortly after, on a visit to them, and was buried in a "bed" between four upright stones, near his son-in-law.

Maca herself is afterwards interred between them. Ciombaot, second in succession from Aod, marries Maca the younger—a princess not less gifted than ambitious: who builds a new palace, second only to Teacmor, for her husband, at this consecrated spot, and calls it in honour of her father, grandfather, and mother, *A bina nimasa*—hence, according to these records, (although a much simpler derivation for the word might be found Ardmagh.

The government, with all the archives of Ullad, is now transferred thither—the queen herself presiding in a splendid bonnet and robe. Her husband then opens a local parliament for Ullad here; but soon after dies, and is buried beside the rest. No male claimant appearing for the national crown at Tarah, Maca his widow ascends that throne, inscribes her own name on the roll of kings, and is crowned and robed—the first female sovereign of Ireland. She survives only a year and a month and a day, and dies lamented; but the new palace and parliament at Ardmagh are ultimate causes of jealousy to Laigean: and thus Ullad bids fair to become a separate kingdom—for which all due provision, in the meantime, is being steadily made.

To chronicle the atrocities of murder among brethren, which followed in the south—not unmixed with the romance of retribution in certain cases—would be out of place for us here. It is more to our present purpose to remark that certain strangers had arrived from the north or north-east on the coast of Ullad, men of gigantic stature and terrible aspect—"round their necks was tied the thong of their swords, and in their right hands they bore a long spear." When first seen, "they stood nigh unto their ships, which floated on the waters;" they spoke a language similar to, but not the same as that of Eri; the chiefs, nine or ten in number, had a numerous retinue of warlike followers, but "there was neither aged man, nor lad amongst them, nor one woman; no provision had they left; and they did call themselves men of Feotar, and Cruithen is their chief." Being hospitably received, they dwell as guests for a year in the north-east of Ullad; they are afterwards introduced to the national assembly at Tarah; are permitted, with some stipulations about inheritance in favour of sons by Irish mothers, to choose wives from among the daughters of the chiefs of Erin; and are then allowed to return, with a covenant of friendship, to their own land—called Cruithen; to which they sail apparently by the North Channel or by the Frith of Clyde. These friendly relations are reciprocated by and by, and wives are afterwards taken by the nobles of Erin from among the women of Cruithen—which, if these records can be relied on, is the earliest connection traceable between the people of Ireland and the native Caledonians of Ayrshire or Argyllshire, and the first instance in which the inhabitants of Erin were permitted to leave the Island. It seems also to have been the first step to a final settlement by the Crutheni in Ireland; who are placed by Tighernac and others, in later ages, partly in Ulster and partly in Galway. But jealousy, as usual, and bloodshed, originate in this connection; and the men of Cruithen, like the Scotch Guards long ago, and the Swiss Guards in France, became objects of aversion to the people—as the next head of our epitome will show.

3 D

14. In 223 B.C., "The portion of Iolar is called *Laigean*," now Leinster, "because of the spears of the Gael of Feotar"—a troop of guards from this very land of Cruithen, brought in by a certain banished prince to recover and maintain his right; who, though partly kindred, as being the sons of Irish mothers, are, with becoming fury, exterminated as "mongrels!" "Now the people of Leinster, and the parts of Mumain contiguous, call a spade *Luige*, pronounced *loyse*"—hence Loynster or Leinster; for the spears of the Feotar resembled a certain kind of spades.

15. In 205, Tarah and Teacmor, which had been deserted, are again resorted to as the seat of government; and Ardri, which had been superseded, is restored as title of the monarch. The Kings of Ullad, however, decline to interfere, and preserve a dignified neutrality. "Is it not good," said Daire, "to preserve one-half of Eri in peace? There is no soul," said he, "in Mumain, neither is there heart or soul in Laigean."

16. From 74 to 67, however, sovereignty returns to Ullad in the person of Ruidruide Mor, that is Roger the Great, or Rory More; "and great was the joy on Tarah, for that a prince of the race of Er sat on the throne of Eri." To provide against mischief, however, he wisely makes a closer league with Oldanmact, and admits that province by representatives to a vote in his own parliament at Ardmagh. It may be somewhat amusing, and by no means inappropriate in present circumstances, to reproduce His Majesty's reflections on this important crisis—"Two hundred and one score and eighteen rings," says he—that is 238 years—"have been completed since Aodmagnmaca hath been built up by Ciombaot and Maca: from the day that she did cease, the sons of Er have not dwelled on Tarah, leaving Mumain and Laigean as Home Rulers! to move to and fro, as passion swayed; howbeit the hawk differeth not more widely from the owl, than the children of *Iber* and *Iolar*. The sons of Iber that is, of Mumain] are vain, without thought, they delight in music and the dance, wisdom hath no charms for them; yet are they brave and generous, and full of wit. The sons of Iolar that is, Laigean] are dark, full of deceit; they think for that Iolar ruled Erinson, Eri should be theirs for ever. In Laigean, the priest is above the king, in Mumain, the bard and minstrels, yea, the dancing-master leads, whither all do follow. . . . Had not Oldanmact stood firm with Ullad, long since would Eri have been under tribute to the good liking of the sons of Iolar; . . . therefore let Ullad and Oldanmact look to themselves betimes. What if the chief and eight of the nobles of the Danan should sit amongst the princes and nobles of Ullad even here, and hold talk, and hold up their hands? and it was so." In addition to which political precaution for approaching disunion, a military school, for the regular training of the youth to arms, is established at Ardmagh; and a body-guard of the younger nobles, called the *Clanna Ruidruide*, in honour of the king, who play a prominent part in the subsequent wars, is organised. During the remainder of the century, the usual disorders prevail in the south—by the selfishness and ambition of Laigean and Mumain; who cease not to destroy one another, and to drench their own half of the Island in blood. What is chiefly worth remarking is, that Ullad assumes more and more the character of an independent kingdom, the capital being still at Ardmagh; and that it was only when the kings of Ullad were forced to interfere, that any interval of peace or prosperity was enjoyed by the people. The most distinguished of these practical dictators after Ruidruide was Factna, his grandson, who chastised the south with tremendous slaughter, and reigned, unmolested thereafter, in all about 23 years. He died accidentally of a chill or fever, 7 B.C., caught by him from having fallen into the sea, when hurrying ashore in Belfast Lough to extinguish some fire among the tents of the people at Carrick-Fergus, but supposed to have been connected with the schools of the Olams there.

At which date, according to their own computation, the Chronicles conclude. According to ours, it should be 93 A.D.; and no reliable record, known to the present writer, exists of events in the north of Ireland, till the epic narratives of Ossian appear. According to Clerk, Vol. I., p. xlii—"The Annals of Tighernac, first published in 1825, agree entirely with Ossian;" and from what we have seen of these, as incidentally cited in our own text—p. 168, it is not impossible they might throw some useful light on this very interval; but the most scrupulous care must be exercised, in correcting and collating their details. In the meantime, however, it is evident from the text of Ossian himself, not only that the south had so far recovered as to carry war into Ullin, but that the Danish or Norwegian sea-kings from Lochlin had invaded that part of the Island.

## APPENDIX.

I. In the foregoing picture, the observant reader can hardly fail to remark that the moral characteristics of the Irish people to this hour, both north and south, are as faithfully reflected as any national features could be in the glass of human history; which is strong proof of its authenticity. But he must be requested yet further to observe, in connection with our present object, that we have already, by imperceptible accumulation, obtained an array of names, facts, and institutions associated with the soil of Ireland, in corroboration of the text of Ossian, as convincing almost as the deposition of living witnesses.

1. As to NAMES—To those already quoted, for example, the names of Usgar, a prince from the west beyond Armagh, and of Toascar, a chief on the coast of Antrim—which, although not introduced in our epitome, occur near the close of the Chronicles—have first to be added, and then we may proceed to remark, 1. that Oldan-mact, by an easy corruption, would become Alnec-macht, or Alnecma, which represents in Ossian's day all beyond Lough-Neagh and the Shannon; '2.' that Erin itself, a name restricted to the remaining three-fourths of the Island, was still further restricted, at his era, to the central and southern divisions; '3.' that Ullad, after practical separation from the south, as we have seen, and still farther separation in itself, becomes the Ullin of his epics—no larger then than Antrim, with a Temora of its own; not *Tea-mer*, as MacPherson fancies, the Assembly Hall of Ireland, but only *Tigh-ruar-ri*, or King's house of the Scottish dynasty in Ullin. '4.' In like manner, Mumain, from Mumo, gives us "the horrid cave of Moma," where conspiracies were being continually hatched among the native princes of Erin against the government of Conar in the north, as they always had been against his predecessors; and the Mur-Olam or Mur-Ollamain, and latterly the military school established in Ullad, are unquestionably identical with those more than once referred to by Ossian as the Halls of Muri or seats of learning in Ullin, where the youth were trained to arms as well as to letters, and innocently translated Muri's hall, by MacPherson, as if they had been the school or schools of one Muri, a teacher. Thus far with respect to the names of localities; but with respect to the names of individuals, we may proceed farther to observe, 5. that Fioun, more than once occurring as a royal personal appearative in the Chronicles, was a name which might well be confounded by the bards of latter times with that of Ossian's father · Usgar again, from the west, reappears in Oscar, the name of Ossian's son by Evirallin, who was a princess from the borders of Connaught; and one Toascar, as we know, is expressly represented in *Conlath and Cuthona* as a chieftain from the coast above Larne. To these, other names—such as Connor, Cairbre, Congal—which occur frequently in his text as the names of Irish heroes extant in his own day, might also be added, as common in the Chronicles of Eri hundreds of years before Ossian was born, but it seems unnecessary.

2. Of FACTS and INSTITUTIONS, we may specify, 1. The knowledge of the metals, and the fabrication of arms—such as swords, spears, shields, &c., of metallic substances, besides bows, arrows, and slings—the slings originally on a short staff called *Cran-Tubsil*, from the seat of their manufacture in Asia Minor, but latterly in the shape of thongs · the cultivation of arts such as carpentry, masonry, mining, shipbuilding of a sort, the fabrication of chariots, smithwork,

and weaving with embroidery, many centuries before the Christian era: so that the use of such arms or implements, and the knowledge of such arts in the days of Ossian should be nothing incredible; yet so ignorant of all this was MacPherson that in quoting the old Irish Bards and Sennachies, and receiving his information exclusively from them, he represents Cuthullin as famous for teaching horsemanship to the Irish, and as "the first who used a chariot in that kingdom" —although the text of Ossian himself almost expressly contradicts such an absurd assertion. When he farther asserts, however, in the same note—*Fingal*, B. II., that Cuthullin was the first who introduced a complete suit of mail into Ireland, there may be some foundation for the statement, for no allusion to panoply occurs in the Chronicles; and it should also be observed that, whereas "shells" are generally mentioned as the drinking vessels among the Scotch at their feasts in the days of Ossian, "horns" are specified in the Chronicles as being everywhere used for the same purpose by the Irish. (2.) The knowledge of letters—that is, of reading and writing—among a certain class in the north; the love of music, skill on the harp, and the cultivation of poetry everywhere, all which corresponds with the testimony of Ossian, as an eye-witness, except as regards the knowledge of letters, on which he is silent. (3.) The great veneration entertained for Minstrels, Bards, and Heralds, who were almost supreme in the estimation of the people, both in Ossian's day and before it; and a corresponding contempt for the priests—that is of Baal, otherwise called Druids—who were not only despised but hated in the north, although in the south their supremacy was maintained. (4.) The elective choice of a king—in the order of succession if possible, but still freely—and government by regencies during the minority of heirs; both principles being capable of the clearest illustration from the text of Ossian—most notably in the case of Cuthullin, who came from Skye to be regent for his relative in Ullin, young Cormac MacArtho, assassinated at Temora. (5.) The prohibition of ships for emigration—a circumstance in strict conformity with the text of Ossian, in which no act of emigration is ever ascribed to the Irish, although many allies or invaders are represented as settling on their shores—the one to plunder, as the Norwegians did; and the other to help the inhabitants, as the Scotch from Morven did. The Irish by nature, and according to these Chronicles of theirs, have always been an emigrant people, wherever tribute was imposed or when starvation occurred—first from the Caspian Sea by Palestine and Spain to Great Britain and Ireland, and thence in more recent times, for the same reasons, publicly assigned, to America. But their fancy for Erin, from the first, was strong; and it is on record in these very Chronicles, that every ship was destroyed to prevent their leaving it. In these circumstances, and on such a fertile soil, it is remarkable that the population was confessedly limited—a fact known to MacPherson from the testimony of Agricola, who says that a single legion was sufficient to overrun the Island, and which MacPherson considers a sufficient argument against their alleged high antiquity. But the fact itself is admitted in the history before us, which claims for them, notwithstanding, the very highest antiquity—the cause of such limitation in their numbers being probably their own internecine wars, and their persistent habit of squatting on the naked soil in tents and hovels. After an interval of comparative increase,

APPENDIX.   xxxvii

the population has again been decimated as before; but how clearly this is to be attributed to their invincible hereditary habits, and to their peculiar mode of life, requiries neither proof nor illustration. (6.) It remains only farther to be noticed, that their funeral obsequies, with the exception of burning, correspond almost exactly to those described in Ossian, as under cairns and mounds, or with stones to mark the silent " bed".—and then to remind the reader, that notwithstanding the numerous and striking coincidences which have now been pointed out between these Chronicles of Eri and the text of Ossian, they must have been absolutely unknown to MacPherson, in as much as the very Chronicles in which they occur had not been given to the world in any form for twenty-five years at least after his death.

II. But we come now, in pursuance of these remarkable revelations, to consider how far the authority itself from which they are derived may be reliable, beyond its evident correspondence to the above extent with the text of Ossian. The correspondence thus established is so far, indeed, a presumption in favour of the record, but the very antiquity alleged for so singular a work among a savage people is a strong argument against it; and we would not be justified in accepting its details, however plausible they may appear, to so remote a period as the Exodus or the Flood, without additional evidence to maintain them. In point of fact, however, there are many considerations, bearing directly both upon its origin and its reliability, which are worthy of serious attention, and which may go far with dispassionate readers to confirm its details, in all important particulars, as a trustworthy historical production, devoted exclusively to the traditions of a people of whom no other trace so remote is to be found in the annals of the world beside.

I. As to its ORIGIN then, in the first place, we remark, (1.) that the book, as it now stands, purports to be a literal translation; and is manifestly such, being characterised throughout by Celtic idioms, so ill adapted as to disfigure their English equivalents everywhere—no more, in this respect, to be compared to MacPherson's work than the composition of a school-boy. (2.) The original, of which a specimen in fac-simile is given, purports to have been the work of various hands, accumulating as the generations succeeded, and copied from generation to generation in the schools of the Olams and Ard-Olams, as the original parchments required. Of this statement, the numerous accidental blanks, the various styles of composition which are often quite dissimilar, and the sort of incidents selected by the different chroniclers for commemoration, are the clearest natural proofs. The earliest written bears to have been made by Eolus, by whom the use of letters, as we have seen, was introduced among the people, about the time of Joshua; before which, the history was traditional, and might therefore be subject to greater inaccuracies. This original document, of course, the Translator does not even pretend to have seen; but only the last official copy of it, made as above explained, on the same principle of conscientious transcript by which other similar documents are preserved. That some of the MSS. kept in the colleges of the Olams, however, or in the archives of the kings, were extremely old, is possible; and the recent reported discovery of a priestly record at Schechem, as old as the commencement of the Christian era, shows that such extreme antiquity is not incredible. These documents, or these last copies of them, fell by right of inheritance to Roger O'Connor, of the O'Connors of Bandon, representative of the Irish monarchy; by whom they were translated, and with whom or whose heirs, after many alleged attempts to destroy them, they remained so late as 1822—O'Connor himself having refused the offer of an Earldom to renounce his claims and surrender them. (3.) In connection with which, it seems proper, under a separate head, to state that these Chronicles are in no way to be confounded with the Annals of Ireland compiled from the Chronicles of Clon-Macnoise and other questionable documents, otherwise called the " Annals of the Four Masters," originally translated by Charles O'Connor of Belanagare, and more recently by the accomplished Dr. O'Donovan; in which, however, many fabulous and miraculous events, or incredible traditions, are mixed up with more reasonable history, thereby discrediting the whole. Neither is the translator, Roger O'Connor, to be confounded with the said Charles O'Connor, who lived long before him, and " who understood the Irish language well, though he always improved on his original, and raised it to the level of his own ' magniloquent style' of English;" or with the Rev. Dr. O'Connor his son, whose Annals are full of " serious errors and defects," " arising partly from the cause just alluded to [contractions in the MS.], but chiefly from ignorance of Irish topography and geography"—thus doubly damaging the already doubtful truth. See O'Donovan's preface to his *Annals*, 1851. (4.) That the style of this original, as manifest in the translation, is equally unpretentious, often weak, and always prosaic; a mere patchwork chronicle, in fact, and no more to be compared with the poems of Ossian, than the Book of Ezra the Scribe is to be compared with the Psalms of David. (5.) That it refers exclusively to the growth of an obscure people—a mere nomad tribe, and to regions of the earth occupied by them in the course of their migrations, absolutely unknown or at least unnoticed by any historian of the time, sacred or profane, beyond their own. Unless its contents, therefore, contradict themselves, they cannot be contradicted by the testimony of any other annals; although they might sometimes be unconsciously confirmed by them, as the reader shall immediately see—a consideration which brings us directly to the question of its RELIABILITY.

2. Whatever the precise origin of the work may have been, its contents fortunately are of such a nature, in many cases, as to admit of independent proof, of which we have already had some incidental illustrations. Thus, for example, the account of the Deluge, as an invasion of barbarians from the East, corresponds with the interpretation of that event long ago given in public by the present writer; and what is of more importance, with the record of the Nineveh tablet as explained by itself in detail—with neither of which, by human possibility, could either the Author or the Translator of these Chronicles have had any acquaintance. Again, as already pointed out, the flight of distressed Phœnicians from Palestine to Spain corresponds so exactly in time and circumstance with the desertion of that country by fugitives from war in the days of David, that no doubt of its reality can be entertained; but on the contrary, many additional interesting particulars—both as to the character, the occupation,

and the resort of the fugitives—in confirmation of the event as recorded in Scripture, are actually made available to complete that history. In singular confirmation of which, and whilst these very words are being written, the following statement appears in the newspapers of the day—October 18, 1873:—

EXTRAORDINARY, IF TRUE—A journal of Bogota, New Granada, the *America*, announces a discovery so strange that confirmation is required before giving credence to it. Don Joaquim de Costa is reported to have found, on one of his estates, a monumental stone, erected by a small colony of Phœnicians from Sidonia, in the year 9 or 10 of the reign of Hiram, contemporary of Solomon, about ten centuries before the Christian era. The block has an inscription of eight lines, written in fine characters, but without separation of words or punctuation. The translation is said to be that those men of the land of Canaan embarked from the port of Aziongaber (Boy-Akubal), and having sailed for twelve months from the country of Egypt (Africa), carried away by currents, had landed at Guayaquil, in Peru. The stone is said to bear the names of the voyagers.—*Galignani*.

By an accurate translation of this curious epigraph, in the Glossary appended, the reader will be able to judge more satisfactorily of its contents than from this newspaper summary, which in some particulars is certainly erroneous.

Whether the fact of the discovery itself, thus alleged, be genuine, we cannot of course affirm; but on the supposition that such a monument has really been found—which there is no reason to doubt—then the circumstances said to be connected with it, and the correctness of its inscription as retranslated, may be easily explained and verified, as the reader will see from the text of the documents we are now investigating, and of which the inhabitants of Guayaquil in Peru could certainly have no knowledge. In like manner, as we have also seen, the famine by drought in Elijah's day, and the atmospheric phenomena which followed, are not only established as facts; but the extent of that extraordinary visitation is illustrated along the whole southern coast of Europe, and the attitude both of priests and people in regard to it, as exemplified in the scenes at Carmel, is corroborated by the unconscious testimony of the chronicler—who knows of nothing else connected with it but the desolation in Spain, and the hurricane that followed from the south-west through the Irish Channel. And lastly, the finding of the Ten Commandments in a corrupt or mutilated form by Eolus, in his visit for educational and scientific purposes to the land of Palestine, about 50 or 100 years after the giving of the Law on Sinai, is a coincidence far too decisive to be explained on any theory of invention, and far too important to be dismissed without the fullest investigation. The Translator himself indeed, although he does not see the force of the fact, comments on it under this very impression—" Should any one fancy," says he, " from their similitude to the Laws of the Hebrews, called the Ten Commandments, that these are of modern date, the compilation of some Christian priests, let the fancy vanish on the recollection of the fact that the *Hebrews* were *Scythians* as well as the *Iberians*, and that the ten laws of the Hebrews and the nine laws of Eri are but the recognition of the original institutions, always in practice, though only at some certain time solemnly acceded to by the people."—Vol. II., p. 239. The simplicity of this explanation, founded on the supposed identity of origin between the Iberians and the Hebrews, to account for the similarity of their moral laws, when according to his own translation, the said moral law was either not known or not acknowledged, until imported by Eolus from Palestine about 100 years after its publication at Sinai, may reasonably provoke a smile; it is at least original and ingenious, and may be acceptable to philologists of the present era. But the circumstances of the discovery itself, known to us only through his own translation, and so palpably significant, seem entirely to have escaped his observation; and this oversight alone, in such an argument, affords the most convincing proof of his honesty.

The facts, as detailed in the Chronicle, are these—(1.) Eolus went to Palestine to acquire the art of writing, and other scientific knowledge; in pursuit of which, he penetrated the country inland from Tyre and Zidon to the southeast—that is, by the borders of Zebulun and Naphtali. But the art of writing was specially known and practised by the tribe of Zebulun, as we learn from Judges, v. 14, at the very time and place assigned for this visit of Eolus in the Chronicles of Eri—a circumstance of which the Translator is utterly oblivious. (2.) Eolus himself believed these inhabitants of Canaan to be of a kindred people with his own, which also corresponds with the account in Judges, chapter iii.; where the mixture of the Israelites with the people of the land is specified and complained of—a coincidence of which the Translator is equally unconscious. (3.) The Law, as there obtained and thence brought home by Eolus, was supposed by him to be corrupt in the four first Commandments—that is, in all that relates to God; which had manifestly been vitiated by the priests of Baal, in support of their own idolatrous superstition still lingering in Canaan, as is everywhere obvious in the Biblical records of the time—more especially in the Book of Judges, chapters i. ii. iii. (4.) The 7th Commandment is also awanting in the Second Table, an omission which seems to have implied a community of wives, and for which there is some foundation in the earlier part of the Chronicles; but which no impostor in the 18th, or any other Christian century, would have dared to make, to the reproach of his own people and the scandal of society. (5.) The Decalogue, so reduced and corrupted, has been supplemented to the number of nine Commandments, according to the number of the priests of Baal, by the addition of moral precepts founded on the 10th, and similar to the teaching of Christ in the Sermon on the Mount, in those portions which seem to be quoted from Leviticus, or were known in the shape of proverbial sayings in the very same region time immemorial before his birth, and which He himself ascribes to "them of old time." Compare Lev., xix. 18; and Tobit, i. 12. (6.) The invention or publication of the 1st, 2nd, 3rd, and 4th Commandments, relating to the worship of God, is by and by hinted at, as the work of an ambitious priest to soothe the conscience of a "bloody-handed" despot, who had slain his own father and two of his brethren, and was distracted with remorse in consequence. Being persuaded by this priest "that he should never cease, but be taken, yet all alive, into the very jaws of raging *Baal*," he agreed to sanction the commands in question to the honour of Baal, that he might escape this vengeance, and thus they were added—the whole being "called the nine laws to the nine priests from the beginning, to which *Eolus*, the wise and good, would not assent"—and so, by his authority as a legislator, they were first suspected or suppressed at the introduction of the law, as we have seen, and then finally struck out. Further, these very commands are said

# APPENDIX.

to have been received by the priest above-mentioned from Baal himself, with whom he spoke "face to face, in a cave within the bosom of vast *Gaba-casa*"; and the "bloody-handed" despot, personal name unknown, by whom they were sanctioned, is represented to have been one and the chief of three rulers by whom the people were overawed and governed in the land of Philè—that is, of Philistia, "in the olden time;" the whole story being obviously a corrupt tradition of the early life and subsequent legislation of Moses, Aaron, and Joshua, and of the judicial or at least mysterious death of Moses on the mount, circulated by the priests of Baal and by the apostate Israelites of Canaan, to account for the obliteration of the First Table of the Law in their hands, and for the neglect or contempt of the authority of Moses, in which they had begun to indulge—expressly detailed, and commented on with indignation, in the Book of Judges. Such mysteries of corruption as these unfolded among an apostate people, unconsciously related by the Author, and innocently reproduced by the Translator, are in fact like a new commentary on the sacred record; and throw a flood of light, hitherto unimagined, not only on the Ten Commandments, in what they have survived; but on the condition of the people to whom they were first committed as by "the ministration of angels," and on the craft and policy of a godless priesthood by whom those people were enslaved, and the very fountains of religion and morality among them were poisoned. No wonder that a cry from Deborah arose, and from Barak son of Abinoam, "to the help of the Lord, to the help of the Lord against the mighty;" that "they fought from heaven" itself against such wickedness; that "the stars in their courses fought against Sisera"—of all which manifest coincidences, we again repeat, the Translator is not only innocent but ignorant; which no impostor, having fabricated such a story, could by possibility have been.

Having thus explained the tradition of the Decalogue, corrupted and defective, by the people of Canaan to the hands of Eolus, and its introduction by him as the foundation of moral law among his own people, 1367-4, B.C., it may be instructive to present it now to the reader precisely as it appears in the Chronicle—

But I, *Eolus*, have not set down the words said by the priests to have been delivered to the nine priests by *Baal* from the beginning, because my understanding cannot give entertainment thereunto; my senses admit not the belief that *Baal* hath at any time held talk with one of the children of this earth.

Afore priests were, have we not heard of the words, spoken by the fathers to their children, as they listened to their voice, beneath the covering of the tents, each of his dwelling, ere the congregations were gathered together, round the habitations of the priests.

Then did each father declare unto those descended from his loins—

Give praise and thanks to *Baal*, the author of light and life.

Shed not the blood of thy fellow, without just cause.

Take not aught belonging unto another secretly.

Keep falsehood from thy lips—falsehood perverts justice.

Keep envy from thy heart—envy corrodes the spirit.

Keep flattery from thy tongue—flattery blinds the judgment.

Pay respect to thy father, conform thyself unto his will, be thou a sure prop to his old age.

Love, honour, and cherish thy mother; let thy hand wait on her eye, thy foot move in obedience to her voice, &c.

In this traditional paraphrase the reader cannot fail to discern at once the 1st Commandment with express adaptation to the worship of Baal, as the fountain of light and life; the 5th, 6th, 8th, and 9th Commandments with reasons annexed, and the 10th with subdivision; to which are added certain moral precepts on brotherly love and unity, kindness and charity to widows, orphans, poor, needy, distressed, and strangers; with a patriotic exhortation to preserve the glory of the race—to die, or live free; which our present object, however, does not require us to quote farther than by the selection of two conjoint prominent precepts—

| | |
|---|---|
| Be merciful to every living creature. Be watchful to keep thy passions in obedience to thy reason in the first place, thereby wilt thou | avoid doing unto another what thou wouldst not have another do unto thee. &c., &c. |

which looks like a traditional quotation of Leviticus, xix. 18—Thou shalt not avenge nor bear any grudge against the children of thy people; but thou shalt love thy neighbour as thyself. *I am* the LORD: explained and enforced by Christ himself, as we have said—Matt., vii. 12—Therefore all things whatsoever ye would that men should do to you, do ye even so to them; for this is the law and the prophets:—with which the reader who has an Apocrypha may compare the express words in Tobit, iv. 14, 15—Be circumspect, my son, in all things thou doest, and be wise in all thy conversation: do that to no man which thou hatest.

In this form, and with such excellent paraphrastic commentary, the general law continued to be rehearsed or read by the Olams from generation to generation among the Sons of Iber for a space of 660 years or thereby, as often as the priests would permit or the people themselves would listen. During the whole of this period, however, there must have been a regular tradition along with it that God himself, that is, Baal, was the author of all the commandments; for, as we have already explained, when the nation came to be consolidated in Ireland, under a federal government at Tarah, and when laws were to be unanimously agreed upon for the regulation of society, these identical commands were again reproduced, the personal or miraculous authorship of Baal in regard to them publicly disallowed, and the names of the very priests to whom he was said to have spoken recapitulated. Five of them were then selected, paraphrased, and engrossed on the statute book as follows:—

WHAT if *Five* of the Laws of the Olden Time only be retained to stand on the roll at the head of the Laws of Eri—not deceitfully as commands from *Baal*, according to the words of the priests, but openly as laws of the land, by consent of all the children thereof?—

BAAL spake not to *Astor*: It is the voice of Reason that crieth aloud, *Let not man slay his fellow*.

BAAL spake not to *Lamas*: It is Justice that directeth, *Let not man take of the belongings of another privately*.

BAAL held not converse with *Soth*: It is the Spirit of Truth that sayeth, *Let not the lips utter what the mind knoweth to be false*.

## APPENDIX. xliii

> BAAL opened not his mouth to *Al:* It is the gentle voice of Tender Pity that whispereth, *Man, be merciful.*
>
> BAAL talked not with *Scar:* It is the tongue of Wisdom that teacheth, *Let man do even as he would be done by.*
>
> What if these five laws stand laws of Eri? And all said, "Yea!"

In which paraphrase, however, and process of ratiocination on the question of their origin, the reader cannot fail to perceive that both the direct form and the divine authority of the old Commandments have been affected for the worse. When thus modified and made the basis of what may be called parliamentary enactment, they cease, in fact, to be commands altogether, as from a higher power, whether God or Baal; and sink at once, in the very act of publication, to the level of mere statutory provisions. "The thunderings, and the lightnings, and the noise of the trumpet, and the mountain smoking," and above all, "the voice of words," have ceased; and what was once the echo of a divine injunction, or the vocal embodiment of an eternal principle as immutable as the foundations of the universe, has dwindled away to a vote in the House, or to the finding of a Social Science Congress at Birmingham or Tarah. It is most observable also, that in this selection the 5th Commandment is deliberately omitted, and the 7th Commandment is not restored—facts which did not augur well for the perpetuity or prosperity of the people.

All this, we must now observe, took place, according to their computation, about 703 B.C.; and at the latest, not later than 600 B.C., of our own. But in reviewing thus, at our leisure, what has been certain matter of fact so many centuries ago in the history of a nation so intimately associated with ourselves, and of a law we all profess to reverence, it is impossible not to remark the similarity of treatment to which that very law is being now subjected by what is called the higher criticism, and the would-be philosophic theology of the present day. As represented by various authorities of distinguished repute—by Bishop Colenso, for example, and his disciples, by way of eminence—this Moral Law or Decalogue, or system of the Ten Words, on which our morality now rests, is but a felicitous accumulation and arrangement of abstract principles; never really spoken or inspired by God, never actually published by Moses, never written on any tables of stone either by electricity or otherwise on the Mount, never enjoined by solemn edict on the people; but surreptitiously got together by pious fraud, after the fashion of the priests, in the name of Moses; cunningly engrossed by Jeremiah in a book, and hidden by him in a place where that book could be easily found again by friends who knew where to seek for it, in the days of Josiah, and so produced before the king as a providential discovery of what really never before existed—is, in fact, a forgery in the name of God and of Moses by a priest at Jerusalem, 629 B.C. of our chronology. But Jeremiah himself, at the date in question, could not be more than twenty years of age, and certainly could not be both at Jerusalem and at Tarah with his forgery at the same time. How then, it may be asked, will Bishop Colenso, with facts so incontrovertible before him, reconcile these dates or explain this coincidence? According to the Chronicles of Eri, this abstract of the Decalogue, as philosophically reasoned on as even the Bishop could wish, was reduced to an Act of Parliament in Ireland more than fifty years before Jeremiah was born; and at the very latest, not later than when he was still perpetrating his so-called forgeries at Jerusalem. According to the same authority, a much better copy, although still imperfect and corrupt, of the same Decalogue, expressly and invariably ascribed to the authorship of Baal himself, one half of it with the public sanction of a man corresponding in many respects to Moses, was in the actual possession of the same people, brought from Palestine by their own king 718 years before Jeremiah saw the light, and not less than 320 before Jerusalem itself was founded. Surely Bishop Colenso, so distinguished for his arithmetical precision in dealing with antiquated records like the Pentateuch, and even with later works like the Prophecies of Jeremiah, must have been ignorant of facts like these, when he ventured on speculations so derogatory to the rank and character of a patriotic Jew, and so subversive of all faith in national history, sacred and profane, yet so easily refuted by the testimony of a heathen chronicle in the name of Baal as reliable as that of his own existence.

3. By a remarkable concurrence of tradition, we are farther reminded at this point, of what has already been stated in the text—pp. 157, 158—that a ship's crew of emigrants from Palestine effected a settlement on the west coast of Scotland and the north coast of Ireland about 728 B.C.; also that, after Jerusalem was destroyed by Nebuchadrezzar, a second ship's crew, with Jacob's pillar and other sacred reliques, under the reputed guidance of Jeremiah, touch land at Carrick-Fergus, are recognised by their brethren of the Dannan there, and supply the coronation stone for a king—570 B.C. If any faith could be reposed in this romantic Legend, or if it was possible that Jeremiah, as an exile, brought the Decalogue as well as Jacob's pillar with him to Ireland, his publication of it there would still have been, according to one reckoning 133 years, and according to another at least 30 years, too late; besides the more important fact that the Decalogue in his hands would have been perfect, whereas the edition adopted at Tarah, and long before in the possession of the people, was deficient in more than five commandments. It is proper to observe, however, that no support whatever is afforded to this curious story by the Chronicles of Eri. According to them, the first landing of emigrants from Spain was effected in Carrick-Fergus bay 1006 B.C.; where they find a people indeed already in possession, called the Danan, who ultimately cede the soil, and retire beyond the Shannon. The fact, therefore, of these Dannan or Danan being there may perhaps be accepted; but the great disparity of dates between Legend and Chronicle almost prevents the possibility of reconciling them—unless the Dannan referred to in the Legend were in fact the Sons of Eri themselves, spoken of by mistake under that name; in which case, there would be no real contradiction. The Legend would then be a supplement to the Chronicle, both would be in harmony with Ossian, and the Lia-fail and spear of Temora might be reliques from Palestine after all. As for the other Lia-fail at Tarah, described as "a mighty

stone, white as snow, round as the head of man, smooth as the arrow for the warrior's bow, borne in a chest drawn by many beasts"—the workmanship and gift of Baal, "to show unto the chief e'en what he ought to be"—&c., no reliance whatever can be placed on the story connected with it—see 8. p. xxxi; and it is worth remarking that none of the kings of Ullad when called to be Ardris, except the first, "would ever sit on [that] Lia-fail, or be present when a king of Mumain or Laigean was inaugurated thereon"—either as if they had some Lia-fail of their own in the north to be preferred, or as if they suspected the validity of the whole proceeding.

4. In another department of evidence, we have the only authentic record extant of the formation of the Scilly Isles, by an earthquake and an irruption of the sea, by which a portion of the original Land's End of Cornwall was separated from the main. This occurred, by their own computation, about 1031 B.C.; that is, about the middle of King Hiram's reign, when the strong currents then prevailing in the Atlantic are said to have carried the Phœnician voyagers to Peru; and long enough certainly before the Roman invasion, to allow the Scilly Isles themselves to be again frequented by the miners of Cornwall in quest of tin, and thus to receive from the Romans, who knew nothing of their formation, the semi-commercial designation of Cassiterides. The event as narrated in the Chronicles, however, is in strict conformity, as we have already stated, both with geological fact and with the remotest traditions of the country. Sir Charles Lyell, who knew nothing of these Chronicles any more than the Romans did, but founded his remarks apparently on the Transactions of the Royal Geological Society of Cornwall, and whose own words we may now quote at length, says

—"The oldest historians mention a celebrated tradition in Cornwall, of the submersion of the Lionnesse, a country which formerly stretched from the Land's End to the Scilly Islands. The tract, if it existed, must have been thirty miles in length, and perhaps ten in breadth. The land now remaining on either side is from two hundred to three hundred feet high; the intervening sea about three hundred feet deep. Although there is no evidence for this romantic tale, it probably originated in some catastrophe occasioned by former inroads of the Atlantic upon this exposed coast."—Lyell's *Geology*, Vol. I., p. 419.

Had Sir Charles consulted the records now before us, which he seems never to have seen, he could have had very little doubt, we think, about the truth of the "romantic tale"—how "the waters of the mighty sea deluged the extremity of *Breotan*, and tore a passage thro' and thro', leaving many fragments in the midst of the waters separated from the land; and many were they who perished in the depths, alas!"—"three hundred feet deep," according to the geologist's own estimate. Had he even been sufficiently acquainted with the language of the original inhabitants, still preserved in local designations by the people, he would not only have been able to accept the tradition, but to understand more clearly how the phenomenon of submergence occurred: for we must now farther observe in the way of evidence, that all the most remarkable and hitherto unintelligible names on that coast are not only most easily, and beyond doubt satisfactorily explained, by the etymologies given in these Chronicles; but, being so explained, convey an account of its physical formation and even of its history nowhere else to be obtained in the annals of the country. Thus, for example, the Lizard Point, to the south, and the Lionnesse, (?) submerged, to the west, in this very neighbourhood, and now under discussion, but hitherto incomprehensible as names, may be interpreted with precision and intelligence. The Lizard, which is but *Lios-ard*, or the lofty stone-fort, was probably a beacon and certainly a landmark for Phœnician sailors on their passage from Spain across the Bay of Biscay—being on the headland of the Cornwall coast nearest Spain, and far enough west to clear the Eddystone Rock, on which the most important pharos in the whole circuit of Great Britain now stands. The Lionnesse, on the other hand, which is but a corruption of *Il-inis-e*—it is a large island, must have been either the central portion of a great irregular peninsula, which sunk entire when the connecting links of rock were severed; or it must have been one of the Scilly Islands themselves, tacked on to the mainland, and ready to be disjoined by the opening of the first chasm, or by the first irruption of the sea. All this, so plainly implied by the mere combination of syllables, rightly pronounced and understood, has been a mystery hitherto to men of science who understood them not; and like a dream of the impenetrable past to the very people themselves, who had corrupted and mispronounced them.

On the same principle throughout, there is scarcely one old local designation along the whole coast of the Mediterranean, and far beyond it—from the Caspian Sea to the Straits of Gibraltar, and from thence along the shores of the Peninsula to the Land's End of Cornwall, including Cornwall itself and all its mines—that is not capable of being explained by the language, and identified with the passage or temporary residence, of these very people, or their fellow-countrymen of Phœnicia. Examples of this, in so far as our present inquiries are concerned, will be found in the Glossary annexed; by which it will be seen that terms hitherto imagined to be Greek or Latin exclusively, and misinterpreted on that supposition, are in reality but Phœnician terms adhering to the soil before either Greek or Roman, properly so called, touched it. But as part of this proof, and supplementing the whole of it, although in no way connected with the Chronicles of Eri as such, we cannot withhold the following express quotation as being almost conclusive in itself—

"In this quarter of the river," says our Translator, referring to the Iber, now called the Ebro, on the south-east coast of Spain, where that river falls into the sea—"Cæsar makes mention of a tribe which he calls Illurgavonenses"—Cæsar himself not understanding the meaning of such term; but which, according to our Translator, is equivalent to, and compounded of the six following descriptive syllables—"Eil-earr-ce-bun-aun-seis, 'the tribe at the other extremity of the land, at the bottom of the river,' in contradistinction to the Bardal-e, at the northern extremity thereof; a name," he continues, "that points out to me as distinctly as an essay on the subject, the seat of this tribe, and must convince the most incredulous man that ever lived, that the language whereby such an assemblage of monosyllables can be at this day accurately and literally explained, must be identic with the language of the people by whom the name had been originally imposed."—*Chron. Eri*, Vol. I., p. ccxlix.

# APPENDIX.   xlvii

Fully to appreciate this evidence the reader must remember, (1.) that the syllables *ce* and *bun* sound *ga* and *von*; (2.) that the exact position of the tribe in question had been fixed in all the oldest classic atlases of Spain precisely as above described, on the south side of the Ebro at its mouth, long before the Chronicles of Eri were known or translated; and (3.) that Cæsar must have met with these people, and probably recorded their strange designation, about 61 B.C. —of which no rational account was ever vouchsafed till the above interpretation appeared in said Chronicles, 1822 A.D., being 1883 years since the day when a Roman general first heard it.

In conclusion, with respect to the people historically, we have only farther to remark that, in strict accordance with the text of these Chronicles, they have been time immemorial Ibers, or Iberians—that is, both in Hebrew and Phœnician, miners, tramps, and squatters; time immemorial, till the present day, they resist the payment of all tax and tribute; time immemorial, they have fought and do fight, in their natural condition, with sticks or shillelaghs; and time immemorial they have sworn, and do swear, by the sun, moon, and stars—that is, unconsciously by Baal with all his host, or the "Blessed Light of Heaven!"

## Glossary to Chronicles of Eri.

ASIA MINOR, IN GEOGRAPHICAL ORDER.

Affreidg-eis—floods of impetuous risings; softened by Greeks to Euphrates.

Teth-gris—sparks of heat; so called from flashes of light on its waters; contracted Tigris.

Iat-da-cal, pron. Id-da-cal—country of the two enclosures; that is, Mesopotamia, between the two above rivers; hence Hiddekel.

Magh-ean-atar, pron. Ma-Senar—the plain of the old men, or fathers; hence Shinar.

Ard-mionn—hill of the solemn oath; since Latinised Armenia; conveys a tradition of God's covenant with Noah after the Flood.

Eis-scir—multitudes or floods from the east; variously called Asshur, and Assyrian.

Eis-amhan, pron. Eis-aun—sea of rivers; corrupted by Greeks to Euxine, with a fanciful derivation —friendly to strangers, because it was *un*friendly!

Eri-caen—headquarters of Eri: hence Hyrcanian Sea; on which they traded—now the Caspian. The word Caen, Cean, Can, Ken, or Khan, occurs in various combinations. The Khan of Tartary, for example, is the Head or Chief of that region: and Og-Eis-caen—the head of the multitude of Og, identical with Ogus-Khan, the celebrated hereditary chieftain of that name.

Gabha-casan, pron. Gow-casan—the Smith's path, made by smelting iron-stone rock in the range, between those two seas: now the Caucasus.

Sagiot, pron. variously, Scict, Scolt, Scyte, Scuit, and Scot—an arrow: hence to shoot: the people who excelled in the use of the bow, and who dwelt beyond the Caucasus.

Sciot-Iath—the land of the Sciot or arrow; the territory inhabited by said people: Greek and Latin Scythia.

Ib-er—land of Er, or land of heroes: name given by the children of Er, a branch of the Sciots, to the land of Tubal; afterwards adopted elsewhere, and Latinised Iberia—hence also Hibernia.

Aoi-magh, pron. Hamah—the land of the plains: Hebrew Hamath.

Sgadan, pron. Zydon—herring-town, of Hamah: the oldest town of Canaan, hence called the Son of Canaan—Can-aan itself being the head of the river. The founder of Zydon, or Zidon, was certainly some great fisherman.

Iard-amhan, pron. Iardaun—the western river, of which Can-aan was the head; western in relation to the Euphrates, and called by us, in our translation from the Hebrews, Jordan.\*

Feiné-ce, pron. Feini-ke—the land of husbandmen; Greek and Latin, Phoiniké and Phœnicia: the whole land of Tyre and Zidon between Jordan and the sea. It was celebrated also for its purple dye—hence called Phoinix. The country, in fact, gave its name to the dye; not the dye to the country. Our classic etymologies in this, as in many other instances, seem really to require some reasonable fundamental revision.

---

\* Jordan-hill, near Glasgow, is an unconscious corruption and reduplication of *Iar-dun*, the western hill—that is, the last distinguishable elevation westward on the northern shore of the Frith of Clyde.

## APPENDIX

### SPAIN TO BRITAIN, IN NAME ORDER.

**Eis-feiné-iath**—land of the tribe of husbandmen, from Feiné: Latinised Hispania, now Spain.

**Globur-ailt-ard**, pron. Gibraltar—the rugged, high, fire-cliff; on which beacons were lighted between the Mediterranean and Atlantic.

**Duor**, pron. Duro—the boundary water; that is, between Hispania proper and Gallicia.

**Gaelag**, now Gallicia—the possession allocated to the Gael of Iber in Spain.

**Ceann-Ib-eir**—the headquarters of Iber; Latinised Cantabria: the region of Spain where the Ebro rises, and where also were the tents of the Iberian chiefs, and the Mount where the congregation assembled, called Ib-er, or the place of Iber.

**Ib-er-uisg**, pron. Iberus—the river which rises at the place of Iber: now the Ebro.

**Bearnas**—the clefts or gaps; now the Pyrenees, remarkable for their narrow defiles: hence also Bearn, and the Bearnese Alps.

**Eochaid-tan**—land of Eochaid, the chief who led a colony beyond the Pyrenees: now Aquitania.

**Sam-ur**—the sun and fire; where was a fire-mount sacred to Baal: a town on the plains of the Duro.

**Bort-I-gael**, pron. Portugal—the haven of the Gael, upon their first landing on the Peninsula.

**Breo-ceann**—the fire-heads, looking across the sea to Britain: Latinised Brigantia.

**BREO-TAN**—the land of flaming fires—partly coast fires, partly furnaces: now BRITAIN.

**Carna-gael**—the cairns or altars of the Gael: now Cornwall. This word has been strangely derived from *Cornu-Walliae*, the Horn of Wales—a combination of Latin and old British; but the region had the name of Carna-Gael, or Carn-vall, 500 years before the Romans were heard of.

**Dun-mia-nae**—the hill of mines; the name originally given to Cornwall and Devon, by the Phœnician miners.

**Scaolead**, pron. Scilly—separated, or torn asunder; Islands so called. Scylla, Sicily, and even Ceylon, which must have been known to the Phœnicians, have probably the same root; and certainly the Skelligs, or Craig-Skellies, on the west coast of Scotland and Ireland—small rocks torn from the shore, have been so called for that reason.

**Casan-tir-eider**—a path between the lands, "torn thro' and thro'." by the sea: corrupted by the Latins to Cassiterides, and applied by them to the Scilly Isles, from which they obtained tin. Compare Gabha-casan, were the same root occurs.

**Lios-ard**, pron. Lizard—the high stone fort: still a well-known landmark on the coast of Cornwall.

**Il-inis-e**: it is a large island;—corrupted, Lionesse: one of the Scilly group. "From Camden," says our Translator, "you must suppose that the place had its name from its being drowned in the sea; but his better informed commentator, Gibson, notes 'There is an island lies before the promontory, which gave occasion to the name.'" In this obscurity, we adhere to the text of the Chronicles.

### IRELAND—PRINCIPAL NAMES.

**Uisg-land**, pron. Eisland—a sea-land, or island: name applied to any large tract surrounded by water. Thus also Eis-land or Iceland.

**Er-i**—the Island of Er: hence ERIN, erroneously derived from Iar-in, the western Island.

**Ullad**—the [royal] burial place: now Ulster.

**Mumain**—respect for Mumo, in allusion to the heap raised over him; now Munster: but neither Ulster nor Munster, as mere words, have any proper meaning in English.

**Laigean**, pron. Loygean—the region of the Spade, now Leinster; so called from Laige or Loy-e, a spade-shaped spear: formerly Gaelen.

**Oldanmact**, equivalent to Connaught: the region beyond the Shannon, to which the Danan were restricted, by special agreement.

**Sean-amhan**—the old river; the Shannon.

**Band' amhan**—the white river; contracted Bandon.

**Buid-amhan**—the yellow river; contracted Boyne.

**TOBRAD**—the hill of election; contracted TARAH or TARA, near the town of Trim, in Co. Meath.

" And they said aloud—
' From this day forth, for evermore,
What if this mount be called
The Hill of TOBRAD?'
and all did say ' Yea.'"
*Chron.* vol. II. 92.

**TEAC-MOHR**—the great house, or Palace; built on Tobrad: but confounded, by MacPherson and others, with the Temora at Connor.

In addition to the above, the reader should now, perhaps, be informed that Father Abbé Pezron, in his curious work *Antiquité Des Gaulois*, Paris, 1703—gives substantially, but not exactly, the same derivation of Portugal; and adds—" Lisbon, in fact, means nothing else than the Habitation of the Lusiens [a mixed tribe of Celtic-Ibers—compare 8. p. xxvi.], and its true name anciently was *Lusibona*; whence was formed *Ulyssibona*, as if it had been the residence of Ulysses in his travels; which is but a fiction of the Greeks, who have filled the whole world with their fables." p. 382. Farther, we have—

**Corabeines**—celebrated musical brotherhood; performers of the war dance to the sound of their own shields: emigrants originally from Palestine, and identical with the Corybantes of Horace—

Non Liber æque, non acuta
Sic geminant Corybantes æra,
Tristes ut iræ:
*Car.* l. xvi.—*Palinodia.*

Not Bacchus, nor the Corybantes so,
Tho' they should clash, with blow on blow,
Their piercing brass, [can work us woe,]
Like savage anger.

" And the warriors danced to the sound of their shields, and the whole host shouted and cried aloud
' *Baal* prosper all the works of the King!'"
*Chron.* II. 358.

## APPENDIX.

Pezron, again, gives a similar account of these performers; but confounds them with the Curetes, who according to our Translator were an entirely different class of men—a sort of gladiators. "These were nothing else," says the Abbé, "than the Druids and Bards so celebrated among the Gauls. . . . . They leaped also and danced so gracefully with their arms, striking their bucklers with their javelins, that it was from this very action, if I may venture so to say, they were called *Curetes*: for it should be noted, that *Curo* of the Celtic tongue is the same as *Kruo* of the Greeks—which has been formed from it by the transposition of one letter— . . . . and signifies to beat, or to clash, one on another." Pp. 106-107.

We mention these facts chiefly to show that Pezron's work and the Chronicles of Eri, published at a distance of 120 years from each other, having so far the same object in view—that is, the origin of the Celtic races from the remotest antiquity in Asia Minor, and agreeing in many important details, are nevertheless entirely independent works, and could not have been borrowed, or in any way adapted, the one from the other.

We have only farther to add that the above Glossary founded upon, and in many particulars taken *verbatim* from the Chronicles, might have been extended to a much greater length, and made to include a philological survey of the countries on both sides of the Mediterranean, and the whole west coast of Europe, from Cape Finisterre to beyond the Bay of Biscay. What has been given, however, may suffice to show, by etymological evidence, not only the track of the emigrants from Asia Minor to the shores of Ireland, but their common origin, along with Greeks and Romans, from a remoter root in the East; and it may suggest also, although we do not now insist upon that, the propriety of discreetly revising our most popular current theories on the origin and development of the classic tongues of Europe.

## The Phœnician Inscription.

[SUPPLEMENTARY TO TEXT AND QUOTATION, P. XXXIX.]

For the benefit of readers who may not be aware, it is proper to state that certain Moabitish Inscriptions, recently discovered, have been subjected to the gravest doubt as fabrications: and in almost all similar inscriptions, whether genuine or not, the writing requires to be first deciphered and then subdivided into words, before it can be translated. In this double process, very much, of course, will depend on the common-sense, experience, and sagacity of the decipherer; for by a wrong subdivision of words, the most contradictory results may be occasioned. In the case before us, without pronouncing in the meantime for or against the authenticity of the document, we shall indicate two readings of the text with their respective translations, and shall then subjoin our own. The first is by Dr. Enting of Strasburg, in No. 110 of the *Academy*, June 13, 1874; who gives a reading and translation on Portuguese authority, but pronounces the whole to be a "clumsy forgery." The second is by Professor Prag of Liverpool, in No. 119 of the *Academy*, August 15, 1874; which differs materially from Dr. Euting's, but implies some emendations or alterations of the text, which seem to us both unwarrantable and unnecessary. These translations, it may farther be observed, are given not according to the sentences or paragraphs, but according

## APPENDIX.

to the mere lines—each corresponding, presumably, to the breadth of the stone on which the inscription was lettered.

| DR. EUTING'S. | PROFESSOR PRAG'S. |
|---|---|
| 1. Canaanites, Sidonians, who set out from the royal city to trade, have erected this stone | 1. We, the sons of Canaan from Zidon, the Royal City; may her commerce |
| 2. without me (?) on this distant, hilly, and unfruitful shore, chosen by the gods (and) | 2. . . . . flourish supporting the high and exalted land chosen by (or for) the supreme (Gods) |
| 3. goddesses in the nineteenth year of Hiram our mighty King. | 3. and supreme (Goddesses). In the nineteenth year of the destruction of our mighty King (or King Abar) |
| 4. And they set out from Ezion-geber in the Reed (*sic*) Sea, and embarked their people in ten ships, | 4. we set out from Accho and conquered in the sea a mariner journeying with ten ships. |
| 5. and were together on the sea two years (coasting) round Africa (Ham); then were they separated | 5. We were together in the sea two years, surrounding a warm and remote land. |
| 6. from their captains, and parted from their companions; and there put in here twice ten (or twelve) | 6. Mighty waters entered the fleet . . . . . our company. We came hither twelve |
| 7. men and three women, on this unknown coast, which I, the servant of the mighty Astarte—(Metuashoret *sic!*) | 7. men and three women into this new (-ly discovered) island, which I mightily enriched (cultivated) |
| 8. took possession of. May the gods and goddesses pity me! | 8. and apportioned. The supreme (Gods) and supreme (Goddesses) be gracious unto us. |

On the above we have only to remark, that Dr. Euting seems to be correct in reading Hiram as a proper name, and that what follows about Ezion-geber, the *Reed* Sea! and Astarte, as he himself admits, is certainly a blunder. Professor Prag, again, seems to be correct about the convoy of ships in the Mediterranean, but wrong about the departure from Accho; for which, according to his own admission, there is no foundation in the text. Adhering to the original, as Professor Prag has reproduced it, but rejecting all emendations or alterations as unnecessary, we translate for ourselves as follows, introducing a few words here and there [in brackets] to explain the sense, and arranging the whole in a continuous paragraph, as it should be.

### INSCRIPTION.

We, sons of Canaan, from Zidon: May commercial enterprise from the Royal City, despatched to the land of rivers [or river-ward], prosper, as a support to the land of lofty ridges [like Lebanon and Carmel] the chosen seat of superintending [gods] and superintending [goddesses.] In the nineteenth year of Hiram our mighty king, we set out from under his sceptre [renounced allegiance,] and overhauled a merchantman at sea getting along with ten ships. After which, we were at sea together two years, coasting round a land of heat [or the land of Ham—that is, of Africa;] and then we separated. Mighty floods of water carried [or lifted up] our company on ship-board [thence,] and we came hither, twelve men in all and three women, to a new island; which I have mightily enriched, and have subdivided. May the superintending [gods] and superintending [goddesses] be propitious to us.

In farther elucidation of which, we have to explain (1.) that the word translated *Hiram* means also *Destruction*—as we say William the Conqueror, and Edward the Hammer, among ourselves. (2.) The word translated *land of rivers*, or

# APPENDIX.

*river-ward* by us, is declared by Professor Prag to be "quite unintelligible." It seems to be only another name for Spain, which was divided into regular provinces by three or four of the largest rivers then known to the Phœnicians, and was by far their most important colony at the date in question. (3.) That no name is given by the inscription, either to the "new island" where the voyagers came ashore, or to any of the voyagers themselves. According to one account the tablet was found in Guayaquil in Peru, where there is an island at the mouth of the river; according to another, it was at Parahyba in Brazil—precise position unknown, which is possibly a reporter's mistake; as is also the "9th or 10th of Hiram," in *Galignani*, which should be the 19th.

In these circumstances, it would be improper to assert the authenticity of the original too confidently, or to found any argument of importance on its truth. As to our translation however, having duly considered all that has been advanced both by Dr. Euting and by Professor Prag in support of their own respectively, we adhere without doubt or difficulty to what we have now given, as the nearest approximation in common English to the necessarily abrupt original in vulgar Phœnician—the work of a piratical peasant, who could not be expected to write, much less to engrave upon stone, with grammatical precision.

Looking carefully now at this curious record as above translated, and with all sorts of presumption against it, we cannot fail to observe (1.) that there is really nothing on the surface, either to suggest or to justify the charge of imposition. Nothing was to be gained by the fabrication of it; the style is indifferent, even to rudeness and vulgarity; and if, as Dr. Euting maintains, it be a "clumsy forgery," then whatever dishonest object was in view has been entirely defeated by the possibility of reading the text on three different principles, and translating it in three different ways. (2.) That, as translated by ourselves without difficulty or prejudice, it presents a wonderful coincidence of dates and facts, both with the Chronicles of Eri and with the Book of Psalms. Some tremendous volcanic surge with a hurricane from the east, strong enough to shake the mountains and to dash fleets to pieces in the Mediterranean, is expressly mentioned in the 46th and 48th Psalms, as a thing that had been both "heard of and seen," at a certain date in Palestine, thus—

God is our refuge and strength, a very present help in trouble. Therefore will not we fear, though the earth be removed, and though the mountains be carried into the midst of the sea: though the waters thereof roar and be troubled; though the mountains shake with the swelling thereof. Ps. xlvi. 1-3.

Immediately after which, it is said—

God is known in her palaces [the palaces of Zion] for a refuge. For, lo, the kings were assembled, they passed by together. . . . Thou breakest the ships of Tarshish with an east wind. As we have heard, so have we seen in the city of the LORD of hosts, in the city of our God. God will establish it [safe from the shocks of earthquakes and the assaults of kings] for ever. Selah! Ps. xlviii. 3-8.

At what date the Psalms now quoted were written, we do not exactly know, but it must have been several years at least after Zion was fortified, and even embellished, by David, as a royal residence. The 48th was written probably after the war with Ammon—that is, about 1030 B.C., the passage of the kings round Zion, before that, being included in the period. If this assumption be correct, the date of the 46th would be a little earlier. This would be about 17 or 18 years after David was crowned at Hebron, and 9 or 10 after he was established at Zion. But according to the Chronicles of Eri, the surge in the Atlantic, which deluged the extremity of Britain, and separated the Scilly Isles from Cornwall, occurred in 1031 B.C., which corresponds exactly—13. p. xxviii. Again, according to the Phœnician Epigraph, as above, the surge by which the pirates from Zidon were carried to Peru was in the 21st, or 19 and 2, of Hiram. But Hiram was a contemporary of David's; was in fact "a lover of David" from the beginning, and honoured and befriended him with gifts when he went up to reside at Jerusalem: he must therefore have been established on his own throne, before David was crowned at Hebron. In short, they were kings together, but Hiram was the elder; so that the 21st of the one might very well correspond with the 17th or 18th of the other. The dates thus harmonise among themselves in an astonishing manner; and the great geological event recorded—some volcanic surge that shakes the mountains of Palestine, rends the coast of Great Britain, destroys navies in the Mediterranean, and sweeps pirates from the Atlantic to Peru—is the same precisely.

In other respects, the circumstances alleged correspond also. (1.) A year or two before this rise of the Atlantic, multitudes of emigrants from Hamath, according to the Chronicles, arrive in Spain and proceed onwards to Britain—see 13. p. xxviii: according to the tablet, the merchantman with his ten ships, and the piratical cruisers themselves, were among the number of these very emigrants. (2.) Zidon, in the Chronicles, is called the "Queen of Ships"—8. p. xxvi: in the tablet, it is called the "royal city of commercial enterprise." (3.) The colonists in Spain were husbandmen and miners from Phœnicia, and were always accompanied by a few women, in their ships: the pirates who were carried to Peru, from the same country, were husbandmen also, as well as artizans, for they greatly enriched by cultivation the newly discovered island to which they had been thus transported; and they were accompanied by women in the proportion of three to twelve.

In short, with every disposition to doubt its authenticity, it seems almost impossible that coinciding to such an extent as it does, when fairly translated, in unsuspected facts, dates, details, and phraseology, with the Psalms and the Chronicles of Eri, this Phœnician tablet can be either false or fictitious. Its falsehood, indeed, would by no means invalidate either the one or the other of these authorities; but its truth, if genuine, would enable us to trace, far beyond its present known limits, the remarkable convulsion so distinctly recorded in them both. It is farther worth observing, that it is immediately after this date the miscalculation already referred to, in the Chronicles of Eri, begins; from which point, 100 years exactly seem to be lost—that is, the narrative goes back to that extent apparently, instead of going forward. In the meantime, however, the dreadful invasion of Sru, or Sesostris, had occurred, by which the whole Peninsula was desolated—p. xxix; which may partly account for the subsequent disorder, and supposed loss of time, in their chronology.

**END OF THE CHRONICLES OF ERI.**

APPENDIX.

liii

# GLOSSARY

AND

## GENERAL GEOGRAPHICAL INDEX,

WITH NOTES SUPPLEMENTARY TO THE TEXT.

In the following catalogue of names applied chiefly to localities and rivers by Ossian, and capable of being identified with modern designations, the reader will find an account of all the most conspicuous occurring in the present work; so that whether quoted from the Gaelig, or referred to under English equivalents, their place in the preceding pages may be ascertained for fuller examination. It is of importance, however, to observe the general principles on which the identification of such names etymologically has been founded; and to note, that where mere etymological identification was difficult or impossible, other means and arguments have been employed to determine the fact.

I. As to Etymology. Gaelig, or the language of the Gael—which means the language of the Tribes, and which has been variously written Gaulic, Gallic, Gaelic, and Gaelig; which latter form has been adopted by us as presumably the best, and appears throughout in the text of the present work, except where quotations from other writers occur—is unquestionably one of the very oldest types of human speech in the world, and is either the root, or intimately connected with the development, of almost every tongue in Europe. The three great varieties of it among ourselves are the Scotch, the Irish, and the Welsh. These dialects have suffered considerable modification in themselves, from accident or usage among neighbouring people of a different origin on the same soil; and still greater modification by passing into common use among such people. In the progress of our researches hitherto, we have had frequent occasion to note these transformations, which it might seem difficult to account for on any uniform principle. It must now be observed however, for the reader's satisfaction in what follows, that the Gaelig language itself, as written and spoken, or spelled and pronounced, seems to strangers like a two-fold dialect. In adapting to their own use terms originally Gaelig, the Scotch and English proceed sometimes according to the spelling, sometimes according to the pronunciation; and thus vary, in more ways than one, without being conscious of it, the same word they adopt after one or other of these fashions. This curious fact not only enables us to explain much that would otherwise be anomalous, but points also conclusively to a much earlier use of written characters among the Celtic people of Scotland than is commonly supposed by philologists; for by speech alone, without writing, the changes we refer to from the spoken tongue could never be accounted for. To whom our forefathers were indebted for this accomplishment—possibly to the Phœnicians—may now be uncertain; but that letters were employed to represent human speech by the inhabitants of Great Britain before the advent of Roman legions in the north, is almost indubitable; and types of these letters, if we only knew how to decipher them, are still to be found on our sculptured stones and on the fragments of canoes dug up in our very rivers.

1. The modes of adapting this primitive language, written or spoken, by successive generations of strangers and others, seem to be as follows:—

(*a*) By pronouncing the word as written, without knowledge of its proper sound.
(*b*) By a selection, where separate vowels occur in the same syllable, of one in preference to the other, and so changing its sound.
(*c*) By omitting certain unnecessary letters, and contracting or softening the rest.
(*d*) By occasionally transposing certain letters or syllables, as the people of a district sometimes capriciously do, even in their own language.
(*e*) By substituting one letter for another, where they slightly resemble, and so ultimately imposing a separate form on the word.

2. There may be other accidental modes than the above, but to enumerate these will be sufficient for our present purpose; and they may all be illustrated by the transformations of a single root, which does not occur in Ossian as a proper name at all, and may therefore be quoted without prejudice. *Chaoille*, or *Coille-dun*, the wooded (not the hazel) height, (1.) translated into Latin according to its written form, and with a Latin termination—*ia*, probably from the primitive *iath*, a country—is *Caledonia;* in which, besides the adoption of the written form, we have the omission of two or three letters in the first part, and the substitution of one letter for another in the second—thus illustrating (*a*) (*c*) (*e*) of the above common processes. (2.) By dropping the final letters of the first part and contracting or softening those which remain, and by substituting E for U in the last part, where the Romans substituted an o, we have *Cowden*—as in the Cowden-hill, or wooded hill, of the Kilsyth range, from which the Kelvin and the Bonny Water flow; or as in the "Broom of the Cowden Knowes," in quite a different part of the country—in both which cases, hill and knowe are mere redundancies of speech by translation of the last syllable into the tongue of strangers. By this process, again, we have (*c*) and (*e*) of the ordinary procedures verified. (3.) By selecting or retaining A, and dropping OI, in the first part, and substituting like the Romans o for U in the second, we have *Caldon*, or *Caldons*, with the same signification as Cowden, and an exemplification of (*b*) and (*e*) in the processes enumerated. (4.) And finally, by substituting E for A in the first part, and transposing the parts themselves, we have Dun-keld, illustrating point (*d*) in our synopsis; and thus multiplying by four the possible transformations of the common root. The reader, however, in examining such derivatives, must be careful not to confound one root with another. *Coille-dun*, the wooded height, although similar to, is by no means identical with *Call-tuin*, the hazel; which is reproduced almost literally in *Calton, Calton-hill, and Calton-mohr*—designations common enough for localities in Scotland.\*

---

\* Thus *Glais-ce*, vulgarly but correctly pronounced *Glais-ke*—the *ce* being identical with the Greek *ghe*, earth—the grey-green earth, sandy soil with a slight covering of verdure, now Glasgow; and *Call-tuin*, the hazel tree, which must have been common on the eastern skirts of it, now the Calton.

II. In many cases, we have been fortunate enough to identify important localities in Ossian by tracing out, in modern designations still adhering to the soil, the very names which are most conspicuous in his text; and which, on examination, are found to correspond unequivocally with the points and places —mountains, rivers, and rocks—described by him. In other cases, where the original name has been entirely superseded by a new designation, and can therefore no longer be traced, topographical evidence, sufficiently strong, has been adduced to identify the subject. The reader, with such two-fold evidence to guide him, can have little difficulty, it is hoped, in ascertaining the scenes referred to, and often the precise spot described; and with such explanatory statements, will be able to understand more easily the bearing and conclusiveness of the derivations which follow. These have been arranged under two separate sections of Scotch and Irish, for facility in reference, and to exemplify also the distinctive peculiarities of change.

## FOR SCOTLAND, THE ORKNEYS, AND ICELAND.

[In most cases, the pages adjoining those quoted should also be examined.]

### RIVERS.

Abhain = Avon, Aven; } Latin {van, ven, vin, von;
Amhain = Amon, Annan;} *Amnis* }a or an, en, in, on, iun or un;—a river; now often a proper name for the river of the district, and in various combinations as under—    PAGE
Balv-a = Auld-ba—the silent river, ... ... ... ...   196, 227
Caol-amon = Cal-or Col-avain, Kelvin—river of narrow stream,   187, 270
Car-avon = Cara'on, Carron—a winding river, ... ... ...   187, 271
Club-a = Cluva—the sheltered water, bay or river, ...   35, 177, 182
Cluth-a = Cluath, Cluad, Clyde—the bending, or as others read, the sheltered river, ...   9, 14, 20, 31, 232, 242, 253, 266, 270, i, ix
Col-dar-onnan = Calder-annan, Calder-water—the stream that separates and encloses; three, which indicate lines of march, ...   253
Con-a = Coan, Coen, Coe—the confluent stream, ... ... ...   196
Cron-a = Crona—dull murmuring stream, ...   187, 210, 262, 324, viii
Dubh-ranna = Deveron, Dovran, Devron—the dark mountain water, ...   347
Fiorth-a = Forth-a, Forth—the river of perennial springs; name not known to Ossian; levels of, in his day, ...   10, 49, 199, iii, viii
Gar-abhain = Garvan, Girvan—the rough-running river, ...   20, 251, xi
Iar-vin = Irvine—the west river; formerly a fiord, ... ...   11, 20
Lor-a = Luvera—the noisy river; some confluent of the Cona, or in that neighbourhood; possibly the Connal, ...   305, 327, 348
Luth-a—the swift-darting river; now the Blackwater in Arran,   60, 71, 274
Strum-on—mountain stream; where? ... ... ... ...   251
Teuth-a = Tuaid—border stream; the Tweed, ... ...   35, 250

Sleaman-an = Slamannan—the smooth-gliding, or slippery tract of the river; descriptive of the parish so called, on the river Avon, in Stirlingshire, ... ... ... ... ... ...   230

## APPENDIX.

### MOUNTAINS, LAKES, LOCALITIES, &c.

|  | PAGE |
|---|---|
| Agnano, Avernus, Quilotoa—Lakes of, | 334 |
| Air or Ayr-shire—arable land; traversed by Comhal and Fingal, | 250, 254, 335 |
| Arran—see also Ben-Varrhain, | 45, 174, 262, 291, 343 |
| Atlantic, drifts from; no reference to ground in, | 271, 291 |
| "Auld Wives' Lifts," a Druidical cairn or cromlech, | 350 |

Baile = Bal—a town :—
    Bal-Clutha—town of the Clyde; at or near Rutherglen,    31, 38. 238, 262, x
    Bal-Mulzie—town of the Heap; a Roman fort,    201
    Bal-Teutha—town of the Tweed; unknown,    35, 250
Bankier—see Caer—the white fort; on Crona,    217
Beinn = Ben, ven; bin, byne, &c.—a hill; the "Bens,"    197, 222
    Ard-ven—the high hill. Three hills so called—
      1, in Stirlingshire, the Kilsyth range,    196, 222, 270
      1, in Argyllshire, not identified,    196
      1, in Arran, probably identical with Ben-varrhain = Ben-varrain, Ben 'arrain; hence Arran; north of Drumadoon,    284
    Mohr-ven = Morven; district in Argyllshire,    34, 153, 266, 271, 280
Brumo, circle of; probably Stones of Stennis,    302, 312, 342
Bute, Shire and Isle of; remains of Sepulture in,    12, 56, 251, vi
Caen = Can or Ken—a head, or head-land :—
    Can-tir (root of Latin *Terra*)—head of the land; Cantyre,    35, 90, 288
    Ken-cath = Cath-Kin—head-land of battle,    243
    Ken-nis—head of the island; now Kennis-head—that is, by reduplication, head of the island-head; see map,    lxv
Caer, or Cathair = Car or Kier—a fortified seat or castle = Roman *Castellum*, or stronghold :—
    Caer-ath-maol = Car-ath-mo, Carthmo, Crathmo,    243
    Car-fin—Castle-Fingal, small town on Clyde,    232, 249
    Castle-Carul = Castle-Cary—Carul's fort,    189, 233, 256, xviii

> There are also two Cor-phins, corruption of *Carfin*, not mentioned in our text—one near Glencoe, the other at Barr in Ayrshire, both indicating unquestionably the presence of Fingal or his people at points so remote from each other; and a Col-fin, close by Culhorn; in strong corroboration of our theory that it was in that neighbourhood the boar was slain by Fingal. See Culdarnu.

Caomala = Comála—maid of the pleasant brow; her rock, her grave,    213, 216
Cave of Thona, and other Sea-Caves,    288
Charraig = Carric, Craig—a steep rock :—
    Carric-Eilse = Craig-Ailsa—the island rock,    290, 294
    Carric-Thura = Craig-Thurwo, or Thuro, in Hoy,    261, 273, 311, xvii
    Carric-nan-iolar—the Eagles' craig, in Arran,    281
Cletes or Cleits—rocky projections, like a feather, from the land into the sea; so called in Arran,    56, 75
Col-amon = Col-am, Colzam, Colzium,    210, 256

> Why *amhain* should be translated *amon*, both by Clerk and MacPherson, in Col-amhain, and only *an* in Carron, does not appear. Possibly Col-am was a separate word, and the designation originally Col-am-avon, contracted in the one case Col-am for place, and in the other Col-vain for river. Col-am or Colzam, otherwise Col-um and Col-an, near Colzium, means, according to the

# APPENDIX.

Editor of Nimmo's *Stirlingshire*, the copper ridge. In point of fact, both iron and coal are found in the neighbourhood, with which copper might once have been mixed; in which case, the name Col-am-avon would be the river of the copper ridge, and allocated by the people afterwards according to its component parts, would give Colam first for the ridge, and then Colvain or Kelvin for the river. The Author may farther state, that whilst these pages are going to press he observes, in literal confirmation of his own view as explained in the text, that Kelvin is derived by the Editor of *Nimmo* from Col-avon, although that learned antiquarian utterly repudiates the idea that Ossian was ever in such a neighbourhood!—thus actually quoting his precise words, without being conscious of their verification.

Col-glan-Crona—narrow glen of the river Crona, (not Cona,) ... ... 191
COMHAL=Cowal, Coul, Coil, Cuil, Kyle—the man of union and strength; Fingal's father, from whom were such names as—
 Cowal, in Argyllshire; and Kyle, in Ayrshire, ... ... 250, x, xvi
 Cuil-hill, in Lanarkshire; Comhal's camp of observation, ... 231, 246

This apparently insignificant ridge—about six miles east from Glasgow, on the banks of the Monkland Canal and close by a railway station so named—is the only point in a straight line between the vallies of the Carron and the Clyde, between Castle-Cary and Castlemilk, between the Kilsyth Hills and the Cathkin Braes, from which they can all be seen at one and the same moment. Compare Map, p. 240. The origin of its name therefore, as Comhal's-hill of observation in his warlike expeditions against the "Strangers" and their allies, cannot possibly be doubted; nor can anyone, who glances at the "trough of the Clyde" from that eminence, fail to understand how Ossian and his people should call the Clyde the Clutha, or the sheltered river, at the very first sight of it. Cuil-hill might be also a British station, although thus appropriated by Comhal; for a Druidical circle under the surface, with stone coffins, funereal urns, and calcined human bones, was discovered in the immediate neighbourhood of it, not very many years ago. A little to the south-east of it also, are two of the Calder-annans, or Calder-waters—one leading to Carfin, the other to Carmyle, on the Clyde; and these would form the natural guides or boundaries for Comhal and for Fingal both, in their expeditions southward of the Wall. To dilate on the strategical sagacity thus manifested by these old "Scotch wanderers on the heath," who had to face "the kings of the world" there, would now be superfluous; but the simple fact above stated, and which was not discovered till after the present volume was in type, is worth a hundred critical arguments not only for the truth, but for the literal topographical accuracy of Ossian, as explained everywhere throughout, in the course of our text.

There is another Cuil-hill in Kirkcudbrightshire, which in like manner commands a view of the Solway and the Nith, and of the range of the Roman Road beyond: and seems to indicate the line and limits of Comhal's expeditions from Inis-huna eastward, through the moors of Galloway. It was within sight of this hill, the magnificent canoe represented on p. xii was discovered; and thus all that was required to confirm the truth of our conclusions on this subject, and on the earliest navigation of the southern Scots from the Solway to Ireland, has in good time been provided. Coilton and Coilsfield also, beyond doubt, imply Comhal's presence in Ayrshire.

Corrie—small circular hollow on the shore:— PAGE
 Corrie-Craobh=Corrie-Craivy—the woody hollow, ... .. 46, 70
 Corrie-Fiun—Fingal's hollow · his grave, ... ... 75, 85, 90, 96
Craca=Cracua, Crega; now Pomona in the Orkneys, ... ... ... 312
Culdarnu=Culhorn, in Wigtownshire, ... ... ... 175, 182, 251
Cumbrae=Cymbri—island of the Cymbri; visited by Fingal, ... 56, 252, vi
 Canoes, where found, ... ... ... ... 37, 177, 200, 252, xi
 Cloud Scenery of the Clyde, ... ... ... ... 270, xviii
Dal=Dale, same as glen in Gaelig, ... ... ... ... 245
Dullator-bog, now drained, ... ... ... ... 204, ix
Dun=Dum—a height; occurs often in combination :—
 Dumbarton=Dun-briton—fort of the British, ... 12, 22, 37, 246, x
 Dum-fin—Fingal's hill; a landmark, ... ... ... ... 226
 Dun-glass—the grey-green hill, ... ... ... 33, 238, 246

# APPENDIX.

|  | PAGE |
|---|---|
| Dum-goyne—hill of wounds, | 224 |
| Dun-i-pace=Dun-i-pacis—hill of peace; that is, of treaties, | 220, 235 |
| Dun-lathmon—Lathmon's hill, near Turriff, | 347 |
| Dun-scaith, in Skye—the Island of Mist, | 293 |
| Fer or Fear= Latin *Vir*—a man, or hero: | |
| Fer-inis= Fereneze—island of the hero; see map, | lxv |
| FION or Fiun=Fin, Fyne, Fan, with Gael—fair-haired clansman; in Stirlingshire, the giant; FINGAL, Ossian's father, | 225, 229 |
| Fin-araich= Finary—Fingal's battle field, | 227 |
| Fin-ard—Fingal's point, or landmark, | 176 |
| Fin-glen= Finglan, Fingland—Fingal's rendezvous; two, | 177, 224 |
| Fin-larig—Fingal's hill-pass, in Perthshire, | 227 |
| Fin-nich, also Finnich-haugh—Fingal's washing-place; two, | 226, 252 |
| Fin-nich-seid= Fannyside—Fin's washing-place with turf between, | 232, 252 |
| Fin-tray= Fintry—Fingal's gathering-place; two, | 228, 252 |
| Fin-trakin, also Entrekin, on route to Roman Road, | 177, x |
| Fyn-loch, also Fin-lochs—Fingal's Lochs, | 177, 227, 232 |
| Fingal's Seat by Right, in Arran; see Note, | 49 |
| Fingalton and Fingart, on route to Rutherglen, | 252 |
| Finthormo, probably Fitful-head; not Gaelig, | 325, 326 |
| Gallovidia= Galloway, name unknown to Ossian; from *Gael-adh-beadh*, pron. Gaul-a-via—the land of provision for the Gael, who followed Fergus from Ireland, | 184 |
| Gallow-flath= Gallow-flatt—hiding place of the hero, | 242, 253 |
| Gare-loch—the short loch; glacial deposits in, | 37 |
| Garscadden= Garsgadan, Gar-sidon—bay of herring on the Clyde, | 27 |
| Gear or Gar-mull= Garmoyle, Carmyle—the short projecting headland; in old frith of Clyde, | 27, 247, 249 |
| Glais-ce—Glais-ke—grey green earth, now Glasgow; see also Clyde, | 13, 249 |
| Glèan= Glen—a hollow, damp, or grassy place: | |
| Glen-cona—Glencoen, Glencoë, Glenco—the glen of confluent waters, | 34, 56, 60, 196, 227, 266, 271, 276 |
| Glen-Fyne, in Cowal; some retreat of Fingal's, | x, xvi |
| Glen-rèidh= Glenree—the smooth clear glen, | 75, 79 |
| Glen-sgor-dale= Glenscordale—glen of sharp-pointed rocks, | 56, 75 |
| Goat-fell= Gaoth-Beinn—the precipice of winds, | 271, 358 |
| Gormal, a hill in Lochlin, now unknown, | 294, 326 |
| "Gathered heap," a Roman fort at Larbert, | 195 |
| Hebrides, one or more of, | 34, 46, 291, 299, 305 |
| Hekla, Mount- | 333, 336 |
| Herman Saul—Herman's Pillar; incorrectly Ermen Sewl, | 255, xix |
| Herculaneum and Pompeii, | 335 |
| I, Inis, Innis= Ins, Insch, Latin *Insula*—an island, | 174 |
| I-thon—islet of the waves; two, Devhar and Sanda, | 37, 287 |
| Inis-huna—I-tuna—the green island, now the Rhinns | 33, 174, 177 |
| Inis-thona—the Island of the Sea, now Iceland, | 325, viii |

# APPENDIX

|   | PAGE |
|---|---|
| Inis-tore—the island of whales, now Hoy in Orkneys, | 225, 311, 314 |
| Isle, the "lonely," now Ailsa Craig: see Index for Ireland. | |
| Isles, the Faroe, and the Zetland, ... ... ... ... | ... 347 |
| Innerkip, route thence to Rutherglen, ... ... ... ... | ... 252 |
| Killin=Kil-ian; not identical with Kil-Fiun, ... ... ... | ... 85 |
| Kilsyth, formerly Moniabrock; explorations from, ... ... | ... 210 |
| Lagg—a low, hollow place: ... ... ... ... ... | 22, 25, 56 |
|    Lagg-an-roan—the Seals' pool on the Lagg, ... ... ... | ... 25 |
|    Lagg-burn, once a fiord in Arran, ... ... ... ... | ... 25 |
| Lang or Long=Loingh—a ship: | |
|    Cambus-lang—the ship's bay, ... ... ... ... ... | 14, 26 |
|    Getthin-a-lang—the ship's point or ridge, ... ... ... | ... 25 |
|    Lang-seid=Langside, the ship's grassy resting place, .. ... | ... 242 |

Close by which, on Camp-hill, are the perfect remains of what has been either a Roman *Castellum* or an old British *Caer*; and which would certainly be a landmark, if not an object of assault to Fingal and his father, in their expeditions through the Land of the Strangers.

| Lano, Lake of; identical with Thingvalla in Iceland, | 266, 300, 332 |
|---|---|
| Lappland and Finnland; whether known to Ossian, ... ... | 338, xxi |
| Lear-bard—Larbart, Larbert—the sea-dyke, or "gathered heap," | 194, 308 |
| Loch—a deep mass of water, an arm of the sea, as contra-distinguished from a lake, which may be shallow: | |
|    Loch-Fyne—Fingal's loch; once Lelamonius, ... ... ... | 36, 48 |
|    Loch-Gilp-head—? chisel-headed loch; passage by, to Crinan, | 37, 45 |
|    Loch-Libo=Loch-leòb—the shattered loch; volcanic, ... ... | ... iv |
|    Loch-Lomond=Loch-Lo-amon—loch like a broad river, ... | 11, 27 |
|    Loch-Tanker, or Tancu, now Kilbirnie Loch, ... ... | 252, iv, xiii |
|    Loch-Trool—? the polluted loch; volcanic, ... ... ... | ... iv |
|    Loch-Winnoch=Loch-Euinach—full of sea birds, ... | 11, 37, 252, iv, xiii |

Otherwise derived from St. Winnoch; but there is another loch of the same name, farther south; and what has once been an island in the valley of the Girvan, still called Enoch, and which has doubtless been the resort of sea fowl. The probabilities are therefore very much in favour of the derivation above suggested, as suitable for all three.

| Lochlin—Sea broken into lochs by projecting headlands, | 266, 313, 326, 337 |
|---|---|

According to MacPherson, is the "Gaelic name of Scandinavia in general; in a more confined sense, that of the peninsula of Jutland:" is called also "the Kingdom of Snow." Lluyd remarks, "by this name 'Llychlyn' we [the Welsh] understood Sweden, Denmark, and Norway."

| Loda, the Scandinavian thunder-god, his residence, | ... 314, 321 |
|---|---|
| Lumon—the bending hill;? the Machers of Galloway, ... | 33, 172, 176, 178 |
| Machrie=magh-rëidh—the clear field, ... ... | 47, 49, 56, 75, 281, 291 |
| Malvina—lovely brow; betrothed to Oscar; her grave, | 59, 261, 274, 344, 354 |
| Maolsmeur=Maulsmyre—marsh of low-lying ridge, ... | 243, 253 |
| Moi-Lutha—the plain of Lutha, now valley of Shisken, ... ... | ... 78 |
| Mora, the heathy ridge between Machrie-burn and Black-water, | 284, 286 |
| Moruth—the great stream or fiord; now Sliddery Water, | 50, 76, 80, 280, 299 |
| Myot=Miad or Miadh—the grassy hill of honour, ... ... | 221, 235 |
| Norway; reference to its snows, ... ... ... ... ... | ... 272 |

## APPENDIX.

|  | PAGE |
|---|---|
| Orkneys; a glance at, | 266, 271, 297, 311, 328 |
| OSCAR=-Usgar—the Jewel, or the jewelled man; son of Ossian; his grave at Moruth, | ...80, 280, 354 |
| OSSIAN—Derivation of name very doubtful; son of Fingal; his tomb at Clachaig, | 51, 309, 354, vi |
| Paisley=Pais-licht—craig-face; or Bas-leac—flat stone shoal, | 14, 20, 37, 250, iii |
| Pentland frith, avoided, | 313 |
| Rathcol, and Rerigonium, | 177, 182 |
| Rathlin, island of, not Ithona. | 290 |
| Renfrew, a Cymbric word; place under water in Ossian's day, | 36, 39 |
| Rhinns—the sharp-pointed peninsula; formerly Inishuna, | 174 |
| ROMANS; where, as known to Ossian, | 187, 199, 210, 226, 238, 305 |
| Forts or Halls, occupied by them, | 194, 217, 230, 233 |
| Road constructed by them, called Watling Street, | 177, 239, 243, 253 |
| Wall, from Forth to Clyde, | 194, 201, 232, 239 |
| Ronan's Cave, now King's Cove, | 46, 168, 281 |
| Rotha's Bay, now Roraheid *neust*, | 314, 318 |
| Runa's Bay, now Reikum, | 330 |
| Ruth-iar-glen=Rutherglen, Ru'glen—point of west valley, | 46, 245, 252, 299 |
| Sandyford=? Sandifiord—the sandy frith, or ford. | 29 |
| SELMA, said to be Dun-Mac-Uisneach, | 35, 348 |
| Shisken, formerly plain of Moi-Lutha, | 61, 71, 79, 281 |
| Solway frith, formerly *Ituna* of the Romans, | 173, 183, 266, 299 |
| Sora—? Sor-oe, in Zealand, | 327 |
| Spain; ships and emigrants from. | 39, xxix |
| Stennis, Stones of, | 352, 355, xvii |
| Stirlingshire; frequent expeditions to and from, | 34. 187, 229, 255, 323 |
| Stobcross; marine formations there, | 14, 18 |
| Stone of Fear, or of Power; otherwise " Dwarfie Stone," | 297, 315, 321, 353 |
| ,, of Mora, monolith at Tormore, | 61, 354 |
| ,, of Renown, on the Crona, | 218 |
| ,, Rocking- of Cromla: see Index for Ireland, | 352 |
| Stranraer, possibly Rerigonium, | 36, 177 |
| Thingvalla; Danish Millennial celebration at, | 337, xx |
| Thon, or Thona—the sea; a wave of the sea: see Inis. | |
| Berra-thon—the rocky promontory of waves, | 325 |
| Troma-thon—the deep-sounding surge of the sea, | 347 |
| Tom—a round hillock; an artificial mound: | |
| Tom-fin—Fingal's mound, in Stirlingshire, | 212, 222, 224, 227 |
| " Tomb"—? " Arthur's Oven," | 220 |
| Tombs; various, | 344, 353 |
| Tor, or Tar,—a fortified mound, or lofty keep, where justice was administered; very common in Scotland: | |
| Tors of Arran; several on west coast of, | 61 |
| Tor-bolton, in Ayrshire, | 250 |
| Tor- or Tar-fin—Fingal's Justice Seat, | 227 |

APPENDIX. lxi

|  |  |  | PAGE |
|---|---|---|---|
| Tor-Lutha, now Drumadoon, | ... | ... | 60, 71, 75, 276, 291 |
| Turriff; see Dunlathmon, | ... | ... | ... ... ... 346 |
| Tyre and Sidon, or Zidon; ships from, | ... | ... | ... 28, 39, xxvi |
| Volcanic ranges in Scotland, | ... | ... | ... 9, 300, 336 |
| West Highlands; Ossian must have lived in, | ... | ... | ... ... 272 |
| Yeskenaby, compared with Roraheid, or Rotha, | ... | ... | 317, xvii |
| Zealand; not Inis-thona, | ... | ... | ... ... 326 |
| Zetland, or Shetland, group of Islands, | ... | ... | 310, 312, 326, 338 |

## FOR IRELAND—MISCELLANEOUS.

[In most cases, the pages adjoining those quoted should also be examined.]

|  |  |  |  |
|---|---|---|---|
| ALBION = Ailbinn—confused heap of hills; Scotland, | ... | ... | 135 |
| Allen, Lough; not same as Bog of, | ... | ... | 139 |
| Alnecma = Alnecmacht, not = Connaught, | ... | 100, 102, 138, 151, 159 |
| Antrim, County—see also Ullin, | ... | ... | 144, 154, 165 |
| ,, Bay of, | ... | ... | 140, 148 |
| Ardglass to Armagh, boundary line, | ... | ... | 179, 262 |
| Armagh; origin of name, | ... | ... | 152, 154, 163, xxxiii |
| Arran; on Fingal's route to Ireland, | ... | 109, 131, 154, 168, 173 |
| Atha—a shallow river; town on,? Armagh, | ... | ... | 100, 153, 183 |
| Avernus, Lake of, compared to Lough Neagh, | ... | ... | 145 |
| Balfosaght = Belfast—entrenched town, | ... | ... | 143 |
| Ballyclare, on Six-mile-water, | ... | ... | 118 |
| Ballylinny, townland of, | ... | ... | 122 |
| Bann, Upper—? Branno, | ... | ... | 141, 152, 180 |
| ,, Lower; see Lara. |  |  |  |
| Bardh, pl. Bàirdh—the Bards; their place of banishment, | ... | ... | 126 |

According to Toland, the Orders of BARDS were as under:—
Pri-vardh, the prince of learniog, or of learned men:
Pos-vardh, otherwise Prydiddion; not an author, but the registrar and teacher of learning:
Arruy-vardh, or Ensign, the genealogist or herald.
In addition, there was also the
Bardh Telyn, or Doctor of players on the harp, and himself the chief harper in the land, whose residence was with the king.
Besides which, there were three kinds of POETS:—
Pruddudh, who treated of Nations, Princes, and Nobles:
Tevluyr, whose themes were jests and pastimes:
Cleruyr, who railed and caricatured, among the lower orders.
These men were all clothed in long garments down to the calf of the leg, or somewhat lower, and of diverse colours.—See *Hist. of Druids*, I., 191. According to other authorities, the Order of public Teachers was different—
Strabo arranges them as—Bards, Vatès, Druids:
Ammianus Marcellinus as—Druids, Bards, Eubages:
The Druids being the highest, educated and exclusive class; the Bards, the popular reciters, who committed all historical records in verse to memory; and the Eubages probably an inferior order. But Toland, who seems to have investigated the matter pretty fully, maintains that this arrangement is a mistake, founded on an imperfect knowledge, in Strabo and Marcellinus, of the Celtic language. *Druids* I. 29.

## APPENDIX

|  | PAGE |
|---|---|
| BOLGA—GAE—the burden, or quiver-bearers; whence? | 153, 161, 171, 182 |
| Boyne water—the yellow river, | 169, 171, 252, xxxi |
| BRITAIN; emigrants from, | 151, 161, 171 |
| Carrick-Fergus, town of, | 110, 144, 157, 169 |
| ,, ,, Bay of, | 138 |
| Cave-hill, | 110 |
| Clyde; voyages from to Ireland, | 109 |
| Connor, village of—see also Temora, | 118, 140, 166 |
| Cormul—Carneal, the Upper and Lower, | 122 |
| Croma—the curved water, now Belfast Lough, | 282 |
| Cromla—Cromleach, a mountain ridge, | 100, 105, 110, 114, 123, 137 |
| Crommal, misty Top of, | 115 |
| Crumlin, town of, | 115 |
| ,, Water-foot, | 142 |
| Culbin, Bay of—behind the hills, | 173, 178 |
| DANAN, the; where settled, | 157, xxx, xliv |
| Divis-mount, in Belfast range, | 110 |
| Dora—Doar, Doagh—the woody side of a mountain, | 104, 110, 122 |
| Drum-a-dora—Drumardo, | 152 |
| DUBLIN, | 151, 167 |
| Duncrue—the hill-fort of blood, | 119 |
| Dundalk, | 109, 151, 153, 178 |
| Dundrum, Bay of, | 178 |
| Duthuma, "horrid cave" of; now cave of Ardtole, | 173 |
| Eagh—eachan—floods of water. In combination— | |
|     Antrim-eagh—Antrim, town of, | 147 |
|     Castle-r'eagh—Castlereagh, | 147 |
|     Iv-eagh, Upper and Lower, | 147 |
|     Kill-eagh, origin of, | 147 |
|     Lough 'n eagh—Lough-Neagh, | 108, 122, 133, 159 |
| Earthquakes; where and when, | 143, 144, 336 |
| ERIN, according to MacPherson—*Iar-in*—western Isle, | 100 |
| ,, ,, Chronicles of Eri=*Er-in*—Island of ER, | 144, 151, 159, 161, xxx |
| Foldath, or Fothadh's grave, | 170 |
| Gabhra, the battle of; where? | 135, 167, 169 |
| Glenhouse, Glinus, or Glenoe, | 121 |
| Hebrides—ean, emigrants from, | 155, 161, 167, 171, 183 |
| Herculaneum and Pompeii, | 145 |
| Inis- or Innis-Fail, according to MacPherson, Island of Falans, | 100 |
| ,, ,, ,, Chronicles of Eri, Island of Fate, | 161 |
| ,, -Owen, in Lough-Foyle, not Inis-thona, | 337 |
| IRELAND; Scots in, | 149, 154, 159, 167, 171, 183, xxxiii |
| Isle-Maghee, apparently Inis-fail, | 106, 178, 160 |
| ,, of Man, Larthon's route to Ireland, | 176, 180 |
| ,, of Skye; Cuthullin, Lord of, | 113, 140, 154, 307, xxxi, xxxvi |
| Isles, "Lonely"—Ailsa Craig and Sanda, | 106, 109, 131, 169 |

## APPENDIX.

|  | PAGE |
|---|---|
| JERUSALEM ; emigrants from, ... ... ... ... ... | 157, xliv |
| Killead or Killeagh, parish of, ... ... ... ... ... | 119 |
| Kilwaughter, ,, ... ... ... ... ... | 165 |
| Lagan, or La'an—the low-lying river, ... ... ... | 141, 143, 152 |
| "Lake of Roes," now L. Mourne, ... ... ... ... | 103, 123 |
| Lamdearg, or—derg, tomb of ; where, ... ... ... | 107, 114, 134, 166 |
| Lara=Larach, river and valley of ; Lower Bann, ... | 137, 141, 149, 151 |
| Lavath, now Glenwherry Water, ... ... ... ... | 105, 136, 160 |
| Lego, Lake of ; now L. Neagh, ... ... 100, 137, 141, 145, 151, 159, 160 |
| LEINSTER, Province of, ... ... ... | 155, 164, 169, xxxiv |
| Lena, heath of, ... ... ... 102, 119, 123, 137, 140, 166, 168, 262 |
| ,, Bay of, now Lough-Larne, ... ... ... ... | 102, 108 |
| LOCHLIN ; expeditions from to Ireland, ... ... ... | 160, 161 |
| Lough=Loch—deep mass of water : |  |
| ,, Beg, or Portmore, ... ... ... ... ... | 140 |
| ,, of Belfast, ... ... ... ... | 110, 144, 151, 160, 171 |
| ,, Foyle, also Swilly, ... ... ... ... | 131, 134, 144, 337 |
| Lubar, Lubhar or Labhar=Luvar, Luvera, Lora— |  |
| the noisy stream ; now Six-mile Water, ... | 100, 104, 108, 115, 166 |
| Meath, County, ... ... ... ... ... ... | 163, 262 |
| Moi-Lena=Magh-Linè—broad valley of Lena, ... | 102, 122, 134, 148, 168 |

Hence also, by slight variety of pronunciation, comes Mauchline, in Ayrshire, Scotland.

|  |  |
|---|---|
| Mora=Slieve-mora, Slimero, hill of, ... ... | 100, 104, 122, 140 |
| Mourne=Muirne, Lake of Lady, ... ... ... ... | 112 |
| Muckamore, parish of, ... ... ... ... ... | 119, 148 |
| Mullingar, town of, ... ... ... ... ... | 164 |
| Mumo, or Moma, "horrid cave" of ; not yet known, ... | 152, 155, 168 |
| MUNSTER, or Mumain ; so called from Mumo, King of, ... | 169, xxxi |
| "Noisy Vale," now Stony Glen, ... ... ... ... | 103, 112 |
| Ollar and Ollarbha, by transposition=Lora and Luvera ... | 165, 168 |
| Orland Water ; why so called, ... ... ... ... | 112 |

It may possibly be alleged that some other origin for this name, than that assigned in our text, could be given: so also, it may be said, for Turloughstown and Dora. But when Mourne and Orland, on one side; Dora and Turloughstown, on the other side; Ollar and Ollarbha, identical with the Lubar and the Larne between; and so many other names in the region, occur all exactly where they should occur according to Ossian—why should any other derivation for them be required? No such correspondence between the nomenclature of a district and the text of a disputed author is to be found elsewhere in Europe; except, indeed, in the case of other localities identified, as we have seen, with those alluded to by Ossian himself.

|  |  |
|---|---|
| Oscar's Grave ; in Arran, not in Ireland, ... ... ... | 136 |
| Palestine, and Phœnicia ; correspondence with, ... ... | xxvi, xl, xliv |
| Quilotoa, Lake of ; exhalations from, ... ... ... | 145 |
| Raths or Forts, several kinds of, ... ... ... | 111, 118, 138 |
| Rocking Stone, Isle Maghee, ... ... ... ... | 114, 123, 161 |
| ROME ; Fingal alleged by Irish to have been sent to, ... | 167 |
| SCOTLAND, emigrants to and from ; Ulster so called, | 142, 150, 158, 183 |
| Selàma, in Ullin, ... ... ... ... ... | 137, 151, 164, 166 |

## APPENDIX.

| | PAGE |
|---|---|
| Selma, in Morven, ... ... ... ... ... ... ... | 155, 158 |
| "Serbonian Bog," compared to L. Neagh, ... ... ... ... | 143 |
| Six-Mile-Water, ... ... ... ... ... ... | 148, 152, 166 |
| Stone of Fate, or *Lia-Fail*, at Connor, ... ... ... ... | 157, 161 |
|   ,, of Lubar, ... ... ... ... ... ... ... | 104 |
| Sulla-tober, or Sallow-well = Sulmalla's well, ... ... ... ... | 112 |
| Tara, or Tarah = Tobrad — hill of Election, in Meath, ... ... ... | 162 |
| Teacmor = Teamohr, the Palace of Ireland, at Tara, ... ... ... | 162 |
| Temora = Tigh-mor-righ, the Palace of Ulster, ... | 105, 140, 146, 161, 262 |
| Ten Commandments; whence? ... ... ... ... | xxvi, xxxi, xxxix |
| Tombs or Pillar Stones, ... ... ... ... ... | 107, 119, 344 |
| Tura = Trué, from *Tuire* — mourning; castle, cave, and bay of, ... | 100, 104, 110, 114, 123, 137, 140, 151, 285 |
| Turloughstown, from Turloch, ... ... ... ... ... ... | 153 |
| Tyre and Zidon, ... ... ... ... ... ... ... | xl, xlvii |
| Ullin, now County Antrim, ... | 100, 106, 138, 146, 150, 154, 160 |
| Ulster, Province of, ... ... ... | 127, 160, 165, 169, 262, xxx |
| Whillan Rocks, or Nine Maidens, ... ... ... ... | 106, 108 |
| Woodburn Water, ... ... ... ... ... ... | 111 |

---

The adjoining map, of the "Trough" or Basin of the Clyde, may be consulted for illustration both of the Text and of the Glossary. Of the numerous tributaries to the chief river, only the four largest—the Leven and the Kelvin on the north, and the two Carts, Black and White, on the south—are fully represented. Of the smaller, only the Levern, near its source at Fer-inis, appears; to which portion alone, at the time, its present name—the Luvar-an, or noisy river—could possibly apply; and that most accurately, one of its branches there being in fact called the Roaring Linn; whereas the rest is almost on a dead level, and would be swallowed in the Frith. This etymological fact alone with respect to the Levern is indisputable evidence that, from Langside to Barrhead, the Frith of Clyde was then a sea; and that a passage by land, along the southern shore of it, could only be obtained by way of Fingalton. The Gryfe also adds its waters to those of the Black Cart, about two miles and a half north-west of Paisley; but the stream is not referred to by Ossian, and to avoid complication is not represented in the Map.

# APPENDIX. lxv

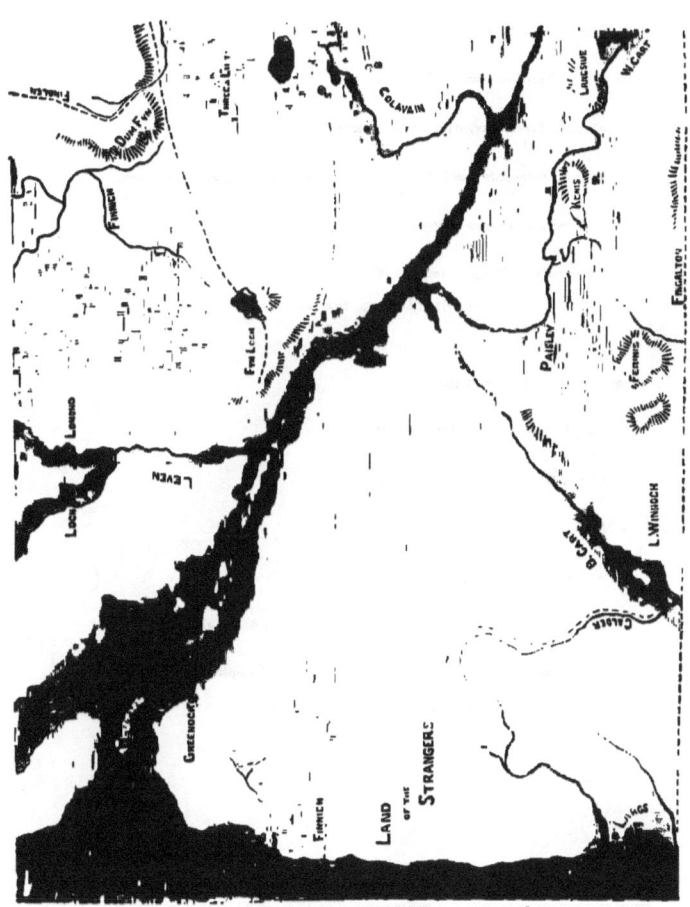

SKETCH MAP OF THE TROUGH OF CLYDE, AS IN OSSIAN'S ERA.

### EXPLANATIONS AND DIRECTIONS.

━ Roman Wall, from Forth to Clyde.

⟵ Roman Road, in Land of the Strangers.

━ Military Tracks; or, with Canoes, Lines of Navigation.

⊙ With B, Balmulzie; with S, Simmerton: Important Stations on the Wall.

▮ Fortified Stations—as Castlecary and Rough Castle.

o Smaller Forts, Places, Camps, or Towns
See also Maps, pp. 124, 208, 240.

✴ Ossian's Tomb, at Clachaig, in Arran.

†† Fingal's Grave, at Corriefiun, in Arran.

△ Oscar's Grave, opposite Glenree, in Arran.

⊙ Malvina's Grave, near Drumadoon, in Arran.

▫ Tor, or Fortified Keep—as Torlutha, &c., in Arran.

· Monolith on Machrie-muir; also at Place of Renown, p. 208.

⋀⋀ Caves—as King's Cove in Arran, and Caves in the Cromla Range, Belfast; p. 124.
See Map, South End of Arran, p. 72.

# POSTSCRIPT.

HAVING thus concluded our researches on Ossian, we have pleasure in stating that we find one man at least, of the highest distinction as a linguist, a scholar, and a critic, who understood the historical sequence and appreciated the harmony of his most important poems. L'Abbate, Melchior Cesarotti, in fact—whose retranslation of MacPherson into Italian verse surprised and delighted all Europe—is the only man who did understand, in anything like reason, the natural sense of Ossian; and it is with singular gratification we now refer to his once celebrated work, as an indication of what required to be done in our own. Without presuming to criticise his translation, which was universally admired on its appearance—Padua, 1763 and 1772—we may with some confidence affirm, that he realised at least the historical continuity of all that related to Ireland—the exact position of the several dynasties there, the rival claims of the various factions for sovereignty, and the extent of Caledonian supremacy in the northern division of that Island. Much of this, as we have seen, was a sort of mystery to MacPherson, but it was not a mystery to Cesarotti; and he distinctly saw, from the text alone, that Temora, the centre of the contest, was in Ulster—which MacPherson never saw. Whereabouts in Ulster this Temora was to be found, he did not see; or how any other locality was to be identified, he did not inquire: but to have seen even so much as this in Ossian, through the bewildering contradictions of MacPherson's notes, was itself a triumph; and it would have been more to the credit of British literature, if its highest authorities on both sides, instead of expending their energies in blind abuse or rhetorical laudation, had endeavoured to form the remotest reliable conception on the subject.

It was not till long after our present investigations had been finished—not, indeed, until after our Preface was in type—that our attention was accidentally directed to Cesarotti's work, or we should have quoted his words with pleasure, when treating of the Campaigns in Ireland. All we can now do, is to refer the student of Celtic and Italian literature alike, for corroboration of our statements, to his own pages.

NOVEMBER 10, 1874.

THE END.

## DIRECTIONS TO BINDER.

Heliotypes—Stobcross No. II. and Stobcross No. III.—to face one another, between Pages 18 and 19: No. III. with lettering to outside, and with tissue paper between them.

Sunnyside Place,
Liverpool.

To Campbell, Esq.

Dear Sir,

I am much obliged for the copy of your handsome work, "Ossian the Strainer," which accompanied your note acknowledging receipt of my book on Ossian and the Clyde. I wish I understood Gaelic, that I might be able to read the collection through; but in ignorance of that language, I must confine myself to the contents and summaries, which are very interesting, with

which you have interspersed the
Selections. Some of the pieces were
substantially known to me before,
through an occasional glance at
the Irish Ossianic translations —
of which, however, you must allow
me to say I have not a very high
opinion.

I notice, of course, the significant
quotation from my own work on the
fly leaf of your valuable volume,
and the short but pithy supplement
with which you have honoured it,
and I am sorry that, in the circumstances, I can neither ask nor

hope for your support in my present arguments. But I must be permitted to say, which I do without hesitation, that your "facts" are not our "facts" — yourselves being judges. Your facts, as against MacPherson, remain all to be proved; our facts, in support of MacPherson and in spite of himself, lie proved already on the very face of the country.

I remain, Dear Sir,
ex parte adversa,
Yours very truly,
P. Hately Waddell C.

July 5th 1875

July 14th 1875.

Millingshill,
by Kilmalcolm,
Renfrewshire.

My dear Sir,

Thanks to Professor Blackie, and a thousand welcomes to you, come when you may; but I would like to know about when, for I will not be permanently at home till the end of August. The question at issue must and should and shall be fought out with somebody, and with yourself by preference to any other. But you greatly mistake: it is not with me a question of merit only by any means, or even chiefly; although even on that ground I might maintain it. Is it not more reasonable to believe that the Dean of Lismore's collection and the preposterous Irish rhapsodies are recent conceptions of a divine original, than that such an original was concocted by a beardless boy from them? But when that alleged concoction is found to be not only coherent and consistent with itself, which theirs is not; but to be in absolute harmony with the very face of nature, of every time and on every inch of ground referred to, without the knowledge and beyond the imagination and contrary to the very words of the alleged concoctor himself, who did not understand it — The question of authenticity must be settled for ever in the faith of all unprejudiced inquirers. That is my position; and I will fearlessly maintain it against all adversaries; not because it is mine, or for the credit of MacPherson's character as an honest man, but because the original geography, the oldest history, and the sublimest poetry of Scotland are involved in it — and these are not to be sacrificed to the lying inventions or the corrupts nept rehearsals of my monk a Sounachie that ever lived. Consider.

Yours affectionately
and devoutly.
P. Hely Hutchinson

What on earth is to be done with such a man but let him alone and devoutly hope he keeps clear of mine.
J. F. Campbell
June 30. 1876

J. F. Campbell, Esq. of Islay.
&c. &c.

www.ingramcontent.com/pod-product-compliance
Lightning Source LLC
Chambersburg PA
CBHW022148300426
44115CB00006B/391